WHO'S WHO IN THE BIBLE

WHO'S WHO IN THE BIBLE

Reader's Digest

The Reader's Digest Association, Inc.
Pleasantville, New York   Montreal

WHO'S WHO IN THE BIBLE

Designed and Edited by Gardner Associates

Editorial Director: Joseph L. Gardner
Art Editor: Howard P. Johnson
Picture Editor: Laurie Platt Winfrey
Associate Picture Editor: Robin J. Sand
Research Editors: Josephine Reidy (chief),
  Robert Melzak (Art), Guadalupe
  Morgan, Sara Solberg
Principal Contributing Writers: Charles
  Flowers, Stephen M. Miller, Thomas L.
  Robinson
Contributing Writers: Jean Callahan,
  Penelope Franklin, Norman Kotker,
  Brian H. Morgan, Gerald T. Sheppard,
  Dennis E. Smith, Harold Kent Straughn
Copy Editor: Felice Levy
Indexer: Cynthia Crippen

Project Staff for Reader's Digest

Senior Editor: Robert V. Huber
Art Editor: Robert M. Grant
Production Coordinator: Tracey
  Grant-Starker

Reader's Digest General Books

Editor in Chief: John A. Pope, Jr.
Managing Editor: Jane Polley
Executive Editor: Susan J. Wernert
Art Director: David Trooper
Group Editors: Will Bradbury, Sally
  French, Norman B. Mack, Kaari Ward
Group Art Editors: Evelyn Bauer, Robert
  M. Grant, Joel Musler
Chief of Research: Laurel A. Gilbride
Copy Chief: Edward W. Atkinson
Picture Editor: Richard Pasqual
Head Librarian: Jo Manning

The credits and acknowledgments that appear on pages 471 and 472 are hereby made a part of this copyright page.

Copyright © 1994 The Reader's Digest Association, Inc.
Copyright © 1994 The Reader's Digest Association
  (Canada) Ltd.
Copyright © 1994 Reader's Digest Association Far East Ltd.
Philippine Copyright 1994 Reader's Digest Association Far
East Ltd.

The Scripture quotations contained herein are from the Revised Standard Version of the Bible, copyright 1946, 1952, 1971 by the Division of Christian Education of the National Council of the Churches of Christ in the U.S.A. Used by permission.

Library of Congress Cataloging in Publication Data
Reader's Digest Who's Who in the Bible: an illustrated
  biographical dictionary.
    p.   cm.
    ISBN 0-89577-618-9
    1. Bible—Biography.   I. Reader's Digest Association
  II. Title: Who's Who in the Bible.
BS570.R43 1994
220.9′2—dc20   94-17591
[B]
Printed in the United States of America
Eleventh Printing, June 2003

ABOUT THIS BOOK

The inspirational record of God's love for humanity, the Bible also contains the stories of countless fascinating men and women: Abraham, chosen by the Lord for greatness; Joseph, who survived a murder attempt to rise to power in Egypt; the inarticulate Moses leading his people to freedom; wise King Solomon deciding an infant's fate; wicked Jezebel, the power behind the throne during the reigns of her two sons; the prophet Elijah, carried off to heaven in a whirlwind; John the Baptist, preaching in the wilderness; Peter, Andrew, and the sons of Zebedee, summoned by Jesus to become fishers of men; Stephen giving his life for the new faith. Through the pages of this book readers can get to know them better.

More than 500 people, Aaron to Job's friend Zophar, are profiled in the alphabetical entries beginning on the next page. At the head of each biography is the pronunciation, original language, and meaning (if known) of the name; following is a summary and interpretation of that person's story, complete with biblical citations and cross-references in **bold** type to related entries. Here are the famous—Noah, David and Bathsheba, the prophets Isaiah and Jeremiah, Mary Magdalene, Herod the Great—as well as the obscure—Tamar, denied a husband by Judah; the harlot Rahab, who helped Joshua capture Jericho; Moabite king Eglon and his assassin, Ehud; Paul's teacher, the rabbi Gamaliel; Ananias and Sapphira, early Christians punished for their greed; the magician Simon, who sought to buy the Holy Spirit's power.

Beginning on page 441 is Everyone in the Bible, a carefully researched listing of the more than 3,400 people named in the Old Testament, the New Testament, and the Apocrypha.

—The Editors

CONTENTS

AARON

(air' uhn) HEBREW: AHARON

meaning uncertain

Although he plays a major role in the early history of the Israelites, Aaron always stands in the shadow of his charismatic younger brother, **Moses**. Moreover, the closer to Moses he stands, the more Aaron's stature rises; whenever he opposes his brother, it plummets.

Aaron first appears in the biblical narrative at the age of 83, trekking from Egypt into the Sinai desert to find Moses, who had left the land of his birth 40 years earlier. Little is known of the first eight decades of Aaron's life. He was born in Egypt, perhaps about 1360 B.C., to a couple from the tribe of Levi named Amram and **Jochebed**. Aaron had an older sister, **Miriam**, who helped save the life of the infant Moses while Aaron was still a toddler. She stood guard when Jochebed put her baby in a basket at river's edge to escape Pharaoh's new death warrant against male Hebrew infants.

According to the genealogy in Exodus 6:16-20, Aaron's father, Amram, was the son of **Kohath** and a grandson of the patriarch **Levi**. Amram married his father's sister Jochebed—a union that would later be prohibited by Mosaic Law but was then apparently legal. Some believe that such biblical genealogies need not be taken literally, and that Aaron and his siblings were simply descendants of Amram and Jochebed, since the family of Amram seems to have been a large clan at the time of the Exodus and since some passages date the Exodus to four centuries after the time of Levi. In the book of Numbers, however, it is said that "Jochebed the daughter of Levi . . . bore to Am-

Speaking for his inarticulate brother, Moses, Aaron asks Pharaoh to let his people go.

ram Aaron and Moses and Miriam their sister" (Num. 26:59).

An elder son, Aaron evidently came to maturity as the leader of his own prominent family and perhaps of the entire tribe of Levi. The younger Moses probably seemed lost to his family and people after he was rescued from the river bank and taken into the house of Pharaoh's daughter. This would have been especially true after he fled from Egypt to avoid punishment for murdering an Egyptian and remained absent for decades. Aaron, however, stayed with his people all through the period of their oppressive slavery to the Egyptians and became known as an eloquent spokesman for the Israelites.

Married to a woman named Elisheba, the daughter of Amminadab, a leader of the tribe of Judah, Aaron had four sons, **Nadab**, Abihu, **Eleazar**, and Ithamar. Later Jewish tradition contains stories of Aaron's long experience as a prophet and peacemaker among the Hebrews in Egypt. Unlike the hot-blooded Moses, Aaron pursued reconciliation and avoided disputes. Thus, a saying of the famous first-century B.C. rabbi Hillel urged, "Be of the disciples of Aaron, loving peace and pursuing peace, loving one's fellow men and bringing them nigh to the Torah."

COMMISSIONED BY THE LORD

Aaron's life changed dramatically at the moment God spoke to him in Egypt: "Go into the wilderness to meet Moses" (Ex. 4:27). Though Moses seemed to have settled permanently among the Midianites, a tribe of sheepherders in the Sinai Peninsula, Aaron heeded God's command and traveled into the wilderness, all the way out to "the mountain of God" (Ex. 4:27)—Mount Sinai—to find his long lost brother. And when he found him, he joyfully greeted Moses with a kiss. Moses told him the amazing story that God had commissioned

ISRAEL'S HIGH PRIEST

From Aaron, the first high priest, to Ananias, the last mentioned in the Bible, the office of high priest spanned more than 1,300 years. As long as the tabernacle or temple stood, the high priest was the unique individual who carried out the most holy act of worship. On the Day of Atonement, the high priest alone entered the presence of God in the Holy of Holies of the sanctuary to make atonement for the sins of the people. He wore a white linen tunic covered by a brilliant blue robe edged with gold bells that rang whenever his bare feet moved. On his chest was a breast piece with 12 precious stones, and on his head a turban and a golden crown with the words "Holy to the Lord."

The high priesthood was handed down within certain clans. At first, it was open to all descendants of Aaron, but later it was limited to descendants of Zadok, the high priest when Solomon built his temple. In the second century B.C. the Hasmonean rulers took over the office; under Herod the Great, it became a political appointment.

Aaron's flowering rod, embroidered in the lower panel of a 16th-century dalmatic

him to deliver the Israelites from slavery, and together the brothers returned to Egypt.

After his 40 years' absence, Moses would have been remembered by few if any among Israel's leaders as a man who had stood among the privileged of Egypt. Aaron therefore took the lead in presenting Moses, who was "slow of speech and of tongue" (Ex. 4:10), to the elders of Israel, putting his own eloquence and his talent for leading at the service of his younger brother and his sacred mission from the Lord. Aaron set out to convince the Hebrew elders, who had never known God to intervene on their behalf in times of hardship, that at long last God had heard their cries. By signs given by God to Moses—turning his staff into a serpent and back, causing his hand to appear leprous and then cleansed—Aaron showed them that God had sent a deliverer, this unlikely man Moses, who had been so long absent from them. In spite of any skepticism on the part of his audience, Aaron was successful: "the people believed" (Ex. 4:31).

Next Aaron and Moses went before Pharaoh—probably Ramses II (1292–1225 B.C.)—to voice the demand of God: "Let my people go" (Ex. 5:1). Aaron served as Moses' prophet, speaking the words and repeating the signs that God had given to Moses.

Although Egyptian magicians were able to match his feat of turning a rod into a serpent, "Aaron's rod swallowed up their rods" (Ex. 7:12). Nonetheless, Pharaoh refused to be swayed by the demands or by the signs wrought by Aaron and Moses.

AT LONG LAST, FREEDOM

It took ten plagues to force Pharaoh to submit to God's will. First, Aaron stretched his rod over the waters of Egypt and they became blood. But Pharaoh did not relent. Nor did Pharaoh capitulate to subsequent plagues of frogs, gnats, flies, a disease that took the Egyptian cattle, boils that afflicted both men and beasts, hail and lightning, locusts, and a darkness lasting three days. "But the Lord hardened Pharaoh's heart," the biblical narrative reveals, "and he would not let them go" (Ex. 10:27). However, the last plague—the death of all the firstborn in Egypt—brought such horror that the Egyptians drove the Israelites from the land.

Once the refugees had crossed into the harsh desert of the Sinai Peninsula, Aaron continued his role as Moses' spokesman and principal aide. Hungry and thirsty, the people became disheartened and "murmured against Moses and Aaron in the wilderness." Moses asked his brother to speak, and as he did so, "the glory of the Lord appeared in the cloud" (Ex. 16:2,10); the people saw that God would care for them, sending miraculous bread called manna and unexpected flocks of quail.

Soon, the Israelites were attacked by desert tribesmen called Amalek, and again Exodus records a miraculous deliverance. While **Joshua** led Israel's warriors, Moses stood on a hilltop holding aloft "the rod of God" (Ex. 17:9); as long as he did so, the Israelities prevailed. When Moses could no longer hold his arms up, Aaron and **Hur**, another of Moses' lieutenants, supported them till the victory was won. The scene of Aaron holding up the arms of Moses is perhaps a fitting symbol of the elder brother's entire life.

The long accounts in Exodus, Leviticus, and Numbers of Israel's encampment at Mount Sinai show both positive and negative elements of Aaron's character. When God manifested himself in thunder and lightning on Mount Sinai, Aaron was the first after Moses to be summoned to the mountain. As the revelations on the mountain continued, Aaron and his two eldest sons, Nadab and Abihu, joined Moses and 70 elders of Israel to experience a remarkable epiphany in which "they saw the God of Israel" (Ex. 24:10) and shared a meal celebrating their covenant with the Lord in the divine presence.

Sometime after this revelation, Moses again ascended Mount Sinai, leaving Aaron

With lamb's blood, Aaron marks a door so the Lord will spare the Hebrews' firstborn from the tenth plague.

and Hur in charge of the people during the 40 days he was absent. The laws Moses received included detailed specifications for the investiture of Aaron and his sons as the priests of Israel. In addition, Moses was instructed to commission "holy garments for Aaron your brother, for glory and for beauty" (Ex. 28:2), and he received commands concerning Aaron's anointing and the sacrifices of ordination that were to be offered in the new tabernacle—a portable altar they were to build.

THE GOLDEN CALF

Ironically, it was at that very time that Aaron and the people were undermining their entire relationship with God. Failing to comprehend the revelations of God that were occurring on the mountain, the Israelites grew impatient as they waited day after day for Moses to return. They came to Aaron demanding idols such as they would have seen in Egypt: "Make us gods, who shall go before us" (Ex. 32:1). At this crucial moment, Aaron utterly failed as Moses' spokesman, unable to explain to them why their demand was impossible. Rather, he joined in their apostasy, gathering their gold—probably booty taken from Egypt— and fashioning it into a calf or young bull. In a parody of the beginning of the Ten Commandments, the cry went up that this was the god who had brought them up out of the land of Egypt. Aaron tried to salvage this disaster somewhat by identifying the bullock as an image of Israel's true God, and he proclaimed a feast to the Lord for the following day. But he had already gone too far.

Moses, burning with anger, descended the mountain and confronted his brother incredulously: "What did this people do to you that you have brought a great sin upon them?" (Ex 32:21). Aaron tried lame excuses but could not escape his guilt. At that moment Moses revealed his true greatness: Despite his outrage at the sins of both Aaron and the people, he asked God to forgive them and even restored Aaron to his role as a leader of the people.

The book of Leviticus records how Aaron and his sons were ordained as priests with all the solemnity and beauty that God had commanded. But tragedy befell Aaron's family in the process. His eldest sons, Nadab and Abihu, presumptuously ignored the laws of holiness God had prescribed for sacrifices in his sanctuary and were miraculously destroyed by fire. The chastened Aaron "held his peace" (Lev. 10:3) as he accepted God's judgment.

Aaron's new role as the chief priest of Israel, however, may have undermined his willingness to accept the leadership of his younger brother. Aaron and Miriam, who had both been designated as prophets of the Lord, challenged Moses' right to act as God's unique spokesman. But the Lord defended Moses emphatically by striking Miriam with leprosy, though he spared Aaron so that he could continue to function as a priest. Aaron showed his penitence by pleading with Moses on behalf of Miriam, and at Moses' request God soon healed her. Thereafter, Aaron and Miriam stood firmly with Moses to the end of their lives.

Numbers relates that God later confirmed his choice of Aaron and the tribe of Levi in their priestly duties through another remarkable miracle. Wooden rods representing Aaron and the other heads of the tribes were placed overnight before the ark of the covenant. Entering the tent of meeting the next morning, Moses saw that "the rod of Aaron for the house of Levi had sprouted and put forth buds, and produced blossoms, and it bore ripe almonds" (Num. 17:8). No one could doubt Aaron's divine calling to be the Lord's priest.

Aaron's faithfulness to Moses also brought its problems. The harsh years of wandering in the Sinai desert repeatedly caused the Hebrews to complain about the leadership of Moses and Aaron. Once, God promised miraculously to provide for the thirsty wanderers by having Moses command a certain rock to give water. Moses and Aaron stood together before the unhappy people and, in exasperation at the incipient revolt, Moses used his rod and twice struck the rock, saying, "Hear now, you rebels; shall we bring forth water for you out of this rock?" (Num. 20:10). Supported by Aaron, Moses had used God's gracious miracle to assert his own power and authority. As a result, the Lord ruled that neither Aaron nor Moses would be allowed to accompany the people into the Promised Land.

A few years later, as the 40 years of wandering drew to a close and the people came to Mount Hor near Edom, south of Canaan, God's judgment on the elder brother was fi-

Cain about to slay Abel, a late Gothic stained-glass window

nally carried out. In full priestly regalia, the 123-year-old Aaron climbed the mountain with his son Eleazar and Moses. Removing the high priest's vestments from Aaron, Moses put them on his nephew, and "Aaron died there on the top of the mountain" (Num. 20:28). Learning of Aaron's death, the people mourned for 30 days.

Later generations looked back to Moses as a unique figure without any real successor. Aaron, however, began a priestly dynasty that in spite of many vagaries continued more than a thousand years, till the Romans put an end to temple worship when they captured and destroyed Jerusalem in A.D. 70.

ABDON

(ab' dahn) HEBREW: AVDON
"service"

The son of Hillel, Abdon was one of the so-called minor judges of Israel (*see* **Tola**). He was from Pirathon, a town to the west of Shechem in the hill country that was wrested from the Amalekites and allotted to the tribe of Ephraim. The 40 sons and 30 grandsons riding on 70 asses mentioned in Judges 12:14 reveal the wealth of Abdon, who judged Israel for eight years.

ABEL

(ay' buhl) HEBREW: HEVEL
"breath" or "vapor"

The second son of **Adam** and **Eve** bore a name that matched his shortened life. Unlike his father and elder brother, **Cain**, who were farmers, Abel became "a keeper of sheep" (Gen. 4:2). In time, the brothers brought offerings to God, Cain's being some of his crops and Abel's being the fat portions of the firstborn lambs, in ancient times considered the very best kind of sacrifice. Somehow it became clear to the brothers that God had accepted Abel's offering but not Cain's. Cain was enraged and, luring his brother into the fields, he struck and killed him. Thus Abel, the first to offer an animal sacrifice, also became the first victim of violence in a religious controversy.

ABIATHAR

(ah bi' uh thahr) HEBREW: EVYATAR
"father is preeminent/abundant"

::::::::::

One of the chief priests of Israel during the reign of King **David**, Abiathar began his religious career at the side of his father, **Ahimelech**, chief priest of the Israelite shrine at Nob. That quiet life of priestly ritual was suddenly interrupted after David, in flight from **Saul**, sought sanctuary at Nob, where Abiathar's father gave him bread from the sacred stores and the sword with which David had slain the giant **Goliath**. When Saul learned that Ahimelech had helped David, he had the entire community of 85 priests and their families at Nob slaughtered. Only Abiathar escaped and fled after David.

In surviving the massacre at Nob, Abiathar was able to rescue the high priest's ephod, not the linen vestment also called an ephod but a box containing lots used by the high priest to discern God's will for the future. Later, Abiathar used the ephod to help David as he "inquired of the Lord" whether he should pursue the Amalekites, who had raided David's town of Ziklag, burned it, and taken captive its children and women—including David's two wives, **Ahinoam** and **Abigail**. "Pursue," Abiathar advised him; "for you shall surely overtake and shall surely rescue" (1 Sam. 30:8). And so it happened.

When David became king, established his capital in Jerusalem, and brought the ark of the covenant there, he appointed Abiathar as one of the two chief priests in charge of the new sanctuary, along with **Zadok**, the son of Ahitub. During the rebellion led by **Absalom**, the two priests were told by David to remain in Jerusalem even after the king withdrew from his capital. Thus, they were able to send information about the uprising to the king through their sons, Jonathan and Ahimaaz. After the rebellion was put down, Abiathar was instrumental in having David restored to his throne.

When David was about to die, Abiathar gave his support and advice to **Adonijah**, David's eldest surviving son and, it was thought, his heir apparent. He was evidently not aware, however, that David had promised his wife **Bathsheba** to put her son **Solomon** on the throne. When Solomon was crowned, he executed Adonijah and his principal supporters and deposed Abiathar. But out of respect for the priest's service to his father, the new king spared Abiathar's life and allowed him to retire to his family estate in Anathoth, northeast of Jerusalem. He was the last of the descendants of **Eli** to serve as high priest of Israel.

BROTHERS IN CONFLICT

Brother against brother—the conflict is as ancient as humanity. In the Bible it is often conflict between an elder and a younger brother, with the younger coming out ahead. It was the younger Abel who surpassed the elder Cain in offering a sacrifice pleasing to God. Cain seemed to recoup by killing Abel, but he was promptly driven away by the Lord and forced to yield his dominance to a still younger brother, Seth.

Isaac was the heir to God's promise to Abraham, though his elder brother, Ishmael, was legally the son of Sarah rather than the surrogate mother, Hagar. Jacob used trickery to get the birthright and blessings due his elder twin, Esau. Joseph's elder brothers hated him so much they sold him into slavery, but he rose to become lord of Egypt, in a position to hold his brothers' lives in his hands.

Abel falls beneath Cain's cruel blow in this 12th-century Italian mosaic.

ABIGAIL

(ab' i gayl) HEBREW: ABIGAYIL
"my father rejoices"

∙∙∙∙∙∙∙∙∙∙

An intelligent, decisive, and beautiful woman, Abigail was the wife first of **Nabal** of Carmel and later of King **David**. When Nabal, a wealthy herder, insulted David—at that time leader of a large outlaw band—Abigail forestalled David's revenge by independently approaching him with a gift of food for his men and an eloquent appeal for his forbearance: "Upon me alone, my lord, be the guilt" (1 Sam. 25:24). David was so impressed by her act of humility that, when Nabal collapsed and died at the news of what his wife had done, David wooed the widow for his own. Abigail faced many dangers from David's enemies and bore him his second son, called Chileab in 2 Samuel 3:3 but Daniel in 1 Chronicles 3:1.

ABIJAH

(ah bi' jah) HEBREW: ABIYAH
"Yahweh is my father"

∙∙∙∙∙∙∙∙∙∙

As the son of **Rehoboam** and grandson of **Solomon**, Abijah inherited a kingdom ruined by the foolishness of his father. From about 915 to 913 B.C. he ruled Judah, a small remnant of the substantial empire built by **David** but by then squandered. He was continually in conflict with the northern kingdom of Israel under **Jeroboam**. Though not the eldest of Rehoboam's 28 sons, Abijah was the first son of Rehoboam's favorite wife, Maacah, who perhaps was the daughter of King David's rebellious son **Absalom**. To show his favor, Rehoboam designated Abijah as his crown prince, while other sons were put in charge of various cities throughout the kingdom. Before he gained the throne of Judah, Abijah had dozens of sons and daughters by his 14 wives. In 1 Kings 14-15, he is called Abijam.

The biblical narrative gives Abijah two contrasting personalities. In 1 Kings 15:3, he is condemned because he "walked in all the sins which his father did before him." The narrative in 2 Chronicles 13, however, presents Abijah as a forceful defender of the Lord and of the temple worship in Jerusalem. In a speech he gave before a battle against Jeroboam, whose army outnumbered his own two to one, Abijah shouted, "God is with us at our head" and warned the northern army not to fight against the Lord "for you cannot succeed" (2 Chr. 13:12). Despite the odds, Abijah won the battle and captured three cities from the north but could not overthrow Jeroboam. Abijah's reign lasted only three years; the cause of his death is unknown. His son **Asa** succeeded him.

Abigail's offering, by David Teniers the Elder (1582-1649)

A woman of Thebez heaves the millstone that crushed Abimelech's head.

ABIMELECH

(ah bim' e lek) HEBREW: AVIMELECH
"my father is king"

The name Abimelech was perhaps the royal title of the kings of Gerar in southwestern Canaan. In Genesis 20, **Abraham visits Gerar and, fearing that the king will kill him to take his wife **Sarah**, pretends that Sarah is his sister, just as he had earlier done in Egypt. Abimelech indeed claims Sarah, but God warns him in a dream that he must die for such a transgression. After protesting his innocence to the Lord, Abimelech upbraids Abraham for his deception and returns Sarah along with a lavish gift. Later, Abimelech made a treaty with Abraham by which he ceded rights to the well at Beer-sheba to the Hebrew patriarch.

ABIMELECH 2

The Abimelech of Gerar in the time of **Isaac** is called king of the Philistines. As his father, **Abraham**, had done, Isaac came to Gerar and out of fear pretended that his wife **Rebekah** was his sister. Abimelech, however, discovered the deception when he saw "Isaac fondling Rebekah" and rebuked him. "Whoever touches this man or his wife," Abimelech warned his people, "shall be put to death" (Gen. 26:8, 11).

ABIMELECH 3

Abimelech the son of **Gideon** was the first to try to make Israel a kingdom. Gideon had founded a huge clan with 70 sons from many wives; Abimelech's mother was a Canaanite concubine from Shechem. Many in Israel had urged Gideon to become king after his victory over the Midianites, but he refused and instead left behind his sons as a dominant oligarchy.

Relying on the desire for monarchy, Abimelech conspired with his mother's clan in Shechem to assassinate all of his brothers and establish himself as king. Only his youngest brother, **Jotham**, escaped the slaughter and fled. But the men of Shechem tired of their king once he moved his residence south to Arumah, and they turned to Gaal son of Ebed, who stirred up rebellion. Abimelech retaliated with a strike at Shechem, razing the city and burning its nearby fortress. He then besieged the rebels at Thebez. But a woman defender atop a tower threw a millstone that struck Abimelech in the head. The wounded ruler ordered his armor-bearer to dispatch him so that no one could say, "a woman killed him" (Jg. 9:54). Abimelech's kingdom lasted three years.

ABINADAB

(ah bin' uh dab) HEBREW: AVINADAV
"my father is noble"

A prominent resident of Kiriath-jearim, a hill town northwest of Jerusalem, Abinadab provided a sanctuary for the ark of the covenant for many years. The Philistines had captured the ark which had been taken from its sanctuary at Shiloh. But when the Lord afflicted them with a plague, the Philistines put the ark on a cart pulled by two cows and sent it back across the border to a town near Kiriath-jearim. Not knowing how to treat such a holy object, the people turned to Abinadab, who was apparently a priest. He brought the ark to his hilltop house and consecrated his son Eleazar "to have charge of the ark of the Lord" (1 Sam. 7:2). The ark remained there 20 years before **David** moved it to Jerusalem.

ABISHAG

(ab' i shag) HEBREW: AVISHAG
"my father is a wanderer"

When King **David** grew "old and advanced in years," Abishag, a beautiful young woman from Shunem, was selected to nurse him. She lay beside David so that her

The ark in the land of the Philistines; a fresco from the third-century A.D. synagogue at Dura Europas in Syria

body would restore warmth and vigor to his, "but the king knew her not" (1 Kg. 1:1, 4)— that is, he did not have sexual relations with her. After David's death, **Solomon** had his elder brother **Adonijah** executed for asking to marry Abishag. Solomon interpreted the request as but the prelude to a demand for the kingdom itself since Adonijah had been passed over for the succession.

ABISHAI

(ah bee' shai) HEBREW: AVISHAI
"father exists" or "father is Jesse"

A warrior to the core, Abishai was one of David's inner circle of military leaders and a staunch defender of the king. He was the eldest of three brothers, the others being **Joab**, who became commander of David's army, and **Asahel**, a soldier known for being fleet of foot. The brothers were David's nephews, sons of his sister **Zeruiah**. Their father is not identified in the Bible.

Abishai seems to have been the first of the three to join his uncle, when David was an outlaw fleeing from King **Saul**. He initially appears as a volunteer who went with David on a perilous mission in which the pair of them crept into Saul's camp, right up to where the king was sleeping. The hotheaded Abishai was eager to kill Saul, to "pin him to the earth with one stroke of the spear," but David forbade him to do so. "Who can put forth his hand against the Lord's anointed, and be guiltless?" (1 Sam. 26:8, 9), David

asked his companion before leading him away from the enemy camp.

After Saul's death, Abishai and Joab developed a blood feud against **Abner**, Saul's chief commander, who had killed their brother Asahel and was then supporting the claim of Saul's son **Ish-bosheth** to the throne. Later, when Abner agreed to a truce with David and was ready to back him as king, Abishai helped his brother Joab take revenge and murder Abner. David was so angry that he gave Abner a state funeral. "These men the sons of Zeruiah," David said, "are too hard for me" (2 Sam. 3:39). Still, David took advantage of what Abishai and Joab had done to consolidate his power over the kingdom.

Once during David's wars with the Philistines, Abishai saved the king's life. David faced one of the Philistine giants in battle and was on the point of being killed, when Abishai "came to his aid" (2 Sam. 21:17) and slew the Philistine. Abishai rose to be a senior commander of David's army and was in charge of the Thirty, an elite corps of warriors in Israel. He became famous for heroic exploits, especially one in which he killed 300 men with his spear.

The writers of the biblical narrative often describe Abishai's tendency toward violence in order to contrast his character with that of the more gentle David. When David was fleeing from the rebel **Absalom** and a man named **Shimei** cursed the weakened king, Abishai was ready to "take off his head" (2 Sam. 16:9), but David restrained him. After

David's victory, Shimei begged David's forgiveness, but Abishai wanted to execute him. Again, the narrators highlight David's compassion. Much of the blame for violence in David's reign is laid on Abishai and Joab, though David often used these fierce warriors to his advantage, as when he sent them in relentless pursuit of another rebel, **Sheba**.

Abishai evidently died before David, since he is not mentioned in the conflicts over the succession in which his brother Joab was on the losing side.

ABNER
(ab' nuhr) HEBREW: AVNER
"my father is the light bearer"

The cousin of King **Saul**, Abner served as commander in chief of Israel's armies and as one of the king's closest advisers. His father, Ner, and Saul's father, Kish, were brothers, leaders of a wealthy clan of Benjaminites that Abner hoped would found a permanent dynasty in Israel. It is ironic, therefore, that Abner's first action described in the biblical narrative is to introduce the youthful **David**, who had just slain the giant **Goliath**, to Saul.

The relationship between David and Saul was profoundly to affect the remainder of Abner's life. Though David was from the rival tribe of Judah, his heroic exploits as a warrior caused Saul to promote him in rank until he was a senior commander under Abner and more celebrated by the people than any other soldier—even the king himself. Then, as Saul's murderous jealousy drove David from court, Abner remained "by Saul's side" (1 Sam. 20:25), more faithful to the monarch even than Saul's own son **Jonathan**, who aided David.

With Abner as his commander and personal bodyguard, the king pursued David through the wilderness. Once David successfully stole into Saul's camp by night and could have killed the king; he later mockingly chided Abner from a distance for not keeping better watch over Saul's safety.

After Saul died at the battle of Gilboa (c. 1004 B.C.), Abner used his military power to support Saul's son **Ish-bosheth** as king, even as David was establishing a breakaway kingdom to the south in Judah. Ish-bosheth, however, was a weak leader, dominated by Abner, who moved him from Gibeah, Saul's capital, across the Jordan and safely out of David's reach.

Civil war flared. At Gibeon, Abner's forces confronted David's men, led by the brothers **Joab**, **Abishai**, and **Asahel**. When the fierce battle went against him,

Abner found himself fleeing from the combat pursued by the swift Asahel. As Asahel was about to catch the older warrior, Abner rammed the butt of his spear through the belly of his pursuer and killed him. From that moment on Abner was marked for death by Joab and Abishai. For the moment, however, Abner and his remaining men were able to retreat across the Jordan.

As the months passed, Abner could not hide his growing contempt for the weak Ish-bosheth. When Ish-bosheth accused Abner of taking Rizpah, one of Saul's concubines, for himself, Abner exploded and renounced his allegiance to Ish-bosheth. Abner opened negotiations with David and eventually met with him in Hebron, while Joab and Abishai were away, and agreed to help unite the kingdom again under David. Shortly after Abner left Hebron, however, the brothers returned and learned what had happened. Secretly, Joab sent messengers to recall Abner for a supposedly friendly meeting. As soon as Abner got back to Hebron, Joab "took him aside . . . to speak with him privately" (2 Sam. 3:27) at the city gate, then murdered him with a blow to the belly that mimicked his brother's death wound.

David was so angry with Joab for killing this powerful man who had just sworn his allegiance that he forced Joab and his men to mourn for Abner in sackcloth while David himself led the funeral lament.

DOUBLETS

What can one make of a story that seems to be told twice or even three times—a literary phenomenon called a doublet. For example, a patriarch goes to a foreign land, pretends his wife is his sister, and nearly loses her. But the deception is discovered, and he is sent away wealthier. This story occurs three times in Genesis—twice for Abraham and once for Isaac—and has caused readers to ask: Did the same basic events simply occur twice or three times or are these different versions of the same story coming from different sources?

ABRAHAM

(a' bruh ham) HEBREW: ABRAHAM

"father of a multitude"

::::::::::

The first great patriarch of the nation of Israel, Abraham is also revered as the epitome of human faith in the will of God by Christians and Muslims. Indeed, Abraham's very name, though of disputed linguistic origin, has been taken to mean "father of a multitude" (Gen. 17:5). His story in Genesis, which seems to be a compilation from three separate and independent original sources, explains how and why the clan of Abraham made its way to Palestine from the Tigris-Euphrates basin, or Mesopotamia.

Yet this towering figure is frankly portrayed in the Old Testament as a flawed, contradictory human being whose personal struggle is a profound and often surprising spiritual drama. Sometimes impatient and deceitful, Abraham comes only slowly to full realization of the true nature of the Lord's revelations and promises to him and to his descendants.

Abraham, originally known as Abram ("exalted father"), was probably born some 4,000 years ago in the famous Babylonian city known as Ur of the Chaldeans, which was situated in what is now Iraq. A direct descendant of **Noah**'s son **Shem**, he was a wealthy man, the head of a seminomadic clan that lived by herding large flocks and by seasonal farming. Perhaps because of an invasion of Ur by the Amorites, Abram's father **Terah** decided to move his family to Haran, a prosperous town 500 miles away from Ur in what is now southeastern Turkey. The two cities may have enjoyed a close relationship, for the inhabitants of both worshiped Sin, a moon god. As the years passed, one great void remained in Abram's prosperous, pastoral life. His remarkably beautiful wife and paternal half sister Sarai (**Sarah**) "was barren; she had no child" (Gen. 11:30).

A PROMISE OF GREATNESS

Abram was given his first test of faith at the age of 75, when God appeared to him and promised that he would become the father of a great nation, but only if he left his homeland and most of his relations behind to strike out for the alien region of Canaan, some 400 miles to the south. "I will bless those who bless you, and him who curses you I will curse," said the Lord; "and by you all the families of the earth shall bless themselves" (Gen. 12:3).

Evidently, Abram's faith at this point was extraordinarily strong, for he immediately gathered up his household and left the set-

THE CALL OF ABRAHAM

The moment when God summoned Abraham to leave his home for an unknown land marks the first great turning point in biblical history. In the earlier narratives of Genesis—from Adam and Eve, to Noah, to the tower of Babel—God was always seen dealing with all of humanity. Even when he saved individuals like Noah and his family, he saved them from a judgment that applied to all the world.

With Abraham there is a difference: God selects a particular man and his family as the recipients of his special revelation, care, and promises. At first, nothing is said of why Abraham was selected; Genesis simply tells the story, thereby beginning a family saga, the history of the chosen people, that continues throughout the Bible. As the narrative progresses, it reveals Abraham as a man of remarkable faith and obedience, who rises to become worthy of God's favor. But God is the principal actor: God decides to call Abraham, leads him to a new land and promises it to his descendants, saves Abraham from his own mistakes and failures, gives Abraham a son and tests Abraham's faith, and continues his covenant with Abraham's descendants. Abraham receives all these gifts, promises, and challenges with faith, gratitude, and a noble submission—truly deserving of being called "the father of us all" (Rom 4:16).

At the head of his clan, Abraham sets out for the Promised Land.

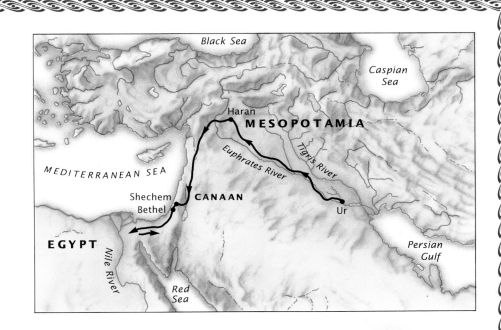

Abraham's caravan en route to the Promised Land, an Italian painting dated c. 1575

tlement of his father and other kinsmen. Sarai joined her husband on this challenging journey, as did his brother's son **Lot**, but the travels and travails of their household had only begun. Wandering through the foreign land of Canaan, Abram may have wondered how it could possibly become the property of his unborn progeny. The area was already well-settled—the Bible mentions ten separate peoples who lived there. But once again, God appeared and explicitly stated, "To your descendants I will give this land" (Gen. 12:7). Abram paused to camp in the region at least twice and set up altars to God: near the oak of Moreh at Shechem and also on a mountain to the east of Bethel. These acts were certainly significant in a country dedicated to worship of the pagan god **Baal**.

As time passed, however, and Abram remained childless and found himself still surrounded in the Promised Land by the pagan Canaanites, it seems that his faith in God's pledge began to waver. For when a severe famine swept through Canaan, he did not wait for the Lord to take care of him and his family. Instead, he immediately pulled up stakes and led his household down into fertile, flourishing Egypt in search of food.

Then Abram revealed still another puzzling aspect of his character. Afraid that he would be killed by some Egyptian eager to seize his beautiful wife, he claimed that Sarai was his unmarried sister and did not object when she was taken into the Egyptian Pharaoh's household. The grateful monarch repaid Abram for this gift with "sheep, oxen, he-asses, menservants, maidservants, she-asses, and camels" (Gen. 12:16). Not until God ravaged the land with severe plagues, which were considered in ancient times to be divine punishment for disobedience or sin, did the unsuspecting ruler discover the truth about Sarai. Appalled, he summoned Abram and cried, "What is this you have done to me? Why did you not tell me that she was your wife? . . . take her, and be gone" (Gen. 12:18-19). Pharaoh swiftly restored Sarai to her husband and encouraged the entire family to return to Canaan.

The story of Abram's reprehensible deception is doubly significant. For one thing, it is another indication that the patriarch was not yet ready to trust completely in the divine promise, which certainly implied that God would ensure his safety, even from foreigners who might be struck by Sarai's beauty. For another, the Lord's response proved that he would forever stand by his chosen servant, even when Abram showed himself to be a fallible human being who had to be rescued from a foolish predicament he had created for himself.

Meanwhile, despite these distractions,

Abram and Lot had acquired so much cattle that the pasturage back in the hills of Bethel was no longer sufficient for them to share by the time they returned to Canaan. When fighting broke out between their herdsmen, Abram generously offered to cede to his nephew whichever area of Canaan he chose. "Is not the whole land before you?" he asked. "Separate yourself from me. If you take the left hand, then I will go to the right; or if you take the right hand, then I will go to the left" (Gen. 13:9). The younger man quickly opted for the best possible site, the extremely fertile Jordan valley, described in Genesis as "well watered everywhere like the garden of the Lord, like the land of Egypt" (Gen. 13:10). Lot removed his household to a city known as Sodom, which was infamous for the degeneracy of its inhabitants.

In this incident, God's chosen one not only demonstrated the benevolence of a clan patriarch toward a younger kinsman, he also parceled out territory with the authority of someone who confidently believed that his descendants would someday inherit all of the land that was still heavily populated by Canaanites. By contrast, Lot is shown in a disagreeably selfish light, probably to compare this ancestor of the Ammonites and Moabites unfavorably with his uncle, the ancestor of the Israelites.

THE PROMISE REPEATED

Perhaps in response to this demonstration of faith, God appeared and specifically repeated the promise, even urging Abram to "Arise, walk through the length and the breadth of the land, for I will give it to you" (Gen. 13:17). For the first time it is made clear that Canaan will be given directly to Abram during his lifetime, not just to his descendants some time in the future. Moreover, God expanded his earlier promise to say that the still childless Abram would father descendants as innumerable "as the dust of the earth; so that if one can count the dust of the earth, your descendants also can be counted" (Gen. 13:16).

Obeying the divine commandment to familiarize himself with the territory, Abram led his household throughout the area and then decided to set up his tents in Hebron, beside the oak trees at a place called Mamre, later described as belonging to an Amorite named Mamre. The site of these oaks assumed great historical significance for Judaism, for the altar that the patriarch built there became an important sanctuary for the Jews' traditional remembrance of the man who later became known as Abraham.

Sometime after the move to Mamre, circumstances forced Abram to go into battle,

the only time this man of peace is shown taking the role of military hero. Four powerful kings from the East joined forces to attack and plunder Sodom, its sister city Gomorrah, and three other Dead Sea settlements, carrying Lot and his household into captivity. Assembling a force of 318 of his own retainers, Abram chased after the interlopers and put them to rout north of Damascus. He not only rescued his nephew and the other captives but was also able to retrieve the valuable booty seized by the four royal invaders.

Upon his return to Canaan, Abram was ritually blessed by **Melchizedek**, the king of Salem, an early name for Jerusalem, and "priest of God Most High" (Gen. 14:18)—in this case, the Canaanite deity El. In addition, the grateful king of Sodom offered to let Abram keep the spoils taken from the city, but he replied, "I have sworn to the Lord God Most High, maker of heaven and earth, that I would not take a thread or a sandal-thong or anything that is yours, lest you should say, 'I have made Abram rich'" (Gen. 14:22–23). In using the phrase "Lord God Most High," Abram was referring not to El but to the Lord.

In other words, it seems that Abram continued to trust fully in God's protection at that point. Soon afterward, however, he was questioning the Lord as to why he and Sarai were still childless, even though ten years had passed since the divine commandment to move to Canaan. "Look toward heaven, and number the stars, if you are able to number them," the Lord replied. "So shall

Melchizedek greets Abraham with bread and wine; a medieval stained-glass window.

your descendants be" (Gen. 15:5). Abram fell into a deep sleep, and God revealed even more of the future, explaining that his chosen people would be held captive in Egypt for 400 years, then be freed at last to return to the land promised to them. But he also confided that Abram himself would not suffer: "As for yourself, you shall go to your fathers in peace; you shall be buried in a good old age" (Gen. 15:15). When Abram awoke, the Lord for the first time revealed the actual extent of the land of promise, which would stretch "from the river of Egypt [the brook of Egypt in the Sinai Peninsula] to the great river, the river Euphrates" (Gen. 15:18).

Astonishingly, Abram must now have become too impatient to believe this latest affirmation of the promise and decided to take matters into his own hands. At Sarai's suggestion, he took her Egyptian maid **Hagar** as a concubine in order to produce an heir. The son of this liaison was named **Ishmael**.

A CHANGE OF NAMES

At this point, the biblical story flashes forward 13 years. When Abram was 99, God appeared and once more repeated his promise of land and descendants. As token of this binding covenant, he changed Abram's name to Abraham, evidently expanding the meaning of the original name from "exalted father" to "father of a multitude." Sarai became Sarah, both words meaning "princess." When the Lord also explicitly pledged that a son would be born to Sarah, Abraham literally fell down laughing at the very idea. "Shall a child be born to a man who is a hundred years old?" he asked. "Shall Sarah, who is ninety years old, bear a child?" (Gen. 17:17) Unmoved, God explained that the boy would be born within the year and should be named **Isaac**, meaning "he laughs."

God also revealed a new ritual requirement for Abraham and all of his promised male descendants: "You shall be circumcised . . . [as] a sign of the covenant between me and you" (Gen. 17:11). Abraham thereupon circumcised himself and then performed the same operation on 13-year-old Ishmael and all of the males in the household. In the future, the ceremony producing this irreversible sign of membership in the Israelite community of the covenant was to take place as soon as a male infant was eight days old. Down to the present, the Jewish circumcision rite or *brith* continues to include the phrase, "entry into the covenant of Abraham our father."

Sometime thereafter, Abraham was resting from the noontime heat in the cool shade of his tent when three strangers suddenly appeared in front of him. As eastern hospitality required, he rushed to welcome them, hastily ordering a small feast to be prepared, including a freshly killed calf. After these heavenly visitors sat down and ate beneath the oaks of Mamre, the Lord revealed his identity by repeating his vow that Sarah would give birth by spring. Listening from inside the tent, she laughed out loud, as her husband had done, saying, "Shall I indeed bear a child, now that I am old?" "Is anything too hard for the Lord?" her visitor countered. Terrified, Sarah denied that she had laughed, but God replied, "No, but you did laugh" (Gen. 18:13-14, 15). For all of its homely and comic touches, this announcement of Isaac's birth was taken by Christian artists of the Middle Ages to prefigure the angelic Annunciation of the birth of **Jesus** in the New Testament.

On this day, it turns out, God had paused on his way to more troubling business, having come to judge Sodom and Gomorrah because of the outcry against their wickedness. When he does Abraham the great honor of sharing this information, his chosen servant, in a moving scene, shows himself worthy to be the father of nations by daring to intercede for these foreigners. "Wilt thou indeed destroy the righteous with the wicked?" he asks (Gen. 18:23). Abraham wins the Lord's agreement to spare the cities if 50 "righteous" can be found, then

Abraham welcoming the three celestial visitors to his tent; an 18th-century Jewish manuscript

As her husband and daughters flee, Lot's wife fatefully turns to view Sodom's destruction; a painting by Raphael.

continues to bargain the number down to a mere ten such people, daring to call down God's wrath on himself in order to save others.

For religious scholars, this determined intercession is profoundly significant, and not simply because Abraham might have come close to winning an argument with the Lord. Rather, he introduced an important new concept: the possibility that sinners could be saved from destruction by the mere existence of even a small number of God-fearing people. Moreover, by trying to rescue the two non-Israelite cities, he was fulfilling God's earlier promise that he would be a blessing to other nations.

But the depraved citizens of Sodom and Gomorrah proved too wicked even for Abraham's intervention. The angels of the Lord could not find even ten righteous persons. Early the next morning, when the patriarch arose and went out to gaze down on the valley of the Jordan where his brother's son had chosen to settle, "the smoke of the land went up like the smoke of a furnace" (Gen. 19:28). In response to Abraham's plea the day before, however, God had warned Lot and his family. Though Lot's wife and sons-in-law perished in the holocaust, Lot and his two daughters survived, eventually settling elsewhere in the eastern highlands.

Not long afterward, Abraham interceded with God again, but this time after he himself had put an innocent man in jeopardy. For some reason that is not given in the Bible, he moved his household from Mamre to Gerar in the Negeb region. There, he introduced Sarah as his sister to the local monarch, King **Abimelech**. As in the similar episode that took place earlier in Egypt, the king brought Sarah into his house but did not sleep with her. Nevertheless, in a terrifying dream, the Lord warned Abimelech, "Behold, you are a dead man, because of the woman whom you have taken; for she is a man's wife" (Gen. 20:3).

The next morning, the stunned king, like the Egyptian Pharaoh before him, summoned Abraham for an explanation. "I did it," he said, "because I thought, There is no fear of God at all in this place, and they will kill me because of my wife" (Gen. 20:11). The pagan Abimelech forthwith returned Sarah to her husband, presented him with slaves and cattle and 1,000 pieces of silver, then assured Abraham that he could settle nearby wherever he chose. Meanwhile, God had punished all of the women in the royal household with infertility. In response to Abraham's prayers, however, they were restored to health and the king was forgiven.

A WELL, AN OATH, A TREE

Despite this episode, the pagan ruler and the ancestor of Israel became firm allies. When Abimelech's servants took sole possession of a well that had been dug by members of Abraham's household, the two leaders made a famous covenant of peace, swearing an oath at the spot. The well was named Beer-sheba, perhaps meaning "well

Abraham sending Hagar and Ishmael into the wilderness;
detail of a 17th-century painting

of the oath." The patriarch then planted a tamarisk tree at the site and worshiped God, thus implying that the area would someday belong to his descendants.

When Abraham reached the age of 100, the son he and Sarah had been craving since the divine promise a quarter century earlier was at last born. As they had been directed, the ecstatic old couple named him Isaac, and he was circumcised by his father on his eighth day of life. Now the household was filled with the laughter of joy, not disbelief. As Sarah put it, "God has made laughter for me; every one who hears will laugh over me" (Gen. 21:6).

Unfortunately, this happiness was eventually marred by domestic strife. Watching the teenaged Ishmael at play with her cherished toddler son, Sarah became jealous and demanded that Abraham cast out the older boy and his slave mother. Abraham was loath to banish his elder son, but God told him to do as Sarah had asked, saying "through Isaac shall your descendants be named" (Gen. 21:12).

BANISHED TO THE WILDERNESS

Early one morning, the patriarch gave Hagar and Ishmael a small ration of bread and water and reluctantly sent them away. Wandering in the desert near Beer-sheba, Hagar became desperate when these provisions gave out and decided to abandon her son beneath a bush, unable to watch as he slowly died of thirst. God, hearing the suffering Ishmael's terrified cries, called down to show Hagar a well and urged her to take

care of the boy, reassuring her that Ishmael would grow up to father a great nation.

This compelling story has been variously interpreted. Some commentators have argued that Ishmael was not suitable to be the instrument of God's promise to Abraham because he was the son of a foreigner and slave. Yet, according to the custom of the day, the boy would have been considered to be Sarah's legal son. Rather, the real obstacle to Ishmael's becoming the heir to the promise was probably the lack of faith that led to his birth. In deciding to use Hagar as a surrogate mother, both Abraham and Sarah had not been willing to wait until the Lord saw fit to present them with a child of their own.

The torments suffered by Ishmael and his mother would pale beside the excruciating ordeal Abraham would be forced to endure once Isaac alone was his heir. One day, without warning, the man who had so often doubted the divine promise, who had waited a quarter century for a son by his wife, was ordered to kill the boy in a blood sacrifice on the mountains of Moriah and to burn his body as an offering to the Lord.

"Take your son, your only son Isaac, whom you love" (Gen. 22:2), said God, at the beginning of a story that not only tested Abraham's faith but has confused and troubled many Jews and Christians since. What did Abraham, who had argued with God to save the lives of sinners in Sodom, think about this apparently cruel command? The Bible is silent on the subject. The aged father is shown getting up in the morning and cutting wood, as he would for an ordinary animal sacrifice. Following God's instructions, he saddled an ass and rode with Isaac and two young retainers until they reached a designated spot on the third day of their mysterious journey.

Leaving the servants to guard the ass, father and son walked farther on, to the place God had chosen for the sacrifice. Isaac carried the wood, Abraham the fire and the knife. When the boy wondered aloud why they had not brought a lamb with them, his father responded with the memorable and heartbreaking answer, "God will provide himself the lamb for a burnt offering, my son" (Gen. 22:8).

Still without revealing his feelings, Abraham erected an altar at the forlorn site and piled the wood upon it. Then he tied Isaac's limbs together, as he would those of any other sacrificial animal, and laid him upon the pyre. Not until he grasped the knife and prepared to slay his son did God intervene. "Do not lay your hand on the lad or do anything to him," the Lord called out, "for now I know that you fear God, seeing you have not withheld your son, your only son, from me" (Gen. 22:12). Nearby was a ram, caught by the horns in a thicket, which Abraham could now offer as an acceptable sacrifice. Then, for the last and most momentous time, God affirmed his promise that this chosen servant would be blessed, would become the ancestor of a posterity beyond numbering, and would be the instrument through which all of the world's peoples would be blessed because he obeyed the terrible command to sacrifice his son.

Thus, Abraham's unforgettable act of obedience becomes the climax of his life story. Remarkably, although neither father nor son speaks openly about his inner feelings, the story is an intensely poignant human drama, revealing that each feels infinite trust in the other and also in the will of God.

To some experts in the history of ancient reli-

gions, the story seems intended to symbolize the Israelites' repudiation of the child sacrifice ritually practiced by some of their pagan neighbors. This interpretation is not universally accepted, however. In mainstream Judaism, the patriarch's acceptance of God's will is considered a model for the faithful as well as a symbol of Jewish martyrdom. To some early Christian theologians, Abraham's obedience throughout this trial was thought to anticipate the submission of Jesus to his death on the cross.

THE FAMILY'S BURIAL CAVE

After this dramatic climax, little more is heard of Abraham, aside from a few particulars about the settling of his earthly affairs. Upon Sarah's death in Hebron at the age of 127, he purchased a family burial cave there, along with an adjacent field, for 400 silver shekels. In this instance, he was legally purchasing a portion of the land that would eventually come to him, and he be-

The angel stays Abraham's hand as he is about to obey the Lord's command to sacrifice Isaac; an early-17th-century painting.

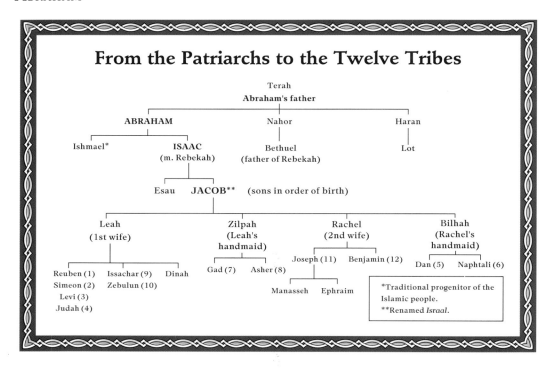

From the Patriarchs to the Twelve Tribes

Terah
Abraham's father

ABRAHAM — Nahor — Haran

Ishmael* — **ISAAC** (m. Rebekah) — Bethuel (father of Rebekah) — Lot

Esau — **JACOB**** (sons in order of birth)

Leah (1st wife) — Zilpah (Leah's handmaid) — Rachel (2nd wife) — Bilhah (Rachel's handmaid)

Joseph (11) — Benjamin (12) — Dan (5) — Naphtali (6)

Gad (7) — Asher (8)

Reuben (1) — Issachar (9) — Dinah
Simeon (2) — Zebulun (10)
Levi (3)
Judah (4)

Manasseh — Ephraim

*Traditional progenitor of the Islamic people.
**Renamed *Israal*.

came owner rather than heir to the promise. The site, known as the Cave of Machpelah, became the final resting place of Abraham and the other patriarchs, as well, and it is revered even today by Jews, Christians, and Muslims as a sacred spot.

Three years after Sarah's death, Abraham bestirred himself to find an appropriate wife for Isaac, who was by then 40 years old. Surrounded by the many alien cultures of Canaan, Abraham was determined that his son marry someone from among his own people. On the one hand, he did not want his heir to be seduced by the pagan religion of the Canaanites, whose fertility rites would become a source of continuing temptation to the incautious Israelites over the centuries.

On the other, he did not want his son to have to leave the Promised Land to find a suitable wife and then settle down with her relatives elsewhere. Therefore, he commissioned the trusted old servant who managed his household to travel back to Haran and select the best candidate from among the eligible women in the kinship network there. The majordomo chose **Rebekah**, who was the young granddaughter of one of the patriarch's own brothers and who fulfilled the requirement of a bride from within the clan that was so important in those times.

Once this responsibility was discharged, Abraham married a woman named **Keturah**, but he took special care that their children and the sons of his concubines did not become a threat

Sarah (left) listens from the doorway as Abraham brings food to his heavenly guests (center) and the sacrifice of Isaac (right); a sixth-century mosaic from Ravenna, Italy

to Isaac's inheritance. These other offspring were well provided for and sent off to live in lands to the east. When Abraham died at the age of 175, Isaac and Ishmael together laid him to rest beside Sarah in the family burial cave. (Eventually, according to tradition, Isaac and Rebekah, their son, **Jacob,** his first wife, **Leah**, and possibly **Joseph** were also interred there.)

References to Abraham are scattered throughout the Old Testament. During the great national crisis of exile in Babylon, he came to epitomize the hope of the expatriates to return one day to their native land and reestablish their nation. In Psalm 105, for example, Israel's national identity is emphatically rooted in God's selection of Abraham as his special servant and in the covenant established between them. "He [the Lord] is mindful of his covenant for ever," writes the psalmist, "of the word that he commanded, for a thousand generations, the covenant which he made with Abraham" (Ps. 105:8-9).

The promise is specifically repeated to his son Isaac, notably in Genesis 26:3: "Sojourn in this land, and I will be with you, and will bless you; for to you and to your descendants I will give all these lands, and I will fulfill the oath which I swore to Abraham your father." God also repeats the promise to Jacob, and both Joseph and **Moses** expect Israel to benefit from it.

FAITH OVER LAW

After the death of **Jesus**, his followers reinterpreted the mission of Abraham, who is mentioned 72 times in the New Testament, more frequently than any other Old Testament figure except Moses. For the apostle **Paul**, the life of the patriarch proves that faith is more important to salvation than Mosaic Law, for Abraham believed in God before he was ordered to undergo the ritual of circumcision. Paul believed that the coming of Jesus made it possible to recapture the pristine faith of Abraham. In other words, God does not require that people follow the laws and rites of religion in order to be considered righteous. In Paul's view, therefore, Abraham is actually the father of all those who have faith in God, not just the father of the nation and religion of Israel. By the same token, Abraham's selection as God's chosen one should be regarded as extending to all others who also have faith in the Lord. Those who have faith are each and every one God's chosen.

From a slightly different perspective, Paul also argues that Gentiles who believe in God receive his blessing through Jesus, who is genealogically the seed of Abraham. "Now

Jesus in the lap of Abraham, from a 13th-century illuminated manuscript

the promises were made to Abraham and his offspring," he wrote. "It does not say, 'And to offsprings,' referring to many; but, referring to one, 'And to your offspring,' which is Christ" (Gal. 3:16). In yet another New Testament interpretation, the author of the letter to the Hebrews argues that Abraham's willingness to sacrifice Isaac proves that the dead will be resurrected by God: "He who had received the promises was ready to offer up his only son, of whom it was said, 'Through Isaac shall your descendants be named.' He considered that God was able to raise men even from the dead" (Heb. 11:17-19). From the very same incident, however, James draws a different moral, arguing that Abraham's conduct on the mountains of Moriah proves that faith in God must be demonstrated by "works" or action. "Do you want to be shown, you shallow man, that faith apart from works is barren?" he writes. "Was not Abraham our father justified by works, when he offered his son Isaac upon the altar? You see that faith was active along with his works, and faith was completed by works" (Jas. 2:20-22).

The well-known phrase "Abraham's bosom" is mentioned only once in the New Testament, when **Luke**, telling the story of the poor man known as **Lazarus**, writes that he "died and was carried by the angels to Abraham's bosom" (Lk. 16:22). The use of this image to refer to heavenly rest for the righteous comes from rabbinic tradition.

The death of Absalom; a 12th-century stone capital from a French church

ABSALOM

(ab' suh luhm) HEBREW: AVSHALOM
"father is peace"

By leading a rebellion against his father, King **David**, Absalom seems to have lived to contradict the meaning of his name. The king's third son, Absalom was born during David's early reign over Judah at Hebron. His mother was Maacah, daughter of the king of Geshur, a nation northeast of the Sea of Galilee. David's second son, Chileab, evidently died young, leaving the handsome, ambitious Absalom second in line of succession after his half brother **Amnon**.

The inevitable tensions between these royal sons of different mothers exploded into a mortal hatred while Absalom was still a youth. Amnon lured **Tamar**, Absalom's full sister, into his house and raped the girl. Devastated, Tamar went to Absalom for protection, while her father, David—though angry—did nothing to punish Amnon for his transgression. Absalom was filled with loathing for Amnon but patiently waited two years before exacting revenge. He invited Amnon with David's other sons to a sheep-shearing festival and, when Amnon was "merry with wine" (2 Sam. 13:28), had him murdered.

Fearing blood vengeance, Absalom fled north to his grandfather's court in Geshur. There he remained three years before **Joab**, commander of the army, was able to persuade David to allow the refugee a safe return. Yet two more years passed before David was willing to meet with his son, and by that time Absalom's resentment had

hardened into a determination to overthrow his father. Absalom used his winning personality and remarkable good looks in a methodical campaign to build a loyal following for himself and to stir resentment against David—in the process, as the biblical text states, "Absalom stole the hearts of the men of Israel" (2 Sam. 15:6).

Absalom sounded the trumpet of rebellion in Hebron, his own birthplace and David's original capital. The popular response was overwhelming. People with any sort of grievance against David flocked to his son's cause—even **Ahithophel**, one of David's most trusted advisers. But David was not without resources. Though he fled Jerusalem, seemingly helpless before the revolt, he left behind loyal followers, such as **Hushai** the Archite, who insinuated themselves into Absalom's confidence. When Ahithophel urged Absalom to send soldiers quickly to assassinate the king, Hushai was able to divert Absalom to a more cautious course in which he would personally lead an army against his father. Hushai's advice allowed David time to muster his battle-tested troops to meet the attack of his rebel son.

The battle took place east of the Jordan River in the dense forest of Ephraim. As the contest turned against him, Absalom fled. His mule ran beneath a spreading oak tree, and Absalom's head with its thick flowing hair became wedged between the branches. Joab again intervened, but this time to dispatch the dangling rebel with three darts through the chest. David, who in spite of everything still loved his son, could not celebrate his victory, but wept openly upon hearing the news: "O my son Absalom, my son, my son Absalom! Would I had died instead of you" (2 Sam. 18:33).

ACHAN

(ay' kan) HEBREW: AKHAN
"troubler"

As the man who stole some of the forbidden spoils of Jericho, Achan the son of Carmi became legendary as "the troubler of Israel" (1 Chr. 2:7). Invading Canaan, Israel was on a mission of holy war and, before Jericho fell, the people were warned that everything in the city was "devoted to the Lord for destruction" (Jos. 6:17).

When Achan hid for himself some silver, gold, and clothing, his act defiled the whole people, and God was so angry that he caused Israel's strong army to be routed by a small force from the town of Ai. God warned **Joshua** that Israel had sinned, and Joshua used a system of lots to identify the culprit. When Achan confessed to the crime, he and his children were stoned to death and all his possessions, including the spoils from Jericho, were set ablaze in order to turn the Lord's "burning anger" (Jos. 7:26) from Israel .

ACHISH
(ay' kish) HEBREW: ACHISH
··········

Fleeing Saul, **David** sought refuge with Achish, the Philistine king of Gath. When David first came to Gath, Achish's men did not trust him because of his reputation for killing Philistines, including the champion **Goliath**, one of their own. David feigned madness and hastily departed from Gath. Later, when David returned with a large band of followers, Achish accepted him and his men as mercenaries and gave them the town of Ziklag to live in. Achish trusted David and even planned to use his force in battle against Israel, but the other Philistine commanders rejected the crafty refugee as an ally.

ADAM
(ad' em) HEBREW: ADAM
"human being" or "mankind"
··········

The book of Genesis provides two versions of the creation of the first man, Adam. In the first chapter, a male and female are created "in the image of God" (Gen. 1:27) on the sixth day of creation. Blessed and set above all of the other animals, this pair is given a specific command: "Be fruitful and multiply, and fill the earth and subdue it; and have dominion over the fish of the sea and over the birds of the air and over every living thing that moves upon the earth" (Gen. 1:28). Furthermore, God makes clear that sufficient food has been provided for all living creatures, humans included, in the form of green plants and fruit-bearing trees. The world thus begins without the need to struggle for survival, with all of creation in perfect balance and harmony.

In the second chapter of Genesis, which is apparently based on a different oral tradition, the creation of all heaven and earth was not yet complete when God scooped up some dust from the

Adam's story is recapitulated in this 15th-century manuscript illumination: the creation of man and then woman from his rib (left background), the temptation by the serpent (center), the expulsion from the garden (right background).

ground (which had been watered only by a terrestrial mist), shaped a man from it, and brought him to life by breathing into his nostrils "the breath of life" (Gen. 2:7). Perhaps the name Adam originated with the Hebrew word *adom*, meaning red, because of the color of the clay used to make him, or from *adamah*, which means earth.

Next, the Creator planted the garden of Eden somewhere "in the east" (Gen. 2:8) and charged his new subject with the task of tilling this fertile paradise, whose flowing stream divided into four great rivers that reached to the corners of the earth—the Pishon, the Gihon, the Tigris, and the Euphrates. The man was granted free use of the garden's fruit trees, with one significant exception: Death was the penalty for eating from the "tree of the knowledge of good and evil" (Gen. 2:17).

Concluding that "it is not good that the man should be alone" (Gen. 2:18), God created the world's animals and birds to be companions and helpers for the lone human, who was given the privilege and responsibility of naming them. When none proved to be a suitable helper for him, however, God put him to sleep, took one of the man's ribs, and used it to form **Eve**, the first woman. "Therefore," comments the writer of this account,

"a man leaves his father and his mother and cleaves to his wife, and they become one flesh" (Gen. 2:24).

These two separate versions of Adam's creation contain significant theological points. In the first, the human is created on the same day as the animals but is purposely set apart, infused with the divine spirit, and given dominance over earthly creation. In both, he is given a life of ease and abundance, blessed as the favorite of the Lord God of the universe.

For ancient readers, the next turn in the story is indicated by the very word Adam, since it was frequently used in ancient Hebrew to mean human being or mankind. In other words, the first created human can be seen as a symbol for all humankind. Therefore, when he decides to commit the first sin and suffers the consequences, Adam represents the plight of all humanity in struggling to be worthy of God's love. Before this sin, Adam and Eve lived together happily in a literal paradise, free from pain, hunger, and thirst. Food was abundant, including the fruit of the "tree of life" (Gen. 3:22), which apparently gave them eternal life. There was no need for clothing, and the animals and birds cooperated with the human pair.

Eventually, however, a serpent seduced Eve into breaking God's commandment by

Adam and Eve in their earthly paradise; an illumination from a 15th-century devotional book

eating the fruit of the forbidden tree "in the midst of the garden" (Gen. 2:3) and sharing it with Adam. Instantly, the couple became conscious for the first time that they were naked. Hastily stitching fig leaves together into aprons, terrified by their guilt, they frantically tried to hide from their creator behind the trees of Eden.

When God saw that they had become ashamed of their nakedness, he knew that they had broken his commandment. Punishment was swift and severe not only for Adam and Eve, but also for all humankind to follow them. Yet the sentence of death itself would not be fulfilled at once. Rather, the lot of the woman would be to suffer increased physical anguish in childbirth and subservience to her husband. The man would now have to earn his food by sweat and heavy labor, wresting it from soil that God cursed and made hostile. Both were expelled forever from Eden and barred from access to the tree of life. Mortal existence would henceforth be burdened with tribulation and woe from cradle to grave, when man would return to the very dust from which God had originally created him.

After the moral disaster of Adam's fall, which would define the relationship of humans to God until the coming of **Jesus**, little more is heard of Adam and his wife in the Scriptures. Their firstborn son, **Cain**, became history's first murderer, killing his pious younger brother **Abel**. A third son, **Seth**, was born when Adam was 130 years old. In the eight centuries that followed before Adam reportedly died at the age of 930, we are told only that he "had other sons and daughters" (Gen. 5:4). After Genesis the only reference to Adam as an individual in the Old Testament is in 1 Chronicles 1:1, where he is placed first in a genealogical table meant to establish the Israelites as God's chosen people.

In the centuries after the Babylonian exile, however, the story of Adam and his sin began to intrigue Jewish thinkers who were trying to understand why God had allowed their nation to suffer defeat and captivity.

The four rivers of Eden appear in this stained-glass depiction of Adam and Eve.

One result was that some Jewish religious writers began to magnify his glory, even describing him as a second angel. He was thought to surpass ordinary human beings in every conceivable way. Indeed, the very concept of the fall was rejected in favor of the belief that he was actually a heavenly figure who is successively incarnated in human form throughout history. Another trend in this speculative pre-Christian scholarship was very different: a newly explicit stress on the disastrous effect of Adam's sin on all generations to follow him, even suggesting that his fall was the origin of all human evil.

Reflection on the meaning of Adam's fall became even more important to the development of Christian belief after the death of Jesus. To place his Gospel firmly in the context of traditional Jewish history, **Luke** traces the ancestry of Jesus back to "Adam, the son of God" (Lk. 3:38). There is one other New Testament genealogical reference to the historical Adam in verse 14 of the letter of **Jude**, the last of the Epistles.

Much more significant, however, is the Christian portrayal of the sinful, fallen Adam symbolically linked with Jesus. **Paul** in particular saw Adam as the father of the old humanity, as the originator of sin and death. By contrast, Jesus made possible a new humanity. He was superior to Adam because he could prevail over the consequences of sin through the grace of God. If death sprang from Adam because of his act of disobedience in the garden, life now sprang from Jesus because he obeyed the will of God and thus earned the salvation of humankind.

This essential distinction between the first Adam and Jesus as the last Adam is used by Paul to explain the resurrection of all believers. "For as in Adam all die," he wrote, "so also in Christ shall all be made alive" (1 Cor. 15:22). The comparison helps explain two inherent aspects of resurrection. In the first place, the linkage with Adam's sin and death showed that the soul would have to have a body for its resurrection to take place. Second, the coming of Jesus showed

*Expelled from Eden (background), Adam is forced to till the soil
as Eve assumes the burdens of motherhood.*

that the body would be new and spiritual rather than the flesh and blood of the old mortality. According to Paul, "The first man was from the earth, a man of dust; the second man is from heaven" (1 Cor. 15:47).

ADONI-BEZEK

(ah doh' nee bee' zek) HEBREW:
ADONI-BEZEK
"lord of Bezek" or "my lord is Bezek"
••••••••••

The ruler of the city of Bezek in southern Canaan who bore the title Adoni-bezek was overthrown soon after the death of **Joshua**, when the tribes of Judah and Simeon attacked Adoni-bezek's forces and apparently defeated them with ease. The king was then sentenced to a punishment he himself had often meted out to those he conquered—his thumbs and great toes were cut off, effectively ending his life as a warrior, since he could no longer use weapons or pursue a fleeing enemy. "As I have done," he admitted, "so God has requited me" (Jg. 1:7). Adoni-bezek died shortly after his men brought him to Jerusalem.

ADONI-ZEDEK

(ah doh' nee zee' dek) HEBREW:
ADONI-ZEDEK
"my lord is Zedek/righteous"
••••••••••

The king of Jerusalem in the time of **Joshua**, Adoni-zedek allied himself with four other local rulers to crush the city of Gibeon, which had made peace with the Hebrew invaders. The beleaguered Gibeonites called on Joshua for aid and, with the miraculous help of a severe hailstorm and a standing still of the sun, the Israelites defeated Adoni-zedek and his allies. The kings were captured and executed, their bodies thrown into the same cave where they had hidden during the battle.

ADONIJAH

(ad' oh nai' juh) HEBREW: ADHONIYAH
"Yah[weh] is my Lord"
••••••••••

While **David** was ruling Judah from Hebron, his fourth son, Adonijah, was born to a little-known woman named Haggith. Adonijah would most likely also have remained an obscure character except for the fact that his three elder brothers all died before their father did—**Amnon** was murdered, Chileab died under unknown circumstances, and **Absalom** was killed as a usurper. Adonijah thus became the crown prince of Israel.

As he neared 40 years of age, Adonijah made no secret of his claim to the throne. David encouraged his royal ambitions both by yielding to his son's actions and never questioning his judgment and by allowing him to establish a personal bodyguard of 50 footmen along with charioteers and horsemen. Although David had not officially designated Adonijah as his successor, "all Israel fully expected" (1 Kg. 2:15) David's eldest surviving son to succeed him.

When David became infirm and near death, Adonijah conferred with the king's senior advisers—**Joab**, commander of the army, and **Abiathar**, one of the two chief priests—to arrange the transfer of government. To solidify support he held a sacrificial meal for David's other sons and his royal officials. But Adonijah did not invite his half brother **Solomon**, who was about 24 at the time, probably because he knew that Solomon himself had royal ambitions and was supported by the prophet **Nathan**, his mother **Bathsheba**, the priest **Zadok**, and the commander of David's personal bodyguard, **Benaiah**.

Adonijah fatally underestimated the strength of Solomon's supporters, who portrayed Adonijah's actions as treasonous and urged the infirm king to fulfill his secret oath to Bathsheba that Solomon would succeed him. David was persuaded and had Zadok and Nathan anoint Solomon as king. When news came to Adonijah that Solomon had been crowned, he fled to the altar of God for asylum, and only with Solomon's assurance of safety did he pledge allegiance to the new king.

Shortly after David's death, Adonijah went to Bathsheba and requested her to ask Solomon to award him David's beautiful young nurse **Abishag** as a wife. Since the royal harem belonged exclusively to the new king, the request was a usurpation of royal prerogatives—an offense for which Solomon immediately had Adonijah executed.

ADONIRAM

(ad uh nai' ruhm) HEBREW: ADONIRAM
"my lord is exalted"

The splendid kingdom of **David** and **Solomon** required not only heavy taxes but also forced labor to keep it running smoothly and to maintain the grandiose construction projects dear to Solomon. Adoniram was the civil servant responsible for raising and maintaining levies of laborers, under David from the Canaanites but under Solomon from the Israelites themselves. It was an unenviable task since it made him the focus of popular hatred. After Solomon's death, Adoniram continued to serve his heir, the foolish King **Rehoboam**. Adoniram was stoned to death in protest against conscripted labor, an action that marked the beginning of the northern tribes' revolt against the house of David.

Adoniram is called Adoram in 2 Samuel 20:24 and in 1 Kings 12:18 and Hadoram in 2 Chronicles 10:18—though some scholars think it is more likely that three separate men with similar names held the office over so long a period of time, perhaps 40 years.

AENEAS

(uh nee' uhs) GREEK: AINEAS
"praiseworthy"

The apostle **Peter** made several journeys to exhort and encourage the faithful of the early church. On a trip to Lydda, a town on the plain of Sharon some 25 miles northwest of Jerusalem, he met a man named Aeneas, who had been paralyzed and bedridden for eight years. Telling Aeneas that "Jesus Christ heals you" (Acts 9:34), Peter cured him—a miracle that converted many.

AGABUS

(ag' uh buhs) GREEK: AGABOS
possibly "locust"

Prophets in the early Christian community, like their Old Testament predecessors, were believed to be divinely inspired. Agabus, a prophet of Jerusalem, was therefore given a respectful hearing when he warned the church at Antioch of an impending famine. The famine indeed took place during the reign of the emperor **Claudius**. Later, Agabus warned **Paul** that the Jews would have him arrested by Roman soldiers if he returned to Jerusalem; this prophecy too was fulfilled.

AGAG

(ay' gag) HEBREW: AGAG
possibly "to flame" or "to become angry"

This name may have been a title for the kings of the Amalekites, a nomadic people who attacked the Israelites immediately after their departure from Egypt. Nearly

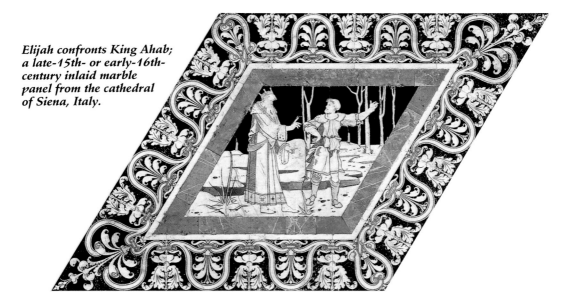

Elijah confronts King Ahab; a late-15th- or early-16th-century inlaid marble panel from the cathedral of Siena, Italy.

two centuries later the prophet **Samuel** sent King **Saul** to destroy the Amalekites as punishment for that attack. Even though Samuel had ordered Saul to destroy every living thing, he spared their king. When Samuel discovered that the defeated king still lived, he himself "hewed Agag in pieces before the Lord" (1 Sam. 15:33). Saul's disobedience triggered the final break between the prophet and the man he had anointed king over Israel.

AHAB

(ay' hab) HEBREW: AHAB
"father's brother" or "the Father [God] is my brother"
....

The son of **Omri**, Ahab ruled the northern kingdom of Israel from about 869 to 850 B.C., a period of renewed vitality and strength. As the defender of Israel against Syria, Ahab is described as a competent leader with widespread support. But he is denounced for religious policies that "did more to provoke the Lord . . . to anger than all the kings of Israel who were before him" (1 Kg. 16:33).

Ahab's father, Omri, formed an alliance with the Phoenicians through the marriage of his son to **Jezebel**, daughter of the Phoenician king Ethbaal. Omri and Ahab also stopped the long war with Judah; their desire for an alliance was later achieved when Ahab married his daughter **Athaliah** to **Jehoram**, the crown prince of Judah.

Apparently, Ahab was primarily a worshiper of Yahweh, Israel's God, and all his children who are identified have names that praise Yahweh. A large part of his kingdom, however, remained Canaanite, and Ahab accommodated these subjects by granting the Canaanite god **Baal** the same standing as Yahweh and allowing Jezebel to support many priests and prophets of Baal.

This policy brought conflict with **Elijah**, who condemned Ahab's tolerance as "limping with two different opinions" (1 Kg. 18:21). The dispute turned violent when Jezebel, who was exclusively devoted to her god, executed many prophets of Yahweh. Elijah pointed to a severe drought as Yahweh's punishment on Israel and asked Ahab to arrange a contest on Mount Carmel between himself and the prophets of Baal. When Elijah won the contest and immediately killed hundreds of Baal's prophets, and when Jezebel in turn swore to kill Elijah, Ahab perhaps saw that his policy of religious tolerance could not survive.

Ahab's greatest military challenge came from **Ben-hadad**, the Syrian king of Damascus, who besieged Samaria. Though Ahab was ready to surrender extensive treasure, he refused to open the city. Guided by a prophet of Yahweh, Ahab sprang a surprise attack on the invaders and overwhelmed them. When Ben-hadad attacked again the next year, Ahab was ready and met him at Aphek east of Galilee. Again, an oracle of Yahweh promising victory was fulfilled.

In 853 B.C., Ahab joined with Damascus and other cities to confront the fierce Assyrian army of Shalmaneser III in the battle of Qarqar. The Assyrians claimed a triumph, but, in reality, their advance south was stopped for several years.

The alliance with Damascus broke down as Ahab built close ties to King **Jehoshaphat** of Judah, with whom he planned a joint campaign to regain Ramoth-gilead from Syrian control. The battle went well until a stray arrow pierced a seam in Ahab's armor and killed him. Jezebel remained powerful during the reigns of their two sons, **Ahaziah** and **Jehoram**.

AHASUERUS

(ah hahz yoo ay' ruhs) HEBREW: AHASWEROS
"mighty one"
••••••••••

The Persian king featured in the book of Esther is better known to history as Xerxes I. The son of **Darius I**, he reigned from 486 to 465 B.C. His domain, according to the Bible, stretched "from India to Ethiopia over one hundred and twenty-seven provinces," and he "sat on his royal throne in Susa the capital" (Est. 1:1-2).

When Ahasuerus rejected **Vashti** as his queen for her refusal to appear at a royal banquet and chose **Esther** to replace her, he unwittingly set in motion events that immortalized Esther and her cousin **Mordecai** and marked his grand vizier **Haman** as one of the Bible's worst villains. The story is celebrated in the Jewish feast of Purim.

In traditional Purim celebrations, Ahasuerus is a somewhat farcical and pathetic figure, remembered for his futile decree requiring wives to obey their husbands and for a command that resulted in Haman's being forced to give Mordecai the triumph he had planned for himself.

What is known about Xerxes (Ahasuerus) outside the Bible may be found in the works of his near contemporary, the Greek historian Herodotus. In addition, Old Persian inscriptions from Xerxes' time purport to reveal the king's own words.

Herodotus tells of Xerxes' invasion of Greece by land and sea in 480 B.C. following his erection of a pontoon bridge to cross the Hellespont, the waterway separating Europe from Asia Minor. However, his fleets soon suffered disastrous losses at Salamis, and a year later his armies were exhausted in an indecisive battle at Plataea. Although hostilities between the rivals continued for 30 years, the invasion was ended. Little is known about Xerxes between his retreat from Greece and his assassination in 465.

Archeologists have uncovered inscriptions attributed to Xerxes that depict his fealty to the Zoroastrian divinity Ahuramazda and also reveal his attitude toward the religions of the peoples he conquered: "Among these countries there was a place where false gods previously were worshiped. Afterward, by the favor of Ahuramazda, I destroyed that sanctuary of the false gods, and I made proclamation, 'The false gods shall not be worshiped!' Where previously the false gods were worshiped, there I worshiped Ahuramazda."

Ahasuerus welcomes Esther to a palace banquet.

AHAZ

(ay' haz) HEBREW: ACHAZ, from JEHOAHAZ
"he [Yahweh] has grasped"

The 11th king of Judah, who ruled c. 735-715 B.C., is described in the Bible as one of the worst examples of an apostate king—one who "even burned his son as an offering" (2 Kg. 16:3). Taking the throne at the age of 20 after several years of coregency with his father, **Jotham**, Ahaz inherited political troubles that overwhelmed his courage and ability. He was vacillating and panicked easily in a time that called for fortitude and faith.

At the beginning of his reign, he was asked to join the alliance of King **Pekah** of Israel and King **Rezin** of Syria to slow the inevitable Assyrian advance. When Ahaz refused, the two kings attacked Judah and besieged Jerusalem in an attempt to replace Ahaz on the throne with the otherwise unidentified "son of Tabeel" (Is. 7:6). Threatened not only by Rezin and Pekah but also by their Edomite and Philistine allies, Ahaz hoped to save Jerusalem by appealing for help to the Assyrian king **Tiglath-pileser III**. As he was about to decide, the prophet **Isaiah** appeared before Ahaz to plead the case against the Assyrian alliance, promising the survival of Judah through a return to worship of Yahweh. Too fearful to trust the prophet, Ahaz hoped to save his kingdom by making the dramatic sacrifice of his son to bring down the wrath of God on his enemies. He also surrendered his independence to Tiglath-pileser, begging the Assyrian king to save him. In response, the Assyrian army marched west in about 732, conquering the Syrian capital of Damascus and portions of Israel before subduing Transjordan and Philistia.

In exchange for protection, Ahaz had appeared before Tiglath-pileser in Damascus to pay tribute in the form of treasure from the temple in Jerusalem and from his own royal palace. While in Damascus, Ahaz was impressed by the great altar that he saw there; he sent construction plans to his high priest **Uriah** with orders to build a replica in Jerusalem. On it were to be offered sacrifices to the "gods of Damascus" (2 Chr. 28:23). The price of political survival was religious surrender to Assyria—and Ahaz is harshly condemned for his apostasy in the books of 2 Kings, 2 Chronicles, and Isaiah.

At his death, the body of Ahaz was "buried with his fathers in the city of David" (2 Kg. 16:20), although it is noted that "they did not bring him into the tombs of the kings of Israel" (2 Chr. 28:27). His son **Hezekiah** began an era of spiritual reform.

AHAZIAH

(ay huh zi' uh) HEBREW: AHAZYA
"Yahweh has grasped"

Ahaziah ruled the northern kingdom of Israel for only two years, c. 850–849 B.C. Like his father and precedessor, **Ahab**, he angered the Lord by worshiping **Baal**, the god of his mother **Jezebel**.

Ahaziah sought to form an alliance with King **Jehoshaphat** of Judah to revive maritime trade with gold-rich Ophir. Jehoshaphat rejected the offer, and Judah's inexperienced fleet was soon destroyed at Ezion-geber. In his second year as king, Ahaziah fell from an upper window at his palace in Samaria. Severely injured, he sent messengers for an oracle from Baal-zebub, the god of Ekron, but they were stopped by the prophet **Elijah**. Twice, a 50-man force was met by Elijah, who invoked a "fire come down from heaven" (2 Kg. 1:10) to consume them. Elijah and a third group of 50 men returned to the ailing king. For his impious act of consulting a foreign god, Ahaziah was told by Elijah that he would not recover from his injuries. Having no son, he was succeeded by his brother **Jehoram**.

AHAZIAH 2

The 22-year-old son of King **Jehoram** of Judah, Ahaziah reigned for only a year, about 842 B.C. Ahaziah joined his uncle **Jehoram**, king of Israel, in an unsuccessful campaign against King **Hazael** of Syria at Ramoth-gilead. Wounded in battle, Jehoram went to Jezreel to recover.

As Ahaziah journeyed to visit his uncle, a revolt broke out in the army at Ramoth-gilead. An army officer named **Jehu** was selected by the prophet **Elisha** to be anointed king of Israel. Jehu promptly left by chariot for Jezreel to punish Jehoram for his idolatrous ways. Warned

The soldiers of Doeg slaughter Ahimelech, the other priests, and their families at Nob.

by watchmen of Jehu's approach, Jehoram and his nephew Ahaziah rode out to meet the rebel at the property of Naboth. After determining that Jehu meant them harm, Jehoram told Ahaziah to flee. Drawing back his bow, Jehu sent an arrow through Jehoram's heart and the king fell dead in his chariot.

Jehu pursued Ahaziah, who was wounded near Ibleam but managed to reach Megiddo, where he died. His servants took his body to Jerusalem for burial in the royal tomb. Ahaziah is called Jehoahaz in 2 Chronicles 21:17.

AHIJAH

(ah hi'jah) HEBREW: AHIYA
"Yah[weh] is my brother"
··········

A prophet from Shiloh, Ahijah lived during the reigns of **Solomon**, **Rehoboam**, and **Jeroboam**. He predicted that the kingdom of Israel would be divided and that Jeroboam the son of Nebat would become king of the larger portion. When he met Jeroboam on a road outside Jerusalem, the prophet tore a new garment into 12 pieces and gave 10 to Jeroboam with the announcement that God would "tear the kingdom from the hand of Solomon, and will give

you ten tribes" (1 Kg. 11:31). Years later, by then old and blind, Ahijah prophesied the downfall of Jeroboam's house and the death of the king's son Abijah.

AHIMELECH

(ah hi' me lek) HEBREW: ACHIMELEK
"my brother is king"
··········

I n the days of King **Saul**, Ahimelech was high priest at the Israelite sanctuary at Nob, just east of Jerusalem. His father, Ahitub, had evidently founded the sanctuary after the Philistines destroyed the shrine at Shiloh where his great grandfather **Eli** had once served. Ahimelech led a community of priests at Nob, while his brother Ahijah was priest in the court of Saul at Gibeah.

One day **David**, fleeing from Saul's attempts to kill him, came to Nob. Telling Ahimelech that he was on a secret mission for Saul, David requested bread for his men and a weapon for himself. Ahimelech trusted David and attempted to comply. On condition that David's men be ritually pure, Ahimelech gave him the holy bread from the sanctuary along with the sword of **Goliath** that was in safekeeping there. Unfortunately, an Edomite named **Doeg** observed this action and reported it to Saul. The king was enraged at this support given to his enemy and charged Ahimelech with treason. Although Ahimelech protested that he thought

THE CONQUESTS OF ALEXANDER

In his comparatively few years of campaigning, Alexander the Great brought under his control much of what was then considered the civilized world. The people of the eastern Mediterranean knew little of Asia and Africa and considered the inhabitants of western Europe as barbarians; the Americas were undiscovered. Whatever vision Alexander had of uniting that world ended with his death.

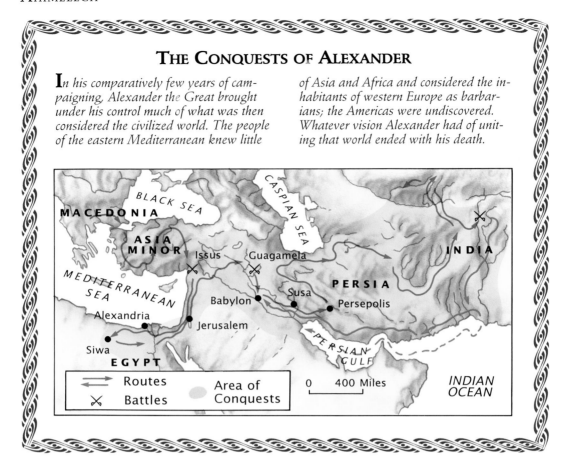

David was still serving the king, Saul had Doeg execute all 85 priests at Nob, including Ahimelech. Only **Abiathar**, Ahimelech's son, escaped.

AHINOAM

(ah hin'oh ahm) HEBREW: AHINOAM
"my brother is delight"

One of **David**'s wives, Ahinoam came from Jezreel in southern Judah. She, along with **Abigail**, joined David on his escape from Saul. Their 16-month-long exile was spent at Ziklag. Having survived capture by the Amalekites, Ahinoam returned with David to Hebron, where he was anointed king of Israel. There she gave birth to David's first son, **Amnon**.

AHITHOPHEL

(ah hith' oh fel) HEBREW: AHITOPEL
"brother of folly"

At first a wise counselor to King **David**, Ahithophel, who came from Giloh in the highlands of Judah, proved disloyal, joining the revolt of **Absalom** against the king. As he fled from Jerusalem, David asked the Lord to "turn the counsel of Ahithophel into foolishness" (2 Sam. 15:31). David's spy **Hushai** infiltrated Absalom's court to counter the advice of Ahithophel—which until that time had been esteemed by both David and Absalom "as if one consulted the oracle of God" (2 Sam. 16:23).

Ahithophel counseled Absalom to attack David immediately with 12,000 men before the king could regroup his weary forces. Hushai suggested caution and dissuaded Absalom from taking Ahithophel's advice. Knowing his position was in jeopardy, Ahithophel returned to Giloh and committed suicide by hanging himself.

ALCIMUS

(al' si muhs) HEBREW: ELYAQIM
"God will raise up"

A Jewish leader of the pro-Seleucid faction in Jerusalem, Alcimus served as high priest from 162 to 159 B.C. A descendant of **Aaron** but not a member of a high priestly family and thus without direct claim to legitimate succession, he nonetheless appealed to King **Demetrius I Soter** of Syria to be appointed high priest. Demetrius granted the request, sending Alcimus to Judea as high priest with a Syrian army led by **Bacchides** to enforce the appointment.

Infuriated by Alcimus's support of Seleucid rule, the rebel **Judas Maccabeus** harassed the high priest until he turned to the Seleucid king for help. Demetrius commanded Nicanor, a prince who detested Israel, to suppress Judas. Nicanor, however, was defeated and killed, and a new 22,000-man force was sent under Bacchides. The Syrian army met the outnumbered forces of Judas at Elasa. Judas was killed, and his army failed to prevent Alcimus's restoration to power.

The following year, Alcimus became paralyzed, apparently from a stroke, and soon died. His sudden death was believed to be an act of divine retribution for having broken down the wall that separated Gentiles from access to the inner courts of the temple that were reserved for Jews.

ALEXANDER THE GREAT

(al' ig zan' duhr) GREEK: ALEXANDROS
"defender of man"
••••••••••

A youth not quite 20 when he came to power in his homeland of Macedonia in 336 B.C., Alexander reshaped his world before he died 13 years later. His life story is told in brief in 1 Maccabees 1:1-7.

Alexander's father, King **Philip II** of Macedonia, trained Alexander to govern, bringing the philosopher Aristotle from Athens to tutor the prince from the age of 13 to 16. At 16 Alexander served as regent and led troops in battle. Two years later he was one of Philip's commanders in the decisive battle that gave the Macedonian ruler control of Greece. King Philip was planning to invade the vast empire of Persia, which for a century had harassed Greece and controlled the Greek cities of Asia Minor, when he was assassinated in 336.

Taking over his father's plan of conquest, Alexander crossed the Hellespont in 334 with some 35,000 Macedonian and Greek soldiers and defeated a Persian army at the river Granicus. He then swept through western Asia Minor to liberate the Greek cities of Pergamum, Sardis, Ephesus, and others. In battle Alexander deployed the most effective army of his day. Its power lay in the use of a concentrated cavalry charge to break enemy lines, to be fol-

lowed by an almost invincible infantry phalanx, thousands of close-ordered fighting men each with a 13-foot spear that made the formation bristle like a porcupine.

In 333 Alexander met the full Persian army under King Darius III at Issus near the northeastern shore of the Mediterranean. The defeated Persian king fled, but his family was captured. A year later Alexander took the island fortress of Tyre after a long siege and marched south through Palestine.

Later legends cited by the Jewish historian Josephus tell how Alexander went up to Jerusalem and was met by the high priest **Jaddua** arrayed in his crown bearing the name of God. Alexander bowed before the name of God and explained that back in Macedonia he had seen a vision of the high priest who had assured him of victory.

Late in 332 Alexander occupied Egypt. There he was crowned as Pharaoh and acclaimed by an oracle as a son of the god Amon-Ra. On the Nile delta he founded the city of Alexandria—the first of many with that name—a city that was to become one of the leading intellectual and political centers of the ancient world.

Moving east toward the heart of Persia in 331, he crossed the Euphrates and Tigris rivers and decisively defeated Darius at Gaugamela. The Persian king again fled but was murdered by his own cousin.

Alexander fought triumphantly across what is now Iran to the borders of India. But his eastward progress was stopped by the refusal of the army to go farther, and Alexander arrived back in Persian Susa in 324. His army had gradually changed from being a Macedonian national force to a personal army owing allegiance to him alone, and the conqueror's success helped to establish the idea of ruler worship in the Mediterranean area. At his request, Greek cities voted him honors as a divinity, evidently to reinforce his political authority. Before he could enjoy his divinity, however, Alexander died of a fever at the age of 33. In the absence of any clear successor, the Middle East was thrown into 40 years of wars among Alexander's generals for control of his legacy. Without naming Alexander, a vision recorded in the book of Daniel foretells his career: "A mighty king shall arise, who shall rule with great dominion and do according to his will. And when he has arisen, his kingdom shall be broken and divided toward the four winds of heaven" (Dan. 11:3-4).

Bust of Alexander executed toward the end of his reign (336-323 B.C.)

ALEXANDER BALAS
(bah' luhs) GREEK: BALAS
possibly a form of Baal, "lord"
··········

Posing as the son of **Antiochus IV Epiphanes**, Alexander Balas (called Alexander Epiphanes in 1 Maccabees 10:1) ruled Syria from 150 to 145 B.C. He was actually of humble origin, born in Ephesus, but nonetheless succeeded in wresting the Syrian throne from **Demetrius I Soter**. In 152, when Alexander began his campaign to usurp the throne, he engaged in a bidding war with Demetrius to secure the allegiance of **Jonathan**, the leader of the Jews. His offer included a purple robe, a gold crown, and an appointment as high priest—though Jonathan was not from a proper high priestly family. Jonathan pledged allegiance to Alexander, rejecting offers from the unpopular Demetrius.

When Alexander was challenged militarily by Demetrius's son, **Demetrius II Nicator**, Jonathan came to his patron's aid. Victorious at Joppa and Azotus, Jonathan was rewarded with the Ekron district. Alexander, however, had ineptly alienated much of the Syrian population.

Amnon lures Tamar to his bedside.

Allied with Ptolemy Philometor of Egypt, Demetrius II eventually took power after a great battle near Antioch. While seeking safety, Alexander was beheaded by Zabdiel of Arabia. The gruesome evidence was sent to Ptolemy three days before he himself died of battle wounds.

AMASA
(ahm' ah suh) HEBREW: AMASA
"to support"
··········

The son of Jether the Ishmaelite, Amasa was military commander under his cousin **Absalom** and his uncle King **David**. He led Absalom's rebel army against the king but was defeated. After David's victory, the king appointed Amasa as his new commander. This gesture served two purposes: it helped reunite the various factions within Israel and sent a message of displeasure to the former commander **Joab** for his killing of Absalom and **Abner**.

In order to suppress the uprising of **Sheba** the son of Bichri, David ordered Amasa to organize the men of Judah within three days. Amasa failed and David called on **Abishai** to accomplish the task. Joined by Joab and David's "mighty men" (2 Sam. 20:7), Abishai was able to quash the rebellion. Amasa had managed to join David's army at Gibeon, but Joab—pretending to greet him with a kiss—disemboweled Amasa in the middle of the road with his sword. At first, the horrible sight stopped the marching troops in their tracks, but soon the body was removed and the army proceeded against Sheba.

AMAZIAH
(am uh zai' uh) HEBREW: AMASYAHU
"Yahweh is strong/mighty"
··········

The eighth king of Judah, Amaziah ascended the throne in 800 B.C. upon the assassination of his father, **Joash**, who had paid a huge bribe to King **Hazael** of Syria in exchange for peace.

Amaziah's first political act was to find and execute his father's assassins, Jozacar and Jehozabad, servants who had joined a palace cabal of those who opposed alliances with nations that did not worship Yahweh. In strict adherence to Mosaic Law, however, Amaziah "did not put to death the children of the murderers" (2 Kg. 14:6).

The king's first military move was the recapture of Edom, bringing the land south and east of the Dead Sea back under Judean rule after a half century of independence.

Flushed with victory, Amaziah challenged Israel's King **Joash** to battle. He responded by sending a messenger with a parable of warning: "A thistle on Lebanon sent to a cedar on Lebanon, saying 'Give your daughter to my son for a wife'; and a wild beast of Lebanon passed by and trampled down the thistle" (2 Kg. 14:9). The message from Joash concluded with an interpretation of the parable: Though emboldened by his victory over Edom, Amaziah should be content with his own kingdom. Heedless of the warning, Amaziah insisted on war. But the Judean armies were routed, Amaziah was taken captive, the walls of Jerusalem were breached, the temple was plundered, and hostages were taken back to Israel.

Joash returned Amaziah to his throne, but as a weakened and humiliated vassal. Amaziah continued to reign for 15 years, until a conspiracy against him forced him to escape to Lachish. He was safe for only a time before his pursuers killed him and returned his body to Jerusalem for burial alongside his forebears.

Amaziah was the father of **Uzziah**, who probably served as coregent during the last part of his father's 17-year reign.

AMNON

(am' nahn) HEBREW: AMNON
"faithful"

David's firstborn son, Amnon was born to **Ahinoam**, a woman of Jezreel, soon after David became king of Judah (c. 1000 B.C.). He is known only for his uncontrollable desire for his half sister **Tamar**. Pretending to be ill, he lured her to his room and raped her. Immediately his lust turned to revulsion and he cast her off. Tamar's full brother **Absalom**, enraged by Amnon's crime, patiently waited two years for an opportunity to take revenge, and then had Amnon murdered while the prince was merrymaking at a sheepshearing festival.

AMON

(ah' muhn) HEBREW: AMON
"trustworthy"

One of the younger sons of King **Manasseh**, Amon ascended the throne of Judah at the age of 22. During his short reign (642–640 B.C.), Amon continued his father's policy of subservience to Assyria and his support of pagan worship. He was assassinated by his servants in a palace plot and succeeded by his eight-year-old son, **Josiah,** who was to enjoy a lengthy reign.

The prophet Amos in an initial letter at the beginning of the book bearing his name; from a 12th-century Bible

AMOS

(ay' muhs) HEBREW: AMOS
"burden" or "burden-bearer"

An enigmatic sheep herder named Amos stands at a unique juncture in the history of ancient Israel. He was the first of the great classical prophets, those who contributed their words in writing to the Scriptures of Israel. Earlier major prophets such as **Elijah** and **Elisha** were known for their deeds rather than their messages, but Amos began the tradition of the writing prophets, a succession of courageous voices that has defined the word "prophet" to the present.

Sometime shortly before the middle of the eighth century B.C., perhaps about 760, Amos became convinced that God had called him to leave the southern kingdom of Judah and travel north to the centers of the kingdom of Israel. There he was to condemn the people for their social injustice, corruption, and shallow religion and to warn them of coming destruction. Following his divine call, he went to Samaria, Bethel, and perhaps other cities—into a society that was to all outward appearances prosperous, peaceful, and militarily strong. He soon became a thorn in the side of the leaders of that society at a time when everyone else seemed to agree that all was well.

Who was this prophet who tried to burst Israel's bubble of self-deception? Amos is known primarily through his prophetic message, and the few facts about his early life given in the book that bears his name seem like meager clues in a detective story—just two brief statements about who he was. In the first verse of his book he is identified as one "who was among the shepherds of Tekoa" (Am. 1:1), a village six miles south of Bethlehem. Later he states, "I am a herdsman, and a dresser of sycamore trees" (Am. 7:14).

These descriptions have often led to the conclusion that Amos was a menial laborer who herded sheep and cattle part of the year and supplemented his income during certain seasons as a farm worker in sycamore groves. The image of Amos as a poor shepherd, cowhand, and tender of sycamore trees seems to fit well with his strong interest in the plight of the poor in Israel and with his attacks on the rich, luxury-loving city dwellers of northern Israel.

Several elements of this portrayal of the prophet cause problems, however. Shepherds and farm laborers in that era would typically have been illiterate, but the prophecies of Amos are cast in beautiful and often fiery language that calls upon a wide variety of types of literature and employs a rich poetic tongue. His oracles show broad knowledge of the history of both Judah and Israel as well as of the kingdoms and empires that surround them— scarcely what one might expect of a farmhand. Moreover, the word translated "shepherd" is not the common Hebrew word for that type of work but a rare word (noqed) that occurs in only one other passage, 2 Kings 3:4, where it identifies a royal sheep rancher. On the basis of these clues, many scholars have concluded that before he became a prophet, Amos may well have been a substantial owner of flocks of sheep and goats and of herds of cattle and may have owned groves of sycamore fig trees that provided his cattle with fodder.

Thus, it was likely a relatively prosperous and well-educated man to whom the call of God came. As Amos succinctly put it, "The Lord took me from following the flock, and the Lord said to me, 'Go, prophesy to my people Israel'" (Am. 7:15).

Amos did not approach his task as a professionally trained prophet or a member of one of the prophetic guilds known as sons of the prophets. "I am no prophet, nor a prophet's son" (Am. 7:14), Amos strongly

asserted. He was not denying that God had indeed called him to prophesy, but he was consciously separating himself from professional prophets who made their living by foretelling the future and who thus could often be corrupted by royal patrons.

Amos trekked north from Tekoa across the border into Israel, entering a kingdom flushed with an era of good feeling, riding high with military expansion, economic prosperity, and a booming religious movement, but one careless of injustice and profound corruption in society. The message of God that came from Amos broke onto Israel's seeming serenity like a charging lion: "The Lord roars from Zion," Amos cried, "and the top of Carmel withers" (Am. 1:2).

When Amos appeared on the scene, **Jeroboam II** had been on the throne for about 25 years. Jeroboam's predecessors had been harassed by the Syrian king in Damascus and by the great power of Assyria farther to the northeast. During the time of Jeroboam's father, **Joash**, however, Assyria had attacked Damascus. As the two powers wore each other down and were consumed with internal dissension, Israel was freed from external pressure in that direction. In addition, Egypt to the south was in decline. Thus, Israel had grown ever stronger, even coming to dominate the kingdom of Judah as senior partner in a forced alliance.

The people had cheered Jeroboam when he recaptured Israel's lost territory east of the Jordan and pushed north to take much of Lebanon. Israel once again ruled territory it had not held since the time of Solomon—a clear sign of God's blessing.

For those who rode the wave of Jeroboam's expansion, it was a time of prosperity such as their region had seldom seen. They could "lie upon beds of ivory" and "eat lambs from the flock," "sing idle songs to the sound of the harp," and "drink wine in bowls and anoint themselves with the finest oils" (Am. 6:4-6). It is hardly surprising that they felt great pride in Jeroboam's accomplishments and believed that they were the objects of God's favor.

In the midst of this prosperity the kingdom of Israel was nothing if not religious. At the shrine of Bethel, Amos observed a con-

BOOK OF THE TWELVE

*A*lthough *the work bearing his name is placed third in the Old Testament's Book of the Twelve, Amos is considered the earliest of the writing prophets—also called the Minor Prophets for the brevity of their writings. Hosea, placed first, actually followed Amos, while the second, Joel, has been dated several centuries later. The last three Minor Prophets— Haggai, Zechariah, and Malachi— are considered contemporaries, all dated to the late sixth century* B.C.

tinuous round of sacrifices. He foresaw, however, that the easy piety, prosperity, and self-congratulation of the times would be overshadowed by a coming catastrophe. Because of that impending shadow, Amos could not stroke Israel's confidence nor praise its piety.

Time proved him right. The death of the canny Jeroboam II about 746 B.C. was matched by the rise of the powerful **Tiglath-pileser III** in Assyria in 745. Israel sank into a morass. Jeroboam's son **Zechariah** reigned only six months before being assassinated; a usurper named **Shallum** lasted a single month. Within 25 years the self-assurance and affluence of Israel was crushed forever beneath the expansionist Assyrian army. But Amos's critique of Israel was not intended to give support to some foreign power; rather, he wanted to reveal the dark underside of the nation's gleaming surface. Israel's wealth was for the few and the powerful; the lowly paid the price.

As Amos walked the streets of Samaria, he observed the destitute living in the shadow of houses inhabited by people absorbed in luxury. His blood boiled: "Behold, the days are coming upon you, when they shall take you away with hooks" (Am. 4:2). Such pronouncements could hardly have made life pleasant for Amos as he challenged the mighty of the northern kingdom.

Ultimately, the rulers of Israel could not allow this stinging gadfly to go unswatted. "The land is not able to bear all his words" (Am. 7:10), complained Amaziah, chief priest of the royal sanctuary at Bethel, who brought charges of treason against Amos. It was a risky matter to condemn a prophet of God, however, and it was decided simply to deport this unwanted voice.

Amos vehemently rebuffed Amaziah, but eventually, when his painful mission was done, he departed. Amos returned to Judah, where he may have compiled the written record of his oracles—almost all his dire

Expelled from Israel, Amos gives a parting warning to the chief priest Amaziah.

words still apparently unfulfilled. It was only a generation later, however, that the warnings and condemnations of Amos proved true and that, in retrospect, the optimistic carelessness of Israel's leaders seemed but a foolish dream.

AMRAPHEL
(am' ra fel) HEBREW: AMRAPEL
〰〰〰〰〰〰

Amraphel, the king of Shinar, a city in Babylonia, joined three other kings to invade Canaan in the time of the patriarchs—possibly to protect or expand their trade with Egypt. During the incursion, Amraphel and his allies kidnapped **Abraham**'s nephew **Lot** and his people. Abraham led a small army of retainers to victory over the kings and rescued Lot—a notable feat for the hitherto peaceful herdsman.

ANAK
(a' nak) HEBREW: ANAQ
"neck" or "necklace"
〰〰〰〰〰〰

A race of giants called the Anakim traced their ancestry to Anak, the son of the Canaanite Arba, founder of Kiriath-Arba (the city later known as Hebron). Anak's descendants were conquered and displaced by **Caleb**, one of the scouts whom **Moses** had sent decades earlier to spy out the land of Canaan. Giants like the Anakim were also known as Nephilim, thought to be superhuman progeny of the sons of God and the daughters of men cited in Genesis 6:4.

Ananias falls dead before Peter; a 16th-century ceramic plate.

ANANIAS
(an uh ni' uhs) GREEK: HANANIAS
"Yahweh has been gracious"
〰〰〰〰〰〰

A Christian in Damascus, Ananias was the unwilling instrument of the Lord, who ordered him to cure the blindness that had stricken Saul while he was traveling to the city to seek out and denounce followers of Jesus. Ananias knew of Saul's relentless persecution of the faithful in Jerusalem and complained of the evils he had done. Nonetheless, the Lord insisted that he had chosen Saul to carry out his divine plan. Ananias fulfilled his mission, seeking out Saul at the house of Judas on "the street called Straight" (Acts 9:11). There he laid hands on him, miraculously curing his blindness. Saul was immediately baptized and began his life's work of preaching to the Gentiles under his Roman name, **Paul**.

ANANIAS 2
〰〰〰〰〰〰

The high priest of the temple in Jerusalem for many years, Ananias was a violent opponent of **Paul**'s attempts to convert the Jewish people. He went so far as to order witnesses at Paul's hearing before the Sanhedrin to "strike him on the mouth" (Acts 23:2). Paul had to be taken into safekeeping by the Roman tribune, who brought him to the governor at Caesarea under heavy escort. Ananias appeared there to further his case against Paul as an agitator and "a ringleader of the sect of the Nazarenes" (Acts 24:5).

ANANIAS 3
〰〰〰〰〰〰

Lying to God before the church brought punishment to Ananias and his wife **Sapphira**, wealthy members of the Christian congregation in Jerusalem. According to the book of Acts, the church at this time, in order to be able to care for the needy, was practicing a policy in which "no one said that any of the things which he possessed was his own, but they had everything in common" (Acts 4:32). In response, many, including **Barnabas**, sold their property and laid the proceeds at the feet of the apostles. Ananias and Sapphira did the same, but, unlike the others, they held back some of their profit while claiming that they had given all. Peter accused Ananias of lying to the **Holy Spirit** and to God. Hearing the apostle's judgment, Ananias fell down and died, as did Sapphira three hours later.

ANDREW
(an' droo) GREEK: ANDREAS
"manly"
∴∴∴∴∴∴

According to the Gospel of John, Andrew (along with an unnamed other) was the first person to become a disciple of **Jesus**. In later Christian tradition he was often called Protokletos, Greek for "first called."

Little is known of Andrew's youth other than that he apparently grew up in Bethsaida, an important town on the north shore of the Sea of Galilee, just east of the Jordan. He was probably born sometime in the first decade B.C. In 4 B.C. Bethsaida had come under the rule of **Herod Philip**, son of **Herod the Great**; Herod Philip had expanded the town and given it the added name of Julias, for Julia, the sister of the emperor **Augustus**. The expanded city evidently had a considerable Greek population and Greek names such as Andrew were not uncommon. The town's older name, Bethsaida, meant "house of the fisherman," an obvious fit for Andrew and his brother Simon **Peter**, who both grew up to make their living fishing the Sea of Galilee.

At some point the brothers apparently moved three miles west across the Jordan to Capernaum, which was under the rule of **Herod Antipas**. They formed a fishing partnership with a man named **Zebedee** and his two sons, **James** and **John**. Andrew lived in a house

Andrew; a 16th-century oak carving

with his brother, who was married and whose wife's mother also lived with them. Archeologists believe they have discovered the ruins of that or a similar house—an extensive structure with room for a clan of several families.

How Andrew came to be a disciple is told in two different ways, in the Gospel of John on the one hand and in the Gospels of Matthew and Mark on the other. John describes Andrew as first a disciple of **John the Baptist**. Before he ever heard of Jesus, Andrew, like many Jews of his day, was filled with expectation of the coming of a Messiah. When reports of John's preaching reached Capernaum, Andrew went with the multitudes to hear him. But unlike most, Andrew stayed with this new prophet and became devoted to his powerful teachings along with a circle of other disciples.

Everything about the Baptist excited the religious expectations of the times, but John himself revealed to those around him that he was not the Messiah. One afternoon Andrew and another disciple were standing with John when Jesus walked by and John said, "Behold, the Lamb of God!" (Jn. 1:35)—a metaphorical reference to the Passover lambs. Andrew and his unnamed companion were intrigued by John's statement and followed Jesus. When Jesus noticed them, he invited them to come to his house, and they spent the rest of the day conversing. The encounter so impressed Andrew that he concluded that his religious quest had been fulfilled. Almost immediately he went to his brother Simon with the news, "We have found the Messiah" (Jn. 1:41), and brought him to meet Jesus. The Gospels of Matthew and Mark provide another account of Andrew's call, emphasizing the authority of Jesus' summons. Both Gospels introduce Andrew and Peter as they are fishing with casting nets along the shore of the Sea of Galilee. Jesus approaches and says simply, "Follow me, and I will make you fishers of men" (Mt. 4:19). Without a word they forsake their nets and obey.

Through most of the Gospel narratives, Andrew simply shares the experiences of the other disciples and does not stand out as an individual. A few episodes, however, highlight his presence. It was in his house, shared with Peter and his wife, that Jesus healed Peter's mother-in-law. When more than 5,000 people were hungry in the wilderness, it was Andrew who found a boy who had five barley loaves and two fish that Jesus used to feed the throng. When certain Greeks who were in Jerusalem wished to see Jesus, they came first to **Philip** and then to Andrew, the two disciples with Greek names, who then informed Jesus of the request.

After Jesus' death and during the early years of Christianity in Jerusalem, Andrew labored with the other apostles, but little is known of his ministry. Many legends about Andrew grew in the second century, and a long, didactic tale called the Acts of Andrew was composed. It told how the apostle preached in Greece, rescued **Matthias**

THE APOSTLES FATES

The 12 apostles, who formed the inner core of Jesus' large following during his public ministry, are listed four times in the New Testament: Matthew 10:2-4; Mark 3:14-19, Luke 6:13-19, and Acts 1:12-14. Traditions are preserved about several of them, telling how they served Jesus and later provided leadership to the first generation of Christian believers. Indeed, their first act, following the ascension of Jesus, was to name Matthias to replace Judas Iscariot so that the sacred number of 12—corresponding to the 12 tribes of Israel—could be restored.

Except for the suicide of Judas Iscariot, and the execution of James the son of Zebedee, recorded in Acts 12:2, the end of every apostle is touched with legend. Peter may have been crucified upside down in Rome as the fourth-century church historian Eusebius records, but the tradition that Andrew died on an X-shaped cross is so late as to be unlikely. Equally dubious are the traditions that Bartholomew was flayed alive in Armenia, that Philip was martyred in Asia Minor, and that Thomas died for his faith in India.

Andrew between the apostles John and Peter, a late 15th- or early-16th-century gilt and painted wood carving

from cannibals, and traveled through Asia Minor and northern Greece working fabulous miracles and preaching celibacy. Finally, it told how Andrew was crucified by a Roman proconsul whose wife refused conjugal relations after Andrew had converted her.

Still later tradition attributed to Andrew the founding of the church in Byzantium (later Constantinople) and in Russia. The supposed bones of the apostle were kept in Constantinople (though an arm was taken to St. Andrews, Scotland) until Crusaders brought them to Italy in 1204. The X-shaped cross was linked to the tradition of Andrew's crucifixion sometime after the seventh century.

ANNA
(an' uh) GREEK: HANNA
"grace"
··········

An elderly and devout widow who was a prophetess and had spent most of her life in prayer and fasting, Anna—along with the aged **Simeon**—witnessed the presentation of the infant **Jesus** in the temple. At the dedication service, she gave a prayer of thanks and carried the news of the child to "all who were looking for the redemption of Jerusalem" (Lk. 2:38).

ANNAS
(an' uhs) GREEK: HANNAS
"merciful" or "gracious"
··········

Annas served as high priest in Jerusalem from A.D. 6 to 15 and continued as head of the high priestly clan for many years thereafter. He figures prominently in the trials of **Jesus** and **Peter** and **John**.

Born into a wealthy and influential family, Annas saw five sons as well as his son-in-law Joseph **Caiaphas** succeed him in the office of high priest. The Jewish historian Josephus relates that in A.D. 6, when the Romans took direct control of Judea, the Roman governor of Syria, **Quirinius**, removed Joezer from the high priesthood and appointed Annas in his place. Some eight years later, Valerius Gratus, the governor of Judea, removed Annas, first substituting Ishmael son of Phabi, but soon replacing Ishmael with Annas's son Eleazar.

As the head of the most prominent high priestly family, Annas stood at the very pinnacle of Jewish aristocracy. A man of wealth and education, he was a leader of the Sanhedrin, or council. He and his family led the aristocratic faction that collaborated with Roman rule and continued to supply most of the high priests appointed by the Roman governors. They were also leading Sadducees, who rejected the doctrine of the resurrection and thus were in opposition both to the Pharisees and to Jesus and the early Christians. Even after Annas was no longer officially high priest, he evidently continued to use the title and receive the deference due the holder of that office.

ANTIOCHUS IV EPIPHANES

(an tie' uh kuhs uh pif' uh neez) GREEK
"opposer"; "illustrious" or "[god] manifest"

The eighth member of the Seleucid dynasty that ruled Syria between 281 and 64 B.C., Antiochus IV is blamed in the book of Daniel for profaning the temple in Jerusalem with "the abomination that makes desolate" (Dan. 11:31). His attempt to destroy Judaism is reported in 1 and 2 Maccabees of the Apocrypha.

Early in his rule (175-164 B.C.), Antiochus intervened in a dispute over the Jewish high priesthood, siding with a hellenizer named **Jason** against his more orthodox brother **Onias**. Then he accepted a bribe from one **Menelaus** to replace Jason as high priest. When an army under Jason attempted to recapture Jerusalem, Antiochus happened to be on the way home from a successful campaign in Egypt. He stopped by Jerusalem to plunder the temple treasures and butcher its inhabitants.

In 167 B.C. Antiochus sent a new force to sack the city and destroy its walls and then issued his infamous edict of religious and cultural conformity, decreeing that "all should be one people, and that each should give up his customs" (1 Macc. 1:41). New rules forbade worship on the sabbath, circumcision, and the observance of dietary regulations. The temple was stripped of all objects associated with ancient worship and a new altar to **Zeus** was installed.

The religious repression brought about the revolt of a priest named **Mattathias**, whose son **Judas Maccabeus** succeeded

in routing Antiochus's armies and restoring temple worship. Preoccupied with other revolts to the north and thus powerless to retaliate, Antiochus withdrew to Persia where he became insane and died.

ANTIOCHUS V EUPATOR

(u pa' tor) GREEK
"born of a noble father"

Only a boy when he succeeded his father, **Antiochus IV Epiphanes**, on the Syrian throne in 164 B.C., Eupator was taken to Palestine the next year by his guardian, **Lysias**, who was attempting to break the siege of Jerusalem by **Judas Maccabeus**. By 162, Lysias and the boy-king were able to muster a large army to attack the rebellious Jews. But when Lysias learned that the official regent, Philip, had returned from Persia, he made peace with the Jews and granted them religious freedom.

Though Lysias was able to defeat Philip at Antioch, the triumph was short-lived. Both he and his charge Eupator were murdered by soldiers of their own army rallying in support of **Demetrius I Soter**.

ANTIOCHUS VI EPIPHANES DIONYSUS

(di uh nee' suhs) GREEK
"the manifest [god] Dionysus"

Not a direct descendant of the Seleucid rulers of Syria, Antiochus VI was the son of **Alexander Balas**, a lowborn Greek who claimed to be the son of **Antiochus IV Epiphanes**. Antiochus VI was put forward by the general **Trypho**, who gained custody of the boy and proclaimed him king in 145 B.C. Having won the support of troops who had been dismissed by the previous ruler, **Demetrius II Nicator**, Trypho ruled in the name of Antiochus VI for three years, then "killed him and became king in his place" (1 Macc. 13:31)

The coins of (from left to right) Antiochus IV Epiphanes; his son, Antiochus V Eupator;
and Antiochus VI Epiphanes, son of the pretender Alexander Balas

ANTIOCHUS VII SIDETES
(si deet ez) GREEK
"born in Sida [a town in Asia Minor]"
....

A ntiochus VII was the second son of **Demetrius I Soter** and the brother of **Demetrius II Nicator**, whom he succeeded as ruler of Syria in 138 B.C. when Demetrius was captured by the Parthians. Antiochus attempted to overthrow the general **Trypho**'s hold on Palestine by granting concessions to the Jewish leader **Simon**. Once he had blockaded Trypho, he revoked the privileges, then had Simon killed for resistance.

Antiochus VII himself led forces into Jerusalem—then held by Simon's son, the high priest **John Hyrcanus**—to restore control. He besieged Hyrcanus at Jerusalem for an entire year, and in 134 razed the city walls, demanded heavy tribute, took hostages among the leading families, and disarmed the Jewish forces. Again he granted the Jews religious freedom, this time with only nominal but stable Seleucid control.

In 129 B.C. Antiochus VII was killed in battle with the Parthians, who were still holding his brother Demetrius II prisoner.

Antiochus VII Sidetes

APOLLOS
(uh pahl' uhs) GREEK: APOLLOS
....

A Jewish convert named Apollos, from Alexandria, Egypt, proved to be an articulate and effective early Christian preacher, missionary, and debater. He is introduced in the New Testament as "an eloquent man, well-versed in the Scriptures," boldly preaching in the Jewish synagogue at Ephesus, where "he spoke and taught accurately the things concerning Jesus, though he knew only the baptism of John" (Acts 18:24, 25). While in Ephesus he encountered **Prisca** and **Aquila,**

coworkers of the apostle **Paul**, who instructed him "more accurately" (Acts 18:26). Apollos then set out for Corinth, where he encouraged fellow believers and soon became as popular as Paul and **Peter**; parties loyal to each began to threaten church unity.

Paul's first letter to the Corinthians addresses the threat: "Each of you says, 'I belong to Paul,' or 'I belong to Apollos,' or 'I belong to Cephas [Peter],' or 'I belong to Christ'" (1 Cor. 1:12). Far from blaming Apollos for the divisions, Paul credits his work and appeals to the true basis for fellowship when he writes: "I planted, Apollos watered, but God gave the growth" (1 Cor. 3:6).

Further indication that Paul and Apollos were not rivals is found in Paul's urging Apollos to revisit the church in Corinth and in his requesting **Titus** to "speed Zenas the lawyer and Apollos on their way; see that they lack nothing" (Tit. 3:13).

AQUILA
(ak' wi luh) GREEK: AKYLAS
"eagle"
....

A quila, a Jew from Pontus in Asia Minor, was married to **Prisca** (called Priscilla in Acts 18). They had been part of the Jewish group in Rome who had come under political suspicion—probably because they were also Christians—and were expelled from the imperial capital by the emperor **Claudius** about A.D. 49.

Moving to Corinth, the couple met **Paul**. Since they, like Paul, were tent makers, the apostle lived and worked with them while he was in Corinth. They became part of his entourage and accompanied him when he left Corinth for Ephesus, where the church met in their house. Both stayed in Ephesus after Paul moved on. When another Christian missionary named **Apollos** came to Eph-

Aquila and other early Christians flank Jesus in this 14th- or 15th-century reliquary casket.

esus, it was Prisca and Aquila who took him aside and instructed him in the gospel "more accurately" (Acts 18:26), meaning they taught him Paul's version of the gospel. Later they apparently returned to Rome, where Paul sent greetings to them and "the church in their house" (Rom. 16:3).

ARCHIPPUS
(ahr kip' uhs) GREEK: ARCHIPPOS

Paul commended Archippus, a leader of the church at Colossae, as a "fellow soldier" (Philem. 2) and urged him to "fulfill the ministry which you have received in the Lord" (Col. 4:17). The term "fellow soldier," which Paul also used of **Epaphroditus** of Philippi, meant not only that Archippus aided Paul in his missionary work, but also that he had probably shared "in suffering as a good soldier" (2 Tim. 2:3) for the faith. Since he, along with **Philemon** and Apphia, is one of three individuals to whom the letter to Philemon was addressed, it is possible that he was a relative of Philemon who shared his house, where the congregation met.

ARETAS
(ah' ruh tuhs) GREEK: HARETAS
"virtuous" or "pleasing"

This was the dynastic name of the kings of Arab Nabatea, the region south of Judea whose capital was at Petra. It was Aretas IV, who ruled from 9 B.C. to A.D. 40, to whom Paul referred in describing his escape from "the governor under King Aretas" in Damascus by being "let down in a basket through a window in the wall" (2 Cor. 11:32, 33). Since Acts 9:25 places this event soon after Paul's conversion, but Paul's own chronology in Galatians 1:17-21 refers to other visits to Damascus, probable dates for the escape range from A.D. 35 to 39 or 40.

ARISTARCHUS
(air i stahr' kuhs) GREEK: ARISTARCHOS
"best ruler"

AJew from Thessalonica in Macedonia, Aristarchus was evidently converted to Christianity by **Paul**, who came to preach in the synagogue there about A.D. 50. The church in Thessalonica subsequently sent

Aristarchus to join Paul's coworkers, and he labored with the apostle throughout Greece, Asia Minor, and Judea, and even accompanied him as a prisoner to Rome.

ARTAXERXES
(ahr tuh zerk' sees) HEBREW: ARTAHSASTA

Artaxerxes I, the son and successor to Xerxes I (**Ahasuerus**), ruled Persia from 465 to 425 B.C. He apparently became acquainted with members of the Jewish community that had been held captive in Babylon since 587 B.C., and in 458 he permitted the scribe **Ezra** to go to Jerusalem as the head of an official delegation.

Artaxerxes gave Ezra unlimited authority to spend money from the Persian treasury to renew temple sacrifices and do "whatever else is required for the house of your God" (Ezra 7:20). However, Artaxerxes temporarily halted the repairing of Jerusalem in response to a letter sent him by local officials who opposed Ezra's work. Construction was resumed about 445 B.C. by **Nehemiah**, a palace servant of Artaxerxes.

ARTEMIS
(ahr' tuh muhs) GREEK: ARTEMIS

The Greek goddess Artemis, known to the Romans as Diana, was celebrated in mythology as the daughter of **Zeus** and the sister of Apollo. As goddess of the hunt, she is often pictured with bow and arrow. In Ephesus, however, she was worshiped as a fertility goddess and depicted in a static pose with multiple breasts. This image was repeated with little variation wherever the cult of the Ephesian Artemis existed, and numerous copies have been found.

When **Paul** was in Ephesus, he came in conflict with the silversmiths who made images of the Ephesian Artemis because his success in converting the populace to Christianity was hurting their business. They became enraged and dragged Gaius and **Aristarchus**, two of Paul's companions, into the theater, threatening them with bodily harm. Had not his prudent friends restrained him, Paul would have joined the pair in confronting the mob. Finally quieted by the town clerk, who warned them that they were "in danger of being charged with rioting" (Acts 19:40), the silversmiths dispersed and there the matter ended.

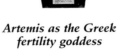

Artemis as the Greek fertility goddess

Asa; a 14th-century English stained-glass window

ASA

(ay' suh) HEBREW: ASA
"he has given"

The son of **Abijah** (also known as Abijam), Asa succeeded his father as king of Judah and ruled for 41 years, from approximately 913 to 873 B.C. He was the fifth king in the line of **David** and the third over Judah after the kingdom was divided. His reign began during the rule of King **Jeroboam** of Israel and ended when **Omri** ruled the rival kingdom to the north.

Because of his program to eradicate the worship of idols from Judah, Asa is praised as one who "did what was right in the eyes of the Lord, as David his father had done" (1 Kg. 15:11). To this end he cast out the male prostitutes of the foreign gods, removed all the idols, and even removed his mother Maacah from her position as "queen mother [probably regent] because she had an abominable image made for Asherah" (1 Kg. 15:13; 2 Chr. 15:16). This effort, however, was only partly successful, since "the high places [pagan shrines] were not taken" (1 Kg. 15:14; 2 Chr. 15:17) from Israel.

On the political front, Asa was credited with winning a significant victory against King **Baasha** of Israel, who was encroaching on the territory of Judah. Asa shrewdly sought an alliance with King **Ben-hadad** of Syria, whom he bribed with "all the silver and the gold that were left in the treasures" (1 Kg. 15:18) of the temple and the royal palace. Ben-hadad then invaded Israel, causing the armies of Baasha to withdraw from Judah. Hanani the seer criticized the alliance with Syria, telling Asa that he had "done foolishly in this" (2 Chr. 16:9) and predicting continued warfare. Asa also scored a notable victory against **Zerah** the Ethiopian after crying to God, "we rely on thee, and in thy name we have come against this multitude" (2 Chr. 14:11).

In the 39th year of his reign, Asa developed a disease of the feet, perhaps gout or dropsy. Failing to call on the Lord, the king "sought help from physicians" (2 Chr. 16:12) and died two years later. He was buried in Jerusalem and was succeeded by his son **Jehoshaphat**.

ASAHEL

(as' uh hel) HEBREW: ASAEL
"God has made"

Along with his brothers **Joab** and **Abishai**, Asahel was one of King **David**'s inner circle of warriors. They were the sons of David's sister **Zeruiah**. Known for being "as swift of foot as a wild gazelle" (2 Sam. 2:18), Asahel appears in the biblical narrative at the moment when that strength proved his undoing.

During David's war with **Saul**'s son **Ish-bosheth**, Joab defeated Ish-bosheth's forces led by the renowned **Abner**. When Abner fled, the younger Asahel pursued him, eager to strike the famous warrior. As Asahel closed on his prey, Abner called on him to take on a younger opponent since he did not wish to risk Joab's anger by smiting his brother. But Asahel ignored him. Just as Asahel was about to seize Abner, the older warrior rammed his spear backward so hard that the butt went completely through his pursuer; Asahel died on the spot. Joab treated Asahel's death as a murder rather than a battle casualty and later killed Abner to avenge his brother's death.

ASAPH

(ay' saf) HEBREW: ASAP
"collector"

A musician to whom King **David** gave major responsibility in the worship at the tabernacle in Jerusalem, Asaph was the son of Berechiah, a Levite and titular ancestor of the guild of musicians known as the sons of Asaph. Twelve of the Psalms (50 and 73 to 83) are linked to Asaph, perhaps written by him or composed in his style.

When David brought the ark of the covenant to Jerusalem, he placed the musical services in the reestablished tabernacle under Asaph, Heman, and Ethan, each representing one of the three great Levitical clans. These three sang and sounded cymbals as the ark was brought to the city. In the dedication service, Asaph led the musicians "to invoke, to thank, and to praise the Lord, the God of Israel" (1 Chr. 16:4).

ASHER

(ash' uhr) HEBREW: ASER
"happy one"

The eighth son of **Jacob**, Asher was the second born to **Zilpah**, also the mother of **Gad**. Since Zilpah was the slave of **Leah**, Jacob's older wife named the woman's son with the exclamation, "Happy am I! For the women will call me happy" (Gen. 30:13). Besides meaning "happy," the name Asher is also the masculine form of the name of the goddess Asherah.

Asher was born in Paddan-aram while Jacob was laboring for his father-in-law, **Laban**. For good and ill, he shared the life of Jacob's growing clan, never separating from his father's family. By the time the clan migrated to Egypt, Asher had four adult sons and a daughter. When the nation of Israel returned to Canaan, the tribe of Asher settled in western Galilee.

ASHURBANIPAL

(ash uhr bahn' i pahl) ASSYRIAN:
ASSURBANIAPLI
"[the god] Ashur creates an heir"

The son of **Esarhaddon**, Ashurbanipal ruled Assyria at its height, from 668 to 627 B.C., but the empire quickly began to decline after his death and fell to the Medes in 612 B.C. Ashurbanipal is not mentioned by his Assyrian name in the Bible, although he is apparently "the great and noble Osnappar" (Ezra 4:10) cited for deporting and resettling conquered peoples. During his reign Judah, the only remaining Hebrew kingdom, was a vassal state. Ashurbanipal may have been the overlord when **Manasseh** was captured and taken in "fetters of bronze" (2 Chr. 33:11) to Babylon since the Assyrian ruler listed Manasseh as one of 22 kings from whom he received tribute.

Although most Assyrian kings were probably illiterate, Ashurbanipal was a learned man. He established an extensive library of cuneiform writings at Nineveh, a part of which has survived and is a major source for our knowledge of Assyrian culture.

ATHALIAH

(ath uh lai' yuh) HEBREW: ATALYAHU
"Yahweh is exalted"

Though she was the daughter of King **Ahab** of Israel, Athaliah became the queen of Judah and its sole ruler from about 842 to 837 B.C. She was evidently born to one of Ahab's many unnamed wives, perhaps before he married **Jezebel**, the princess of Sidon. (In some translations of the Bible, she is called the daughter of **Omri** and would thus have been Ahab's sister.) Athaliah, however, was strongly influenced by Jezebel, and she became an ardent devotee of Jezebel's god **Baal**.

In 867 B.C. Ahab concluded an alliance with King **Jehoshaphat** of Judah, ending 50 years of hostility between the two kingdoms. The treaty was sealed by the marriage of Athaliah to **Jehoram**, the prince of Judah. During the following years, though Jehoshaphat actively promoted the worship of Yahweh in the south, Athaliah maintained her ties to her family in the north and her devotion to Baal.

Her husband Jehoram was made governmental regent by Jehoshaphat about 852. Some three years later Athaliah became queen of Judah when her husband succeeded Jehoshaphat; at about the same time her brother, also named **Jehoram**, became king of Israel.

Ashurbanipal hunting from a chariot; a seventh-century B.C. stone carving

Judah became divided religiously. Jehoram, as a descendant of David, represented the worship of Yahweh, but he was tolerant of Athaliah's promotion of Baal. After eight years Jehoram died of a painful illness, cited by his opponents as a plague from God, and Athaliah's son **Ahaziah** became king; Athaliah was the power behind the throne.

The next year, bitterness engulfed Athaliah's life. Her son Ahaziah was with her brother Jehoram of Israel, when an army commander named **Jehu** assassinated them both in the name of Yahweh. Jehu soon had Athaliah's extended family executed or murdered; 70 of her half brothers, Ahab's sons, were slaughtered in Samaria, as were the priests and worshipers of Baal.

In response to this holy war against her family and religion, Athaliah attacked the Davidic dynasty that had been the mainstay of the worship of Yahweh. After executing all possible Davidic successors, she assumed the throne herself, apparently hoping to reestablish in Judah the dynasty that had been destroyed in Israel.

A single infant escaped the queen's wrath: **Joash**, one of her grandsons, who was raised in secret by the priest **Jehoiada** in the temple. Opposition to Athaliah's draconian rule remained underground for six years, so that she was taken by surprise when the priest brought forth Joash and proclaimed him king. Athaliah rushed to the temple to try to stop this rebellion but was captured and executed.

AUGUSTUS

(aw guhs' tuhs) LATIN: AUGUSTUS
"revered"

The designation Augustus was a title given by the Roman Senate in 27 B.C. to Gaius Julius Caesar Octavianus (Octavian), the great-nephew and adopted son of Julius Caesar. It recognized the power and almost divine authority of the man who was the founder of the Roman empire and its sole ruler from 31 B.C. to A.D. 14.

Born in 63 B.C., Octavian impressed Julius Caesar with his keen abilities, and in his will Caesar made the young man his principal heir. Octavian was only 19 when Caesar was assassinated, but he showed a remarkable combination of political acumen and total ruthlessness in navigating his way through the chaos of civil war. First he combined with Caesar's lieutenant, Mark Antony, to crush the forces of the assassins, Cassius and Brutus, in 42 B.C. But growing conflict with Mark Antony, who married Cleopatra VII, queen of Egypt, led to a new civil war that ended with the battle of Actium in 31 B.C. Octavian was victorious, and Antony and Cleopatra committed suicide to avoid the ignominy of capture.

During the following years Octavian, under his new title Augustus, carefully used the powers of republican offices and the Roman tradition of patronage to create a web of authority that gave him complete political, military, and social control over the Roman realm. He was also able to maintain a peace that facilitated travel, trade, and prosperity throughout his sprawling empire. However, Augustus had great difficulty in establishing a successor for his office. He ultimately adopted his stepson **Tiberius**, whom he personally disliked, as the official recipient of what became the hereditary title of Roman emperor.

Augustus is mentioned in the Bible only in Luke 2:1, which tells of his decree when **Quirinius** was governor of Syria "that all the world should be enrolled" for taxation.

Augustus heroically depicted by a contemporary sculptor

BAAL

(bay' uhl) HEBREW: BAAL
"lord"

The deity most commonly worshiped by the ancient Canaanite peoples, Baal was a god of fertility and also of storms. The Hebrew word *baal* simply means "lord" and is often used to mean owner, master, husband, or even man. But as a religious term, Baal was the title given the god Hadad—although in the Bible, Baal is always used in place of the god's proper name. By calling their deity Baal instead of Hadad, the Canaanites emphasized their belief that their god was lord and owner of the land and its people. He supplied them with the rain that made the land fertile and thus bestowed life and prosperity on all the people. Therefore, they spoke of him as "the prince, the lord (Baal) of the earth."

In Canaanite mythology, Baal was part of an extended pantheon. The distant high god was the creator El, a name that means "god." El's brother was **Dagon**, god of grain, and Baal was Dagon's son. Baal's sister and wife, Anath, played an important role in the story of his rise to power.

According to the myth, Baal gained his preeminence in Canaanite worship by overcoming forces that sought to destroy the equilibrium and security of the world. The first of Baal's feats was a battle with the god of waters, Yam, sometimes called Prince Sea and other times Twisting Serpent. When Prince Sea demanded Baal's submission, even the gods in El's council were intimidated by the ruler of the chaotic seawaters. Using divine weapons, Baal was able to rout and defeat Prince Sea, and the cry went up, "Hail, Baal the Conqueror!" In celebration of this great victory, a temple was built for Baal the Conqueror.

But the myths tell of an even stronger challenge to Baal from El's son Mot, or Death, a being whose strength lay in his ability to induce sterility and famine. When even Baal, the protector of human life, had to surrender to the power of Mot, the gods mourned, "Baal is dead: what will happen to the peoples?" Indeed, their fate was a deadly drought that lasted until Anath, by her love for Baal, was able to wrest her brother-husband from the grip of Mot and return him to life. And with him, all nature blossomed anew. In the agricultural society of Canaan, the people saw these myths played out in the cycles of nature and celebrated them in seasonal festivals.

In the Bible, Baal is seen as a rival to Israel's God. Not surprisingly, nearly every reference to Baal in the Scriptures is negative, bearing witness to the harsh fact that the Israelites were continually attracted to his worship. Indeed, **Ahab** and **Jezebel** made Baal the principal deity of Israel for a time. Even in more orthodox Judah, the prophet **Jeremiah** noted, Jerusalem's altars, where incense was burned to Baal, were "as many as the streets" (Jer. 11:13).

ISRAEL'S BAAL

There **is** some evidence in the Old Testament that Israel's God, Yahweh, was also known as Baal. One of the "mighty men" (1 Chr. 12:1) who joined David at Ziklag was Saul's kinsman Bealiah, whose name means "Yahweh is Baal." Some 300 years later Hosea declared that the Lord, in renewing his covenant with Israel, demanded, "you will call me, 'My husband,' and no longer will you call me, 'My Baal'" (Hos. 2:16).*

BAASHA

(bah' uh shuh) HEBREW: BASHA
"Baal hears"
••••••••••

Starting early in the ninth century B.C., rival clans fought each other for rule over the kingdom of Israel. Baasha the son of Ahijah, from the tribe of Issachar, began the destructive custom of gaining the throne of the northern kingdom by assassinating the current king. In the midst of a war against the Philistines, Baasha killed King **Nadab**, son of **Jeroboam**, and then proceeded to murder the entire royal family in order to become the third ruler of the northern kingdom.

During his reign (c. 900-877 B.C.) Baasha formed an alliance with Syria to the north and tried to strangle Judah's trade by fortifying the city of Ramah, five miles north of Jerusalem. King **Asa** of Judah responded by bribing King Ben-hadad of Syria to switch sides and attack Israel. After Baasha lost extensive territories in the regions of Dan and Naphtali, north and west of the Sea of Galilee, he was forced to surrender Ramah to Judah.

Baasha remained in power more than 20 years. But he provoked opposition from prophets such as **Jehu** the son of Hanani, who predicted the destruction of his dynasty—a prediction that came true with the assassination of Baasha's son and successor, **Elah**, in the second year of his reign.

BACCHIDES

(back' uh deez) GREEK: BAKCHIDES
"child of [the god] Bacchus"
••••••••••

In 161 B.C., during the Maccabean revolt, Bacchides, a close adviser of King **Demetrius I Soter** of Syria and governor of the regions west of the Euphrates River, was chosen to lead an army into Judea and to install **Alcimus** in the office of high priest. Bacchides accomplished his mission but alienated many by killing a group of pious Jews.

A year later, after **Judas Maccabeus** had defeated a Syrian force, Bacchides was sent back with a much larger army and managed to defeat the dispirited Jewish troops and kill Judas. Bacchides again engaged the Jewish forces in 157 B.C. but eventually concluded a peace treaty with the Jews that recognized **Jonathan**, the brother of Judas, as their legitimate leader.

The ageless frustration of a man, like Balaam, astride a recalcitrant donkey; a 16th-century bronze figurine

BALAAM

(bay' luhm) HEBREW: BILAM
possibly "devourer"
••••••••••

Balaam, a non-Israelite prophet whose home was Pethor, near the Euphrates River in northern Mesopotamia, is one of the most curious figures in the entire Bible. His fame was such that, when King **Balak** of Moab was confronted with the arrival of the Israelites en route to the Promised Land, he sent an embassy to Balaam asking the seer to curse the invaders so that the Moabites could defeat them.

Balaam apparently did not know the nation that Balak wanted him to curse, the Moabite ruler having described them only as "a people . . . come out of Egypt; they cover the face of the earth" (Num. 22:5). Though Balak's emissaries offered him rich fees, he summarily dismissed them after God had forbade him to curse this people. But at night God commanded Balaam to "rise, go with them; but only what I bid you, that shall you do" (Num. 22:20). Yet God did not specify what he would ask Balaam to do, and it may be imagined that Balaam departed in the hope of cursing Balak's unknown enemies. The narrative seems to assume this, since without explanation it states that God was angry at Balaam for going.

As a further warning to Balaam, the Lord sent an angel with a drawn sword to block his way. But only Balaam's donkey could see the divine messenger—perhaps a symbol of how little this seer could really see of the situation he was about to encounter—and refused to proceed. When the frustrated Balaam beat the animal, Yahweh allowed the donkey to speak in protest and finally let Balaam see and talk to the angel, who sent him on, warning him to speak only "the word which I bid you" (Num. 22:35).

When the delegation accompanying Balaam arrived in Moab, Balak was hopeful of getting help from the renowned seer. But Balaam warned the king that he had no power in himself: "The word that God puts in my mouth, that must I speak" (Num. 22:38). Nonetheless, elaborate rites were performed. At three different locations seven altars were built and seven bulls and seven rams were sacrificed. But each time, when all was ritually ready for the powerful curse from God on Balak's enemies, the Lord put in Balaam's mouth a resounding blessing on Israel.

When Balak exploded in anger at Balaam, the prophet added oracles that foretold Israel's eventual truimph over its enemies, including Moab, and then returned home.

The text proceeds to describe a period during which the Israelites worshiped **Baal** and intermarried with Moabites and Midianites and tells of a miraculous plague that killed thousands of the apostates. Only several chapters later does the text again mention Balaam, abruptly reporting that he was killed by Israel in a battle with Midian.

BALAK

(bay' lack) HEBREW: BALAQ
"destroyer" or "devastator"

Moab's King Balak was justifiably terrified of the Israelites. Under **Moses** they had already dispossessed the neighboring Amorites and killed both their king, **Sihon**, and King **Og** of Bashan, both of whom had sought to stop their advance toward the Promised Land through the lands east of the Dead Sea; suddenly, they were encamped on his border. Confronted with this uncomfortable fact, Balak sent emissaries to the Mesopotamian soothsayer **Balaam**, offering him generous fees if he would curse the Israelites. But God would only allow Balaam to speak the words he put in his mouth, and so the seer blessed rather than cursed the Israelites.

BARABBAS

(buh rab' uhs) GREEK: BARABBAS
"son of the father/teacher"

All four Gospels describe **Pilate**'s offer to the crowd during the trial of **Jesus** to free one prisoner—a customary favor bestowed by the Roman governor at the time of the Passover feast. The choice given was Jesus or Barabbas, a man who had been arrested for insurrection and murder and was a notorious prisoner. Urged on by their leaders, the people clamored for Barabbas to be freed and for Jesus to be executed.

Barabbas may have been a leader of the Jewish militants who wanted to throw off the

In a narrow Jerusalem street, Roman soldiers seize Barabbas, who has just murdered one of their comrades.

Roman yoke by force. As an insurrectionist, Barabbas would have been sentenced to death by crucifixion as a warning to others. Some ancient manuscripts give Barabbas's first name as Jesus, a not uncommon name of the time. This would have made Pilate's offer even more poignant: "Whom do you want me to release for you, [Jesus] Barabbas or Jesus who is called Christ?" (Mt. 27:17).

BARAK

(bay' rack) HEBREW: BARAQ
"lightning"

The son of Abinoam, Barak was from Kedesh, a city of refuge in the northern region of Naphtali. He was evidently a tribal leader, known for his military prowess.

In the 12th century B.C., the Israelites in the north were dominated by Jabin, the Canaanite king of Hazor, who fielded chariots of iron, while the Israelites were largely unarmed. The prophetess **Deborah**, who was judging in the hill country of Ephraim to the south, summoned Barak and commanded him in the name of Yahweh to muster an army at Mount Tabor and confront Jabin's forces under his general **Sisera**. Aware of Israel's weakness, Barak refused to do so unless Deborah herself would accompany him. She agreed but warned Barak that for his reluctance he would lose to a woman the personal glory of defeating Sisera. Barak led militias mobilized from the northern tribes to crush Sisera's chariots in the muddy, rain-drenched plains by the river Kishon. But true to Deborah's word, Sisera escaped, and a woman named **Jael** gained renown by killing him.

BAR-JESUS

(bahr' jesus) GREEK: BARIESOUS
"son of Jesus"

A Jewish magician also known by the Greek name Elymas, Bar-Jesus became involved in a confrontation with **Paul** and **Barnabas** in which the apostle caused him temporarily to lose his sight. The encounter occurred at Paphos, capital of Cyprus, where Bar-Jesus was employed by the Roman proconsul Sergius **Paulus**.

On a journey to Barnabas's native country, the two missionaries attracted the attention of Paulus, who granted them a public audience. Bar-Jesus opposed their preaching, fearing his influence would be diminished if the proconsul embraced the Christian faith. Paul, however, exposed the magician's motives, condemned him for

The scribe Baruch, his scroll unfurling from a 14th-century Italian roundel

"making crooked the straight paths of the Lord" (Acts 13:10), and struck him blind. The severity of the rebuke was apparently sufficient to evoke the proconsul's belief.

BARNABAS

(bahr' nuh buhs) GREEK: BARNABAS
"son of encouragement"

A native of Cyprus and member of the tribe of Levi, who perhaps served in the temple, Barnabas was a crucial early link between Jewish and Gentile Christians. **Luke** introduces him in the book of Acts as a generous man who sold land to support the growing church.

Barnabas soon vouched for a new convert named Saul of Tarsus (**Paul**), who was viewed with suspicion by those who only recently had been targets of Saul's persecution. Shortly thereafter, Jerusalem church leaders sent Barnabas to Antioch where the congregation contained both Jews and Gentiles. Under Barnabas, the church grew so quickly that Barnabas went to Tarsus and asked Saul to join him. Together Barnabas and Saul worked successfully for a year; in Antioch at this time "the disciples were for the first time called Christians" (Acts 11:26).

In another effort to build harmony, Barnabas helped organize a relief drive during a widespread famine. Gifts were taken to Jerusalem by Barnabas and Saul—the order in which the names appear in Acts 11:30 is intentional and reflects the order of leadership at this point. The Antioch church subsequently sent Barnabas, Saul, and John **Mark**, Barnabas's cousin from Jerusalem, on a tour to preach to Gentiles. Their first stop was Cyprus, where Roman proconsul Sergius **Paulus** was converted. Here Luke stops calling Saul by his Jewish name and begins referring to him by his Roman name, Paul. After this, the order of names in Acts is generally reversed to read Paul and Barnabas (the first time in Acts 13:43), suggesting a change in leadership.

In further travels Paul and Barnabas preached in synagogues, where they drew receptive listeners as well as opponents. In the city of Lystra, their preaching and healing caused some to hail them as Greek deities. Soon adulation turned to attack, however, and Paul was nearly killed.

Barnabas's last major role in Acts was at a conference in Jerusalem called to decide whether Gentile converts had to become full proselytes to Judaism (including being circumcised) before they could be Christians. **Peter** spoke first, then Barnabas and Paul. Finally, **James** the brother of **Jesus** urged that all follow only certain requirements that were held to be older than **Abraham** and thus binding on both Jews and Gentiles. Neither circumcision nor the dietary laws need be observed. Paul and Barnabas returned to Antioch with a letter explaining the decision, which restored peace.

Paul, Barnabas, and Mark planned one more trip together, to revisit the sites of their first successes. However, Paul did not want to take Mark, saying he had abandoned the first mission after they left Cyprus. Unable to agree, Paul and Barnabas went their separate ways.

BARTHOLOMEW

(bahr thah' luh myoo) GREEK:
BARTHOLOMAIOS
"son of Tolmai/Talmai"
•••••••••

One of the lesser known of the 12 apostles, Bartholomew is named in all four New Testament lists of **Jesus'** inner circle of disciples: Matthew 10:3, Mark 3:18, Luke 6:14, Acts 1:13. Since the ninth century many have proposed that Bartholomew and **Nathanael** were the same person. This is because the Gospel of John (1:45-51) links Nathanael to **Philip** but fails to mention Bartholomew, whereas Matthew, Mark, and Luke name Bartholomew after Philip but omit Nathanael from their lists. Today, however, the tradition is questioned as an effort to fuse existing evidence. Many scholars now prefer to treat Bartholomew and Nathanael as separate figures, since the sources nowhere say they are the same, and no events are ascribed to both.

BARUCH

(bah rouk') HEBREW: BARUKH
"blessed"
•••••••••

The royal scribe Baruch sacrificed his own rising career to assist the prophet **Jeremiah**. At Jeremiah's dictation, he set down the first collection of his friend's oracles in 605 B.C. and later read them publicly at the gate of the temple—King **Jehoiakim** having banned the prophet from the sanctuary. After the scroll was confiscated and personally destroyed by the king, Baruch and Jeremiah went into hiding to avoid arrest but were able to make a new and expanded copy of the prophecies. Many scholars believe that Baruch was the author of the historical narrative included in the book of Jeremiah.

BATHSHEBA

(bath shee' buh) HEBREW: BATSHEBA
"daughter of abundance"
•••••••••

So great was Bathsheba's beauty that it drove **David**, the Lord's anointed king, to adultery and murder. While Bathsheba's husband, **Uriah** the Hittite, was away in

From a palace window, David sees Bathsheba at her bath.

battle, David saw her bathing and summoned her to his quarters. Without apparent protest, she joined the king in adultery and married him after he arranged for Uriah to be killed in battle. Though her first son died, she made David promise that her second son, **Solomon**, would succeed him. When David was near death, she used this promise to block the elevation of his eldest surviving son, **Adonijah**. In 1 Chronicles 3:5, Solomon's mother is called Bath-shua.

BEL

(bel) HEBREW: BEL
"lord"

The title Bel was given by the Babylonians to their idol Marduk (or Merodach) to show that he was their chief god. Bel-Marduk is equivalent to the Canaanite deity

Baal. In Mesopotamian mythology, Bel won kingship among the gods by defeating Tiamat, the goddess of chaotic waters. His ascension symbolized Babylon's political dominance of the region. But prophets of Judah foretold the fall of Bel along with Babylon: **Jeremiah** speaks of a time when "Babylon is taken, Bel is put to shame, Merodach is dismayed" (Jer. 50:2).

In Bel and the Dragon, a second-century B.C. addition to the book of Daniel, the foolishness of the Babylonian belief that "Bel is a living God" (Bel 6) is revealed by **Daniel**. The Babylonians, according to this tale, set a feast each day before their idol and believed that Bel came at night to consume it. But one night Daniel secretly sifted ashes on the floor of the temple, and the next morning he pointed out priests' footprints to the king, proving the food had been secretly carried away.

THE BELOVED DISCIPLE

One of the most intriguing figures in the New Testament is the unnamed disciple who appears only in the Gospel of John and plays a major role in the final events of Jesus' story. He is introduced at the Last Supper: "One of his disciples, whom Jesus loved, was lying close to the breast of Jesus" (Jn. 13:23).

The beloved disciple next appears standing with Jesus' mother at the crucifixion site. From the cross Jesus said to his mother, "Woman, behold, your son!" and to the disciple, "Behold, your mother!" The Gospel adds, "From that hour the disciple took her to his own home" (Jn. 19:26-27). Just after Mary Magdalene reported that Jesus' tomb was empty, the beloved disciple ran to the tomb with Peter and seeing, believed—the first to accept Jesus' resurrection. Later, the beloved disciple was in the group that went fishing with Peter in Galilee. When Jesus appeared on the shore, the beloved disciple was the first to recognize him.

Since the second century tradition has identified the beloved disciple as the apostle John, the son of Zebedee, and has attributed the fourth Gospel to him. Some scholars believe that the tradition is partly or wholly correct; others, however, think it unlikely that the author would give himself such a flattering title and note that

the Gospel portrays the beloved disciple as a man with home and acquaintances around Jerusalem rather than as a Galilean fisherman like John.

***Jesus and the beloved disciple;
a 14th-century painted wood statue***

Belshazzar sees the handwriting on the wall; detail of a 1635 painting by Rembrandt.

BELSHAZZAR

(bel shaz' uhr) HEBREW: BELTESASSAR
"Bel protects the king"

••••••••••

The book of Daniel describes Belshazzar as the son and successor of King **Nebuchadnezzar** of Babylon, and two of **Daniel**'s visions are placed in the first and third years of his reign. The book also contains a vivid narrative of the last night of Belshazzar's life.

On that night Belshazzar "made a great feast for a thousand of his lords" and served them wine from the holy vessels "his father had taken out of the temple in Jerusalem" (Dan. 5:1-2). In answer to this sacrilege, a disembodied hand suddenly appeared writing mysterious words on the wall; only Daniel was able to interpret the sign. He castigated the king for misusing the holy vessels and revealed that the words—"MENE, MENE, TEKEL, and PARSIN" (Dan. 5:25)—predicted Belshazzar's overthrow. "That very night," the text recounts, "Belshazzar the Chaldean king was slain," overthrown by **Darius the Mede** (Dan. 5:30).

According to Babylonian records, Belshazzar was actually the son of Nabonidus, a Babylonian noble who in 556 B.C. overthrew Labashi-Marduk, the third ruler after Nebuchadnezzar. Nabonidus was the last king of the Babylonian empire, and during part of his reign shared power with his son. Nabonidus and Belshazzar in turn were overthown by **Cyrus II** of Persia in 539.

BENAIAH

(ben i' uh) HEBREW: BENAYA, BENAYAHU
"Yahweh has built"

••••••••••

The commander of King **David**'s guard of Cretan and Philistine mercenaries, Benaiah was instrumental in ensuring that the royal succession passed to **Solomon** after David's death. Benaiah and his troops supported Solomon's party against the expected heir, **Adonijah**. When Solomon became king, he ordered Benaiah to kill those who had opposed him, including Adonijah and David's army commander **Joab**. Benaiah was rewarded for the bloody deeds by being named the supreme commander of Solomon's army.

Noted for his heroic exploits, Benaiah one day bravely entered a pit to dispatch a lion. Another time, carrying only a staff, he faced down an Egyptian soldier who was armed with a spear. Benaiah grabbed the spear away and killed his enemy with it.

BEN-HADAD

(ben hay' dad) HEBREW: BEN-HADAD
"son of [the god] Hadad"

••••••••••

Ben-hadad was the name of two or possibly three kings of Syria. The second of that name ruled in Damascus for some 20 years, starting about 860 B.C., and made Syria the region's dominant power by playing off the small rival kingdoms of Judah and Israel against each other. But when Ben-hadad tried to force King **Ahab** of Israel to join an alliance against the Assyrians, the Israelite defeated him in battle and even captured Ben-hadad himself. Ahab spared his opponent's life but forced Ben-hadad to return captured cities and grant commerical concessions to Israel. Although it is disputed, some scholars think it was also the second Ben-hadad who sent his court official **Hazael** to request a cure of **Elisha**. Told by the prophet that he would soon rule Syria, Hazael murdered the king on his return.

Unable to conceal his emotion at seeing Benjamin, Joseph turns from his gift-bearing brothers.

BENJAMIN
(ben' juh muhn) HEBREW: BINYAMIN
"son of the right hand"

As **Rachel** was dying in childbirth, she named her second son Ben-oni, which means "son of my sorrow"; but his father, **Jacob**, gave him a more propitious name: Benjamin, meaning "son of the right hand." As the youngest son and the son of Jacob's beloved wife, Benjamin was the favorite of his father, particularly after Rachel's other son, **Joseph**, was sold into slavery.

Long after Joseph had risen from slavery to become a power in Egypt, the famine that he had predicted struck Canaan as it had Egypt. Jacob sent his sons to Egypt to buy grain, which was plentiful there thanks to Joseph's foresight. Since Joseph was in charge of Egypt's food supply, his brothers had to plead with him for grain, although they failed to recognize him. After selling them food, Joseph accused his brothers of being spies. Holding **Simeon** as a hostage, he insisted they return with Benjamin.

Jacob was afraid to let Benjamin go, but **Judah** swore to assume responsibility for Benjamin's safety. When Benjamin finally got to Egypt, Joseph first tricked his brothers by planting a silver cup among the youngest son's belongings; then, after a dramatic confrontation, he revealed his true identity.

The tribe of Benjamin later inhabited the strategic territory between Judah and the other northern tribes.

BERNICE
(buhr nees') GREEK: BERNIKE

A daughter of **Herod Agrippa I**, Bernice plays only a small role in the Bible; she is present when **Paul** is summoned by the procurator **Festus** to defend himself before her brother, **Herod Agrippa II**. But ancient historians have left us a great deal of information about Bernice's life, very little of it admirable.

After her first husband died, Bernice was given in marriage to her own uncle and bore him two sons. Following his death, she wed an Anatolian king named Polemo to quell rumors that she and her brother were involved in an incestuous relationship. But this marriage did not last long. Bernice eventually became the mistress of Titus, who commanded Rome's war against the Jews, destroyed Jerusalem in A.D. 70, and later became emperor.

BETHUEL
(buh thoo' uhl) HEBREW: BETUEL
"dweller in God"

The son of **Abraham**'s brother **Nahor**, Bethuel remained near Haran when the patriarch left for the Promised Land. In his old age, Abraham feared that his son **Isaac** might marry a Canaanite woman, so he sent a servant—possibly **Eliezer**—bearing gifts to find Isaac a wife among his kindred in Mesopotamia. Bethuel's daughter **Rebekah** appeared at the well of the city of Nahor, where the servant was waiting for a sign from the Lord. After she identified herself and was rewarded with gifts, Rebekah ran home to announce the stranger's arrival.

Brought to Bethuel's house for food and shelter, the servant told of his search. Hearing the story, Bethuel and his son **Laban** said, "Rebekah is before you, take her and go" (Gen. 24:51). Rebekah's relatives proved useful later, when **Jacob** went to "the house of Bethuel" (Gen. 28:2) to escape his brother **Esau**'s rage and also to find a wife.

BEZALEL

(bez' uh leel) HEBREW: BESALEL
"in the shadow [protection] of God"
••••••••••

When **Moses** needed master artisans and craftsmen to work on the tabernacle of the tent of meeting, the Lord called Bezalel, son of Uri, and "filled him with . . . ability and intelligence, with knowledge and all craftsmanship" (Ex. 31:3). Bezalel and his assistant Oholiab led a large group of workers who designed and worked in fine metals, precious stones, rare wood, and luxurious cloth of blue, purple, and scarlet. All these were needed for the splendors of the tabernacle, including its furnishings and the "finely worked garments" for **Aaron** and his sons "for their service as priests" (Ex. 31:10). Even the metal mirrors of the ministering women were used to form the great bronze laver. More than 300 years later, in the time of **Solomon**, it was said that Bezalel's altar still stood in the temple.

BILDAD

(bil' dad) HEBREW: BILDAD
possibly "son of strife"
••••••••••

One of the three friends of **Job** ironically described as his comforters, Bildad the Shuhite came with **Eliphaz** and **Zophar** to condole with Job on his horrible sufferings. Bildad was a traditionalist who saw suffering as a direct punishment for sin. In his first speech he blamed the deaths of Job's children on their own sins. In his second discourse, Bildad described in horrific detail the punishment and ultimate destruction of the wicked, implying that Job's suffering proved him to be one "who knows not God" (Job 18:21). Finally, he reminded Job that man is merely a maggot and a worm, who cannot "be righteous before God" (Job 25:4). When Job was restored to favor, Bildad and his friends were ordered to atone for their mean-spirited words.

BILHAH

(bil'hah) HEBREW: BILHA
possibly "simplicity" or "modesty"
••••••••••

When **Rachel** was unable to conceive a child, she sent her maid Bilhah to **Jacob** as a surrogate for herself. Bilhah's sons by Jacob were **Dan** and **Naphtali**. Their names were given them not by Bilhah but by Rachel, who had authority over them as if they were her own children. Much later, Jacob's eldest son **Reuben** committed adultery with Bilhah.

BOAZ

(boh' az) HEBREW: BOAZ
"strength" or "might"
••••••••••

A wealthy man of Bethlehem in Judah, Boaz followed the Israelite law that required farmers to leave the edges of their fields unharvested and its gleanings ungathered so that the poor might reap them. During the barley harvest, the young widow **Ruth** came into Boaz's field to glean. When he learned that her deceased husband was a distant kinsman, Boaz invited her to eat with him and asked her to glean only in his field, instructing his farm workers to leave sheaves of barley especially for her to gather. At the urging of her mother-in-law, **Naomi**, Ruth later went to Boaz to remind him of his right and obligation as a relative of her late husband to marry her. They did marry and their son, **Obed**, became the grandfather of King **David**.

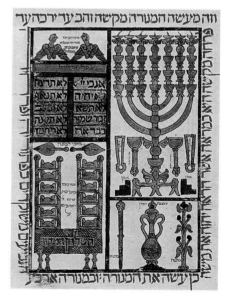

Items crafted for the temple by Bezalel, as depicted in a c. 1315 book of knowledge

CAIAPHAS

(kay' uh fuhs) GREEK: KAIAPHAS

As high priest, Caiaphas presided over the first trial of **Jesus** before the Sanhedrin, the Jewish court. The historian Josephus twice notes Caiaphas's life and career, but he is named nowhere else outside the New Testament. Josephus first mentions Caiaphas's appointment as high priest by Valerius Gratus, the Roman governor of Syria, about A.D. 18. Josephus later reports that Caiaphas was deposed by the Roman procurator Vitellius in 36/37 and was replaced by Jonathan, son of **Annas**. Caiaphas's 18-year tenure brought rare stability; when appointed, he was the fifth high priest in four years.

The Gospel of John introduces Caiaphas shortly after Jesus raised **Lazarus** from the dead. The excitement caused by the miracle drove the worried members of the Sanhedrin to pressure Caiaphas: "What are we to do? For this man performs many signs. If we let him go on thus, every one will believe in him, and the Romans will come and destroy both our holy place and our nation." Then came Caiaphas's famous rejoinder: "You do not understand that it is expedient for you that one man should die for the people, and that the whole nation should not perish" (Jn. 11:47-48, 50).

All four Gospels make the trial a preliminary hearing, before Jesus is bound over to **Pilate**. After Caiaphas heard the accusations against Jesus and noted his silence, he ordered Jesus to say whether he claimed to be the Son of God. The Gospel accounts of the reply vary: "You have said so" (Mt.

Caiaphas rending his garments in horror at what he considers Jesus' blasphemy; detail of a 14th-century painting for the cathedral of Siena, Italy

26:64); "I am" (Mk. 14:62); "You say that I am" (Lk. 22:70).

Did Jesus actually claim to be the Son of God or did he attribute the claim to others? If the latter, how could it be construed as blasphemy? And if Jesus was charged with blasphemy, how would Pilate be expected to agree, since it was not a crime under Roman law? Some scholars consider the first and third answers as proof of an illegal trial; others point to the apparent inconsistencies as the varying emphasis intended by each Gospel author. Regardless, the official reaction was the same: Jesus had uttered blasphemy, a capital offense according to Mosaic Law. In keeping with a pious custom on hearing blasphemy, Caiaphas ritually tore his garment.

Questions remain about Caiaphas. Why does Matthew name him as high priest yet Mark does not do so, while John presents a trial before Annas, but not Caiaphas? Other curiosities: Why were Annas and Caiaphas linked as high priests during the time of **John the Baptist**, while years later, when **Peter** and **John** were arrested, Annas is called the high priest but Caiaphas is not? Outside records that may have clarified such puzzles were lost in the destruction of Jerusalem in A.D. 70.

CAIN

(kayn) HEBREW: QAYIN
"smith"

The firstborn son of **Adam** and **Eve**, Cain was a farmer and the older brother of the shepherd **Abel**. When Cain offered in sacrifice the produce of the field (stintingly given, according to tradition, though the Bible does not say that), God disdained the offering, preferring Abel's sacrifice of the firstborn sheep of his flock. This enraged Cain, who summoned his brother out to a field and killed him. Legend supplies an-

God banishes Cain for murdering Abel; an 11th-century ivory carving.

other detail omitted from the bare biblical narrative: The murder weapon was a stone.

Calling Cain to account for the first murder in human history, the Lord asked him, "Where is Abel your brother?" Refusing to accept responsibility for the deed, Cain claimed not to know. "Am I my brother's keeper?" (Gen. 4:9) he replied, with words that are among the most familiar of biblical quotations. But, as it turned out, that was not a satisfactory answer. "The voice of your brother's blood is crying to me from the ground" (Gen. 4:10), the Lord told him.

Because of his crime, Cain was sentenced to wander the earth and, if he did settle anywhere to farm, his labors would be futile; the ground into which Abel's blood had flowed would refuse to produce crops for him. Fearing that he himself would be killed by anyone who encountered him, Cain begged for mercy. "My punishment is greater than I can bear" (Gen. 4:13), he pleaded. God showed his forgiveness and mercy by promising to protect him with a mark (unexplained in Genesis but perhaps a skin blemish or a tattoo) that would ward off attackers. It was a sign that the Lord himself would demand vengeance if Cain were killed. Then Cain started his wanderings, "in the land of Nod, east of Eden" (Gen. 4:16)—the very word Nod meaning "wandering." According to tradition, he built a city named for his son Enoch; his descendants are said to have included the earliest tent-dwelling herdsmen, metalworkers, and musicians.

Cain is mentioned twice in the New Testament. Christians are warned "not to be like Cain" (1 Jn. 3:12); ungodly people are said to "walk in the way of Cain" (Jude 11).

CALEB

(kay' leb) HEBREW: KALEB
"dog" or "slave"

While the Israelites were camped in the wilderness after fleeing from Egypt, **Moses** sent out 12 men, one from each of the tribes, to inspect the Promised Land and assess its fruitfulness and the strength of its inhabitants. Representing the tribe of Judah was Caleb.

Most of the spies were intimidated by Canaan's inhabitants, returning with "an evil report of the land" (Num. 13:32), as well as with ample evidence of its fertility—figs, pomegranates, and an enormous cluster of grapes. But Caleb was bolder, urging the Israelites to invade and occupy Canaan. Despite his testimony, the frightened report of the other spies prevailed. "We are not able to go up against the people," they said; "for they are stronger than we" (Num. 13:31). Losing faith that the Lord would protect them, the Israelites "murmured against Moses and Aaron," saying to one another, "Let us choose a captain, and go back to Egypt" (Num. 14:2,4). When Caleb and **Joshua**, the spy representing Ephraim, urged the Israelites to maintain their faith in the Lord's protection and move ahead into Canaan, they were pelted with stones. God punished the Israelites by making them remain in the wilderness for decades longer until the disobedient generation—excepting only Caleb and Joshua—died out.

After the years of desert wandering were over and when Canaan was being parceled out among the Israelite tribes, Caleb was allotted land and villages in the vicinity of Hebron. By then 85 years of age, Caleb claimed to be as strong as he had been a generation earlier when he first traveled through Canaan as a spy—and proved his prowess by driving out the inhabitants. Either Caleb or his immediate descendants intermarried with Canaanites or with Edomites to the south since the clan is described later in the Bible as being of mixed origin. Nonetheless, these people were assimilated into the tribe of Judah and in 1 Chronicles are given a genealogy traced back through **Judah** to **Jacob**.

CANAAN

(kay' nan) HEBREW: KENAAN

The son of **Ham** and grandson of **Noah**, Canaan was the ancestor of the Canaanites, a loose grouping of peoples who proved troublesome to the Israelites during the period of settlement in the Promised Land. It was Ham who "saw the nakedness" of the drunken Noah, but Canaan who received the curse: "a slave of slaves shall he be to his brothers" (Gen. 9:22, 25).

The curse seems to have been realized when the Israelites "put the Canaanites to forced labor" (Jg. 1:28). Among the descendants of Canaan listed in Genesis 10:15 were Heth (the Hittites), the Jebusites (a people who lived in the vicinity of Jerusalem), the Amorites (people of the Palestinian hill country), and the Hivites (perhaps the Horites or Hurrians).

CHLOE

(kloh' ee) GREEK: CHLOE
"tender shoot"

Chloe was a woman, presumably a Christian, of either Corinth or Ephesus. Writing to the Corinthians from Ephesus, **Paul** noted that he had heard of dissension in their church from "Chloe's people" (1 Cor. 1:11), possibly her slaves who had converted to Christianity. Chloe is not mentioned anywhere else in the Bible.

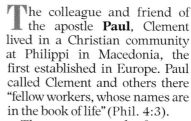

A first-century A.D. bust of the Roman emperor Claudius

CLAUDIUS

(klaw' dee uhs) GREEK: KLAUDIOS

For thirteen years, from A.D. 41 to 54, Claudius was emperor of Rome. He is mentioned by name twice in the book of Acts and referred to a third time simply as Caesar. The phrase "in the days of Claudius" (Acts 11:28) was one commonly used by Roman subjects to indicate an indefinite date during that particular emperor's reign. The second reference tells something about the emperor himself: "Claudius had commanded all the Jews to leave Rome" (Acts 18:2).

Two Roman historians report an event similar to the one mentioned in Acts. Dio Cassius (c. 155–235) wrote that Claudius forbade Jews to hold meetings—a restriction that would have forced them to leave Rome to practice their religious rites. Writing somewhat closer to the event, Suetonius (c. 69–140) tells a different story. According to him, "Since the Jews constantly made disturbances at the instigation of Chrestus, Claudius expelled them from Rome." Suetonius appears to have confused the Christian movement with the person of Christ, mak-

ing it sound as if **Jesus** were still alive, in Rome, and stirring up trouble. Among those exiled were **Aquila** and **Prisca**, who later were **Paul**'s hosts in Corinth.

During an earlier quarrel in Thessalonica a crowd of Jews attacked Christians, accusing them of "acting against the decrees of Caesar, saying that there is another king, Jesus" (Acts 17:7). Claudius is the Caesar referred to in this passage.

CLEMENT

(klem' ant) GREEK: KLEMENTOS
"mild"

The colleague and friend of the apostle **Paul**, Clement lived in a Christian community at Philippi in Macedonia, the first established in Europe. Paul called Clement and others there "fellow workers, whose names are in the book of life" (Phil. 4:3).

There are scattered references in the Old Testament to a heavenly registry of God's elect, but Paul may have been drawing an analogy between civic registries of the time and a divine list of believers, residents of what he called "our commonwealth [that] is in heaven" (Phil. 3:20). Early authorities confused the Clement of Philippi with **Peter**'s third successor as bishop of Rome, author of a first-century letter to Corinth included in some early Bibles.

Clement; a 14th-century icon

CLEOPAS

(klay' oh puhs) an abbreviated form
of GREEK: KLEOPATROS
"renowned father"

Two disciples, Cleopas and an unnamed
other, were walking from Jerusalem to
Emmaus, a town seven miles to the northwest, on the day of the resurrection. They
were dejected and disillusioned as they dis-
cussed the terrible events of the past few
days. When a stranger joined them expressing ignorance of the story that so moved
them, they explained about the crucified
Jesus and how they "had hoped that he was
the one to redeem Israel" (Lk. 24:21).
Asked to join Cleopas and his companion at
their evening meal, the stranger revealed
himself as Jesus by blessing and breaking
bread; he immediately vanished. Hastening
to Jerusalem, the two carried the news to
the other disciples—at which time Jesus appeared again to them all.

Cleopas is often confused with Clopas,
whose wife Mary stood by Jesus' cross—
though the names are of different origin.

CORNELIUS

(kor neel' yuhs) GREEK: KORNELIOS

The Roman centurion Cornelius was ap-
parently the first Gentile to become a
Christian. In the book of Acts, **Luke** dwells
on the story of Cornelius's conversion by
Peter, placing it just after the conversion of
Saul (**Paul**)—though the mission to the
Greeks in Antioch may have taken place
somewhat earlier.

Even before his conversion, Cornelius was
sympathetic to the Jews among whom he
was stationed and worshiped one God. In a
vision at Caesarea, an angel appeared to the
centurion and told him to summon Peter,
who was then staying in Joppa. The next
day, Peter himself had a vision, which occurred three times and which he interpreted
as meaning that it was permissible for him
to eat foods that Jews considered unclean.
He then concluded that, just as no food was
unclean, no person could be considered unclean either: Gentiles were as free as Jews to
receive **Jesus**'s teachings.

Peter was taken by the centurion's messengers to Caesarea, where Cornelius told
him of the angel's summons. While Peter
was preaching about Jesus, Cornelius and
his fellow Gentiles began "speaking in
tongues and extolling God" (Acts 10:46), a
demonstration that they had been visited by
the **Holy Spirit** and thus chosen for baptism. The brethren in Jerusalem were scan-

*The supper at Emmaus; detail of a painting
from the church of Santa Croce, Florence*

dalized by Peter's association with the un-
circumised, but he silenced their criticism
by saying, "who was I that could withstand
God?" (Acts 11:17).

COZBI

(koz' bi) HEBREW: KOZBI
"voluptuous"

Toward the end of their period of wandering in the wilderness, the Israelites
stopped at a place called Shittim. There they
began to intermarry with the people of the
land and to worship the local god, **Baal** of
Peor, so that "the anger of the Lord was kindled against Israel" (Num. 25:3). When
Zimri brought the Midianite woman Cozbi
into his household, **Aaron**'s grandson
Phinehas slew them both for this crime
against the Lord "and made atonement for
the people of Israel" (Num. 25:13). Ironically, Cozbi was of the same tribe as **Moses'**
wife **Zipporah**, the daughter of the Midianite priest who had befriended Moses when
he was a fugitive.

CRISPUS

(kris puhs) GREEK: KRISPOS
"curly"

One of **Paul**'s converts, Crispus was a
Jew of Corinth in Greece and head of
that city's synagogue—a natural place from
which to spread the gospel. Although many
of the Jews "opposed and reviled" Paul,

Crispus "together with all his household" (Acts 18:6, 8) came to believe in **Jesus**. The church at Corinth subsequently became racked with dissension, leading Paul to write to the Christians there: "Is Christ divided? . . . I am thankful that I baptized none of you except Crispus and Gaius; lest any one should say that you were baptized in my name" (1 Cor. 1:13, 14-15). Paul made it clear that he wanted followers not for himself but for Jesus.

CUSHAN-RISHATHAIM

(koo' shan ri sha thay' im) HEBREW: KUSAN RISATAYIM

"Cushan of double wickedness"

A monarch of Mesopotamia, Cushan-rishathaim ruled over the Israelites for eight years until the first of the judges, **Othniel**, led a successful rebellion against him. Scholars have been unable to identify this ruler, nor are they sure that he really came from Mesopotamia. Some identify Cushan as one of the Kassites who governed Mesopotamia between the 16th and 12th centuries B.C. Others refer to him as a ruler from Cush, a region under Egyptian control, located along the Nile in the modern country of Sudan; as the head of a nomadic tribe, also called Cush, living in the desert region south of Othniel's own tribe of Judah; as an Edomite chieftain; or as a Syrian monarch who conquered the Israelites around 1200 B.C. as his army moved across their territory to seize Egypt.

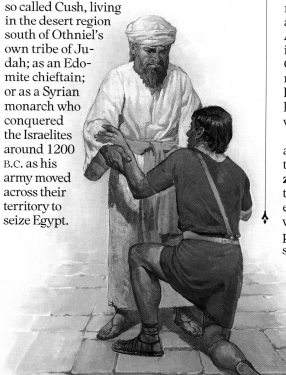

Peter raises the kneeling Cornelius, his first Gentile convert.

CYRUS II

(si' ruhs) HEBREW: KORES

King of Persia from 559 to 530 B.C., Cyrus permitted the exiled Jews to return from Babylon to Jerusalem, thus fulfilling the prophecy of **Jeremiah**: "When seventy years are completed for Babylon, I will visit you, and I will fulfil to you my promise and bring you back to this place" (Jer. 29:10).

After uniting all the Persian tribes living in what is now southern Iran, Cyrus moved against the Medes, a closely related group who had established a kingdom powerful enough to have overthrown the Assyrians. Cyrus himself was half-Mede: his mother was the daughter of the Median king Astyages; his father was a vassal to that ruler. In the revolt against his grandfather and overlord, Cyrus allied himself with Babylon and was aided by a turncoat Median army. By subsequently defeating the Medes, Cyrus gained control over much of the land lying within the borders of modern Iran as well as the Median provinces of Assyria, Mesopotamia, Syria, Armenia, and Cappadocia.

Cyrus next defeated Croesus of Lydia in Asia Minor—a king whose very name has come to symbolize wealth. This victory made Cyrus master of most of Asia Minor and overlord of the Greek cities on the Aegean coast, setting the stage for Persia's invasion of Greece in the fifth century B.C. Cyrus then moved to subjugate all the remaining Iranian tribes to the east, as far as India. In the process he established the largest empire the world had yet seen, for which he is known as Cyrus the Great.

But Cyrus's place in the Bible depends on another exploit, his conquest in 539 B.C. of the Babylonian empire that **Nebuchadnezzar** had ruled. That conquest gave him control of the city of Babylon, where Jerusalem's exiles lived, as well as of Jerusalem itself. It was Cyrus's policy to allow conquered peoples to return to their homelands and resume their local worship; the application of this policy to the Jews is described in 2 Chronicles 36:22-23: "The Lord stirred up the spirit of Cyrus king of Persia so that he made a proclamation . . . 'The Lord . . . has charged me to build him a house at Jerusalem which is in Judah. Whoever is among you of all his people . . . . Let him go up.'" In obedience to Cyrus's decree, exiled Jews did indeed leave Babylon for Jerusalem, where they began rebuilding the temple.

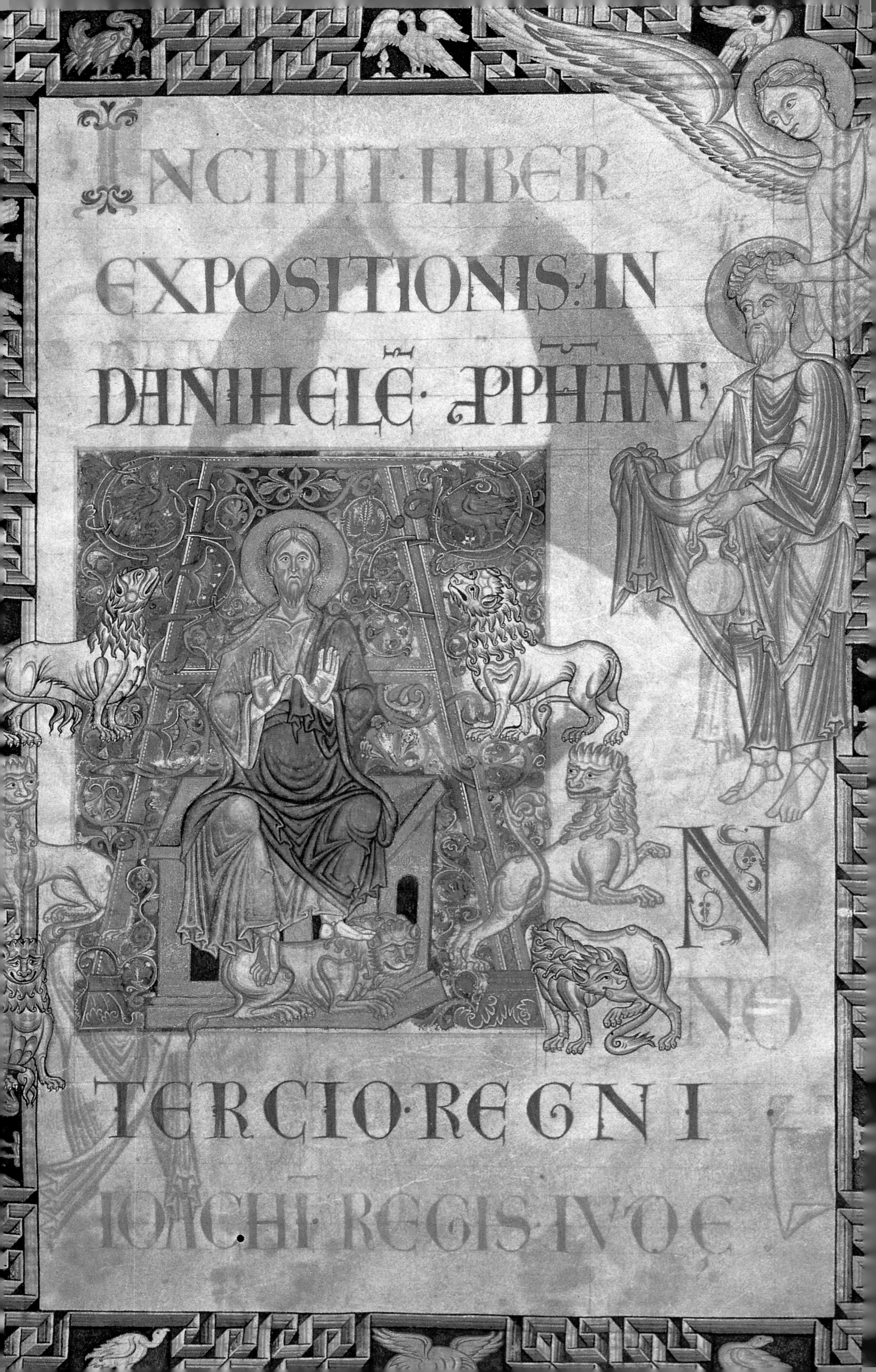
INCIPIT LIBER
EXPOSITIONIS IN
DANIHELE PPHAM
N
NO
TERCIO REGNI
IOACHI REGIS IVDE

DAGON

(day' gahn) HEBREW: DAGON
"grain"

An ancient Semitic fertility god representing seed and vegetation, Dagon
was adopted as a god by the Philistines.
Congregated to worship this deity, the
Philistines mocked their blinded captive
Samson as he stood between the pillars
supporting Dagon's temple at Gaza. With
his hair grown back and his strength restored, Samson pushed down the pillars,
killing himself and destroying both Dagon's
temple and his own tormentors.

In a later period, the Philistines brought
the captured ark of the covenant to their
temple at Ashdod and set it next to the statue of Dagon. The following morning they
found the idol flat on its face before the ark.
Though they restored the statue, the next
morning they again found it toppled—this
time with both head and hands cut off. This
was but the beginning of the troubles that
eventually caused the Philistines to return
the ark. On another occasion, when King
Saul was killed in battle, the triumphant
Philistines cut off his head and set it before
Dagon's idol in the temple at Beth-shan.

DAMARIS

(dam' uh ris) GREEK: DAMARIS
possibly "wife" or a variant of Damalis, "heifer"

When **Paul** preached at Athens about
the resurrection of the dead, some
mocked him. But a woman named Damaris
was among those who "joined him and believed" (Acts 17:34). The fact that she, along

*In this 12th-century illumination, an angel
hovers above St. Jerome (upper right), awaiting Daniel's emergence from the lions' den.*

with **Dionysius** the Areopagite, was mentioned by **Luke** suggests that she was a
woman of some prominence. Moreover, it
indicates that the gospel was meant for
women as well as men.

DAN

(dan) HEBREW: DAN
"he judged"

In his deathbed blessing **Jacob** described
his fifth son, Dan, as "a serpent in the
way, a viper in the path" (Gen. 49:17). This
may refer to the difficulties the small tribe of
Dan encountered in the settlement period,
before migrating to the north and seizing
territory there: "The Danites came to Laish,
to a people quiet and unsuspecting, and
smote them with the edge of the sword, and
burned the city with fire. . . . And they rebuilt the city and dwelt in it. And they
named the city Dan, after the name of Dan
their ancestor" (Jg. 18:27-29). The phrase
"from Dan to Beer-sheba" (Jg. 20:1) denotes the entire north-south expanse of the
land claimed by the Israelites.

Dan was the first son born to **Rachel**'s
maid **Bilhah**. The childless Rachel named
him, saying, "God has judged me, and has
also heard my voice and given me a son"
(Gen. 30:6). No traditions about Dan himself have been preserved.

DANIEL

(dan' yel) HEBREW: DANIYEL
"God is my judge"

The hero of the book that bears his name,
Daniel was a wise man, a courtier, an
interpreter of dreams, and a visionary during the period of the Babylonian exile. His
story takes place between the time when
Nebuchadnezzar, king of Babylon, conquered Jerusalem in 597 B.C. and began

taking Jews into exile and the time when the Jewish captivity ended under **Cyrus II** of Persia in 538—and perhaps beyond. As preserved and handed down, the narrative inspired later generations to be faithful to God's law in times of trial by showing that such faithfulness can bring success even under the most adverse of circumstances.

Daniel was a member of the late-seventh-century B.C. aristocracy of Judah; he was a nobleman and may even have been part of an extended royal family. He was evidently born during the reign of King **Josiah** (640–609 B.C.) and grew out of childhood during the reign of King **Jehoiakim** (609–598 B.C.). In that period the weak kingdom of Judah was dominated first by Egypt and then by the rising Neo-Babylonian empire. Shortly after Jehoiakim died and was succeeded by his 18-year-old son **Jehoiachin** (who was perhaps about Daniel's age), Nebuchadnezzar besieged Jerusalem and the young king surrendered. Nebuchadnezzar looted both the king's palace and the temple and took into exile "all the princes, and all the mighty men of valor, ten thousand captives, and all the craftsmen and the smiths; none remained, except the poorest people of the land" (2 Kg. 24:14).

Daniel, one of the prophets Michelangelo depicted in his famed frescoes for the Vatican's Sistine Chapel

TRAINED FOR THE COURT

It was the practice of the Babylonians continually to search the empire for talented young men to be trained as wise courtiers for the imperial court. Therefore, when Nebuchadnezzar conquered Jerusalem, he assigned a high officer of his court to pick out the best and the brightest from the Jewish nobility: "youths without blemish, handsome and skilful in all wisdom, endowed with knowledge, understanding learning, and competent to serve in the king's palace" (Dan. 1:4).

Among the chosen were Daniel and three of his companions, Hananiah, Mishael, and Azariah. Their training was under the direction of Ashpenaz, the king's chief eunuch, who gave them each a Babylonian name. Daniel became Belteshazzar, and the others **Shadrach**, Meshach, and Abednego. The youths embarked on a three-year education that began with learning to speak and write Aramaic and covered all the scientific and diplomatic skills, perhaps including astrology and magic, that a courtier needed to work effectively in the rarefied atmosphere of the most powerful court of the day. Their privileged position entitled these youths to a portion of the food prepared for the king himself—the best in the land—so that they would mature in health and strength worthy of their intended roles in the empire.

Daniel, however, immediately showed himself to be remarkably confident and disciplined in his allegiance to the traditions of his people. Although he did not resist the call to serve as a courtier to the king, he insisted that "he would not defile himself with the king's rich food or with the wine which he drank" (Dan. 1:8). The narrator does not indicate precisely how the food would have defiled Daniel—whether it was from unclean animals or contained blood or included meat from pagan sacrifices or was in some other way contaminated—but he allows the rich food to typify the enticing and corrupting compromises with pagan life that challenged many a faithful Jew in a foreign land. It is perhaps noteworthy that Jehoiachin himself did not maintain the same standard when he was captive in Babylon but "dined regularly at the king's table" (2 Kg. 25:29).

Since the main sources of food defilement were from meat, Daniel asked Ashpenaz that he and his companions be fed on vegetables and water. The narrator tells how God caused Ashpenaz to listen favorably and to give these Jewish youths a ten-day trial of their seemingly ascetic diet. Ashpenaz was so surprised and pleased when the vegetarian diet left them "better in appearance and fatter in flesh" (Dan. 1:15) than the other youths that he allowed them to continue their strict regimen. Faithfulness to God was thus shown to be a superior way of life, even as judged by pagan standards. God blessed the four youths with scholarly learning and great wisdom and gave Daniel "understanding in all visions and dreams" (Dan. 1:17). At the end of the three years, Nebuchadnezzar not only found the four better than all other youths, they were also ten times wiser than any of his royal magicians and enchanters.

The second major story of the book depicts Daniel, with God's help, as a powerful interpreter of dreams. The theme repeatedly stressed is that all true wisdom belongs only to God, who alone "reveals deep and mysterious things" (Dan. 2:22). Like **Joseph** in the book of Genesis, Daniel had abilities far beyond those of pagan wise men; and, as with Joseph in Egypt, Daniel eventually enjoyed high honors in Babylon.

One day Nebuchadnezzar summoned his magicians and sorcerers to reveal that he had been troubled by a dream. They asked the king to tell his dream, but he demanded that they both tell him the dream and interpret it or they would be "torn limb from limb" (Dan. 2:5). Although confident that they could interpret the dream, they begged him first to reveal its content. When Neb-

uchadnezzar threatened them further, they despaired: "There is not a man on earth who can meet the king's demand . . . . none can show it to the king except the gods, whose dwelling is not with flesh" (Dan. 2:10-11).

True to his threat, Nebuchadnezzar commanded the execution of all the wise men of Babylon, a vast company that by then included Daniel and his compatriots. When Daniel learned of the situation, he begged the king to appoint a time for him to reveal the interpretation. Returning home and exhorting his friends to pray, Daniel received a night vision of the king's mysterious dream. When the moment of truth arrived, Daniel made clear to the king the meaning of the events: "No wise men, enchanters, magicians, or astrologers can show to the king the mystery which the king has asked, but there is a God in heaven who reveals mysteries" (Dan. 2:27-28).

Daniel then proceeded to describe Nebuchadnezzar's dream. He had seen a colossal statue: "The head of this image was of fine gold, its breast and arms of silver, its belly and thighs of bronze, its legs of iron, its feet partly of iron and partly of clay" (Dan. 2:32–33). Suddenly a stone untouched by human hands struck the image and broke it into dust that the wind scattered while the stone grew into a mountain. The interpretation Daniel gave was both good and bad for the Babylonian king. He was the head of gold in the dream, Daniel assured him, but his dynasty would not last. Lesser kingdoms would succeed him, represented by silver and bronze (the Medes and the Persians). But those would be broken by a fourth kingdom of iron (the Greeks under **Alexander the Great**), which in time would be divided like the feet of iron and clay (as Alexander's kingdom was divided between the Seleucids and Ptolemies). In the final period, Daniel asserted, "the God of heaven will set up a kingdom which shall never be destroyed" (Dan. 2:44), much like the stone that became a mountain.

Nebuchadnezzar was so astonished at Daniel's revelation that he did homage to Daniel with incense, confessed that the God of the Jews was "God of gods and Lord of kings" (Dan. 2:47), and placed Daniel over all Babylonian wise men and over the entire province of Babylon itself.

HISTORICAL PUZZLES

*B*iblical scholars have noted a number of apparent discrepancies in the book of Daniel: Nebuchadnezzar's siege of Jerusalem is dated to the third year of Jehoiakim's reign (606 B.C.), a year before Nebuchadnezzar actually became king of Babylon; not Belshazzar but his father, Nabonidus, was the last ruler of Babylon; Nabonidus was overthrown by Cyrus II of Persia rather than the otherwise unknown Darius the Mede. But a story similar to the one about Nebuchadnezzar living in the wild has been found in the Dead Sea Scrolls, where the demented king is identified as Nabonidus.

SAVED FROM THE FURNACE

The third story of the book does not involve Daniel at all but rather his three compatriots, Shadrach, Meshach, and Abednego. Nebuchadnezzar had forsaken his devotion to Daniel's God and become a raging tyrant demanding idol worship and the burning to death of those who did not comply. The miracle that saved Daniel's companions in a blazing furnace, however, converted Nebuchadnezzar once again so that he threatened death to any who spoke against the God of the Jews.

The fourth story of the book is presented as a letter from Nebuchadnezzar to his domain: "all peoples, nations, and languages, that dwell in all the earth" (Dan. 4:1). Here the king bore witness to the eternal power of God and the dominion of God's kingdom and rule over any powers on earth by recounting a remarkable dream and its aftermath. He had told his dream to the usual enchanters and astrologers but none could make sense of it till Daniel arrived, a man "in whom is the spirit of the holy gods" (Dan. 4:8). Daniel listened while Nebuchadnezzar told of seeing a huge tree in the center of the world with its top in heaven, visible to the whole earth. An angelic being had the tree cut down and its stump left in the wild for seven years.

With dismay Daniel interpreted the fallen tree as representing the mighty king himself. "You shall be driven from among men, and your dwelling shall be with the beasts of the field," he warned, "till you know that the Most High rules the kingdom of men, and gives it to whom he will" (Dan. 4:25). Sure enough, a year later when the king was feeling self-satisfied with his own might and majesty, a voice from heaven rebuked him, and he fell to eating grass and living with the wild animals. After seven years the demented monarch had learned his lesson: His reason returned, he praised God for his absolute dominion, and he resumed his role as king.

The fifth story in the book is set at the very end—indeed on the final day—of Baby-

A pensive Daniel between two tamed lions; an 11th-century stone carving

lonian rule. A new king, **Belshazzar**, was holding a vast feast for a thousand of his nobles and drinking wine with his wives and concubines from the sacred vessels that "Nebuchadnezzar his father had taken out of the temple in Jerusalem" (Dan. 5:2).

The narrator is appalled at the horrific image of Belshazzar drinking wine from the holy temple vessels while he "praised the gods of gold and silver, bronze, iron, wood, and stone" (Dan. 5:4). But God immediately responded with a miraculous sign: A man's hand appeared and wrote with its finger on the palace wall. Belshazzar was terrified and offered royal robes and vast power to anyone who could read and interpret the words. But none of the royal enchanters or astrologers could decipher the writing, so the queen reminded Belshazzar about Daniel, whom his father, Nebuchadnezzar, had made chief of the magicians.

Summoned to appear before the king, the now aged Daniel reminded Belshazzar of Nebuchadnezzar's punishment for not honoring God and warned him that, by abusing the temple vessels, he had set himself "against the Lord of heaven" (Dan. 5:23). He read the mysterious words, "MENE, MENE, TEKEL, and PARSIN" (Dan. 5:25), and interpreted them to mean that Belshazzar's kingdom was at an end, about to be taken by the Medes and Persians. Belshazzar tried to reward Daniel's amazing abilities, but to no avail. Before the night was out, **Darius the Mede** had invaded Babylon and taken the kingdom; Belshazzar himself was dead.

FAITHFUL TO HIS GOD

The most famous of all the Daniel stories—Daniel in the lions' den—is set during the reign of Darius the Mede. The narrator shows that Daniel's great authority under the Babylonian kings continued under Darius. Then about 80 years old, Daniel was the most distinguished of three presidents who directed 120 satraps, or governors, who ruled the empire for the king. Indeed, Darius planned to "set him over the whole kingdom" (Dan. 6:3). The Jewish courtier's preeminence made him the object of envy, and Daniel's rivals contrived to have Darius sign a self-flattering edict that no one could petition any god or man but Darius alone for 30 days on pain of being cast into the den of lions. Once the document was signed, according to the law of the Medes and Persians, it could not be changed even by the king himself.

As he had been in his youth, so Daniel in old age was unswerving in his loyalty to "the law of his God" (Dan. 6:5). In spite of the edict, he continued to pray three times each day before an open window facing Jerusalem. Immediately his rivals brought charges against him to the king, who was distressed when he recognized their plot. But in view of the unchangeable law he had no choice but to give Daniel to the lions. Darius spent a night of sleepless fasting and worry for his chief minister and at daybreak returned to the den in anguish. Daniel, however, was alive and completely calm. "My God sent his angel and shut the lions' mouths" (Dan. 6:22), he told the king. Then the royal wrath was vented on Daniel's rivals, who were themselves thrown to the lions and killed instantly. Soon Darius wrote a universal letter commanding all to "fear before the God of Daniel, for he is the living God, enduring for ever" (Dan. 6:26).

During the later years of his life, Daniel experienced visions and dreams that laid out the course of future events through vivid images. The visions focused on the years of the persecution of the Jews under the Syrian king **Antiochus IV Epiphanes** in 167-164 B.C. This focus probably points to the actual period in which the extensive traditions about Daniel's life were put into their final form in the book of Daniel.

DARIUS I

(dah ri'uhs) HEBREW: DAREYAWES
"he who upholds the good"

Though authorized by King **Cyrus II** of Persia in his edict of 538 B.C., the rebuilding of the temple at Jerusalem progressed little beyond the laying of the foundation until 520, when work was resumed. The governor of the province "Beyond the River" (Ezra 5:3), Tattenai, reported the activity to his master, Darius I, who had come to the Persian throne the previous year. A search in the royal archives produced Cyrus's decree, and Darius reissued it—generously providing that all costs should be met from royal revenues.

Darius was not a direct descendant of Cyrus and for the first two years of his reign had to suppress rebellions from Central Asia to the Aegean Sea. A Median general

Darius I of Persia

who defied him had his nose, ears and tongue cut off; then he was impaled. A ghostwritten royal autobiography justifying Darius's claim to the throne was sent throughout his empire to be read to his subjects and inscribed at the site where his armies had crushed rebels.

Under the protection of his god, Ahuramazda, Darius imposed a comprehensive law code, based on Babylonian precedents, on his empire. He extended his conquests to India, Libya, Thrace, and Macedonia, standardized his empire's weights and measures, dug a canal from the Nile to the Red Sea, and built a vast new capital at Persepolis, where he ruled until 486 B.C.

DARIUS THE MEDE

In the book of Daniel, the king who deposes **Belshazzar** and orders **Daniel** thrown into the lions' den for refusing to worship him instead of the Lord is called Darius the Mede. However, no such ruler is known to have existed. Scholars propose that the name is an alternate for **Cyrus II**, the Persian monarch who actually overthrew the last Babylonian ruler. If this hypothesis is correct, Daniel 6:28 could be translated: "So this Daniel prospered during the reign of Darius, namely the reign of Cyrus the Persian."

DATHAN

(day' than) HEBREW: DATAN
"strong/heroic"

A member of the tribe of Reuben, Dathan and his brother Abiram were among the leaders of a revolt against **Moses** and **Aaron**. Refusing Moses' summons, they grumbled: "Is it a small thing that you have brought us up out of a land flowing with milk and honey, to kill us in the wilderness, that you must also make yourself a prince over us?" (Num. 16:13). The enraged Moses called down a curse on the brothers, "and the earth opened its mouth and swallowed them up" (Num. 16:32). The Sheol into which the brothers and their households disappeared is a Hebrew word meaning "abode of the dead."

DAVID
(day' vid) HEBREW: DAWID
"beloved"
....

Shepherd, warrior, musician, outlaw, faithful friend, empire builder, sinner, saint, failed father, ideal king! Who in the Bible but David appears in so many roles? His name occurs more than 1,000 times in the Old and New Testaments, more than any other. He has a prominent place not only in the political and military history of his people but also in their theology and poetry and even in their hopes for the future.

David is introduced in the Bible during the time when Israel was adjusting to the new institution of monarchy, the people having long lived in a tribal confederation without any centralized government. Previously, regional judges had risen in moments of crisis and dispensed justice for particular areas. But the weakness and uncertainty of this organization led the people to call for a king, and **Samuel**, a prophet and the last of the judges, had chosen **Saul** from the tribe of Benjamin. Samuel anointed Saul with oil and "the spirit of God came mightily upon him" (1 Sam. 10:10).

As a charismatic ruler empowered by that spirit, Saul led the tribal militias in a valiant struggle against the Philistines and other opponents. But when Saul forfeited Samuel's support by his usurpation of religious duties and his failure to pursue a ruthless holy war, "the Spirit of the Lord departed from Saul, and an evil spirit from the Lord tormented him" (1 Sam. 16:14). Realizing his loss, Saul became despondent.

The story of David's rise begins just as Saul loses his divine mandate. Three successive episodes introduce the rising star of Judah. The first occurred in secret as God instructed Samuel to accept Saul's failure and sent the seer to a man of Bethlehem named **Jesse**, because, God said, "I have provided for myself a king among his sons" (1 Sam. 16:1). Since such an action would be traitorous to the sitting king, God instructed Samuel to cover his real purpose under the guise of a special sacrifice.

In Bethlehem, Samuel invited Jesse, the elderly scion of a prominent family of Judah, and his sons to the sacrifice. Samuel viewed in turn each of Jesse's seven noble sons, surprised that God rejected each one. Outward appearance did not matter, God reminded him, because "the Lord looks on the heart" (1 Sam. 16:7). When Samuel asked if there were any more sons, Jesse told him that his youngest was tending the sheep. The youngest, of course, was David, a handsome youth with ruddy skin and beau-

tiful eyes. When David arrived from the fields, Samuel "anointed him in the midst of his brothers, and the Spirit of the Lord came mightily upon David from that day forward" (1 Sam. 16:13).

The second and third introductory episodes provide narratives of David's coming into the service of Saul, each emphasizing a different strength of the future king. To relieve Saul of his despondency, his servants urged him to find a musician whose melodies on the lyre might drive away his depression. Saul agreed, and one of his men recommended David, describing him as "skilful in playing, a man of valor, a man of war, prudent in speech, and a man of good presence"—adding, "and the Lord is with him" (1 Sam. 16:18). David, about 18 years of age, was summoned and became not only Saul's personal musician but also his permanent armor-bearer or squire, and "Saul loved him greatly" (1 Sam. 16:21).

The third episode—the famous story of David and **Goliath**—introduces David, the warrior for God, and offers another account of how David and Saul met. The armies of the Philistines and Israelites confronted one another from opposite sides of the valley of Elah, west of Bethlehem. Every day a Philistine champion stepped out into the valley to insult the Israelites and challenge any warrior to single combat, with national victory or servitude hanging in the balance. The

SHEPHERDS

Shepherds with flocks of sheep and goats were common sights on the hills of southern Palestine where the rough terrain made most farming impractical. The shepherd had to face the rigors of weather and predators for several months of the year caring for the flock and guiding it in search of pasture. The fact that many of the great men in Israel's history had been shepherds helped make the image of the shepherd a metaphor for God's care for his people. "He will feed his flock like a shepherd," wrote Isaiah, "he will gather the lambs in his arms" (Is. 40:11).

Philistine was a giant named Goliath of Gath, nearly ten feet tall and sheathed in all the finest armor and weaponry of the time. He was so fearsome that not even Saul, a mighty warrior who stood head and shoulders taller than the other Israelites, dared to meet his challenge.

When David arrived at the front lines, he heard Goliath's challenge and boldly expressed contempt for such a man who "would defy the armies of the living God" (1 Sam. 17:26). Brought before Saul, David volunteered to fight the Philistine. Though Saul was at first bemused by this unheralded young shepherd, he listened to him boast of killing lions and bears and of his trust in God. Amazingly, with the whole war at stake, Saul finally allowed this youth to go against the mighty giant. David refused the conventional armor and sword Saul proffered him, instead choosing his own familiar weapon— a sling and smooth stones.

David's youthful appearance and lack of armor infuriated Goliath: "Am I a dog that you come to me with sticks?" he blustered (1 Sam. 17:43). The noble dignity of David's response encapsulated the fundamentally religious meaning he saw in the battle: "You come to me with a sword and with a spear and with a javelin; but I come to you in the name of the Lord of hosts" (1 Sam. 17:45). With lethal efficiency, David ran at Goliath and slung a single stone that embedded itself in the forehead of the giant warrior. As David took Goliath's own sword to behead his victim, the astonished Philistine army took flight, pursued by the jubilant Israelites.

THE KING'S JEALOUSY

Immediately, David moved to center stage in Israel. Saul began to use David for important missions, which he always successfully completed, and gave the young warrior command over a thousand troops. Meanwile, David found a kindred spirit in Saul's noble son **Jonathan** and the pair formed a covenant of friendship that lasted till death. But in his recurring bouts of despondency, Saul could not help brooding on his suspicion that David, for all his winning ways, ultimately meant to overthrow him. Even David's victories on Saul's behalf became a threat to the king, as cheering crowds sang triumphantly, "Saul has slain his thousands, and David his ten thousands" (1 Sam. 18:7). Saul's suspicion was both

David triumphant over Goliath; a late-15th-century gilt bronze figurine

founded and unfounded. It was untrue that the loyal David had any conscious intention to overthrow Saul's dynasty, but it was true that he was destined to do just that and found his own royal house.

Saul's jealous rage seemed to wax and wane. At one moment he offered David his eldest daughter, **Merab**, as wife, if David would lead his troops in battle. Behind the offer was Saul's real hope that David would be killed fighting. But when David was victorious, Saul withdrew his offer and gave Merab to someone else. Another daughter, **Michal**, fell in love with David, and Saul agreed that she should marry him. But he required David, as the price for his royal bride, to slaughter 100 Philistines—again hoping his youthful rival would be killed in the process. David, however, claimed his bride with proof that he had killed 200 of the enemy.

Even as David became Saul's son-in-law, his fame and success made him ever more the object of Saul's mortal fear. At one point, Saul explicitly ordered his guards to kill David, but at Jonathan's pleading rescinded the order. After David won a great victory over the Philistines for Saul, the king attempted to murder him in private—viciously trying to pin David to the wall with his spear as the young man played the lyre for him. Next, he sent guards to kill David at home, but Michal helped him escape by putting a decoy in his bed to delay the assassins.

David fled to Samuel in Ramah, 20 miles northwest of Gibeah. Saul sent men to arrest him, but when they saw Samuel and his company of prophets, "the Spirit of God upon the messengers of Saul" (1 Sam. 19:20) and the ecstasy of prophecy turned them aside from their purpose. The same happened to a second and third group of messengers. Finally, Saul came to arrest David himself, but he too was captured by the ecstatic Spirit and "stripped off his clothes . . . and lay naked all that day and all that night" (1 Sam. 19:24). And so David escaped arrest.

Still, Jonathan hoped to reconcile his father, whom he could not forsake, and his dearest friend, whose innocence he clearly saw. Jonathan met David in secret and made plans to find out at an upcoming feast the depth of his father's enmity and to let

David summoned to soothe King Saul with his lyre playing; detail of a 16th-century Flemish painting

David know. The result was far worse than Jonathan had imagined. Saul was implacably determined on David's death and cursed Jonathan for defending him. In fierce anger and grief, Jonathan left the feast to inform David. As they said goodbye, David and Jonathan swore friendship between themselves and their descendants forever.

Alone and uncertain about the future, David headed south from Gibeah to the town of Nob just east of the Jebusite city of Jerusalem. There a community of priests maintained a sanctuary for the worship of the Lord. Pretending to be on a secret mission for Saul, he intimidated the high priest **Ahimelech** into giving him the sacred bread of the sanctuary and allowing him to take as a weapon the sword of Goliath that had been kept in the sanctuary. With these supplies David fled southwest to the Philistine city of Gath, out of Saul's reach. The threat from Saul, however, was replaced by the more immediate danger of Philistine hatred for a warrior whose fame was built on killing Philistines. David recognized his mistake and feigned madness in order to escape back into the Judean wilderness.

AN OUTLAW LEADER

Just at the moment when he seemed most alone and without resource, David's fortunes began to turn. First, his own brothers joined him in his hideaway. His situation became known, "and every one who was discontented, gathered to him; and he became captain over them" (1 Sam. 22:2). Thus, as the leader of a growing band of 400

outlaws, David became a formidable presence in southern Judah.

The people of southern Judah soon found themselves caught between David, the local hero and leader of a personal army, and Saul, who commanded the larger intertribal army. One day at a desert spot on the shore of the Dead Sea picturesquely called Wild Goats' Rocks, David's moment for revenge came. Lurking in the back of a cave, David and his men saw Saul himself enter the front of the cave to relieve himself. A single javelin throw from the darkness might have ended David's troubles, but he refused his men's whispered urgings—instead, stealing up behind Saul to cut off a part of his robe. He refused to kill his adversary because, as he said, "he is the Lord's anointed" (1 Sam. 24:6). After Saul was some distance away, David emerged and, shouting to Saul, held up the scrap of robe to show that he could have killed him. "I have not sinned against you," he protested, "though you hunt my life to take it" (1 Sam. 24:11). Moved by David's gesture, Saul called off his vendetta for the moment and allowed David to return to his desert stronghold.

Saul soon renewed his pursuit and David, finding he could not be safe in Judah, once again fled to the Philistines. This time **Achish**, king of Gath, gave the town of Ziklag near the border with Judah to David and his band of 600. For more than a year David convinced Achish that he was raiding Israelite settlements while in fact he was annihilating towns of the Amalekites and various Canaanite tribes. He shared his spoils with the towns of Judah so as to make friends even though he was allied with Israel's enemies. Achish so trusted David that, as the Philistine warlords were massing for a major battle with Saul at Mount Gilboa, he planned for David to fight in the Philistine army. Other Philistine commanders were less trustful of David, however, and insisted that he be sent home.

Thus David was back in Ziklag when the fateful news arrived that the Philistines had won an overwhelming victory at Gilboa. Saul was dead, as were Jonathan and two other royal sons.

The disaster at Gilboa left Israel in grave danger of becoming subjugated to the Philistines, who had come to dominate central Canaan west of the Jordan. Saul's powerful commander **Abner**, who survived Gilboa, tried to salvage the dynasty by installing Saul's son **Ish-bosheth** as king in Israelite territory east of the Jordan. Although Ish-bosheth was weak and dominated by Abner, he gained at least the tacit allegiance of all the northern tribes. Meanwhile David moved with his troops from Ziklag to Hebron, the central city of Judah. The people of Judah rallied around David, the most famous warrior of their tribe, and anointed him their king. No doubt the Philistines thought the situation ideal: Israel was split; a weak king ruled the north; and an ally of theirs ruled the south.

The unstable situation could not last. Mustering his northern troops, Abner crossed the Jordan and came to the town of Gibeon in Benjamin, Saul's home territory, just north of Judah. There he was met by David's troops under the command of **Joab**, David's nephew. The two sides first tested each other in a duel between 12 champions from each side. But when all 24 warriors were killed in the fray, a general battle broke out, and Abner's men were beaten and forced to flee the field.

A RIVAL ELIMINATED

War between north and south continued with David growing ever stronger until Abner became alienated from the ineffectual Ish-bosheth and decided to betray his master and deliver the northern tribes to David's rule. David and Abner met and agreed to an alliance, but their plans were forestalled when the hot-headed Joab murdered Abner to avenge the death of his brother **Asahel**. Though David was outraged at this spiteful killing, the intent of his agreement with Abner was soon fulfilled by other means. Two of Ish-bosheth's captains thought to ingratiate themselves with David by assassinating their king during his afternoon siesta and bringing his head to David at Hebron. Their efforts gained them execution for murder.

With Saul's dynasty effectively at an end, the elders of the northern tribes assembled at Hebron in about 1000 B.C. and installed David as king over all Israel. Thus, the destiny foretold by Samuel's secret anointing years earlier finally came to fulfillment. The powerful Philistines were apparently content to have their former ally and vassal in control. But David had no intention of remaining a subservient neighbor to the Philistines. With a united nation behind him and a large army of battle-hardened troops, he soon gave rein to his genius for conquest and expansion. He intended to be king of an empire not a chieftain over tribes.

To be such a ruler, David needed a capital city, and he chose one that belonged to no tribe—the Jebusite city of Jerusalem on the border between Judah and Benjamin. Surrounded by Israelites, the Jebusites had remained independent for centuries, believing themselves impervious to attack. But David soon found a chink in their defenses

Bathsheba by Rembrandt

THE WOMEN IN HIS LIFE

While David was still at Hebron, he took six wives: Ahinoam, Abigail, Maacah, Haggith, Abital, and Eglah. Each bore him a son: Amnon, Chileab, Absalom, Adonijah, Shephatiah, and Ithream.

All that is known of Ahinoam is that she, along with Abigail, was briefly taken captive by the Amalekites when David left the two women at Ziklag to join the Philistines. Before being claimed by David, Abigail was the wife of the foolish Calebite Nabal. David's marriage to Maacah, the daughter of the king of Geshur, was a political alliance. Nothing is known of the other three wives.

After withdrawing the offer of his daughter Merab as a wife to David, Saul agreed to the marriage of another daughter, Michal, to his young rival. When David fled his court, Saul gave Michal to another man, Palti. By the time David reclaimed her, their love had faded and Michal died childless.

Upon establishing his capital at Jerusalem, David took other wives and concubines. The only one named is Bathsheba, the mother of Solomon.

and conquered the city, making it his own personal capital: "the city of David" (2 Sam. 5:9). Not content with a rustic fortress like Saul's at Gibeah, David made an alliance with **Hiram**, the Canaanite king of Tyre, and obtained the material and craftsmen to build Israel's first royal palace in the new capital city of his realm.

The Philistine warlords were disconcerted at this independent behavior by David, and they determined to shorten his leash. When they massed their forces in the valley of Rephaim, just west of Jerusalem, David recognized that he must either conquer them or fall. In the ensuing battle, David's forces broke through the enemy lines "like a bursting flood" (2 Sam. 5:20), and the Philistines fled the battlefield. Soon David was able to drive the Philistines back into their own territory and free his land from their domination. Israel had not only gained its independence; Philistia had become Israel's vassal.

In the aftermath of this victory, David also consolidated control over the rest of Canaan by subjugating the numerous Canaanite cities that the Israelites had never taken.

He did not destroy the Canaanites but incorporated them into his kingdom as a subject people. It was evidently in this period that David carried out the military census of Israel described at the end of 2 Samuel. Such a census was so contrary to ancient Israelite law and tradition that even Joab and the other army commanders opposed it. As a result, Israel was struck with a plague, which David knew was his fault. In remorse he purchased a hilltop threshing floor just north of the city of David as the location for an altar. That site became the religious center of the Israelite nation; on it David's son and successor, **Solomon**, would build his temple.

David understood the power of Israel's deep spiritual traditions, and he sought to consolidate them in a way that would strengthen his kingdom. Saul had become alienated from Samuel the prophet and had slaughtered the priests at Nob for Ahimelech's aid to David. Learning from his predecessor's mistakes, David strove to make the king the chief patron of Israel's religion rather than its enemy.

The greatest symbol of Israel's faith was the ark of the covenant, containing the stone tablets of the Ten Commandments, by then more than two and a half centuries old. It had sat neglected for most of Saul's reign in a private shrine in the little town of Kiriath-jearim. If David could bring the ark to his new capital, his own throne and the throne of God would be associated in the same location—a powerful symbol for a revitalized kingdom of Israel.

The first attempt to transport the ark to Jerusalem on an ox-drawn cart failed when one of the oxen stumbled, and an attendant named **Uzzah** reached out to steady the ark. Because he had transgressed the untouchable holiness of the sacred object, Uzzah "died there beside the ark of God" (2 Sam. 6:7). David waited three months before making another attempt. With careful sacrifices and joyful rituals of dancing and music, David brought the ark to Jerusalem, the king himself dancing before the ark wearing a priestly ephod (in this instance, a sacred vestment). The traditional tabernacle had been destroyed, but David installed the ark in a new tent, like the Mosaic tent of meeting, and furnished it with everything required for sacrifices and priestly rituals. Ahimelech's son, **Abiathar**, and a newly elevated priest named **Zadok** became the chief priests of the new national sanctuary.

It may have been in this period that David began to collect psalms for Israel's worship. It is not known how many of the 73 psalms

David dances before the ark being brought into Jerusalem

that are linked to David's name were actually written by him, but he certainly attained a reputation as "the sweet psalmist of Israel" (2 Sam. 23:1).

THE HOUSE OF DAVID

David was dissatisfied with the ark being kept in a tent, however, and hoped to build a real temple—a house for the ark of God. But the prophet **Nathan** informed him that God did not want David to build him a house but would allow his son to do so. Rather, Nathan said, God would build a house for David: He would "establish the throne of his kingdom for ever" (2 Sam. 7:13). Later generations saw in this covenant with David an inviolable promise from God that David's "line shall endure for ever, his throne as long as the sun" (Ps. 89:36). Some of the prophets also interpreted the covenant as the basis for the hope that an ideal king—the Messiah—would one day sit on David's throne in Jerusalem.

With Israel united and the Philistine and Canaanite cities subjugated, David was able to deal with foreign threats and seek new lands for conquest. The large empires of Assyria to the north and Egypt to the south were both languishing under weak rulers and internal conflicts that provided an opening for Israel's expansion. A conflict between David and the Moabites east of the Dead Sea led to a brutal war, which left two of every three Moabite soldiers dead and the people of Moab burdened with paying tribute to Israel. The Israelites also subdued the Edomites south of Moab and the Ammonites east of the Jordan.

David's successes, however, roused the Syrians under the leadership of **Hadadezer** of Zobah to attack Israel from the north. David himself led the army that confronted this threat, and his infantry-based army convincingly overwhelmed the chariots and horsemen of the Syrians. Though the Israelites captured hundreds of chariots and thousands of horses, David had no desire to shift his mode of warfare. The Israelites

THE KINGDOM OF DAVID

The rise of King David not only changed the fortunes of Israel in his own time but left its mark on the soul of his nation for all time. David took a weak, dispirited nation and made it an empire.

Saul had nominally united the 12 tribes, but his kingdom was but a loose confederation beset by powerful enemies throughout his reign. Taking advantage of the fact that the great empires of Assyria and Egypt were in decline, David used his years of military experience to forge the Israelites into a powerful fighting nation. He expanded the kingdom's borders to engulf Moab, Edom, and Ammon and pushed north through Syria to the Euphrates River. The tribute from the conquered nations reduced taxes at home and brought prosperity to his people.

Equally important, David captured Jerusalem and established the city as the royal and religious capital of Israel. The

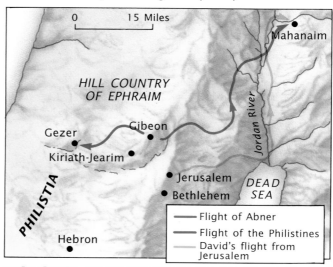

hamstrung most of the horses and kept only a few chariots, evidently for display.

All of Syria was now subject to David or allied with him, opening to Israel vast areas for trade and providing extensive natural resources such as copper from the mines of northern Syria. His empire extended from the Gulf of Aqabah and the border of Egypt in the south, through all of Canaan between the Arabian desert and the Mediterranean Sea, north through Syria to the Euphrates—by ancient standards a very respectable empire.

It was during the war against Ammon that David's affairs began to turn sour at home. He had at least six wives while he ruled in Hebron and had taken several more following his move to Jerusalem. One afternoon he looked out from his roof and saw a beautiful woman bathing. Inquiring about her, he learned that she was **Bathsheba**, the daughter of Eliam and the wife of **Uriah** the Hittite. Both men were members of David's elite royal guard called the Thirty and were then at the battlefront. Accus-

tomed to having whatever he wanted, the king called Bathsheba to his quarters and "lay with her" (2 Sam. 11:4). She soon discovered she was pregnant.

To prevent the impending scandal, David summoned Uriah home on a pretense, so that he would sleep with his wife and believe the child was his own. But Uriah was a faithful warrior who knew that Israelite soldiers engaged in a holy war were required to keep away from women, and he refused to go home. Next David sent Uriah back to the front with a secret message for Joab, his commander, ordering him to expose Uriah to unnecessary danger in battle so that he would be killed. When word arrived back in Jerusalem that Uriah was dead, Bathsheba mourned her soldier husband the required period and then married the king. The royal crime appeared to have succeeded.

David, however, had not counted on the prophet Nathan. He came to David to report the crime of a rich man with many flocks who had stolen and butchered the one little

city of David would later be expanded to take in the site where his son Solomon would build his temple.

David's personal character came to represent the ideal ruler to later generations: God's faithful anointed king, the heroic deliverer, dispenser of justice, poet and psalmist. Even when the biblical narrative tells how David succumbed to lust and power, he is presented as a repentant sinner. Power did not harden David's heart or keep him from recognizing his own sins with deep sorrow.

Finally, David established a dynasty that lasted nearly half a millennium. Though the northern tribes rebelled against his grandson, Rehoboam, David's descendants continued to reign in Jerusalem until the exile to Babylon in 587 B.C. The prophet Nathan told David that God had made a covenant with the king, promising "Your throne shall be established forever" (2 Sam. 7:16). And even when the southern kingdom was destroyed, that promise laid the foundation for the continuing hope for the coming of a descendant to save Israel, the Messiah.

JERUSALEM — Mt Moriah, TYROPOEON VALLEY, CITY OF DAVID, KIDRON VALLEY, HINNOM VALLEY

A stone fragment from Israel with the only nonbiblical reference to David

David enthroned; a tenth-century plaque

---

who gained the king enough time to regroup his forces. As the two sides met in battle, David was confident of victory, but urged his commanders to "deal gently for my sake with the young man Absalom" (2 Sam. 18:5). But Joab killed Absalom despite his orders, and the heartbroken David could not bring himself to celebrate his victory.

Before David could return to Jerusalem to consolidate his position, another rebellion broke out; it was led by a man of Benjamin named **Sheba** who wanted to split the northern tribes away from David's rule. David's men pursued Sheba to the northern reaches of the kingdom where they besieged him in the town of Abel. A woman of the city negotiated with Joab to spare Abel; the price was Sheba's head thrown over the wall.

THE DISPUTED SUCCESSION

The nemesis of family strife pursued David to his dying day. As the king grew old, **Adonijah**, David's eldest surviving son, was preparing to succeed his father, and indeed was conferring with Joab and Abiathar to form a government. The prophet Nathan, however, preferred Solomon as David's successor. He brought Bathsheba to the king to warn him that Adonijah was ready to seize the kingdom and to remind David of his secret promise to leave the kingdom to Bathsheba's son. David acted decisively to anoint Solomon immediately as king over Israel. Despite all the troubles he had experienced, David rejoiced that God had allowed him to see one of his sons sitting on his throne.

The book of 1 Chronicles greatly expands the account of the end of David's life by telling of his extensive advice to Solomon and his detailed instructions about building the temple at Jerusalem and organizing its numerous clergy. It recounts that David had amassed vast quantities of material for construction, including 100,000 talents of gold. In about 961 B.C., after a 40-year reign, "David slept with his fathers, and was buried in the city of David" (1 Kg. 2:10).

David was no doubt a hero of faith, but a hero tempted by the intoxication of power and desire, who paid dearly for his shortcomings. The biblical writers knew that no human being could be perfect and that no king should be deified like an Egyptian Pharaoh; they were dedicated to showing their hero's warts as well as his beauty. Nevertheless, David's virtues of devotion to God, valor in war, loyalty even under mistreatment, magnanimity in victory, and faithfulness in friendship were so striking that, in spite of his many faults, he was seen as an ideal king, a man after God's own heart.

lamb of a poor man in order to feed an unexpected guest. David, quite properly, was outraged, till Nathan looked at him and said, "You are the man" (2 Sam. 12:7). Because of his crime, Nathan warned, God would raise up evil against David from his own house. The first child of David and Bathsheba died shortly after birth, but soon a second was born and named Solomon. David evidently promised Bathsheba in secret that this son would supersede his elder brothers and inherit the kingdom.

More trouble was not long in coming to David's house as competition and hatred flared among his sons and daughters by different wives. **Amnon**, David's eldest son and heir apparent, raped his half-sister **Tamar**, David's daughter by a Canaanite princess from Geshur. **Absalom**, Tamar's full brother, plotted for two years before assassinating Amnon and fleeing to the court of his grandfather, the king of Geshur.

By the time he returned, Absalom was thoroughly alienated from David. Extremely handsome and outgoing, Absalom worked stealthily but effectively to convince the people of Israel that he would be a better king for them than his father. His broad success revealed that David's support among many of his subjects was shallow.

When Absalom proclaimed his rebellion, so many flocked to his cause that David was forced with great sadness to abandon Jerusalem to the rebels and flee across the Jordan. But even in his pain, David did not lose his will to survive and prevail. He planted spies among Absalom's advisers,

DEBORAH

(deb' aw ruh) HEBREW: DEBORA
"bee"
··········

The story of Deborah is told twice in the book of Judges: first in prose and then in "The Song of Deborah," thought to have been composed in the latter half of the 12th century B.C., shortly after the events it describes took place, and therefore the earliest extensive fragment of Hebrew poetry. Seated beneath a palm tree "between Ramah and Bethel in the hill country of Ephraim" (Jg. 4:5), Deborah responded to questioners who came to ask her help in resolving disputes and adjudicating law cases. Nothing is known of her husband, Lappidoth, not even his tribe. Nor is it known how, in that patriarchal society, a woman rose to judge the Israelite tribes and, even more, became a war leader.

It has been suggested that Deborah's prominence resulted from her religious fervor. Indeed, she provides one of the Bible's earliest examples of charismatic leadership. It was Deborah—according to the

prose version—who summoned the general **Barak** to gather an army to battle the Israelites' oppressor, Jabin, the Canaanite king of Hazor. She even told Barak where to lead that army against Jabin's general, **Sisera**, and predicted the outcome of the battle, an outcome that would depend not on Barak's military skills, but on the intervention of the Lord.

At Deborah's command, Barak called 10,000 warriors from two Galilean hill tribes, Naphtali and Zebulun, to meet at his own birthplace, Kedesh, southwest of the Sea of Galilee. But Barak was reluctant to go there himself unless he was joined by Deborah. Her presence would ensure victory; her influence would turn the campaign into a holy war. Although she agreed to accompany the army, Deborah told Barak that his hesitation would cost him a personal victory over Sisera—that honor going to a woman.

From Kedesh, Barak marched his army to Mount Tabor. The summit of this isolated promontory gave the general a wide view of the plain beneath, across which the enemy would soon be approaching,

Deborah commissions Barak to rid Israel of Canaanite oppression.

riding out over the level ground in iron-wheeled chariots. The Israelites had no chariots; nor did they have either spears or shields. Armed only with short swords, they were posted in the woods on the mountainside where the Canaanite chariots could not reach them. Because the Israelites could not be seen, Barak was able to time the attack to his own advantage.

The Canaanite general made the mistake of concentrating his forces at the foot of the mountain close to the river Kishon. When a sudden downpour changed the river into a torrent and turned the valley floor to mud, Sisera's chariots were immobilized. The Israelites ran down from the mountainside and slaughtered the enemy. Sisera himself fled for refuge to the tent of a man he thought was an ally, **Heber** the Kenite. There, in fulfillment of Deborah's prophecy that Sisera would fall to a woman, he was killed by his ally's wife, **Jael**, who drove a peg through his forehead while he was asleep in her tent.

"The Song of Deborah" differs somewhat from the prose version—for example, naming other tribes who joined Barak and those who withheld their support; placing the battle at "Taanach, by the waters of Megiddo" (Jg. 5:19); saying that Sisera was killed while standing and drinking rather than while asleep; and adding the pathetic figure of the Canaanite general's mother waiting in vain for her son's return from the battlefront with the spoils of victory.

Although Deborah was the only woman to judge Israel, other Israelite women were prophets, most notably **Miriam**, the sister of **Moses**, and **Huldah** who, in the seventh century B.C., verified the authenticity of a newly discovered scroll of the Mosaic Law.

DELILAH

(de li' lah) HEBREW: DELILA
"temptress"

Delilah, the wily woman unwisely loved by **Samson**, came from the valley of Sorek in northern Philistia and was presumably a Philistine. Offered a large payment by the lords of that land to discover the source of Samson's great strength, she was three times given a false clue by her wary lover. At last, she enticed the secret from him: "If I be shaved, then my strength will leave me" (Jg. 16:17). Delilah arranged for a man to cut Samson's hair while he slept, then woke him and delivered him to the Philistines. She was rewarded with 1,100 pieces of silver from each of the lords, while Samson was blinded and put to work in the prison at Gaza.

Delilah betraying Samson; a Limoges enamel dated c. 1575

DEMAS

(dee' muhs) GREEK: DEMAS

One of **Paul**'s fellow-workers, Demas shared the apostle's two-year house arrest in Rome (A.D. 61–63) and was included in greetings sent by Paul during that period to the Colossians and to **Philemon**. Eventually, Demas—"in love with this present world" (2 Tim. 4:10)—deserted Paul and went to Thessalonica.

DEMETRIUS

(di mee' tree uhs) GREEK: DEMETRIOS
"belonging to [the goddess of agriculture] Demeter"

Selling to tourists was big business even in biblical times. Demetrius, a silversmith of Ephesus, crafted silver shrines—probably miniature temples or statues of the goddess **Artemis**—to sell to visiting pilgrims. Demetrius was concerned that **Paul**'s arrival in Ephesus would lead to a decline in sales, for in his Asian travels the apostle cautioned that "gods made with hands are not gods" (Acts 19:26). The silversmith incited his fellow artisans to drag Paul's traveling companions into the theater, where Paul would have joined them but for the restraints imposed by his friends. The town clerk was able to control the riotous crowd, advising Demetrius and the others to bring charges against the newcomers in the courts. However, they apparently failed to do so, and Paul left town.

DEMETRIUS I SOTER

(so' ter) GREEK: SOTER

"savior"

As a boy of about ten, Demetrius was sent as a hostage to Rome by his father, King Seleucus IV Philopator of Syria, to satisfy one of the requirements imposed by the peace treaty of Apamea. From that vantage point, he learned of his father's assassination and the decline of Syria under his uncle, **Antiochus IV Epiphanes**, who was going insane. In 163 B.C., when the crown shifted to his nine-year-old cousin **Antiochus V Eupator**, Demetrius petitioned the Roman senate twice for permission to return to Syria and take his rightful place on the throne. The senate rejected him, preferring a weak ruler to the capable Demetrius.

With the help of the Greek historian Polybius, Demetrius escaped to Syria. Learning that the boy-king and his guardian **Lysias** were unpopular, he gained the support of the army, seized power, and had his two rivals killed. In short order, he named **Alcimus**, a hellenized Jewish reformer, as high priest and launched a military campaign against Judea, ordering his general **Bacchides** and Alcimus to march on the Judeans under **Judas Maccabeus**. On the way, the force was approached by a group of Hasidic scribes seeking peace. After agreeing not to harm them, Alcimus had 60 of them murdered and left unburied.

Bacchides placed Alcimus in charge of Judea and returned to the king, who next dispatched Nicanor, a general "who hated and detested Israel" (1 Macc. 7:26), to crush the Maccabean revolt. Instead, Nicanor was defeated and killed at Adasa; his severed head and right hand were put on display at Jerusalem. Demetrius wasted no time in returning Bacchides and Alcimus to combat. In 160 the Syrian army gained control of Judea with the defeat and death of Judas at Elasa.

As the years passed by, Demetrius's support waned, and a new challenger for the throne of Syria appeared. He was the pretender **Alexander Balas**, claiming to be the son of Antiochus IV. As he prepared to confront Alexander, Demetrius sent **Jonathan**, the brother of Judas Maccabeus and the newly elected leader of the Judeans, a "let-

Coins of Demetrius I Soter and his son, Demetrius II Nicator

ter in peaceable words" (1 Macc. 10:3). Thus began a series of concessions to gain Jonathan's support. Demetrius promised that hostages would be freed and that authority to recruit and arm troops would be granted to the Jews. Alexander countered with an offer of friendship and appointed Jonathan high priest, sending him a purple gown and gold crown. An anxious Demetrius answered this move with still more concessions: exemptions from payment of tribute, taxes, and levies for all Jews. However, numerous other offers failed to convince Jonathan of Demetrius's sincerity, and the Jews allied themselves with Alexander instead. In battle with Alexander's forces in 150 B.C., Demetrius died as his horse became mired in a deep swamp.

DEMETRIUS II NICATOR

(nee' kay tor) GREEK: NICATOR

"victor"

Son of **Demetrius I Soter**, Demetrius had a turbulent life, battling pretenders for the throne of Syria. Until the age of 14, he lived at Cnidus in Asia Minor to avoid his father's adversary **Alexander Balas**. In 147 B.C., with Alexander growing unpopular, Demetrius arrived in Syria with mercenaries from Crete. He was well received by the populace, except for Judeans, and formed an alliance with Ptolemy VI Philometor of Egypt, whose daughter Cleopatra III he married. In 145 the combined forces defeated Alexander near Antioch. Alexander escaped to Arabia where he was beheaded, Ptolemy died of battle wounds, and Demetrius became king of Syria.

The inexperienced monarch, still a teenager, granted many concessions to the Judean rebel leader **Jonathan**. Among them, were the right to annex the districts of Aphairema, Lydda, and Rathamin. In the emerging peace, however, Demetrius initiated military cutbacks that angered his army. Alexander's former commander, Diodotus **Trypho**, organized the disaffected troops and claimed the throne for Alexander's son, **Antiochus VI Epiphanes Dionysus**. Jonathan sided with Trypho, but he was later killed by the deceptive general, who next dispatched Antiochus VI and claimed the crown for himself. These acts drove **Simon**, Jonathan's brother and successor as leader of Judea, to Demetrius, who in 142 granted independence to the Jewish state.

On an expedition to Media seeking allies, Demetrius was captured by King Arsaces VI of Parthia. During Demetrius's ten-year imprisonment, his brother **Antiochus VII Sidetes** ruled Syria. Upon his release from captivity and the death of his brother, Demetrius reclaimed the throne but faced yet another challenge, this time from Egypt. Demetrius was defeated at Damascus and murdered at Tyre in 125 B.C.

DINAH
(di' nuh) HEBREW: DINA
"justice"

The daughter of **Jacob** by **Leah**, Dinah was born in Paddan-aram. As a young woman in Canaan, she was seduced by **Shechem**, the son of Hamor the Hivite. When Shechem asked to marry Dinah, the sons of Jacob plotted revenge by agreeing to the match only if all the males of the city were circumcised. On the third day after the procedures—when all the men "were sore" (Gen. 34:25)—Dinah's brothers **Simeon** and **Levi** led an attack against the city and killed Shechem, his father, and all the other townsmen. The city was plundered and all the women, children, and animals were taken. Jacob cursed the brothers' anger; the decline of the tribes of Simeon and Levi can be traced to this event. Dinah is later mentioned as going with her father to Egypt.

The Greek deity Dionysus, grapevines twining above his porpoise-shaped boat

DIONYSIUS
(di uh nee' si uhs) GREEK: DIONYSIOS

When the apostle **Paul** brought the gospel to Athens, he was asked, "May we know what this new teaching is which you present?" (Acts 17:19). Paul climbed the rocky hill to the Areopagus, the high court of justice, and spoke to a gathering there. Some mocked him and some deferred judgment, but Dionysius—an influential member of the Areopagite council—was among those who believed. According to tradition, the Athenian had studied in Egypt where he observed an eclipse at the time of Jesus' crucifixion and surmised that God was suffering. It is possible that Dionysius became the first bishop of Athens.

DIONYSUS
(di uh nee' suhs) GREEK: DIONYSOS

A Greek deity of Thraco-Phrygian origin, Dionysus is best known as the god of wine and the grape harvest, who communicated his power to followers through intoxication. The only biblical references to him occur in the Apocrypha. On one occasion, King **Antiochus IV Epiphanes** of Syria forced the Jews to participate in the feast of Dionysus, "wearing wreaths of ivy" (2 Macc. 6:7). On another, the Syrian general Nicanor threatened to replace the Lord's house in Jerusalem with "a splendid temple to Dionysus" (2 Macc. 14:33) if the priests did not hand over **Judas Maccabeus**.

Dionysus was said to have been born at Thebes, the son of Zeus and the Theban princess Semele. But his mother died while still carrying Dionysus so that Zeus had to nurture the unborn child, keeping it at his side until birth. Dionysus was then given over for raising to the nymphs of Nysa. In one of his many encounters, Dionysus came upon the abandoned princess Ariadne on the island of Naxos. He rescued her, fell in love with her, and, upon her death, placed her crown among the stars.

Like wine itself, Dionysus had a dual nature: Worship of him centered on ecstatic joy and savage brutality. Those who tried to resist the cult usually met with unfortunate ends. When Dionysus himself was murdered, pomegranates grew where his blood flowed. The annual celebrations of his death and rebirth mirrored the vegetation cycle: death with the coming of winter and resurrection with the return of spring. Eventually, worship of Dionysus spread as far as Persia and India. To the Romans, the god was known as Bacchus.

CHRISTIANITY'S ENEMY

The emperor Domitian is not named in the New Testament but has nevertheless left a stamp on the Bible. He was a persecutor of Christians, and it was under his reign that John was exiled to Patmos and wrote the book of Revelation. Domitian came to power in A.D. 81 at the age of 30. He was already bitter, however, because his predecessors, his father, Vespasian, and his older brother, Titus, had not trusted him and had excluded him from power. He immediately showed himself to be a ruthless autocrat and within a few years insisted on being called "lord and god."

Roman emperor Domitian

Fearful of conspiracies all around, Domitian made the latter years of his rule into a reign of terror, until his own wife helped to murder him in A.D. 96.

Little specific is known about Domitian's persecution. The early church historian Eusebius tells that he banished a woman named Flavia Domitilla, niece of a Roman consul for her "testimony to Christ." Domitian's attitudes and actions helped to solidify an official condemnation of Christianity, later expressed in numerous executions of believers early in the second century.

DOEG

(doh' eg) HEBREW: DOEG
"anxious"

The Edomite Doeg was **Saul**'s chief herdsman. After **David** fled from the king, Doeg saw him receiving aid from **Ahimelech**, a priest of Nob, and informed Saul of the incident. Saul's guard refused his order to kill the priests of Nob, and the king turned to Doeg, who slaughtered 85 priests and destroyed Nob and its inhabitants. Only Ahimelech's son **Abiathar** escaped the destruction and took refuge with David. According to rabbinic lore, Doeg was a learned man who turned his knowledge toward selfish ends. At age 34, he was confronted by three angels of destruction who took his learning, burned his soul, and scattered his ashes.

DORCAS

(dor' kuhs) GREEK: DORKAS
"gazelle"

Also known as Tabitha, Dorcas was a Christian living in Joppa. She was known for her acts of charity, including the making of tunics and other garments for the poor. When Dorcas became ill and died,

many mourned her. Learning that **Peter** was only 10 miles away in Lydda, the disciples sent two men to ask him to come to Joppa. Upon reaching the town, Peter secluded himself in an upper room with the body of Dorcas, prayed, said, "Tabitha, rise," and—when she opened her eyes and extended a hand to him—called the others and "presented her alive"(Acts 9:40, 41). The raising of Dorcas, the first such miracle by an apostle, gained many believers.

DRUSILLA

(droo sil' uh) GREEK: DROUSILLA

Born in A.D. 38, Drusilla was the beautiful daughter of **Herod Agrippa I** and Cypros. As a teenager, she was promised in marriage to Epiphanes, prince of Commagene, but the arrangement was canceled when the groom refused to convert to Judaism. Later, Drusilla was married by her brother **Herod Agrippa II** to Syrian King Azizus, who agreed to be circumcised. In A.D. 53, less than a year into her marriage, a Jewish magician persuaded her to leave Azizus and marry Antonius **Felix**, the Roman procurator of Judea; they had a son named Agrippa. Drusilla was with Felix when **Paul** spoke of his faith to the procurator.

EBER

(ee' buhr) HEBREW: EBER
"[from the] region beyond"

The great-grandson of **Noah**'s eldest son **Shem**, Eber is considered to be the person for whom the Hebrews were named, as in the phrase "all the children of Eber" (Gen. 10:21). The names Eber and Hebrew share the same root, a verb meaning "to cross over." Since **Abraham** came from Haran beyond the Euphrates River, scholars suggest that the name signifies the origin of the Hebrews, who would have crossed over the river to reach the Promised Land. In Luke's genealogy of **Jesus** (Luke 3:23-38), Eber is Shem's great-great-grandson, the name Cainan being added.

EGLON

(eg' lahn) HEBREW: EGLON
"young bull" or "circle"

Early in the 12th century B.C. King Eglon of Moab allied himself with the Ammonites and Amalekites to attack Israel. He crossed the Jordan and captured the land around Jericho, then penetrated farther into Israel, subjugating the tribes of Benjamin and Ephraim for 18 years. The Israelites were spared Eglon's oppression by the "deliverer" (Jg. 3:15) **Ehud**.

EHUD

(ee' hood) HEBREW: EHUD
"united"

By assassinating King **Eglon** of Moab, the Benjaminite Ehud delivered Israel from 18 years of foreign rule. Being left-handed, Ehud could conceal his sword on

Pretending to deliver a secret message, Ehud draws his sword to slay the obese Eglon.

his right thigh and not arouse suspicion from guards. Thus armed and bearing tribute, Ehud gained a private audience with Eglon by saying, "I have a secret message for you, O king" (Jg. 3:19). Told that the message was from God, Eglon rose in respect to receive the special words. At that moment, Ehud buried his double-edged sword to the hilt in the fat belly of the monarch. Locking the door behind him so that his deed would not quickly be discovered, Ehud escaped from the scene, rallied the armies of Israel, and slaughtered a 10,000-man Moabite force on the western bank of the Jordan. His deed brought 80 years of peace.

ELAH

(ee' lah) HEBREW: ELA
"oak"

The son of **Baasha**, Elah reigned as king of Israel for two years (877–876 B.C.) and provoked the Lord's anger by continuing his father's sinful idolatry. While "drinking himself drunk" (1 Kg. 16:9), Elah was murdered at Tirzah, the northern kingdom's capital city. The killer, a commander of the royal chariots named **Zimri**, struck down the king while the Israelite army was away, attacking the Philistines at Gibbethon. Zimri then had Baasha's entire household murdered; "he did not leave him a single male of his kinsmen or his friends" (1 Kg. 16:11). A week later Zimri, besieged at Tirzah by the army commander **Omri**, took his own life.

ELDAD

(el' dad) HEBREW: ELDAD
"El [the god] has loved"

Along with a companion named Medad and 68 others, Eldad was chosen by **Moses** to help govern the people and was endowed with some of the Lord's spirit. As the 68 other elders gathered around the tent of meeting with Moses, Eldad and Medad lingered in the wilderness camp, "the spirit rested upon them," and they prophesied. Moses' aide-de-camp **Joshua** was angered by their unauthorized behavior and asked that they be stopped. Moses responded, "Would that all the Lord's people were prophets, that the Lord would put his spirit upon them" (Num. 11:26,29). The Bible does not reveal their prophecies, though the Aggadah reports that they predicted "Moses shall die, and Joshua shall bring Israel into the [Promised] Land."

Samuel reveals his prophetic mission to the aged priest Eli; detail from a 1780 painting by John Singleton Copley.

ELEAZAR

(el ee ay' zer) HEBREW: ELAZAR
"God has helped"

Aaron's third son, Eleazar married a daughter of Putiel who bore him a son, **Phinehas**. Eleazar was consecrated to the priesthood along with his father and three brothers, and, during his father's lifetime, he became "chief over the leaders of the Levites" (Num. 3:32)—his two older brothers, **Nadab** and Abihu, having been punished with death for making an unholy offering to God. In his expanded role, Eleazar supervised the carrying of the ark.

Upon the death of Aaron at Mount Hor, Eleazar was appointed high priest. After the plague sent by God as punishment for the Israelites' apostasy, **Moses** and Eleazar carried out a census of the people on the plains of Moab, east of the Jordan and opposite Jericho. Later, the Lord instructed Moses to invest **Joshua** as his successor, and ask him "to stand before Eleazar the priest and all the congregation" (Num. 27:19).

Following the conquest of Canaan, Eleazar joined Joshua "and the heads of the fathers' houses" (Jos. 14:1) in administering the division of Canaan by lot among nine and a half tribes of Israel—Moses having given land east of the Jordan to the other two and a half tribes. Eleazar was buried at Gibeah, a town belonging to Phinehas in the hill country of Ephraim.

In King **David**'s day, 16 of the 24 priestly houses were descended from Eleazar, including the family of the high priest **Zadok**.

ELI

(ee' lie) HEBREW: ELI
"[God is] exalted"

High priest in the sanctuary at Shiloh during the period of the judges, Eli was likely descended from **Aaron**'s fourth son, Ithamar. During his tenure at Shiloh, the shrine housed the ark of the covenant. Eli also served as a judge for 40 years and had two sons, **Hophni** and Phinehas.

One day while Eli sat by the door of the temple, he observed **Hannah** weeping as she prayed and at first thought she was drunk. But Hannah, who had accompanied her husband Elkanah on his annual pilgrimage to worship and sacrifice at Shiloh, was anguished because "the Lord had closed her womb" (1 Sam. 1:5). After learning of her desire for a son, the priest invoked God to grant her wish. When that son, **Samuel**, was born and weaned, Hannah brought him to Shiloh to serve with Eli as she had promised God she would do.

While Eli was devout and caring, especially with Samuel, he lacked the firmness to control his sons. Hophni and Phinehas were worthless, corrupt men who may have promoted ritual prostitution at the shrine, where "they lay with the women who served at the entrance to the tent of meeting" (1 Sam. 2:22). But Eli's protests against their behavior were ineffective. As the "sin of the young men was very great in the sight of the Lord" (1 Sam. 2:17), a man of God visited Eli, prophesying the downfall of his house and the violent deaths of his sons—all on the same day. The prophecy was confirmed to Samuel in a vision while he was lying down in the temple.

Because Israel was in a desperate struggle with the Philistines at Ebenezer, the people asked for the ark to be brought from Shiloh to the battlefield. Hophni and Phinehas escorted the ark to the scene, but they were among the 30,000 Israelites slaughtered during a rout in which the Philistines captured the ark. When news of the disaster reached Eli, the 98-year-old stout, blind priest—sitting by the road in dread anticipation—fell over backward and broke his neck.

ELIEZER

(el i ee' zer) HEBREW: ELIEZER
"my God is help"

One of the many of this name in the Bible, Eliezer of Damascus was **Abraham**'s old and faithful servant. When the Lord promised Abraham a great reward, he reproachfully said, "thou hast given me no offspring; and a slave [Eliezer] born in my house will be my heir" (Gen. 15:3). It was an accepted practice in the ancient Near East for the childless to adopt a servant as heir, and Eliezer would thus have come into Abraham's wealth—and inherited his covenant with the Lord—had it not been for the unexpected birth of **Isaac**. Eliezer is probably the trusted servant, "the oldest of

By her offer of water to Abraham's servant Eliezer, Rebekah identifies herself as the bride appointed by the Lord for Isaac.

his house, who had charge of all that he had" (Gen. 24:2), whom the patriarch sent to Mesopotamia to find a bride for Isaac so that his son would not marry a Canaanite woman.

ELIHU

(ee lie' hyoo) HEBREW: ELIHU
"he is my God"

Perhaps a descendant of **Abraham**'s brother **Nahor**, Elihu the Buzite was the young man who challenged the long-suffering **Job** and his three friends. They were, he said, "wise in their own conceit" (Job 37:24). He accused Job of having "justified himself rather than God" (Job 32:2) and chided him for his arrogance, empty talk, and sinful words. Elihu's harsh speeches serve as an introduction to the Lord's answer to Job—both illustrate divine omnipotence and the gulf between the wisdom of man and his creator. "God thunders wonderously with his voice," Elihu explained; "he does great things which we cannot comprehend" (Job 37:5).

ELIJAH

(ee lie' juh) HEBREW: ELIYAHU or ELIYA
"my God is Yahweh"

The first great prophet of the northern kingdom of Israel, Elijah gained a reputation as one who appeared and disappeared like the wind—as though the spirit of God both deposited and snatched him away. The narrator of 1 Kings certainly fosters that reputation by introducing the prophet without a word of background.

In a time when **Baal**, the Canaanite god of storm, rain, and fertility, was gaining allegiance throughout the kingdom, Elijah broke upon the scene with the brash and confident assertion that the God of Israel held control over the generative powers of nature. "As the Lord the God of Israel lives," Elijah announced to King **Ahab**, "there shall be neither dew nor rain these years, except by my word" (1 Kg. 17:1). The dramatic message was clear: If the word of a single prophet of Yahweh could negate all the claims of Baal to give fertility and moisture, clearly Baal was not a god deserving either worship or fear.

KNOWN FOR HIS DEEDS

The biblical account of Elijah's mission spans some 15 years, from about 865 to 850 B.C. The stories of the prophet's courageous deeds were handed down by word of mouth from generation to generation for some 300 years, until they were finally incorporated into 1 and 2 Kings, originally a single work completed about 550, a decade after the last events described in the book. Unlike the records of later prophets—usually filled with their teachings—the biblical narrative emphasizes the works rather than the words of Elijah. Thus, his ministry is filled with conflict and wondrous deeds. He and his disciple and successor **Elisha** are the greatest miracle workers in Scripture between **Moses** and **Jesus**.

Elijah was probably born sometime in the decade before 900 B.C. and reared in the village of Tishbe, a settlement so far from the center of Israelite life or so undistinguished that it is mentioned nowhere else in the Bible. Tishbe was located in Gilead, a harsh region east of the Jordan on the edge of the great Arabian desert. Little influenced by the more affluent, even luxurious life-style of central Canaan, the people of Gilead tended to maintain Israel's strict ancient traditions derived from their nomadic years in the wilderness. They were devoted to Yahweh alone and scorned the fertility cults and many gods of the Canaanites.

Hiding from King Ahab by the brook Cherith, the prophet Elijah is fed by ravens.

During the years that Elijah was growing to maturity, political turmoil racked the northern kingdom, which was also engaged in a destructive and debilitating war against the southern kingdom of Judah. Peace and political stability finally came to Israel when **Omri** seized the throne about 876 B.C. and negotiated a collaborative accord with Judah. Since Omri's lands included a large Canaanite population, he formed a close alliance with Canaanite Phoenicia, sealing it by marrying his son Ahab to the Phoenician princess **Jezebel**, daughter of King Ethbaal of Sidon. With trade flowing easily north and south, the kingdom of Israel entered a period of prosperity such as had not been known for nearly a century or since the early reign of **Solomon**.

Though Omri was, at least formally, a worshiper of Yahweh, he did not reject other gods, allowing and even fostering the worship of Baal. In time his son would build a substantial temple to Baal in the new capital at Samaria, perhaps to rival the shrines to Yahweh at Bethel and Dan. Apparently, Omri and his son wanted Yahweh and Baal to be equally honored and worshiped. For people like Elijah, who were steeped in Israel's strict monotheism, such a situation was intolerable.

JEZEBEL'S BANEFUL INFLUENCE

Ahab succeeded Omri in about 869, when Elijah was perhaps in his mid- to late 30's. Whether Elijah had already begun his work as a prophet, perhaps as part of a prophetic guild, is unknown. The religious crisis in Israel deepened, however, as Jezebel, Ahab's queen, made her presence felt. She had grown up with the Phoenician worship of Baal and the goddess Asherah, and her advocacy of Baal appears to have been almost as strong as Elijah's devotion to Yahweh. Not only did she financially support hundreds of prophets of Baal and Asherah at the royal court, she also worked to suppress the rival worship of Yahweh by abrogating the influence of his prophets there, driving many into hiding and executing others. This was the situation when Elijah suddenly appeared at court to utter his prophecy of doom, sentencing Israel's agriculture-based economy to years of drought. Immediately thereafter, Elijah vanished.

Ahab believed the prophet's words enough to hold him responsible for the famine that ensued, and he made Elijah the object of an international manhunt. God, however, sent Elijah into hiding by a brook called Cherith (exact location unknown) east of the Jordan, out of Ahab's immediate reach. Though the prophet was alone and

As the prophets of Baal cringe, Elijah summons the Lord's fire to consume his water-drenched offering; a painting by Albert Moore (1841-1893).

totally without resources, God miraculously provided for his needs. "Ravens brought him bread and meat in the morning, and bread and meat in the evening" (1 Kg. 17:6), while the brook provided water—much as in Moses' day God had provided food and water for Israel in the wilderness.

The brook also served to mark the increasing severity of the drought. When it dried up, Elijah was sent north to the town of Zarephath in Sidon, Jezebel's homeland, a region supposedly loyal to Baal. There Elijah found a Canaanite widow gathering sticks at the town gate and requested her to bring him bread and water. The woman and her son, however, had been devastated by the drought—Baal could not protect even his own territory from the power of Yahweh. She had only enough oil and meal to bake a few final morsels for them; when that was gone, she said in resignation, they must starve and die. Still the prophet challenged her to bring food first for him, trusting the God of Israel to provide her with sustenance. The woman obeyed and, sure enough, for the duration of the famine her "jar of meal was not spent, neither did the cruse of oil fail" (1 Kg. 17:16).

Later, however, God's life-giving power seemed to falter when the widow's son contracted an illness "so severe that there was no breath left in him" (1 Kg. 17:17). Both the widow and the prophet understood this to be God's doing. But when Elijah "stretched himself upon the child three times, and cried to the Lord," God's om-nipotence was again manifested, and "the soul of the child came into him again, and he revived" (1 Kg. 17:21-22).

In the third year of the drought, God sent Elijah back to the territory of Israel to challenge Ahab. "Is it you, you troubler of Israel?" (1 Kg. 18:17), Ahab shouted. Elijah responded that the king himself was Israel's troubler because of his policy of support for Baal and proposed a contest, summoning the 450 prophets of Baal and 400 prophets of Asherah to meet him at Mount Carmel. This promontory overlooking the Mediterranean Sea had evidently been the site of an altar to Baal from ancient times. But during the early monarchy, when the whole territory was consolidated under Israelite rule, an altar to Yahweh had also been built here. That altar had been abandoned and lay in ruins—symbolic of the religious situation of Israel. Hordes of people gathered at the mountain to see 850 Canaanite prophets with the king and a prominent altar of Baal on one side and a single prophet of Yahweh and an altar in ruins on the other.

THE UNANSWERED SUMMONS

Elijah emphatically repudiated Ahab's policy of accommodation between Yahweh and Baal. A choice must be made: "How long will you go limping with two different opinions? If the Lord is God, follow him; but if Baal, then follow him" (1 Kg. 18:21). The people were silent, uncertain. To decide the issue, Elijah proposed that the two sides prepare sacrifices but not burn them. Each side would pray, "and the God who answers by fire, he is God" (1 Kg. 18:24).

The rites began in the morning, with an appeal to Baal. Surging in motion together, hundreds of prophets performed a ritual dance in which they bent their knees and hopped from one foot to the other in a virtual parody of the limping beliefs for which Elijah had castigated Israel. Their cries to Baal went unanswered. As the hot sun reached high noon, Elijah could not help but be amused; perhaps Baal was meditating, he taunted, or relieving himself, or on a journey, or asleep; they must cry louder to rouse him. With a disappointed monarch and restless people watching, the prophets became more frenzied, in ecstatic ravings gashing themselves till they were covered in blood. But "no one answered, no one heeded" (1 Kg. 18:29).

As the time for the afternoon sacrifice approached, the crowds turned from the clotted mass of Baal's failed prophets to Elijah, who began quietly to repair the broken altar of Yahweh. He used 12 stones to symbolize the reunited people of the 12 tribes, the altar thus becoming a symbol of Israel's true identity. Although he laid out the wood and sacrificial bull in proper fashion, Elijah mysteriously dug a deep trench around the altar. He then called for four jars to be filled with water but, instead of using them for rites of purification as some might have expected, ordered them poured over the sacrifice and the wood. Twice more the jars were filled and emptied till the trench was filled and the altar was drenched.

When the proper moment arrived, Elijah approached the altar alone and addressed Yahweh: "God of Abraham, Isaac, and Israel . . . . answer me, that this people may know that thou, O Lord, art God, and that thou hast turned their hearts back" (1 Kg. 18:36-37). As he spoke, flames consumed everything—sacrifice, wood, stones, even the water. Elijah's question was answered, not by the people but by God himself. Immediately, Elijah urged the people to seize the prophets of Baal. Defeated enemy in a holy war, all were condemned to death in strict enforcement of the ancient Israelite law against apostasy: "Whoever sacrifices to any god, save to the Lord only, shall be utterly destroyed" (Ex. 22:20).

A TRIUMPH UNREWARDED

Elijah had demonstrated Baal's impotence as the giver of either rain or fire and had shown that Yahweh alone sends fire. Next the prophet had to establish that Yahweh was also the giver of rain and its fertility. Boldly Elijah announced to Ahab that he heard "a sound of the rushing of rain" (1 Kg.

18:41), but then he went to the top of Mount Carmel and humbled himself before God, kneeling with his face between his knees. Seven times he prayed, and each time told his servant to go look west to the sky over the sea. Only after his seventh prayer did his servant report seeing "a little cloud like a man's hand" (1 Kg. 18:44). Elijah sent word to the king that he should leave with his chariot immediately, before rain turned the parched ground to impassable mud. Elijah, however, perhaps unwilling to leave the announcement of the amazing events at Mount Carmel to the hostile monarch, ran the nearly 20 miles to the gates of the northern capital at Jezreel and arrived with the news before the king.

It might be expected that, following the contest on Mount Carmel, all of Israel would immediately return to faithful worship of Yahweh. The sequel indicates the opposite. When Queen Jezebel heard of the slaughter of her favored prophets, she not only failed to abandon her faith in Baal, she swore to have Elijah executed immediately. The triumphant but exhausted prophet now had to flee for his life rather than enjoy his victory. How he escaped the city of Jezreel is not said; perhaps it was under cover of the sudden thunderstorm. Elijah traveled south, out

Elijah races ahead of King Ahab to bring news of the drought's end to Jezreel.

B. Gallego

of Jezebel's reach, passing through Judah to Beersheba, where he left his servant and went on alone into the Sinai desert. As his dreams of transforming his people and restoring their faithfulness to Yahweh appeared crushed by Jezebel's power, despair overshadowed the fugitive's faith. Under a lonely broom tree in the desert the dispirited prophet sat exhausted.

At that moment an angel of the Lord touched Elijah and gave him water and bread baked on the hot stones of the desert. The prophet ate and drank but sank again into despairing thought. Again the angel came and fed him, but this time he also instructed Elijah to travel farther south. Strengthened

by the heavenly messenger's food, Elijah was able to make the 40-day journey to "Horeb the mount of God" (1 Kg. 19:8)— known also as Mount Sinai. It was as if the prophet had retraced Israel's 40 years in the desert and had returned to the place of God's original revelation on the sacred mountain of the covenant. There Elijah rested in a cave reminiscent of the cleft rock where Moses hid while God passed by and revealed his glory to him.

Even after encountering the angel, Elijah was in the grip of despair, darkened by self-pity. But before the prophet could raise himself, amazing events began to occur outside his cave. Just as God had first appeared to

The chariot and horses of fire take Elijah up to heaven in a whirlwind; an inlaid marble image from the cathedral of Siena.

Israel on Mount Sinai in fire, smoke, thunder, and earthquake, so now the physical world marked a divine epiphany. But this time, somehow, Elijah sensed a difference. A mighty wind, strong enough to break the rocks, tore at the mountain, but Elijah knew that God was not in the wind. Next a great earthquake, then a blazing fire occurred, but Elijah recognized that the Lord was not in them either. These were the traditional signs of theophany, or divine manifestation—signs also claimed by Baal. Yahweh could easily have manifested them, but he could never be identified with them as were the pagan gods.

As the fire died away, however, Elijah heard a whisper in the silence, "a still small voice" (1 Kg. 19:12), and something within the prophet told him that in that sound of gentle stillness was the true voice of God. He could no longer sit, consumed by his own sadness, but wrapped his mantle around his face to shield his eyes and went forth from the cave to meet God. Then the voice confronted Elijah forcefully, "What are you doing here, Elijah?" The prophet immediately began to defend himself, speaking of his own zealousness for God and of the apostasy of others. "The people of Israel have forsaken thy covenant, thrown down thy altars, and slain thy prophets with the sword; and I, even I only, am left; and they seek my life, to take it away" (1 Kg. 19:13-14). Eli-

jah had been engaged so long in the battle for his faith, that he had come to think of it as inextricably linked to his personal victories and defeats.

A NEW COMMISSION FOR ELIJAH

But the unique epiphany of God on the mountain had pointed in a different direction. The fact that God was not in the mighty demonstrations of nature's power like those that were claimed for Baal, but was present only in a whisper breaking the silence, intimated that Yahweh was on an entirely separate plane from Baal. There could be no true competition between Baal, who was hardly more than a personification of those natural forces, and the true and mysterious God of Israel, who encompassed and surpassed all natural power. In spite of what Elijah imagined, God's survival did not depend solely on him, and there was no cause for despair.

God, however, did not reject his prophet, but gave him a new commission, one allowing him to see that the divine purpose was much broader than the defeat of Baal. God sent him to anoint new kings for both Syria and Israel, so that the political power structure would not remain in the hands of Ahab, Jezebel, and their ilk. Elijah was also to anoint a new prophet, Elisha, to take his own place; no one was indispensable. These new figures would carry out God's plan to punish the apostasy that so troubled Elijah. The time was not yet ripe for the anointing of new kings in Israel and Syria, but Elijah set about fulfilling the third part of his commission immediately. He traveled up the Jordan valley till he came to the town of Abel-meholah, where he found Elisha plowing in a field. When Elijah "cast his mantle upon him" (1 Kg. 19:19), Elisha bade farewell to his parents and became Elijah's new servant and apprentice.

In this very period Ahab seemed at the height of his career, facing down military challenges from the Syrians, regaining long-lost cities, establishing advantageous trading agreements. These successes, however, made him eager to expand his royal lands and, with Jezebel's help, he confiscated the property of a neighbor named **Naboth** after having had him executed on trumped-up charges of blasphemy and treason. As Ahab entered his new property, Elijah met him. "Have you found me, O my enemy?" (1 Kg. 21:20) Ahab cried, suspecting what was coming. Elijah would not let Ahab forget that he was guilty of a judicial murder and foretold the complete destruction of Ahab's dynasty and the shameful death of Jezebel. The fire of Elijah's words was so intense that it melted even the steely heart of Ahab: He tore his royal robes, put on sackcloth, and

began to fast. His apparent reversal of attitude brought a delay in the destruction of his house but could not undo the effects of his transgressions and those of Jezebel. Not long after these events, Ahab was fatally wounded in battle at Ramoth-Gilead, and was succeeded by his son **Ahaziah**.

HIS FINAL PREDICTION

Elijah's last indirect contact with a king of Israel came after Ahaziah had been injured in a fall. The king wanted an oracle to foretell his recovery and sent messengers to "Baal-zebub, the god of Ekron" (2 Kg. 1:2). Elijah, however, met them and turned them back with the terse message that the king would die. When the messengers reported the incident, Ahaziah recognized the description of Elijah and sent 50 soldiers to arrest him. The troop was powerless against the prophet, who called down fire from heaven to destroy both them and a second 50 sent in their place. Finally, Elijah came to the faithless king in person and pronounced his doom. Ahaziah died childless and his brother **Jehoram** succeeded him.

The final episode in the story of Elijah merges his narrative with that of his successor, Elisha. The time had come "when the Lord was about to take Elijah up to heaven by a whirlwind" (2 Kg. 2:1), and the old

THE TRANSFIGURATION

A week after Jesus had accepted Peter's acknowledgment that he was the Messiah, he took Peter, James, and John to the top of a mountain. There they saw Jesus "transfigured before them, and his face shone like the sun" (Mt. 17:2). Beside Jesus stood two men, somehow recognizable to the disciples as Moses and Elijah.

Both men had departed from earth in amazing ways. After Moses died on a mountaintop, the Lord buried him in a secret place. According to one ancient author, this meant a cloud had suddenly descended upon Moses and he disappeared. Elijah, of course, was taken up to heaven by a whirlwind. On the mountain, Moses and Elijah spoke to Jesus about the "departure, which he was to accomplish in Jerusalem" (Lk. 9:31)—that is, his death. Their conversation with Jesus certified the unity between Jesus' message and the Law and the prophets of the Hebrew Scriptures. It also showed that Jesus' fate

was not simply in the hands of the high priests or the Roman governor. All was already known to these celebrated figures, sent from heaven as witnesses that Jesus was, indeed, God's "beloved Son" (Mk. 9:7).

Jesus flanked by Moses and Elijah

prophet tested the mettle of the new. Setting out on a journey, Elijah thrice urged Elisha to remain behind. But thrice Elisha declared he would not leave his mentor. When the pair reached the Jordan, Elijah parted the waters with a blow of his rolled up mantle so they could cross on dry ground—just as the Israelites had done so long ago in the days of **Joshua**.

The moment of farewell drew near, and Elijah offered his follower a final gift. Elisha asked only to be like an eldest son and receive "a double share of your spirit" (2 Kg. 2:9). As they walked and talked, they were suddenly separated by the chariot and horses of fire that took Elijah to heaven. Elijah was gone, but his disciple took up the mantle that had fallen from him—as he would then take up Elijah's sacred mission.

As one who did not die, Elijah captured the thoughts and prophetic hopes of later generations. The prophecies of **Malachi** in the fifth century B.C. conclude the Old Testament by telling how God would send Elijah to restore his people before "the great and terrible day of the Lord comes" (Mal. 4:5). **Jesus Ben Sira**, in the Apocrypha, notes that Elijah stands ready to "restore the tribes of Jacob" (Sir. 48:10). In the New Testament, both **John the Baptist** and Jesus were associated with Elijah. John was said to act "in the spirit and power of Elijah" (Lk. 1:17) and even wore Elijah's distinctive haircloth tunic and leather belt. Likewise, the Gospels report that some thought Jesus was Elijah restored to life on earth.

ELIMELECH

(ee lim' eh lek) HEBREW: ELIMELEK
"El [God] is king"

A native of Bethlehem, in Judah, Elimelech married **Naomi** and had two sons. Because of famine, "in the days when the judges ruled" (Ru. 1:1), the family was forced to resettle in the land of Moab. After Elimelech's death, the two sons married Moabite women, **Orpah** and **Ruth**. When the sons died, Naomi told her daughters-in-law to return to their mothers' houses, as she intended to go back to Bethlehem. Ruth insisted on accompanying Naomi to her homeland, however, and subsequently married Elimelech's kinsman **Boaz**. His purchase of Elimelech's land not only allowed Boaz to claim Ruth but also ensured that the estate would remain in the family.

ELIPHAZ

(el' i faz) HEBREW: ELIPAZ
possibly "God is fine gold" or "God is victorious"

Given precedence among **Job**'s three friends, perhaps because of his age, Eliphaz the Temanite was a wise and sympathetic man. In his first speech to Job, he asked with polished courtesy, "Who that was innocent ever perished?" (Job 4:7). Job's continued obduracy in the face of Eliphaz's counseling, however, led him to a horrible depiction of what would befall the wicked man who "has stretched forth his hand against God and bids defiance to the Almighty" (Job 15:25). He ended his third

Using the mantle he has received from Elijah (left), Elisha parts the Jordan waters (center); later, he curses jeering boys, who are devoured by bears (right).

discourse with a plea to Job: "Agree with God and be at peace" (Job 22:21)—that is, Job should admit that his punishment at the hands of the Lord was just retribution. But Eliphaz's wisdom, based only on his own experience and understanding of God, was not applicable to Job's plight and ultimately displeased the Lord, who commanded him and his two friends to sacrifice seven bulls and seven rams in atonement.

ELISHA

(ee lie' shuh) HEBREW: ELISA
"God is salvation"

The disciple of **Elijah**, Elisha was a powerful prophet in his own right, a miracle worker, a master of prophetic guilds, and the dominant religious figure in Israel during the second half of the ninth century B.C. He may have become Elijah's apprentice as early as 861 or 860, but his own prophetic career did not begin until the end of Elijah's work, about the year 850. Though Elisha continued the work of his mentor, he was less a lonely, isolated voice and more a prophet among people.

As generation after generation listened to the stories handed down about Elisha, the people especially loved to hear how God manifested his power through the words and deeds of the prophet. Most of the first half of 2 Kings, written about 250 years after the death of Elisha, is devoted to preserving traditions about him.

Elisha was the son of a farmer, a man named Shaphat, from the ancient town of Abel-meholah in the fertile Jordan River valley. When Elijah found him, he was at work at his plowing—perhaps in hope of the first good crop of grain after the long years of drought—and seems to have had no thought of a career as a prophet. Elisha was evidently directing 11 other plowmen as they drove yokes of oxen through a field that was to be planted. As driver of the 12th yoke, Elisha was able to oversee the others. If all 24 oxen belonged to his father, his family would have been quite prosperous. But after Elijah cast his rough mantle over Elisha, anointing him a prophet as he had been instructed during his encounter with God on Mount Horeb, the young man's life changed dramatically. Asking only to kiss his parents good-bye, Elisha immediately ran after the prophet. Before leaving, however, he showed his break with the farmer's life by butchering his working oxen, cooking them on a fire made by burning their yokes, and sharing the meat with his neighbors. Wealthy or not, he was to be a people's prophet.

SONS OF THE PROPHETS

The prophetic guilds known as sons of the prophets were an important part of Israel's religious life from before the time of Samuel. By Elijah's day, these men often lived and ate together as members of distinctive communities. They regarded Elijah as a beloved father, which explains their persistence in seeking the prophet after his disappearance—though acknowledging Elisha as his successor. It was largely through their efforts that the heroic deeds of both Elijah and Elisha were collected and handed down from generation to generation until incorporated in the Scriptures centuries later.

When Elijah was about to depart from the world, Elisha refused to be separated from the older man, no matter how often Elijah suggested that he stay behind. But after Elijah had led his apprentice across the Jordan, he told Elisha to "ask what I shall do for you before I am taken from you"; Elisha requested "a double share of your spirit" (2 Kg. 2:9)—the inheritance of a firstborn son. Elijah responded that his follower's wish would be granted only if he saw him depart, suggesting both that Elisha must be faithful to the end and that God must grant him the vision. Sure enough, as they proceeded on their way, Elisha saw the event: They were separated by a fiery chariot and horses, and Elijah was swept up to heaven by a whirlwind. As the prophet ascended, however, the mantle that he had originally cast around Elisha to summon him as a disciple fell to earth. Elisha picked it up, ripped his own cloak in two, and—as Elijah had done earlier—used the mantle to part the waters of the Jordan. The miraculous work of Elisha as heir to both the mantle and spirit of Elijah had begun.

SALT FOR A SPRING

West of the Jordan, a band of the so-called sons of the prophets immediately recognized that "the spirit of Elijah rests on Elisha" (2 Kg. 2:15). Staying with these men at Jericho, Elisha performed his first miracle of practical aid. Jericho's oasis spring had become

Elisha restores the Shunammite's son

*Elisha raises a woman's son to life (above),
as his mentor Elijah had done before (below,
detail of a painting by Ford Madox Brown)
and as Jesus would do in the future.*

polluted and was causing crop failure, miscarriages, and death. When the people asked for help, Elisha ordered that a new bowl be filled with salt, which he cast into the spring. Then he announced that Yahweh had "made this water wholesome" (2 Kg. 2:21); the spring was restored.

The next miracle takes the reader by surprise. On his way to Bethel, the prophet was jeered at for his baldness—perhaps a form of tonsure—by a group of boys. The prophet cursed the mockers in the name of Yahweh, and two bears "came out of the woods and tore forty-two of the boys" (2 Kg. 2:24). This story, which seems so troubling, evidently conveyed to the ancient hearers a sense of the holiness that the prophet embodied. Like the ark of the covenant, which could bring death to any who touched it, Elisha's holiness could not be mocked without dreadful consequences.

HELPING THE POOR

Most of the traditions preserved about Elisha, however, reveal him as a man of compassion who brings with him the power to overcome any difficulty. Several narratives, for example, include brief scenes of life among the sons of the prophets, communities primarily made up of poor families.

When one of the sons of the prophets died in debt, his widow and two children were left destitute, at the mercy of creditors ready to sell the children as slaves. The widow begged help from Elisha, who saved the children by using the only thing she owned, a jar of oil. At the prophet's word, the jar poured out its valuable contents until it had filled every available container in the community. The oil was sold and the creditors satisfied. On another occasion, a famine forced the sons of the prophets in Gilgal to share Elisha's pot of stewed vegetables made with wild herbs. When someone accidentally added poisonous wild gourds to the common stock, the whole group might have been killed. Elisha, however, saved the day. Just as he had earlier purified a spring by pouring salt into it, so Elisha preserved the food by throwing ground meal into the poisoned pot. On yet another occasion a man brought a gift of 20 small barley loaves to Elisha as part of his first fruits of harvest, and with the loaves the prophet miraculously fed a hundred men—and even had leftovers. Nearly a thousand years later, similar miracles would be attributed to **Jesus**.

In some places, at least, the impoverished prophetic guilds lived in common quarters under the direction of the great prophet. Once they told Elisha that "the place where we dwell under your charge is too small for us" (2 Kg. 6:1) and announced they were going to the Jordan River to cut logs from trees that grew near its banks for a new dwelling. Fortunately, the prophet himself decided to go along. When one of the men was felling a tree with a borrowed ax and the valuable iron head flew off its handle and disappeared into the water, the prophet cut a stick and threw it into the river at the place where the tool had sunk. The iron ax head bobbed up to the surface and was easily retrieved by the man who had lost it.

GIVING AND RESTORING LIFE

In addition to the numerous pithy miracle stories of only a few sentences, 2 Kings also includes some more extended narratives that read like concise dramas with several scenes and fully developed characters. The first and perhaps most prominent of these is the account of Elisha's dealings with a wealthy woman from the town of Shunem, just north of Jezreel. She and her husband decided to aid the prophet's work by giving him room and board on his regular travels across the land of Israel. Wishing to reward their generosity and discovering that the couple had no heir for their considerable wealth, the prophet promised the Shunammite woman a son within the year. With understandable skepticism she begged the prophet not to toy with her, but nonetheless Elisha's promise came true.

The next scene takes place several years later. By then the boy was old enough to accompany his father into the fields. But suddenly the boy cried out, "Oh, my head, my head!" (2 Kg. 4:19) and collapsed with an apparent sunstroke. The boy was taken to his mother and was lying on her lap when he died. In bitter sorrow she laid the boy out on the bed in Elisha's room and departed for Mount Carmel, one of the places where Elisha regularly stayed. There she seized the prophet's feet and begged for help. At first, Elisha sent his servant **Gehazi** to touch the child with the prophet's staff, but the Shunammite woman refused to leave until the prophet himself returned with her.

The scene shifts back to the woman's home in Shunem. Gehazi having been unable to raise the child, Elisha had to deal with the death personally. He prayed to God and stretched his body out fully over the small corpse, "putting his mouth upon his mouth, his eyes upon his eyes, and his hands upon his hands" (2 Kg. 4:34), and with his own body warmed the child's cold one. Then Elisha got up, walked back and forth, and again stretched out on the boy. This time the child sneezed seven times and opened his eyes. Elisha reunited the boy and his grateful mother.

The final scene of the drama again takes place a few years later. Elisha had warned the woman, by then apparently a widow, of an impending seven-year famine. She trusted the prophet enough to abandon their home and take her son outside Israel to the land of the Philistines for the duration. When she returned home, she appeared before the king to request the restoration of her

ANIMALS SERVING GOD'S PURPOSES

The two bears who punished the boys for insulting Elisha are part of a fascinating biblical tradition stretching back to the clever serpent in the garden of Eden: animals used by God to serve his divine purposes.

The dove released from the ark by Noah brought confirmation that the Flood had ended. For Abraham, a ram caught in a bush was God's substitute for the sacrifice of Isaac. Moses' and Aaron's staffs turned to snakes as a sign for Pharaoh, and God struck Egypt with plagues of frogs, gnats, flies, and locusts. In the desert, God provided the Israelites with quail to eat, but later punished them with fiery serpents. When Balaam tried to curse Israel, his ass saw an angel and spoke to the seer. In Canaan, God helped Samson kill a lion with his bare hands. Lost asses caused Saul to find Samuel, who anointed him Israel's first king. When the prophet Elijah hid during a drought, ravens brought him food. Dogs licked up the blood of Ahab and ate the flesh of Jezebel until no more of her was left than skull, feet, and the palms of her hands. Jonah was swallowed by a great fish; later a worm ate his shade tree. When Daniel was thrown among lions, an angel stopped their mouths so that he survived the ordeal.

property. Remarkably, at that very moment the king was listening to Gehazi's account of Elisha's miracles. Since the woman and her son were living proof of the prophet's powers, the king was impressed enough to grant her request. This extended account is intended to show that God's power worked through Elisha to give life, to restore life, and to preserve life. Though the scenes themselves are filled with colorful details, the miracles are never performed so as to build up the fame or following of the prophet. And the final scene stresses that even such great miracles were intended to be kept private; only long after the fact do circumstances converge so that the king or the public are able to learn of the great things Elisha had done.

AN AFFLICTION TRANSFERRED

The second major narrative about Elisha in 2 Kings concerns **Naaman**, a Syrian general, who came to the prophet for healing, for "he was a leper" (2 Kg. 5:1). In ancient times leprosy was the name used for a variety of skin diseases and was not limited to Hansen's disease, as in modern usage. In spite of all Naaman's resources, it was one of those whom he had enslaved, a maid from the land of Israel, who held the knowledge that could relieve this potentate of his affliction. She told his wife of a prophet who could give him the cure that the gods of his own land could not provide.

Naaman was a man used to wielding authority. Though he was in need of help, he would go to the prophet only after his visit had been arranged through royal channels and endorsed with a letter from the king of Syria. He expected that the prophet would meet him personally and would directly

Sent to wash in the Jordan by Elisha, the Syrian general Naaman is cured of leprosy.

carry out the healing. Further, he expected to pay handsomely for everything he received and so incur no sense of debt for the prophet's aid. Thus, laden with wealth, he set off to visit the king of Israel. Everything went awry. Israel's king, who evidently was not fully aware of Elisha's powers, did not know what to make of the Syrian monarch's request to heal his general: "Am I God, to kill and to make alive?" (2 Kg. 5:7). He assumed the worst, that Syria was seeking to provoke a conflict.

Eventually Elisha heard of Naaman's pilgrimage and sent for him. The supplicant arrived at the prophet's door with the horses and chariots that bespoke his mighty position. But again things did not go as expected. Elisha did not so much as come out to greet him or wave his hands over him. Rather, he sent his servant out with strange instructions: "Go and wash in the Jordan seven times, and your flesh shall be restored, and you shall be clean" (2 Kg. 5:10).

Naaman was flabbergasted. He wanted personal service, a clear display of power, even some great deed for himself to perform, but not to be hustled off to a little local river to perform ordinary rites with no clear purpose. Again, however, his slaves rescued the mighty man and convinced him to go along with the prophet. When he followed "the word of the man of God," we are told, he was not only healed, he was rejuvenated so that "his flesh was restored like the flesh of a little child" (2 Kg. 5:14). As the next scene opens, Naaman is a changed man, a pagan now convinced that the God of Israel is the one true God.

The final scene of the drama develops a striking contrast between the transformed foreigner and Gehazi, the greedy servant of the prophet. When Gehazi saw that Elisha refused Naaman's lavish gifts, it was more than he could bear. He ran after Naaman and pretended that the prophet had changed his mind and now wanted some of the gifts. Naaman was happy to give even more than had been requested. But when Gehazi tried to hide his deed from Elisha, the prophet condemned him to suffer the very ailment that had been removed from Naaman. As the drama ends, the greedy servant is seen departing, his skin "white as snow" (2 Kg. 5:27) with the disease.

WAR COUNSELOR AND KINGMAKER

From early in his ministry, Elisha was involved with affairs of state. When King **Jehoram** went to war to subdue an uprising by his vassal **Mesha**, king of Moab, he made an alliance with King **Jehoshaphat** of Judah and with the king of Edom.

Marching through the desert to attack Moab from the south, the three kings feared that their armies would run out of water. After Jehoshaphat suggested that they consult a prophet of Yahweh, the allies went to visit Elisha. At first, the prophet refused to have anything to do with Jehoram, because of the support his parents, **Ahab** and **Jezebel**, had given the prophets of **Baal**. But for the sake of the king of Judah, who was more faithful to the worship of Yahweh, Elisha agreed to help. The prophet summoned a musician and "when the minstrel played, the power of the Lord came upon him" (2 Kg. 3:15). Elisha delivered an oracle promising that water would appear in the desert and that Israel would conquer the Moabites. The next day, indeed, abundant water was inexplicably flowing; and, at first, the campaign was successful. But then, facing defeat, Mesha sacrificed his eldest son on the city wall. The Moabites considered the terrible sacrifice an act of devotion to their god Chemosh, whose wrath would now be stirred against the attackers. Fearful of the Moabite god's anger, the Israelites withdrew to their homeland.

Sometime later, carrying out a commission that God had originally given to Elijah at Mount Horeb, Elisha is said to have instigated two political revolutions, one in Syria and one in Israel. The Syrian revolution began when Elisha told **Hazael**, minister to the king **Ben-hadad**, that his lord would die and that "you are to be king over Syria" (2 Kg. 8:13). Hazael made the prophecy come true by murdering Ben-hadad and usurping the throne.

The second revolution took place after Hazael had begun his attacks on the northern kingdom. After a battle in which King Jehoram was wounded and had to withdraw, Elisha sent one of the sons of the prophets secretly to **Jehu**, an Israelite commander, to pour a flask of oil over his head with the words, "Thus says the Lord, I anoint you king over Israel" (2 Kg. 9:3). When this act by Elisha's delegate became known, the other generals unanimously acclaimed Jehu as king. In short order, Jehoram was assassinated, his mother Jezebel was thrown from a high window and her body eaten by dogs, and 70 other sons or grandsons of Ahab were killed.

Elisha evidently lived to a great age, perhaps 80 or 90 years, and his mission extended until about the beginning of the eighth century. Even on his deathbed his powers are said to have been in full force. Coming to visit the stricken prophet, King **Joash** of Israel cried out to him, "My father, my father! The chariots of Israel and its

The birth of John the Baptist to the aged Elizabeth, by Jean Fouquet, c. 1455

horsemen!" (2 Kg. 13:14), repeating the words Elisha himself had spoken when his mentor Elijah had been taken up to heaven. But Elisha did not escape the fate of mortality as his predecessor had, though even death could not limit the power of his words or the holiness of his person. As he lay near death, Elisha told the king of the future course of his conflict with Syria.

Elisha's last reported miracle was perhaps the most astounding of all, since it was performed after he was dead and as a funeral procession passing near his grave was attacked by Moabite marauders. In panic the mourners cast the corpse they were carrying into a nearby grave, which happened to be Elisha's. When the corpse touched the bones of Elisha, it was as if life surged forth from the prophet. The man revived, it is recorded, and stood up. The prophet was a giver of life to the end.

ELIZABETH
GREEK: ELISABET; HEBREW: ELISHEBA
"God is [my] oath" or "Sheba is my god"

Elizabeth was the wife of the priest **Zechariah** and the mother of **John the Baptist**. Both she and her husband were descendants of **Aaron** and therefore members of a priestly family. The couple, "advanced in years" (Lk. 1:7), had no children, much to their sorrow. But one day while Zechariah was burning incense in the temple, an angel appeared to announce that a son who would "be great before the Lord" (Lk. 1:15) would be born to Elizabeth. After Elizabeth conceived, "for five months she hid herself" (Lk. 1:24).

In the sixth month of Elizabeth's pregnancy, her kinswoman **Mary** heard from the angel **Gabriel** that she, too, would bear a child, and the young virgin set out to visit the older woman. At the sight of Mary, Elizabeth cried out, "Blessed are you among women, and blessed is the fruit of your womb!" (Lk. 1:42). As she heard Mary's words of greeting, the infant in her womb leaped for joy—perhaps the first stirring that confirmed life. When her son was born, Elizabeth's relatives and neighbors joined her in rejoicing but could not understand why she insisted that the baby be named John, saying, "None of your kindred is called by this name" (Lk. 1:61). After the temporarily dumb Zechariah endorsed the choice in writing, Elizabeth had her way. There is no further mention of Elizabeth or Zechariah in the New Testament; the cryptic note that their child "was in the wilderness till the day of his manifestation to Israel" (Lk. 1:80) suggests to some that John was given over for raising to an austere religious sect, perhaps the Essenes.

ENOCH

(e' nok) HEBREW: HANOK
"initiated," "follower," or "dedicated one"

Enoch was a member of "the generations of Adam" (Gen. 5:1), the incredibly long-lived group that extended from **Adam** to **Noah**. At age 65 Enoch became the father of **Methuselah**, and later he had other sons and daughters. He "walked with God" (Gen. 5:22)—that is, he was in close spiritual communion with the Lord. After 365 years of this holy life (a relatively short span for these men), Enoch was taken by God. The anonymous author of Hebrews explains: "Enoch was taken up so that he should not see death" (Heb. 11:5) because his faith was pleasing to God.

Enoch's supernatural disappearance led to the belief that he became privy to the divine secrets. These heavenly secrets were purportedly revealed in the noncanonical books of Enoch, probably compiled during the second and first centuries before **Jesus**. Familiar to both Jews and Christians, the writings predicted, among other things, the end of the world, the last judgment, the resurrection of the just, and the establishment of the messianic kingdom.

Elizabeth saluting Mary; detail of a late-15th- or early-16th-century painting

EPAPHRAS

(ep' uh fras) GREEK: EPAPHRAS (contraction of Epaphroditus)
"charming" or "handsome"

A native of the town of Colossae in Asia Minor, Epaphras had been commissioned by **Paul** to preach to the citizens there. Epaphras also "worked hard for . . . those in Laodicea and Hieropolis" (Col. 4:13) and later (c. A.D. 61–63) was imprisoned with Paul in Rome, where he had gone to report to the apostle on a crisis in the church Paul had founded in his hometown. Paul's letter to the Colossians in response to the news of dissension praised Epaphras highly as his "beloved fellow servant," "a faithful minister of Christ," and "a servant [slave] of Christ Jesus" (Col. 1:7; 4:12). The designation "servant," which Paul several times applied to himself, was used for only two others: **Timothy** and **Tychicus**.

EPAPHRODITUS

(e paf ro di' tuhs) GREEK: EPAPHRODITOS
"charming" or "handsome"

A member of the church at Philippi in Macedonia (the first established by **Paul** in Europe), Epaphroditus was charged with carrying gifts from the congregation to the imprisoned apostle in Rome. In acknowledgment, Paul wrote gratefully to the Philippians of Epaphroditus, "my brother and fellow worker and fellow soldier" (Phil. 2:25). Epaphroditus became seriously ill in Rome; indeed, according to Paul, he had been near death, having risked his life to complete his service. To reassure the anxious Philippians about the health of the beloved Epaphroditus, Paul sent him back with the letter, requesting them to "receive him in the Lord with all joy" (Phil. 2:29).

EPHRAIM

(ee' free uhm) HEBREW: EPHRAYIM
"fruitful"

Born in Egypt to **Joseph** and Asenath, the daughter of an Egyptian priest, Ephraim was later adopted by **Jacob**, along with his brother **Manasseh**, and became the ancestor of one of the 12 tribes of Israel. Ephraim's name refers to his birth during the seven years of plenty that his father had foreseen before the seven years of famine.

After Genesis, on most of the occasions when the Bible mentions Ephraim, the name refers not to Joseph's son but to the tribe of Ephraim—one of the most powerful among the 12—or to the territory where the tribe dwelt, the densely forested hill country that lay to the east of the site of modern Tel Aviv. "You are a numerous people and have great power," Joshua said to the descendants of Joseph; ". . . the hill country shall be yours, for though it is a forest, you shall clear it and possess it" (Jos. 17:17-18). One Ephraimite tribal leader was **Joshua**, whose exploits, some commentators maintain, were transferred in the telling from being events in the history of his own tribe to being events describing the history of the entire Israelite nation.

It was in the territory of Ephraim, at Shiloh, that one of the central shrines of the Israelite tribes came to be located. That shrine had an enormous impact on biblical history because from there **Samuel** ruled the Israelites. Loyal to Israel's first king, **Saul**, the Ephraimites never reconciled themselves to the Judahite **David** as his successor; three generations later, it was an Ephraimite, **Jeroboam**, who led the secession of the ten tribes to establish the separate kingdom of Israel in the north. Eventually, the prophets came to use the name Ephraim to stand for

Enoch, like Elijah, was spared death and taken up to heaven.

the northern kingdom, which continued to be dominated by the Ephraimites.

Centuries later, after they had conquered the region around Bethel and sent most of the Israelites into exile, the Assyrians promoted the use of the shrine at Bethel. This helped discourage the few remaining Israelites from using the temple at Jerusalem, which lay outside Assyrian control.

EPHRON

(e' fron) HEBREW: EPRON
"gazelle"

Because **Abraham** was a seminomadic chieftain, not a landowner, he had no family tomb in which to bury his wife **Sarah**, when she died at Hebron at the age of 127. He therefore asked "the Hittites, the people of the land" (Gen. 23:7) of Canaan, for a burying place, and with Eastern courtesy they offered him the choicest of their sepulchers. Equally courteous, Abraham asked to buy the cave of Machpelah, which belonged to Ephron, son of Zoar. But Ephron offered the cave as a gift: "My lord, hear me; I give you the field, and I give you the cave that is in it; in the presence of the sons of my people I give it to you" (Gen. 23:11). But Abraham refused the gift and instead paid Ephron 400 shekels for the property "in the presence of the Hittites" (Gen. 23:18); the public nature of the transaction gave Abraham legal title to Ephron's land. Abraham himself, **Isaac**, **Rebekah**, **Jacob**, and **Leah** were all buried in Ephron's cave; only **Rachel** of the first three patriarchal generations was interred elsewhere.

ESARHADDON

(es ahr had' duhn) HEBREW: ESARHADDON
"Ashur has given a brother"

Succeeding to the throne of Assyria in 681 B.C. after his father **Sennacherib** had been assassinated by two other sons, Esarhaddon had to fight for his inheritance, although his brothers had earlier taken an oath to support his succession. Victorious over his brothers, Esarhaddon marched his army southward to conquer Egypt, which had frequently supported uprisings by Assyria's vassals. One vassal, King **Manasseh** of Judah, was shrewd enough not to rebel. Although he regularly sent tribute to Esarhaddon, Manasseh suffered the humiliation of being taken captive to Babylon to profess his loyalty to his Assyrian overlord. Esarhaddon boasted that in Egypt he fought bloody battles daily, wounding Egypt's ruler

five times and then carrying him and his family away as captives to Assyria. But the conquest of Egypt was only temporary. After a rebellion there, Esarhaddon had to march off to Egypt again. This time, however, he died en route in the 12th year of his reign.

Following Assyrian custom, Esarhaddon removed conquered people from their homelands and settled them in other territories. Among the people so treated were the ancestors of the Samaritans. They were moved into the land once occupied by the ten northern tribes of Israel, the so-called ten lost tribes, who had themselves been resettled in Assyria after their own kingdom was destroyed by **Sargon II**.

HOSTILE NEIGHBORS

The Hebrews lived at a crossroads of commerce and conflict. From the time of Moses until the first century A.D., their nation was surrounded by potential enemies, many of whom were believed to be descendants of Israel's own patriarchs.

The Midianites of the Sinai Peninsula, who provided Moses with his wife, Zipporah, but became mortal enemies of the Israelites, were descendants of Midian, the son of Abraham by Keturah. The Amalekites in the same region, who attacked Israel when they left Egypt, were descendants of Amalek, the great-grandson of Isaac through Esau, Jacob's twin and rival. Just south of the Dead Sea were the Edomites, also direct descendants of Esau; their long and bitter conflicts with Israel were expressed in rejoicing over Babylon's destruction of Jerusalem. In the first century B.C. their descendants in Idumea gave Israel the ruthless King Herod the Great. The Moabites and Ammonites, who dominated the area east of the Dead Sea and the Jordan River, were disdained by Israel as descendants of Abraham's nephew Lot by incest with his daughters. Both nations worked to subdue Israel during the period of the judges but were reduced to vassal status within David's empire.

ESAU

(ee' saw) HEBREW: ESAW
"hairy"

Isaac and **Rebekah**'s firstborn son, Esau was given his name because his body was covered with hair when he was born. A moment later his twin, **Jacob**, emerged, holding onto his heel. Even in their mother's womb, the two had struggled, and their struggle continued in life.

Esau became a hunter; Jacob, a herdsman. Returning one day from a hunt, Esau encountered his brother cooking lentil soup, and asked for some. He was told he could have it only if he swore to sell his birthright to Jacob, handing over whatever might accrue to him as Isaac's firstborn. Famished and exhausted, Esau agreed to the sale with the words, "I am about to die; of what use is a birthright to me?" (Gen. 25:32). The effects of his oath became apparent only later.

Aged, dying, and nearly blind, Isaac asked Esau, the hunter, to bring him some meat to eat; then he would give Esau his blessing. Rebekah, who favored Jacob over Esau, heard this and arranged for Jacob to receive the blessing instead. Dressed in fleece to appear hairy like Esau, Jacob brought a dinner of meat to his father. The trick worked: Jacob received the blessing meant for his brother; and once the blessing was given, it could not be recalled. The incident echoed practices in Rebekah's native Mesopotamia, where inheritances sometimes bypassed the firstborn son, and fulfilled the prophecy made to her during her troubled pregnancy: "The elder shall serve the younger" (Gen. 25:23). Years later, when Jacob became rich and returned home with his wife, children, and flocks, he feared Esau's revenge and sent gifts to assuage him. But Esau had no need of Jacob's wealth and he forgave him.

Esau's descendants, listed in Genesis 36, were the Edomites, who lived just south of Canaan. The prophets used Esau's name to symbolize Edom. "How Esau has been pillaged!" **Obadiah** exclaims; "There shall be no survivor to the house of Esau" (Ob. 6, 18). **Malachi** describes how Esau's heritage has been left "to jackals of the desert" (Mal. 1:3). Esau's name appears in the New Testament too. **Paul** cites Esau in Romans 9 as an example of those not elected by God, and the anonymous author of Hebrews enjoins his readers not to be "immoral or irreligious like Esau, who sold his birthright for a single meal" (Heb. 12:16).

ESTHER

(es' tuhr) HEBREW: ESTER
"star"

The Jewish wife of King **Ahasuerus** of Persia (known to history as Xerxes I, 485–464 B.C.), Esther is the heroine of the biblical book bearing her name, a work that is considered one of the masterpieces of storytelling in ancient world literature.

Esther's Jewish name was Hadassah, the Hebrew word for myrtle. Born in Susa, the former capital of Elam, which had been absorbed by Persia, she was orphaned at an early age and brought up by an older

Esau (left) greets his returning brother, Jacob, in friendship; a painting by Peter Paul Rubens (1577-1640).

Esther, by Andrea Castagno (1421-1457)

---

cousin named **Mordecai**. His family had been taken captive from Judah years earlier, after the fall of Jerusalem to **Nebuchadnezzar** in 586 B.C.

After his wife **Vashti** embarrassed him by refusing to make a command appearance at a royal banquet, Ahasuerus ordered a search for a new queen to replace her. Esther, a maiden "beautiful and lovely" (Est. 2:7), was among the many young women brought into the harem and put in the custody of the king's eunuch Hegai. But Mordecai continued to keep an eye on his ward—then known by her Persian name, Esther, from the word for star—and charged her not to give away her Jewish identity. For a year Esther was trained in the arts of the harem, and when she finally made her first appearance before the king, he "loved Esther more than all the women, and she found grace and favor in his sight more than all the virgins" (Est. 2:17). Ahasuerus promptly named Esther his queen.

One day as Mordecai was lingering near the palace, he overheard two guards discussing a plot to kill the king. Quickly, he passed the word to Esther, who told the king, and the two guards were hanged. Soon thereafter the king named **Haman** the Agagite as his grand vizier. When Mordecai alone among the spectators at the palace gate refused to bow in obeisance as Haman rode by, the furious grand vizier plotted the destruction not just of Mordecai but of the entire Jewish population of the kingdom. To obtain an auspicious date for the pogrom to begin, he cast lots and came up with the 13th day of the 12th month, Adar.

When the terrible decree was published, Mordecai appealed to Esther to intervene with the king. She took the risk of appearing unsummoned before the king, but was warmly received and told that any request she made would be granted. She first asked the king to invite Haman to a banquet she was giving that evening. Haman accepted, enjoyed himself, and was invited to another banquet the following evening. His elation at this newfound favor with the queen was ruined when he again met an unrepentant Mordecai at the palace gate.

Ignoring his previous announcement of the date for killing the Jews, Haman decided to go after Mordecai at once. He ordered a huge gallows built, and went to the palace to obtain permission to hang Mordecai on it. Coincidentally, however, the king was having trouble sleeping and had asked that the royal journal be read to him. Fortuitously, he learned how Mordecai had earlier saved his life and realized that he had never been rewarded. When Haman appeared, the king asked his advice: "What should be done to the man whom the king delights to honor?" (Est. 6:6). Smugly assuming that the king meant him, Haman suggested a royal procession in his honor. The king then ordered Haman to "do so to Mordecai the Jew who sits at the king's gate" (Est. 6:10).

A REVERSAL OF FORTUNE

That evening after the second dinner with Haman, Esther revealed her Jewish identity, then told of the plot to kill her people, climactically pointing out Haman as the person behind the murderous scheme. Enraged, the king stalked from the room to consider an appropriate fate for Haman. Throwing himself at the queen's feet, the terrified grand vizier made a pathetic appeal to Esther for his life. The king returned to the room, thought Haman was attacking the queen, and ordered him taken out and hanged immediately—on the very gallows he had built for Mordecai. The king rewarded Esther with all of Haman's estate, bestowed Haman's signet ring on Mordecai, meaning that he was to replace Haman as grand vizier, and revoked Haman's edicts against the Jews.

On the day chosen by Haman for their deaths, the Jews of Persia took their revenge, slaying their enemies in Susa and throughout the land. The next day, the 14th, became a day of festivities, one still celebrated as Purim, in ironic reference to the twist of fate dealt the Jews by Haman's casting of lots (*pur* in Akkadian).

The story of Esther is one of the most widely known in the Bible, partly because it has been read around the world wherever Jews celebrate Purim. Another reason is its narrative style; scholars long have noted the many captivating techniques used throughout: exotic setting, fast-paced action, humor, intrigue, suspense, sudden reversals, delicious ironies, and a happy ending.

A LEGEND RETOLD?

It is, in fact, precisely its style that leads some scholars to count it as a work of fiction. The very use of the names Esther and Mordecai, goes this argument, links the story with the Babylonian deities Ishtar and Marduk (also cousins) and may well hint at a Persian legend, which Jews living in captivity began to retell with a different purpose. Others, however, see a basis in history for the story because of its detailed knowledge of customs and practices and its careful attention to names for even marginal figures. They also cite the archeological evidence for a Persian official named Marduka who lived about the time of Esther. A further argument for authenticity is that the book contains the conventional opening of an historical account and an ending with the typical reference to sources, as is found in other Old Testament historical books.

In reply, critics say that no evidence has been found for a queen for Xerxes named either Vashti or Esther. They also argue that many of the narrative forces are more typical of the folk literature of the time than surviving historical records. As evidence, they cite Esther's delay in presenting her request to the king; the precise reversal of the fortunes of Haman and Mordecai; the graphic violence as the people take their revenge—each a device used by a good storyteller to make his message more memorable.

Whatever the type of literature, the author was probably someone with a fair knowledge of Persian customs, most likely someone who lived before the overthrow of Persia by **Alexander the Great** in 331 B.C. The Talmud ascribes authorship of the book of Esther to returnees from Babylonian captivity who reestablished worship in Jerusalem and began rebuilding the temple in the time of **Ezra** and **Nehemiah**.

Another, even more wide-ranging debate has occurred over the religious purpose of the story. In fact, the book of Esther was one of the last to be accepted in both the Hebrew and Christian canons of Scripture. One reason: It and the Song of Solomon are the only books in the Bible where the name of God is not used and where specific religious activities are not at the center. Possibly as an attempt to meet these objections, a longer version of the book of Esther appeared ear-

A medieval French gilt bronze garment clasp, said to represent Esther and Ahasuerus

ly on, with six additional passages containing 107 verses not found in the Hebrew text of Esther. The additional material includes frequent mentions of God and prayer, his covenant with Israel, and denunciations of Gentiles; a dream by Mordecai foretelling his discovery of the plot against the king and the deliverance of the Jews; and the "actual" words of the decrees of Ahasuerus. In some instances contradicting the older text, these so-called Additions to Esther were never in the Hebrew Bible and today are collected in the Old Testament Apocrypha.

Ahasuerus chooses Esther as queen; detail of a painting by Filippino Lippi (c. 1457-1504).

EUTYCHUS

(yoo' tuh kuhs) GREEK: EUTYCHOS
"fortunate"

A young man of Troas in Asia Minor, Eutychus was present at a meeting conducted by **Paul**, who was on his third missionary journey. Falling asleep during the apostle's lengthy discourse, Eutychus fell from a third-story window "and was taken up dead" (Acts 20:9). But Paul, descending to where the youth lay, embraced Eutychus and was able to revive him. The group then broke bread in the Lord's supper and "took the lad away alive, and were not a little comforted" (Acts 20:12).

Some argue that Eutychus had not died from the fall but was merely knocked unconscious; others claim that **Luke**—writing in the first person at this point—was apparently an eyewitness and, as a physician, would have recognized the state of death.

Eve, by Lucas Cranach (1472-1553)

Paul's action in restoring life to Eutychus by his embrace echoes the acts of the prophets **Elijah** in 1 Kings 17:17-24 and **Elisha** in 2 Kings 4:32-37.

EVE

(eev) HEBREW: HAWWA
"life" or "life-giving"

As the first woman and wife of **Adam**, Eve plays a leading role in the drama of the early chapters of Genesis. The name Eve is actually the third designation given to the first woman. In Genesis 1 and 5, God creates male and female together and in the latter chapter calls them by the single Hebrew word *adam*, meaning human being: "Male and female he created them, and he blessed them and named them Man [*adam*]" (Gen. 5:2). In Genesis 2:23, however, the female receives a separate designation: "She shall be called Woman [*ishshah*], because she was taken out of Man [*ish*]." Her third name, Eve, is given by her husband as the couple is about to leave the garden of Eden and is a play on the Hebrew verb *hayya*, meaning to live. The woman will bear her husband's children and thus be "the mother of all living" (Gen. 3:20). In the same context, the word *adam* begins to be used as the proper name for the first man.

The well-known story of the separate creation of woman comes from Genesis 2. God had made a single human being from dust and had given the human a garden in which to live. But the creature was lonely. God, therefore, created the animals but could not find among them a helper fit for the human. (The Hebrew word translated here as helper also means partner or ally. It implies no subordination and is most often used in the Bible to refer to God as Israel's ally.) No animal could fit the role; the true partner must come from within. Therefore, God took a small inner part of his creature—a rib—and miraculously expanded it into a whole person. When God brought the two together, they were perfectly matched. "This at last is bone of my bones, and flesh of my flesh" (Gen. 2:23), the man said. God had made the single human into man and woman.

Living in the garden, the two were innocent of the knowledge of good and evil, for God had lodged that knowledge within a tree in the center of the garden, warning them not to eat the fruit, "for in the day that you eat of it you shall die" (Gen. 2:17). One day the woman met a serpent, described as the cleverest of God's creatures, and they struck up a conversation about the forbidden fruit. The serpent told her that the fruit would not kill her but rather offered special wisdom. "Your eyes will be opened, and you will be like God, knowing good and evil" (Gen. 3:5), the tempter promised.

As the woman weighed the dangers of the fruit against its supposed benefits, she crossed a divide to make the first moral choice—a wrong one. She ate the fruit and shared it with her husband. Their eyes were indeed opened but not to see that they were gods. Rather they saw that they were weak, naked, and afraid. God rebuked them; but, instead of imposing the immediate death he had threatened, he forced the pair out of the garden and punished the woman with the pain of childbirth and made her subject to her husband.

The story of Eve is nowhere else mentioned in the Old Testament, partly because the doctrine of the fall of man had not yet been developed when the Hebrew Bible was written down. From the second century B.C. onward, however, reflections on the origin of evil led to teachings that blamed either Eve or Adam or both for the appearance of sin and death in the world. In later Christian theology, Eve was called the devil's gateway and was often seen as the negative counterpart to **Mary**, the mother of **Jesus**.

EVIL-MERODACH

(ee' vil mare oh´ dahk) HEBREW: EWIL MERODAK; BABYLONIAN: AMEL-MARDUK
"man of Marduk [chief god of Babylon]"

The son and successor to **Nebuchadnezzar** as king of Babylon, Evil-merodach released his father's captive King **Jehoiachin** of Judah from prison in the 37th year of his custody. This mark of favor probably celebrated Evil-merodach's accession to the throne in 562 B.C. He continued his kindness to Jehoiachin, giving him a place above that reserved for other captive kings and allowing him to dine "regularly at the king's table" (2 Kg. 25:29). In the third year of his reign, Evil-merodach became the victim of a conspiracy led by his brother-in-law Neriglissar, possibly the Nergal-sharezer of Jeremiah 39:3 and 13.

EZEKIEL

(e zee' kyel) HEBREW: YEHEZQEL
"God strengthens" or "may God strengthen"

The priest Ezekiel was among the 8,000 exiles taken to Babylon after the siege of Jerusalem in 598-597 B.C. In the fifth year of exile he was called to be a prophet through a dazzling vision. Appearing with

Borne by strange creatures, God appears to Ezekiel in this painting by Raphael (1483-1520).

the brightness of a rainbow and seated in a wheeled chariot borne by four grotesque creatures, God told Ezekiel to speak his "words of lamentation and mourning and woe" (Ezek. 2:10) to the rebellious Israelites. The message he was to deliver was handed to him on a scroll. "Eat this scroll that I give you and fill your stomach with it," the Lord commanded; to the prophet's relief, it was "as sweet as honey" (Ezek. 3:3).

During the 22 or more years he prophesied, Ezekiel was to do many other bizarre things. They are vividly described in the book that bears his name, a work rich with the imagery of a fertile mind. And yet these acts do not in themselves give us a glimpse into Ezekiel's personality because they were symbolic, performed at times as street drama to convey his prophetic message. What may shed more light on Ezekiel as a person are his extraordinary visions and how he interpreted them. Beneath the surface of these amazing accounts lie his own sober and sincere efforts to guide Israel, with both criticism and hope, past its devastating defeat by the Babylonians and toward a new and more glorious future.

Immediately after his call, the Spirit lifted up Ezekiel and deposited him among a

The prophet Ezekiel, a 15th-century German stained-glass roundel

group of exiles living near the river Chebar, actually an irrigation canal along the lower Euphrates River. He was so shaken by these events that he "sat there overwhelmed among them seven days" (Ezek. 3:15). The Spirit next told Ezekiel to become a recluse in his own house, warning him that he would be unable to speak other than to deliver an occasional prophecy. And, in fact, he did not regain his speech until seven and a half years later, when news arrived that Jerusalem and the temple had been totally destroyed.

During his period of withdrawal, Ezekiel was told to lie on his left side 390 days and on his right side 40 days while contemplating a brick replica of the siege of Jerusalem—the 390 days in token of the punishment of Israel; the 40 in token of the punishment of Judah. His diet was to be barley cakes baked on human dung (amended, after Ezekiel's protest, to cow dung). He was to cut his hair and beard with a sword and burn the clippings, scatter them about, or weave them into his robe. Understandably, Ezekiel's neighbors gossiped mercilessly about him, at times relegating him to the status of an entertainer, "like one who sings love songs with a beautiful voice and plays well on an instrument" (Ezek. 33:32). People around the prophet were also confused about the message he wanted to give them. When Ezekiel's wife died, God told him to go about his daily chores as if nothing had happened, with no signs of mourning. His puzzled neighbors asked, "Will you not tell us what these things mean for us, that you are acting thus?" (Ezek. 24:19). For Ezekiel himself it was simple: He was "a watchman for the house of Israel" (Ezek. 33:7).

Whatever the confusion about Ezekiel's actions and pronouncements, the fulfillment of his prediction of the fall of Jerusalem in 586 B.C. finally convinced the people that he ought to be taken seriously as a prophet. But after the temple was destroyed, his message shifted radically from the earlier doom and gloom to one of promise that the exiles would return to the land and rebuild the temple. The people, therefore, must seek to do justice according to the covenant God had made with them. In fact, his optimism about the future appears unbounded. In the last chapters of his book, Ezekiel describes a temple to be rebuilt that far exceeds anything that ever would exist in the future of Jerusalem. For example, a freshwater stream would flow from under the temple in such abundance that fruit trees would blossom in the barren wilderness of Judah and the brine of the Dead Sea would be made sweet.

In all parts of his prophetic discourse, outside of the temple vision in the last chapters, Ezekiel employs such recurrent phrases as "I, the Lord, have spoken" (Ezek. 5:13) or "you shall know that I am the Lord" (Ezek. 6:7) to express the need to recognize God's presence in the world. Both the judgments and the promises that Ezekiel delivers emphasize God's freedom to act and to be known and worshiped by the exiled Judeans, as well as by other nations. More than did the earlier prophets, Ezekiel insisted on the responsibility of each individual to obey God's commands. He chided against the common rationalization that the present generation suffered merely because of an earlier generation's disobedience, and confidently argued that individual acts of justice in the present could undo the punishment brought on by past injustices.

A MESSAGE OF HOPE

The content of Ezekiel's message has created special problems for close readers of the Bible. Not only is his description of God among other heavenly beings in the first chapter shocking, it seems to contradict the biblical statement that "there has not arisen a prophet since in Israel like **Moses**, whom the Lord knew face to face" (Dt. 34:10). Even more troubling is what Ezekiel is inspired to say about the Law: "I gave them statutes that were not good and ordinances by which they could not have life" (Ezek. 20:25). Ezekiel's own transmission of "the law of the temple" (Ezek. 43:12) differs in many details from the Law of Moses. Some later rabbis sought to explain this discrepancy by arguing that the laws in Ezekiel were pertinent only to a messianic age yet to come; others warned that children should not try to read the book of Ezekiel and considered it unsuitable for public reading during worship in the synagogues.

According to one ancient Jewish tradition, Ezekiel should not be placed in his proper chronological order, after the other two Major Prophets, **Isaiah** and **Jeremiah**. The arrangement of the three books should rather be: Jeremiah, who represents doom; Ezekiel, who begins with doom and ends with consolation; and Isaiah, who is all consolation. Certainly, Ezekiel is a transitional figure, one who marks the divide between Israel's religion before and after the exile. And he speaks not only to the Jews in their time of exile and despair, but also to them in their time of restoration.

Perhaps the most graphic instance of Ezekiel's message of hope occurs in his prophecy to a valley of dry bones. "Can these bones live?" God asked, likening the exiles to the grim remains of a battlefield; and Ezekiel answered wisely, "O Lord God, thou knowest." And as Ezekiel prophesied to the skeletal congregation, "there was a noise, and behold, a rattling; and the bones came together, bone to its bone." And after sinew, flesh, and skin covered the bones, God called breath from the four winds so "they lived, and stood upon their feet, an exceedingly great host" (Ezek. 37:3, 7, 10). In these words of a glorious future for a persecuted people, early Christians were later to find the seeds of their faith in the resurrection of the body and in life after death in a city not made with human hands.

EZRA

(ez' rah) HEBREW: EZRA
possibly "[Yahweh] helps"

A descendant of Israel's first high priest, **Aaron**, Ezra was "a scribe skilled in the law of Moses" (Ezra 7:6) who lived in exile in Babylon. He was among those Jews who returned to their homeland following the proclamation of King **Cyrus** of Persia in 538 B.C., probably in advance of **Nehemiah**.

Ezra's achievements are recorded in two books of the Bible, Ezra and Nehemiah, which originally comprised a single work written sometime around 400 B.C.; later editors of the Bible divided it and altered the historical chronology. Jewish tradition maintains that it was Ezra himself who composed the book bearing his name and some modern scholars agree. Others suggest a single author—often referred to as the Chronicler—for 1 and 2 Chronicles as well as for Ezra and Nehemiah. If the author was not Ezra himself, it is likely that the writer was at least a contemporary of his.

Together, the books of Ezra and Nehemiah describe the return of the exiled Jews to the devastated capital of Jerusalem where—in the face of opposition from the Samaritans whom the Assyrians had settled north of the city and from others who were eager to keep the Jews from regaining power—they started rebuilding the temple. Despite interference, the reconstruction was completed by the year 515 B.C.

Actually, there were several returns encompassing several generations. The first was led by the royal prince **Sheshbazzar**; a

Dry bones are restored their flesh and bodies their breath;
Ezekiel's vision is the subject of this third-century A.D. synagogue
fresco from Dura Europas, Syria.

second, by his nephew **Zerubbabel**, who is credited with the temple's reconstruction. Ezra's return was one of the later ones. Armed with a commission from King **Artaxerxes** of Persia, Ezra was specifically charged with the task of overseeing the religious conduct of all Israelites both in Jerusalem and throughout the western province of the Persian empire. Because there were two kings named Artaxerxes, the first ruling from c. 465 to 425, and the second, his grandson, ruling from c. 404 to 358, fixing a date for Ezra's return is problematic.

The best scholarly estimate, however, is that Ezra arrived in Jerusalem sometime around 458 B.C. and that Nehemiah reached the city some years later. Whatever the date, Ezra was given permission to receive contributions from Babylonian Jews to support the rebuilt temple and to draw on royal funds as well.

Gathering a party of Jews from the surroundings of Babylon and preparing them for their journey with fasting and prayer, Ezra left in April and traveled west during the hot summer months. Although he was traveling during a time of instability in the Persian empire and feared attacks on his caravan, he refused to take along a military escort. Employing an escort, he felt, might give the impression that he did not trust God alone to help him. The journey took four months. But once Ezra had arrived in Jerusalem, the former exile set to work carrying out his mission.

After handing over the treasure he had brought for the rebuilt temple, Ezra made burnt sacrifices to the Lord there and delivered the Persian king's commission to the local governors. But he soon received disturbing news: Forsaking the ethnic purity that had sustained them during their exile, returning Jews had taken pagan wives, "so that the holy race has mixed itself with the peoples of the land" (Ezra 9:2). Tearing his garments and pulling hair from his head and beard, Ezra slumped to the ground in shock and rose only toward evening to confess the sins of the people. As a heavy winter rain fell, the assembled Israelites vowed to put aside their foreign wives, asking only for time to do so since this was not "a work for one day or for two" (Ezra 10:13). A few among the assembly refused to go along with this reform, but the book of Ezra ends with a lengthy list of those Israelites, among them priests and Levites, who agreed to divorce their idolatrous wives and made guilt

Ezra reads the Law to the returning exiles; a translator is to his left.

offerings for their transgressions in marrying them.

Ezra's story is continued in Nehemiah 8 and 9. The scribe had brought along with him from exile a scroll of the Law. On the first day of the seventh month, Tishri (September/October)—a traditional Israelite day of convocation that Jews still celebrate as Rosh Hashanah, the New Year—Ezra was summoned to read the Mosaic Law before the Israelites who had left their hometowns and, as was traditional, had gathered in Jerusalem to celebrate the holiday. Standing on a wooden pulpit above the crowd assembled in a public square before the city's water gate, Ezra held up the scroll and read from it from early in the morning until noon; "and the ears of all the people were attentive to the book of the law" (Neh. 8:3).

Ezra was reading in Hebrew. By then most of the people were using Aramaic in their daily speech and Ezra's words had to be translated so that all could understand him. His audience was so moved that they wept on hearing what Ezra read; but Ezra and those assisting him urged them to stop mourning: "This day is holy to the Lord your God; do not mourn or weep" (Neh. 8:9). And so, rejoicing in what they heard, the people celebrated with food and drink.

ESTABLISHING THE JEWISH RELIGION

On the following day, the heads of households, the priests, and the Levites joined Ezra for a closer study of the Law. From it, the Jews learned that they were commanded to celebrate the Feast of Booths shortly after the New Year. The custom of bringing branches of olive, myrtle, palm, and other leafy trees from the countryside to fashion into booths in which they could temporarily dwell had fallen into disuse from the time when the Israelites had first entered the Promised Land. Now it was revived; and every day for the seven days that the holiday lasted, Ezra continued to read from his scroll. On the eighth day, he finished his reading and there was, as the Law commanded, a solemn assembly. (On the eighth day after Rosh Hashanah, contemporary Jews still celebrate the completion of the annual reading of the Law.) Two weeks later, at another assembly in Jerusalem, Israelites dressed in sackcloth and standing with dirt on their heads as a sign of mourning "stood and confessed their sins" (Neh. 9:2).

Ezra's ceremonies were, in effect, the establishment of the Jewish religion as it was to be until the destruction of the temple in A.D. 70. After he completed his work, Israel no longer meant merely a group of people united by a common residence or a common

Ezra, seated within the letter "E" of a medieval manuscript illumination

EZRA'S SCROLL

When Ezra stood before the returned exiles in Jerusalem to read the Law, he was revealing what many had long forgotten or never heard of: the now familiar words of the Bible. Some scholars believe that the scroll he brought with him from Babylon contained only the priestly code, various laws relating to the temple and its sacrifices found in Exodus, Leviticus, and Numbers, which had been preserved in the foreign city. Others maintain that Ezra's scroll included the entire Pentateuch, the first five books of the Bible, which Jews today call the Torah—or some variation of those books since they had not yet reached their final, canonical form.

According to Jewish legend, the scroll that Ezra carried back to Jerusalem was an ancient copy of the Torah, which had been written by the priest Eli and later buried under the threshold of the temple in Jerusalem. Placing manuscripts in building foundations was not an unusual custom in the ancient Near East. When the temple was destroyed in the capture of Jerusalem that ended the kingdom of Judah in 586 B.C., Eli's scroll—in this tale—was somehow rescued and taken to Babylon.

descent, or even a common devotion to Yahweh. Now it came to mean the Jews, a people marked primarily by adherence to the Torah, the first five books of the Bible. Exile in Babylon had gone a long way toward redefining Israel, for even without their temple ritual Israelites had the commandments of the Bible. But it was not until Ezra's time that the religion of Judaism was firmly linked to obedience to the Law.

One measure of Ezra's significance is the fact that so many ancient books were written about him. Most important, of course, are Ezra and Nehemiah, which were canonized when the final number of books in the Old Testament was fixed (with just a few exceptions) around 300 B.C. Among other books about Ezra are the first two books of the Apocrypha—1 Esdras and 2 Esdras. (Esdras is the Greek form of the Hebrew name Ezra.) 1 Esdras is, for the most part, a Greek translation of the biblical story of Ezra, though it contains some material that does not appear in the Bible. Scholars have suggested that both it and 2 Esdras (an apocalyptic book) may be based on an ancient Hebrew version of the book of Ezra-Nehemiah, which no longer exists. 1 Esdras was probably written around 150 B.C.; 2 Esdras, considerably later. Originally composed in Hebrew sometime after A.D. 70, it shows signs of containing a Christian anti-Jewish polemic added on to an older Hebrew text. Outside the biblical canon are such works as the Apocalypse of Ezra, the Questions of Ezra, the Revelation of Ezra, and the Vision of Ezra.

FELIX
(fee' liks) LATIN; GREEK: PHELIX
"happy"

A former royal slave, Antonius Felix was a favorite of Roman emperor **Claudius** and his successor Nero. Named procurator of Judea by Claudius in A.D. 52, Felix owed his post in part to his marriage to **Drusilla**, daughter of **Herod Agrippa I**, and to his alleged sympathy with the Jews. Nevertheless, according to ancient sources, Felix proved himself treacherous, cruel, and desperately ambitious and was responsible for the murder of the high priest Jonathan and the sending of a number of priests to Rome for trial on various charges.

In 58, **Paul** was in Jerusalem for the last time. Accused by Jews of profaning the temple, he was arrested and brought before the tribune Claudius Lysias for examination. Learning of a plot to kill Paul, a Roman citizen, the tribune promptly sent him under guard to Felix at Caesarea. Five days later, the high priest **Ananias** and other elders arrived to accuse Paul before Felix, describing him as "a pestilent fellow, an agitator among all the Jews throughout the world, and a ringleader of the sect of the Nazarenes" (Acts 24:5). Felix put off these accusers but ordered Paul to be kept in custody, though giving him some liberty and allowing him to receive visitors.

Subsequently, Felix, who already had "a rather accurate knowledge of the Way [the early Christian movement]," brought his wife Drusilla to hear Paul "speak upon faith in Christ Jesus" (Acts 24:22, 24). When Paul touched on future judgment, however, Felix grew alarmed and sent him away.

Although never charged with any crime, Paul remained in Felix's custody for two years, during which time the two often conversed. The procurator apparently hoped to be bribed to release his prisoner, but no money was offered. And, when Felix was recalled to Rome to answer for his misdemeanors as governor, he kept Paul in prison, "desiring to do the Jews a favor" (Acts 24:27). Felix himself barely escaped severe punishment in Rome, where his powerful brother Pallas had to intervene with Nero to spare his life.

FESTUS
(fes' tuhs) LATIN; GREEK: PHESTOS
"joyful"

A ppointed by Nero to succeed **Felix** as procurator of Judea, Porcius Festus was far superior to his predecessor. Although he served in his provincial post for only a short time (A.D. 60—62), Festus was effective in utterly destroying a group of Jewish bandits called *sicarii* (dagger-wielders) who had been terrorizing the land.

Another of his priorities was to visit Jerusalem, where the chief priests and Jewish leaders reminded him that **Paul** was still in prison in Caesarea by order of Felix. The Jews asked Festus to have Paul brought to Jerusalem for trial, "planning an ambush to kill him on the way" (Acts 25:3). Festus replied that he intended to return to Caesarea shortly and invited their representative to go with him.

Some ten days later, back in Caesarea, Paul was brought to him and the unfounded but serious charges of the Jews were made. Paul denied them: "Neither against the law of the Jews, nor against the temple, nor against Caesar have I offended at all" (Acts 25:8). When Festus asked if he wished to go to Jerusalem to be tried, Paul said, "I am standing before Caesar's tribunal, where I ought to be tried; . . . no one can give me up to them. I appeal to Caesar." Festus answered, "You have appealed to Caesar; to Caesar you shall go" (Acts 25:10-12).

When King **Herod Agrippa II** and his sister **Bernice** came to Caesarea to welcome the new procurator, Festus described Paul's case to them. The three decided to hear Paul's defense, which he concluded by saying, "Christ must suffer, and that, by being the first to rise from the dead, he would pro-

claim light both to the people and to the Gentiles." At this, Festus cried out, "Paul, you are mad; your great learning is turning you mad" (Acts 26:23-24). Agrippa, Bernice, and Festus all agreed on Paul's innocence; in their opinion, he had done nothing to deserve death or imprisonment. "This man could have been set free if he had not appealed to Caesar" (Acts 26:32), Festus concluded before unwillingly dispatching the apostle to Rome. Two years later, Festus died suddenly while still in office.

Standing in chains before Festus, Herod Agrippa II, and Bernice, the apostle Paul argues his case.

GABRIEL

(gay' bri uhl) HEBREW: GABRIEL
"strong man of God" or "God is my warrior"

The angel Gabriel is one of only two such celestial beings named in the Bible; the other is **Michael**. But two more angels, **Raphael** and **Uriel**, are mentioned in the Apocrypha. Gabriel appears in both the Old Testament book of Daniel and in the New Testament Gospel of Luke.

As **Daniel** is pondering his dream of the two-horned ram overpowered by the single-horned he-goat, there suddenly stands before him "one having the appearance of a man"; a voice calls, "Gabriel, make this man [Daniel] understand the vision" (Dan. 8:15-16). Fearful, Daniel falls into a trance, but the messenger of God rouses him and explains the revelation: The kings of Media and Persia will fall to **Alexander the Great**, whose empire will ultimately be divided among four successors—just as in the vision the he-goat's horn is broken and replaced with four horns.

Later, in response to the prayer of Daniel, Gabriel returns "in swift flight at the time of the evening sacrifice" (Dan. 9:21) to interpret **Jeremiah**'s prophecy of an end to Jerusalem's desolation in 70 years, saying that it would be 70 weeks of years, or 490 years, before the coming of the messianic kingdom. By implication, at least, the being "having the appearance of a man" (Dan. 10:18) who comes to interpret Daniel's vision of the last days is also Gabriel. Such an appearance by an angel to explain the vision of a seer is not uncommon in the Old Testament. However, it is unusual to give the heavenly messenger a name.

The angel Gabriel tells the virgin Mary that she is to conceive a son by the Holy Spirit; a painting by Federigo Barocci (1528-1612).

Twice in the Gospel of Luke, Gabriel comes to announce the birth of a son: first to the aged **Zechariah** burning incense in the temple at Jerusalem and then to the virgin **Mary** in Nazareth. In each instance the angel names the child to be born: **John [the Baptist]**, for the son of Zechariah and his wife, **Elizabeth**; **Jesus**, for the son of Mary. "I am Gabriel," the angel tells Zechariah, "who stand in the presence of God; and I was sent to speak to you, and to bring you this good news" (Lk. 1:19). Luke's story is also in keeping with traditional biblical appearances of angels. The births of both **Ishmael** and **Samson** are heralded by an angel, although in their stories the angel is not named.

In Genesis and other pre-exilic biblical writings, angels tend to represent the visible presence of God among humans and are not given names. In post-exilic Jewish literature, such as the book of Daniel, however, angels are perceived as personal beings and are given names. Jewish and Christian traditions, both biblical and nonbiblical, speak of seven angels, or archangels, who are the highest ranking of all and who stand in the very presence of God. In the pseudepigraphal books of 1 and 2 Enoch (ancient writings not included in any canon of the Bible), Gabriel is given such status, while other nonbiblical traditions name him as the angel who will blow the trumpet at the end of time to announce the final judgment.

GAD

HEBREW: GAD
"fortune"

When **Leah**, who thought she had ceased bearing children herself, heard that her maid **Zilpah** had given birth to a son of **Jacob**, she exclaimed, "Good fortune!" (Gen. 30:11) and gave the child his name, Gad. Virtually nothing is known of Jacob's sev-

Gad, his brother Asher, and four of their half brothers gather on Mount Ebal for Moses' curse. Jacob's six other sons appear in the companion piece to this 14th-century manuscript illumination shown on page 400.

enth son, though Gad's own seven sons are listed among those accompanying their grandfather to Egypt.

In Jacob's deathbed blessing of his sons, he says, "Raiders shall raid Gad, but he shall raid at their heels" (Gen. 49:19). This recognition of a powerful and warlike spirit, which was passed on to the tribe of Gad, is reiterated in the blessing of Moses: "Gad couches like a lion . . . . He chose the best of the land for himself" (Dt. 33:20-21)—actually a reference to the future tribal land east of the Jordan River.

GAD 2

The prophet and seer Gad first appears in the Bible to persuade the fugitive **David** to leave his place of safety in Moab and return to Judah, where an insanely jealous King **Saul** awaited him. Much later, Gad gave David a choice of punishments from the Lord for his rash act in carrying out a census. When the three-day plague that David had chosen as the least of the evils took 70,000 lives, Gad told David, "Go up, rear an altar to the Lord on the threshing floor of Araunah the Jebusite" (2 Sam. 24:18). The burnt offerings from this altar, the future site of **Solomon**'s temple, caused the Lord to halt the pestilence.

Gad is also cited in 2 Chronicles 29:25 as an authority, along with David and the prophet **Nathan**, for the placement of musicians in the temple. His lost writings were a source for the author of 1 and 2 Chronicles.

GALLIO

(gal' lee oh) GREEK: GALLION

Lucius Junius Gallio Annaeanus was named Roman proconsul of Achaia in Greece by the emperor **Claudius** in A.D. 51. Since **Paul** is known to have been in Corinth during Gallio's term of office, it is possible to date the apostle's sojourn there with **Aquila** and **Prisca** from about late A.D. 50 to the early summer of 52.

Arguing "in the synagogue every sabbath . . . . [and] testifying to the Jews that the Christ was Jesus" (Acts 18:4-5), Paul was eventually brought before the Roman tribunal by Jews who claimed he was breaking their Law. Gallio calmly rejected their suit, saying, "Since it is a matter of questions about words and names and your own law, see to it yourselves; I refuse to be a judge of these things" (Acts 18:15). Gallio likewise ignored the action of an angry crowd that followed up his disdainful ruling by beating **Sosthenes**, the synagogue ruler.

Gallio returned to a consulship in Rome but was subsequently implicated, along with his brother, the philosopher Seneca, in a conspiracy against the emperor Nero. He died, possibly having been ordered to commit suicide, in A.D. 65.

GAMALIEL

(guh may' lee yuhl) GREEK: GAMALIEL
"God is my recompense/reward"

Despite a warning from the religious authorities not to do so, the apostles **Peter** and **John** continued to preach in the temple at Jerusalem in the days following Pentecost. They were arrested and brought before the Sanhedrin, the ruling court or council of the Jews, to be questioned. Most of the council members were Sadducees, members of the priestly party, but among them was the Pharisee Gamaliel, a man renowned for his wisdom and tolerance. He was perhaps a grandson of the great rabbi Hillel, a figure still revered by Jews today.

Gamaliel rose in the council meeting to advise against prosecuting the disciples. Citing other recent prophetic movements among the Jews, he reminded his hearers that these had faded away. This new movement might very well disappear too, he said, and its followers also might be scattered. "But if it is of God," he added, "you will not be able to overthrow them" (Acts 5:39). Since Gamaliel was widely respected, his colleagues heeded his advice and released the apostles, but only after a beating had been administered to them.

Gamaliel's statement confirms the Pharisees' belief that, when there are divergent versions of the truth, both sides should be heard and recorded; neither side should be suppressed. Some of Gamaliel's legal opinions survive in the compendium of debates that makes up the Jewish Talmud. Like Hillel and like his own grandson, also named Gamaliel, he was a leader of the liberal wing of the Pharisees, rabbis who distanced themselves from the strictest interpretations of the Law. A number of Gamaliel's legal decisions are prefixed by the words "for the benefit of humanity." Several of these were designed to better the situation of women, among them one permitting a widow to remarry, even if only one witness appeared to testify that her husband was deceased, and another prohibiting husbands from annulling divorce proceedings without their wives' knowledge. Gamaliel also concerned himself with the Hebrew calendar, writing letters to notify Jews in distant lands when it was time to have a leap year; knowledge of the proper date was important to make sure that traditional holy days were celebrated at the proper time.

The only other mention of Gamaliel in the Bible is in **Paul**'s testimony that he had been a student of his, "educated according to the strict manner of the law of our fathers" (Acts 22:3). In contrast to his teacher, however, Paul (as Saul) did not at first grant tolerance to Christians.

GEDALIAH

(ged uh lai' uh) HEBREW: GEDALYAH or GEDALYAHU
"Yahweh is great"

After the army of **Nebuchadnezzar** had destroyed Jerusalem and carried off its inhabitants to exile in Babylon, a few towns in the kingdom of Judah survived unscathed and a few farmers were allowed to remain in the vicinity of the capital. With Judah defunct and almost depopulated, the Babylonians named Gedaliah governor over the meager population. He was a man they could trust to do their bidding.

Although Gedaliah was powerless to act independently, he was not merely a Babylonian puppet. A moderate and a friend of the prophet **Jeremiah**, who had warned Judah's rulers against resisting Nebuchadnezzar, and the son of a man who had been an important counselor of the pious King **Josiah**, Gedaliah had the trust of the people he ruled. When the Babylonians freed Jeremiah, telling him that he could either go into exile in Babylon or remain at

The rabbi Gamaliel appears to be admonishing a lazy student in this 11th-century manuscript illumination.

RABBIS

The **term rabbi** never appears in the Old Testament and in the New Testament it is used only for Jesus and John the Baptist—though the Pharisee Gamaliel can be called a rabbi. Derived from the Hebrew word *rab*, meaning "great," the appellation was used in the sense of "master." In Jesus' time it was a term of respect, somewhat like the word "sir," but considerably stronger, and inscriptions from that time show that it was often used simply for men of high social standing. The word came to be applied more and more, however, to the teachers of the Torah. After the destruction of the temple in A.D. 70 and the rise of so-called rabbinic schools in the second century, rabbi became a title for an ordained teacher. By the Middle Ages the term referred to the spiritual head of a Jewish community.

home, the prophet chose to stay with his friend Gedaliah.

With Jerusalem destroyed, Gedaliah set up his capital seven miles north of its ruins, at Mizpah; and to him, as reported in the book of Jeremiah, came Jews who had fled Judah to find refuge southward in Edom and across the river Jordan among the Ammonites and Moabites. But then a member of Judah's royal family named Ishmael, spurred by the Ammonite king, entered Mizpah and assassinated Gedaliah, his advisers, and his Babylonian guards. Gedaliah's followers, fearing that they might somehow be blamed by their Babylonian masters for the slaughter, swiftly fled to Egypt, taking Jeremiah with them despite the prophet's plea that they trust in the Lord's protection and remain in Judah. The Jewish calendar retains a day of fasting to commemorate Gedaliah's assassination.

GEHAZI

(guh hay' zai) HEBREW: GEHAZI
"valley of vision" or "valley of avarice"

As the devoted servant of **Elijah**, **Elisha** had inherited his master's prophetic powers when Elijah ascended to heaven in a chariot of fire. But Elisha's own servant Gehazi, because of greed, proved to be unworthy of continuing the tradition. Gehazi was, however, involved in some of his master's miracle-working. Most notably, he suggested that a childless Shunammite woman, who had greatly helped Elisha, be granted a son even though her husband was elderly; and when a son was born to her and later sickened and died, Gehazi was sent by his master to place Elisha's staff upon the corpse in an attempt to revive the boy. But the boy failed to come to life until Elisha himself breathed into his mouth and lay upon him to give him bodily warmth.

Gehazi's selfish nature is revealed in the story of Elisha's healing the Syrian general **Naaman** of leprosy. Though the prophet refused payment, Gehazi ran after Naaman and demanded one talent of silver and two festal garments. Naaman gratefully gave him two talents of silver and the garments. But when Gehazi brought the reward home, Elisha saw the deception and punished Gehazi by decreeing that "the leprosy of Naaman shall cleave to you, and to your descendants for ever" (2 Kg. 5:27). According to a rabbinic tradition, the four lepers in 2 Kings 7:3-10 who discovered the supernatural rout of the Syrians, looted the abandoned camp, and then reported news of the enemy's flight, were Gehazi and his three sons.

Elisha's greedy servant Gehazi

GERSHOM

(ger' shuhm) HEBREW: GERSOM
"a sojourner there"

When **Moses** fled from Pharaoh after killing an Egyptian, he found refuge with a priest of Midian named **Jethro**. Descendants of **Abraham** and his second wife **Keturah**, Midianites were kinsmen of the Israelites. The priest gave his daughter **Zipporah** in marriage to Moses, and their child was called Gershom because, Moses said, "I have been a sojourner [ger in Hebrew] in a foreign land" (Ex. 2:22). In Exodus 4:25, Zipporah circumcises her son to avert the Lord's wrath from the presumably uncircumcised Moses. Gershom's descendants included **Jonathan**, a priest of the idolatrous shrine at Dan, and Shebuel, the officer in charge of King **David**'s treasuries.

GERSHON

(ger' shuhn) HEBREW: GERSON
meaning unknown, possibly "sojourner"

The oldest of **Levi**'s three sons, Gershon is also called Gershom in 1 Chronicles 6. He was born in Canaan before the entire family traveled to Egypt to be reunited with the long-lost **Joseph**. Generations later, in Sinai, the Gershonites encamped "behind the tabernacle on the west"; their charge was the tabernacle, the tent and its covering, the door screen of the tent court, the hangings of the court, and "all the service pertaining to these" (Num. 3:23, 26). After the conquest, the Gershonites received 13 cities in the north of Canaan. In the time of **David**, a Gershonite was among those "put in charge of the service of song in the house of the Lord" (1 Chr. 6:31). Later still, Gershonites participated in the cleansing of the temple initiated by King **Hezekiah** in the first year of his reign.

GESHEM

(geh' shuhm) HEBREW: GESHEM, also GASHMU
possibly "important man"

When **Nehemiah** arrived to restore Jerusalem, he found enemies there who were ready to oppose his efforts. Among them was Geshem, an Arab chieftain who presumably governed the Persian province south of Judah. He and his friends **Sanballat** and **Tobiah** ridiculed Nehemiah's plans to rebuild the walls of the city. When the walls were completed, despite danger and difficulty, Geshem and his cohorts first conspired to harm Nehemiah and then threatened to report him to the Persian ruler, saying, "You and the Jews intend to rebel; that is why you are building the wall; and you wish to become their king" (Neh. 6:6). Supremely confident, Nehemiah ignored their threats and carried on with his work. No more was heard from Geshem.

GIDEON

(gid' ee uhn) HEBREW: GIDON
"slasher" or "hewer"

A farmer turned military leader, Gideon is one of the great folk heroes of the Israelite people. Like other farmers of his time, he was forced to hide from the Midianites, desert warriors who invaded the northern Israelite farm country every year around harvest time to take whatever they could. "Coming like locusts for number" (Jg. 6:5), the raiders eventually forced farmers to abandon their fields and seek safety in caves

Gideon asks the Lord for a sign—fleece left overnight on the threshing floor to be wet, then dry—before undertaking his campaign against the Midianites.

By observing how the volunteers drank from a spring, Gideon selected 300 men for his attack.

and other mountain strongholds. Gideon himself took refuge in a wine press while he threshed his grain by hand rather than with oxen and sledge in a hilltop field.

Earlier in the 12th century B.C., Israelite warriors led by the judge **Deborah** had overthrown the Canaanite rulers of Galilee. However, the Israelites' newfound freedom also robbed them of the protection those rulers had provided. With no strong power in control of the region, the Midianites were emboldened to ride in for plunder, arriving regularly each year as soon as the harvest was gathered and the pickings were good. The raiders were part of a confederation of desert tribes living east of the Jordan and south of Canaan's well-settled hill country. Traveling all the way from Mesopotamia to southern Arabia, these tribes carried on a trade in spices and incense. For mobility the Midianites depended on the camel, an animal with which the Israelites were unfamiliar: To them the camel was a large and terrifying beast, best avoided when employed by their enemies in combat.

THE LORD APPOINTS A DELIVERER

One day an angel appeared to Gideon and urged him to deliver the Israelites from their Midianite oppressors. "The Lord is with you," the messenger declared, "you mighty man of valor" (Jg. 6:12). Gideon pointed out that his clan—the Abiezerites—was the

weakest in the tribe of Manasseh and pleaded for a sign that would demonstrate heaven's favor toward him, an insignificant member of his family. After Gideon offered a repast to his mysterious visitor, the angel made it disappear in fire. The farmer, realizing he had seen an angel of the Lord, erected an altar on the spot.

That night the Lord commanded Gideon to demolish the altar that his father had erected to honor **Baal** and to cut down the Asherah beside it. (The Asherah was most likely a wooden pole dedicated to the fertility goddess of that name.) After these tasks were completed, Gideon was ordered to build a new altar in place of the pagan one and to sacrifice on it to Yahweh, using the wood of the Asherah to build the sacrificial fire. Gideon did as he was told but he did it secretly, at night, because he was afraid of a hostile reaction from his relatives and from the townsmen. Indeed, they were outraged, even to the point of threatening to punish Gideon with death. But his father pointed out that Baal could very well defend himself if he was indeed a god. And that very day Gideon was given a new name, Jerubbaal— "Let Baal contend against him" (Jg. 6:32).

Gideon sounded the trumpet to summon members of his clan and sent messengers asking for volunteers from the other northern tribes—Asher, Zebulun, Naphtali, and probably Issachar (though Issachar is not mentioned in the biblical account)—to make war against the Midianites. But before he launched his campaign, Gideon sought additional reassurance that God was with him. First he asked for dew to appear overnight on fleece left on the threshing floor but not on the floor itself; the next night he asked for dew to appear only on the floor while the fleece remained dry. And so it was done.

KEEPING HIS ARMY SMALL

Thousands of men answered Gideon's call. But the Lord ordered him to decrease the size of his army to keep the Israelites from boasting that their own power, not that of God, had beaten the Midianites. So Gideon dismissed "the fearful and trembling" (Jg. 7:3). But the force was still too large, and the Lord commanded him to lower their number by means of a test. Arraying his troops in front of water—most likely the spring of Harod by which they were then encamped—Gideon ordered the men to drink. Those who knelt down to drink and lapped water the way a dog would were sent away. But those who cupped their hands and brought water to their mouths were chosen to stay, leaving Gideon with a force of only 300 men. Scholars have found no evidence that this test was a means of separating the brave or alert from the fearful or incautious; rather, they contend, it was an arbitrary method of reducing the army to a size that would magnify the Lord's subsequent achievement in providing victory for the Israelite army.

Gideon divided his 300 men into three companies, equipping them with trumpets and with empty pottery jars, into each of which was placed a lighted torch. To decrease his enemy's military advantage, Gideon planned an attack by night and arranged his men so that they could charge the enemy camp from three sides simultaneously. Between ten P.M. and midnight, after the Midianites had changed the guard of their camp, Gideon and his men blew their trumpets and smashed their jars, shouting, "A sword for the Lord and for Gideon" (Jg. 7:20). The surprise was complete; all but surrounded

with noise and with flickering torches, the Midianites fled eastward.

Gideon pursued his terrified enemy, asking the men of Ephraim to block fords along the Jordan River. Although two Midianite commanders were captured and killed at the fords, the routed troops managed to get across the river and head for home. Gideon's men pursued them into the desert and, finding them off guard in what they thought was a secure encampment, seized two Midianite kings and "threw all the army into a panic" (Jg. 8:12). Savoring victory, Gideon paused on his way home to punish the inhabitants of Succoth and Penuel, non-Israelite towns east of the Jordan that had refused him supplies during the pursuit for fear of reprisal by the Midianites.

Unlike the other heroes of the book of Judges, Gideon is not described as judging Israel—the term used to describe leadership in the premonarchical period. However, because Gideon's success ended raids by camel-riding nomads on the lands west of the Jordan and brought 40 years of peace, his followers urged him to become ruler over the Israelites and inaugurate a royal dynasty. In some ways, he already lived like a king. He had, the Bible reports, many wives and 70 sons. But Gideon disdained the offer of kingship. "I will not rule over you, and my son will not rule over you," he replied, adding the traditional Israelite theocratic belief: "The Lord will rule over you" (Jg. 8:23).

Gideon's story ends with a disturbing and prophetic event. Rejecting a crown, the victorious warrior asked for a reward: the gold earrings his men had taken from the slain Midianites. From this booty he made an ephod, apparently some sort of pagan image, which he placed in his city of Ophrah. "And all Israel played the harlot after it there; and it became a snare to Gideon and his family" (Jg. 8:27). Indeed, the price for Gideon's apostasy would be paid in the time of his son **Abimelech**, who contrived to become king.

Gideon's famous victory nonetheless entered Israelite tradition; centuries later the prophet **Isaiah** recalled the liberation from Midianite oppression as an example of the

---

JUDGES

The Hebrew word rather misleadingly translated in the English Bible as "judge" is from a verb that can also mean "decide," "rule," "govern," "vindicate," or "deliver." Thus, the warrior judges, such as Othniel, Gideon, and Jephthah, might better be termed "deliverers," since they rid Israel of its oppressors. The role of the so-called minor judges— Tola, Jair, Ibzan, Elon, and Abdon—is uncertain, since so little information has been preserved about them. It is possible, however, that they performed an actual judicial role in the modern sense of the word judge.

The 17th-century Italian painter known as Guercino called this work "The Eternal Father."

freedom that the Messiah would bring. And in the New Testament book of Hebrews, Gideon is cited as one of many Old Testament figures who triumphed through faith.

GOD

The opening words of the Bible, "In the beginning God" (Gen. 1:1), announce the fundamental premise of the entire book. God's existence is assumed at the very outset and only seldom thereafter is argued or disputed. Indeed, the Bible as a whole *is* the story of God, the central personality and driving force both in the background and the foreground of all that is recorded in its pages. The first chapter (Genesis 1) describes how God by his word created the heavens and the earth—the sum of existence. The last chapter (Revelation 22) poetically portrays the throne of God from which flows a river of life through a world where "night shall be no more . . . for the Lord God will be their light" (Rev. 22:5).

Between Genesis and Revelation is a vast tapestry of literature, written during more than a millennium. Through history, biography, prophecy, law, prayer, song, proverb, oracle, epistle, vision, and other expressions, the Bible recounts the extraordinary story of God's interaction with humanity. Though people often speak of this timeless work as the story of the human quest for God, the Bible portrays it as just the reverse—God's quest for humanity.

The Bible, moreover, contains warnings that no human being can know God in essence: "Can you find out the limit of the Almighty? It is higher than heaven—what can you do? Deeper than Sheol—what can you know?" (Job 11:7-8). Knowing such an unimaginably glorious Being is possible only because God in his own chosen ways and in his own chosen times desired to make himself known. God's times stretch across history; his ways vary vastly—from the concerned creator worrying about **Adam**'s loneliness; to the quiet speaker directing **Abraham** to the Promised Land; to the mysterious trumpet, thunder, and fire on Mount Sinai; to the voice from heaven at **Jesus**' transfiguration; to the startling visions of **John of Patmos**. Always, the revelations concern the relationship between God and humanity. Thus, the Bible is also permeated with human responses to God, with awe and worship, disobedience and rebellion, trust and love—God and humanity reaching out to each other in a vast drama played out across the centuries.

Often historians try to tease out of the biblical fabric strands of early tradition and strands of later tradition in order to distinguish between people's developing conceptions of God. But the Bible is concerned less with people's conceptions of God and more with the changing ways in which God reveals himself. What is important is God's unfolding story punctuated by great moments of illumination: the creation of the world, the call of Abraham, the revelations to **Moses**, the rise of **David**, the cries of the great prophets, the coming of Jesus, the vision of **Paul** on the road to Damascus, and many others.

The early chapters of Genesis begin the process of revealing God by showing his power in relationship to the entire world, both as the giver of life and the slayer of the wicked. To an earth that is a dark, formless turmoil, devoid of life and order, God simply spoke: "'Let there be light'; and there was light" (Gen. 1:3). Without opposition or conflict, God's word set the chaotic mass into majestic motion. Day followed night, the dome of heaven appeared; land and sea separated; plants rose from the earth; sun and moon began to shine; and water, air, and land swarmed with life. Finally, God decided to make man "in the image of God . . . male and female" (Gen. 1:27). Thus, from the void God's powerful and awesome word brought forth time, order, beauty, self-sustaining life, intelligence—a world that God could recognize "was very good" (Gen. 1:31).

THE GIFT OF CHOICE

In the character of what he created, the character of the creator was revealed. The creation account in Genesis 2 stresses God's intimate concern for humanity. It begins with God seeming to stoop down to mold from dust a human form and to breathe into its nostrils "the breath of life" (Gen. 2:7). God planted a marvelous garden for the new human to care for but decided that the human should not be alone. As possible partners for the human, he created all the animals but found none adequate. God therefore took a portion from within the human, a rib, and fashioned a perfect partner, and the two became man and woman.

God gave these humans one more gift, which no other part of his creation received. He gave them a choice and allowed them the freedom to make that choice for good or ill—though he knew the strengths and weaknesses of the precarious creatures he had formed. And so God created a tree whose lovely fruit tantalizingly offered "the knowledge of good and evil" (Gen. 2:17). When the couple, prodded by the subtle serpent, ate its forbidden fruit and tasted the bittersweet knowledge of good and evil, human life as we know it began—outside the paradise of Eden, a continual mix of good and bad.

Again, the character of God is revealed by his actions. He desired a relationship with his creatures that was based on their own moral freedom, even if that freedom could lead to disaster. God did not create robots to do his will, nor did he leave humans in the amoral innocence of Eden. By planting that famous tree, God created the conditions that led them outside Eden so that God could say that the humans had "become like one of us, knowing good and evil" (Gen. 3:22). In

many ways, the rest of the Bible is based on that fundamental correspondence between God and humanity as moral beings in the struggle between good and evil.

The Bible is quick to show the tremendous power of evil. **Cain** killed **Abel** and received God's curse. Eventually, the whole family of humanity followed the way of Cain, and "the earth was filled with violence . . . for all flesh had corrupted their way upon the earth" (Gen. 6:11-12). God bestowed his verdict on such human conduct by sending a devastating torrent to return creation to chaos— but he allowed life to continue from the tiny remnant of human and animal existence preserved with **Noah** aboard the ark. After the Flood, God made a covenant with Noah, promising never again to destroy the earth by waters but to preserve its regularity and order. He did not, however, change the moral freedom of humanity, which could and would again lead to disaster.

In the story of the tower of Babel—the last episode in which God deals with all of humanity together—the contrast between the power of God and humanity's self-absorbed pride and presumption is made clear. United humanity thought to build a tower to the sky. But with pointed irony, Genesis shows that this supposedly vast enterprise was so tiny from God's perspective that the Lord had to descend from heaven even to see it. God con-

A benevolent God surveys his creation.

125

THE NAME OF GOD

In both Hebrew *(elohim)* and Greek *(theos)*, the words for god are basic terms that can be used for pagan gods as well as for the God of Israel. Although the Hebrew term is plural, implying majesty or comprehensiveness, it is used with singular verbs. The singular Hebrew term for god *(el)* is much less commonly used, perhaps because El was the name of the chief Canaanite god. However, it is occasionally used for the God of Israel, especially in poetry, and is sometimes joined with a second word to form a special title, such as God Most High *(El elyon)* or God Almighty *(El shaddai)*.

By far the most distinctive term for God in the Hebrew Scriptures is the personal name of God: Yahweh. This name is sometimes called the tetragrammaton, meaning "four letters," since the Hebrew consists of four consonants, YHWH (sometimes written JHVH), while the vowels are usually not written. The name could be shortened to Yah or Jah when part of a longer word or phrase, such as Elijah, meaning "my God is Yahweh."

Though the name Yahweh was extensively used in the Hebrew Old Testament—more than 6,800 times—and is by far the most frequently used name in the Bible, it is often completely removed from modern translations. By the third century B.C. the name came to be considered so holy that pious people no longer pronounced it aloud, but rather substituted for it the Hebrew word for Lord *(Adonai)*. Most modern English translations transform the name Yahweh into a title, "the Lord." Only a few translations use the name Yahweh, while a few others use the word Jehovah, a term created by combining the Hebrew consonants JHVH with the Hebrew vowels of the word for Lord.

founded human arrogance by confusing languages and scattering humanity across the face of the earth.

Instead of continuing to deal directly with all humanity, God chose to establish a relationship with a faithful individual in order to create through him a new way of blessing all people. He sent the elderly Abraham to a far-off country and promised, "I will make of you a great nation, and I will bless you . . . and by you all the families of the earth shall bless themselves" (Gen. 12:2-3). The ensuing story shows how God again and again had to intervene so that his promises could be fulfilled.

COVENANTS AND PROMISES

Through a long series of appearances and repeated promises, God made himself known to Abraham with such intimacy that on occasion Abraham even felt bold enough to argue with him. For his part, Abraham "believed the Lord" even when God's pledge that Abraham would have many descendants seemed incredible to the childless old man. Seeing his faith, God decided to make a special covenant with Abraham and his descendants. In return for his promise of the land of Canaan, God required them to circumcise all their male children as "a sign of the covenant" (Gen. 17:11). God also promised Abraham a special son to be born to his aged and apparently barren wife **Sarah**. But once their child was born, God tested Abraham by making the emotionally and theologically astonishing demand that Abraham sacrifice his son **Isaac** as a burnt offering. When Abraham trusted the Lord and set out to obey him, God responded by establishing an irrevocable covenant, renewing his relationship with all humanity through Abraham. "By myself I have sworn," says the Lord, "because you . . . have not withheld your son, your only son, I will indeed bless you . . . and by your descendants shall all the nations of the earth bless themselves" (Gen. 22:16-18).

Through these covenants and promises, God established the basic pattern of his relationship with humanity, as shown in the Bible. Everything depends on God's initiative and everything occurs to achieve his purposes. People respond in trust toward God and are guided by his will. They both follow his immediate demands and trust in the future that God offers.

The next great moment of divine revelation came through Moses. After the people of Israel descended into a long period of servitude and apparent hopelessness in Egypt, God revealed himself as the deliverer of the oppressed by calling Moses to lead the powerless slaves out of bondage. "I have seen the affliction of my people," the Lord told Moses from the burning bush. "I know their sufferings, and I have come down to deliver them" (Ex. 3:7-8). He identified himself as "the God of Abraham, the God of Isaac, and the God of Jacob" (Ex. 3:15)—emphasizing continuity with the past—but showed that he wished to create from this enslaved people a whole nation in covenant with himself.

Through astonishing signs at the hand of Moses (including ten plagues, parted seas, and bad water made potable) and despite obstinate Egyptian resistance, God, by his power alone, delivered Israel from Egyptian oppression and led the people to Mount Sinai. The events at Sinai define all of God's subsequent relationships with Israel. There the Lord reached out to deliver and save, and that salvation created a relationship and a covenant that carried with it expectations and demands. People have no claim on God that he does not freely give them; but because they are God's creation and recipients of his deliverance, God has an absolute claim on them.

God's claim was expressed at Mount Sinai through the Law, starting with the Ten Commandments. And the first of those commandments is "I am the Lord your God, who brought you out of the land of Egypt, out of the house of bondage. You shall have no other gods before me" (Ex. 20:2-3). The Law continues through three biblical books, Exodus, Leviticus, and parts of Numbers, with a reiteration in a fourth, Deuteronomy. By traditional count, 613 laws, positive and negative, were laid upon Israel. Religious, moral, ethical, criminal, and civil statutes were so mingled together as to show that God laid claim to every part of Israel's life, from the sublime to the mundane. Exodus tells how, through numerous manifestations, the Lord revealed to Moses and the people his character as "a God merciful and gracious, slow to anger, and abounding in steadfast love and faithfulness . . . forgiving iniquity and transgression and sin, but who will by no means clear the guilty" (Ex. 34:6-7). The history that follows Sinai shows how these characteristics of God were revealed. With steadfast love and faithfulness, God preserved and

Speaking from the burning bush, God tells Moses to remove his shoes because he is standing on hallowed ground.

chastened a people who repeatedly rebelled.

The biblical narrative shows God continually interacting with his people through all the vagaries of their history—disciplining them in the wilderness wandering, fighting for them in the conquest of Canaan, warning them of the temptation to follow other gods, chastising them with times of oppression, redeeming them through periods of deliverance, and even yielding to their desires to establish a monarchy for the nation.

But the Bible's next major moment of revelation and covenant—a supplement to the covenant at Sinai—comes with the promises of God to **David**. From obscurity he picked David as "a man after his own heart" (1 Sam. 13:14) and anointed him to rule Israel in place of the rebellious **Saul**. Although David had shown great qualities of loyalty, courage, and trust in God, he also had weaknesses, such as his callous taking of **Bathsheba**. Nevertheless, when David desired to build a temple to house the ark of the covenant, which symbolized God's presence among his chosen people, the Lord redirected the king's desires in a way that would change the religious history of Israel forever. Instead of David building a house for him, God promised to make a dynasty for David. "Your house and your kingdom shall be made sure for ever before me," the Lord said; "your throne shall be established for ever" (2 Sam. 7:16).

HOPES FOR A MESSIAH

God's covenant with David played an important role in the history of Israel, for even when the nation divided into northern and southern kingdoms, the legitimacy of tiny

Judah was maintained by David's descendants for four centuries. But more important for the faith of Israel, God's promises to David laid the foundation for the expectation of a Messiah, an anointed king like David. And even when the faithlessness and foolishness of its kings led to ruinous war and foreign oppression, trust in God brought hope for renewal.

God had not forsaken his people even during the long and difficult period of the dual monarchy, when Israel's faith often seemed trapped within the structures of royal courts, an official temple priesthood in Jerusalem, and rival shrines in the north. Rather, God created new prophetic voices to make his will known. In the northern kingdom of Israel, the Lord thundered through the voice of **Elijah** to challenge the power of the Canaanite god **Baal** and his hundreds of royally supported prophets. Later, he spoke through **Amos** and **Hosea** to correct Israel's corrupt ideas of worship. The prophets served as

God's trumpet to call his faithless people back to him. But they failed to heed him, and the northern kingdom fell to Assyria in 721 B.C.

Later God sent **Isaiah**, **Micah**, and **Jeremiah**, among others, to the southern kingdom of Judah with much the same message, combining the threat of disaster and hope of renewal. He chose to speak only through a handful of outsiders, each in his own way, like Elijah, a "troubler of Israel" (1 Kg. 18:17), who often suffered derision, deprivation, and even the threat of death for serving as God's spokesmen. The Lord's presence was not always pleasant for them. "There is in my heart as it were a burning fire, shut up in my bones," Jeremiah said, "and I am weary with holding it in" (Jer. 20:9).

While Judah descended into the pit of seemingly hopeless dissolution, ending with the conquest by **Nebuchadnezzar** in 586 B.C. and the exile of Jerusalem's population to Babylon, God spoke through the prophets in new tones of compassion and hope. As he showed to the prophet **Ezekiel** in a vision, God wanted to breathe new life into the dry bones of Judah's destroyed people, and he urged Isaiah to "comfort, comfort my people . . . speak tenderly to Jerusalem and cry to her that her warfare is ended, that her iniquity is pardoned" (Is. 40:1-2). And through the spiritual perception of these prophets, God powerfully expressed the truth of monotheism that Israel so often forgot: "Turn to me and be saved, all the ends of the earth! For I am God, and there is no other" (Is. 45:22).

The biblical narrative of God enters a long period of quiet after the Lord restored his people to their land under **Zerubbabel**, **Ezra**, and **Nehemiah**. During the long centuries of subservience to such foreign powers as Persia, Macedonia, Egypt, Syria, and finally Rome, the ancient covenants with God took on new importance and meaning. Obedience to the Law as given to Moses became a focus of devotion as never before. At the same time God's ancient promises to David became the foundation of intense expectations for a Messiah.

The New Testament bears witness to the belief that God intervened in human history in the most dramatic way possible—in the life, death, and resurrection of Jesus. The Gospel of John describes how Jesus as "the Word" was "in the beginning . . . with God" and indeed "was God"

The dove of the Holy Spirit hovering at his shoulder, God cradles his crucified son; a Flemish painting attributed to Robert Campin (c. 1375-1444).

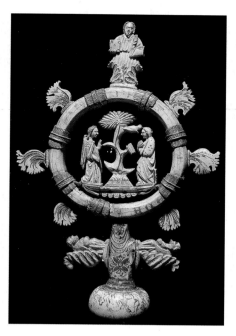

God surmounts an Annunciation scene in this 14th-century Venetian carved and painted ivory pastoral staff.

and "all things were made through him" (Jn. 1:1-3). That divine Word, John says, "became flesh and dwelt among us, full of grace and truth" (Jn. 1:14). Later John recounts how Jesus told his disciples, "He who has seen me has seen the Father" (Jn. 14:9), and he prayed that his disciples "may be one; even as thou, Father, art in me, and I in thee" (Jn. 17:21).

The other Gospels are less explicit in portraying the divinity of Jesus, but they nevertheless show how his story is in a profound sense a continuation of God's own story. It was the **Holy Spirit** who descended at Jesus' baptism, God's voice announcing, "This is my beloved Son, with whom I am well pleased" (Mt. 3:17). God was active throughout Jesus' ministry and showed his presence at Jesus' death by signs—darkness fell at noon and, as he died, "the earth shook, and the rocks were split" (Mt. 27:51). But above all God manifested himself in the resurrection. "By the hands of lawless men," Jesus died, **Peter** proclaimed on Pentecost. "But God raised him up, having loosed the pangs of death" (Acts 2:23-24).

Early Christians saw God's direct action and the revelation of God's character in every aspect of Jesus' story. Searching the Scriptures, they found numerous connections between Jesus and God's prophetic words of old that confirmed Jesus' role as Messiah. But it was especially the surprising, wholly unexpected element of Jesus' story—his death as a

condemned and crucified Messiah—that became for them the greatest revelation of God. What Paul called "the word of the cross" seemed "a stumbling block" and "folly" to some, but was in fact "the power of God and the wisdom of God" (1 Cor. 1:18, 23-24).

God also chose, through Jesus, to establish a newly intimate relationship with those who have faith in Christ. Because Jesus was God's son, Christians taught, God also adopts as his own child the one who trusts in Jesus. Thus Paul wrote, "When the time had fully come, God sent forth his Son . . . so that we might receive adoption as sons. And because you are sons, God has sent the Spirit of his Son into our hearts, crying, 'Abba! Father!'" (Gal. 4:4-6). "Abba" was a familiar term expressing the intimacy that God wished to reestablish with his creatures.

The fulfillment of God's purposes on both a cosmic and personal scale leads ultimately to the final vision of the Bible as its story of God's actions is completed. The vision, expressed in the apocalyptic images of Revelation, shows "a new heaven and a new earth" that calls to mind the moment of creation in the beginning. Now "the dwelling of God is with men" and we see him tenderly "wipe away every tear from their eyes" (Rev. 21:1, 3-4). In the vision, God reigns with the Lamb, symbolizing Christ, over a marvelous jeweled city, the "new Jerusalem" (Rev. 21:2) that shines from within with the glory of God. All that is false, destructive, violent, corrupt, and deadly has been removed from God's presence. Life, light, truth, and beauty surround God's throne. There, the vision assures us, God "shall reign for ever and ever!'" (Rev. 22:5).

By including this final vision that reaches beyond all of history to a new world, the Bible makes it clear that the whole course of humanity's struggles through the centuries lies within the biblical story of God. The God who is exalted beyond all time, history, and imagination and yet who is personal and intimate enough to listen to a single heart crying, "Abba! Father!"—this is the God who reveals himself through the books of the Bible.

GOG

HEBREW: GOG
"valuable gold object"
••••••••••

Speaking in the Lord's voice, the prophet **Ezekiel** foretells a crushing defeat for "Gog, of the land of Magog, the chief prince of Meshech and Tubal" (Ezek. 38:2), who was to come with allies from the distant north to make war against the Israelites. Scholars have been unable to identify Gog, though some suggest Gyges, a seventh-cen-

Armed only with a sling, the shepherd David confronts the Philistine giant Goliath.

tury B.C. Lydian king. In his oracle of hope issued after the fall of Jerusalem to **Nebuchadnezzar** in 586 B.C., Ezekiel seems to have linked an earlier prediction, that "out of the north evil shall break forth" (Jer. 1:14), with God's promise to defeat the enemy "and upon my mountains trample him under foot" (Is. 14:25). Ezekiel's vivid image of putting hooks through an enemy's jaws is derived from an Assyrian practice of leading captive kings on rings inserted in their lips.

In the final book of the New Testament, Gog and Magog represent nations "at the four corners of the earth" (Rev. 20:8) who will gather under **Satan**'s command for a final battle against the saints before being consumed by fire from heaven.

GOLIATH

(guh lai' uhth) HEBREW: GOLYAT
possibly "ravaging spirits"
∙∙∙∙∙∙∙∙∙∙

As the army of **Saul** formed a battle line against the invading Philistines, a champion named Goliath stepped out from the enemy camp. Heavily armed, nearly ten feet tall, he challenged the Israelites to send a man against him in single combat to decide which side would claim victory—such combat being a tradition in the ancient Near East. "Dismayed and greatly afraid" (1 Sam. 17:11), the Israelites did nothing for the 40 days, morning and evening, that the taunt was repeated. Finally, however, the young shepherd **David** arrived on the scene with provisions for three older brothers in the ranks, heard and accepted the challenge, and slew the giant with a single stone from his slingshot. As David cut off Goliath's head with the giant's

own sword, the Philistine army fled in panic.

In 2 Samuel 21:19, the slaying of Goliath is attributed to one Elhanan and takes place during David's reign. This, however, appears to be a mistake in transcription; in 1 Chronicles 20:5, it is Goliath's brother, Lahmi, who is dispatched by Elhanan. Although some early texts give Goliath's height as only about seven feet, giants in the vicinity of Gath are mentioned in both accounts of Elhanan's feat. It has been suggested that they were not true Philistines but rather conscripted descendants of the remarkably tall Anakim described in the books of Deuteronomy and Joshua.

GOMER

(goh' muhr) HEBREW: GOMER
∙∙∙∙∙∙∙∙∙∙

Ordered by the Lord to take "a wife of harlotry and have children of harlotry" (Hos. 1:2), the prophet **Hosea** sought the prostitute Gomer as a bride. (She was possibly a cult prostitute at a Canaanite temple.) Her three children—Hosea is specifically called the father only of the first—were a son named Jezreel, a reference both to the city where **Jehu** brought down the house of **Ahab** and the valley where Jehu's dynasty in turn was destroyed; a daughter named Not pitied, as the Israelites were not to be pitied; and another son named Not my people, since the Lord was disowning his chosen people for their transgressions.

Though Gomer left Hosea for other lovers, he bought the adulteress back from a paramour. The entire story appears to be an analogy for the Lord's forgiveness of an errant Israel, which he promised to betroth "in righteousness and in justice, in steadfast love, and in mercy" (Hos. 2:19).

GORGIAS

(gor' gee uhs) GREEK: GORGIAS
∙∙∙∙∙∙∙∙∙∙

To suppress an uprising by his Jewish vassals after he had declared their religion illegal, Syria's king **Antiochus IV Epiphanes** sent an army southward in 165 B.C. Gorgias was one of three "mighty men among the friends of the king" (1 Macc. 3:38) who were chosen to command Antiochus's army, a force greatly outnumbering the army of the rebel leader, **Judas Maccabeus**. The two armies met near Emmaus, west of Jerusalem, and the Maccabees were victorious. Gorgias was forced to retreat and his camp was destroyed. A few years later, he had his revenge when he defeated another Jewish army that had rashly attacked him in disobedience to the orders of Judas.

HABAKKUK

(huh bak' kuhk) HEBREW: HABAKKUK
"embrace" or "embracer"
··········

Like the tormented **Job** and like the prophet **Jeremiah**, Habakkuk wrestled with the ancient religious question: Why do the evil prosper? "O Lord," he pleaded, ". . . why dost thou look on faithless men and art silent when the wicked swallows up the man more righteous than he?" (Hab. 1:12, 13). His attempt to justify the ways of God, incorporated in the prophetic book that bears his name, has been subject to a number of scholarly interpretations. All biblical commentators agree, however, that "the Chaldeans, that bitter and hasty nation" (Hab. 1:6), were the neo-Babylonians who overthrew the Assyrians and ruled the Near East from 612 to 539 B.C.

This identification makes it possible to date Habakkuk, about whom nothing else is known, to the late seventh century B.C., in a time when one oppressor of the kingdom of Judah had been replaced with another. The wicked Chaldeans, Habakkuk pointed out, were not only the instrument of divine anger sent to punish the persecutors of his countrymen, but also an evil force itself deserving of punishment.

There are only 56 verses in the book of Habakkuk, but one of them—"the righteous shall live by his faith" (Hab. 2:4)—underlies all of the Bible's commandments, according to one Talmudic sage. Quoted by Paul in Romans 1:17 and in Galatians 3:11, it is a verse that was to have an enormous effect on Christian theology.

Habakkuk is the eighth of the Old Testament's 12 Minor Prophets. His book falls easily into three sections, each corresponding more or less to one of its three chapters. The first section is the prophet's lament over the evils of his time and the apparent triumph of the wicked over the righteous, an anguished protest cast in the form of a dialogue with God. The second section contains the prophet's vision of the retribution that wrongdoers will certainly encounter, eventually if not at once. In five clusters of verses, Habakkuk proclaims five "woes" in store for such transgressors. Plunderers will themselves be plundered; those who seek gain from evil will forfeit their lives; those who are guilty of bloodshed will be overwhelmed by the glory of Yahweh; the violent will themselves be subjected to violence; and idol-worshipers will be struck dumb before the Lord in his temple.

The third section of the book is a prayer that bears many resemblances to the psalms that were sung during temple rituals; it even contains a final instruction to the temple's choirmaster that it is to be accompanied by stringed instruments. Habakkuk's prayer, possibly a later addition, portrays Yahweh as a warrior, riding out against his enemies in a chariot and armed with a bow and arrows and with a spear whose brightness outshines the sun and the moon.

Habakkuk appears again in the apocryphal book Bel and the Dragon. In the second of two tales, he is told by an angel to carry a bowl of pottage and some bread to feed the prophet **Daniel,** who had been cast

The prophet Habakkuk

The 12th-century German artist who fashioned this ivory plaque interpreted Habakkuk's prayer as a prophecy of the ascension of Jesus.

into a lion's den. When Habakkuk answered that he did not know where to find the lion's den, the angel "lifted him up by his hair and set him down in Babylon" (Bel 36). After feeding Daniel, the prophet was returned home.

HADAD

(hay' dad) HEBREW: HADAD
"thunderer" or "the one who smashes"

As a child, Hadad, a member of the royal house of Edom, witnessed the occupation of his homeland by King **David**. Although many of his countrymen were killed, Hadad managed to escape and make his way to Egypt. There "Hadad found great favor in the sight of Pharaoh" (1 Kg. 11:19), who not only gave him land, a house, and an allowance of food, but also the hand of his wife's sister in marriage—possibly because he thought Hadad might eventually be used as a bargaining chip with Israel. Hadad bided his time in Egypt until, after David's death, he returned to his country, where he is recorded as "doing mischief" (1 Kg. 11:25) against King **Solomon**.

HADADEZER

(hay dad ay' zuhr) HEBREW: HADAD-EZER
"Hadad [Baal] is help"

The powerful Syrian ruler Hadadezer, king of Zobah, north of Damascus, met the forces of King **David** in battle a number of times. In a rivalry that had begun during

Saul's reign, Hadadezer repeatedly rallied coalitions to fight against Israel. Three battles involving Hadadezar are recounted in 2 Samuel: In 8:3-12, Hadadezar's army is said to be totally defeated, and his territory subjugated by David; in 10:6-15, his soldiers are listed as mercenaries in the Ammonite force defeated by **Joab** and his brother **Abishai**; and in 10:16-19, Hadadezer brings troops from beyond the Euphrates as David in person joins a battle in which the Syrians are definitively defeated. Authorities disagree on whether these accounts describe the same or different battles and on the order in which they occurred—the biblical narrative not necessarily being chronological.

HAGAR

(hay' gahr) HEBREW: HAGAR
"emigration," "flight," or "wandering"

Since **Sarah** had failed to bear a child to **Abraham**, she gave her husband the Egyptian slave Hagar to conceive an heir in her place. (Hagar was possibly one of the maidservants Pharaoh had given Abraham at the time he took Sarah into his house, having been told she was the patriarch's sister, not his wife.) But when Hagar became pregnant, "she looked with contempt on her mistress" (Gen. 16:4). Abraham refused to intervene in the conflict; and Sarah began to

---

SURROGATE MOTHERS

Providing her husband with an heir was considered a woman's duty in the ancient Near East. Thus, when Sarah remained barren until she had apparently passed her childbearing years, she offered her maidservant Hagar to Abraham as a surrogate, or substitute, for herself. The child born of such a liaison was legally hers.

The tradition of providing surrogate mothers continued with Jacob's two wives, Leah and Rachel, each of whom offered a maid to bear children during a period of infertility. By each servant, Zilpah and Bilhah, Jacob had two additional sons.

Abraham sends Hagar and their son Ishmael into the wilderness; detail of a 17th-century Dutch painting.

treat Hagar so harshly that she finally fled into the wilderness. There, by a spring, an angel appeared and urged her to return to her mistress, telling her that the child she was to bear would be named **Ishmael** ("God has heard") and that he would "be a wild ass of a man" (Gen. 16:12) and produce a multitude of descendants.

Hagar returned and, 14 years after Ishmael's birth, Sarah at last bore a son, **Isaac**. At a feast given to celebrate Isaac's weaning, Sarah saw Ishmael "playing with" (Gen. 21:9) Isaac—perhaps mocking or laughing at the child. She grew concerned that Hagar's son would share Isaac's inheritance and appealed to Abraham to expel the servant woman and her child. Abraham overcame his reluctance to do so only after God assured him that such an expulsion would serve the divine purpose, because Abraham's main line of descent was to be through Isaac.

Sent into the wilderness with only a small amount of bread and water to sustain her and her son, Hagar soon realized that they would die of thirst and placed the boy under a bush to avoid seeing his death. But as her child wept, an angel called to Hagar, saying that Ishmael would survive to produce a great nation. Opening her eyes, she saw a well from which she drew water for her son.

When Ishmael grew up, Hagar found an Egyptian wife for him.

The story of Hagar was used as an allegory by the apostle **Paul** in the New Testament. He pictured the slave Hagar and her son, "born according to the flesh," as representing the restrictions of the old covenant, whereas Christians "like Isaac, are children of promise. . . . [children] of the free woman" (Gal. 4:23, 28, 31).

HAGGAI
(hag' ee ai) HEBREW: HAGGAY
"festal"

❚❚❚❚❚❚❚❚❚❚

One of the 12 Minor Prophets whose short books bring the Old Testament to a close, Haggai—along with his contemporary **Zechariah**—was instrumental in getting Jerusalem's Jews to rebuild the temple following their return from exile in Babylon. Haggai began his prophecies in August of 520 B.C., the second year in the reign of Persia's King **Darius I**. On that day, the first day of the Hebrew month of Elul, Haggai told **Zerubbabel**, the governor of Judah, and the high priest Joshua the reason for the people's inadequate harvests, their hunger, thirst, and cold: God was dissatisfied with them for neglecting to restore his house of

Ham discovers his drunken father, Noah.

worship. "Is it a time for you yourselves to dwell in your paneled houses, while this house [the temple] lies in ruins?" (Hag. 1:4) Haggai asked.

Continuing to speak in the name of the Lord, Haggai commanded them to go into the hills surrounding Jerusalem—hills now almost bare but then well-wooded—and cut down enough lumber to rebuild the temple. Among his listeners there may have been some who, apparently like the prophet himself, were old enough to remember how beautiful the original temple had been before it was plundered and burned by the neo-Babylonians 67 years earlier. The rebuilt temple, Haggai promised in a subsequent prophecy, would be filled with silver and gold, as had been the old; in splendor it would surpass **Solomon**'s magnificent edifice. Although little is known about the so-called second temple, which was built following Haggai's exhortation, it was to survive for nearly 600 years, two centuries longer than had the first temple.

"Take courage, all you people of the land . . . ; work, for I am with you" (Hag. 2:4), Haggai exhorted in the name of the Lord. And they did work, beginning their labors about three weeks after Haggai's first prophecy. On December 18, the 24th day of the 9th month, the Hebrew month of Chislev, the stone foundation for the new building was laid. Soon thereafter, the

prophet asserted, the faithful would see the results: barns filled with grain and ample yields from the vines and from the fig, pomegranate, and olive trees.

HAM
HEBREW: HAM
"warm" or "hot"
••••••••••

Although he is always listed between his two brothers, **Shem** and **Japheth**, Ham was apparently the youngest son of **Noah**. All three brothers and their wives accompanied their father on the ark. After the floodwaters receded, Noah planted a vineyard, and one day Ham came upon his father naked and intoxicated in his tent. He told his brothers of Noah's condition, and they carefully covered their father, walking backward so as not to see his body, since Israelite tradition prohibited viewing the nakedness of a parent.

When Noah recovered from his drunkenness and realized what had happened, he said, "Cursed be Canaan; a slave of slaves shall he be to his brothers" (Gen. 9:25). Interpreters differ as to the reason why Noah cursed **Canaan**, who was one of Ham's sons, rather than Ham himself. However, in the Bible it is not uncommon for children to be punished for the sins of their parents. Some of Canaan's descendants, the Gibeonites—in line, apparently, with Noah's prophecy—were told by **Joshua**, "You shall always be slaves, hewers of wood and drawers of water" (Jos. 9:23).

Ham's sons were Cush, Egypt, Put, and Canaan. The descendants of three—the Cushites, the Egyptians, and the Canaanites—figure prominently in the Bible. Put apparently engendered the people of either Libya or the Horn of Africa, areas that are mentioned less often in the Scriptures.

HAMAN
(hay' muhn) HEBREW: HAMAN
"well disposed"
••••••••••

After he named Haman the Agagite grand vizier, the Persian king **Ahasuerus** ordered the entire court to bow down to him. But **Mordecai**, a Jew who was one of the king's gatekeepers, refused to prostrate himself; as a Benjaminite, he could not so honor the descendant of King **Saul**'s enemy **Agag**. Enraged at this flouting of the king's order, Haman vowed his revenge not only on Mordecai but upon all his people as well, and persuaded the king to decree that on a given day Jews throughout the kingdom should be killed. He then built a gallows especially for Mordecai.

But before Haman's orders could be carried out, Ahasuerus learned that Mordecai had never been rewarded for thwarting an assassination plot against him. Summoning Haman, the king asked his minister to suggest what could be done for "the man whom the king delights to honor" (Est. 6:6). Haman proposed a gift of fine clothes and a horse from the royal stable—assuming the man to be honored was himself. Thus clothed and mounted, he suggested, the honoree should be led through the city in triumph. To his dismay, Haman was told that Mordecai was the man cho-

sen for the honor, and had to endure the humiliation of giving his enemy the reward he had proposed for himself.

During the course of a subsequent banquet to which Haman had been invited, Mordecai's cousin **Esther**, who was the wife of Ahasuerus, revealed to the king that the vizier's plot was against her own people and pronounced Haman her enemy. As he begged for mercy, Haman fell upon Esther's couch, leading Ahasuerus to believe that he was trying to assault the queen. Furious, the king ordered Haman hanged on the same gallows that he had built for Mordecai and decreed that, on the day originally set for their destruction, the Jews would be allowed to take revenge on their enemies.

Haman's ten sons were among those killed in the ensuing bloody retaliation, and Mordecai was awarded Haman's estate and position. To this day, Jews commemorate this deliverance as the holiday of Purim.

HAMMURABI
(ham uh rah' bee) also: HAMMURAPI

According to a once popular but now discredited theory, King **Amraphel** of Shinar, one of the four monarchs defeated by **Abraham** near the Dead Sea, is the same person as Hammurabi, who ruled Babylon for 42 years beginning in 1728 B.C. Although Hammurabi was a near-contemporary of Abraham and his domain included Shinar, the biblical name for Sumer and Akkad, there is no evidence that his military campaigns extended nearly as far south as the Dead Sea. Hammurabi's importance to biblical studies rests with his law code, which had an enormous influence on later legal codifications throughout the ancient Near East, including those of the Hebrews that were enshrined in the Bible.

One surviving copy of Hammurabi's law, inscribed on an almost eight-foot-tall diorite stele discovered by French archeologists in 1901, shows the king receiving his laws from Shamash, the

Haman forced to give Mordecai the triumph he planned for himself

135

Hammurabi receiving his laws from the god Shamash, top of an 18th-century B.C. stele

sun god who was also worshiped as the god of justice. In the prologue to the laws, Hammurabi calls himself "the exalted prince" and describes his aim as "to cause righteousness to prevail in the land, to destroy the wicked and the evil, to prevent the strong from injuring the weak, . . . to enlighten the land, and to further the welfare of the people." There follow 282 laws concerning adoption, wills, debts, personal injuries, dowries, slavery, and numerous other matters important to Babylonian society.

Among the laws of Hammurabi that have biblical parallels are those spelling out punishments for various kinds of personal injury. For example, Hammurabi's law 196, "If an aristocrat has destroyed the eye of a member of the aristocracy, they shall destroy his eye," will be familiar to Bible readers since it is echoed in Exodus 21:24, Leviticus 24:20, and Deuteronomy 19:21. But there is nothing in the Bible like Hammurabi's law 198, which abandons the principle of "an eye for an eye" to provide a fine of 500 grams of silver for destroying a commoner's eye. And, according to law 199, whoever destroys a slave's eye is liable for half the worth of the slave's entire value. Throughout Hammurabi's code, distinctions are made according to the social class of both the perpetrator and the victim. The Bible is more egalitarian: "Life for life, eye for eye, tooth for tooth, hand for hand, foot for foot, burn for burn, wound for wound, stripe for stripe" (Ex. 21:23-24).

Hammurabi's code punishes certain cases of kidnapping with death. So does the Bible. In both the Babylonian code and the Bible, anyone sold into slavery for failure to pay a debt is allowed to go free after serving a certain amount of time. Both law codes call for the execution of a man who rapes a betrothed virgin and both recognize the victim's innocence. Both contain long lists of kinfolk with whom it is forbidden to have sexual relations. Both the Bible and Hammurabi deal with the problems arising from a goring ox, holding its owner responsible if the ox was known to be a gorer and, in the case of the Bible, condemning the ox to death by stoning. But there are more substantial differences: Hammurabi allows a wronged husband to spare the life of his adulterous wife, whereas the Bible insists that both she and her lover be put to death.

Hammurabi's laws were not necessarily a reflection of the legal practices current in his time. They were rather an ideal, showing what the king aimed for and what he and, ostensibly, his god desired. It was not until much later that the Israelites actually melded ideal and real behavior so that their laws truly showed how their society operated.

HANANIAH

(ha nuh nai' uh) HEBREW: HANANYAHU
or HANANYAH
"Yahweh has been gracious"

Contradicting **Jeremiah**, who believed that Judah's continued submission to Babylon was God's will, a prophet from Gibeon named Hananiah predicted Judah's freedom from "the yoke of the king of Babylon" (Jer. 28:2). Within two years, he claimed, the treasure taken from the temple by **Nebuchadnezzar** would be returned to Jerusalem. Hananiah then seized and broke the symbolic wooden yoke Jeremiah wore. Jeremiah, calling Hananiah a false prophet, declared that the wooden yoke would become one of iron and correctly predicted Hananiah's death within the year.

HANNAH

(han' uh) HEBREW: HANNA
"grace"

The first wife of Elkanah, a man from the hill country of Ephraim, Hannah was mocked by her husband's second wife, Peninnah, because she had borne no children. Though her husband tried to comfort her, saying, "Why is your heart sad? Am I not more to you than ten sons?" (1 Sam.

1:8), Hannah was mortified by her infertility and often wept or fasted in her distress. Finally, on one of her family's annual pilgrimages to the temple at Shiloh, she made a vow to God that if she was granted a son, she would dedicate him to the Lord for life.

Seeing Hannah moving her lips silently as she prayed, **Eli**, the priest at Shiloh, accused her of drunkenness. But when Hannah protested that she was merely "pouring out my soul before the Lord" (1 Sam. 1:15), Eli blessed her and asked God to grant her petition. Hannah returned home and in time gave birth to a son, whom she named **Samuel**. When her child was weaned, Hannah brought him to Shiloh. There she reminded Eli of their earlier meeting and gave her son over for service to the Lord. The song of Hannah recorded in 1 Samuel 2:1-10 is a precursor of **Mary**'s song of thanksgiving in Luke 1:46-55.

Each year thereafter Hannah visited Samuel, offered a sacrifice at the temple, and gave him a robe to wear. She later bore three other sons and two daughters.

HANUN
(hay' nuhn) HEBREW: HANUN
"favored"
∙∙∙∙∙∙∙∙∙∙

U pon the death of his father, Nahash, Hanun assumed the throne of Ammon, a land northeast of the Dead Sea. When King **David** sent messengers with condolences, Hanun suspected that they were spies and ordered that their beards be shaved half off and their garments cut around the hips—thus robbing them of a symbol of virility and indecently exposing them. The gross insult brought war with David, who defeated the Ammonites and their Syrian allies, enslaved the population, and seems to have placed Hanun's brother Shobi on the throne of Ammon.

HAZEL
(hay' zuh el) HEBREW: HAZAEL
"God has seen"
∙∙∙∙∙∙∙∙∙∙

T he usurper Hazael, king of Syria from about 842 to 800 B.C., was a powerful enemy of the Israelites—ironically chosen for his throne by the Lord, who ordered the prophet **Elijah** to anoint him. Years later, when the Syrian king **Ben-hadad** was ill, he sent his court official Hazael

Hannah with her son Samuel, detail of a painting by Rembrandt

This carved ivory figure adorned Hazael's ninth-century B.C. bed.

with 40 camel loads of gifts in search of the prophet **Elisha** (Elijah's successor) to learn whether he would recover. Although Elisha asked Hazael to tell the king that his health would improve, the prophet revealed that he knew Ben-hadad was to die. Gazing at Hazael, Elisha wept—for the prophet also knew that Hazael would assume power over Syria and wage a ruthless war against Israel. The day after he returned to Damascus with the supposedly good news, Hazael suffocated Ben-hadad with a wet cloth and seized power.

Early in his reign Hazael defeated King **Jehoram** of Israel and King **Ahaziah** of Judah at the battle of Ramoth-gilead and, after deflecting Assyrian attacks from the north in 841 and 837 B.C., returned south to seize Israelite territory east of the Jordan. Eager to gain control of trade routes in Philistia, Hazael next moved down the coast to seize Gath and "set his face to go up against Jerusalem" (2 Kg. 12:17). But he was dissuaded from taking the capital by King **Joash** of Judah, who stripped treasure from the temple and the royal palace and offered it as a bribe.

HEBER

(hee' buhr) HEBREW: HEBER
"associate"
∙∙∙∙∙∙∙∙∙∙

A descendant of **Moses'** father-in-law **Jethro**, Heber lived apart from other Kenites (a nomadic clan closely associated with the Israelites) at the oak in Zaanannim near Kedesh. After the destruction of his army by the prophetess **Deborah** and her commander **Barak, Sisera**, the leader of the Canaanite forces, took sanctuary in Heber's supposedly neutral tent. Thinking he was safe, Sisera fell asleep—only to be assassinated by Heber's wife, **Jael**.

HERMES

(huhr' meez) GREEK: HERMES
"rock" or "cairn"
∙∙∙∙∙∙∙∙∙∙

One of the Olympian deities of the Greeks, Hermes was especially known as the messenger god and herald of **Zeus**, who was both the king of the gods and his father. According to a popular story told by the Latin poet Ovid (who refers to them by their Roman names of Jupiter and Mercury), Zeus and Hermes once descended from their home on Mount Olympus, disguised themselves as humans, and appeared as travelers at the door of a poor elderly couple named Baucis and Philemon. The old people invited the strangers into their home, offering them food. When their modest repast was miraculously increased, the surprised hosts discovered that they were

Winged boots and helmet identify the messenger god Hermes in this fifth-century B.C. painted vase from Greece.

dealing with immortals, who promptly rewarded Baucis and Philemon for their exemplary hospitality.

This pagan tradition lies behind the story in Acts 14:8-18. In response to a healing miracle by **Paul**, the people of Lystra proclaimed, "The gods have come down to us in the likeness of men!" They then designated Paul's coworker **Barnabas** as Zeus and Paul himself, since he was the "chief speaker" (Acts 14:11,12), as Hermes. Paul and Barnabas responded to this unwanted tribute by tearing their garments in despair and going out among the people to preach a sermon on the true nature of God.

HEROD THE GREAT

(hair' uhd) GREEK: HERODES
∙∙∙∙∙∙∙∙∙∙

According to the two Gospels that record the event, the birth of **Jesus** took place during the reign of Herod the Great. Other than to place his narrative "in the days of Herod, king of Judea" (Lk. 1:5), **Luke** tells us nothing about the notorious monarch. Matthew, on the other hand, has more to say about Herod.

After Jesus was born in Bethlehem, Matthew writes, "wise men from the East came to Jerusalem" searching for the one "who has been born king of the Jews" (Mt. 2:1-2). Herod heard of their quest and asked the scribes where the birth might have taken place. They answered by quoting the prophet **Micah**, who had foretold that a new ruler of Israel would come out of "you, O Bethlehem Ephrathah, who are little to be among the clans of Judah" (Mic. 5:2).

Summoning the wise men to determine when the star that guided them had first appeared, Herod was able to calculate the infant's approximate age. With the request that they let him know when they found the child so that he too could come and worship him, he sent the strangers on their way to Bethlehem. But after presenting their gifts, the wise men returned home without notifying Herod, for they had been warned in a dream to avoid him. Fearful of any rival, Herod ordered the death of all male children under the age of two in Bethlehem. Jesus escaped the massacre because **Joseph**, also warned in a dream, had fled with **Mary** and her child to Egypt.

Although historians have found no clear evidence outside the Gospel of Matthew for Herod's slaughter of the children, the story certainly fits the well-known character of Herod, who reigned from 37 to 4 B.C. His importance to the world of the New Testament, however, goes far beyond the meager

The three wise men before Herod, a 14th-century mosaic from the basilica of San Marco in Venice

references in the two Gospels. Herod established a highly successful form of client kingship within the Roman empire and founded a dynasty that dominated Palestinian politics through most of the first century of the Christian era. His rule was one of great prosperity during which magnificent building programs were undertaken, but it was also marred by fierce family quarrels and acts of extreme brutality. And he was never popular with the local populace.

WINNING ROME'S TRUST

To most Jews, Herod was an outsider. His homeland, Idumea, a tribal state located to the south of Judea, had come under the rule of the Hasmonean kingdom of Judea established by the Maccabean revolt in 167 B.C.; and his aristocratic family was among those Idumeans forcibly converted to Judaism during the reign of **John Hyrcanus** (134-104 B.C.). Both Herod's grandfather, Antipater, and his father, also named Antipater, had served as military commanders of Idumea under the Hasmoneans. The second Antipater advanced his career by shrewdly adjusting to changing political currents—a skill he passed on to Herod. Although Antipater was a close adviser to the Hasmonean ruler Hyrcanus II, he successfully switched his allegiance to Rome when Judea was conquered by the legions of Pompey. Then, after

fighting with Julius Caesar in his Egyptian campaign against Pompey in 48-47 B.C., Antipater was granted Roman citizenship and named procurator of Judea. He made his son Herod governor of Galilee. When Antipater was killed by poisoning in 43 B.C., Herod began to emerge as his father's political heir—though he was still under 30.

The young man had made a name for himself by putting down a rebellion in Galilee and suppressing further dissent in Jerusalem. Such actions fit the Roman ideal for their client rulers, for they valued keeping order above all else. In gratitude for his actions, the Roman Senate named Herod king of the Jews. But he was king in name only, since the last Hasmonean ruler Antigonus II, still claimed the throne of

In deference to the Jews, no images appeared on the coins of Herod the Great.

Judea and was backed by the Parthians, who were enemies of Rome.

Meanwhile, a power struggle was under way in Rome to fill the leadership gap left by the assassination of Julius Caesar in 44 B.C. Eventually the contest was narrowed to one between Mark Antony, who was allied with Queen Cleopatra of Egypt, and Julius Caesar's grandnephew and heir, Octavian. Since Antony had established his power base in the eastern Mediterranean and was therefore the Roman leader in control of all regions surrounding Judea, Herod secured his patronage and, with the help of Antony's legions, was able to defeat Antigonus and claim his throne in 37 B.C. Thus began Herod's 33-year rule as king of Judea.

The Jews did not willingly accept Herod's rule, and many of their leaders derisively referred to the king as a half-Jew. Indeed, Herod was neither very well informed about the Jewish religion nor particularly observant. Though he considered himself the protector of the Jews and promoter of their religion—and later spent a great deal of time and money rebuilding the temple—he often took actions that offended the religious sensibilities of the populace. His way of dealing with his alienated subjects was to cow them into obedience—beginning by ordering the execution of 45 Jewish noblemen who still supported Antigonus and seizing their property. He bestowed favors on other potential detractors and eventually won the grudging support of enough Jewish leaders, including important Pharisees, to rule without fear of a serious rebellion.

ALLIANCE BY MARRIAGE

Since they were still regarded respectfully by the populace, the remaining members of the Hasmonean family had to be treated with special care. To create an alliance with the Hasmoneans, Herod took as his second wife Mariamne, a granddaughter of Hyrcanus II. She became not only the great love but also the great tragedy of his life.

The marriage did not entirely resolve Herod's problems with the Hasmoneans. His primary adversary was his mother-in-law, Alexandra, who opposed his appointment of a Jew from Babylonia named Hananel as high priest and proposed her son Aristobulus for the position. After Alexandra won the endorsement of both Cleopatra and Antony, Herod gave in and replaced Hananel with Aristobulus. But the king soon grew jealous of Aristobulus's growing favor with the people and responded to this threat in a way that would become typical of his rule. Inviting the young man for a swim in the palace pool at Jericho,

Herod had his servants drown Aristobulus, but made the death look like an accident and feigned grief at the loss.

Two subsequent events significantly affected Herod's destiny: the outbreak of war between Antony and Octavian in 32 B.C. and a border war with the Nabateans. Herod had wanted to bring his army to the aid of his Roman patron. But, at the instigation of Cleopatra, Antony instead ordered him to fight the Nabateans. When Antony was defeated at the battle of Actium the following year, Herod was suddenly bereft of his primary Roman sponsor.

Once more, Herod displayed his consummate political skill by successfully switching his allegiance from Antony to Octavian. At a meeting he requested with Octavian on Rhodes in 30 B.C., he pointed out that he had not actually joined Antony's side in the civil war and argued that as he had proved himself a good ally of Antony's, so would he be with Octavian. Recognizing Herod's usefulness and accepting his assurance of loyalty to Rome, Octavian allowed Herod to continue as king of Judea. Soon to become the emperor **Augustus**, Octavian later bestowed on Herod additional territories, including those that had once been given to Cleopatra.

With his rule firmly endorsed by Rome, Herod could deal more directly with the problems in his own household. It was characteristic of Herod throughout his long reign to be suspicious of all who surrounded him, including members of his own family, and to be ruthless in dealing with anyone suspected of disloyalty. Many of his advisers had been telling him for some time that his wife Mari-

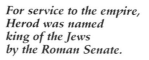

For service to the empire, Herod was named king of the Jews by the Roman Senate.

amne was not to be trusted, for she was a proud, beautiful woman of noble blood who often asserted her will with Herod. Finally, after he had once again received charges that she was unfaithful and had conspired to have him killed—accusations brought this time by his sister Salome—Herod had Mariamne charged with treason and executed in 29 B.C.

The execution of Mariamne became a greater burden for Herod to bear than any other atrocity he committed, for he apparently loved her deeply. Following her death, he spent much time wallowing in self-pity and engaging in extended drinking bouts—activities that soon affected his health. After Herod took to his bed, Alexandra began a campaign to take over her son-in-law's power. But he heard of it and had her put to death as well.

If Herod's first decade in power was marked by ruthlessness and unbridled ambition, the second period of his reign was a time of peace and prosperity as his kingdom and his control of it reached their peaks. During these years—roughly 27 to 13 B.C.—he further solidified his ties with Rome, strengthened his hold over the people, and undertook elaborate building programs throughout his kingdom.

Herod came to exemplify what Rome expected of a client king. Though his people were known to be troublesome and difficult to rule, Herod kept order throughout his kingdom and was rewarded with additional territories, so that his domain eventually reached the size of the Hasmonean kingdom at its greatest extent.

THE KINGDOM OF HEROD THE GREAT

After capturing Jerusalem in 63 B.C., the Roman general Pompey dismembered the Hasmonean kingdom established by the Maccabean revolt. A quarter century later, Herod the Great reassembled the pieces into a sturdy domain that anchored the Roman empire to the eastern shore of the Mediterranean Sea. His kingdom stretched from Galilee in the north through Samaria to Judea and embraced Perea to the east of the Jordan River and his homeland of Idumea southwest of the Dead Sea.

A consummate politician, Herod managed faithfully to serve his Roman masters and skillfully placate his restless Jewish subjects. After the initial struggles to consolidate power, his 33-year reign (37-4 B.C.) was one of stability and general prosperity. This allowed him to undertake ambitious, if not grandiose, building projects—most notably the rebuilding of Jerusalem, but also including the construction of the port city of Caesarea and the rebuilding of the ancient capital of Samaria, which he renamed Sebaste.

Because of his insane jealousy, Herod was unable to pick a single successor. Thus, under the terms of his final will, the Jewish state was once more fragmented. The title king of Judea and the core of Herod's sprawling kingdom went to Archelaus, his son by a Samaritan wife, Malthace. Antipas, Archelaus's younger brother, had to settle for the lesser title of tetrarch (literally, governor of a fourth part of a province) and the two separate territories of Galilee and Perea. Their half brother Herod Philip was named tetrarch of the mainly Gentile areas north and west of the Sea of Galilee (continuing well beyond this map), a large though relatively poor area. Herod's ambitious sister Salome laid claim to the coastal areas around Jamnia and Azotus and the inland city of Phasaelis. Such hellenized cities as Gaza, Gadara, and Hippus were placed under the jurisdiction of the governor of Syria.

0   20 Miles

Archelaus's inheritance
Antipas's inheritance
Philip's inheritance
Salome's inheritance

By controlling all of the major institutions of the Jews, Herod maintained a tight rein on domestic affairs. Early on, he had taken over the appointment of the high priest, an unauthorized and much-resented incursion into the religious affairs of the Jews. To this post he appointed subservient individuals; if they could not be manipulated, he had them deposed or killed. He also took over the Sanhedrin, the Jewish high tribunal, stacking it with his own appointees so that it became a rubber stamp for his own decisions.

Much of the populace was grateful to Herod for the stability of his regime if not devoted to or trustful of him. Pious Jews, in particular, never accepted him as a legitimate ruler, considering him to be a pagan usurper of the Jewish throne. Yet, the pagans under his rule also resented him, because they perceived him as a Jew who played favorites with his Jewish constituency. In actuality, Herod in many ways tried to mollify the Jewish majority under his rule. In deference to Jewish restrictions on graven images, he avoided placing human or animal images on his coins. He is even said to have forbidden the women in his family to marry any man who would not submit to circumcision.

In other respects Herod, like most of the Jewish aristocracy, was quite hellenized—that is, he leaned toward Greek culture. Most of his closest advisers were men of Greek education, and Herod sent his sons to Rome to be educated in the Greek and Roman manner. Locally, Herod sought favor with the pagan subjects of his realm by building pagan temples in predominantly Greek cities. Herod, however, was a study in contrasts. Though he followed strict Pharisaic restrictions in rebuilding the temple in Jerusalem, he allowed a Roman eagle to be placed at the temple gate—his lapse causing a great uproar. Such inconsistencies served to support the general perception that Herod's espousal of Judaism was simply a political convenience.

OUTDOING SOLOMON

Herod's true legacy, however, was not to be political but rather architectural, for he spent lavishly to make his kingdom one of the finest in the ancient world. The cities of the New Testament in which Jesus and his disciples walked had been reconstructed on a magnificent scale: Public buildings were placed everywhere; splendid palaces and villas for the king dotted the countryside; and a variety of temples—including especially the temple of the Jews in Jerusalem—were remodeled or built anew.

Herod extensively renovated his capital, Jerusalem, and there he placed the jewel in his architectural crown, the temple that Jesus first visited at the age of 12 and to which he returned during his final days. The first temple on the site, built by **Solomon**, had been destroyed by the Babylonians in 586 B.C. The second temple, a modest structure begun in 520 B.C. under the leadership of **Zerubbabel** after the return from exile, had fallen into disrepair by Herod's time. Herod's ambitious renovation resulted in a substantially new structure; in Jesus' day it had come to be known as Herod's temple.

Since Herod was careful to follow biblical injunctions in his rebuilding project, the actual temple structure was limited to its traditional size, small by the standards of the period. But the temple mount, the stone platform on which the temple and its associated structures were built, was of massive size and made the complex truly an architectural marvel of its day. Part of the Herodian temple mount still survives in the form of the so-called Wailing Wall, where pious Jews to this day gather to mourn the temple's destruction in A.D. 70 by the Romans.

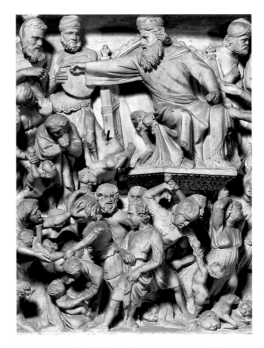

Herod ordering the massacre of the innocents, detail from a 14th-century marble carving from the cathedral of Siena

Augustus had granted Herod the rare privilege of naming his own successor, and the last decade of the king's reign was marred by intrigue among his sons and other relatives vying for the throne. Herod married ten times and had children by all his wives (see The Family of Herod, page 145). Although such multiple marriages were not considered unlawful at the time, Herod's actions were nevertheless considered inappropriate. The eventual contenders for the crown were Antipater, his eldest son by his first wife, Doris; Alexander and Aristobulus, sons of his second and favorite wife, the Hasmonean princess Mariamne, whom he had executed; **Herod Archelaus** and **Herod Antipas**, sons of his Samaritan wife, Malthace; and **Herod Philip**, son of his fifth wife, Cleopatra of Jerusalem.

THE STRUGGLE FOR SUCCESSION

Favorites of their father, Alexander and Aristobulus were sent to Rome to be educated. After their return, the two appeared to enjoy a special status with the people because of their Hasmonean blood. This aroused the jealousy of Antipater and of Herod's sister and brother, Salome and Pheroras. The three conspired against the two brothers, whose ill-concealed resentment against Herod for killing their mother did not help their cause. Finally succumbing to the pressures from their rivals, Herod brought charges of treason against Alexander and Aristobulus before the emperor. The fortunes of the two brothers fluctuated wildly until Herod got the emperor's permission to deal as he wished with his troublesome sons. In 7 B.C. he had the two tried before a Roman tribunal; found guilty of treason, they were executed by strangulation. Meanwhile, Herod had named Antipater as his heir in 13 B.C., in the second of what would be six wills.

Although Antipater was heir apparent, his fortunes too rose and fell. But the unraveling of his alliance with Salome and Pheroras proved to be his undoing. Salome, perhaps hoping to put her own son on the throne, fanned Herod's suspicions of his eldest son. And when Pheroras died of poison supposedly intended for Herod himself, Antipater was accused, recalled from Rome, where he was lobbying for confirmation of his succession, tried and convicted of the crime, and placed in prison to await execution. Herod, in his 70's and in failing health, changed his will again to name Antipas as his sole heir. Then, just days before his own death, Herod had Antipater executed and made a sixth and final will, dividing his kingdom among three of his sons rather than choosing a sole successor. He named Archelaus king of Judea; Antipas tetrarch of Galilee and Perea; and their half brother Philip tetrarch of Gaulanitis, Trachonitis, Batanea, and Paneas. The administration of the will was entrusted to Augustus.

"I would rather be Herod's pig than his son," Augustus is supposed to have said. Whoever made it, the remark accurately reflects Herod's complex character. Because of the Jewish prohibition, he refused to eat pork. Yet his reputation for vicious dealings with members of his own family was widely known. Herod considered himself the legitimate king of the Jews and took pride in his protection of the Jewish religion, land, and people. By most objective standards, his rule would have been considered highly successful and prosperous. Yet, in the end, his excesses outshone his accomplishments—for what lingered most about Herod in the memory of Romans, Jews, and Christians alike was his ruthless ambition and barbaric cruelty.

HEROD AGRIPPA I

(uh' grip uh) GREEK: AGRIPPAS

⋅⋅⋅⋅⋅⋅⋅⋅⋅⋅

As a child, Herod Agrippa I was sent to Rome to be educated at the imperial court, following the execution of his father Aristobulus and shortly before the death in 4 B.C. of his grandfather, **Herod the Great**, who had ordered the execution. In Rome he made important political connections, especially with two future emperors, Caligula and **Claudius**.

Agrippa's early business ventures in Rome met with little success, and at one point he had to return to Judea to seek help from **Herod Antipas**, who had married his sister **Herodias**. But Agrippa was humiliated by the dependence on his brother-in-law and went back to Rome. His fortunes improved after Caligula became emperor in A.D. 37, for his old friend named him king over the former tetrarchies of **Lysanias** and **Herod Philip**. Three years later Caligula awarded him Galilee and Perea, regions belonging to the tetrarchy of Herod Antipas, who had been deposed and exiled in A.D. 39. After the assassination of Caligula in A.D. 41, Agrippa aided Claudius in gaining the imperial throne; and the new emperor further increased Agrippa's kingdom by giving him the provinces of Judea and Samaria. Thus, Agrippa came to rule over virtually the same territory as had his grandfather, uniting these lands for the first time in nearly half a century.

As a ruler, Agrippa seems to have honored Jewish traditions and pursued a policy of Jewish nationalism. In the Bible, however, he is more infamously known as a persecutor of the early Christians, one who "laid violent hands upon some who belonged to the church" (Acts 12:1). He ordered the execution of **James** the son of **Zebedee** and, seeing this pleased the Jews, arrested and imprisoned **Peter**.

In A.D. 44, at the age of 54, Agrippa died suddenly in Caesarea after he had made a public appearance with great pomp and had been acclaimed by the crowds as a god. Both the Jewish historian Josephus and **Luke** in Acts attribute Agrippa's death to divine punishment brought on by his excessive pride, the latter noting that "he was eaten by worms" (Acts 12:23) before his untimely death.

Unlike Herod the Great, Herod Agrippa I (top) and Herod Agrippa II allowed portraits on their coins.

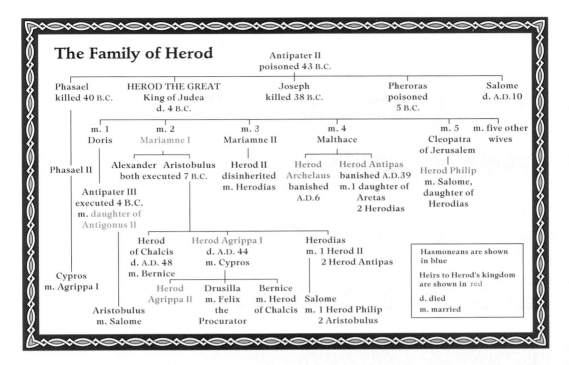

The Family of Herod

Antipater II
poisoned 43 B.C.

Phasael	HEROD THE GREAT	Joseph	Pheroras	Salome
killed 40 B.C.	King of Judea	killed 38 B.C.	poisoned	d. A.D.10
	d. 4 B.C.		5 B.C.	

m. 1 Doris — m. 2 Mariamne I — m. 3 Mariamne II — m. 4 Malthace — m. 5 Cleopatra of Jerusalem — m. five other wives

Phasael II

Alexander Aristobulus
both executed 7 B.C.

Antipater III
executed 4 B.C.
m. daughter of
Antigonus II

Herod II
disinherited
m. Herodias

Herod
Archelaus
banished
A.D.6

Herod Antipas
banished A.D.39
m.1 daughter of
Aretas
2 Herodias

Herod Philip
m. Salome,
daughter of
Herodias

Herod
of Chalcis
d. A.D. 48
m. Bernice

Herod Agrippa I
d. A.D. 44
m. Cypros

Herodias
m. 1 Herod II
2 Herod Antipas

Cypros
m. Agrippa I

Herod
Agrippa II

Drusilla
m. Felix
the
Procurator

Bernice
m. Herod
of Chalcis

Salome
m. 1 Herod Philip
2 Aristobulus

Aristobulus
m. Salome

> Hasmoneans are shown in blue
>
> Heirs to Herod's kingdom are shown in red
>
> d. died
> m. married

HEROD AGRIPPA II

Like his father **Herod Agrippa I**, Marcus Julius Agrippa (to give him his Roman name) was raised in the imperial court at Rome. When his father died suddenly in A.D. 44, Agrippa was only 17 and, according to the emperor **Claudius**, too young to inherit the kingdom, which instead was placed under direct Roman administration. Six years later, however, Claudius named the young man ruler of Chalcis, a small kingdom in present-day Lebanon; the previous king, Herod of Chalcis, was Agrippa's uncle and also the husband of his sister **Bernice**. Then, in A.D. 53, Agrippa surrendered Chalcis in order to receive the tetrarchies formerly held by **Herod Philip** and **Lysanias**. In A.D. 61 the emperor Nero, Claudius's successor, granted him portions of Galilee and Perea as well.

Herod Agrippa II appears in the book of Acts as one of the rulers before whom the apostle **Paul** defended himself. About A.D. 56, Paul was arrested in Jerusalem for inciting a riot. He presented his defense first before the Jewish Sanhedrin in Jerusalem, next before the Roman procurator Antonius **Felix** in Caesarea, then two years later before Felix's successor Porcius **Festus**. Since Agrippa and his sister Bernice, who had come to live with him following the death of her husband, were visiting Caesarea, Festus informed them of the case. "I should like to hear the man myself" (Acts 25:22), Agrippa told the procurator. The next day Paul was brought before them so that they could help Festus decide what charges were to be pressed against the apostle.

Paul's defense included a review of his life with an emphasis on his conversion and his call to preach to the Gentiles. But he opened with an appeal to Agrippa's knowledge of Jewish customs and closed with a rhetorical question: "King Agrippa, do you believe the prophets? I know that you believe." Agrippa was so favorably impressed that he replied, "In a short time you think to make me a Christian!" (Acts 26:27-28). Agrippa recommended that Paul be released, agreeing with the governor that Paul deserved neither death nor imprisonment. But, since the apostle had already appealed to Caesar, he had to go to Rome for final judgment.

In Rome under Claudius, Agrippa had defended Jewish causes, and later, as king in Jerusalem, he undertook costly improvement of the temple. However, his true loyalty was to Rome. When the Jews rebelled against Rome in A.D. 66, Agrippa, like many other Jewish leaders, judiciously sided with the Romans. After the rebellion had been suppressed, Agrippa was rewarded with additional territories to expand his kingdom. Although he continued to rule until his death in A.D. 93, Agrippa lived in Rome for much of his last two decades. Bernice, with whom Agrippa is said to have had an incestuous affair, was for a time the mistress of the Roman emperor Titus. Since Agrippa never married and was childless, he was the last of the Herodian dynasty.

Jesus brought before Herod Antipas, by Duccio di Buoninsegna (c. 1255-1319)

HEROD ANTIPAS

(an' ti puhs) GREEK: ANTIPAS

When **Herod the Great** died in 4 B.C., the Roman emperor **Augustus** ratified Herod's final will dividing the kingdom among three of Herod's sons: the brothers **Herod Archelaus** and Herod Antipas and their half brother **Herod Philip**, also known as Philip the tetrarch. Raised in Rome along with Archelaus, Antipas was once favored to succeed his father but he had to share the kingdom, his portion being Galilee and Perea. Antipas is the Herod who is most prominent in the Gospels during the ministry of **Jesus**—though he is sometimes called king rather than tetrarch, his actual title.

Antipas's reign was marked by ambitious building programs and a general strengthening of the region. Although he complied with some of the tenets of Judaism, he built his new capital, Tiberias, on an old burial ground, making it unclean for devout Jews; he also decorated his palace with animal figures in defiance of the law. He further invited political strife and scandal by divorcing his first wife, the daughter of King **Aretas** of Nabatea, and marrying **Hero-**

dias, the wife of a half brother. The marriage was not only greatly criticized by the populace, it also incurred the wrath of Aretas and prompted a border war, which Antipas lost.

The union with Herodias also led to conflict with **John the Baptist**, who told the tetrarch, "It is not lawful for you to have your brother's wife" (Mk. 6:18). In his denunciation, John was holding the Herodian family subject to Jewish law that clearly stated, "If a man takes his brother's wife, it is impurity" (Lev. 20:21). John's accusation especially angered Herodias, who prevailed upon Antipas to seize the Baptist and imprison him. However, because of John's popularity with the people, Antipas resisted his wife's demand that John be executed. Soon afterward, Antipas gave a feast celebrating his birthday and was so entranced by the dance of Herodias's daughter **Salome** that he promised the girl anything she wanted. Prompted by her mother, Salome asked for John's head on a platter. Antipas "was exceedingly sorry; but because of his oaths and his guests he did not want to break his word to her" (Mk. 6:26). After receiving the head of John, Salome gave the grisly trophy to her mother.

When Antipas first heard of Jesus' ministry, he feared that John had been raised from the dead. Later, learning that Antipas was bent on killing him too, Jesus sent a message to "that fox" that he would continue to cast out demons and heal the sick until "I finish my course" (Lk. 13:32). After his arrest, Jesus appeared before Antipas. According to **Luke**, the Roman prefect **Pilate** learned that Jesus was from Galilee and therefore technically under the jurisdiction of Herod Antipas, who was in Jerusalem for the Passover. Pilate sent Jesus to Antipas to be judged. "When Herod [Antipas] saw Jesus," Luke reports, "he was very glad for he had long desired to see him, because he had heard about him, and he was hoping to see some sign done by him" (Lk. 23:8). Although Antipas questioned Jesus extensively, he got no answer. But after the chief priests and scribes bitterly denounced Jesus, Antipas and his soldiers "treated him with contempt and mocked him" (Lk.

23:11). Arraying Jesus in apparel befitting one who was accused of claiming to be the king of the Jews, Antipas sent the prisoner back to the prefect—refusing to pass judgment himself. Ominously, Luke notes that Herod Antipas and Pilate became friends from that day, thus implying the tetrarch's complicity in the prefect's ensuing sentencing of Jesus.

Though he was responsible for the death of John and was possibly a coconspirator in the death of Jesus, Antipas is nevertheless treated in the Gospels as something of a tragic figure. When he arrested John the Baptist, he is said to have done so under pressure from Herodias. When he was tricked into beheading John, he is said to have done so reluctantly. And his initial reaction to Jesus was favorable, though he ended up mocking him and sending him back to Pilate for eventual execution.

When Caligula succeeded **Tiberius** as emperor of Rome in A.D. 37, Herodias's brother **Herod Agrippa I** was given the title of king over certain regions bordering Galilee. Jealous of the younger man's advancement, Antipas departed for Rome to seek the same title for himself. Instead, he was discredited by Agrippa, who accused him of treason against the emperor. In A.D. 39 Antipas was deposed and exiled to southern France. Though Caligula spared

Herodias because of her relationship to his favorite, Agrippa, she joined her husband in an exile from which they never returned. What remained of the tetrarchy of Antipas was added to Agrippa's kingdom.

HEROD ARCHELAUS
(ahr kuh lay' uhs) GREEK: ARCHELAOS

In his last will, written only five days before his death in the spring of 4 B.C., **Herod the Great** named his eldest surviving son, Archelaus, as principal heir to his kingdom—though alloting two other sons, **Herod Antipas** and **Herod Philip**, portions of the domain. Archelaus sailed for Rome—as did Antipas—to dispute the will before Roman emperor **Augustus**. Although the emperor confirmed Archelaus's largest share, he withheld the title of king, naming him instead ethnarch, a less prestigious title used for a local ruler appointed to govern on Rome's behalf. Significantly, however, Galilee was not included in his domain.

In the only reference to Archelaus in the New Testament, **Joseph** hears that he has succeeded his father as ruler of Judea and "afraid to go there . . . [Joseph] withdrew to the district of Galilee" (Mt. 2:22), where he settled in the city of Nazareth. Archelaus, it seems, was more threatening to Joseph than

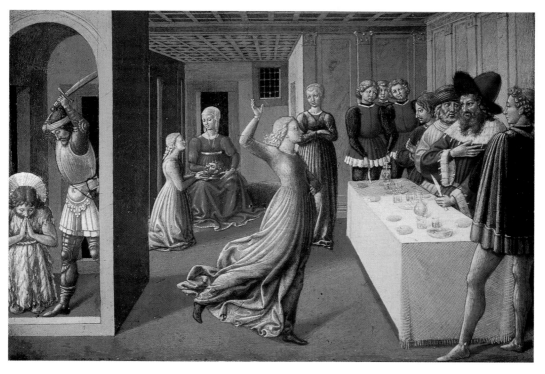

Having won John's execution (left) with her dance (right), Salome presents the Baptist's head to her mother (background).

Herodias with her grisly trophy

Herod Antipas, who had been awarded Galilee. And so, as Matthew notes, **Jesus** would be known as the Nazarene, in fulfillment of an Old Testament prophecy.

Of all Herod's successor sons, Archelaus was the most brutal, at the very outset of his reign suppressing an incipient rebellion at the cost of 3,000 lives. In time, he so alienated the populace that a delegation of Jews and Samaritans brought charges against him before the emperor. Summoning Archelaus to Rome, Augustus deposed and banished him to Gaul in A.D. 6. His kingdom was reduced to a Roman province and placed under the rule of a prefect, a Roman governor usually chosen from the imperial equestrian ranks.

HERODIAS

(her oh' dee uhs) GREEK: HERODIAS

A granddaughter of **Herod the Great** and the sister of **Herod Agrippa I**, Herodias married her paternal half uncle Herod II (whom Matthew and Mark call Philip and seem to identify with **Herod Philip** the tetrarch) and bore him a daughter, **Salome**. But she deserted her first husband to marry another half uncle, **Herod Antipas**. This union was condemned by **John the Baptist**, who said to Antipas, "It is not lawful for you to have her" (Mt. 14:4).

Infuriated by the Baptist's accusation, Herodias sought to have John killed. But Antipas hesitated because of John's popularity. She got her wish, however, as a result of a notorious incident at Antipas's birthday feast. Antipas was so taken by Salome's dance at the banquet that he promised to give her whatever she wished. After consulting with her mother, Salome asked for the head of John the Baptist—which Antipas gave her and which she presented to her mother. The first-century A.D. Jewish historian Josephus also held Antipas responsible for the death of John, but he did not mention the banquet scene or the complicity of Herodias and Salome.

Herodias encouraged Antipas to go to Rome to seek advancement commensurate with that of her brother, Agrippa I. But instead of advancing him, the emperor Caligula deposed her husband and banished him to southern France in A.D. 39. Although the emperor offered to spare her, Herodias chose exile with her husband and there disappears from the pages of history.

HEROD PHILIP

GREEK: PHILIPPOS

A lso known as Philip the tetrarch, Herod Philip was a son of **Herod the Great** by his fifth wife, Cleopatra of Jerusalem. Upon the death of Herod in 4 B.C., the emperor **Augustus**—as administrator of the old king's will—divided the kingdom among Philip and two of his half brothers, **Herod Archelaus** and **Herod Antipas**. Philip's portion was the territories northeast of the Sea of Galilee largely inhabited by non-Jews.

According to the Jewish historian Josephus, Philip was married to **Salome**, the daughter of **Herodias**. In the Gospels of Matthew and Mark, however, it is not the husband but the father of Salome who is named Philip. This individual, the first husband of Herodias and a half brother of her second husband, Antipas, is simply called Herod by Josephus. After many attempts to dispel the confusion, scholars have come to believe that Herodias's first husband was Herod II, a son of Herod the Great by his third wife, Mariamne.

Philip the tetrarch is mentioned in the Gospel of Luke as one of the local rulers in the time of the emperor **Tiberius**, when **John the Baptist** began preaching in the wilderness. His long and peaceful reign—he died in A.D. 34, leaving no heirs—was noted for two building projects. He enlarged a settlement near the source of the Jordan River and renamed it Caesarea Philippi; there **Peter** professed the messiahship of **Jesus** and was given the charge to found the church.

Philip also rebuilt the fishing village of Bethsaida close to where the Jordan empties into the Sea of Galilee and renamed it Julias. Near this town, Jesus fed the 5,000 and restored the sight of a blind man.

HEZEKIAH

(hez uh kai' uh) HEBREW: HIZQIYAHU
"Yahweh strengthens"
••••••••••

Coming to the throne of Judah in 715 B.C., at a time when the southern kingdom was subservient to Assyria, Hezekiah spent much of his 29-year reign struggling to regain his nation's independence and to purge its religion of pagan elements. His father and predecessor, **Ahaz**, had not only taken gold from the temple and palaces of Jerusalem to pay in tribute to Assyria, but had also brought the worship of Canaanite gods to his nation—giving homage to them, the prophets **Isaiah** and **Micah** implied, out of conviction as much as out of necessity. But unlike his father, Hezekiah was a faithful adherent of the ancient Israelite religion, one who "held fast to the Lord; he did not depart from following him" (2 Kg. 18:6).

Hezekiah's first political test came only a year after his succession to the throne at the age of 25. Encouraged by Egypt, which was always eager to counter Assyrian influence in the region, the Philistine city of Ashdod withheld tribute demanded by its Assyrian overlords, and other Philistine cities followed suit. But Hezekiah wisely refused to join in the rebellion, heeding the counsel of Isaiah, who dramatically stripped off his clothing and walked naked and barefoot around Jerusalem as a demonstration of what would happen to the people when King **Sargon** of Assyria exacted his vengeance.

Having avoided a military catastrophe, Hezekiah turned to religious reform, ordering his scribes to copy out a collection of proverbs attributed to **Solomon** (now incorporated in the book of Proverbs) and reinstituting the traditional levitical musical services in the temple. But he did not dare expel

Two Judeans of Lachish led by their Assyrian captor, detail from a bas-relief at Sennacherib's palace in Nineveh

the Canaanite cult from his capital, which could have sparked open rebellion in the kingdom, and he diplomatically retained the great pagan altar that Ahaz had erected in the temple.

The king did, however, rid the temple of various other pagan elements that had been introduced. An ancient bronze serpent that, it was believed, dated back to the time of **Moses** and before which the Israelites customarily burned incense was removed and broken into pieces. He also cleared the temple of wooden images of the Canaanite fertility goddess Asherah, and resanctified for sacrifice to the Lord the altar and temple utensils that had been used in pagan worship. To ensure the primacy of the temple, Hezekiah destroyed the "high places and the altars" (2 Chr. 31:1) throughout the land and sent messages inviting Israelites living outside the boundaries of his own kingdom to return to worship at the temple.

But Hezekiah could not ignore the ever-present danger of Assyria. Only a few years before he succeeded Ahaz, an Assyrian army had attacked Israel and, after a long siege of its capital, Samaria, had destroyed the northern kingdom and sent its inhabitants into exile. To avoid a similar fate, Judah was required to pay an enormous tribute to Assyria; it would have been disastrous to skip paying it for even a year. Yet slowly and cautiously, Hezekiah prepared for his own independence.

In the year 705 Sargon was killed in battle, to be succeeded on the throne of Assyria by his son **Sennacherib**. As Assyria's vassals rose in rebellion again, Hezekiah decided that the time had come to join them. He sent ambassadors to Egypt to negotiate a treaty of support and formed alliances with rebellious Phoenician and Philistine cities. In the year 701 B.C., Sennacherib embarked on a campaign to put down the rebels. He marched an army westward and south along the Mediterranean coast, where he ousted the king of Tyre, a leader of the anti-Assyrian coalition. Everywhere along his army's route, rebel kingdoms surrendered.

Only three held out: the Philistine cities of Ashkelon and Ekron and Hezekiah's Judah. Just as the allies had hoped, an Egyptian army headed north to rescue them. But the Assyrians met and defeated it and subjugated both rebellious Philistine cities. Hezekiah stood alone.

The resourceful king of Judah had been making his kingdom ready for the inevitable Assyrian onslaught. Among the measures he took was building a tunnel—some 1,750 feet long and cut through solid rock—to carry spring water to a pool inside Jerusalem's walls so that the city could withstand a siege. It was one of the greatest engineering feats of antiquity.

The king not only arranged to have water in his own capital, but also took measures to make sure that the invading Assyrian army went without it, ordering wells and springs stopped up throughout Judah. He strengthened Jerusalem's walls and built up stocks of armaments, ordering "weapons and shields in abundance" (2 Chr. 32:5). The Assyrian army's march southward is recorded in Sennacherib's annals: "As to Hezekiah, I laid siege to 46 of his strong cities and conquered them by means of well-stamped earth ramps and battering rams. Himself I made a prisoner in Jerusalem, his royal residence, like a bird in a cage."

One of Sennacherib's conquests was the well-fortified Judean town of Lachish. Assyrian bas-reliefs show the campaign against Lachish, with defenders on the wall shooting arrows at the attackers and Assyrian bowmen, protected by body-size wicker shields, climbing a ramp to the city gate.

Isaiah points to the sun's shadow miraculously moving back up the steps as a sign God has spared the ailing King Hezekiah from death.

With Hezekiah trapped, Sennacherib demanded and received a sizable tribute—according to 2 Kings 18:14, 300 talents of silver and 30 talents of gold. To pay it, Hezekiah had to strip gold from the temple doors and doorposts. Assyrian annals record an even larger tribute. Both sources agree on the gold but Sennacherib claimed that he also received 800 talents of silver, plus precious stones and other treasures—including Hezekiah's daughters.

After his men had finished off Lachish, Sennacherib sent reinforcements to the army besieging Jerusalem. Commanding these troops were three officials: a man the Bible calls Tartan (the Assyrian word for commander in chief is *turtanu*); the chief eunuch, Rabsaris; and Sennacherib's chief steward, Rabshakeh. These three men held a parley with Hezekiah's officials outside Jerusalem's walls, urging them to surrender. Failure to do so, they were warned, would bring destruction to the city. Many of Jerusalem's inhabitants stationed themselves on the city walls to watch the encounter and to find out what was going on. To guard their morale and keep them from understanding the negotiations, Hezekiah's officials urged the Assyrians to speak Aramaic, the diplomatic language of the day. But the Assyrians failed to oblige. Rabshakeh "called out in a loud voice in the language of Judah [Hebrew]: . . . . 'Do not let Hezekiah deceive you, for he will not be able to deliver you out of my hand'" (2 Kg. 18:28-29). He urged the people of Jerusalem to make a separate agreement with him and be taken to a land of plenty where they would live, not die. But they remained silent as Hezekiah had ordered.

The Assyrians may have been bluffing, perhaps unwilling to repeat the siege of Samaria, the capital of Israel, which had lasted three years. All they really wanted to do was to collect tribute and leave. The prophet Isaiah assured Hezekiah that the Assyrians "shall not come into this city or shoot an arrow there, or come before it with a shield or cast up a siege mound against it" (2 Kg. 19:32). And indeed, an angel of the Lord came in the night and killed 185,000 Assyrian soldiers. Sennacherib was forced to abandon his siege and flee.

Biblical scholars have vigorously debated the origin of this story. Some claim that it should be dated long after 701 B.C., to the year 688, when the Assyrians returned. These scholars maintain that the verses describing the miraculous destruction of the Assyrian army somehow got attached to the story of Sennacherib's earlier siege of Jerusalem. The Greek historian Herodotus relates a tantalizingly similar tale. According to him, Sennacherib's army, heading toward Egypt, was stopped by a plague of mice that attacked it at the frontier. It has been suggested that the mice were really plague-bearing rats and that the army was stricken by bubonic plague.

Meanwhile, Hezekiah's son **Manasseh** had been named coregent at the age of 12 in 697 or 696 B.C. And the old king was enjoying a new lease on life. Having fallen ill and been told by Isaiah that he would die, Hezekiah prayed to be spared, reminding the Lord "how I have walked before thee in faithfulness and with a whole heart, and have done what is good in thy sight" (Is. 38:3). Speaking through the prophet, God granted the faithful Hezekiah 15 more years of life and promised to defend Jerusalem against the Assyrians. As a sign of his favor, the Lord made the setting sun's shadow retreat up the steps on which it had fallen.

HIEL

(hai' uhl) HEBREW: HIEL
"God is brother"

After the walls of Jericho had fallen down, **Joshua** placed a curse on "the man that rises up and rebuilds this city" (Jos. 6:26). He added the prediction that the firstborn and youngest son of anyone who defied the curse would die in punishment for the deed. Centuries later, during the reign of King **Ahab** of Israel, a man of Bethel named Hiel ventured to defy the curse and rebuild Jericho—but only "at the cost of" (1 Kg. 16:34) two of his sons. The phrase implies a payment, suggesting that the sons were foundation sacrifices, ritually killed in keeping with Canaanite customs. Whether or not this was the case, Joshua's curse was fulfilled.

HILKIAH

(hil kai' uh) HEBREW: HILQIYAHU
"Yahweh is my portion"

When the temple was being repaired by order of Judah's King **Josiah**, the high priest Hilkiah discovered the lost book of the Law and sent it to the monarch. As it was read to him, Josiah "rent his clothes" (2 Kg. 22:11), seeing how far current practice had diverged from the ancient Israelite religion. At his command, Hilkiah cleared **Solomon**'s temple of all traces of pagan worship. The scribe **Ezra**, who labored to establish orthodoxy after the return of the Israelites from Babylon, was a descendant of Hilkiah.

HIRAM

(hi' ruhm) HEBREW: AHIRAM
"my brother [god] is exalted"
··········

An ally of the Israelites, Hiram ruled the Phoenician port city of Tyre from 970 to 936 B.C. With no external threat from Mesopotamia or Egypt, his kingdom prospered; and wealth from trade with colonies on Cyprus, Sicily, and Sardinia allowed Hiram to enlarge and beautify his city and its many temples.

When King **David** built a palace in Jerusalem, he relied on Hiram for its construction, importing both timber and carpenters who knew how to work it. Upon succeeding his father, **Solomon** asked help from Hiram (called Huram in 2 Chronicles) in building a house for the Lord: "As you dealt with David my father and sent him cedar to build himself a house to dwell in, so deal with me" (2 Chr. 2:3). In exchange for Israel's agricultural products, Hiram sent

Judith about to lop off the head of Holofernes, by Donatello (c. 1386-1466)

rafts of cedar and cypress logs south along the seacoast from Tyre. The cedar was used to build the walls and rafters of Solomon's temple; the cypress, its floor. As a result of such extravagant construction projects, Solomon apparently ran short of cash and had to cede 20 cities to Hiram in exchange for 120 talents of gold (a sum worth perhaps $3.6 million dollars).

Solomon's fortunes greatly improved after Hiram furnished him with Phoenician sailors, "seamen who were familiar with the sea" (1 Kg. 9:27), to man a new fleet that was built and based at Ezion-Geber on the Gulf of Aqabah. From that port, Solomon's ships sailed down the Red Sea to the mysterious land of Ophir—its location remains unknown—to bring back gold, precious stones, ivory, rare wood, and exotic animals. These trading voyages greatly enriched Solomon's Jerusalem as they had previously enriched Hiram's Tyre.

HIRAM 2
··········

Variously called Hiram, Huram, or Huram-abi, and not to be confused with **Hiram**, king of Tyre, this skilled artisan was brought from Tyre to work on King **Solomon**'s temple. He cast in bronze two pillars, called Jachin ("God will create") and Boaz ("come, O strong one"), to be placed at the vestibule; the "molten sea" mounted on 12 oxen in which the priests washed; 10 stands for washbasins; and so many vessels that "the weight of the bronze was not found out" (1 Kg. 7:43, 47).

HOLOFERNES

(hol uh fur' neez) GREEK: OLOPHERNES
··········

In a tale dating from long after the events it describes, the general Holofernes leads an army of 120,000 infantrymen and 12,000 cavalry to enforce both the rule and the worship of **Nebuchadnezzar** in the lands between the Red and Mediterranean seas. (Nebuchadnezzar is mistakenly identified in the apocryphal book of Judith, where the story is found, as an Assyrian rather than a neo-Babylonian king.)

When Holofernes invades Judah, a beautiful and pious widow named **Judith** puts aside her mourning clothes, bedecks herself in finery, and makes her way to the enemy camp. There she offers to guide the general past her people's defenses, but instead he invites her into his tent to "drink wine and be merry" (Jdt. 12:13). After Holofernes falls asleep from too much drink, Judith takes

THE TRINITY

Controversies over the nature of God first broke out in the second century, as Christians tried to reconcile New Testament references to Jesus and the Holy Spirit as God with the ancient belief in only one God, monotheism. Some defended monotheism by asserting that Jesus was a human being adopted by the one God as his son; others held that the one God manifests himself in different modes as Father, Son, and Spirit. In the third century both ideas were rejected by Tertullian, who spoke of a "trinity" consisting of three persons of one substance. But the most strenuous debate was only beginning.

A teacher named Arius asserted that the Son was begotten by God before creation but had not always existed and thus was not fully divine. Bishop Athanasius of Alexandria adamantly opposed Arius, holding that Father and Son were of identical substance and the Son was fully divine and eternal.

The first ecumenical council, meeting at Nicaea in A.D. 325, rejected Arius and confirmed Athanasius's view, but many ambiguities remained. Eastern theologians tended to emphasize the three persons; western theologians, the one deity. But all agreed that both must somehow, paradoxically be affirmed. St. Augustine wrote, "The Father is God, the Son is God, the Holy Spirit is God . . . yet we do not say that there are three gods, but one God, the most exalted Trinity itself."

A 13th-century enamel and copper gilt dove to hold the Eucharist

---

his sword and cuts off his head. Upon discovery of their general's headless body, the Assyrian army flees, and Judith's countrymen repossess their land.

HOLY SPIRIT

HEBREW: RUACH; GREEK: PNEUMA
"breath" or "wind"
••••••••••

The word spirit literally means "breath" or "wind," but it can be used to refer metaphorically to a variety of nonbodily entities, including the human spirit and unclean spirits. When it is specified in the Bible as the Holy Spirit, or the Spirit of God, however, it refers to a particular manifestation of the Deity. It is the Spirit of God that is said to animate creation, including humankind; to inspire the prophets and other leaders; and in general to empower individuals or communities with abilities they would not otherwise possess in order to bring about the will of God. Depending on needs and circumstances, God's will can be accomplished in different ways. Consequently, the manifestation of the Holy Spirit can vary; persons who are filled with the Holy Spirit experience a wide variety of phenomena.

The concept of the Holy Spirit grows and develops throughout the Bible. In the Old Testament, the Spirit is usually identical with the activity of God. It is only in the New Testament that the Holy Spirit begins to take on the sense of a person who can be referred to as he. This development reaches its culmination in the doctrine of the three persons of the Trinity formulated in the early centuries of Christianity.

Although the term Holy Spirit is rare in the Old Testament—occurring only three times (Psalms 51:11; Isaiah 63:10, 11)—it is understood to be equivalent to the much more common Spirit of God, which imbues Israel's heroes with extraordinary powers. Thus, when **Othniel** became a judge of Israel, it is said that "the Spirit of the Lord came upon him" (Jg. 3:10). So also **Samson** was able to accomplish his renowned deeds when "the Spirit of the Lord came mightily upon him" (Jg. 14:6, 19; 15:14). It is the Holy Spirit that also confirmed the kings of Israel. When **Samuel** anointed **David**, "the Spirit of the Lord came mightily upon [him]." But since the Spirit "departed from Saul" (1 Sam. 16:13,14) at the same time, kingship is seen as a divine right to rule, bestowed or withdrawn from an individual at the will of God.

As prominent figures filled with the Holy Spirit, the Old Testament prophets represented the will of God to the people and their

The Holy Spirit in the form of a dove at the Annunciation to Mary

rulers and addressed his words to them. "I am filled with power, with the Spirit of the Lord, and with justice and might," the prophet **Micah** proclaimed, "to declare to Jacob his transgression and to Israel his sin" (Mic. 3:8). Thus, the prophet, like the judge and the king, is a hero called forth by God and fortified by his Spirit to guide the people to his will. These spirit-empowered heroes of the Bible are characters in a larger drama, the history of God's chosen people. In some cases, the community itself is said to be filled with the Spirit. For example, God "put in the midst of them his holy Spirit" in order to lead his people and make for them "a glorious name" (Is. 63:11, 14). But the dominant way in which the Spirit is present in the community is through leaders called forth by God—namely, the judges, kings, and prophets.

The connection of the Holy Spirit with the king, as seen in the story of David's anointing, became a part of Israel's messianic expectations. The prophet **Joel** speaks an oracle of God about the day when "I will pour out my spirit on all flesh; your sons and your daughters shall prophesy, your old men shall dream dreams, and your young men shall see visions" (Jl. 2:28). These words are quoted by **Peter** on Pentecost to show that the messianic age had arrived.

The four Evangelists share a basic story of **Jesus** and the Holy Spirit and then, each in his own way, expand on it. The core story

can most easily be read in Mark's Gospel, the shortest and generally believed to be the earliest. Jesus' ministry begins with his baptism when the Spirit descended upon him "like a dove" and immediately thereafter "drove him out into the wilderness . . . [to be] tempted by Satan" (Mk. 1:10-12). From this point on, the Spirit is thought of as being continually present in the person of Jesus. His entire ministry is one that manifests the Spirit's power. Unlike **John the Baptist**, Jesus baptizes "with the Holy Spirit" (Mk. 1:8). "It is by the Spirit of God that I cast out demons" (Mt. 12:28), Jesus announces, making it clear that in him is found the fulfillment of messianic promises. Reading from the book of Isaiah in the synagogue at Nazareth, Jesus testifies that "the Spirit of the Lord is upon me, because he has anointed me to preach good news to the poor" (Lk. 4:18). Moreover, in their accounts of the birth of Jesus, both Matthew and Luke emphasize that **Mary** conceived by the Holy Spirit.

Matthew, Luke, and John all give special attention to how the Holy Spirit functions in the church after the death of Jesus. In Matthew, the apostles receive from the resurrected Jesus the commission to "make disciples of all nations, baptizing them in the name of the Father and of the Son and of the Holy Spirit" (Mt. 28:19). In Luke, the apostles are told to stay in Jerusalem "until you are clothed with power from on high" (Lk. 24:49). The story is continued in the book of Acts when, on the day of Pentecost, "they were all filled with the Holy Spirit and began to speak in other tongues, as the Spirit gave them utterance" (Acts 2:4).

Throughout Acts, it is the Holy Spirit that guides the growth of the church. While all who are baptized receive "the gift of the Holy Spirit," it is the leaders chosen by God who are deemed to be "full of the Spirit" and who "spoke the word of God with boldness" (Acts 2:38, 6:3, 4:31). Thus, the heroes of faith are defined in the story of the church much as they were in the story of Israel, as individuals whose ability to lead the community is based on the power given them by the Holy Spirit. The Holy Spirit also functions as a distinct character in Acts, shaping events according to the will of God. Thus, the Holy Spirit guides **Philip** to the Ethiopian eunuch and Peter to the Gentiles, appoints **Barnabas** and **Paul** as missionaries, and later inhibits Paul from entering Bithynia. Often speaking to individuals and telling them what should be done, the Holy Spirit begins to take on characteristics of an independent personality. Moreover, it is precisely these events in which the Spirit appears that are turning points—intensely controversial ones—in the history of the church. For Acts emphasizes that the spread of the gospel to the Gentiles, an issue that divided early Christians, was undertaken by divine guidance.

In his Gospel, John contributes another dimension to the Holy Spirit. "Receive the Holy Spirit" (Jn. 20:22), the resurrected Jesus says to his disciples before he departs. His presence among them is to be replaced by the Holy Spirit. Earlier, John had clarified how this could be—in the process giving the Holy Spirit a new name, Counselor. In his extended last discourse with the disciples, Jesus emphasized that the Counselor "will teach you all things"; "will bear witness to me"; and "will guide you into all the truth" (Jn. 14:26, 15:26, 16:13). The church would continue to be inspired by and operate under the authority of Jesus through the power of the Holy Spirit in its midst.

Besides playing such a prominent role in the story of the church, the Holy Spirit is also seen acting in the lives of individual Christians. In Paul's writings, the foundation of a moral life is the Holy Spirit, for Christians are admonished to "walk by the Spirit . . . [for] the fruit of the Spirit is love, joy, peace, patience, kindness, goodness, faithfulness, gentleness, self-control" (Gal. 5:16, 22-23). It was the Spirit that

would set them "free from the law of sin and death," Paul counseled the Romans. "If the Spirit . . . dwells in you, he who raised Christ Jesus from the dead will give life to your mortal bodies" (Rom. 8:2, 11). A Christian's body could therefore be spoken of as "a temple of the Holy Spirit" (1 Cor. 6:19). In addition, the presence of the Holy Spirit would provide an intense experience of God, enabling the believer to speak to God with the affectionate "Abba! Father!" (Rom. 8:15).

Paul taught that the Holy Spirit can enter all Christians equally, though the Spirit could still be manifested in certain individuals in distinct, extraordinary ways, such as speaking in tongues and prophecy. In Corinth, this became a problem, because the "varieties of gifts" (1 Cor. 12:4) was causing divisions in the church. Here Paul reminded the faithful that the purpose of the Holy Spirit's gifts was for service to the church, not for individual self-fulfillment. Therefore such gifts should not be used unless they benefited the community. This meant that extraordinary manifestations of the Spirit bring with them moral responsibilities.

Paul's discussion in 1 Corinthians 12-14 emphasized the idea that the Holy Spirit acts in the name of God and his son, Jesus. This is not far from the point in John that the Holy Spirit would not act independently of the authority

Tongues of fire from the Holy Spirit descend upon the disciples gathered at Pentecost.

of Jesus. As this point developed further in the church, it came to be related to the idea that the Holy Spirit spoke through the authority of the church itself. Thus, the reception of the Holy Spirit in some contexts took place only by the laying on of hands of authoritative church leaders. "Rekindle the gift of God that is within you through the laying on of my hands," Paul wrote **Timothy**; "for God did not give us a spirit of timidity but a spirit of power and love and self-control" (2 Tim. 1:6).

HOPHNI

(hof' nee) HEBREW: HOPNI
"tadpole"
• • • • • • • • •

Hophni and his brother Phinehas were priests of the sanctuary at Shiloh. Unlike their father, the pious high priest **Eli**, the two "were worthless men; they had no regard for the Lord" (1 Sam. 2:12) and used their office for gain. They gorged themselves on meat brought to the altar for sacrifice, taking it by force if necessary; they "treated the offering of the Lord with contempt" (1 Sam. 2:17). The brothers also sinned with the women serving at the sanctuary, ignoring Eli's reproaches. They were killed carrying the ark of the covenant in battle against the Philistines, and for their crimes the ark was exiled for years.

A sixth-century B.C. relief of Pharaoh Hophra

The prophet Hosea, a 12th-century German enamel plaque

HOPHRA

(hof' ruh) HEBREW: HOPRA; GREEK: APRIES
"happy-hearted is [the sun god] Ra"
• • • • • • • • •

A 26th-dynasty Pharaoh, Hophra (589-570 B.C.) was determined to re-create Egypt's former greatness. When **Nebuchadnezzar** laid siege to Jerusalem, he sent a relief army in reply to the appeal of King **Zedekiah** of Judah, but the Egyptians retreated in the face of a Babylonian counterattack. "The Chaldeans [Babylonians] shall come back and fight against this city," **Jeremiah** warned; "they shall take it and burn it with fire" (Jer. 37:8). Following Nebuchadnezzar's annexation of Judah, the Pharaoh allowed Judean refugees to settle in his land. Nonetheless, Jeremiah prophesied against Hophra: "Behold, I will give Pharaoh Hophra king of Egypt into the hands of his enemies" (Jer. 44:30). In a civil war brought on by another unsuccessful foreign adventure, Hophra was deposed and later put to death after he supported an abortive Babylonian invasion of Egypt.

HOSEA

(hoh zay' uh) HEBREW: HOSEA
"he [God] has helped/saved"
• • • • • • • • •

Sometime late in the reign of King **Jeroboam II** of Israel (c. 786-746 B.C.), the prophet Hosea appeared on the scene to warn of the external threat from Assyria. He also predicted that the nation would be plunged into anarchy, and claimed that all these impending troubles were the result of Israel's betrayal of its covenant with the Lord. The book that contains Hosea's curious biography and his dire oracles is first in the Old Testament section known as the Book of the Twelve, the twelve also being called the Minor Prophets.

The first three chapters of the book of Hosea give the only biographical information we have about the prophet himself; the remaining eleven chapters contain a series of discourses, perhaps written after Jeroboam's death, at a time when—as Hosea proclaimed—"a vulture [Assyria] is over the house of the Lord, because they [the Israelites] have broken my covenant, and transgressed my law" (Hos. 8:1).

Hosea compared Israel to an unfaithful wife who could be divorced and cast out of her home. Images of marriage and divorce, of an adulterous wife and a wronged husband, play a major part in the prophet's warnings. The Israelites, he declares, had sworn to be faithful to Yahweh, faithful as a bride; and they had sealed their vow in the covenant by which they had agreed to worship only him. But in Hosea's time the people had abandoned their vow, taking the bounty God had provided and lavishing it on the Canaanite god **Baal**; they were, in effect, guilty of committing adultery.

The theme of adultery is introduced in the very first chapter, in which God makes the prophet's marriage a mirror of Israel's transgression. "Go, take yourself a wife of harlotry and have children of harlotry," he commands Hosea, "for the land commits great harlotry by forsaking the Lord" (Hos. 1:2). Obediently, Hosea finds and weds a prostitute, a woman named **Gomer**, who bears three children—only the first of which is explicitly said to be his. Following an ancient tradition in which infants were named in commemoration of the circumstances surrounding their birth, these children were given names symbolizing God's rejection of the Israelites after they had rejected him.

The firstborn was a son. He was named **Jezreel** ("God sows") in recollection of the deeds of **Jehu**, founder of the dynasty that was to end with the brief reign of Jeroboam's son **Zechariah**. The second child, a daughter, was giv-

en the name Not pitied, an affirmation of God's stern attitude toward a wayward people. The third child, another son, was called Not my people, "for you are not my people and I am not your God" (Hos. 1:9). An adaptation of the traditional statement of divorce, the name of the third child further emphasized God's break with his chosen people.

The Lord, however, is a merciful God; Israel's punishment was not necessarily final. As a deceived husband might forgive a faithless wife, God would lure back the errant nation. "I will have pity on Not pitied, and I will say to Not my people, 'You are my people'" (Hos. 2:23). And so, in the third chapter, Hosea is commanded to buy back his adulterous wife from her paramour, chastise her, and once more offer her his love and protection.

Hosea's ministry followed soon after that of **Amos,** a southerner who came to warn the outwardly prosperous but inwardly corrupt northern kingdom of impending disaster. By the time Hosea was delivering his final oracles, disaster was at hand. In relatively short order, Zechariah and three of his four successors as king of Israel were assassinated; **Hoshea**, installed as a vassal of the Assyrian monarch **Tiglath-Pileser**, was to be the last ruler of the northern kingdom. "They made kings, but not through me," the Lord proclaimed in Hosea's voice. "They set up princes, but without my knowledge. . . . they sow the wind, and they shall reap the whirlwind" (Hos. 8:4, 7). As Hosea completed his warnings of catastrophe, Israel still maintained a precarious independence. But in 721 B.C. the Assyrians captured the capital of Samaria after a three-year siege; the northern kingdom was no more.

Hosea holding a prophecy, a medieval manuscript illumination

Over the centuries biblical commentators have devoted a considerable amount of study to the book of Hosea. Part of this attention is due to the complexity of the language as it has been transmitted. It was written in a northern dialect unfamiliar to later translators and has survived only in a partly garbled version. A more compelling reason for the scholarly debate, however, is the Lord's distasteful command that the prophet take as his wife a prostitute.

Ancient rabbis had no difficulty in accepting

the instruction as literally true, but medieval Jewish commentators found it deplorable. They got around the problem by claiming that the marriage had never taken place; the verses in which Hosea describes it, they maintained, were expressions of a dream or a prophetic vision. Christian scholars have also had trouble with the concept of marriage with a harlot. Thomas Aquinas tried to deal with the problem of Gomer's immoral behavior by suggesting that she was not Hosea's wife at all but merely a concubine. Martin Luther proposed that the reason Hosea's wife and children were linked to adultery was not because of the woman's actual failings but only because the prophet wished to make a point about fidelity to God. Whatever their response to the puzzling story in the first three chapters, all biblical commentators agree that it proves that God's love is so great that even infidelity will be forgiven.

HOSHEA
(hoh shee' uh) HEBREW: HOSEA
"may Yah[weh] save"

Hoshea seized the throne of Israel by murdering King **Pekah** in 732 B.C. He was the 19th and last ruler of the northern kingdom, by then a shrunken domain that included little more than the capital of Samaria and the surrounding hill country of Ephraim. Indeed, Hoshea was but a puppet of Assyria's **Tiglath-Pileser**, who had divided much of Israel into subjugated provinces, exiled many of its inhabitants, and imported new settlers from other parts of his empire. Subject to heavy tribute his impoverished nation could ill afford to provide, Hoshea nonetheless seems to have shared the destructive self-confidence of his predecessors.

After Tiglath-Pileser died in 727 B.C., Hoshea stopped paying tribute to Assyria and turned to So, an unidentified king of Egypt, for help in regaining Israel's independence. But Egypt was in no position to help anyone, least of all a pathetic vassal like Hoshea. The new Assyrian ruler, **Shalmaneser**—no doubt hearing of Hoshea's overtures to Egypt—promptly took his treacherous vassal prisoner, annexed what was left of Israel, and lay siege to Samaria. At the end of three years, "the ninth year of Hoshea king of Israel" (2 Kg. 18:10), the capital fell; Shalmaneser's brother and successor, **Sargon**, proclaimed it as a great victory for Assyria and deported Samaria's population.

The circumstances of Hoshea's death are unknown. "He did what was evil in the sight of the Lord,

As instructed by God, Hosea buys back his wife from her paramour for 15 shekels of silver.

yet not as the kings of Israel who were before him" (2 Kg. 17:2). Whatever were Hoshea's redeeming qualities, the sins that led to Israel's destruction are clearly specified in the Bible: forsaking the commandments of the Lord, making molten images, serving **Baal**, sacrificing their sons and daughters as burnt offerings, and turning to divination and sorcery. Angry with his chosen people, the Lord "removed them out of his sight; none was left but the tribe of Judah only" (2 Kg. 17:18).

HULDAH

(huhl' duh) HEBREW: HULDA
"weasel"

Huldah, the wife of King **Josiah**'s wardrobe keeper, is the only prophetess mentioned in the monarchical period. She was of such high repute that the king sought her advice when the book of the Law was found in the temple. Huldah foretold that the Lord would "bring evil upon this place and upon its inhabitants . . . . because they have forsaken me and have burned incense to other gods" (2 Kg. 22:16-17), but that the king would die peacefully. Josiah in fact died in battle; but the rest of Huldah's wrathful prophecy came true: In little more than two decades following the king's death, Jerusalem fell to the Babylonians.

HUR

(her) HEBREW: HUR
possibly "child"

A trusted associate of **Moses** during the wilderness period, Hur was perhaps the grandfather of **Bezalel** and either the husband or son of **Miriam**. During the battle with the Amalekites, Hur and **Aaron** held up the hands of the aged Moses as he overlooked the battle till Israel prevailed. Hur and Aaron later judged the Israelites during Moses' absence on Mount Sinai.

HUSHAI

(hoo' shai) HEBREW: HUSHAY
"my brother's gift"

The royal counselor Hushai came to meet King **David** on the Mount of Olives "with his coat rent and earth upon his head" (2 Sam. 15:32) as a sign of mourning over the revolt of David's son **Absalom**. David instructed his faithful friend to return to Jerusalem to thwart the advice of the rebel's adviser **Ahithophel**, whose counsel was taken as seriously "as if one consulted the

Hur and Aaron support Moses' arms at the battle with the Amalekites.

oracle of God" (2 Sam. 16:23). Pretending allegiance to Absalom, Hushai convinced him to postpone an immediate pursuit of David—as Ahithophel had proposed. The delay gave the fugitive king time to flee across the Jordan River and regroup his forces for the subsequent victory in which David regained his throne.

HYMENAEUS

(hai muh nee' uhs) GREEK: HYMENAIOS
from Hymen, the Greek god of marriage

The heretical Christian Hymenaeus is mentioned in two epistles. He and a coppersmith named Alexander are said to "have made shipwreck of their faith" by ignoring their consciences and therefore had been "delivered to Satan that they may learn not to blaspheme" (1 Tim. 1:19-20)—a punishment conjectured to be either excommunication or some form of supernaturally inflicted bodily pain. Hymenaeus and another comrade, Philetus, were also accused of spreading "godless chatter . . . [that] will eat its way like gangrene"; their sin lay in "holding that the resurrection is past already" (2 Tim. 2:16-18). Unable to accept the resurrection of the body after death, they may have proposed that resurrection took place when baptism freed a person from sin.

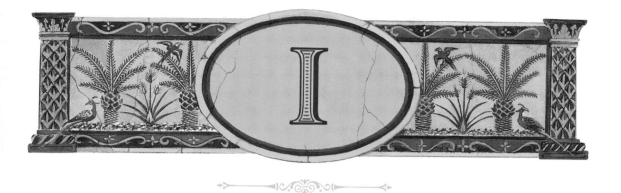

IBZAN

(ib' zan) HEBREW: IBTSAN
"swift"

The tenth judge of Israel named in the Old Testament book of Judges, Ibzan was a native of Bethlehem, a town a few miles northwest of Nazareth (not the later Bethlehem of Judah, where **Jesus** was born). Ibzan was evidently a man of wealth and high social standing, since he was able to marry all of his 30 daughters "outside his clan" (Jg. 12:9) and bring in wives for all of his 30 sons—which would have entailed substantial gifts to the brides' families. Like the rest of the so-called minor judges (the first of whom was **Tola**), Ibzan seems to have fulfilled a truly judicial role rather than the warlike one of the better known judges. After judging for seven years, Ibzan died and was buried in his native town.

ICHABOD

(ik' uh bahd) HEBREW: IKABOD
"alas for the glory"

The pregnant wife of Phinehas heard several pieces of dreadful news simultaneously. Her husband, her brother-in-law **Hophni**, and her father-in-law, the priest **Eli**, had all just died violently, and the ark of the covenant was in the hands of the Philistines. The shock caused her to give birth. She lived only long enough to name her child Ichabod, saying, "The glory has departed from Israel, for the ark of God has been captured" (1 Sam. 4:22). In the only other reference to Ichabod in the Bible, he is identified as the uncle of Ahijah, one of the men with **Saul** at Gibeah.

Stopped from sacrificing Isaac, Abraham spies the ram provided for his offering; a painting by Andrea Mantegna (1431-1506).

IMMANUEL

(im man' yoo el) HEBREW: IMMANU-EL
"God is with us"

The prophet **Isaiah** foretold the birth to a young woman of a son she would call Immanuel. "He shall eat curds and honey when he knows how to refuse the evil and choose the good" (Is. 7:15), Isaiah added, predicting hard times to come when the child to be born reached the age of reason. In the Gospel of Matthew the same text is used to show how the birth of Jesus fulfilled the prophecy.

Isaiah was addressing King **Ahaz** of Judah. Threatened with war by an alliance between the northern kingdom of Israel and Syria, the king had decided to seek help from Assyria. Isaiah urged Ahaz to avoid the foreign entanglement and, instead, to trust in the Lord. The birth of the child Immanuel, he said, would be a sign from God. While the child was still young, the prophet continued, Israel and Syria would cease to be a threat; the danger in the future would come from Assyria. Shunning Isaiah's advice, Ahaz made a fateful alliance with the Assyrians.

The prophecy of Isaiah does not specify a miraculous birth to a virgin. The Hebrew word used to describe the mother merely means "maiden" or "young woman"; a different term would have indicated a virgin. But in the Greek translation of the Hebrew Bible known as the Septuagint (or by the acronym LXX, Roman numerals for 70), the word used is "virgin." It was this version that Matthew quoted when he applied Isaiah's original prophecy to the birth of **Jesus**: "Behold, a virgin shall conceive and bear a son, and his name shall be called Emmanuel [the Greek spelling]" (Mt. 1:23). Unlike Isaiah, Matthew does not say that the young woman would name her child but rather he would be called by that name. Thus, there is no conflict with a previous verse: "You shall call his name Jesus" (Mt.

An angel of the Lord stays Abraham's sword in this late 19th-century enameled gold pendant set with precious stones.

1:21)—the idea being that the parents would name him Jesus, but the world would recognize him as Emmanuel.

Matthew sees this text, like all of the many prophecies he quotes, as a messianic reference regardless of its use in the Old Testament. This does not mean that he ignored or overlooked the original context. Rather, he was applying the principles of biblical interpretation of his day, whereby prophecies were considered to have more than one valid meaning.

Scholars argue over the fulfillment of Isaiah's prophecy—some suggesting an immediate fulfillment, perhaps a son born to the king in order to perpetuate the house of David, as well as the distant fulfillment in the birth of Jesus, a descendant of that house. Others suggest that the son referred to was Isaiah's after the prophet "went to the prophetess [his wife], and she conceived and bore a son" (Is. 8:3). That son, however, was given the name **Maher-shalal-hash-baz**, which means "the spoil speeds, the prey hastes"—a prediction of the destruction of Israel and Syria by Assyria.

ISAAC

(i' zik) HEBREW: YISHAQ
"he laughed"

The second patriarch of ancient Israel, Isaac is a strangely colorless figure in the Old Testament, perhaps because few ancient traditions about him have survived. Born when his father **Abraham** was 100 years old, he stands in the older man's im-

mense shadow, giving rise to an ironic adage: "An Abraham is apt to be followed by an Isaac." As a youth, Isaac was passively acquiescent in the greatest drama of his life, when God commanded his father to make of him a burnt offering. Throughout his life, he tended to avoid potential conflict by distancing himself from his adversaries. In his old age, weakened and nearly blind, he was helpless when his final wishes were thwarted by his wife and younger son, **Jacob**. Isaac nonetheless stands out as an exemplar of piety, kindness, and gentleness, and he provides a direct link between the crucial figures of Abraham and Jacob.

Descendants had been promised for 25 years to an increasingly skeptical Abraham. In fact, Isaac's name is variously explained in Genesis as recalling his father's sardonic laughter or that of his mother, **Sarah**, at the very idea that a 90-year-old woman could bear a child. In the meantime, at Sarah's urging, the dubious Abraham, desperate for an heir, had begotten his son **Ishmael** with the slave woman **Hagar**. Another suggested explanation for Isaac's name is that the older boy laughed at his half brother or, in other words, made fun of him. Biblical experts generally prefer still another interpretation, "may God laugh," a phrase asking that the Lord look upon Isaac with affection. Whatever the reading, Isaac would never have his name changed, as did the other patriarchs, because he had been named by God before he was born.

Earlier, Abraham's household, including the 13-year-old Ishmael, had followed the divine command to be circumcised as a token of their faith. Isaac would become the first descendant of Abraham to be circumcised when he was eight days old, a Jewish tradition observed to the present day. Eventually, whether because Ishmael actually harassed Isaac or posed a threat in her mind, Sarah persuaded Abraham to send the growing boy and his mother away in order to ensure that her son would be her husband's sole heir.

For Isaac, however, the greatest apparent danger would arise from a commandment of the Lord some years later. When Isaac was a lad, or perhaps even a young man, God ordered Abraham to take his son up to Mount Moriah and sacrifice him there. The son's voice is heard only once. When they arrive at the place of sacrifice, Isaac asks, "Behold, the fire and the wood; but where is the lamb for a burnt offering?" (Gen. 22:7). To Abraham's cryptic reply that God himself will provide the offering, the boy responds with a profoundly affecting and submissive silence. Both Abraham and Isaac are rewarded for their faith when an angel prevents the father from slaying his son and points out an alternative sacrifice nearby, a ram caught in a thicket.

This famous story has both inspired and troubled Jews and Christians throughout the ages. Perhaps for that reason, one nonscriptural Jewish tradition explains that a 37-year-old Isaac himself proposed the sacrifice to prove that he was more virtuous than his older brother Ishmael, who bragged that his faith was superior because he had been old enough to choose whether or not to be circumcised when he participated in the rite. This story was linked with the nonbiblical tradition that the proposed sacrifice caused Sarah's death, since Isaac was indeed 37 when she died.

A BRIDE FROM THE HOMELAND

Three years later, Abraham sent his trusted household servant, likely **Eliezer**, back to the family's ancestral lands in northern Mesopotamia to find a suitable wife for Isaac, a woman who would maintain the clan's integrity. Above all, Abraham did not want Isaac to "take a wife . . . from the daughters of the Canaanites" (Gen. 24:3). The account of the old servant's mission demonstrates that God intervened in the selection of **Rebekah**, the daughter of one of Abraham's nephews. Eliezer had asked for a sign that the chosen bride be the first woman to give him water from a spring and offer to draw some for his camels. Rebekah did exactly that; Eliezer identified himself and revealed his mission; and the young woman's family, recognizing the hand of

God, allowed Rebekah to leave with him.

The story of the first meeting between Isaac and Rebekah is beloved for its simplicity and unspoken feeling. Having gone out one evening to meditate, perhaps eagerly awaiting the arrival of his father's servant, Isaac caught sight of a camel caravan. Rebekah, spying a man walking to meet her, dismounted to ask who he was. When she learned Isaac's identity, she immediately veiled herself—as would have been proper for a maiden appearing before her betrothed. No sooner were they introduced than "Isaac brought her into the tent, and took Rebekah, and she became his wife, and he loved her" (Gen. 24:67).

A blight on their union, however, was Rebekah's apparent infertility, like that of Sarah before her. Once again, God's promise that Abraham would be the progenitor of a great nation was brought into question. Unlike his father, Isaac showed patience without making protest or taking rash action. Trusting God, Isaac prayed, and his prayers were answered after some two decades with the birth of twin sons when he was 60 years old.

Ominously, the infants scuffled with each other in the womb. The Lord explained her distress to Rebekah: "Two nations are in your womb, and two peoples, born of you, shall be divided; the one shall be stronger than the other, the elder shall serve the

CHILD SACRIFICE

*A*lthough their Law forbade it, the Israelites were known to practice human sacrifice—especially of children. Having vowed to sacrifice the first to greet him upon his return from victory over the Ammonites, the judge Jephthah was forced to slay his only daughter. As late as the seventh century B.C., King Manasseh of Judah made burnt offerings of his sons—but one of his many transgressions. Moreover, the potency of such dreadful offerings was acknowledged by the Israelites when they lifted their siege after King Mesha of Moab sacrificed his eldest son.

younger" (Gen. 25:23). When the firstborn **Esau** emerged, he was covered in red hair; Jacob followed, gripping his older brother's heel. As the years passed, Esau became a skilled hunter and outdoorsman, loved by his father. Jacob, a quiet and contemplative boy, became Rebekah's favorite. Yet again, God's promise seemed endangered because of the gathering conflict within the family.

For some years, however, this danger seems to have been ignored. When Isaac considered going to Egypt to escape a famine, as his father had done in a similar crisis, he received his first vision. "Do not go down to Egypt," the Lord warned; ". . . Sojourn in this land, and I will be with you, and will bless you; for to you and to your descendants I will give all these lands, and I will fulfil the oath which I swore to Abraham your father" (Gen. 26:2-3).

BLESSED BY THE LORD

Isaac obeyed, staying in Gerar, an area settled by the Philistines. As his father had done years before, he tried to pass off his beautiful wife as his sister, fearful that he would be killed for the sake of Rebekah. When the Philistine monarch **Abimelech** found out the truth, he was furious but warned his subjects not to harm Isaac or Rebekah on pain of death. Thereafter, the Lord blessed Isaac so abundantly that his crops reaped "a hundredfold" and he "gained more and more until he became very wealthy" (Gen. 26:12-13). This phenomenal prosperity sparked so much envy among his

Deceived by his wife and his younger son, Isaac bestows the patriarchal blessing on Jacob rather than Esau.

neighbors that Abimelech asked him to move elsewhere. First at Esek and then at Sitnah, he settled his household beside an old well that had originally been dug by Abraham but since filled with earth by Philistines. When his servants reopened these wells, however, the pagans living nearby claimed them for their own. Twice, Isaac pulled up stakes and moved on. When he found and reopened a third well, there were no arguments. Recognizing that this was a sign from God that he should settle there, Isaac named the spot Rehoboth, meaning "broad places."

When Isaac went to Beersheba, where Abraham had also dug a well and made his pact with Abimelech (perhaps an earlier ruler), the Lord again appeared to Isaac to reaffirm the essential promise that he would be blessed with numerous descendants. Soon thereafter, Abimelech and his chief advisers, convinced by then that Isaac was under God's protection, journeyed to Beersheba to swear an oath of peace with him. This covenant marked the summit of Isaac's public achievements as the hero and patron of the surrounding region.

DECEIVED BY HIS WIFE AND SON

The patriarch is next seen in old age, his faculties dimmed, as the foil in a sad and sordid domestic drama that fulfilled the oracle given to Rebekah before her twin sons were born. Worried that he might soon die, the feeble patriarch decided to give his blessing to Esau, the firstborn twin and favorite son. To appreciate the intensity of this story, it is necessary to understand that this paternal blessing was no mere formula of words but a powerful act that conveyed leadership of the clan upon the recipient. Moreover, as everyone involved knew very well, the blessing, once bestowed, could not be withdrawn or given to another, for it came from God.

Having made his decision, Isaac asked Esau to hunt down game and prepare a savory dish for him before he gave the blessing. Rebekah overheard her husband's instructions and swiftly devised a subterfuge to benefit her beloved Jacob. She told him to select choice young goats from the household flock so that she could prepare a stew. Further to deceive her nearly blind husband, she outfitted the young man in his older brother's best clothing and covered his smooth hands with bits of goatskin. Puzzled that Esau had so quickly killed and cooked his game, Isaac asked Jacob to come near. "The voice is Jacob's voice," he said, dubious, "but the hands are the hands of Esau" (Gen. 27:22). After eating the stew and drinking wine that Jacob brought, the old man smelled the familiar garments of his older son and, finally convinced, gave his blessing. Not long afterward, Esau appeared with the fresh meat he had prepared, eager for the blessing that was his due. When he found out that his brother had already gained the patriarchal benediction, he determined to kill him. For this reason and because they did not want Jacob marrying among the Canaanites, as Esau had, Rebekah and Isaac sent their younger son away to live with her father's clan and find a wife there.

Isaac lived 70 years longer and, when he died "old and full of days" (Gen. 35:29), his sons came together to bury him. The Old Testament frequently refers to the God of Abraham, Isaac, and Jacob (or Israel); and the prophet **Amos** goes so far as to use the name Isaac to stand for the nation of Israel. According to scriptural accounts, Isaac is the only patriarch to marry only once, to keep no concubines, and to succeed in agriculture. In traditional Jewish literature, he is revered as the model for martyrs and intercedes with God for Israel more often than the other patriarchs.

Paul saw in Ishmael and Isaac an allegory of, respectively, God's old and new covenants. In other words, Ishmael represented the Jews, while Isaac represented Christian believers, the "children of promise" (Gal. 4:28). The fathers of the Christian church would discover even more parallels between the patriarch's life and the story of **Jesus**. They interpreted Isaac's miraculous birth as prefiguring Jesus' birth to a virgin. For many Christians, Isaac's obedience and trust in his father at the time of the sacrifice on Mount Moriah is a powerful symbolic portrait of the obedience Jesus shows to his heavenly father. Finally, the substitution of a sacrificial ram for Isaac was seen as the Old Testament counterpart of Jesus' sacrifice on behalf of humanity.

ISAIAH

(i zay' ah) HEBREW: YESHAYAHU
"Yah[weh] is salvation"

During the last four decades of the eighth century B.C., the prophet Isaiah gave hope of salvation to the people of Judah at a time when the northern kingdom of Israel was falling prey to Assyria. His mission spanned the reigns of four kings: **Uzziah**, **Jotham**, **Ahaz**, and **Hezekiah**. But Isaiah's prophetic vision looked far beyond those times of trouble. His hopeful words offered comfort to a future generation, fol-

Raphael (1483-1520) depicted Isaiah with a Hebrew scroll; a painting from the church of San Agostino in Rome.

lowing Babylon's capture of Jerusalem and exile of its populace nearly two centuries later, and promised them a release from captivity and the restoration of their holy city.

Born perhaps shortly before 760 B.C., Isaiah is initially identified simply as "the son of Amoz" (Is. 1:1). Later Jewish tradition suggests that Amoz may have been the brother of King **Amaziah** of Judah, making the prophet a cousin of Uzziah. Most of the stories about Isaiah preserved in the Bible concern his interaction with kings, and the sheer eloquence of his language may indicate that he acquired a royal education. However, no direct textual or historical evidence exists of noble origins. Indeed, little is known about Isaiah, and modern scholars agree that the book bearing the prophet's name was heavily edited in the centuries following his death. Most believe that certain traditions belong to later disciples of Isaiah, referring to such unknown prophets as a post-exilic Second Isaiah or an even later Third Isaiah. Whatever the scholarly argument about the authorship of the book of Isaiah, the prophet emerges from the pages of the Bible as a real person, a messenger of God with his own distinctive voice, one that clearly distinguishes him from other biblical prophets.

The first datable event in the life of Isaiah refers to "the year that King Uzziah died" (Is. 6:1)—sometime around 742 B.C., when Isaiah was apparently still a young man. Come to worship at the temple, he experienced a

*The Lord appears to a slumbering Isaiah;
a 12th-century manuscript illumination.*

sudden, extraordinary vision of God sitting on a throne. So immense was the divine manifestation that just the train of God's robe filled the huge sanctuary. Discovering that he was witness to a council where God was deliberating with the heavenly host and aware that profane human beings could not survive such grandeur, Isaiah screamed, "Woe is me! . . . for my eyes have seen the King, the Lord of hosts!" (Is. 6:5). Immediately, a six-winged seraph soared to his rescue to place a burning coal from the altar upon his lips. Absolved of all mortal guilt and sin, Isaiah could then remain safely at the divine conclave. And when the Lord asked who would be his messenger, Isaiah, without a moment's hesitation, volunteered: "Here am I! Send me" (Is. 6:8). God accepted the offer but warned that the message would fall on deaf ears. Isaiah asked how long this would be and received a disheartening reply: "until cities lie waste without inhabitant . . . and the land is utterly desolate" (Is. 6:11)—that is, to the period in the future when the kingdom of Judah would fall to Babylon.

Indeed, throughout his entire ministry, Isaiah would find his sermons rarely understood, and he experienced a deepening awareness that the prophecies that he himself recorded in "a book that is sealed" (Is. 29:11) would remain incomprehensible to most of his own generation—with but few exceptions, most notably King Hezekiah. Nonetheless, despite Isaiah's disappointment at how poorly his message was received, he always spoke confidently of a

time in the future when "the ears of those who hear will hearken" (Is. 32:3). In most of what scholars refer to as First Isaiah, chapters 1 to 39, the prophet appears as a messenger of God whose rhetoric rarely wins a congenial response and whose gifted art of persuasion cannot break through a wall of dogmatic resistance by his contemporaries. However, the second part of the book of Isaiah, chapters 40 to 66—called Second or Second and Third Isaiah—reveals the full acceptance of Isaiah's message in the period following the return from exile.

Although audiences may not have accepted his message, Isaiah was not alone, for he had the full support of his family. Some years after he received his commission, Isaiah mentioned his wife as "the prophetess" (Is. 8:3), without writing anything about either how she became a prophetess or what, if anything, she might have contributed to his own book. Modern historians speculate that she could have been the unnamed "young woman [who] shall conceive and bear a son and shall call his name Immanuel" (Is. 7:14). The importance of Isaiah's family to his prophecy is further illustrated by the naming of his children according to parts of his message—Shearjashub, "a remnant shall return"; perhaps **Immanuel**, "God is with us"; and certainly, **Maher-shalal-hash-baz**, meaning "the spoil speeds, the prey hastes."

CONFRONTING THE KINGS

Many of Isaiah's oracles addressed ordinary people and lesser leaders. But the biblical narrative focuses on the prophet's confrontation with the kings of Judah. Despite the lack of prophecies explicitly dated to their reigns, it can be assumed that Isaiah was supportive of both King Uzziah and his son and successor, Jotham. During the last ten years of Uzziah's long reign (783-742 B.C.), Jotham served as coregent. In this period, Assyria became a major military power in Mesopotamia, eventually posing a threat to Judah. Jotham maintained his father's anti-Assyrian policies; but, when Assyria appeared ready to conquer Judah's immediate neighbors to the north in 736-735 B.C., many of Jotham's subjects voiced their concern over attempts to resist the juggernaut. Still in his early 40's when he died in 735, Jotham was succeeded on the throne by his 20-year-old son Ahaz.

During Ahaz's rule, Isaiah directly opposed the king's foreign policies. The northern kingdom of Israel had formed a coalition with Syria to revolt against Assyria. When Ahaz refused to join them, the kings of Syria and Israel threatened to re-

PROPHETS, MAJOR AND MINOR

The terms *Major Prophets* and *Minor Prophets* apply to two sections of the Old Testament in English. The Major Prophets are the five books from Isaiah to Daniel; the Minor Prophets are the twelve books from Hosea to Malachi. The groups are primarily distinguished by the lengths of the books, not the importance of the prophets in history. In fact, prophets of major importance, such as Elijah and Elisha, left no writings at all—though their deeds are amply recorded in 1 and 2 Kings.

However, the two categories—Major and Minor—are only partially appropriate for the books they describe. Isaiah and Jeremiah are certainly "major" from any point of view. But Lamentations, for example, is included among the Major Prophets because of a tenuous tradition that Jeremiah wrote it. It is not, however, a book of prophecy but a series of five acrostic psalms lamenting the fall of Jerusalem.

The Hebrew Bible is traditionally divided into three parts: the Law, or Torah, the Prophets, and the Writings. Here, too, the prophets are divided into two groups, the Former and Latter Prophets rather than Major and Minor Prophets. The Former Prophets include historical books from Joshua through Kings, which were often thought to have been written by prophets. The Latter Prophets include both Major and Minor Prophets: Isaiah, Jeremiah, Ezekiel, and the twelve Minor Prophets counted as a single book. The books of Daniel and Lamentations are included not among the Prophets but among the Writings. The Writings also include books of poetry, wisdom, and history that were among the last to be added to the canon of Hebrew Scripture.

move him from the throne and replace him with a son of someone named Tabeel, who would be sympathetic to their cause. God sent Isaiah to Ahaz with a message: "Take heed, be quiet, do not fear, and do not let your heart be faint because of these two smoldering stumps of firebrands" (Is. 7:4). Isaiah promised Ahaz that if he remained firm, God would deliver him from the threat of Israel and Syria.

As evidence that his word would prove true, the prophet offered to give Ahaz a sign. In a cynical show of false piety, the king refused on grounds that it would test the Lord. Furious, Isaiah accused him of not only wearying his subjects but also wearying God. Over Ahaz's objection, Isaiah gave him a sign anyway. A young woman would soon bear a child; and, by the time that child was weaned, Syria and Israel would be defeated. But to this good news Isaiah added a series of threats introduced by the phrase, "In that day" (Is. 7:18, 20, 21, 23). Those words, as in the metaphor of the prophet's commission, anticipated the exile of the nation two centuries later. The child named Immanuel would be a sign of both an end to the present threat as well as a sign of the end to the later devastation of Judah. Moreover, the prophet also promised that a light would be cast into the gloom and darkness of the future nation-

al disaster and would be accompanied by the birth of a messianic child, "and the government will be upon his shoulder" (Is. 9:6)—that is, the house of **David** would be reestablished in a time of endless peace.

Ahaz remained unconvinced and furtively sent messengers to Assyria, agreeing to make his nation a vassal of Assyria and pay tribute

From the walls of the Borgia apartment in the Vatican, Isaiah as portrayed by Pinturicchio (1454-1513)

in exchange for protection from his two northern neighbors. The policy provided temporary security to Judah at a high price, for it allowed Assyria a free hand to annihilate Israel and exile its survivors in 721 B.C.

A MONARCH WHO HEEDED

Hezekiah, Ahaz's son and successor, apparently served as coregent with his father from about 727 and served alone from 715 to 687 B.C. Surprisingly, he held views opposite from those of his father and was the only king to obey Isaiah's message. Despite some pro-Babylonian tendencies of which Isaiah disapproved, this king excelled almost all others in the Old Testament as one who listened to the prophets and obeyed the Law of God. Hezekiah aggressively sought to destroy elements of Canaanite religion that compromised the Israelite faith. Returning to the more neutral political position of Uzziah and Jotham, Hezekiah broke completely with Assyria in 705. He secured territories around Judah and built a magnificent tunnel to guarantee water supplies for the city of Jerusalem during times of siege.

Isaiah carved in stone; from a 12th-century church porch in Moissac, France

Hezekiah's greatest challenge came when he faced intimidation from the Assyrian forces of **Sennacherib** in 701. Isaiah encouraged him to be brave and to trust in God. The king followed Isaiah's advice and "the angel of the Lord went forth" to slay the Assyrians in their camp and the next morning, "behold, these were all dead bodies" (Is. 37:36). In this same period, when Hezekiah became critically ill, Isaiah told him that he ought to prepare to die. But the king bitterly pleaded with God for a longer life: "Remember . . . how I have walked before thee in faithfulness" (Is. 38:3). Speaking through Isaiah, God gave Hezekiah assurance that he would live for 15 more years. The promise was accompanied by a sign: The shadow cast by the sun on a stairway leading to the roof moved back up the ten steps down which it had descended.

The last story involving Isaiah concerns Hezekiah's hospitality to the envoys of a foreign king, **Merodach-baladan** of Babylon, then a minor power located south of mighty Assyria in Mesopotamia. The visit was entirely friendly, occasioned by the happy news of Hezekiah's recovery from his critical illness. After the foreigners depart-

ed, Isaiah learned that the king had showed them the magnificence of his palace and everything of value in his storehouses. Isaiah then prophetically announced that in the future some of Hezekiah's own children would see all of these things taken as spoil by these same Babylonians, who would come to conquer Judah and destroy Jerusalem. Pathetically pleased, Hezekiah mused, "There will [at least] be peace and security in my day" (Is. 39:8).

This episode is the last explicitly linked to Isaiah within his book, and it most likely recalls an event that preceded historically the threat of the Assyrians in 701 B.C. There is no biblical evidence that Isaiah lived into the reign of the next king, Hezekiah's less faithful son **Manasseh**. Yet, according to a later Jewish-Christian tradition, Isaiah died as a martyr by being sawed in two by Manasseh. This tradition is preserved in a first-century A.D. book called the Ascension of Isaiah, echoed perhaps in Hebrews 11:37. Otherwise, nothing is known about the death of the prophet, nor is it known in what year he died.

Isaiah's prophecies, throughout the long book that bears his name, show remarkable flexibility, great breadth, and surprisingly fresh expression. Even when expecting a disappointing response, Isaiah ingeniously found ways to get his message across. "Let me sing for my beloved a love song concerning his vineyard" (Is. 5:1), Isaiah writes, assuming the guise of a bride at a public celebration, perhaps an engagement ceremony. But the song soon takes a disturbing turn: The owner of the vineyard expected it to yield plump and delicious grapes while it produced only wild or sour ones. The vineyard, Isaiah explains, is Judah, which the Lord will allow to be laid waste as punishment for the people's faithlessness.

The prophet employed other devices to shock the people into attention. When the Assyrian army captured cities on the nearby coastal plain, an unnamed king of Judah was tempted to make a treaty with Egypt for protection. In response, God told Isaiah to "loose the sackcloth from your loins and take off your shoes from your feet" (Is. 20:2); and, in obedience, the prophet walked barefoot and naked for three years as a portent of the fate of the Egyptians and as a warning against relying on their help rather than God's.

An outstanding characteristic of Isaiah's message occurs in his repeated and deceptively simple command: Do not fear! By these words, the prophet condemned all efforts to defend the kingdom through alliances with enemies, to compromise faith in the Lord, and to rely on desperate political strategies rather than on God. This admonition recurs throughout his ministry in different circumstances and at very different times and places: in the oracle he gives to Ahaz, in the message God gives to Isaiah himself, in Isaiah's prophecy to Hezekiah and his addresses of comfort to the exiles.

Isaiah's life and ministry carries this central message: that all human activity motivated by fear of anything but God is contrary to faith and will almost always lead the faithful astray. This message, which people found hard to believe in Isaiah's lifetime, became integral to the faith by which Jews survived the exile to Babylon and endured many other historical catastrophes in the generations to come. Christians, finding in Isaiah the essential promises fulfilled in the Gospels, have often called him the Evangelist of the Old Testament.

ISH-BOSHETH

(ish boh' sheth) HEBREW: ISH-BOSHETH
"man of shame"

Ish-bosheth, one of **Saul**'s sons, tried unsuccessfully to continue the dynasty when his father and three older brothers were all killed in the battle on Mount Gilboa

with the Philistines in about 1004 B.C. Only Ish-bosheth, two younger half brothers, the young son of his brother **Jonathan**, and five sons of his sister **Merab** were left as potential successors to Saul. The king's cousin and army commander **Abner**, who had escaped alive from the fateful battle, hurriedly sought Ish-bosheth—most likely finding him at Saul's stronghold at Gibeah—and took him across the Jordan to Mahanaim in Gilead. Because the Philistines then controlled central Canaan and were allied with **David** in the south, quick action was required if Saul's dynasty was to be maintained. Abner had Ish-bosheth acclaimed king immediately and was able to gain recognition of his candidate from the regions of Gilead, Benjamin, Ephraim, Asher, and Jezreel, and at least nominally from the other northern tribes.

The statement that Ish-bosheth was "forty years old when he began to reign over Israel" (2 Sam. 2:10) seems to be a scribal error; Jonathan, Saul's eldest son, was only about 30 at his time of death. Since Ish-bosheth did not fight at Mount Gilboa, he was probably just 20 (the age of military conscription) at the outset of his two-year reign.

During the following months of warfare with David's rebel state in Judah, Abner began to gather power into his own hands. When he began to show contempt for Ish-bosheth by taking one of Saul's concubines, the young king challenged his mentor, but the enraged general threatened Ish-bosheth so fiercely that he feared for his life. Nonetheless, Ish-bosheth was willing to

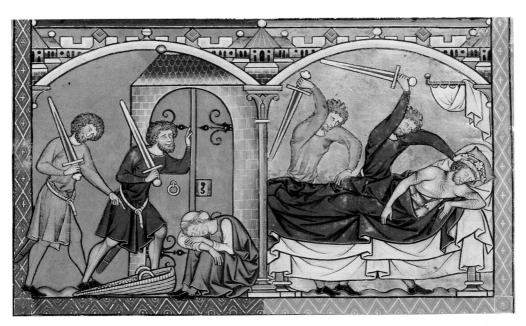

As Ish-bosheth naps, two captains of his own army steal in to assassinate him.

make peaceful gestures to David, even allowing him to reclaim his sister **Michal** as his wife. But when he heard that Abner had been murdered in Hebron while selling out his cause to David, Ish-bosheth knew that his struggle was lost and "his courage failed" (2 Sam. 4:1). The end was not long in coming. Two captains from his own army, Rechab and Baanah, arrived one day as Ish-bosheth took a noontime rest, entered his bedchamber, and beheaded him—bringing their gruesome trophy to David. Showing respect for the house of Saul, David had the assassins killed and the head buried in Abner's tomb at Hebron.

Although 2 Samuel consistently calls him Ish-bosheth, his name originally was Eshbaal, which means "man of the Lord." Here, the word *baal* carried its simple meaning,

"lord," but in later times the word was so linked to the hated Canaanite god **Baal** that scribes often put the word *bosheth*, "shame," in its place. Thus, Eshbaal became Ishbosheth, "man of shame."

ISHMAEL
(ish' may uhl) HEBREW: YISMAEL
"God has heard"

In his early years Ishmael, the son of **Abraham** and the Egyptian maidservant **Hagar**, was the focus of conflict between his mother and **Sarah**, Abraham's wife. Although God had told Abraham that he would father "a great nation" (Gen. 12:2), Sarah remained childless and had grown old. As was her responsibility in keeping

An angel comforts Hagar and her son Ishmael in the wilderness; a painting by Mattia Preti (1613-1699).

with ancient Middle Eastern customs, she gave her servant Hagar to Abraham to conceive and bear a child in her place. But when Hagar became pregnant, she behaved rudely to her mistress, who in turn treated her so harshly that Hagar fled into the wilderness. There, by a spring, she was visited by an angel who told her to go back to her mistress and predicted a great future for her unborn child—a son to be named Ishmael. He would, the angel added, "be a wild ass of a man" (Gen. 16:12) and have numerous descendants.

Hagar returned to give birth to Ishmael, who was raised in his father's household and was brought into the covenant of circumcision at the age of 13. However, the "everlasting covenant" (Gen. 17:7, 19), relating to ownership of land, was not extended to Ishmael.

Fulfilling God's promise, Sarah miraculously became pregnant and gave birth to **Isaac** a year later. At Isaac's weaning ceremony, Sarah became furious at the sight of her son playing with his half brother Ishmael. Determined that Isaac should not have to share his inheritance, Sarah urged Abraham to banish Ishmael and his mother. Abraham hesitated, but God told him he should do as Sarah said, because Isaac was to continue Abraham's line, while Ishmael was destined to father another nation. Giving them only a bit of bread and water as sustenance, Abraham sent Hagar and Ishmael into the wilderness of Beersheba. When her meager provisions ran out, Hagar laid Ishmael under a bush and went to sit a bowshot's length away, so that she would not have to "look upon the death of the child" (Gen. 21:16). But again an angel appeared, giving her water and assurance that God had heard her plea. Ishmael, the angel said, would survive and prosper.

Ishmael grew up in the eastern Sinai Peninsula, fulfilling the prophecy that he would be fierce and independent as a wild ass (a prime game animal that was greatly admired). He became a skillful archer and, after Hagar arranged for him to marry a woman of her own country, Egypt, he fathered 12 sons and a daughter who grew up to marry **Esau**. As did many another honored patriarch, Ishmael lived to an advanced age, 137. His numerous descendants, supposedly the nomadic Bedouins of Arabia, share his love of the freedom that comes with dwelling in a wilderness.

The apostle **Paul** used the story of the half brothers Ishmael and Isaac as an allegory of the conflict between Judaism and early Christianity, telling his converts that "we are not the children of the slave but of the free woman" (Gal. 4:31).

ISSACHAR
(is' uh kahr) HEBREW: YISSAKAR
"man of reward" or "hired man"

After the birth of her fourth son, **Judah**, Jacob's wife **Leah** seemed to be barren. Then her oldest son, **Reuben**, found some mandrake roots, which were widely used as a remedy for infertility. Leah and her younger sister **Rachel**, Jacob's second—and beloved—wife, quarreled over the roots but agreed that Leah should be the first of the two to try the effectiveness of the herb. That night, as a result, Issachar was conceived. Leah took his birth to indicate divine favor; thus, one interpretation of his name is "man of reward." Subsequently, Leah gave birth to a sixth son, **Zebulun**, and a daughter, **Dinah**.

Each of Jacob's 12 sons, including Issachar, became the ancestor of one of the 12 tribes of Israel. The tribe of Issachar, generally closely linked to that of Zebulun, settled in the fertile valley of the Jezreel River, a western tributary of the Jordan, and in the low hills southeast of Mount Tabor. In the blessing of Jacob, Issachar is described as "a strong ass" who "became a slave at forced labor" (Gen. 49:14-15)—perhaps an indication that the tribe of Issachar may have been subject at one time to the Canaanites of their region and also an explanation of the alternate interpretation of the name Issachar, "hired man."

All that is known of Issachar's own life is that he fathered four sons, all of whom joined him in the migration of Jacob's family to Egypt, where Issachar died and was buried. From the tribe of Issachar came the minor judge **Tola** and two kings of Israel, **Baasha** and his son **Elah**.

ITTAI
(it' ai) HEBREW: ITTAY

The leader of a band of 600 Philistine soldiers employed by **David** at the time of the rebellion of his son **Absalom**, Ittai showed remarkable loyalty to the king. When fleeing Jerusalem, David magnanimously told Ittai that he did not need to follow him into exile. Ittai vowed to remain with David, however, and later served as one of the principal generals in the victorious battle against Absalom.

JABIN

(jay' bin) HEBREW: YABIN
possibly "discerning"

After hearing of Israelite victories under Joshua in southern Canaan, King Jabin of Hazor, a city in upper Galilee, organized a massive confederacy to fight the invaders. Although Jabin and the other Canaanite kings assembled large numbers of men, horses, and chariots—"in number like the sand that is upon the seashore" (Jos. 11:4), the Israelites defeated them at the waters of Merom near Hazor. Jabin was killed and his city put to the torch.

Some scholars suggest that this Jabin and the Canaanite king by that name in the time of **Deborah** were the same person. It is more likely, however, that Jabin was a dynastic title of the kings of Hazor and that the king defeated by **Barak** was a later ruler.

JACOB

(jay' kab) HEBREW: YAAQOB
"may God protect/God has protected [him]"

Sly, duplicitous, and occasionally timorous, **Isaac**'s second son would seem an improbable choice to embody the fulfillment of God's promise to the nation of Israel. In fact, as the Old Testament and rabbinical tradition clearly show, it was the very human fallibility of the third patriarch that helped prove that it was divine will, not human initiative or individual merit, that established the Israelites in their Promised Land and in other ways shaped their national destiny. Today most biblical scholars believe that Jacob lived sometime between the years 2000 and 1700 B.C.

Esau (left) selling his birthright to Jacob; a late-16th-century Flemish tapestry

Like his father Isaac, Jacob and his older twin brother **Esau** were born to a mother who had been barren for a long time. Isaac prayed fervently for his wife **Rebekah** to conceive a son, a plea the Lord granted when he was already 59 years old and she had failed to conceive for the first 19 years of their married life. Even in the womb, however, the twins wrestled furiously with each other, causing their distraught mother to cry out, "If it is thus, why do I live?" (Gen. 25:22). She sought an oracle from God, whose explanation to her was prophetic of a troubled future for the family: "Two nations are in your womb, and two peoples, born of you, shall be divided; the one shall be stronger than the other, the elder shall serve the younger" (Gen. 25:23). Indeed, at the moment of birth, Esau emerged first, his heel firmly clasped by Jacob.

From the moment of birth, the differences between the boys were echoed in their relationship with their parents. Esau, the elder, was considered to be his father's son, an active, uncomplicated individual and a skilled hunter. Jacob, who preferred to stay home among the tents of the family compound and pursue the life of a shepherd (*ish tam*, meaning "plain" or "quiet man," is the phrase used in the Bible to describe him), became his mother's favorite. Of Jacob's childhood years, nothing is known; but the first biblical anecdote about the two brothers, which takes place when they were young men, illuminates their contrasting characters and their mutual hostility.

Stumbling home famished and exhausted from the hunt one day, Esau found his younger brother boiling pottage, in this case a thick red lentil soup. When he asked for some, Jacob replied without hesitation, "First sell me your birthright" (Gen. 25:31). Obviously, he felt cheated by the accident of birth that condemned him to the inferior status of a younger brother. And so Jacob not only took unfair advantage of his broth-

Angels on Jacob's ladder; a silk embroidery dating to about 1660

character of the recipient—in this instance, irrevocably designating the recipient as clan leader. Before performing this important ritual, Isaac asked his beloved Esau to hunt down some fresh game and prepare a savory meat dish. Rebekah, having overheard this plan, ordered Jacob to fetch two young goats from the household flock so that she could cook a counterfeit dish and deceive her husband into giving the blessing to her younger son. Jacob, characteristically cautious, hesitated because he saw an obstacle. "My brother Esau is a hairy man," he objected, "and I am a smooth man. Perhaps my father will feel me, and I shall seem to be mocking him, and bring a curse upon myself and not a blessing" (Gen. 27:11-12).

His mother was not to be deterred. After preparing a stew from the kids and baking fresh bread, she dressed Jacob in his older brother's best clothing, then covered his smooth neck and hands with the skins of the slaughtered animals. Thus coached and abetted by his mother, the young man carried the hot, tasty food to his father, boldly identifying himself as Esau. When Isaac, suspicious, asked how he had killed and cooked wild game so quickly, Jacob replied, "Because the Lord your God granted me success" (Gen. 27:20).

Still uncertain, the old man asked his visitor to draw nearer. In a memorable line, he mused, "The voice is Jacob's voice, but the hands are the hands of Esau" (Gen. 27:22). Even after eating the meal and drinking wine, Isaac may have had his doubts. But when he asked his son to kiss him before receiving the blessing, he was convinced by the smell of Esau's garments, which were imbued with the natural fragrances of the fields and woods. And thus, Isaac unwittingly gave his patriarchal blessing to his younger son. According to the beliefs of the day, the blessing, once spoken, could not be retracted or transferred. For the second time, Jacob had been able to swindle Esau out of a major part of his natural patrimony as the elder son.

In the case of this very special family, the blessing had enormous significance. Not only did it include the right to inherit the land of Canaan, it also passed on the divine promise to become the patriarch of the entire nation of Israel, the promise originally given to **Abraham** and reaffirmed for Isaac. Ironically, Jacob's deceit was itself a fulfillment of the divine plan; the flaws in his character were no impediment to God's long-range purposes for his chosen people.

Learning what had happened, the enraged Esau threatened to kill his brother as soon as their father died. Rebekah there-

er's hunger and naïveté; he also went to the heart of the jealousy between them, in effect bargaining to become the firstborn. Esau did not resist the bluff, blithely saying, "I am about to die; of what use is a birthright to me?" (Gen. 25:32). Even so, his exacting brother demanded that he swear away his birthright before getting any food.

Later in the history of Israel, it became illegal to transfer a birthright from the elder son to anyone else, but the practice was apparently widely accepted throughout the Middle East in the time of the patriarchs. One ancient document records that a younger brother had been allowed to buy his eldest brother's birthright for three sheep. In another, a father testifies that he is restoring the birthright of a son whom he had disinherited. Despite the unpleasant nature of this encounter between Esau and Jacob, the selling of the birthright fulfilled God's prophecy to Rebekah.

GAINING A FATHER'S BLESSING

Whatever Esau's remorse about so casually relinquishing his birthright, the next incident involving the brothers drove him to a homicidal rage. Isaac, aged and virtually blind, began to realize that death was approaching, and he was determined to pass on his patriarchal blessing to his firstborn. The Israelites, like other ancient peoples, believed that deathbed blessings could powerfully affect both the destiny and the upon decided to remove Jacob from harm's way. Using the argument that their younger son might marry a pagan Canaanite girl, as Esau already had, she urged Isaac to send the young man to live with her brother **Laban** in Haran, the area of northern Mesopotamia where she had spent her childhood. He agreed, this time freely bestowing his blessing on Jacob.

It was on this journey that Jacob experienced an astonishing heavenly vision. As he sank down in exhaustion one night in the wilderness some 12 miles to the north of the future site of Jerusalem, resting his head on a rock, he dreamed that he saw angels ascending and descending a ladder suspended between heaven and earth. At the top rung, God himself stood and directly affirmed the promise made to Jacob's grandfather Abraham and his father Isaac: "The land on which you lie I will give to you and to your descendants; and your descendants shall be like the dust of the earth" (Gen. 28:13-14). Jacob awoke, awestruck, and the following morning he anointed his stone pillow with oil, thus setting it apart for God's use, and named the place Bethel, meaning "the house of God." He also vowed to give the Lord one-tenth of his earnings, or a tithe, if he was able to return safely to Canaan.

When Jacob neared Haran, he encountered his beautiful young cousin **Rachel** tending her father Laban's flock and immediately fell in love. Laban agreed to let Jacob marry her but only after working for him for seven years. When the time came, there was the traditional wedding feast with the veiled bride, who continued to wear her veil during the wedding night. Only the next morning did the shocked Jacob discover that he had been deceived into marrying Rachel's older, less attractive sister **Leah**. When Jacob objected, Laban blithely explained that local custom required that the elder daughter be married first. For Rachel's hand, Jacob would have to agree to work another seven years with his uncle's flocks—though the lovers were allowed to marry after waiting only a week. Yet again, a deception turned out to be instrumental in God's plan for Jacob and his descendants. Leah, the unloved wife, proved to be fertile while the cherished Rachel did not conceive for some years. Leah's sons included **Levi**, ancestor of Israel's priesthood that guarded its spiritual traditions, and **Judah**, whose descendant **David** came to symbolize the monarchy that embodied its temporal power.

RETURN TO CANAAN

After the 14 years of indentured servitude, Jacob decided to continue working as a shepherd for his uncle, and it became apparent that these two men deserved each other. First, Jacob asked that he be paid with all of the dark-colored sheep and speckled or streaked goats. Laban agreed, then had his sons spirit away every one of those animals. Jacob countered by setting up peeled, white-streaked stakes of fresh poplar, almond, and plane tree limbs at the flock's watering troughs. The visual suggestion was supposed to encourage the goats and sheep to bear dark, speckled, or streaked offspring. He also made certain that only the healthiest and strongest of Laban's animals watered near the streaked stakes, thus ensuring the genetic superiority of his share of the flock.

As his own flocks grew larger and stronger, he became more prosperous than his kinsmen, exciting their envy. Also, it became clear that Laban no longer felt much regard for

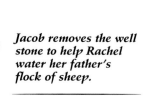

Jacob removes the well stone to help Rachel water her father's flock of sheep.

him. At the Lord's suggestion, Jacob decided to return to Canaan. In the 20 years since he had first laid eyes on Rachel, he had fathered six sons and a daughter with Leah, two sons with Leah's maid **Zilpah**, and two sons with Rachel's maid **Bilhah**. And, after years of infertility, his beloved Rachel had finally given birth to a son, **Joseph**. In fact, 11 of the 12 ancestors of the 12 tribes of Israel were born during this period of exile, making it the formative period for the development of the nation. Only Jacob's youngest son, **Benjamin**, had not been born before the patriarchal household left Haran.

Characteristically, Jacob tried to avoid any possible dispute by leaving while Laban was away shearing sheep. But when his uncle returned home three days later, he was furious, feeling insulted that Jacob had left surreptitiously and not allowed him to say farewell to his daughters and grandchildren. Worse yet, his *teraphim*, the images of his household gods, were missing. After a seven-day pursuit, Laban and his kinsmen caught up with Jacob's party on Mount Gilead in the hill country west of the Euphrates River, where uncle and nephew had a testy confrontation. The younger man was indignant at being accused of stealing the idols and told Laban to search at will through his tents. What neither knew was that Rachel had taken the gods and hidden them in the saddlebags of her camel. During the search, she sat firmly upon the bags, pleading she could not rise, "for the way of women is upon me" (Gen. 31:35). And so the theft went undetected.

Following some mutual recriminations, the two men agreed to make a pact of peace and, according to traditional usage, set up a mound of stones to mark the occasion. Jacob called this spot Galeed, or "the heap of witness," a name that was later modified to Gilead. The cairn also acted as a boundary marker between the two households. After this important compact, the Bible drops its references to Mesopotamia and the kinship connections there that play so critical and recurring a role in the patriarchal history to that point.

After Laban headed back northward, Jacob sent a conciliatory message to Esau, who was living in a part of Edom, the semi-arid land of Seir near the Dead Sea. But when a messenger returned with the news that his older brother was coming to greet him along with a company of 400 men, Jacob panicked. First, he packed off a huge present to Esau, including hundreds of sheep and goats and scores of cattle and camels. Next, he hustled his household and remaining goods back across the Jabbok, a tributary of the Jordan River.

A DIVINE ANTAGONIST

Later that night, alone on the south bank of the Jabbok in the midst of this apparently grave crisis, Jacob proved his mettle in one of the most enigmatic episodes in the Bible. Alone and in the dark, he found himself wrestling with a mysterious stranger. Unable

To increase his flocks, Jacob puts peeled rods in the watering troughs; a 14th-century painting.

The head of a considerable clan, Jacob sets out for Canaan in this painting by Raphael (1483-1520).

to bring Jacob down, this other being touched the hollow of Jacob's thigh and sprained it. Still Jacob dominated in the struggle. When the stranger asked to be released because the sun was about to rise, Jacob refused—unless he first received a blessing. His adversary replied, "Your name shall no more be called Jacob, but Israel, for you have striven with God and with men, and have prevailed" (Gen. 32:28). As Jacob limped away the next day, he realized that he had been face to face with God yet survived. And so he called the spot Peniel, or "the face of God."

This strange, compelling story has fascinated generations of Jews and Christians alike. In general terms, the wrestling match that earns a divine blessing is seen as characteristic of the Israelites in their persistent struggles with the Lord. Curiously, a Christian interpretation common in the Middle Ages was that Jacob's bout with the stranger represented the battle that every human being must undergo with the forces of evil. Yet at the same time, early Christian art clearly portrayed God as the antagonist in the mystical bout.

In the worldly sphere, Jacob enjoyed another kind of victory, for his fears of Esau were unfounded. When they met, his openhearted older brother ran joyously to him and kissed him. Although Esau wanted Jacob and his household to join him in Seir, the younger brother decided to travel on to Canaan. He settled for a time at Succoth or "booths," so named for the booths he set up

for his cattle, then moved to the hills of central Canaan near the town of Shechem. There he bought land from the prince of the city, Hamor, and set up an altar to the God of Israel. But the rape of Jacob's daughter **Dinah** by Hamor's son **Shechem** led to a massacre that put the Israelites in jeopardy. At this point God intervened, ordering Jacob to move farther southward to Bethel, the site of the vision of the angels on the ladder, where he restored the altar he had built about 20 years earlier. Once again, God appeared to him there, repeating the promise made to Abraham and to Isaac, and reminded him that he was no longer Jacob but Israel.

A BIRTH, TWO DEATHS

After all these years, Isaac was still alive in Hebron, despite his earlier fears that he would die before giving his patriarchal blessing. Jacob decided to visit him, but on the way, not far from Bethlehem, Rachel went into labor and died giving birth to her second son, Benjamin. She was buried near the town, according to the account in Genesis, although another Jewish tradition places her tomb north of Jerusalem in an area later associated with the tribe of Benjamin. Isaac, now 180 years old, died soon after and was buried by his twin sons, who never saw each other again.

The latter part of Jacob's life in Canaan, dwelling where his father and his grandfather Abraham had lived in accordance with the divine plan, was uneventful except for

Joseph brings his sons to Jacob for the patriarchal blessing; detail of a painting by Rembrandt (1606-1669).

WHY JACOB BECAME ISRAEL

*I*n the Bible a name change marks a turning point in a person's life—a major alteration of character, direction, or status. Abram became Abraham when God promised to make him "the father of a multitude of nations" (Gen. 17:4). After Jacob wrestled with the mysterious stranger south of the Jabbok River, his adversary told him that henceforth his name would be Israel, meaning "he strives with God." The remaining chapters of Genesis devoted to Jacob portray him as a changed man, dedicated to the Lord.

A name change also signifies that the one doing the naming assumes power over the one named. Thus, when Pharaoh Neco placed Josiah's son Eliakim on the throne of Judah, he named him Jehoiakim, "Yahweh will establish."

the dramatic events surrounding his favorite son, Joseph. Rachel's firstborn did not endear himself to his older half brothers by sharing dreams that apparently prophesied his eventual ascendance over them. Exasperated with his supposed impudence, the brothers conspired to kill Joseph, but the eldest, **Reuben**, persuaded them to throw the boy into a pit instead, hoping to rescue Joseph later. But in Reuben's absence the other brothers sold their detested rival to slave traders who happened by.

To cover up their crime, Jacob's sons killed a goat and splattered Joseph's coat with its blood. When they showed their father this garment, he immediately jumped to the conclusion they hoped for: "A wild beast has devoured him," the old man wailed; "Joseph is without doubt torn to pieces" (Gen. 37:33). Distraught, Jacob tore his own clothes and vowed to mourn until he himself died.

In the ensuing years, Joseph, who had been sold into the household of the Egyptian captain **Potiphar**, rose to the powerful position of governor. When one of the periodic famines struck, Jacob sent his ten oldest sons to Egypt to buy wheat, keeping Rachel's only other surviving child, Benjamin, at home. Curiously, he did not migrate to the Nile valley himself, as his grandfather had chosen to do in a similar crisis, but went to Egypt only when he learned that his long-lost favorite son was alive there.

A REUNION IN GOSHEN

On the journey southward, the 130-year-old Jacob paused at Beer-sheba to offer sacrifices to God at the altar associated with his father Isaac. During the night, the Lord appeared in a dream to reassure him: "Do not be afraid to go down to Egypt; for I will there make of you a great nation. I will go down with you to Egypt, and I will also bring you up again" (Gen. 46:3-4). His descendants did not return to Canaan until about four centuries later, when **Moses** led them out of the bondage into which they had fallen.

Jacob's migrating household numbered 70 people covering three generations, in addition to servants. This band with its flocks and numerous possessions no doubt followed the seacoast route to reach Goshen, the area given them by Joseph in the eastern section of the Nile River's fertile delta. When they arrived at their destination, Joseph rode eagerly out to welcome them, fell upon Jacob's neck, and wept. Equally moved, Jacob said that he was ready to die, having seen the face of his long-lost son. In fact, he thrived another 17 years in the land of

Goshen, a revered patriarch whose other sons had been placed in charge of the royal cattle at Joseph's suggestion.

On his deathbed at age 147, with all 12 of his sons beside him, Jacob pronounced his famous and strikingly poetic blessing, a catalogue of the distinguishing traits of each of these men. Traditionally, these characteristics came to be associated with the Israelite tribe named after each son, and some sound more like reproaches than blessings. For example, Reuben was praised for his strength and pride but also criticized for being as "unstable as water" (Gen. 49:4). **Simeon** and Levi were described as cruel and angry, **Asher** as skilled in agriculture, and Benjamin as aggressive as a wolf. The longest section, not surprisingly, is directed toward Joseph, who is blessed by God Almighty and by his loving earthly father.

For many reasons, scholars now suspect that this supposed parental blessing was composed long after Jacob died. The different sayings about each brother (or tribe) seem to originate in different periods: The use of language varies from simple and straightforward to obscure, and more than one type of poetic form is employed. Yet this extraordinary document is invaluable as an historical and theological source, providing the only surviving information about some of the tribes during biblical times.

Joseph arranged for Egyptian physicians to embalm Jacob's body and joined with the rest of his brothers and prominent members of the Egyptian court in accompanying a great funeral procession back to Hebron. There Jacob was buried alongside his first wife, Leah, his parents, Isaac and Rebekah, and his grandparents Abraham and **Sarah** in the hallowed cave of Machpelah. From then on, the 12 tribes descended from his sons were collectively known as the children of Israel or the house of Jacob. The patriarch's importance to the national religion is clear from the many scriptural references to the Lord as the God of Jacob. His identification with his descendants is further stressed in later comparisons between his essential character, flawed but faithful to God, and the equally contradictory behavior of the Israelites themselves on many occasions.

In addition, his personal struggles became symbolic of the conflicts between the Jews and their principal antagonists; that is, Esau, Laban, and even the mysterious stranger of the nocturnal wrestling match were thought to represent or prefigure the Romans and, later, the Christians. According to rabbinical writings, Jacob was the only one of the three patriarchs who continued to be personally involved in the fate of his descendants, even after his death. One traditional belief held that, like the nation

In this manuscript illumination, Jacob's burial is given a 14th-century Italian setting—complete with an unlikely procession of monks.

Jael reveals Sisera's corpse to Barak; a painting by James Tissot (1836-1902).

itself, Jacob was immortal. In modern times, the name given him by God reappeared in 1948, when the Jews of Palestine declared their independence and named their new state Israel.

JADDUA

(jad' ooa) HEBREW: YADDUA
"known"

The last of the high priests named in the Old Testament, Jaddua is said to have served "until the reign of Darius the Persian" (Neh. 12:22), identified by historians as Darius III Codomannus, who was overthrown by **Alexander the Great**. According to a legend recorded by the first-century A.D. Jewish historian Josephus, Alexander visited Jerusalem en route to Egypt in 333 B.C. and there met Jaddua, who showed him a prophecy of **Daniel** that could be taken as foretelling Alexander's conquests.

JAEL

(jay' el) HEBREW: YAEL
"mountain goat"

In one swift, gruesome act, Jael, the wife of Heber the Kenite, rid the Israelites of a powerful enemy. It happened at the time when **Deborah** was fighting to free her nation from 20 years of oppression by Jabin, the Canaanite king of Hazor. Deborah directed her commander **Barak** to assemble a large force that would challenge Jabin's army, led by **Sisera**, prophesying that "the Lord will sell Sisera into the hand of a woman" (Jg. 4:9).

Although the Canaanite army was superior—it was said to have 900 iron chariots—the Israelites under Barak's command ultimately achieved victory in battle at the river Kishon. As the chariots were swept away in the rain-swollen river, the only man to escape was Sisera. Fleeing from the battle zone on foot, he sought refuge in Jael's settlement; she welcomed him into her tent with milk and a bowl of curds. But Jael's hospitality was merely a trick. She covered the exhausted Sisera with a rug and promised to stand guard against his enemies at the door of her tent. Then, as soon as he was asleep, she took a hammer and quickly drove a tent peg into his temple. When Barak arrived searching for Sisera, Jael showed him the commander's body and was hailed as a heroine.

Jael's exact motives for killing Sisera are unclear. Her tribe—nomadic metalworkers said to be descended from **Cain**—was at peace with the Canaanites, but they may have had no choice; they were probably dependent on King Jabin for trade and land on which to pitch their tents. But as a group, they had suffered greatly under his rule and were generally sympathetic to the Israelites. Moreover, Jael's husband was a descendant of **Moses'** father-in-law, **Jethro**. In any case, by helping Canaan's conquerors, Jael ensured that the Kenites in the future would have good relations with the newly powerful nation of Israel. In the Song of Deborah, which recapitulates the narrative of Judges 4, Jael is celebrated as "Most blessed of women . . . of tent-dwelling women most blessed" (Jg. 5:24).

JAIR

(jay eer') HEBREW: YAIR
"may God shine/enlighten"

A man from Gilead, east of the Jordan, Jair followed **Tola** as the second of the so-called minor judges of Israel in pre-monarchical times; he served for 22 years. Jair's wealth and power are revealed by the statement that he had "thirty sons who rode on thirty asses; and they had thirty cities" (Jg. 10:4). The name of these cities, Havvoth-Jair, actually means "villages of Jair." They are mentioned in Numbers 32:41 as having been conquered and given that name by another Jair, the son of **Manasseh**; and in Joshua 13:30 they are said to have numbered 60.

JAIRUS

(jay' uh ruhs) GREEK: IAIROS

The synagogue official Jairus was the father of a girl who was raised from the dead by **Jesus**, an event recorded in all three Synoptic Gospels. The desperate father knelt before Jesus in the midst of a great crowd and begged him to come at once to his home, where his only daughter, age 12, lay dying (in Matthew's account, she is already dead). Accompanied by his disciples, Jesus set out; but before he reached his destination, a messenger came from Jairus's house to say that his daughter had died—there was no longer any reason to bother Jesus. Nonetheless, Jesus urged the man to have faith and continued on to his house. When he arrived, he told the grieving family not to mourn the girl, "for she is not dead but sleeping" (Lk. 8:52). Going to her bedside, he took her hand and commanded her to rise. When she did so, he asked that she be fed but warned the amazed parents to keep the miracle a secret. The two other raisings from the dead attributed to Jesus are those of the widow's son at Nain (see Luke 7:11-17) and of **Lazarus**.

THE WOMAN FROM BEHIND

In all three Synoptic Gospels, the story of the raising of Jairus's daughter is interrupted by a poignant vignette. As Jesus set out to heal the girl, he was approached from behind by a woman who had suffered from a hemorrhage for 12 years; no doctor had been able to help her. In her great faith, she had but to touch Jesus' garment to be instantly cured. Sensing the power flowing from him, Jesus turned to ask who had touched him. While his disciples were insisting it was only the jostling of the crowd, the frightened woman came forward to tell her story—whereupon Jesus commended her faith and told her to go in peace.

With her parents and three disciples witnessing, Jesus restores Jairus's daughter to life.

JAMES

GREEK: IAKOBOS, derived from
HEBREW: YAAQOB (JACOB)
••••••••••

James the son of **Zebedee**, along with his brother **John**, was one of the original 12 apostles. According to the Gospels of Matthew and Mark, they were among the first to be summoned by **Jesus**. Walking beside the Sea of Galilee just after he had begun his public ministry, Jesus first called Simon (**Peter**) and **Andrew** as they were "casting a net in the sea . . . . And immediately they left their nets and followed him." Then "going on a little farther, he saw James the son of Zebedee and John his brother, who were in their boat mending the nets" (Mk. 1:16, 18-19). Jesus called them, too, and they also followed him—leaving their father without a backward glance. According to **Luke**, the sons of Zebedee were partners of Peter and had been fishing all night without luck in a separate boat when Jesus first spied them. Before calling them, Jesus demonstrated his mastery of nature by filling their nets to bursting with fish. "Do not be afraid," he said; "henceforth you will be catching men" (Lk. 5:10). These four—Peter, Andrew, James, and John—were not only the first called but are always named first in lists of the 12 apostles and tend to be the most prominent in the Gospels.

When James and John are mentioned together, James is usually named first, which probably means that he was the elder of the two. Since the two are often referred to simply as the sons of Zebedee, their father must have been a person of some reputation and, because he had hired servants, apparently one of some means. Their mother is also prominent in the Gospels, being listed as one of the women who witnessed the crucifixion and discovered the empty tomb on the third day. Mark calls her **Salome**.

Peter, James, and John were the apostles closest to Jesus, for it is they who, on several occasions, were taken aside from the others to be special witnesses to a miracle or lesson of Jesus. The first time was at the raising of the daughter of **Jairus**, a ruler of the synagogue who had sought out Jesus because his daughter was at the point of death. By the time Jesus arrived on the scene, the girl had already been pronounced dead. Nevertheless, Jesus went in to her, specifying that only Peter, James, John, and the girl's parents be present when he brought her back to

life. Later, Jesus took the three "up a high mountain apart . . . [where] he was transfigured before them," and a voice from heaven proclaimed, "This is my beloved Son; listen to him" (Mk. 9:2, 7). Finally, following his last meal with the apostles, Jesus once more took Peter, James, and John aside to accompany him to where he would pray in the garden. Although he asked them to "remain here, and watch" (Mk. 14:34), the three apostles could not stay awake and slept while he prayed in agony. Interrupted by the arrival of **Judas** and the soldiers, they were among those who fled when Jesus was arrested. Thus, even though these three had been given special knowledge about Jesus, their understanding still fell short. Only when they came to comprehend the meaning of his death did the faith of these men become complete.

Though James and John were best known as the sons of Zebedee, Jesus gave them another surname, Boanerges, or "sons of thunder" (Mk. 3:17)—a name thought to refer to their fiery personalities. In fact, on more than one occasion, the brothers exhibited their impetuosity. When the Samaritans failed to show hospitality to Jesus, they

The sainted James with the scallop shell emblem of his earlier vocation as a fisherman; a ceramic roundel by Luca della Robbia (c. 1400-1482)

inquired, "Lord, do you want us to bid fire come down from heaven and consume them?" (Lk. 9:54). But Jesus summarily rebuked them. On another occasion, they asked Jesus to place them "one at your right hand and one at your left" (Mk. 10:37) when he came into his kingdom. (In Matthew 20:20-21, the request is made by their mother.) The demand provoked Jesus to explain that true greatness consists rather in serving others, as he was doing, for "the Son of Man also came not to be served but to serve, and to give his life as a ransom for many" (Mk. 10:45). Jesus informed them that they would share his fate, for "the cup that I drink you will drink" (Mk. 10:39). As if in fulfillment of that prophecy, James was put to death by **Herod Agrippa I**; his death, reported in Acts 12:2, is the only martyrdom of one of the 12 apostles that is recorded in the New Testament.

According to a later tradition, James brought the gospel of Jesus to Spain. He is the patron saint of that country, and his supposed place of burial, Santiago de Compostela, became a great goal of pilgrims from the early centuries of the Middle Ages.

Jesus summons James and John, the sons of Zebedee, from their father's boat.

James baptizing a convert; a stone carving from a 12th-century Nazareth church

JAMES 2

James the son of Alphaeus is named as one of the 12 apostles in all four New Testament lists: Matthew 10:1-4; Mark 3:14-19; Luke 6:13-16; and Acts 1:13. Since Levi (**Matthew**) is also called a son of Alphaeus in Mark 2:14, it has been suggested that he was a brother of James. But the two are never referred to as brothers, whereas other brothers are consistently mentioned in that way—namely **Peter** and **Andrew**, and **James** and **John** the sons of Zebedee. Nothing is known about this James and he does not appear in any of the stories of the apostles in the book of Acts. He is often identified with one of the others named James, such as **James** the brother of **Jesus** or **James** the brother of Joseph (or Joses), but most scholars consider him to be a distinct character.

JAMES 3

A mong those known as the brothers of **Jesus**, the one named James became the most prominent. The Gospels refer to several siblings of Jesus. When Jesus returned to his homeland to preach in the synagogue there, he was met with skepticism. "Is not this the carpenter's son? Is not his mother called Mary? And are not his brothers James and Joseph [Joses in Mark

6:3] and Simon and Judas? And are not all his sisters with us?" (Mt. 13:55-56). Of these members of Jesus' family, only James and **Judas** are mentioned by name elsewhere in the New Testament—James as a leader of the early church in Jerusalem and as the possible author of the letter of James; and Judas as the possible author of the letter of **Jude**. The brothers of Jesus, however, are mentioned as a group at several additional places in the New Testament.

Since the rise of the belief in the perpetual virginity of **Mary**, which was proclaimed church dogma in A.D. 451, the concept of brothers and sisters of Jesus has been in dispute among Christian scholars. Several alternative interpretations have been proposed. One is that these were only stepbrothers and stepsisters, referring to the nonbiblical tradition that **Joseph** was a widower with children when he married Mary. Another is that the word commonly translated as "brother" could mean "cousin." Proponents of this theory note that another **Mary**, "the mother of James the younger and of Joses" (Mk. 15:40), was present at the crucifixion and was among those women who discovered the empty tomb. This individual could be identical with Mary the wife of Clopas, whom John places at the crucifixion and calls the sister of Mary the mother of Jesus—meaning that, in reality, James was a cousin of Jesus, called "brother" according to Jewish custom.

Other interpreters simply point to the widespread metaphorical use of the terms "brothers and sisters" in those times and suggest that these were associates of Jesus who were so close that they were considered family. Most Protestant scholars today, however, accept these references to siblings of Jesus as being literally true.

The Gospels hint that the family of Jesus was skeptical of his ministry. On one occasion his mother and brothers stood outside and called to him while he was preaching—perhaps concerned for his safety or even worried about his sanity. "Who are my mother and my brothers?" Jesus asked and then answered his own question. "Whoever does the will of God is my brother, and sister, and mother" (Mk. 3:33, 35). Thus, for the sake of his ministry, Jesus limited their familial claim. And when the brothers of Jesus tried to manipulate him by urging that he speak more openly than he had been doing, he rejected their plea: "My time has not yet come" (Jn. 7:6).

The presence of Jesus' mother and brothers in the upper room in Jerusalem with the 11 apostles (the 12 minus **Judas Iscariot**) after his death and resurrection implies that the family had become believers. In addition, **Paul** says that the resurrected Jesus "appeared to James, then to all the apostles" (1 Cor. 15:7), including him among those who could testify to Jesus' triumph over death. And, as the story of the church unfolds in the book of Acts, James emerges as the most prominent of Jesus' brothers. Some suggest that, since he is mentioned first in the list of brothers, James must have been the eldest. But his importance seems to have derived mostly from his closeness to Jesus, for he continues to be identified as "the Lord's brother" (Gal. 1:19).

When Paul went to Jerusalem three years after his conversion, he visited only two of the church's leaders there, **Peter** and James. Fourteen years later, on the occasion of another visit to Jerusalem, Paul said that James, Peter, and **John** the son of Zebedee "were reputed to be pillars" (Gal. 2:9) of the church. Since **James** the son of Zebedee, one of the 12 apostles, had already been

killed by **Herod Agrippa I** when Paul noted this tribute, it is clear that it is James the brother of Jesus who was meant. Incidentally, Paul also indicated that the other brothers of Jesus played some form of leadership role in the early Christian church when he referred to them as examples of those who served the Lord and had wives: "Do we not have the right to be accompanied by a wife, as the other apostles and the brothers of the Lord and Cephas [Peter]?" (1 Cor. 9:5).

CONSERVATIVES VS. LIBERALS

As a leader of the church at Jerusalem, James came to represent the conservative position of converts to Christianity who still maintained certain Jewish traditions. Often they had to contend with the liberalizing influence of those Jewish Christians, like Paul, who preached the gospel to Gentiles. The controversy came to a head at the Jerusalem conference, an event that is described from different perspectives in Acts 15 and, in a first person account by Paul, who was there, in Galatians 2:1-10. The leaders of the Jerusalem church had heard reports that the missionaries in Antioch were having great success among the Gentiles but had not required their male converts to be circumcised. Up to that point, Christianity had been such a part of Judaism that circumcision was assumed, as it was for any Jew under the covenant. Christianity without circumcision was unexpected, and one of its proponents, Paul, went to Jerusalem to consult with church leaders, including James. On that occasion, James took a moderate stand on the issue of whether Gentiles needed to be circumcised in order to become Christians, acknowledging the right of Gentiles to be church members without first converting to Judaism. But another problem soon arose.

Paul recorded that soon after the Jerusalem conference Peter was in Antioch sharing the fellowship of Gentile Christians without observing any dietary restrictions. But then "certain men came from James" (Gal. 2:12), evidently representatives of the Jerusalem church who believed that the Mosaic Law was still to be followed by Jew-

Peter and the sons of Zebedee, unable to stay awake as Jesus prays in Gethsemane; a 14th-century painting

ish Christians in all respects, especially in regard to circumcision and dietary practices. Jews would not eat at the same table with the Gentiles unless they kept the dietary laws, and Peter evidently urged the Gentile Christians to yield to the newcomers in this restriction. James continued to be firmly identified with a group of Jewish Christians who maintained close obedience to the Mosaic Law. Members of this group would have seen adherence to the Law to be consistent with Jesus' own mission, which had been concentrated almost entirely on the Jews of his homeland, and only rarely, and somewhat accidentally, reached out to the Gentile world beyond.

According to the Jewish historian Josephus, James was martyred in Jerusalem a few years before A.D. 70, the year of the destruction of the temple. The remnants of Jewish Christianity were driven out of Jerusalem, but continued to exist as a minority movement in Christianity for several generations.

The author of the letter of James identifies himself as "a servant of God and of the Lord Jesus Christ" who was writing to "the twelve tribes in the Dispersion" (Jas. 1:1). An early tradition identified the author as the brother of Jesus. However, many scholars today doubt this because the letter exhibits an exceptional command of Greek that stands out from that of other writers of the New Testament and seems inconsistent with the thorough Jewishness of James.

Nevertheless, the tone of the letter is in accord with the reputation of James, for it is a letter in which Jewish traditions are strongly upheld against a form of preaching that sounds like the radical message of Paul.

JAMES 4

This James was one of two sons of the **Mary** who was among the women present at the crucifixion and who later discovered the empty tomb; her other son was Joseph, also known as Joses. He is referred to as James "the younger" (Mk. 15:40), an adjective that could be translated as meaning youthful or small. In Christian tradition, this James is called "the Less" to distinguish him from **James** the son of Zebedee, called "the Great." It is possible that he is identical with **James** the son of Alphaeus, who was one of the 12, or perhaps with **James** the brother of **Jesus**; but most scholars believe him to be a separate individual. Nothing else is known about him.

JANNES AND JAMBRES

(jan' iz, jam' briz) GREEK: IANNES, IAMBRES

In writing to his helper **Timothy**, the apostle **Paul** named the Egyptian magicians Pharaoh summoned to match the miracles of **Moses** and **Aaron**. "As Jannes and Jambres opposed Moses," Paul warned about those resisting the gospel, "so these men also oppose the truth." But like the sorcerers, he continued, "they will not get very far, for their folly will be plain to all, as was that of those two men" (2 Tim. 3:8, 9).

In Exodus 7:11-12, where the story is found, the magicians are not named. Paul, however, was drawing upon rabbinical tradition, which contained a rich collection of stories about the magicians who repeatedly opposed Moses and Aaron. Like Aaron, Pharaoh's magicians were able to turn rods into serpents, but when Aaron's serpent swallowed theirs, the magic of Jannes and Jambres was shown to be inferior. Yet even when Moses turned the Nile waters into blood, they were able to duplicate that feat to Pharaoh's satisfaction. Nevertheless, the Lord's power eventually prevailed. Stories about these magicians were popular over the centuries since they demonstrated the vulnerability of secular magic, the persistence of which troubled both Jews and early Christians.

Pharaoh's magicians duplicating Aaron's feat by turning their rods into serpents; a late-16th-century French ceramic plate

JAPHETH

(jay' feth) HEBREW: YEPET
"may God enlarge"

In Genesis 5:32 and three subsequent passages, Japheth is listed as the last of **Noah**'s three sons. However, some scholars consider him to be the second son or—according to his place in the table of nations (Genesis 10:1-32)—even the first. Along with his two brothers, **Shem** and **Ham**, and their wives, Japheth and his wife escaped the Flood on the ark Noah had built at the Lord's command. Afterward, he and Shem covered their drunken father's nakedness, while Ham violated tradition by looking at him. For this considerate act the two brothers received Noah's blessing, whereas the descendants of Ham were cursed.

Japheth had seven sons and seven grandsons and was the ancestor of many nations. Although the descendants of Shem and Ham are mentioned throughout the Bible, Japheth's progeny—outside the genealogies in Genesis and 1 Chronicles—appear mainly in the books of Isaiah and Ezekiel.

JASON

(jay' suhn) GREEK: IASON, for HEBREW:
JOSHUA or JESHUA
"healing" or "salvation"

Jason, the Jewish historian of the Maccabean revolt, came from Cyrene on the North African coast. His five-volume history, written late in the second century B.C., began at the time of the high priest **Onias III** and concluded with the defeat of Nicanor. A fine example of Judeo-Hellenistic literature, the books survive only in the condensation crafted by the unknown compiler of the apocryphal book 2 Maccabees. Jason may have traveled widely, as his name is inscribed on the temple of Pharaoh Thutmose III in Egypt.

JASON 2

The son of **Simon II** and brother of **Onias III**, Jason was high priest from 175 to 172 B.C., during the reign of **Antiochus IV Epiphanes**. Jason had purchased the position from the king during his brother's absence. The new high priest proceeded to establish "the Greek way of life" (2 Macc. 4:10) in the kingdom and enrolled all Jerusalem's men as citizens of Antioch. Jason angered many by constructing a gymnasium that placed importance on Greek values, thereby weakening tradition-

Noah's sons help build the ark; detail from a medieval silver church panel.

al Jewish culture. During the games held at Tyre, Jason sent envoys with 300 silver drachmas as an offering to the god Hercules. When Antiochus visited Jerusalem on his way to Phoenicia, Jason organized a lavish welcome for him. Despite all his efforts, Jason was finally ousted by **Menelaus**, who could pay more for the position of high priest, and he sought refuge with the Ammonites east of the Jordan River. In 169 B.C., crediting false rumors of the king's death, Jason led a 1,000-man army into Jerusalem in an unsuccessful attempt to regain power, and then withdrew once more to Ammon. Ultimately, Jason "met a miserable end" (2 Macc. 5:8). He was tried by the Nabatean ruler Aretas, spent years as a wandering outcast, and was en route from Egypt to Sparta when he died at sea.

JEHOAHAZ

(juh hoh' ah haz) HEBREW: YEHOAHAZ
"God has grasped"

The northern kingdom of Israel was in sharp decline during the reign of Jehoahaz (815-801 B.C.); for the first three years he served as coregent with his aging father, **Jehu**. At that time, Israel was in servitude to Aram, which controlled all of Syria and Palestine. The Syrians under King **Hazael** and his son Ben-hadad III left Jehoahaz with only "an army of [no] more than fifty horsemen and ten chariots and ten thousand footmen; for the king of Syria had destroyed them and made them like the dust at threshing" (2 Kg. 13:7). Assyrian campaigns into northern and central Syria during the later years of Jehoahaz's reign weakened Israel's northern neighbor, but this ultimately brought Israel under the yoke of that far stronger power.

JEHOAHAZ 2

The son of King **Josiah** of Judah, Jehoahaz assumed the throne when his father was killed battling Pharaoh **Neco** at Megiddo. As the fourth son, Jehoahaz was not first in the line of succession, but "the people of the land" (2 Kg. 23:30) chose him over his older brothers. Only 23 years old that summer of 609 B.C., Shallum (Jehoahaz's proper name) reigned but three months before Neco returned from campaigns against the Medes and Chaldeans in Assyria and ordered Jehoahaz to be arrested in Jerusalem and brought to his headquarters at Riblah on the Orontes River. The young king of Judah was deposed and replaced by his older brother Eliakim, renamed **Jehoiakim**. To emphasize that Judah was then firmly under the thumb of Egypt, Neco exacted a tribute of "a hundred talents of silver and a talent of gold" (2 Chr. 36:3) from Jehoiakim. Jehoahaz was taken as a captive to Egypt and died there without ever seeing his homeland again. He was the last independent king of Judah, which was henceforth to be subjected to one or another of its powerful neighbors.

JEHOIACHIN

(juh hoy' ah kin) HEBREW: YEHOYAKIN
"Yahweh will uphold"

As King **Nebuchadnezzar** of Babylon was preparing to besiege Jerusalem in December of 598 B.C., Jehoiachin (who is also called Jeconiah) succeeded his father, **Jehoiakim**, on the throne of Judah. He was only 18 years old. But by the following March, Jehoiachin was forced to surrender and was taken to Babylon along with thousands of other Jewish captives. Nebuchadnezzar named Jehoiachin's uncle **Zedekiah** the new king.

Jehoiachin spent at least 37 years in Babylon, retaining a leadership role over his fellow exiles and enjoying varying degrees of freedom during Nebuchadnezzar's reign. Administrative documents unearthed in Babylon reveal deliveries of oil to Jehoiachin during the exile; and it is known

from 1 Chronicles that he eventually had seven sons during his captivity. Even after his exile, many Jews considered Jehoiachin still to be the king of Judah and continued to date events by the years of his reign.

The deposed king of Judah outlived Nebuchadnezzar, who died in 562 B.C. and was succeeded by his son **Evil-merodach**. To mark his accession, the new Babylonian king pardoned Jehoiachin and "gave him a seat above the seats of the kings who were with him in Babylon. So Jehoiachin put off his prison garments. And every day of his life he dined regularly at the king's table" (2 Kg. 25:28-29). During his captivity, Jehoiachin is said to have erected a mausoleum at the grave of the prophet **Ezekiel**.

JEHOIADA

(juh hoy' ah dah) HEBREW: YEHOYADA
"God has known"

Upon the death of her son King **Ahaziah** of Judah, the queen mother, **Athaliah**, seized power and ordered a massacre of the royal family. But Ahaziah's sister Jehosheba rescued the king's infant son **Joash** and gave him over to the care of her husband, a priest named Jehoiada. The boy was sheltered in the temple for six years before Jehoiada decided to risk challenging the queen. With the aid of Carite mercenaries, he had Joash publicly crowned and anointed. Surprised and enraged at this unexpected restoration of the house of **David**, Athaliah stormed into the temple, shouting, "Treason! Treason!" (2 Kg. 11:14). But Jehoiada ordered her dragged from the house of the Lord and killed.

Jehoiada served as adviser to Joash during his youth, and together they initiated policies to destroy the cult of **Baal** and repair the temple in Jerusalem. Jehoiada made a covenant between "the Lord and the king and people" to ensure that all would be "the Lord's people" (2 Kg. 11:17). Much later, when the repair of the temple had not progressed in 23 years, the king summoned Jehoiada for a financial report. It seemed that the priests were not allocating money from assessments and donations for repairs. So Jehoiada devised what may have been history's first collection box. Those entering the temple were encouraged to deposit money into a hole bored into a chest kept near the altar. When the chest was full, the money was counted and given directly to the carpenters, masons, and stonecutters in order for the work to be resumed.

Jehoiada served the king until he "grew old and full of days" (2 Chr. 24:15) and

In this manuscript illumination Judah's King Jehoiachin is led off to captivity in Babylon, accompanied by the prophet Ezekiel.

died at the age of 130; his good deeds earned him a burial among the kings in the city of David. The author of 2 Chronicles wrote that Joash "did what was right in the eyes of the Lord all the days of Jehoiada the priest" (2 Chr. 24:2)—testimony that the king's character deteriorated in the years following his protector's death.

JEHOIAKIM
(juh hoi' uh kim) HEBREW: YEHOYAQIM
"Yahweh will establish"
∙∙∙∙∙∙∙∙∙∙

When his younger brother **Jehoahaz** was ousted by Pharaoh **Neco** after only three months on the throne of Judah, 25-year-old Eliakim was chosen in his place and his name changed to Jehoiakim. For the first few years of his reign (609-598 B.C.), Jehoiakim remained a vassal of Egypt, which effectively controlled all the territory north through Syria. Using slave labor, the king expanded the royal palace in the Egyptian style and was condemned by the prophet **Jeremiah** for "practicing oppression and violence" (Jer. 22:17). He was accused of committing murder, incest, rape, and theft, and he openly defied the traditions of Israel's Law: "He did what was evil in the sight of the Lord, according to all that his fathers had done" (2 Kg. 23:37).

In 605 B.C., Jeremiah prophesied the destruction of Judah by the Babylonians. The

papyrus scroll containing his oracles as written down and read by **Baruch** was confiscated and brought to Jehoiakim. Sitting by a fire, Jehoiakim listened to the prophecies. As several were read, he cut the text columns from the scroll and burned them, then repeated the process. That very year an Egyptian army was defeated by Babylonian forces under the heir apparent **Nebuchadnezzar** at Carchemish on the Euphrates. The balance of power had shifted, and for three years Jehoiakim paid tribute to Babylon and endured military incursions by Babylon's allies.

Still harboring pro-Egyptian tendencies, Jehoiakim rebelled against Nebuchadnezzar in 600 B.C. after a bloody Babylonian–Egyptian confrontation on the frontier. Nebuchadnezzar did not retaliate immediately against Judah, but instead reorganized his army and saw to other matters. By 598 B.C., however, Nebuchadnezzar was ready to pursue a vigorous attack on his rebellious vassal state. The Babylonian army marched on Judah aided by Chaldean, Moabite, and Ammonite forces. In December, just before the siege of Jerusalem, Jehoiakim died. The exact circumstances of his death and burial are uncertain, although it seems likely that he was assassinated. His 18-year-old son and successor, **Jehoiachin**, held on until March of 597 B.C.

A surviving tablet from the seventh year of Nebuchadnezzar tells of the fall of Jerusalem: "In the month Kislimu [December], the king of Akkad called up his army, marched against Syria, encamped against the city of Judah and seized the town on the second day of Adar [March/April]. He captured the king. He appointed there a king of his own choice. He took much booty from it and sent it to Babylon." Along with the booty, Jehoiachin and thousands of captives were taken to Babylon.

JEHORAM
(juh hoh' ruhm) HEBREW: YEHORAM
"Yahweh is exalted"
∙∙∙∙∙∙∙∙∙∙

The last of the dynasty of **Omri**, Jehoram (also called Joram) succeeded his brother **Ahaziah** on the throne of Israel about 849 B.C. and is said to have ruled for 12 years. The actual length of his reign is somewhat uncertain since many passages in 2 Kings purporting to cover that period refer only to "the king of Israel" and not to Jehoram by name. He is best known for military exploits he achieved in association with two kings of Judah.

When King **Mesha** of Moab refused to deliver his annual tribute, Jehoram enlisted the support of King **Jehoshaphat** of Judah for an attack through the subject state of Edom south of the Dead Sea. The combined force destroyed city after city, until Mesha was besieged at Kir-haraseth. Facing certain defeat, the Moabite ruler sacrificed his eldest son as "a burnt offering upon the wall" (2 Kg. 3:27). The attackers withdrew in horror and the Moabites were freed permanently from Israelite control.

Jehoram also sought to control the disputed frontier post of Ramoth-gilead, east of the Jordan, which was under attack by the Syrian king **Hazael**. His ally this time was Jehoshaphat's grandson King **Ahaziah** of Judah, the son of his sister (or possibly his aunt) **Athaliah**. Jehoram was wounded in that action and took refuge in his palace at Jezreel to recuperate, being joined there by Ahaziah. Meanwhile, the prophet **Elisha**—determined to avenge the transgressions of Jehoram's parents, **Ahab** and **Jezebel**—sent a disciple to anoint an army commander named **Jehu** as the new king of Israel. Acclaimed by his troops, Jehu raced off to the capital of Jezreel before word of his coronation could spread. As Jehoram and Ahaziah came out in chariots to meet him, Jehu treacherously shot Jehoram through the heart with an arrow. Ahaziah fled but was pursued and also killed.

Jehoram is judged less harshly in the Bible than his parents because he "put away the pillar of Baal which his father had made" (2 Kg. 3:2), thus somewhat diminishing the cult introduced by Jezebel. Jehoram was also probably part of an anti-Assyrian coalition that confronted Shalmaneser III on three campaigns of westward expansion launched during his reign.

JEHORAM 2

The firstborn of King **Jehoshaphat**'s seven sons, Jehoram (also called Joram) was king of Judah from 849 to 842 B.C. He assumed the throne at the age of 32, probably at first serving as coregent with his father. During his father's reign, Jehoram was married to **Athaliah**, the daughter (or possibly the sister) of King **Ahab** of Israel, to cement the alliance between the two kingdoms. Thus, the cult of **Baal**, which had been flourishing in the northern kingdom, was introduced into Judah's royal family.

Jehoshaphat had been generous with his other sons, showering them with silver, gold, and property. However, when Jehoram took power, "he slew all his brothers with the sword, and also some of the princes of Israel" (2 Chr. 21:4). The young king also "made high places [pagan shrines] in the hill country of Judah, and led the inhabitants of Jerusalem into unfaithfulness" (2 Chr. 21:11). This earned him a letter of rebuke from the prophet **Elijah**, who said that the Lord would bring a great plague on the people and a severe illness to their king. In time, both prophecies were fulfilled.

Politically, Jehoram faced two revolts in

Jehoshaphat announces the birth of his firstborn son, Jehoram; the marriage alliance the king made for Jehoram with Ahab brought the worship of Baal to Judah.

the south—from Edom and Libnah. When these subject states broke free of Judah, trade routes to Arabia were disrupted and the economy of the country was seriously weakened. The Lord's anger next took the form of an attack by Philistines and Arabs, who carried off all the king's possessions and family, except for his youngest son, Jehoahaz (**Ahaziah**). Despite his grief, Jehoram suffered still more. The Jewish historian Josephus relates that he came to a horrible death in fulfillment of a prophecy of Elijah, "that he should die of a disease of the intestines after a long period of torment, when from the excessive corruption of his inward parts, his bowels would fall out, so that he would look on his own misery."

The wickedness of Jehoram's reign is evidenced by the report that "His people made no fire in his honor . . . . and he departed with no one's regret" (2 Chr. 21:19, 20). The Bible contains conflicting information on whether Jehoram was buried in the royal tombs at Jerusalem.

JEHOSHAPHAT

(juh hoh' shuh fat) HEBREW: YEHOSHAPHAT
"Yahweh has judged"

During his more than two-decade reign as king of Judah (873-849 B.C.), Jehoshaphat solidified the peace that had ended years of constant warfare with the northern kingdom of Israel, perhaps by subordinating himself to King **Ahab**. His alliance with the former rival state was cemented by the marriage of his son **Jehoram** to **Athaliah**, Ahab's daughter (or perhaps his sister).

A balance of power thus achieved, Jehoshaphat focused on internal matters. With a "heart . . . courageous in the ways of the Lord" (2 Chr. 17:6), he removed pagan shrines from his kingdom and, in his third year, sent teachers throughout Judah with the book of the Lord's Law. In foreign affairs, Jehoshaphat pursued a policy of peace-through-strength, organizing Judah's large standing army into an effective fighting force. Feared and honored, he became wealthy from tribute. The Philistines brought him silver and the Arabs thousands of rams and male goats. Judah was an important part of the economic partnership between Tyre and Israel, since the southern kingdom controlled the land trade routes between the Mediterranean ports and the Red Sea to the south.

When Ahab asked Jehoshaphat to join him in an attack against the Syrians at Ramoth-gilead, he responded "I am as you

are, my people are as your people, my horses as your horses" (1 Kg. 22:4). The ill-fated military expedition left Ahab mortally wounded and Jehoshaphat retreating to Jerusalem. Admonished by the seer **Jehu** for his alliance with the sinful Ahab, Jehoshaphat renewed his campaign to counter the influences of the cult of **Baal**. The king also reformed the judicial system of his kingdom, appointing Levites, priests, and heads of family to hear disputed cases in Jerusalem and sending judges to other cities, telling them, "Take heed what you do, for there is no perversion of justice with the Lord our God, or partiality, or taking bribes" (2 Chr. 19:7).

Militarily, Jehoshaphat continued to assist Israel. When the subject Moabites under **Mesha** rebelled by refusing to deliver the annual tribute of lambs and wool to Ahab's son and successor **Jehoram**, both kingdoms again took to the battlefield. With his army suffering great losses, Mesha sacrificed his eldest son to the god Chemosh—at which the opposing armies retreated in fear and horror. In another action, in which he faced an enemy host from Ammon and Moab, Jehoshaphat proclaimed a fast and sought the help of the Lord. "Fear not, and be not dismayed," he was told, ". . . for the battle is not yours but God's" (2 Chr. 20:15). The next day, the people watched as the attackers destroyed each other. For three days, the men of Judah searched the bloody field for the spoils of victory, then returned to Jerusalem for joyful celebration.

Not everything went so well for Judah. Eager to expand trade through the Red Sea, Jehoshaphat established a shipyard at Ezion-geber on the Gulf of Aqabah. However, the venture failed when the ships were wrecked before they could reach Ophir, a source of gold no longer identifiable.

Jehoshaphat died at the age of 60, and according to the Jewish historian Josephus, "was buried in a magnificent manner in Jerusalem, for he had imitated the actions of David."

JEHU

(jay' hoo) HEBREW: YEHU
"he is Yahweh"

A crafty and ruthless monarch, Jehu ruled the northern kingdom of Israel for 28 years (842-815 B.C.), founding a dynasty that lasted for nearly a century. Jehu was an army commander based at Ramoth-gilead, an important point on the north-south trade route between Damascus and the Gulf of Aqabah. While in a meeting with other offi-

A defiant Jezebel peers from her palace window as the victorious Jehu thunders into Jezreel; a 19th-century painting.

cers, Jehu was approached by a messenger of the prophet **Elisha** and summoned into an inner chamber, where the young man poured oil on his head and anointed him king. He was told to destroy the house of **Ahab** and rid the country of the cult of **Baal**, which had been promoted by the queen mother, **Jezebel**.

After celebrating with his men, Jehu set out for Jezreel where King **Jehoram** was recuperating from wounds received while

battling the Syrians under **Hazael**. With his visiting nephew King **Ahaziah** of Judah in a chariot alongside his own, Jehoram rode out to hear the news from Ramoth-gilead. Speaking with Jehu, the two kings learned of his treacherous plans and turned to flee. Jehu shot Jehoram with an arrow through the heart and ordered his men to hunt down Ahaziah and kill him as well. Entering the gate of Jezreel, Jehu heard the mocking words of Jezebel as she peered out from a window of the palace, and he shouted to her attendant eunuchs, "Throw her down" (2 Kg. 9:33). Jezebel's blood colored the walls and the horses that trampled her body. The deed done, Jehu took food and drink, ordering Jezebel to be buried as befitted a king's daughter—but her corpse had already been devoured by dogs.

With the main players eliminated, Jehu focused on the 70 sons of Ahab residing in Samaria. As the rulers and elders of Samaria trembled in fear of Jehu, they were commanded to "take the heads of your master's sons, and come to me at Jezreel" (2 Kg. 10:6). The next day, baskets containing the 70 heads were brought to Jehu, who placed them in two large piles at the town's main gate. The house of Ahab was exterminated, but Jehu completed his mission by slaying all of Ahab's leaders, family friends, and priests in Jezreel. On the way to Samaria, Jehu encountered a group of Ahaziah's kinsmen who knew nothing of the massacre. Jehu slew all 42 of them at a place called Beth-eked.

In Samaria, Jehu's "zeal for the Lord" (2 Kg. 10:16) caused him to devise a plan for the supporters of Baal. Pretending to serve the Phoenician god, Jehu summoned all worshipers to gather so that "the house of Baal was filled from one end to the other" (2 Kg. 10:21). Assured that the shrine contained no servants of the Lord, Jehu made burnt offerings and, when he was finished, called in 80 soldiers to put all the worshipers to death. The house and cult pillar were demolished and the site was thereafter used as a latrine. The Lord rewarded Jehu's actions by declaring, "your sons of the fourth generation shall sit on the throne of Israel" (2 Kg. 10:30).

With the collapse of the dynasty founded by Ahab's father, **Omri**, former alliances with Judah and Phoenician cities ended. Politically savvy, Jehu knew that he must bolster his isolationist position in light of the growing strength of Hazael of Damascus. The harsh economic policy of the Omrides, including heavy military expenditures, had not been popular with the people. Jehu therefore opted for vassal status and made overtures to Assyria. The annals of Shalmaneser III record his campaigns against Syria and the payment of tribute by the king of Israel, while a stela from the Assyrian capital of Nimrud shows Jehu bowing before the Assyrian monarch. In an event not mentioned in the Bible, the Assyrian ruler has preserved the following payment: "The tribute of Jehu, son of Omri; I received from him silver, gold, a golden saplu-bowl, a golden vase with pointed bottom, golden

tumblers, golden buckets, tin, and a staff for a king." The Assyrian campaigns against Syria were crucial to Jehu as he sought to consolidate his power after the coup. However, as internal strife intensified within Assyria, Hazael was able to launch successful attacks against Israel, seizing much of the territory east of the Jordan.

Jehu apparently died of natural causes and was buried at Samaria. He was succeeded by his son **Jehoahaz**. Although Jehu's seizure of power is legitimized in the account in 2 Kings, the prophet **Hosea** later condemned "the house of Jehu" (Hos. 1:4) for his bloody deeds and named his firstborn son for the slaughter at Jezreel.

JEHU 2

Jehu the son of Hanani was a prophet during the rule of King **Baasha** of Israel. He rebuked the monarch for his sinful leadership, warning that the king and his house would be condemned by the Lord. Any who died in the city, he said, "the dogs shall eat"; and those who died in the country "the birds of the air shall eat" (1 Kg. 16:4). Though Baasha reigned nearly a quarter century, his son and successor **Elah** was assassinated after two years on the throne and all males of his family were killed.

Years later, Jehu protested the alliance of King **Jehoshaphat** of Judah with the evil King **Ahab** of Israel against the Syrians. The biography of Jehoshaphat was said to be recorded in now lost chronicles of Jehu.

Jehu bows before Shalmaneser III in this detail from an Assyrian stone carving.

JEPHTHAH

(jef' thuh) HEBREW: YIPTAH
"opened" or "opener"

As the child of a harlot, Jephthah was scorned by his father's legitimate sons, who drove him from the family home in Israelite Gilead when they reached maturity. With no personal resources or hope of an inheritance, he fled to the land of Tob, a border region far east of the Jordan, where he gathered about him a group of "worthless fellows" (Jg. 11:3). Small roving bands of disenfranchised youths like Jephthah were common from the early settlement period up to Roman times. While making alliances with local inhabitants who felt overtaxed or mistreated by their nominal rulers, these lawless frontiersmen sustained themselves by plundering merchant caravans and raiding other settled communities. Jephthah, however, rose above these inauspicious beginnings to judge Israel for six years; he was the ninth in a series of primarily military heroes who led temporary armies summoned to defend Israelite villages under attack from enemy nations in the premonarchical period.

When their hostile neighbors the Ammonites sought to regain territory seized by the Israelites, the elders of Gilead turned to Jephthah—obviously impressed with his martial skills despite their earlier disdain for him. But he responded angrily to their plea for help: "Did you not hate me, and drive me out of my father's house? Why have you come to me now when you are in trouble?" (Jg. 11:7). Nonetheless, he agreed to lead the fight after the elders promised to make him their ruler when "the Lord gives them [the Ammonites] over to me" (Jg. 11:9).

Upon taking command of the Israelite forces, Jephthah sent messengers to negotiate a settlement with the Ammonites. But the enemy demurred; they were determined to reappropriate territory that Israel had taken from them during their migration from Egypt to Canaan. In a lengthy speech Jephthah set forth Israel's right to the Transjordan region, pointing out that his people had been refused permission to pass peacefully through these foreign lands. Israel's possession of the territory, he argued, was sanctified by the Lord—just as the earlier claim of the Ammonites had been endorsed by their deity.

With the collapse of these negotiations, Jephthah turned to God, vowing that he would sacrifice whoever first appeared at the door of his house if he were allowed to return in triumph from war. Jephthah may have expected to see an animal at the door, since the ground floor in dwellings of that period served to shelter livestock while people usually lived on the second floor of their houses. To Jephthah's horror, it was his only child, his daughter, who greeted his victorious return "with timbrels and with dances" (Jg. 11:34). Although human sacrifice was repugnant and in violation of religious law, the warrior's oath apparently took precedence over the ban. In despair, Jephthah granted his daughter's request for two months in which to mourn her maidenhood, but subsequently fulfilled his vow to sacrifice her. The women of Israel later commemorated this tragic event with an annual four-day period of lamentation.

In the New Testament, Jephthah is remembered—along with **Gideon**, **Barak**, **Samson**, **David**, **Samuel**, and the prophets—as one who "through faith conquered kingdoms" (Heb. 11:33). However, both Jews and Christians have expressed their ethical concerns about a story in which a father is willing to kill his own daughter in order to fulfill a vow.

Before his six years of judging Israel had ended, Jephthah had to put down an uprising by the men of Ephraim, fellow Israelites incensed by his failure to summon them to join the fight against the Ammonites. With apparent ease, he defeated the Ephraimite attack across the Jordan and cut off their retreat by stationing troops at the fords of the river. Realizing that Ephraimite soldiers looked no different from his own, he told his men to demand that each person crossing the fords be asked to say "Shibboleth" (ear of grain). Ephraimites were unable to pronounce the *sh* sound, so the word came out "Sibboleth." Thus, the Gileadites were able to identify their enemy and, the Bible reports, slew 42,000 Ephraimites who

Horrified at the prospect of fulfilling his terrible vow, Jephthah falls to his knees as his daughter dances out to meet him.

failed to pass this simple verbal test. In modern English the word "shibboleth" has come to be a catchword devoid of an actual meaning but serving to identify a particular group of people.

JEREMIAH

(jair uh mi' uh) HEBREW: YIRMEYAHU
possibly "Yah[weh] founds/exalts/loosens/throws"

A boy of only 12 or 13 when he was called to be a prophet in 627 B.C., Jeremiah witnessed the final resurgence of the kingdom of Judah and its ultimate destruction. Only a few years after Jeremiah's call, the rediscovery of the Law (probably the book of

Deuteronomy) within the temple precincts in Jerusalem sparked the religious reforms of King **Josiah**. Coincidentally, the disintegration of the Assyrian empire allowed Josiah to reassert Judah's independence after nearly a century of vassalage. Unfortunately, both reform and independence were short-lived—which accounts for the intense personal stress Jeremiah experienced in his 40-year career as a prophet under Josiah and his four successors. The lengthy biblical book that bears his name is essentially a collection of oracles against Judah and its foreign enemies dictated by the prophet to his aide, the scribe **Baruch**.

Jeremiah was born about 640 B.C. to a priestly family in Anathoth, a village some

three miles north of Jerusalem. His father, Hilkiah, was a landowner of some means and was perhaps a descendant of the priest **Abiathar**, who had been banished to Anathoth by King **Solomon** for failure to side with him in his struggle for the throne against his older brother **Adonijah**.

A RELUCTANT PROPHET

According to Jeremiah's own account of his call, God knew him even "before I formed you in the womb" and had appointed him to be "a prophet to the nations" (Jer. 1:5) before he was born. But at the time of his call, Jeremiah did not think he was ready for such a role, protesting, "I do not know how to speak, for I am only a youth" (Jer. 1:6). Jeremiah's story thus parallels that of **Samuel,** who also as a "boy ministered to the Lord" (1 Sam. 2:11). And his reluctance to serve recalls **Moses,** who also had resisted his summons, claiming, "I am not eloquent . . . I am slow of speech and of tongue" (Ex. 4:10). God overcame Jeremiah's objections by telling the youth not to be afraid and by assuring his new prophet that the Lord was with him. Then, by touching Jeremiah on the mouth, God indicated that he would give the prophet the words to say. The message was the Lord's intention "to pluck up and to break down, to destroy and to overthrow" (Jer. 1:10) the kingdom of Judah for its faithlessness.

To clarify the message, the Lord gave Jeremiah two visions. In the first, he asked the prophet to describe what he saw; Jeremiah answered, "a rod of almond." God said, "You have seen well, for I am watching over my word to perform it" (Jer. 1:11-12). The Hebrew word for "almond" is *shaqed*, and God interpreted it for him as a play on *shoqed*, meaning "watchman." Like a solitary watchman on a high tower above the ordinary events of life below, Jeremiah must stand guard over the word that God had given him as those predictions were enacted in world affairs. In the second vision, Jeremiah saw a boiling pot tilted away from the north toward the south, ready to spill out its scalding contents. God explained its significance in terms of the triumph of an enemy "out of the north" (Jer. 1:14)—that is, Babylon, which he would employ for the de-

The prophet Jeremiah, by Donatello (c. 1386-1466)

struction of Judah. Within his call to Jeremiah, however, God offered a note of hope, saying he aimed "to build and to plant" (Jer. 1:10)—a reference to the restoration of the nation after its destruction in 586 B.C.

The first 18 years of Jeremiah's ministry were perhaps the happiest for him as the pious Josiah "began to seek the God of David his father" (2 Chr. 34:3). But when Egyptian Pharaoh **Neco** led his army up through Israel to aid Assyria against the burgeoning power of Babylon, Josiah unwisely tried to stop him and was fatally wounded in battle at Meggido in 609 B.C. Neco appointed Josiah's older son, **Jehoiakim**, king of Judah, instead of a younger son, **Jehoahaz**, who had been chosen by the people.

To signal his disapproval of the new king's apostasy, the Lord commanded Jeremiah to speak his words in the temple: "If you will not listen to me, to walk in my law which I have set before you, and to heed the words of my servants the prophets whom I send to you urgently . . . I will make this city a curse for all the nations of the earth" (Jer. 26:4-6). First a puppet of Egypt, Jehoiakim was later forced to pay tribute to a triumphant Babylon and maintained a fragile independence throughout the rest of his reign (609-598 B.C.). When Jeremiah and some other prophets announced that Babylon was actually an agent of God's judgment and would successfully invade Judah, Jehoiakim responded by killing the prophet **Uriah** as others sought Jeremiah's death. Citing Jeremiah's divine inspiration, his defenders won a reprieve.

Prohibited from speaking in the temple, Jeremiah dictated his oracles to Baruch and sent him to read the scroll in the sacred precincts. When some of the king's associates heard these words, they advised Baruch to go into hiding with his master, but demanded that he first hand over the scroll to them so it could be brought to the king. As he heard each oracle read to him, Jehoiakim cut off a portion of the scroll with a penknife and threw it into the fire of a brazier until the entire manuscript was burned. In obedience to the Lord, Jeremiah dictated a second scroll that not only preserved the original message but also added harsh words of judgment on the king: "His dead body shall be cast out to the heat by day and the

In this medieval fresco from the Vatican, crude letters spell out the prophet's name in Latin: HYEREMIAS.

frost by night. And I will punish him and his offspring and his servants for their iniquity" (Jer. 36:30-31).

In 598 B.C., Jehoiakim died and was succeeded by his 18-year-old son, **Jehoiachin**. But within three months King **Nebuchadnezzar** of Babylon had conquered Jerusalem, looted the temple and royal treasury, and carried away most of the royal family and other leaders into exile. Babylonian records mention Jehoiachin among the captives. In 597 Nebuchadnezzar installed a third son of Josiah's, **Zedekiah**, on the throne of Judah; he was to be the last ruler of the southern kingdom.

About this time God gave Jeremiah a vision of two baskets of figs, one good and the other bad. The good figs signified the people of Judah who had gone into exile with Jehoiachin, for they would be restored to the land. The bad figs represented Zedekiah and other leaders who remained behind in Judah. Thus, Jeremiah revealed that some people in captivity would preserve and continue to obey the Law of God. From this remnant would come the faithful who would repopulate the land and restore the nation.

Jeremiah confirmed God's promise of restoration by a provocative act. As Nebuchadnezzar laid siege to Jerusalem, the Lord told Jeremiah to purchase some property his cousin owned at Anathoth. How foolish it must have seemed to buy land that would soon belong to the Babylonians, for Jeremiah himself had predicted the fall of Judah. Nonetheless, the prophet went through all the red tape of a property transfer, including the making of two copies of the deed and the preservation of the copies in an earthenware jar, so that no one could dispute the ownership. Embarrassed, Jeremiah complained to God, and God replied that the prophet had just given witness to everyone that someday land would be bought and sold in Judah again. By this act, the prophet was expressing a promise for future generations that few of his contemporaries could understand.

Any number of Jeremiah's actions must have made him appear unconventional. When everyone else went to the house of mourning to express their despair over Babylonian attacks on Judah, the Lord demanded that Jeremiah not lament but go about his daily activities as if nothing had happened. When people appeared heedless of the impending danger, God told Jeremiah to cut off his hair to express humility and mourning. And as a symbol of the hopeless future of Judah, God told Jeremiah not to marry or have children. On one occasion, he bought a new linen waistcloth, wore it, and then went to the banks of the Euphrates River to hide it in a cleft of rock—all as commanded by the Lord. After Jeremiah retrieved the garment sometime later, he showed everyone that "the waistcloth was spoiled; it was good for nothing" (Jer. 13:7). Whether or not he actually walked the 700 miles to the Euphrates and back or dramatized the journey on a smaller scale, Jeremiah demonstrated the consequences of exile in Babylon. On another occasion, he bought a new pot. After inviting several priests and elders to accompany him outside the city to the valley of Hinnom, he shattered the pot to illustrate the gravity of the Lord's coming judgment against Judah.

TIMELESS ADVICE

Most of Jeremiah's words are recorded without reference to a specific date or circumstance, and this gives them a timeless quality, far removed from the original period and place of delivery. The prophet raised serious objections to pious behavior devoid of introspection, repentance, and change. Ritual observance, he contended, is only as authentic as the inner conviction the worshiper brings to it. In his view, the temple had degenerated from being a house of prayer into a "den of robbers" (Jer. 7:11)—a phrase **Jesus** would adopt in driving out the money changers. He questioned the efficacy of sacrifices unless they were combined with a willingness to hear and obey the word of God. Rather than submitting to circumcision to satisfy the ritual demand, Jeremiah told men, it would be better to "remove the foreskin of your hearts" (Jer.

4:4). Rather than entertaining false promises of peace when the world was in flames, it would be better to hear the harsh words of faithful prophets. Rather than merely possessing a book of revealed teaching, it would be better to understand and obey God.

Although Zedekiah publicly opposed Jeremiah, he secretly sent messengers to the prophet to inquire of God what next to expect from Nebuchadnezzar and to pray for the nation's deliverance. At least once, Zedekiah himself met privately with the prophet to seek his help but made him swear that he would tell others the visit had been at Jeremiah's own request. And when Zedekiah made a trip to Babylon in the fourth year of his reign—apparently to profess loyalty to Nebuchadnezzar—Jeremiah sent a book of prophecies with the king's quartermaster and, coincidentally, Baruch's brother, Seraiah. Jeremiah instructed Seraiah to read these oracles against Babylon, then bind the book to a stone and cast it into the Euphrates. "Thus shall Babylon sink," Seraiah was to cry out, "to rise no more, because of the evil that I am bringing upon her" (Jer. 51:64).

Jeremiah frequently stood opposed to the king's favored prophets, men who offered alternative words of advice and admonition and whom Jeremiah described as pretenders leading corrupt private lives and prophesying for money. The Lord had instructed Jeremiah to wear a wooden yoke while he was telling the people of Judah to submit to the yoke of Babylon. **Hananiah**, one of the king's prophets, confronted Jeremiah in the temple by announcing that God would remove "the yoke of the king of Babylon" and in two years return the vessels of the temple that Nebuchadnezzar had taken away. Jeremiah simply said, "Amen! May the Lord do so" (Jer. 28:2, 6). But when he expressed his doubts, Hananiah pulled the yoke off Jeremiah's shoulders and broke it to illustrate his disagreement. Sometime later, God gave Jeremiah a new message for Hananiah: "You have broken wooden bars, but I will make in their place bars of iron. . . . I have put upon the neck of all these nations an iron yoke of servitude to Nebuchadnezzar" (Jer. 28:13-14).

Despite Jeremiah's warnings, Zedekiah defied the Babylonians by refusing to pay tribute. Nebuchadnezzar retaliated by reconquering Jerusalem in 586 B.C. After killing Zedekiah's sons in front of him, the victors blinded the king and marched him off in chains, with most of the remaining able-bodied persons in the city, to reside in exile in distant Mesopotamia.

During an interlude in the final siege of Jerusalem, Jeremiah was apprehended as he sought to return to Anathoth on personal business and was placed in prison. Later, the king permitted him to stay in the guards' court. Also during these final days, the prophet was thrown in an abandoned cistern for having preached surrender, but was rescued from almost certain death by an Ethiopian named Ebed-melech.

After the fall of Jerusalem and the exile to Babylon of most of its inhabitants, Jeremiah withdrew to Mizpah, a town some seven miles north of the city, where Nebuchadnezzar had installed a puppet governor named **Gedaliah** to rule the remnant of Judah. But when Gedaliah was assassinated, some

Jeremiah is drawn out of the abandoned cistern, where he had been left to die.

198

of the remaining people proposed flight to Egypt to avoid Babylonian retaliation. Speaking the words of God, Jeremiah urged that they stay: "If you will remain in this land, then I will build you up and not pull you down; I will plant you, and not pluck you up; for I repent of the evil which I did to you" (Jer. 42:10). Not only did the people ignore the prophet by leaving for Egypt, they took Jeremiah and Baruch with them. In Egypt, Jeremiah had to contend with the exiles' worship of the goddess Ishtar and ended his oracles by predicting that this remnant of Judah would die in their land of refuge. And, indeed, they as well as Jeremiah himself soon disappeared from the pages of history.

Because Jeremiah "uttered a lament for Josiah; and all the singing men and singing women have spoken of Josiah in their laments to this day" (2 Chr. 35:25), the book of Lamentations has traditionally been ascribed to Jeremiah. However, the psalms in Lamentations mourn the destruction of Jerusalem, not the death of a king, and in concept and style they are so unlike Jeremiah's oracles as to suggest another author or authors. The so-called Letter of Jeremiah in the Apocrypha is an injunction against idolatry based on Jeremiah's oracle that "the gods who did not make the heavens and the earth shall perish from the earth and from under the heavens" (Jer. 10:11). It dates to perhaps 300 years after the prophet's time.

Rembrandt used his father as a model for this portrait of Jeremiah.

JEROBOAM
(jair uh boh' uhm) HEBREW: YAROBAM
"may the people be great"

Although he rose to power as the hero of a rebellion against the oppression of King **Solomon**, Jeroboam is better known as the apostate king who divided and weakened the Israelite nation. The authors of 1 and 2 Kings used his name nearly 20 times in passing judgment on later rulers who were said to have "walked in all the way of Jeroboam the son of Nebat, and in the sins which he made Israel to sin" (1 Kg. 16:26).

As a young man, Jeroboam left his home in the hill country of Ephraim to find work on Solomon's new public building projects in Jerusalem. His ability and diligence quickly drew the attention of the king, who "gave him charge over all the forced labor of the house of Joseph" (1 Kg. 11:28). But as an overseer for Solomon, Jeroboam was in a position to observe his people's deep resentment—not only at labor carried out under slavelike conditions, but work so organized as to break down tribal loyalties and center all power in the monarchy at Jerusalem.

Leaving the city for unexplained reasons, Jeroboam met the prophet **Ahijah** of Shiloh. In a ritual act the prophet tore his robe into 12 pieces and told Jeroboam to take 10 of them. Speaking on behalf of the Lord, Ahijah prophesied that upon Solomon's death Jeroboam would be granted leadership over ten tribes, while only one tribe (other than his own) would be left to Solomon's heir. The prophecy ended with the promise that Jeroboam's dynasty would endure, as would the house of **David**—but only if he remained loyal to Israel's God.

A PETITION REJECTED

Solomon soon heard about Ahijah's prophecy and ordered Jeroboam killed. To escape the king's wrath, Jeroboam fled to Egypt, where he came under the protection of Pharaoh **Shishak,** one of the few foreign potentates with whom Solomon had not made a marriage treaty. At Solomon's death, leaders of the northern tribes of Israel sent word to Jeroboam asking him to return and lead their delegation to meet with the king's son and heir, **Rehoboam,** before his coronation. The decisive meeting, at which they petitioned Rehoboam to reduce the onerous burdens imposed by his father, took place at the ancient shrine of Shechem.

After conferring with his advisers, Rehoboam contemptuously rejected the appeal of the northerners: "My father chastised you with whips, but I will chastise you with scorpions" (1 Kg. 12:14). Israel's delegation refused to acknowledge Rehoboam's accession and returned home, defiantly chanting their war cry: "What portion have we in David? We have no inheritance in the son of Jesse. To your tents, O Israel! Look now to your own house, David" (1 Kg. 12:16).

In an inept attempt to restore unity, Rehoboam sent the northern tribes a new taskmaster, Adoram, but the people summarily executed him by stoning. Then they crowned Jeroboam king over Israel. Possibly this was the moment when the name Jeroboam was bestowed. In fact, the parallelism of the names Jeroboam and Rehoboam may indicate that both were given when the two kings ascended their thrones, a common custom. Both names stress the power of the people against that of a king.

Rehoboam's last attempt to gain control ended in futility when, in the midst of mustering an army from the tribes of Judah and Benjamin, he was confronted by the prophet **Shemaiah**. The prophet told him not to attack his Israelite kinsmen, adding a demoralizing word from the Lord: "Return every man to his home, for this thing is from me" (1 Kg. 12:24).

A TROUBLED NATION BUILDER

From the very outset of his reign (C. 922-901 B.C.), Jeroboam faced great challenges in trying to create a new religious and political order. Worried that any continuing loyalty to temple worship in Jerusalem might cause his subjects to overthrow him and return to Rehoboam's fold, Jeroboam thought to revive an older form of worship centered at ancient northern shrines. First, he rebuilt Shechem and made it his capital, gaining for the new nation an ancient site associated with **Abraham** and the other patriarchs as well as with the entry of **Joshua** into the Promised Land. He next claimed Penuel, the place where **Jacob** wrestled with an angel and was given the new name Israel. Finally, he placed golden calves in the shrines at Bethel and Dan. The objects were probably not at first thought of as idols but as symbolic pedestals of the deity; inevitably, later generations made the golden calves objects of veneration.

Jeroboam also dismissed the priestly tribe of Levi and appointed new priests representing all strata of society. Occasionally, the king even officiated at the altar himself. Not surprisingly, most Levites defected to Jerusalem. And to compete with the great celebration in Jerusalem, Jeroboam reorganized the religious calendar, moving the Feast of Booths from the seventh to the eighth month.

The nation-building came to a halt in the fifth year of Jeroboam's reign, when Pharaoh Shishak invaded

The prophet Ahijah rips his garment to foretell Jeroboam's rise to power over the ten northern tribes of Israel.

first Judah and then Israel. Apparently, the protection earlier extended to Jeroboam by Shishak counted for naught, since archeological evidence indicates that Shishak was even harder on the north than on the south. Weakened by invasion, Jeroboam's reign was sapped by endless border disputes with Judah. Even after the death of Rehoboam, the southerners kept up their offensive against the breakaway state to the north, first under Rehoboam's son and successor, **Abijah**, then under his grandson **Asa**.

The disturbing appearance at Bethel of an unidentified man of God signified the beginning of the end. As the king was preparing to burn incense at the altar, the prophet cried out: "O altar, altar, thus says the Lord: 'Behold, a son shall be born to the house of David, Josiah by name; and he shall sacrifice the priests of the high places who burn incense upon you'" (1 Kg. 13:2). Jeroboam ordered his servants to seize the man, but as the king was gesturing, his arm became paralyzed. Ingloriously, he had to beg the prophet to restore his arm. Nonetheless, Jeroboam remained firm in his rupture with Jerusalem, and his inflexibility proved to be the breaking point: "This thing became sin to the house of Jeroboam, so as to cut it off and to destroy it from the face of the earth" (1 Kg. 13:34).

The judgment was not long in being carried out. When Jeroboam's son Abijah fell sick, the king asked his wife to disguise herself and consult Ahijah, who had prophesied his ascent to the throne. Recognizing her in spite of the disguise, Ahijah uttered a prediction of unrelenting doom: The moment she returned to the city, he said, her child would die. Not only that, but the entire lineage of Jeroboam would meet ignominious deaths, their bodies devoured by scavengers. Shortly thereafter, Jeroboam died. His son **Nadab** reigned for only two years before being assassinated by the usurper **Baasha**. Jeroboam's dynasty had ended within a quarter century.

JEROBOAM II

A seal dating to the time of Jeroboam II

More than a century after the reign of **Jeroboam**, the first ruler of the northern kingdom of Israel, his namesake (but not a descendant) Jeroboam II regained control over more of King **David**'s realm than had any monarch since the division between Jeroboam and **Rehoboam**. The great-grandson of **Jehu**, Jeroboam II ruled during one of the most prosperous, yet also one of the most maligned, periods in Israel's history. Although his reign lasted 41 years (786-746 B.C.), the Bible makes only a few summary statements about Jeroboam II, most notably that "he did what was evil in the sight of the Lord; he did not depart from all the sins of Jeroboam the son of Nebat" (2 Kg. 14:24).

Ancient sources outside the Bible reveal a region temporarily free from menacing foreign powers, with Assyria particularly weak at the time. For years Assyrian kings had exacted tribute from all the nations of the area, including Israel under Jeroboam's father, **Joash**. Now Jeroboam took advantage of the vacuum to recover territories lost in the preceding two generations. He also took virtual control of Judah in the south, and ruled "from the entrance of Hamath [the northern limit of King Solomon's realm] as far as the Sea of the Arabah [the Dead Sea]" (2 Kg. 14:25).

The expansionist activities of Jeroboam were supported by some religious figures, including **Jonah** the son of Amittai (the prophet remembered long afterward in the book bearing his name). A northerner, Jonah took a traditional view of the expansion and prosperity as proof of God's blessing. However, his views were opposed by others, notably the prophets **Amos** and **Hosea**. Amos was a sheep breeder from the south, called to prophesy at the northern shrine of Bethel. There he condemned the Israelites, whose wealth came from crops grown on property seized from the poor and from trade with peoples of the newly acquired lands. For Amos, the agricultural and trade policies of the newly rich were to blame for both the rise of social injustice and the deplorable resurgence of **Baal** worship in the northern kingdom.

Amos cried out against the greed and immorality of Jeroboam's kingdom: "They sell the righteous for silver, and the needy for a pair of shoes . . . A man and his father go in to the same maiden [cult prostitutes] . . . They lay themselves down beside every altar . . . and in the house of their God they drink the wine of those who have been fined" (Am.

THE DIVIDED MONARCHY

The rise of Jeroboam marked the permanent division of the tribes of Israel along a fault line of old and persistent rivalries. Northern Israel was dominated by the large tribes of Ephraim and Manasseh, while the south was peopled mostly by the tribe of Judah. King Saul had pulled them together at least partly because he came from the small tribe of Benjamin and did not represent the ascendancy of either rival. At Saul's death the kingdom split. The north followed Saul's son Ishbosheth while Judah made David, one of its own, king. David was such a powerful figure that, when Ish-bosheth was assassinated, he was able to reunite the tribes. Yet even under David, the forces of dissolution were powerful. Absalom led a nearly successful rebellion, and the northern tribes later supported a Benjaminite named Sheba in a short-lived uprising.

Solomon turned Judah's dominance into an oppression of the north through conscripted labor and heavy taxation. Jeroboam, a man of great ability from the tribe of Ephraim, rebelled against Solomon and fled to Egypt to escape arrest. When Solomon died and was succeeded by the hotheaded Rehoboam, the ancient fault line between north and south gave way in an earthquake that permanently divided the nation.

THE KINGS OF JUDAH AND ISRAEL

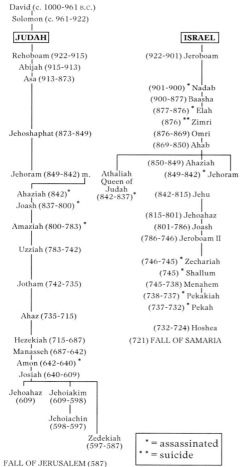

David (c. 1000-961 B.C.)

Solomon (c. 961-922)

JUDAH

Rehoboam (922-915)
Abijah (915-913)
Asa (913-873)

Jehoshaphat (873-849)

Jehoram (849-842) m.

Ahaziah (842)*
Joash (837-800)*

Amaziah (800-783)*

Uzziah (783-742)

Jotham (742-735)

Ahaz (735-715)

Hezekiah (715-687)
Manasseh (687-642)
Amon (642-640)*
Josiah (640-609)

Jehoahaz (609)   Jehoiakim (609-598)

Jehoiachin (598-597)

Zedekiah (597-587)

FALL OF JERUSALEM (587)

ISRAEL

(922-901) Jeroboam

(901-900)* Nadab
(900-877) Baasha
(877-876)* Elah
(876)** Zimri
(876-869) Omri
(869-850) Ahab

(850-849) Ahaziah
(849-842)* Jehoram

(842-815) Jehu

(815-801) Jehoahaz
(801-786) Joash
(786-746) Jeroboam II

(746-745)* Zechariah
(745)* Shallum
(745-738) Menahem
(738-737)* Pekahiah
(737-732)* Pekah

(732-724) Hoshea

(721) FALL OF SAMARIA

Athaliah
Queen of
Judah
(842-837)*

* = assassinated
** = suicide

0   20 Miles

MEDITERRANEAN SEA

PHOENICIA

ISRAEL

SYRIA

•Dan
Abel-beth-maacah
•Hazor
Chinnereth
Sea of Galilee

Tirzah
Samaria• •
Shechem

Jordan River

**Border between
Judah and Israel**

Bethel•
Gezer•   Jericho•
Gibbethon• • • • •Geba
Aijalon •Ramah
Mizpah
Jerusalem

PHILISTIA

JUDAH

Dead Sea

AMMON

MOAB

EDOM

Jeroboam sacrificing to the idols, detail of a painting by J. H. Fragonard (1732-1806)

2:6-7). Perhaps the most eloquent words of Amos are those portraying God's abhorrence of piety that neglects social justice: "I hate, I despise your feasts, and I take no delight in your solemn assemblies. Even though you offer me your burnt offerings and cereal offerings, I will not accept them . . . . But let justice roll down like waters, and righteousness like an ever-flowing stream" (Am. 5:21-24).

Hosea was from the north and prophesied near the end of Jeroboam's long reign. He neither supported the prosperity nor attacked it without pity. Rather, his message blended a penetrating critique of social injustice with a promise of forgiveness: "I will not again destroy Ephraim; for I am God and not man, the Holy One in your midst, and I will not come to destroy" (Hos. 11:9).

Thus, during the time of Jeroboam II, more than ever before, prophets challenged the link between prosperity and divine favor. Wealth by unjust means would be short-lived, they argued. As it happened, Jeroboam's reign marked the beginning of the end for Israel. Four of the five kings who ruled Israel in the 15 years following Jeroboam were assassinated, including his son, **Zechariah,** and Zechariah's killer, **Shallum**. And the kingdom itself fell to Assyria in 721 B.C.

JESHUA
(jesh' oo uh) HEBREW: YESHUA
"Yahweh is salvation"

A high priest of Judah, Jeshua (also called Joshua) was born during the exile of the Jews in Babylon (587-538 B.C.). Before the exile, high priests had been subordinate to the kings of Judah. But when King **Cyrus II** of Persia permitted the Jews to return to Jerusalem and rebuild their temple, Jeshua assumed a major leadership role along with the Jewish governor **Zerubbabel**, who remained subject to the Persian ruler. Together, the pair saw to it that an altar was erected and worship restored in Jerusalem. In the second year of the return, the Jews began rebuilding the temple foundations and city walls, but these efforts were frustrated by the successors to Cyrus, who discouraged the reconstruction of the city. Later, under the rule of the humane Persian king **Darius I**, and at the urging of the prophets **Haggai** and **Zechariah**, the work was resumed. The temple was finished about 515 B.C.

Jeshua appears in two of Zechariah's visions. In one, his "filthy garments," symbolic of the people's sins that had led to the exile, are replaced by "rich apparel" (Zech.

3:3,4) to indicate purification and restoration. In another, Jeshua is designated as the one who "shall bear royal honor" (Zech. 6:13)—though some scholars suggest that a textual error here makes Jeshua and not Zerubbabel the messianic ruler. In an earlier passage, the prophet calls Jeshua and Zerubbabel "the two anointed who stand by the Lord of the whole earth" (Zech. 4:14). Some members of Jeshua's family appear on the list in Ezra 10:18 of those who married foreign wives and were ordered by Ezra to give them up.

JESSE

(jes'ee) HEBREW: YISHAY
meaning unknown

The prophet **Samuel** was told by the Lord that he would find a successor to King **Saul** among the sons of an elderly farmer of Bethlehem named Jesse. Consequently, the prophet invited Jesse to a sacrifice and asked him to present each of seven sons to him. But when none was revealed as the chosen one, Jesse said that there was an eighth son, "the youngest, but behold, he is keeping the sheep" (1 Sam. 16:11). This son, **David**, was sent for and was promptly anointed by Samuel as Israel's new king.

Later, as Saul began suffering from a mental illness, messengers were dispatched to Jesse to ask that David come to play the lyre to soothe the king, for David was "skilful in playing" (1 Sam. 16:18). Provided with gifts of bread, wine, and a young goat, David arrived at court, where he was successful in calming the king and was allowed to remain there by his father. In a subsequent narrative, Jesse sent David with supplies for his three oldest sons, who were with Saul's army fighting the Philistines. "See how your brothers fare," Jesse said, "and bring some token from them" (1 Sam. 17:18). At the battlefront David heard the challenge of the giant **Goliath** and was the only man brave enough to meet and kill him. But when Saul later became jealous of David's fame, the youth fled for his safety, hiding his father and his mother with the king of Moab.

Biblical prophecies such as "there shall come forth a shoot from the stump of Jesse" (Is. 11:1) are often interpreted as predicting the coming of the Messiah. In support of this prediction, both Matthew and Luke list Jesse among the ancestors of **Jesus**. The so-called tree of Jesse is an illustration of this genealogy, with the figure of Jesse, a tree sprouting from his body, at the bottom and Jesus uppermost among his descendants lining the branches.

JESUS BEN SIRA

Ecclesiasticus is the longest and one of the earliest books of the Apocrypha and the only one in which the author gives his name: "Jesus the son of Sirach, son of Eleazar" (Sir. 50:27). A sage, scribe, and teacher, Ben Sira (Hebrew for "son of Sirach") composed his work sometime between 198 and 175 B.C. Taking the Hebrew manuscript with him to Egypt in about 132 B.C., a grandson translated the book into Greek and published it about 15 years later.

The final significant work of so-called wisdom literature, represented in the Old

The tree of Jesse, a 13th-century stained-glass window from Chartres cathedral, France

Testament by Job, Proverbs, and Ecclesiastes, Ben Sira's lengthy collection of maxims, sacred songs, and reflections on the life and customs of his times influenced the subsequent development of rabbinical Judaism. Christians also adopted the book, which in the third century A.D. came to be known as Ecclesiasticus, Latin for "the church book," because of its use in the liturgy and possibly also as an instruction manual for converts. (It is now generally referred to as the Wisdom of Jesus the son of Sirach, or simply Sirach, to avoid confusing it with the Old Testament book of Ecclesiastes.)

Ben Sira wrote at a time when Palestine was dominated by the successors of **Alexander the Great**—first the Ptolemies of Egypt, then the Seleucids of Syria. Both foreign dynasties sought to impose Greek culture on their subjugated lands. All about him, Ben Sira would have seen Jews struggling to maintain their faith against formidable pressure to adopt a Greek life-style, which included Greek philosophy and religion. His book was a response to that challenge, a work that found inspiration in the ancient literature of Israel but also embraced many ideas found in pagan writings.

PORTRAIT OF THE AUTHOR

Ben Sira seems to have been describing his own life when he wrote that the person "who devotes himself to the study of the law of the Most High will seek out the wisdom of all the ancients, and will be concerned with prophecies; he will preserve the discourse of notable men and penetrate the subtleties of parables" (Sir. 39:1-2). God willing, such a man would be empowered to "pour forth words of wisdom and give thanks to the Lord in prayer"; his reward would be universal praise and a name that would "live through all generations" (Sir. 39:6, 9).

From elsewhere in the text, scholars have concluded that the author was an aristocrat, a traveler, and a book lover, a man who enjoyed good food and good company and who relished music. He was pious and sympathetic to the poor and the oppressed. However, typical of his times, he was distrustful of women. Still, good marriages pleased him and he advised men not to be jealous of their wives—for that would only inspire them to be jealous too.

As an aristocrat, Ben Sira appears to have looked down a bit on merchants and ordinary farmers and on artisans, though he advised that artisans be complimented on their work when it deserved praise. Though his life was far removed from that of ordinary merchants, he knew something about business, including sharp practices. "A

Jesus Ben Sira appears within the letter "O" in this medieval manuscript of his book.

merchant," he wrote, "can hardly keep from wrongdoing, and a tradesman will not be declared innocent of sin. . . . As a stake is driven firmly into a fissure between stones, so sin is wedged in between selling and buying" (Sir. 26:29, 27:2).

Some of Ben Sira's suggestions ring oddly to the modern ear. Don't laugh with your son or play with him, he advises. Teach him obedience by beating him. But on the whole, his book is filled with good advice, much of it merely common sense: Don't boast, gossip, lie, or meddle. Be cautious in choosing friends and beware of enemies who appear to be friendly. Forgive your neighbor and hold no grudges. Give to the poor, visit the sick, avoid strife. Avoid harlots and other men's wives. Don't overeat or be the first one in a crowd to reach for the food. "When a powerful man invites you, be reserved," he writes; "and he will invite you the more often. Do not push forward, lest you be repulsed; and do not remain at a distance, lest you be forgotten" (Sir. 13:9-10). Underlying this advice is his basic message: "Good things and bad, life and death, poverty and wealth, come from the Lord" (Sir. 11:14).

Ben Sira had a tough, no-nonsense view of the world. "An enemy will speak sweetly with his lips," he wrote, "but in his mind he will plan to throw you into a pit" (Sir. 12:16). "When the rich man speaks all are silent, and they extol to the clouds what he says. When the poor man speaks they say, 'Who is this fellow?' And should he stumble, they even push him down" (Sir. 13:23). That practical outlook on life may have been the reason that Ben Sira's book is quoted no fewer than 82 times in the Talmud and that it was also accorded such respect by the early Christian church.

Panels illustrating Jesus' birth (left) and baptism (right) flank the central image of his resurrection in this triptych by El Greco (c. 1548-1614).

JESUS

GREEK: IESOUS; form of
HEBREW/ARAMAIC: YESHUA
"Yahweh is salvation/has saved"

For Christians, Jesus is the central figure of the Bible: His life fulfilled God's promises made through the Old Testament prophets; the good news that he brought mankind was God's offer of a new covenant of salvation. His is a story so important that it is told four times over in the New Testament, and the brief years of his public life transformed the entire course of Western civilization.

Jesus is called the Christ, the equivalent of the Hebrew term Messiah, meaning "God's anointed one," and Christians confess him as the Son of God, expressing faith in his divinity. Many other titles also surround his name: Lord, Savior, Son of man, the Word, Son of David, Lamb of God, King of Kings. All stem from the belief that in the life, death, and resurrection of Jesus, God was showing his love for the world and saving humanity from sin and death. Thus, the New Testament story of Jesus is never presented as a simple human biography but always as a continuous interplay of the divine and the human. The narrative is filled with miraculous deeds, revelations of God's will, and events of cosmic significance.

Virtually everything known of the life of Jesus comes from four remarkable documents, the Gospels of Matthew, Mark, Luke, and John. There are scattered references to Jesus in the works of Jewish and Roman historians, certainly sufficient to establish beyond doubt that he was a living person; but those references add no specific information that is not in the New Testament. The four Gospels, however, are full of information and insight into Jesus' life. They pulse with brief, vivid, revealing episodes that flash before the reader like dozens of snapshots from life. Jesus is seen walking the dusty roads of ancient Palestine, helping the poor, teaching his followers, healing the sick, telling stories, performing miracles, and engaging in controversies.

Written between 40 and 60 years after Jesus was crucified by Roman soldiers, the Gospels record incidents that no doubt had been told and retold hundreds of times by early Christians. Almost immediately after Jesus' death, his disciples faced the challenge of explaining why they believed their slain master had been raised from the dead and why they continued to follow his teachings. By the time the first Gospel—evidently that of Mark—was written, there was no need for the author to introduce Jesus; rather, he gathered what he considered significant information from the great wealth of accounts that had doubtless been widely known for decades. Thus, the Gospel of Mark is made up of scores of pithy vignettes brought together in a narrative leading up to Jesus' death and resurrection.

The Gospels of Matthew and Luke build on Mark's narrative but expand it with more examples of Jesus' teachings and deeds; they also add narratives of his birth and his post-resurrection appearances. Because of their common structure, these three are called the Synoptic Gospels, meaning that they can be viewed together. The Gospel of John, with its own distinctive style, is largely independent of the Synoptic Gospels. It is filled with longer discourses, conversations, and dramatic encounters from Jesus' life and follows its own chronology, though all four Gospels overlap at many points.

THE BIRTH NARRATIVES

As prologue to Jesus' ministry, the Gospels of Matthew and Luke recount the story of his birth. Both describe how Jesus was miraculously conceived by the virgin **Mary**, betrothed to a man named **Joseph**, and how the child was born in Bethlehem as a descendant of King **David**—all in fulfillment of ancient prophecies. The two Evangelists place these events during the reign of King **Herod the Great**, who died in 4 B.C. Since Matthew also implies that Jesus was born at least two years before the death of Herod, his birth can be dated to about 7 or 6 B.C.

In addition, each of the two Gospels provides other distinctive information that helps show the significance of Jesus' birth. Matthew looks at events through Joseph's eyes, recording how angels appeared to him in dreams to guide his actions. Matthew also emphasizes Jesus' royal ancestry, listing kings in the house of David among his forebears and telling of a miraculous star that announced the coming of a new "king of the Jews" (Mt. 2:2). He also introduces "wise men from the East" (Mt. 2:1) who recognized the star's meaning and brought Jesus gifts of gold, frankincense, and myrrh, while Herod mounted a vicious attempt to destroy his newborn rival, but succeeded only in killing innocent infants.

Luke, on the other hand, emphasizes the humility of Jesus' birth—the irony of divine power manifested in lowly surroundings. He views the story from Mary's perspective, describing the angel **Gabriel**'s appearance to announce Jesus' birth and including Mary's song of celebration (the Magnificat), in which she praises God for having "scattered the proud" and having "exalted those of low degree" (Lk. 1:51, 52). Mary and Joseph were drawn to Bethlehem as poor Jews forced to register for taxation by command of the distant Roman emperor. They had so few resources that they had to sleep in a stable, where Jesus was born—his first bed an animal feeding trough. Luke traces Jesus' ancestry through nonroyal descendants of David; his birth is announced not to the powerful but to shepherds in the field.

Gabriel appearing to Mary, as painted by Peter Paul Rubens (1577-1640)

Thus, the two birth narratives in different ways help to interpet the meaning of Jesus' later life by placing it in a context of Old Testament prophecy, divine power, and human hopes.

THE HIDDEN YEARS

Practically nothing is known of Jesus' childhood, youth, and early adulthood except that he was reared at Nazareth in Galilee. Luke alone tells of the journey to Jerusalem at Passover time, when the 12-year-old Jesus remained behind in the temple, absorbed in discussions with teachers of the Law, while his parents started back to Nazareth. In that year, most likely A.D. 5 or 6, Jerusalem was a hotbed of religious fervor. **Herod Archelaus**, a son of Herod the Great, had just been deposed for misrule; and Judea, Samaria, and Idumea (united as the province of Judea) had come under direct Roman rule. Many patriotic Jews called for revolt against paying taxes to foreign masters. Luke, however, does not mention whether Jesus' youthful discourse in the temple "sitting among the teachers" (Lk. 2:46) touched on the volatile religious and political situation.

During the 18 or so remaining years before he began his public ministry, Jesus evidently had a normal Jewish education in the synagogue at Nazareth and became a village carpenter under the tutelage of Joseph. As a carpenter, he would have been

The devil challenges Jesus to turn stones into bread; a 15th-century German manuscript illumination.

a general woodworker supplying whatever needs local people had—yokes for oxen, wooden plows, threshing boards, winnowing forks, benches, tables, beds, boxes, and carts. The carpenter's shop would probably have been a room open to the village street with Jesus' family living above. Years of observation of the everyday life that flowed through his shop no doubt provided Jesus with many of the vivid images he used in his parables and other teachings. During those years, the province of Judea continued to be a Roman stronghold, while Galilee, where

THE WISE MEN

Although the Gospel of Matthew does not specify their number, tradition holds that there were three wise men—one for each gift. And, as early as the sixth century, names were given to them, with physical attributes coming somewhat later. Thus, the bearer of gold was said to be Melchior, an elderly Persian with a long beard; a young and beardless Indian named Caspar offered fragrant frankincense; a black Arabian named Balthasar brought myrrh, the bitter gum resin valued for its medicinal properties.

En route home from China at the end of the 13th century, Marco Polo reported that he visited the wise men's graves near Tehran —though a century earlier the Holy Roman emperor claimed to have moved their bodies to Germany for preservation. The most scholars will say about the wise men is that, being guided by the star, they were probably astrologers from Persia.

The three wise men worship Jesus; detail of a painting by Albrecht Durer (1471-1528).

Jesus lived, and the region of Perea, east of the Jordan River, were ruled by **Herod Antipas**, another son of Herod the Great.

Jesus' life came to a dramatic turning point when he was about 30 years old. A prophet named **John the Baptist**, a distant kinsman of his, had begun preaching in the wilderness region around the Jordan, drawing large crowds from the towns and cities of Judea. John proclaimed the coming of God's judgment, challenged everyone to repent, and baptized the people in the river as a sign of their preparation for God's judgment. For Jesus the news of John's prophetic work was evidently a sign to begin a new phase of his own life.

The Gospels do not explain Jesus' decision for doing so, but one day he abandoned the obscurity of Nazareth and traveled south to join the crowds seeking to be baptized by John. When John recognized him as the Messiah and resisted baptizing him, saying it was he who needed to be baptized, Jesus insisted that he "fulfil all righteousness" (Mt. 3:15). After his baptism, the heavens split open; the **Holy Spirit** descended on Jesus like a dove; and he heard a voice from heaven, saying, "Thou art my beloved Son; with thee I am well pleased" (Mk. 1:11).

As Jesus left the crowds that surrounded John, that Spirit caused him to seek the loneliness of the nearby desert and undertake a period of fasting. There he confronted the temptations of Satan to serve and exalt him rather than God, to grasp power and domination for himself rather than to accept the sacrifice that was his destiny. These tests were meant to subvert Jesus' future ministry, but he emerged from the 40 days of solitude even more empowered by the Spirit.

WATER INTO WINE

The Gospel of John tells how John the Baptist bore such striking testimony to Jesus, calling him "the Lamb of God" (Jn. 1:29), that some of John's own followers, including a Galilean fisherman named **Andrew**, went to listen to Jesus and became convinced that he was the Messiah. Andrew, in turn, brought his brother Simon to meet Jesus, who gave him a new name, **Peter**, the "rock." Andrew and Peter thus became the first of Jesus' circle of disciples.

Shortly thereafter, according to John, Jesus returned to Galilee and first manifested

The wedding at Cana, from an early-15th-century devotional book

his remarkable mastery of nature at a marriage feast in the town of Cana, north of Nazareth. This celebration was evidently for one of Jesus' friends or extended family, and he, his mother, and his disciples were invited to attend the feast, an affair that probably continued for several days. The wine that the host had prepared ran short, and the festive joy of the occasion was in danger of being dissipated. Mary informed Jesus of the situation, but at first he seemed to resist getting involved, saying mysteriously, "My hour has not yet come" (Jn. 2:4). Prompted by Mary, however, he had the household servants fill with water six stone jars, each holding 20 to 30 gallons. He then sent a sample of their contents to the master of ceremonies of the feast, who tasted and discovered that it was a delightfully fine wine, better than what had been offered earlier. Hardly anyone realized what had occurred except Jesus' new followers. To them the miraculous wine carried them beyond being impressed with Jesus' words; they now began to see his glory.

Jesus had been baptized by John, but he did not become John's disciple; rather, for a time, his ministry apparently grew alongside John's but with a fundamentally different character. Whereas John was an ascetic, "the voice of one crying in the wilderness"

Seeking to have Jesus cure the man, friends of a paralytic lower him through a roof opening.

(Mt. 3:3), Jesus served and taught the people where they lived, in the villages and cities. Being in the midst of human life with its suffering and pains as well as its joys was basic to his work.

For the first 30 years of his life, Jesus had evidently seldom traveled from the town of Nazareth except to go to Jerusalem for festivals and perhaps to visit surrounding villages for carpentry work. Once his ministry began, however, he was almost continuously on the road, taking his message to villages and towns throughout Galilee and to Judea.

PROCLAIMING GOD'S KINGDOM

To the villagers of Galilee he brought a powerful message of hope and challenge: "The time is fulfilled, and the kingdom of God is at hand; repent and believe in the gospel" (Mk. 1:15). In speaking of the kingdom of God, Jesus was referring to the ancient belief in Israel that, no matter who the current human ruler might be, God is the true king both of Israel and of his entire creation. Though God's right to rule the lives of his people had often been usurped by tyrants, foreign potentates, or even demonic powers, he would reclaim his rightful place and would overthrow the usurpers—through his Messiah. Jesus challenged the people to expect God's reign and to change their lives to fit God's will. But he refused to limit God's kingdom to any particular religious reform or institution, or equate it with any political program, social transformation, or even with the end of the world. He could speak of the kingdom as something in the future and also as present in his own ministry.

He could even tell his attentive listeners that "the kingdom of God is not coming with signs to be observed"; rather "the kingdom of God is in the midst of you" (Lk. 17:20, 21).

Jesus often preferred to define the kingdom of God by the kinds of people to whom it belonged. "Blessed are you poor," he said, "for yours is the kingdom of God" (Lk. 6:20). "Let the children come to me," he told his disciples, "for to such belongs the kingdom of God" (Mk. 10:14). "Unless one is born anew," Jesus advised the Pharisee **Nicodemus**, "he cannot see the kingdom of God" (Jn. 3:3).

It was through parables, the many brief, colorful stories that are so distinctive in his teaching, that Jesus characteristically revealed the kingdom of God. In those parables the common people who made up the throngs around him could recognize everyday things: seeds, yeast, vineyards, fishnets, farmers, servants, shepherds, widows,

JESUS' WORLD

The life of Jesus, in Christian belief, marks the greatest turning point of all history. In sixth-century Europe, that belief was made official as a scholarly monk named Dionysius Exiguus attempted to establish all dates from the year of Jesus' birth. Although Dionysius' calculations were off by four to seven years, the principal purpose of his system was nevertheless clear. All time before Jesus became B.C., "before Christ." Every year since his coming was A.D., anno domini, "the year of the Lord."

The worldwide impact of Jesus' life is remarkable in its contrast to the small scale on which his life was lived. Though Matthew tells that as an infant Jesus was carried for a short time to Egypt, by far most of his childhood and adulthood was spent in the little-known village of Nazareth in the hills of Galilee, and his travels were evidently confined to festival pilgrimages to Jerusalem, about 70 miles away. During the brief period of his ministry, Jesus was almost continually on the move—teaching in villages and countryside, healing the sick, training his disciples, arguing with opponents—but bridesmaids. By using a succinct story, Jesus could draw his hearers to a better understanding of the kingdom of God without the weight of theological discourse.

The clarity and absolute authority with which Jesus spoke took people by surprise and amazed them. And the power of his word extended into his actions: His word or touch could heal the sick, raise up the lame, or bring those who were possessed by what were called unclean spirits or demons back to their right minds.

When Jesus began to teach in the synagogue in Capernaum on the north shore of the Sea of Galilee, a deranged man cried out in the assembly. Without any magical incantation of exorcism, Jesus simply commanded, "Be silent, and come out of him!" The man was healed, and the amazed observers said, "What is this? A new teaching! With authority he commands even the unclean spirits, and they obey him" (Mk. 1:25, 27). With the same simplicity and complete

Jesus cleanses a leper; this panel and the one opposite are from a 12th-century Greek book of the Gospels.

all within a limited radius. The full range of his travels never exceeded about 130 miles—from the region of Tyre and Sidon to Jerusalem—an area considerably smaller than Vermont.

Jesus made no attempt to establish a base of influence in the great cities of the Roman empire nor to make his message attractive to the wealthy and powerful. Quite the opposite. He stayed near home and drew his closest followers from humble folk. The Synoptic Gospels emphasize Jesus' ministry in Galilee, while the Gospel of John focuses on the time he spent in Judea, but in neither case do the Gospels attempt to give an unbroken itinerary. Rather, they provide vignettes along the way, insights into Jesus' remarkable message and deeds among the people. It was only as the opposition to Jesus heated up and was brought to white-hot intensity in Judas's betrayal and Jesus' execution by Pontius Pilate that the full meaning of Jesus' message was seared into the hearts of his followers. When they came to the realization that God had raised the crucified Jesus, the power of that faith broke the geographical confines within which Jesus had lived, and began to spread throughout the world.

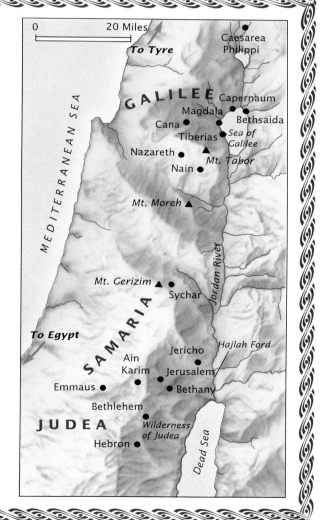

confidence Jesus could go to the bedside of Peter's mother-in-law, who lay burning with fever, touch her hand, lift her up, and make her fever disappear. Such deeds brought throngs from the surrounding countryside—people who listened to his teachings and hoped to be healed. It was the fulfillment of **Isaiah**'s words: "He took our infirmities and bore our diseases" (Mt. 8:17).

GATHERING HIS DISCIPLES

Jesus' sympathies were with the crowds that came to him; he understood their lives and spoke their language. Yet he wanted to create a community of friends and close associates whom he could teach in greater depth and draw into his understanding of God's kingdom. Thus, as he began to travel through the towns and countryside, he gathered a group of disciples about him. The word disciple means "learner," and the relationship of a teacher to his disciples was considered important by Jews in ancient times. Pharisaic teachers, Sadducees, and scribes all had disciples; John the Baptist had disciples. It was from teacher to disciple that the traditions of Jewish law, religion, and society were handed down and preserved. Usually, a young man who wished to become a learner would find a rabbi whose teaching he admired and arrange to study with him, serve him, and be trained by him to become a rabbi in turn.

Jesus turned the process around, actively calling those whom he desired to be part of his traveling band. He did not summon them for professional training in the Law, however, but to become personally identified with his ministry and with himself. Peter, Andrew, **James** and **John**, the sons of **Zebedee**, all fishermen, and **Matthew**, a tax collector, simply dropped their livelihoods, left family behind, and began to travel with this wandering teacher when he called, "Follow me" (Mt. 9:9). Jesus' band of disciples was unusual for that period of history in that it also included a number of women—for example, **Mary Magdalene** and **Joanna**, the wife of Herod Antipas's steward Chuza—who traveled with him and his disciples in Galilee, accompanied them to Jerusalem, and "provided for them out of their means" (Lk. 8:3). All who joined the band took up the hard life of their master, who said, "Foxes have holes, and birds of the air have nests; but the Son of man has nowhere to lay his head" (Mt. 8:20).

Peter struggles ashore after Jesus has rewarded the unsuccessful fishermen with a miraculous draft of fish; henceforth, he told them, they would be fishers of men.

As the ministry of Jesus developed, the disciples around him formed several groupings. The three closest to Jesus were Peter and the brothers James and John. At crucial moments, such as at Jesus' transfiguration or in the garden of Gethsemane, Jesus took these three aside. The three were also part of the larger group known as "the twelve" (Mk. 9:35), whose number symbolized the renewal of Israel's 12 tribes. Fairly early in his ministry, Jesus chose them from his followers "to be with him, and to be sent out to preach and to have authority to cast out demons" (Mk. 3:14-15). The twelve became known as the "apostles," or emissaries. The number 12 was so important for the symbolic role of this group that after **Judas Iscariot** betrayed Jesus, another disciple, **Matthias**, was chosen to fill his place.

Jesus showed the purpose of his ministry by the kinds of disciples he chose. They were not scholars with noteworthy credentials but "uneducated, common men" who came to new boldness and faith because "they had been with Jesus" (Acts 4:13). Besides the two pairs of brothers who were fishermen and the tax collector Matthew, the only disciple whose background is noted is **Simon** the Zealot. Simon's designation as a Zealot links him to groups of Jews who were committed to the overthrow of the Romans and their client kings, such as Herod Antipas. Simon and other disciples (Judas

Iscariot, for example) likely hoped that Jesus' preaching of the kingdom of God would eventually come round to a political program to rid the country of the Romans. They certainly would normally have felt only loathing for a tax collector like Matthew. Nevertheless, Jesus' own understanding of the kingdom was inclusive enough to enfold carpenters, fishermen, tax collectors, and Zealots.

Around the twelve Jesus also gathered a large number of other committed disciples from whom on one occasion he commissioned 70, sending them out "into every town and place where he himself was about to come" (Lk. 10:1). They were to carry no money, food, extra clothing, or weapons, but were simply to travel two by two, preaching the kingdom of God and healing by Jesus' authority. By the end of his ministry, the core of Jesus' disciples numbered about 120 and included his mother and brothers. Around this core was a larger circle of at least 500.

Some months after his baptism, Jesus journeyed south to Jerusalem for Passover.

There he confronted the temple authorities and worked among the villages of Judea. After John the Baptist was arrested, Jesus returned to Galilee through Samaria, where he met a woman at the well of the village of Sychar. In Galilee he visited Nazareth and Cana again, healed an official's son at Capernaum, and solidified the circle of disciples around him. As the throngs who came to hear him grew, he traveled more in the countryside and taught in rural settings, including a hillside near the Sea of Galilee where he delivered what came to be known as the Sermon on the Mount.

MORE THAN OBEDIENCE

In many ways Jesus' message could be seen as similar to calls for renewal in Judaism that had been sounded from many quarters for decades, even centuries. A common thread in most of the renewal movements was a call for purity and rigorous obedience to Mosaic Law. The Pharisees of Jesus' time were especially influential as they strived to develop precise definitions of how the Law was to be implemented—purification rites,

With a simple gesture, Jesus summons Matthew to leave the tax office; this painting by Jan Sanders Van Hemessen is dated 1536.

The multiplication of the loaves and fish; an early-16th-century ivory panel from Ravenna, Italy

saying, "Rise, take up your pallet, and walk" (Jn. 5:8). The Pharisees were outraged, first because Jesus had told the man to pick up his pallet on the sabbath and then because he had healed the man. Jesus rebuffed the criticism, however, since God had granted the healing. "My father is working still," Jesus said, "and I am working" (Jn. 5:17). On another occasion, Jesus was criticized by certain Pharisees when some of his disciples plucked and ate some heads of grain on a sabbath. Jesus cited the story of David eating sacred bread that was prohibited in order to show that the Pharisees' highly restrictive view of what constituted unlawful activity was not warranted. "The sabbath was made for man," he asserted, "not man for the sabbath" (Mk. 2:27).

exact forms of work to be banned on the sabbath, and tithing, for example—in order to make careful obedience possible and to maintain a life separate from the impure and sinful.

Jesus similarly made rigorous demands of his disciples, but he refused to interpret those demands solely in terms of obedience to the Law. To the Pharisees, who often served as religious teachers in the synagogues, Jesus seemed to flout the Law and even encourage disobedience to it. The Gospels record numerous controversies that led many Pharisees to become ever more vigorous opponents of Jesus. One sabbath when Jesus was in Jersualem, he healed a man who had been an invalid for 38 years,

As Jesus' attitude about the sabbath became known, some opponents tested him by confronting him in the synagogue with a man whose hand was withered. Jesus recognized the test and demanded, "Is it lawful on the sabbath to do good or to do harm, to save life or to kill?" (Mk. 3:4). He simply refused to concede that doing the good of healing constituted unlawful work. "Grieved at their hardness of heart" (Mk. 3:5), Jesus healed the man and confirmed his opponents' suspicions about him. Similarly, Jesus refused to remain separate from people who were notorious for not keeping the Law, such as tax collectors, men considered to be traitorous, dishonest, and irreligious. After he summoned the tax collector

Peter founders in attempting to walk across the water to Jesus; a 12th- or 13th-century Armenian manuscript illumination.

Matthew (also called Levi) to be a disciple, Jesus went to a dinner at which "many tax collectors and sinners came and sat down" (Mt. 9:10) with him and his disciples. The affair became a scandal, and soon Jesus was tagged with the damning title, "friend of tax collectors and sinners" (Mt. 11:19), to show his disregard for the Law. Jesus cited the prophet **Hosea** and said that his opponents needed to "go and learn what this means, 'I desire mercy and not sacrifice,' for I came not to call the righteous, but sinners" (Mt. 9:13).

Jesus and his disciples also disregarded such pious practices as fasting that were important not only to the Pharisees but also to the followers of John the Baptist. Jesus insisted that he and his disciples were enjoying a life of celebration, like a wedding feast, and would not fast. His message was like "new wine" that "must be put into fresh wineskins" (Lk. 5:38). If they tried to make the message of the kingdom of God dependent on the old pious observances, both would be destroyed. Thus, through one controversy after another, Jesus' radical reformulation of piety and obedience to God emerged. Many, such as the Pharisees, who were seeking to call the people to strict observance of the Mosaic Law, found themselves deeply offended by Jesus' seemingly cavalier attitude toward piety and increasingly saw him as a dangerous force that must be opposed and stopped.

THE MASTER OF NATURE

Jesus evidently went to Jerusalem again at the autumn Feast of Booths. There he healed an invalid by a pool in the city and sparked an extended controversy over healing on the sabbath. Returning to Galilee, he continued his ministry in the villages during the winter months. When a seasonal storm struck his boat on the Sea of Galilee, he stilled the wind and waves in a dramatic demonstration of his mastery of nature.

Such nature miracles were not uncommon in Hebrew Scripture, of course, and ranged from **Moses'** parting the Red Sea to **Joshua's** calling for the sun to stand still at Gibeon. Thus, when the Gospels tell of Jesus changing water into wine, walking on water, or filling nets with a miraculous draft of fish, they place him within an ancient biblical tradition in which God's power is especially visible when nature does not follow its expected course. The Gospels recount these stories in order to strengthen belief in Jesus. John regularly calls Jesus' miracles "signs," meaning that they point beyond themselves to a deeper understanding of Jesus and his mission.

SERMON ON THE MOUNT

The best known single body of Jesus' teaching appears in Matthew 5-7, the Sermon on the Mount. Many scholars view it more as an anthology of Jesus' sayings than as a single sermon, but it has a powerful unity that establishes the basic themes of all his teaching. Both the content of Jesus' message and the characteristic way in which he conveyed that content are important.

After pronouncing a series of blessings, the beatitudes, Jesus turned to the great issue that concerned every Jewish teacher: the Law and its fulfillment. He asserted that his purpose was to fulfill the Law and the prophets, at the same time claiming the authority to speak in a way that went beyond the Law and indeed challenged it. Jesus laid out six contrasts between his own teaching and that of traditional law; each opened with the phrases "You have heard that it was said. . . . But I say to you" (Mt. 5:21, 22). Though Jesus cast his language in the style of legal formulations, his intent and effect was radically to move away from a law intended to be enforced by judicial authorities toward a standard of thought and commitment that could only be applied internally to one's own heart and life.

Jesus offered antitheses between the old and the new as he dealt with difficult topics of anger, adultery and covetousness, divorce, lying and oaths, retaliation, and resisting evil. Finally, he came to the heart of his teaching, a commitment to love without boundaries. Jesus rejected the common attitude of loving one's neighbor and hating one's enemies, asking them to "love your enemies and pray for those who persecute you" (Mt. 5:44).

For many modern readers, however, miracles that seem to involve a violation of the laws of nature sometimes become more an obstacle to belief than a help. They view the miracles as divine interventions to overturn or change natural laws or processes. For the writers of the Gospels, the matter was precisely reversed: The miracles confirmed and demonstrated the way the world truly works all the time. God created the world and controls it at every moment; he "clothes the grass of the field" and not a single sparrow "will fall to the ground" apart from God's will (Mt. 6:30; 10:29). Thus, the wonder of the nature miracles is that they bring God's hidden guidance of all things clearly and amazingly into view.

Jesus and his disciples traveled into the Gentile region of the Decapolis, southeast of Galilee, where Jesus healed a man so deranged with demons that he lived naked among the tombs. Jesus again returned to Galilee, where he raised **Jairus**'s daughter from the dead, but he was received with skepticism and distrust when he visited Nazareth. After feeding a throng of more than 5,000 with a few loaves and two fish, Jesus traveled extensively, visiting Phoenicia and later Caesarea Philippi. It was there Peter dramatically confessed him to be the Messiah.

By then Jesus had reached a milestone with his disciples. Traveling with them to one of the sources of the Jordan River, he asked them about speculation as to whether he was one of the prophets raised from the dead, perhaps **Elijah** or John the Baptist, who had been executed by Herod Antipas. Then he asked them directly, "Who do you say that I am?" Peter responded just as directly for the twelve, "You are the Christ" (Mk. 8:29). Their understanding of his ministry was as yet by no means perfect—they had no conception of a suffering Messiah—but still Peter's words were an important step. A week later Jesus took Peter, James, and John up a mountain to pray. And there "his countenance was altered, and his raiment became dazzling white" (Lk. 9:29), and the three disciples saw him in glory, talking to Moses and Elijah.

By early autumn, at the time of another Feast of Booths, Jesus made the fateful decision to return south to Jerusalem to confront his opponents. After attempts were made to arrest Jesus in the temple and he

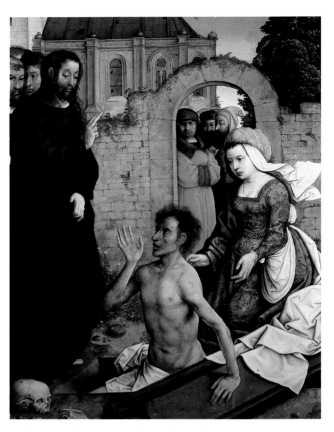

Jesus calls Lazarus from the tomb; the 16th-century Flemish artist placed skeptical observers behind the cemetery portal.

became the center of increasingly bitter controversies, he withdrew from Jerusalem and crossed the Jordan into the region of Perea, where he spent some time extensively instructing his disciples. Again in the winter he went to the temple briefly for Hanukkah, the Feast of Dedication. But once more facing death threats from those who considered him to be a blasphemer, Jesus left the city.

THE FINAL DAYS

Very early in the new year, Jesus was informed that his friend **Lazarus** was deathly ill. By the time Jesus arrived at Lazarus's home in the village of Bethany just outside Jerusalem, Lazarus had been dead four days. But Jesus told Lazarus's sister **Martha** that he was "the resurrection and the life" (Jn. 11:25)—and so he proved to be as he raised Lazarus from the dead.

Opposition to Jesus' popular movement had become so strong among the priestly aristocrats of Jerusalem, however, that the report of this amazing wonder served only to harden it. Even **Caiaphas**, the high priest who had been appointed by the Roman governor and who had worked closely with the

Romans for 12 years, had become alarmed, fearing Jesus might gain such a following as to precipitate conflict with Rome. "It is expedient," Caiaphas asserted, ". . . that one man should die for the people, and that the whole nation should not perish" (Jn. 11:50). Meanwhile, Jesus had withdrawn one last time from Jerusalem, remaining out of view to the religious authorities there, teaching in Judea and Perea through the rest of the winter. But as Passover approached, he was prepared for the final conflict.

The end was near and Jesus knew it. He had told his incredulous disciples that he "must suffer many things, and be rejected by the elders and the chief priests and the scribes, and be killed, and after three days rise again" (Mk. 8:31). But the statement seemed to them impossible to reconcile with what they expected the Messiah to be and do, and they could scarcely credit it. The disciples apparently often misunderstood Jesus' pronouncements about the kingdom of God as promises of great glory to come. James and John even tried to preempt the other disciples by requesting to sit at Jesus' right and left hand in his kingdom. Knowing how difficult his mission was for them to understand, Jesus did not condemn their petition but used it to teach them: "Whoever would be great among you must be your servant . . . . For the Son of man also came not to be served but to serve, and to give his life as a ransom for many" (Mk. 10:43, 45).

Approaching Jerusalem, Jesus passed through Jericho, where he restored the sight of a blind man named Bartimaeus and imparted new ethical insight to the tax collector **Zacchaeus**. As he arrived at Beth-

any, Passover pilgrims were flowing into Jerusalem a few days before the feast.

On the Sunday before Passover, Jesus reentered Jerusalem—consciously fulfilling the well-known prophecy from **Zechariah** that described a triumphant but deferential king who comes to Zion "humble, and mounted on an ass" (Mt. 21:5). The Passover crowds, fired as always with messianic zeal, recognized the prophecy in Jesus' actions and were electrified. They carpeted the road before Jesus with their garments, waving palm branches symbolizing victory and crying, "Hosanna! Blessed is he who comes in the name of the Lord! Blessed is the kingdom of our father David that is coming!" (Mk. 11:9). Those who feared Jesus' influence among the people were aghast.

FACING HIS OPPONENTS

On Monday, according to Mark (Sunday in the Gospel of Matthew), Jesus sharpened the edge of his prophetic message against the way the temple was governed by Caiaphas and other members of the aristocratic priesthood. He decried the fact that the sacred courts had become vast markets for trade in sacrificial animals and profiteering by money changers. Again he dramatized his prophetic message by action, overturning the tables of the money changers and driving out the animal sellers. One can only imagine the din as coins skittered across the stone pavement and people shouted as they scrambled to retrieve as many animals as possible. To make his point clear, Jesus quoted Isaiah and **Jeremiah**: "Is it not written, 'My house shall be called a house of prayer for all the nations?' But you have

Scourge in hand, Jesus overturns a money changer's table.

made it a den of robbers" (Mk. 11:17). Not surprisingly, such actions hardened the opposition of the priests and others who made a living from the temple.

All day Tuesday Jesus was in the temple teaching and facing his opponents. The chief priests demanded of him proof of his prophetic authority, but Jesus refused to offer any and turned the question into a condemnation of the priests because they had refused to recognize John the Baptist as a prophet. Pharisees and Sadducees tried unsuccessfully to trap Jesus in his talk with slippery questions about paying taxes to Caesar and about the resurrection. Jesus was so surrounded by crowds who hung on his words, however, that his opponents were powerless to stop his teaching. Jesus finished the day by warning his disciples about the hard days ahead—times of persecution, struggle, and intense suffering before their mission would be fulfilled.

He ended his public teaching with a vivid vision of the last judgment, when the King would judge all people by the same standard—whether they fed the hungry, aided strangers, clothed the naked, cared for the sick, helped those in prison. The King, Jesus said, would count such service "to one of the least of these my brethren" (Mt. 25:40) as having been done to him.

On Wednesday, Jesus remained outside Jerusalem in Bethany, where he ate at the

Jesus cradles the beloved disciple under his arms in this 15th-century Last Supper scene.

house of a man called **Simon** the leper. (The Gospel of John places this meal four days earlier in the house of Lazarus and his sisters, Martha and **Mary**.) During the meal a woman entered the room with an alabaster flask, opened it, and poured an expensive ointment over Jesus' head. Though she said nothing, the woman's actions sparked an argument as some disciples protested such a waste of money. Jesus, however, interpreted her act positively: "She has done a beautiful thing to me. . . . she has anointed my body beforehand for burying" (Mk. 14:6, 8). One person left the dinner in disgust. Judas Iscariot went, apparently almost immediately, to the chief priests of the temple and arranged to help them arrest Jesus. The Gospels do not fully explain Judas's motives. Perhaps greed played a part, but the traitor was more likely disillusioned that Jesus really had no intention of fulfilling the widespread expectation that a messianic king would cast out the Roman oppressors and restore Israel's glory.

Jesus knew that only hours remained for his labors. On Thursday, he prepared to return to Jerusalem for his last meal with his disciples. An upper room was found, and he sent two disciples to make arrangements for the evening meal. Here a historical puzzle intrudes. The Synoptic Gospels are explicit in treating this evening meal as a Passover banquet, but the Gospel of John is equally insistent that Thursday evening was the day before Passover. On the Jewish calendar a day begins at sundown; thus, if the Last Supper was a formal Passover meal, then the arrest of Jesus, his interrogation before the high priest, and his crucifixion all took place on Passover, when all work was strictly banned. Such a procedure would have been illegal and practically unthinkable for the chief priests. Therefore, many historians consider John's chronology more likely, though Jesus may well have treated the Last Supper as a Passover meal since he was aware of Judas's betrayal and anticipated his arrest that very evening.

HIS BODY, HIS BLOOD

What forever fixed that banquet in the minds and hearts of the disciples was what Jesus did during the meal. Their revered master and teacher took a basin of water and washed the disciples' feet as though he were their slave. This action was so startling that at first Peter refused to allow it until Jesus insisted. "Do you know what I have done to you?" Jesus asked. "I have given you an example, that you also should do as I have done to you" (Jn. 13:12, 15).

The disciples were again startled when

Jesus took the bread of the meal, blessed it, and said, "Take, eat; this is my body." Similarly, he took a cup of wine and said, "Drink of it, all of you; for this is my blood of the covenant, which is poured out for many for the forgiveness of sins" (Mt. 26:26-28). Jesus' words of blessing were to be remembered and regularly repeated by early Christians as the Last Supper became the Lord's Supper, an observance directly linking each believer to Jesus.

When the disciples looked back on that evening, they must have realized how little they had understood at the time. They had heard Jesus predict that one of them would betray him, but could not believe it. When Judas left the banquet, they thought he was going on some errand for Jesus. And when Jesus foretold that Peter would deny him that very night, they all stood with Peter in asserting their unwavering loyalty even unto death. They had heard Jesus tell them of his commandment to love each other, but found themselves arguing over who was the greatest among them and showing him the swords they were carrying. Finally, when Jesus led them out to Gethsemane on the Mount of Olives, they had no

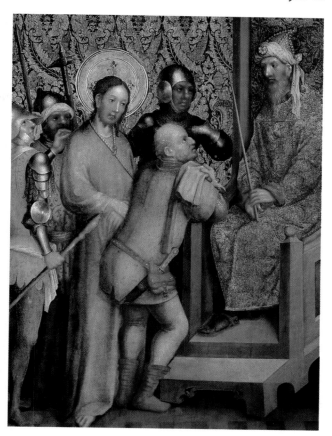

Jesus before the high priest; a painting from c. 1450

idea of the struggle he was enduring; they knew only that they were tired and fell asleep while he prayed. At last stirred from their stupor, they saw Judas arriving with a mob to arrest Jesus, and they fled in panic.

It was a turbulent night, and the confusion and disorientation of the disciples during those troubled hours seems to have left its mark on the records of Jesus' trial. All four Gospels agree that the decisive trial in which Jesus was condemned to be crucified took place Friday morning before Pontius **Pilate**, the Roman governor. But what happened during the night is described variously. Matthew and Mark report a midnight hearing before the Sanhedrin, the supreme Jewish judicial court, presided over by the high priest Caiaphas, in which there was a seemingly desperate effort to marshal incriminating witnesses against Jesus. Finally, in frustration, the high priest asked Jesus, "Are you the Christ, the son of the Blessed?" And Jesus answered, "I am; and you will see the Son of man seated at the right hand of Power, and coming with the clouds of heaven." That was blasphemy enough for members of the council, and "all condemned him

as deserving death" (Mk. 14:61-62, 64).

Luke, on the other hand, indicates that Jesus was held in the courtyard of the high priest throughout the night and was given a hearing only in the morning, but with similar results. In addition, Luke says that Pilate sent the prisoner to Herod Antipas since, as a Galilean, Jesus was technically under Antipas's jurisdiction. Antipas questioned Jesus "at some length; but he made no answer" (Lk. 23:9). After mocking the captive and dressing him in finery befitting one who seemed to be claiming he was king of the Jews, Antipas sent Jesus back to Pilate. By contrast, John describes only an interrogation of Jesus by **Annas**, a former high priest and Caiaphas's father-in-law. John mentions no trial before the Sanhedrin or Caiaphas but indicates that early Friday Jesus was taken to Pilate for trial.

A CHOICE OF PRISONERS

The Jewish trial, hearing, or interrogation ultimately made little difference, however, since it was the Roman governor who had the final word on Jesus' fate. When Jesus was brought before Pilate, probably at the governor's mansion, the old palace of Herod

In this painting by Lorenzo Lotto (c. 1480-1556), Jesus stoically endures the pain and humiliation of carrying his cross.

Jews?" Jesus responded, "You have said so," and refused to say more (Mk. 15:2). Pilate's contempt for the Jews led him to discount any charges the Jewish authorities brought against Jesus, and yet he had no use for a troublemaker like Jesus either.

But before condemning Jesus, Pilate offered the people a choice of amnesty or death between Jesus and **Barabbas**, a rebel who had led an insurrection against Rome. Pilate apparently harbored the vain hope that Jesus' popularity as a prophet, so apparent a few days earlier, would lead the people to condemn Barabbas. When the people shouted for the release of the rebel, Pilate—true to his reputation for injustice—sent Jesus away to be scourged and crucified, though he knew that the prisoner was guilty of no capital crime.

Pilate's quick verdict offered no possibility of appeal, and the sentence was carried out immediately. By 9:00 A.M., Jesus had already been taken outside Jerusalem to a spot called Golgotha, "the skull," and was being crucified—nailed through the wrists to a heavy crossbeam and raised to the top of a vertical post, to which his feet were nailed. Jesus' cross stood between those of two insurrectionists, considered robbers and criminals by the Romans—men whom Pilate had likely intended to crucify with Barabbas. Pilate had a sign put over the condemned man's head calling him "the King of the Jews" (Mk. 15:26)—thereby combining the official charge against Jesus with mockery of Jewish aspirations for their own ruler.

the Great, the trial was simple enough. Pilate was described by a contemporary, **Herod Agrippa I**, as a man of "vindictiveness and furious temper" who had carried out numerous "executions without trial" and did not "wish to do anything which would please his subjects." With obvious disdain, he asked Jesus, "Are you the King of the

THE TWO ROBBERS

*A*ll four Gospels report that two criminals were crucified alongside Jesus—one to his right, the other to his left. Only Luke, however, distinguishes between the two, recording that one mocked him while the other recognized Jesus' innocence. If Jesus were indeed the Messiah, said the first, he could prove it by saving himself and them. The other rebuked his companion for the outburst, declared Jesus to be blameless, and acknowledged his own guilt. Finally, the repentant criminal asked to be remembered by Jesus when he inherited his kingdom. For his compassion and faith,

the second man was rewarded with the promise of joining Jesus in paradise that very day.

An early Arabic narrative identified the good thief as Titus who, along with his evil companion Dumachus, had attempted to rob Mary and Joseph some 30 years earlier as they were fleeing to Eygpt with the infant Jesus. When Titus bribed Dumachus to spare the holy family, Jesus predicted their end on crosses flanking his. Early Christians gave the good robber the name Dismas, from the Greek word for dying, and made him the patron saint of prisoners and penitent criminals.

Crucifixion was a well-known form of humiliating torture. A victim would typically hang for 36 hours of excruciating pain, bleeding, naked, and helpless before passersby. The Evangelists did not need to describe the horrors of Jesus' crucifixion to their contemporary readers, but rather concentrated on details that helped to interpret the dark and troubling event. They highlighted small particulars like the wine mingled with myrrh, the soldiers casting lots for Jesus' garment, and observers wagging their heads, because these details echoed words of the Scriptures and thus helped to place the crucifixion within the framework of God's purposes.

As with every crucifixion, the scene around Jesus' cross was confusion: soldiers, gawkers, passersby, enemies, family, and friends all mingled. Groans of the dying competed with jeers of enemies, wailing of friends, and jokes of soldiers. The sky grew inexplicably dark about noon and remained so till 3:00 P.M.

The Gospels record a few words of Jesus on the cross that provided meaning to the events. Matthew and Mark saw the power of Jesus' death in the dark loss and absolute loneliness in which he died, forsaken by the fawning crowds and even by his nearest disciples. In the end Jesus experienced the depth of human suffering, expressed in his mysterious cry, echoing Psalm 22: "My God, my God, why hast thou forsaken me?" (Mt. 27:46). Luke emphasized Jesus' serene trust in God as he forgave his tormenters, promised paradise to the penitent man crucified beside him, and chose the moment of his death, saying, in the words of Psalm 31, "Father, into thy hands I commit my spirit" (Lk. 23:46). Similarly, John highlighted Jesus' calm control of events, even on the cross. Jesus cared for his mother's future, entrusting her to the beloved disciple; he said, "I thirst," in order "to fulfil the scripture"; and, when the full purpose of his life was completed, he simply said, "It is finished," and then "bowed his head and gave up his spirit" (Jn. 19:28, 30).

Thus the challenging, joyful, authoritative, reinvigorating, hopeful ministry of Jesus ended on Golgotha—or so it seemed at the time. Jesus' body was hurriedly removed from the cross before the sabbath began at sundown and placed in a tomb by **Joseph of Arimathea**, a secret disciple.

THE EMPTY TOMB

Many of Jesus' disciples were so despondent over his crucifixion that his story also might have ended at Golgotha had not remarkable events occurred early on Sunday morning, following the sabbath observance. Coming to the place of burial, three women followers found the tomb empty.

The Evangelists as well as the apostle **Paul** joined in recording a great variety of subsequent appearances of Jesus to his followers, experiences that convinced them completely that Jesus had risen from the dead. According to Matthew, Mark, and John, Jesus first appeared to Mary Magdalene, either alone or with another woman disciple. Paul stated that Jesus "appeared to Cephas [Peter], then to the twelve. Then he appeared to more than five hundred brethren at one time . . . . Then he appeared to James, then to all the apostles. Last of all, as to one untimely born, he appeared also to me" (1 Cor. 15:5-8).

Luke described appearances in the vicinity of Jerusalem, ending with Jesus' ascension to heaven; Matthew and John related appearances in Galilee. John recounted the

Jesus on the cross, by Rubens

*As the Roman guards doze, Jesus rises in triumph
from his tomb; a 12th-century French
enamel and gilded copper plaque.*

poignant scene when Jesus met several of the disciples beside the Sea of Galilee after their night of unsuccessful fishing, filled their nets to bursting, and shared breakfast with them on the shore. He thrice asked Peter, "Do you love me?" and commissioned him to "feed my sheep" (Jn. 21:15-17). Matthew told how from a mountain in Galilee Jesus sent the apostles out to "make disciples of all nations" and promised, "I am with you always, to the close of the age" (Mt. 28:19-20).

These experiences of Jesus' resurrection as well as the memories of his teachings and ministry transformed his disciples. The testimony and proclamation of Peter, James, John, and the other disciples became a veritable explosion of faith in the Roman empire. Jesus, the wandering teacher who had proclaimed the kingdom of God and called people to repentance and love, became the center of this new faith. Not only his message but also his person and especially his death and resurrection became the focus of Christian belief. His influence, which his opponents had sought to quash by so cruelly executing him, became more powerful and universal through their unsuccessful efforts to silence him. The results for the history of the world have been incalculable.

JESUS JUSTUS
(juhs' tuhs) GREEK: IESOUS HO
LEGOMENOS IOUSTOS
"Jesus called just/lawful"

An associate of **Paul**, Jesus Justus was with the apostle during his imprisonment by the Romans. In writing to members of the Christian church in the small town of Colossae in Asia Minor, Paul listed Jesus Justus along with **Aristarchus** and **Mark**. These three, Paul said, "are the only men of the circumcision [Jews] among my fellow workers for the kingdom of God, and they have been a comfort to me" (Col. 4:11). Jesus Justus is mentioned nowhere else in the New Testament.

JETHRO
(jeth' roh) HEBREW: YITRO
"preeminence"

When the young **Moses** fled Egypt after killing a man he caught beating a Hebrew, he went to the land of Midian in the Sinai. As descendants of **Abraham** by his second wife, **Keturah**, the Midianites were his distant blood relatives. Stopping to rest at a well, Moses encountered seven young

222

women, the daughters of a priest named Jethro, who were drawing water for their father's flocks. Moses defended the women from shepherds seeking to drive them away; in gratitude, Jethro invited him to a meal. The fugitive stayed in Midian, becoming a shepherd for Jethro and marrying one of his daughters, **Zipporah**, by whom he had two sons, **Gershom** and Eliezer.

Many years later, when God spoke to Moses out of a burning bush and commanded him to return to Eygpt to deliver his people from bondage, Moses asked and received permission from his father-in-law to depart on his great mission. Upon learning of the Israelites' safe escape from Egypt, Jethro brought Zipporah and her sons to Moses in the wilderness, and there he heard what God had done for his chosen people. "Now I know that the Lord is greater than all gods" (Ex. 18:11), Jethro exclaimed. In his capacity as a priest, Jethro made a burnt offering to God and shared a sacrificial feast with the elders of Israel.

The following day, Jethro witnessed Moses settling disputes among the people, a task that took all day. Concerned that Moses would exhaust himself, Jethro suggested that his son-in-law establish a hierarchy of judges to hear cases according to their seriousness. After instructing them in the law, Moses should decide only the most difficult cases himself. Jethro's wise advice to Moses set forth important standards for the government of Israel, standards that have been used by many other nations since. For he taught the difference between making laws and judging actions, and the importance of delegating authority and appointing leaders of integrity.

Jethro is called Reuel in Exodus 2:18 and Hobab in Numbers 10:29 and Judges 4:11.

JEZEBEL
(jez' uh bel) HEBREW: IZEBEL
possibly "Where is the prince?"

An ambitious, strong-minded woman, the Phoenician princess Jezebel became an active partner of her husband, King **Ahab** of Israel, and maintained her influence after his death, during the reigns of her sons, **Ahaziah** and **Jehoram**. Jezebel was the daughter of Ethbaal, king of the Sidonians; her marriage to Ahab had been arranged to strengthen an alliance between Israel and Phoenicia.

After he married Jezebel, Ahab adopted her worship of the god **Baal**. Although it was common for a foreign wife to continue honoring her own gods, Jezebel was not only an active promoter of her native religion, but also an adversary of Israel's God. Out of the royal treasury, she supported 450 prophets of Baal and 400 prophets of the goddess Asherah while she opposed the prophets of Yahweh, killing many of them

Moses and the daughters of Jethro; detail of a 19th-century British painting

The death of Jezebel, from a 10th-century Spanish illuminated Bible

death. She then seized the dead man's property and presented it to her husband. Speaking through Elijah, the Lord told Ahab that Jezebel would be punished: "The dogs shall eat Jezebel within the bounds of Jezreel" (1 Kg. 21:23).

In keeping with Elijah's prophecy, Jezebel's end was an ignominious one. A commander named **Jehu** led an insurrection against the royal family and killed Jezebel's son Jehoram as he was fleeing toward Jezreel. When she heard the news, Jezebel "painted her eyes, and adorned her head" (2 Kg. 9:30)—probably to emphasize her royalty—and taunted Jehu from her palace window as he entered the gates of Jezreel. Jehu told her eunuchs to throw her from the window, then left her body for dogs to devour. Later he ordered that she be buried, since she was a king's daughter. "But when they went to bury her, they found no more of her than the skull and the feet and the palms of her hands" (2 Kg. 9:35).

If Jezebel's name means "Where is the prince?" or "The prince exists," it refers to a traditional story of Baal's death and return. But an alternate reading of the final syllable is not "prince" but "dung"—making Elijah's earlier judgment on the queen a play on words: "The corpse of Jezebel shall be as dung . . . so that no one can say, 'This is Jezebel' " (2 Kg. 9:37).

Old Testament writers generally blamed Jezebel for the idolatry practiced by her husband, children, and in-laws (her daughter—possibly her sister-in-law—**Athaliah** became queen of Judah and introduced the worship of Baal there). It is possible that they were merely using Jezebel as a symbol of the danger of Canaanite cults in general, but she may actually have been a priestess with considerable spiritual influence over the people. In any case, her misdeeds were religious as well as political. Only centuries later was her name attached to the concept of a shameless seductress.

JEZREEL

(jez' reel) HEBREW: YIZREEL
"God saves" or "God sows"

At God's command, the prophet **Hosea** named his first son Jezreel. The name could be taken as a reference to the overthrow of the house of **Ahab** by **Jehu**, which happened in the town of Jezreel about a century before the child's birth. In thus naming his son, Hosea was condemning that immoral seizure of power and implying that the present king—Jehu's great-grand-

and forcing 100 into hiding. The Lord punished Israel for the queen's sinful actions by inflicting a serious drought, which was broken after the prophet **Elijah** challenged the prophets of Baal to a contest at Mount Carmel. The outcome showed the people that Elijah's God was the one true deity. But when Jezebel heard that Elijah had executed all the rival prophets, she threatened him with death, saying, "So may the gods do to me, and more also, if I do not make your life as the life of one of them by this time tomorrow" (1 Kg. 19:2). Understandably frightened, the prophet fled to Judah.

Jezebel viewed the powers of the monarchy as absolute, in keeping with the tradition of her homeland. The story of **Naboth**'s vineyard is an example of the lengths to which she would go to uphold that viewpoint. When Naboth rebuffed the king's attempt to buy his vineyard, which adjoined the palace in Jezreel, Jezebel intervened. "Let your heart be cheerful," she told her despondent husband; "I will give you the vineyard" (1 Kg. 21:7). Immediately she set about destroying Naboth, having him unfairly denounced and ultimately stoned to

son, **Jeroboam II**—was not a lawful ruler. Hosea predicted that, in vengeance, God would destroy Jehu's dynasty in the valley of Jezreel. However, the name Jezreel also carried the promise of a hopeful future for Israel: "God saves."

Joab dispatches the helpless Absalom.

JOAB

(joh' ab) HEBREW: YOAB
"Yahweh is father"
┄┄┄┄┄┄┄┄┄

A powerful and fearless military man, Joab became King **David**'s commander in chief and confidant. His family connection—he was the son of David's sister **Zeruiah**—undoubtedly helped him reach his position, but his fierce loyalty, unbridled ambition, and unparalleled leadership abilities ensured that he would hold it.

Joab is first mentioned during David's war with **Abner**, in a battle at the pool of Gibeon. David's army won the battle, but Joab's brother **Asahel** was killed by Abner. Later, while Joab was away, Abner switched loyalties and formed an alliance with David—a move that Joab protested, charging that Abner's motives were deceitful. Without informing the king, Joab sent for Abner and killed him, thus eliminating a possible rival and avenging Asahel's death. When David discovered the trickery, he was furious. He cursed Joab and his descendants, saying, "the sons of Zeruiah are too hard for me" (2 Sam. 3:39), and forced the offending commander to wear sackcloth and publicly mourn his victim.

Despite this humiliation, Joab remained loyal to David and went to great lengths to please him. During the war with the Ammonites, Joab helped David eliminate **Uriah**, the husband of **Bathsheba**, so that the king could marry the woman he had made pregnant. Joab also intervened on behalf of David's son **Absalom**, who had been in exile for several years since killing his half brother **Amnon**. Joab arranged for a wise woman to bring a complaint before the king; she then chastised him for his treatment of Absalom, as Joab had instructed her to do. Although the king gave his son permission to return to Jerusalem, he refused to see him until Joab once again interceded.

When Absalom led a revolt against his father, David fled to Mahanaim, east of the Jordan, but sent his army, partly under the command of Joab, to fight the rebel forces. "Deal gently for my sake with the young man Absalom" (2 Sam. 18:5), the king told his generals. In the wake of the victory for David, a messenger told Joab that Absalom, in trying to escape, had become caught by his hair in the branches of a tree. Defying the king's order, Joab killed the helpless man. Hearing the news, David grieved uncontrollably instead of celebrating his army's victory—for which Joab strongly rebuked him. Angry, David replaced Joab as commander with **Amasa**, another of his nephews. But the ruthless Joab was soon able to eliminate this new rival and regain his position. During preparations for a battle against a rebel named **Sheba**, Joab approached Amasa as if in friendship, drew a concealed weapon, and killed him in cold blood. He then dealt quickly with Sheba, pursuing him to the city of Abel-beth-macah and getting its inhabitants to kill the fugitive and throw his head over the wall.

In the succession struggle, Joab backed **Adonijah**, David's oldest surviving son. But the king instead designated **Solomon** as his heir. Unable to forget Joab's misdeeds, David told Solomon not to "let his gray head go down to Sheol in peace" (1 Kg. 2:6). Knowing that he was marked for death, Joab sought sanctuary at the tent of the Lord. But Solomon sent a man named **Benaiah** to kill the vexatious general, thus removing from David's house the guilt for the murders of Abner and Amasa.

Joab's treacherous murder of Amasa; a 13th-century stained-glass window from Strasbourg cathedral, France

JOANNA

(joh an' uh) GREEK: IONANA
feminine of John
••••••••••

Joanna was one of the "women who had been healed of evil spirits and infirmities" (Lk. 8:2) by **Jesus** and who then accompanied him and his disciples on their travels to spread the Gospel. She was apparently a woman of means, the wife of Chuza, **Herod Antipas**'s steward. Along with **Mary Magdalene** and **Susanna**, she helped provide the entourage with food and other necessities. That Jesus welcomed women into his inner circle was another example of his break with the rigid social distinctions of his day.

Joanna was also one of those who traveled with Jesus on his last journey from Galilee to Jerusalem and, after his crucifixion, was present at his burial. Later, Joanna went with several other women to Jesus' tomb with spices and ointments to anoint his body, discovered that his tomb was empty, and went to tell the apostles.

Since Joanna is mentioned only by **Luke**, it is thought that she may have been one of the evangelist's original sources.

JOASH

(joh' ash) HEBREW: YOAS, variant of YEHDAS
"Yaweh has bestowed"
••••••••••

While he was still an infant, Joash (also called Jehoash) narrowly escaped being murdered by order of his grandmother. The boy's father, King **Ahaziah** of Judah,

and his great-uncle, King **Jehoram** of Israel, had both perished in a recent uprising. With her family displaced in Israel, Joash's grandmother, the former Omride princess **Athaliah**, ordered a massacre of the rest of the royal family in an attempt to eradicate the house of **David** so that she could rule unchallenged over Judah. Her plans were thwarted, however, when Joash's aunt Jehosheba, the wife of the high priest **Jehoiada**, "stole him away from among the king's sons who were about to be slain" (2 Kg. 11:2).

For six years, Joash was kept secretly in the temple, tutored by Jehoiada, a man of high moral principles. Then, when the time was right, the high priest presented the boy to the palace guards and commanded them to protect the legitimate heir. During a sabbath festival, with the guards forming a wall of protection around him, Joash was crowned ninth king of Judah in a joyful ceremony. It was about the year 837 B.C. When Athaliah heard the noise, she rushed in, "rent her clothes, and cried, 'Treason! Treason!'" (2 Kg. 11:14). But she was quickly removed from the temple and killed.

The reestablishment of the dynasty was symbolically celebrated by bringing out David's shields and spears, and a new covenant was made among God, the king, and the people. The cult of **Baal**, which had flourished under Athaliah, was banished, and its priest was killed. Since Joash was only seven years old when he assumed the throne, Jehoiada acted as regent for a time, and the priesthood became more influential than ever before.

Joash was determined that the temple, which had been plundered under Athaliah, be repaired. By the 23rd year of his reign, however, it had become clear that the work was not being done because the priests were in the habit of taking the temple funds for themselves. Joash remedied this by placing a collection box at the entrance of the temple and insisting that donations be put directly into it. The king's secretary and high priest were in charge of counting the money and giving it to those overseeing the work. In this way the restoration of the temple was ultimately well financed.

Following the death of his mentor Jehoiada, Joash's rule weakened. He came into increasing conflict with the nobility, who demanded more freedom of worship than Jehoiada had allowed. Joash gave in to them, and idols were erected throughout the kingdom. But when **Zechariah**, Jehoiada's son, warned that disaster would follow, Joash in retaliation ordered him stoned to death. The king's power was further eroded when King **Hazael** of Syria threatened an attack. In order to buy peace, Joash was forced to surrender all the gold and valuables of the temple and palace.

After a reign of nearly 40 years, Joash was killed by his servants, possibly backed by the priests; his assassins were put to death by his son, **Amaziah**.

JOASH 2

The 12th king of Israel, Joash (also called Jehoash) was the son of **Jehoahaz** and the grandson of **Jehu**, who had toppled the Omride dynasty. During Joash's years on the throne (c. 801-786 B.C.), Israel began to regain its lost power and prosperity. The defeat of Syria by Assyria set the stage for this comeback. With his northern neighbor thus weakened, Joash was able to recover the cities taken from Israel by Syria during his father's reign.

On his deathbed, the prophet **Elisha** had predicted Joash's military successes. Receiving the king during his final illness, Elisha told Joash to shoot an arrow out the window; as he did so, Elisha declared it to be "the Lord's arrow of victory, the arrow of victory over Syria!" (2 Kg. 13:17). Then he told Joash to strike the ground with his other arrows. The king struck the ground three times, angering Elisha, who told him that each strike of the arrows portended a victory over Syria. Had he struck five or six times, he would have eliminated the Syrian threat altogether, but Joash's restraint assured him of only three victories .

At first Joash resisted the challenge to fight King **Amaziah** of Judah. But when pressed, he led his army into battle at Beth-shemesh, where he defeated the forces of Judah and captured Amaziah. Joash entered the city of Jerusalem in triumph, tore down part of the wall, and took hostages and treasure from the temple and palace back with him to Samaria. Judah was much reduced in status, and Israel regained its position of importance.

JOB

(johb) HEBREW: IYOB
possibly "Where is the Father [God]?" or "an enemy/persecuted one"

According to the prophet **Ezekiel**, Job was one of the three most righteous mortals who ever lived—the others being **Noah** and **Daniel**. As Noah had escaped drowning in the Flood and Daniel had emerged unscathed from the lions' den, so Job survived an undeserved, catastrophic destruction of his family, his health, and his

Job's wife cools the tormented man's fevered agony with a bucket of water; a painting by Albrecht Dürer (1471–1528).

227

JOB'S STORY

hemes similar to those in the book of Job occur in many ancient Near Eastern literary works dating to the second millennium B.C. or even earlier. For example, "The Protests of the Eloquent Peasant," an Egyptian document written in the 21st century B.C., contains a series of complaining speeches addressed to a deified Pharaoh. Secretly recorded for the entertainment of the court, the man's complaints ultimately bring relief. The Canaanite epic of Keret tells of a man, like Job, who loses a wife and sons but obtains a new family after regaining the favor of the gods.

Unjust suffering is the subject of at least four Mesopotamian texts. The most exact parallel to the biblical book is found in *"Man and His God,"* sometimes called the Sumerian Job. Though none of these related literary traditions carries the name Job, that name is found in several ancient Near Eastern documents outside the Bible, indicating that such a person or his story was widely known.

An 18th-century B.C. tablet containing the poem of the so-called Sumerian Job

wealth—all the while eloquently protesting his innocence in the midst of virtually indescribable agony.

There is but meager information in the Bible about the identity, homeland, and time of Job, who is merely referred to as "a man in the land of Uz" (Job 1:1). A person by the similar name of Iob is listed in Genesis 46:13 as a grandson of **Jacob**. And, indeed, certain details in the book of Job—such as the inventory of his wealth, the Hebrew word used for the piece of money referred to in the last chapter (*qesitah*), and the long life he is granted—suggest the patriarchal period.

A CENTURIES-OLD TALE

Oral traditions about Job may have been handed down for centuries, but were most likely not written in Hebrew before the time of **David** and **Solomon** (c. 1000-922 B.C.). Some scholars date the book of Job later, to the time of King **Hezekiah** (715-687 B.C.); others suggest that the poetic dialogue that forms the core of the book was composed during the sixth-century B.C. exile in Babylon. All are agreed on the complexity of the language; Job contains more rare words than any other book in the Bible.

The location of Job's country, the land of Uz, is no longer known with certainty—though **Jeremiah** listed it among the nations that were to drink the "cup of the wine of wrath" (Jer. 25:15). The Jewish historian Josephus thought Uz was among Aramean or Syrian territories north of Palestine. The old Greek translation of the book of Job indicates another possibility, that Uz lay on the border between Edom and Arabia, and that Job's home city was called Dennaba. If so, the remains of the city could be a mound, Sheikh Sa'ad, about 23 miles east of the Sea of Galilee. While place-names are uncertain, at least one of Job's three friends, **Eliphaz**, clearly came from Edom, from the region of Teman, and the character **Elihu** is from an Aramean family.

Although Job is not presented as an Israelite, he exhibited a devotion to God and to wisdom that Jews had always admired. The absence of references to beliefs distinctive to Israel's Law and its prophets suggest that Job was a figure who represented perennial issues faced by people everywhere.

What can be learned most clearly about Job from the biblical book is that he lived out his life in an earthly arena, with no access to what God was doing in the heavenly grandstand. The narratives at the beginning and the end of the book report things Job never knew, while the poetic core of the book contains his response to what has

The suffering Job, from a 15th-century Spanish choir stall

sit in silence with him for seven days and nights, waiting to hear how Job will respond to his suffering. His first words are nearly a scream, an eerie and indirect prayer to God. Job wishes the day of his birth could be wiped from the calendar or that he had perished as soon as he was born. His soliloquy arrives at the blunt conclusion, "the thing that I fear comes upon me, and what I dread befalls me" (Job 3:25).

His three concerned friends believe that Job should not protest his innocence but rather confess his sins, for they think some wrongdoing on his part must lie behind so much personal loss. Their words of comfort begin as general admonitions but soon become harsh arguments, more typical of prosecuting attorneys than of empathetic friends. In three cycles of challenge and response, Job defends his innocence against the criticisms of his friends, while summoning God to judge his case. At the end of this debate, a young bystander named Elihu again castigates Job, interpreting human illness as a refining experience and questioning Job's verbose self-righteousness.

Suddenly God appears "out of the whirlwind" (Job 38:1) to criticize Job for pretending in the course of his protestations to know things only God could know. Job repents of his arrogance, and God rewards him with a new family and an estate twice as large as the one taken from him. At God's suggestion, Job offers sacrifices to redeem his three friends who erred so badly in their counsel to him. The happy ending of this story is blunted by a reminder of what Job has experienced and lost despite God's restoration. Job's relatives and friends attend a feast at his new house, where they "comforted him for all the evil that the Lord had brought upon him" (Job 42:11).

ENDURANCE, NOT PATIENCE

In the New Testament, James refers to Job's well-known reputation as he gives advice to wait patiently for the coming of the Lord: "You have heard of the steadfastness of Job" (Jas. 5:11). However, the modern cliché about the "patience of Job" misses the point. A friend chides Job for having counseled others to remain calm in times of trouble, but, "now it has come to you, and you are impatient" (Job 4:5). Job retorts, "What is my end, that I should be patient?" (Job 6:11). Job provides less an example of patience than of a tenacity by which he "holds fast to his integrity" (Job 2:3) under catastrophic personal experiences.

Job thus offers a model of endurance in faith in order to overcome the terrors of undeserved suffering. Despite his friends' ad-

happened to him. In effect, the reader knows more about Job than he knows about himself, because the reader is permitted to sit for a few moments in the grandstand with God and hear conversations that have a bearing on Job's circumstances.

In heaven God greets the adversary **Satan** and points out Job as "a blameless and upright man, who fears God and turns away from evil" (Job 1:8). Satan, appearing here more like the serpent in the garden of Eden than the devil of later Jewish and Christian tradition, asks God a question that may be paraphrased: "Is Job's faith nothing more than gratitude for all the good things you let him experience?" God decides to prove Satan wrong by allowing him to remove Job's family and estate and, finally, to rob him of health. God allows Satan to "destroy him [Job] without cause" (Job 2:3).

And, thus, in the arena, unaware of what has happened in heaven, Job sits in an ash heap, scraping his painful open sores with a potsherd. Job's wife proposes that he "curse God, and die," but he refuses to "sin with his lips" (Job 2:9-10). Then, his three friends—Eliphaz, **Bildad**, and **Zophar**—

vice to confess sin, Job properly knows that these calamities are not due to his own wrongdoing—as God eventually affirms. To confess uncommitted sin in the face of adversity can be as much a foolish exercise in bad faith as to refuse to confess sin under other circumstances. The wisdom of Job helps clarify the difference.

JOCHEBED

(joh' kee buhd) HEBREW: YOKEBED
possibly "Yahweh is glory"

Born during the Israelites' 400-year sojourn in Egypt, Jochebed married her nephew Amram—a relationship that would have been prohibited under later religious law. She became the mother of **Moses**, **Aaron**, and **Miriam**.

Before Moses was born, the Pharaoh had ordered all male Hebrew children killed because "the people of Israel are too many and too mighty for us" (Ex. 1:9). Jochebed hid Moses until he was three months old, then devised a clever plan to save his life. She put the infant in "a basket made of bulrushes . . . and placed it among the reeds at the river's brink" (Ex. 2:3), posting his sister as a sentinel to find out what happened. When Pharaoh's daughter discovered the basket, Miriam stepped forth and offered to find a Hebrew woman to nurse Moses—and thus Jochebed was paid to care for her own son until he was weaned. She then returned Moses to the Pharaoh's daughter, who raised him as her own.

JOEL

(johl) HEBREW: YOEL
"Yah[weh] is God"

Other than the fact that he was "the son of Pethuel" (Jl.1:1)—a person nowhere else mentioned in the Bible—nothing is known about the prophet Joel. The book that bears his name is the second of the so-called Minor Prophets, immediately following that of **Hosea**. From clues contained in the book, it appears that Joel lived in Judah during the postexilic period, 538-331 B.C.; but scholars disagree on more precise dates.

The book of Joel falls into two parts: a call to lamentation and repentance for a terrifying locust plague and drought that symbolized national destruction (Jl. 1:2-2:27); and the promise of complete restoration following an apocalyptic war with other nations (Jl. 2:28-3:21). In this alteration of national fortunes can be seen the fate of the kingdom of Judah, whose people were taken into exile by the Babylonians and later, under the Persians, allowed to return to Jerusalem to rebuild the temple.

Fearful of Egyptians coming to seize her infant, Jochebed makes a basket to send Moses to safety.

The plague of locusts described in the opening verses well conveys this type of natural calamity in the ancient Middle East. But there is a hint that the plague is but a prelude to a unique historical catastrophe when the prophet compares the locusts to an invading army: "Like warriors they charge, like soldiers they scale the wall" (Jl. 2:7). The later reference to "the northerner" (Jl. 2:20) extends the symbolism to other nations—Tyre, Sidon, Philistia, Greece—that had stolen temple treasures and taken the people into captivity.

If Joel prophesied early in the period following the return from exile, he would have been a near contemporary of the prophets **Haggai** and **Zechariah**. But if his book was written later—after the rededication of the temple in 515 B.C.—the name Joel might refer to a figure of that period to whom older traditions were ascribed. The prophet's call for a ritual of repentance by the people before the priests and his prophetic announcement of salvation in response to their prayers indicate Joel's strong devotion to the temple cult and liturgy. He may have worked alongside the priests as a member of the temple staff in Jerusalem.

Despite the division between the prophecy of doom and the promise of restoration, the book of Joel appears to belong to one person whose distinctive human voice rings throughout it. The prophet summons the people to "awake," "lament," "sanctify a fast," and "blow the trumpet" (Jl. 1:5, 8, 14; 2:1). But his panic and anxiety are suddenly alleviated when "the Lord became jealous for his land and had pity on his people" (Jl. 2:18). The locusts are driven from the land; the lost grain, wine, and oil are restored; the theme of darkness is replaced by divine deliverance. All this takes place "So you shall know that I am the Lord your God, who dwell in Zion" (Jl. 3:17). Never again will strangers violate Jerusalem, the Lord promises his chosen people.

Joel's prophecy is also remarkable because it contains a striking description of a lament performed by an entire community. Children and elders gather at the temple; nursing mothers bring their infants with them to the sanctuary; bridegroom and bride cancel their wedding plans to join the solemn assembly, where priests openly weep as they loudly pray "between the vestibule and the altar" (Jl. 2:17). Joel's words show that the prophets of Israel hoped that their diatribes would provoke such repentance that their messages could be changed from judgment to blessing.

In the Old Testament Joel's prophecy has been placed strategically between the books

The prophet Joel; a ninth-century ivory carving

of Hosea and **Amos**, both dated to the eighth century B.C. And thus the timeless words of Joel are heard as if in conversation with them across the centuries. In this way, the oracle of Joel the prophet is not anchored to a single historical period but rather establishes a pattern of God's judgment and promise that is pertinent to future times and places. In support of such a wide audience for the book are the words at the very beginning: "Tell your children of it and let your children tell their children, and their children another generation" (Jl. 1:3). The introduction is a reminder that the message of the book is far more important than the irretrievable biography of its prophetic messenger.

JOHANAN

(joh hay' nan) HEBREW: YOHANAN
"Yahweh is/has been gracious"

After the destruction of Jerusalem and the deportation of its inhabitants in 586 B.C., the Jewish military leader Johanan allied himself with **Gedaliah**, who had been appointed by the Babylonians to govern the remaining population of Judah. Hearing of a plot against Gedaliah, Johanan informed the governor of the danger and offered to murder the would-be assassin, Ishmael. But his warning went unheeded. Gedaliah was killed, along with Jewish members of his entourage and his Babylonian guard; and many hostages were taken. Johanan pursued the fleeing assailant and freed the prisoners, though the killer himself es-

John the Evangelist, from the Lindisfarne Gospels, dated about 698

ANCIENT BAPTISM

The baptism John offered was not unique, nor was Christianity the first religion to immerse its members in water. Worship of Mithras, Isis, and other pagan gods involved ceremonial baths. But as a Jew, John may have patterned his ritual after those he had seen and practiced while growing up as the son of a Jerusalem priest. Jews took a ritual bath to cleanse themselves of impurities caused by a variety of defilements: contact with a corpse, menstruation, childbirth, nocturnal emissions. In addition, brides took a ritual bath before the wedding, and men were required to be purified before taking part in religious services. The Essenes, a Jewish sect at Qumran near Jerusalem in John's day, took purifying baths every day.

Perhaps the closest parallel with John's baptism was the ritual that formally initiated converts into the Jewish faith.

caped. Johanan and the other survivors of the massacre, fearing they would be blamed by their Babylonian overlords for the slaughter, consulted the prophet **Jeremiah**, who warned them to stay in Judah. If they fled to Egypt, he said, they would "die by the sword, by famine, and by pestilence" (Jer. 42:17). But Johanan and the people he had saved seized the prophet and took him with them as they sought refuge in Egypt.

JOHANAN 2

The high priest Johanan was a younger contemporary of **Nehemiah**, the governor of Judah in the period following the return of the Jews from exile in Babylon. In Nehemiah 12:11 he is called Jonathan, a somewhat similar name in Hebrew; he is also said to be the same person as Jehohanan the son of Eliashib mentioned in Ezra 10:6. In that passage **Ezra** is described as retiring to Jehohanan's chamber to fast after he had discovered the faithlessness of the returned exiles and demanded that they make a new covenant with God.

The Jewish historian Josephus, writing around the year A.D. 90, claimed that the high priest Johanan murdered his brother Jeshua in the temple to prevent him from taking over the priesthood.

JOHN
short for HEBREW: JOHANAN;
GREEK: IOANNES
"Yahweh has been gracious/shows favor"

John and his brother **James**, the sons of **Zebedee**, were among the first disciples called by **Jesus**. Along with **Peter**, these three fishermen formed an inner circle of men who witnessed events that were not shared by the other apostles, including the raising of **Jairus**'s daughter, the transfiguration, and Jesus' prayer in the garden of Gethsemane. According to the Gospel of Luke, it was John and Peter who were sent to prepare the Passover meal (the Last Supper) on the eve of Jesus' crucifixion.

Apparently in reference to their fiery temperaments, Jesus called the brothers Boanerges, meaning "sons of thunder" (Mk. 3:17). True to his nickname, John once told Jesus, "Teacher, we saw a man casting out demons in your name, and we forbade him, because he was not following us" (Mk. 9:38). He and James also asked permission to punish the Samaritans with fire from heaven for their inhospitality to Jesus. Later they urged Jesus to give the two of them places of honor in the kingdom to come, a request that understandably aroused the ire of the other apostles.

Though his brother James was the first apostle to be martyred, John continued for some time as a prominent leader in the early Christian church. **Paul** lists John as one of the "pillars" (Gal. 2:9) of the Jerusalem church, along with Peter and **James** the brother of Jesus. His prominence is also recorded in the book of Acts, where he is said to have accompanied Peter on important missions. On one occasion, they healed a lame man and thus encountered the opposition of the Jewish authorities. On another occasion, they were dispatched to Samaria to impart the **Holy Spirit** to those who had "received the word of God" (Acts 8:14).

Church tradition identifies John as the author of the fourth Gospel and the three letters of John, works that are similar in literary style and in their teaching, as well as the book of Revelation (see **John of Patmos**). But many scholars consider it to be unlikely that John wrote anything, since he was known to be an unlettered man. Tradition further identifies John with the otherwise unnamed figure in the Gospel of John known as the beloved disciple (see page 56). The fate of John is unknown. Some traditions state that he lived to an old age in Ephesus; others, that he was martyred early in life as had been his brother.

JOHN THE BAPTIST

In introducing John the Baptist as the precursor of **Jesus**, all four Evangelists quote the prophet **Isaiah**: "A voice cries: 'In the wilderness prepare the way of the Lord, make straight in the desert a highway for our God'" (Is. 40:3). John's mission, according to Mark, also fulfilled the oracle of **Malachi**: "Behold, I send my messenger to prepare the way before me" (Mal. 3:1). Thus, John is presented as one chosen by God to announce the coming of the Messiah. Yet John's disciples, and perhaps the Baptist himself, seem to have understood his mission differently. During his life and even after his death, his disciples existed as a group separate from and even competing with the disciples of Jesus. Consequently, though

John the Baptist, by Donatello

John remained a central figure in early Christian preaching, he was nevertheless something of an enigma—both essential to, yet distinct from, the ministry of Jesus.

John was the son of **Zechariah**, a priest "of the division of Abijah," one of 24 groups that regularly served at the temple in Jerusalem; his mother, **Elizabeth**, was "of the daughters of Aaron" (Lk. 1:5) and thus also of priestly lineage. Zechariah and Elizabeth were an elderly couple who had no children. One day while Zechariah was burning incense in the temple, he was greeted by the angel **Gabriel**, who told him that Elizabeth would bear a child to be named John and who would "make ready for the Lord a people prepared" (Lk. 1:17). When Zechariah questioned how this could be, he was told that he would lose his voice until the child was born as punishment for doubting the word from God.

Six months later the same angelic messenger told the betrothed virgin **Mary** that she also would bear a son and informed her of her kinswoman Elizabeth's pregnancy. Mary hastened to visit Elizabeth, whose child "leaped in her womb" (Lk. 1:41) at the younger woman's greeting. Later, after John was born, Zechariah's voice was restored, and he spoke of the divine redemption that was to be bestowed on "the house of his servant David," referring to the coming Messiah, and of the future mission of his own son: "And you, child, will be called the prophet of the Most High; for you will go before the Lord to prepare his ways" (Lk.1:69,76). By telling the stories of the births of John and Jesus in this way, **Luke** presents the two as having parallel missions, with John as the prophetic forerunner of Jesus. He also gives special importance to John by showing how his birth echoes those of such noteworthy Old Testament figures as **Isaac**, **Samson**, and **Samuel**, all born to women thought to be barren. The story of the birth of John is Luke's alone, however; none of the other Evangelists show any knowledge that John was so closely linked to Jesus before the latter's baptism.

Luke concludes his story of John's birth with the cryptic remark that, after the child grew, "he was in the wilderness till the day of his manifestation to Israel" (Lk. 1:80). Since this was most likely the arid region bordering the Dead Sea on the west just below where the Jordan River empties into it, some scholars have suggested that John may have been in contact with the Essenes, a Jewish sect that had settled in that area and whose history has become widely known through the discovery of the Dead Sea Scrolls and the excavation of their settlement at Qumran. The Essenes, some of whom claimed priestly descent, like John, opposed the current line of priests in the temple. Like John, they

The baptism of Jesus, from the 13th-century Ingeburg Psalter

preached a message full of warnings of divine judgment. Although there are similarities between the message of John and the beliefs of the people of Qumran, there are also clear differences, and it is unlikely that he was a member of their movement.

AN UNEXPECTED MESSAGE

By the time Jesus appeared on the scene, John had already attracted a considerable following. He preached a message of final judgment and a call to repentance. "You brood of vipers!" he said. "Who warned you to flee from the wrath to come? Bear fruits that befit repentance . . . . Even now the axe is laid to the root of the trees; every tree therefore that does not bear good fruit is cut down and thrown into the fire" (Lk. 3:7-9). But when he defined the fruits of repentance, they were not issues of purity or of priestly ritual, as his listeners might have expected to hear. Rather, John emphasized issues of social justice: "He who has two coats, let him share with him who has none; and he who has food, let him do likewise" (Lk. 3:11).

Consistent with his harsh message of repentance and judgment, John chose to locate his ministry not in the more comfortable population centers but in a harsher area, the "wilderness of Judea" (Mt. 3:1). He also wore rough garb reminiscent of **Elijah**'s "garment of haircloth, with a girdle of leather about his loins" (2 Kg. 1:8); moreover, John's spartan and unusual diet of locusts and wild honey recalled the Old Testament prophet's ability to survive on meager rations. No wonder the curious asked if John was Elijah returned from the heavens to which he had been taken by a chariot of fire in a whirlwind.

The first-century A.D. Jewish historian Josephus compared John favorably with other political preachers of the era, individuals such as **Judas** the Galilean and **Theudas**, whom Josephus regarded as frauds. These men railed against the injustices of the Romans and their Jewish sympathizers and called down the judgment of God upon them. Also responding to the social oppression of the time, these prophets preached armed revolution; John's preaching suggested only a revolutionary change of the social order. But to the Jewish establishment both types of messages were considered politically dangerous; and so, like both John and Jesus, many of these messianic prophets met violent deaths at the hands of the government authorities.

The Synoptic Gospels agree that Jesus' ministry began with his baptism by John. It was then that the divine announcement was made: "This is my beloved Son, with whom I am well pleased" (Mt. 3:17). Very soon after his baptism Jesus returned to Galilee to pursue his own ministry, taking with him some members of John's entourage as his first disciples.

John continued preaching even after Jesus began his ministry, and the two were often compared. Though their messages were similar, they emphasized different aspects of it, worked in different mission fields (John in the countryside, Jesus in the towns), and followed different life-styles. Jesus himself made the distinction: "John the Baptist has come eating no bread and drinking no wine; and you say, 'He has a demon.' The Son of man has come eating and drinking; and you say, 'Behold, a glutton and a drunkard, a friend of tax collectors and sinners!' Yet wisdom is justified by all her children" (Lk. 7:33-35). John and Jesus shared a common ministry, Jesus was saying, though each approached it differently. Indeed, John was often taken to be the Messiah and, similarly, Jesus was later thought to be the resurrected Baptist.

PRAISE FOR EACH OTHER

The relation of John to Jesus is complex and puzzling. John is said to have clearly proclaimed that he was the forerunner and that after him would come "he who is mightier than I, the thong of whose sandals I am not worthy to stoop down and untie" (Mk. 1:7). The Baptist also spoke with certainty of the identity of Jesus when he proclaimed, "Behold, the Lamb of God, who takes away the sin of the world!" (Jn. 1:29). Yet the Gospels also note that John was unsure about Jesus toward the end of his life. While he was in prison, John sent his disciples to inquire, "Are you he who is to come, or shall we look for another?" (Lk. 7:20). Perhaps even more telling is the fact that he still had disciples of his own. Clearly, John's ministry continued on its independent way even after Jesus began his. Jesus spoke in high praise of John. "Among those born of women none is greater than John," Jesus said; but he added, "yet he who is least in the kingdom of God is greater than he" (Lk. 7:28). The idea Jesus was expressing was that a new period of history had begun with him; John, however, was still part of the earlier period.

John's disciples and Jesus' disciples were also often compared. For example, Jesus was once asked why John's disciples fasted and his did not. On another occasion, his disciples asked Jesus to teach them to pray as John had taught his disciples. The followers of John continued to revere him after his death, and for a time their movement apparently coexisted with early Christianity. **Apollos**, a Jew from Alexandria, came to Ephesus, where "he spoke and taught accurately the things concerning Jesus, though he knew only the baptism of John" (Acts 18:25). The point made here is that such persons had to be brought into line with the teachings of Jesus. Underlying this story is an indication that there was some rivalry between the two groups. This can also be surmised from other references in the New Testament. For example, Matthew makes it clear that John did not see himself as superior to Jesus even though he baptized him. Luke emphasizes John's subordination to Jesus even in the womb. John's Gospel records that the Baptist denied vehemently that he was the Christ. The Gospels were written at a time when there probably was still competition between the followers of John and the followers of Jesus, and the Evangelists were apparently trying to set the record straight as to the relationship between the two.

John was imprisoned by **Herod Antipas**, whose anger he had especially provoked by accusing him of breaking Jewish law in marrying a half brother's wife, **Herodias**. Later, at a banquet given by Antipas, the daughter of Herodias danced for the king and pleased him so much that he promised her whatever she might ask. At the

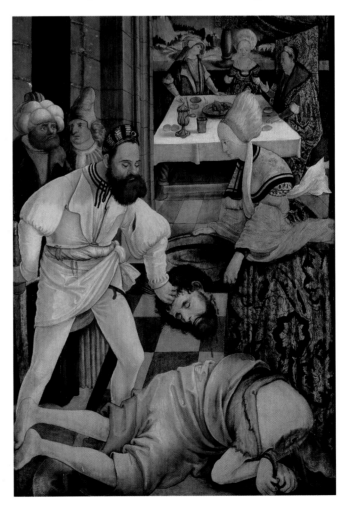

The beheading of John the Baptist; a 16th-century German painting

instigation of her mother, who hated John for his accusation, the girl asked for John's head. Reluctant but bound by his promise, Herod had John beheaded and gave the head to his stepdaughter on a platter.

JOHN OF PATMOS

The author of the book of Revelation identifies himself by name at the outset: "The revelation of Jesus Christ, which God gave him to show to his servants what must soon take place; and he made it known by sending his angel to his servant John." The book, he later reveals, was written while he "was on the island called Patmos on account of the word of God and the testimony of Jesus" (Rev. 1:1, 9). John apparently had been exiled to the island during a Roman persecution of Christians in Asia Minor. The most likely date for this would have been during the reign of Domitian (A.D. 81-96), since he was an emperor who demanded to be worshiped as a god and seems to have persecuted Christians. Church tradition gives a date for John's exile to Patmos: the 14th year of Domitian's reign, or A.D. 95.

Patmos is a small island in the Aegean Sea just off the coast of Turkey, located about 37 miles southwest of the ancient city of Miletus. It is in the general region of the "seven churches that are in Asia" (Rev. 1:4) named by John: Ephesus, Smyrna, Pergamum, Thyatira, Sardis, Philadelphia, and Laodicea. This must have been the area where John practiced his ministry.

Though the author's name is known, it is not clear which John he was, for this was a common name in the early church, and there are several individuals of that name who could have written the book. Church tradition prefers to identify him as **John** the son of Zebedee, one of the 12 apostles, who is also often named as the writer of the fourth Gospel and the three letters of John. However, this identification is problematic since John of Patmos does not refer to himself as an apostle and even seems to speak of the 12 in the past tense: "And the wall of the city had twelve foundations, and on them the twelve names of the twelve apostles of the Lamb" (Rev. 21:14). It is quite probable, therefore, that John of Patmos was a distinct individual in the early church who is known only through his writing.

What kind of individual was John of Patmos? Since he calls his work a "prophecy" (Rev. 1:3), he must have been one of those early Christian prophets who offered various forms of inspired utterance in the name of God or **Jesus**. Some, like **Agabus**, were itinerant preachers; others, like the Christian prophets in Corinth, were identified with a specific locale. John appears to have been an itinerant prophet, since he had apparently visited all of the seven churches to which he wrote. However, there is no evidence that he had ever been a resident of any of those communities.

John was an apocalyptist, one who wrote in a style quite popular in the centuries just before and after Jesus. Revelation is the only such book in the New Testament; Daniel is the best known Old Testament apocalyptic book, 2 Esdras in the Apocrypha being another. Many other such books were once known and widely read by both Jews and Christians, though they remained outside the biblical canon. Apocalyptic literature was a response to persecution and oppression. These writings invariably presented divinely inspired visions in which the evils of the present were explained in terms of God's plans for the end of the age—called eschatology by theologians, from the Greek word *eschatos*, for "last" or "end." At that time God would defeat evil, assert his full power and authority over the world, and relieve the righteous of their suffering and restore them to their proper position of blessedness. In presenting this message, the prophet, or seer, would utilize a rich tradition of symbolic language. His purpose was to provide comfort to those who were in the midst of suffering at the hands of a power that was beyond their control.

John drew on this literary tradition to give solace to the seven churches then suffering severe persecution. He mentioned in the letter to Pergamum that one of their number, Antipas, had already died for the faith; others faced imprisonment as well as possible death—in part, for their refusal to offer a sacrifice to the image of the emperor, a simple act required of all good citizens. John described a state of affairs in which the government was "drunk with the blood of the saints and the blood of the martyrs of Jesus" (Rev. 17:6) and called for endurance, assuring Christians that "blessed are the dead that die in the Lord" (Rev. 14:13). Ultimately, he presented a vision that the evil government would come to an end and that God would triumph by creating a new heaven and a new earth.

The persecution of Domitian did eventually come to an end, but the fate of John is unknown. According to some traditions, he was released from exile and continued for some time as a leader of the church in Ephesus. Whatever his fate, his book survives as a testimony to a faith that can endure no matter how catastrophic the circumstances.

JOHN HYRCANUS
(her ka' nuhs) GREEK: HYRKANOS
"of Hyrcania"
****

Following the assassination of his father, **Simon**, John Hyrcanus succeeded to the high priesthood in 134 B.C., three decades after his grandfather **Mattathias**

had raised the flag of revolt against the Seleucid kings of Syria. Hyrcanus confirmed the independence Simon had won for the Jews and greatly expanded the domain that the Hasmonean dynasty was to rule for the next century.

The country Hyrcanus inherited was still subject to Syrian attack, however, and he was forced to pay a heavy tribute to the Syrian king **Antiochus VII Sidetes**, who seized the cities of Joppa and Gazara and lay siege to Jerusalem. In the ensuing peace settlement, Hyrcanus allowed the city walls to be torn down but was able to avoid having a Syrian garrison reestablished in Jerusalem. The Jews' hard-won independence appeared at an end. But Antiochus's successor, **Demetrius II Nicator**, was weakened by internal political strife, and Hyrcanus took advantage of the situation to renew an alliance with Rome that confirmed Jewish rule.

Hyrcanus immediately set about to consolidate his power and strengthen the kingdom. He opened a link to the sea, seized the town of Medeba east of the Jordan River, and captured the Samaritans' capital of Shechem and destroyed their temple on Mount Gerizim. He also invaded Idumea to the south and forced many of its inhabitants to convert to Judaism, among them the ancestors of **Herod the Great**. Hyrcanus seems to have been the first Hasmonean to mint coins bearing his name: "John the high priest and head of the community of the Jews." It was also during his rule that the rival religious factions of the Pharisees and Sadducees achieved prominence. When the former expressed displeasure that the

On his island of exile, John of Patmos receives the visions that inspired the book of Revelation; a painting by Hans Memling (c. 1430-1495).

Coins dating to the second-century B.C. reign of John Hyrcanus

high priest was exercising secular power, Hyrcanus sided with the Sadducees and restricted the activities of the Pharisees.

After a prosperous rule of 31 years, Hyrcanus died in 104 B.C. and was succeeded by his son Aristobulus. Following Aristobulus's death within a year, another son, Alexander Jannaeus, ruled from 103 to 76 B.C. But with Hyrcanus died the driving religious zeal of the Maccabees, as the subsequent generations of Hasmonean rulers were to prove.

JONADAB
(joh' nuh dab) HEBREW: YONADAB
"Yahweh is noble/liberal"

Described in the Bible as "a very crafty man" (2 Sam. 13:3), Jonadab devised the ruse by which **David**'s son **Amnon** seduced his half sister **Tamar**. Learning of his friend's illicit desire for the young woman, Jonadab told Amnon to feign illness, then ask that Tamar be sent to prepare a meal and feed it to him. Amnon did as Jonadab suggested and, once he was alone with Tamar, "being stronger than she, he forced her, and lay with her" (2 Sam. 13:14).

Jonadab is mentioned again at the end of this tragedy. Two years later Tamar's brother **Absalom** took revenge for his sister by killing Amnon. When a messenger erroneously told David that Absalom had slain all of his sons, Jonadab reassured him: "Let not my lord the king so take it to heart as to suppose that all the king's sons are dead; for Amnon alone is dead" (2 Sam. 13:33).

A son of David's brother Shimeah, Jonadab may be the same as the Jonathan who slew one of the giants of Gath; in some ancient manuscripts the two names are used interchangeably. It is also possible that Shimeah had two sons.

JONADAB 2

As founder of the conservative Rechabite sect, Jonadab (also called Jehonadab) joined **Jehu** in bloody raids against the remnants of King **Ahab**'s rule. Jonadab's followers were faithful to Yahweh and violently opposed to the **Baal** cult that had flourished under Ahab and his wife **Jezebel**. Unlike the settled Israelites, they embraced a nomadic life and boasted that "we have no vineyard or field or seed; but we have lived in tents, and have obeyed and done all that Jonadab our father commanded us" (Jer. 35:9-10). Speaking through the prophet **Jeremiah**, the Lord praised the Rechabites' adherence to Jonadab's commands—in sharp contrast to the disobedience of the people of Judah.

JONAH
(joh' nuh) HEBREW: YONA
"dove"

Jonah was an eighth-century B.C. prophet from Gath-hepher, a small Galilean town near Nazareth. He first appears in the Bible to foretell that King **Jeroboam II** of Israel will restore the borders of the nation "from the entrance of Hamath as far as the Sea of the Arabah [Dead Sea]" (2 Kg. 14:25)—that is, to the approximate northern limit of the kingdom under **Solomon** but not as far south as Solomon's had stretched.

The book of Jonah, which contains the well-known story about him, was probably written much later, between the sixth and fourth centuries B.C., at a time when its central

Jonah cast overboard, from a 15th-century manuscript

idea—that God is concerned with all nations, not just Israel—had become an important theme in Jewish religious life. Jonah is unique among the 12 Minor Prophets in that his book contains little prophecy; its single oracular statement, "Yet forty days, and Nineveh shall be overthrown!" (Jon. 3:4), requires only eight words in the English translation. Instead of prophecies, the book tells how Jonah was swallowed by "a great fish" and survived "in the belly of the fish three days and three nights" (Jon. 1:17).

The tale begins with the Lord's command to Jonah: "Arise, go to Nineveh, that great city, and cry against it; for their wickedness has come up before me" (Jon. 1:2). Nineveh, the capital of the powerful Assyrian empire, a city so large it took three days to cross, was called "the bloody city, all full of lies and booty" (Nah. 3:1) by the prophet **Nahum**. Wicked it certainly was to the Israelites, whose northern kingdom fell to Assyria in 721 B.C. But Jonah decided to disobey God. He went to the seaport of Joppa and boarded a ship heading for Tarshish, located perhaps at the western end of the Mediterranean, in the hope of traveling as far away as possible from Nineveh—and from the reach of the Lord.

As the ship sailed across the sea, God sent a great storm that threatened to break it apart. The seamen prayed to their own gods for salvation, and the captain went below to rouse Jonah from sleep and demand that he do likewise. When the crew cast lots to find out if any passenger was responsible for the storm, Jonah was revealed as the guilty party. Realizing that God had sent the storm because of his disobedience, Jonah begged to be thrown overboard. His wish was reluctantly granted and, as soon as he was cast into the sea, the storm abated.

Swallowed by the fish, Jonah cried out to God for deliverance. Heeding the prophet's anguished prayer, "the Lord spoke to the fish, and it vomited out Jonah upon the dry land" (Jon. 2:10). Again God ordered Jonah to preach in Nineveh. This time, he obeyed. On his very first day in the city, Nineveh's king and people repented, dressing themselves and even their animals in sackcloth as a sign of remorse. In response to the contrition of Nineveh's residents, "God repented of the evil which he had said he would do to them" (Jon. 3:10); he decided not to destroy the city.

Jonah was infuriated. He had originally fled the Lord's command because he feared that at the end of his mission God would be merciful. Sitting in the hot sun, Jonah pleaded with God to end his life; but God created a plant to shade him. The next day,

In this 12th-century enamel, sailors thrust Jonah directly into the fish's mouth.

when the plant withered, Jonah was left in the hot sun again. Angry because God had sent a worm to destroy the plant, Jonah again asked to die. The final lines of the book bring home its message: "You pity the plant," the Lord said to Jonah. "And should not I pity Nineveh, that great city, in which there are more than a hundred and twenty thousand persons?" (Jon. 4:10, 11).

Jesus was later to draw a parallel between the "three days and three nights in the heart of the earth" (Mt. 12:40) he would face after the crucifixion and Jonah's days and nights inside the fish.

JONATHAN

(jon' uh then) HEBREW: YONATAN/YEHONATAN
"Yahweh has given"

A grandson of **Moses**, Jonathan traveled as a young man to the hill country of Ephraim, where he became a priest in the house of **Micah**. Soon after, five scouts from the tribe of Dan stopped at Micah's shrine on their way to find a new homeland for their people. When they asked Jonathan for an oracle for their mission, he said, "The journey on which you go is under the eye of the Lord" (Jg. 18:6). After the scouts found a suitable place to settle, the entire tribe headed north. Six hundred men stopped at Micah's home to steal the holy objects and images from his shrine and persuaded Jonathan to accompany them and become their priest. "Is it better for you to be priest to the house of one man, or to be priest to a tribe and family in Israel?" (Jg. 18:19), they asked. Jonathan gladly agreed and traveled with them to Laish, a Canaanite city in the far north that was destroyed, rebuilt, and renamed Dan. There he and his sons were priests until the fall of the northern kingdom and the dispersion of its people in 721 B.C.

JONATHAN 2

A prince who combined bravery and boldness with modesty and nobility of heart, **Saul**'s son Jonathan might well have been one of the great kings in Israel's history. But he became trapped between the rashness and paranoia of his father and his friendship and loyalty to **David**, the rising hero of Israel whom Saul came to fear and hate.

When Jonathan is first mentioned at the

beginning of Saul's reign, he is already grown, a valiant soldier, capable of leading a garrison of 1,000 soldiers stationed at Saul's stronghold of Gibeah. Though the Israelites had long been under the heels of the Philistines, Jonathan instigated a challenge to the oppressors by attacking and capturing a Philistine garrison near Gibeah. Saul, however, took credit for his son's victory and used the enthusiastic response it brought to raise an Israelite army. The Philistines reacted to this provocation by mustering a vast force of chariots, cavalry, and infantry—"like sand on the seashore in multitude" (1 Sam. 13:5)—to punish the Israelites. Because the Philistines had banned iron production in their land, Israel was almost totally without armor or weapons, and Saul's army was not strong enough to meet the attack. His soldiers deserted in droves until his force of several thousand was reduced to a few hundred.

Jonathan reversed the apparently hopeless situation by a daring stroke. Alone, he and his armor-bearer attacked what was thought to be an unassailable Philistine garrison in a mountain pass between two rocky crags. Through surprise and valor they

Jonathan shoots an arrow beyond a running boy, the signal to David, hiding behind a heap of stones, that he must flee the wrath of Saul.

Jesse brings his son David to play the lyre for King Saul (left); the friends Jonathan and David clasp hands behind the throne (right)—two panels from a tenth-century illustrated Bible.

defeated the 20-man outpost. This coup sent a shock of panic through the Philistine camp and so roused the flagging Israelites that Saul was able to turn his own likely defeat into a rout of the enemy. However, Saul had foolishly pronounced a curse on any soldier who ate before the Philistines were totally defeated. As the battle wore on, the Israelites became famished and exhausted. Not having been told of the curse, Jonathan ate some honey and was refreshed. When Saul learned that Jonathan had eaten, he was ready to have him executed—apparently having grown jealous of his own son. But the people refused to allow the rash king to kill the hero whom God had blessed with victory. The entire incident did not bode well for Saul's reign, a fact that Jonathan evidently recognized.

A few years later, when the Philistines again asserted their domination over the Israelites, the young soldier David emerged as the hero of the war. Jonathan had found a kindred spirit and "the soul of Jonathan was knit to the soul of David, and Jonathan loved him as his own soul" (1 Sam. 18:1). At first Saul exalted David, making him an army commander and giving him **Michal**, Jonathan's sister, as a wife. But the fearful jealousy of Saul turned from his son and with even greater ferocity was directed against David. Jonathan was caught between them. Initially he defended David to his father and at one point thought that he had fully reconciled them. But when Saul tried to murder David, Jonathan knew that he must help his friend escape the king's irrational wrath. At one point Saul even exploded in curses at what he considered Jonathan's treason and tried ineffectually to kill him with a throw of his spear.

Saul's behavior convinced even Jonathan that the dynasty of Saul could not endure, but Jonathan never left his father to join David's outlaw band. He stayed with the despondent king as the Philistine armies surged around them at Mount Gilboa. When David was informed that both Saul and Jonathan had fallen, he mourned for them: "How are the mighty fallen! . . . Saul and Jonathan, beloved and lovely! In life and in death they were not divided; they were swifter than eagles, they were stronger than lions" (2 Sam. 1:19, 23).

JONATHAN 3

The youngest of the five sons of **Mattathias**, Jonathan succeeded to the leadership of the Maccabean revolt after the death of his brother **Judas Maccabeus** and the destruction of the Jewish army in 160 B.C. The Maccabees, as the family is known, supported Jewish rule of Judea and a strict interpretation of all religious laws. They were opposed by hellenized Jews, who had adopted Greek culture and favored cooperation with the Seleucid kings of Syria.

Consecutive scenes in the Joseph story: sent to his brothers in the field (top center); cast in the well (bottom left); sold into slavery (right); bound for Egypt across the Red Sea

With the backing of the Syrian army, the hellenized Jews had been able to gain the high priesthood for **Alcimus**, one of their own. But meanwhile Jonathan had rebuilt the Maccabean army into a powerful military force that the Syrians were reluctant to engage in battle.

Jonathan was shrewd enough to take advantage of a weakened Syrian central government as various pretenders fought for the throne after the death of **Antiochus IV Epiphanes**. First, **Demetrius I Soter** granted Jonathan the right to raise an army in return for his support. Then Demetrius's opponent, **Alexander Balas**, awarded the office of high priest to Jonathan in 152 B.C. following the death of Alcimus. From this point on, the Hasmoneans (as the dynasty founded by the descendants of Mattathias were to be known) held the high priesthood, never again relinquishing it to their rivals, the hellenized Jews.

As king of Syria, Alexander Balas became a generous patron of Jonathan's. But when **Demetrius II Nicator**, a new claimant to the Syrian throne, appeared, Jonathan found himself in a tenuous position. However, he was able to utilize the threat of his military strength to secure concessions from Demetrius after he became king in 145 B.C. Demetrius failed to honor his promises, and Jonathan then went over to the side of Demetrius's new opponent, **Antiochus VI Epiphanes Dionysus**, and his general **Trypho**. Wary of the growing power of the Jewish army, Trypho tricked Jonathan into making a friendly journey into his territory, convinced him to dismiss his army, and took him prisoner. Jonathan's older brother **Simon** attempted to secure his release, but Trypho put Jonathan to death before he could do so. Claiming the body, Simon buried Jonathan in the family tomb at Modein and assumed leadership of the revolt.

JOSEPH

HEBREW: YOSEP
"may he [God] add [other sons]"
••••••••••

The story of Joseph's pampered adolescence, near-murder, and eventual rise to power in Egypt is symbolically important for two reasons. First, the mature Joseph, who had learned through adversity to be virtuous and wise, was considered by the ancient Israelites to be the ideal for all administrators or figures of authority. Second, he was able to reconcile the discord between brothers that had scarred the patriarchal generations down to his own strife-torn family. Significantly, God no longer needed to appear frequently in order to renew promises or visibly intervene, as he had done with Joseph's ancestors in Canaan. On the contrary, Joseph in the land of Egypt himself took the actions and made the decisions that brought peace to the troubled, bickering family of Israel, even as those actions and those of his brothers inevitably fulfilled a divine plan.

Joseph was born to **Jacob**'s second wife and first love, **Rachel**, after years of barrenness. The long-awaited infant, hailed by his relieved mother as a sign that "God has taken away my reproach" (Gen. 30:24), had been preceded by ten half brothers; his full brother, **Benjamin**, was born later. Although the Scriptures tell nothing of the boy's childhood, it can be inferred that he was reared in a tense family atmosphere of jealousy and resentment.

Neither Joseph nor his father handled this potentially explosive situation with good grace. The first time Joseph is mentioned after the report of his birth, he is a 17-year-old tattletale eagerly running home with an "ill report" (Gen. 37:2) of his brothers. Meanwhile, Jacob had treated this "son of his old age" (Gen. 37:3) with undisguised favoritism, giving the boy a fabulous robe while his older brothers wore the simpler garb of working shepherds.

THE BROTHERS PLOT REVENGE

Adding fuel to the sibling rivalry was Joseph's habit of brashly revealing dreams that predicted he would reign over his brothers someday. In one dream, his sheaf of wheat stood upright as theirs gathered round and submissively bowed down. (This indicates to biblical scholars that Jacob's family had become seminomadic, farming as well as herding sheep.) In another, the sun, moon, and 11 stars gave homage to him. Even Jacob balked at that particular dream, since he and Rachel seemed to be the sun and the moon.

Eventually, the brothers had enough. When Jacob sent Joseph out to the fields one day to report on their activities, they saw him approaching. Nine brothers reacted as one: "Here comes this dreamer. Come now, let us kill him" (Gen. 37:19-20). Only **Reuben**, Jacob's eldest son and traditionally the brother who should have been treated as the favorite, objected to this plan. He demanded that no blood be shed, perhaps because of the ancient belief that the blood of a victim would literally cry out for vengeance, publishing the deed. Intending to return later and rescue Joseph, he suggested that his despised brother be cast into a dried up natural cistern and left to die there in the wilderness of Dothan without water. When the young man reached his brothers and their flocks, they ripped off his robe and threw him into the pit.

Sometime later, when Reuben was away and the other brothers had calmly sat down to eat, a caravan of Ishmaelites appeared on the horizon, evidently plying the traditional trade route from Syria to Egypt. Immediately, **Judah** recognized a twofold opportunity. By selling Joseph into slavery, he noted, they would evade responsibility for his fate: "Let not our hand be upon him, for he is our brother, our own flesh" (Gen. 37:27). Also, the sale would earn them 20 shekels, or the average price for a slave at the time.

After Joseph was well on his way south-

DREAMS

*I*n biblical times, a dream was more than just a dream; many believed it was one way the supernatural world communicated with humans. Some people desperately sought these revelations by sleeping in a temple or another holy place. Jews, Egyptians, Assyrians, and Greeks all had professional dream interpreters, often aided by handbooks.

Through dreams God warned Joseph of Herod's plot to kill the child Jesus. Elsewhere in the Bible God delivered messages through dreams of such unlikely people as Nebuchadnezzar and Pilate's wife, who warned her husband against condemning so righteous a man as Jesus.

ward, Reuben returned and learned the shocking news. He rent his clothes in anguish, but he also joined his brothers in concealing their crime, for selling someone into slavery was a punishable offense. They dipped the troublesome robe in fresh goat's blood and brought it back to their father, asking with feigned innocence if he recognized it. Jacob leapt to the conclusion they intended: "It is my son's robe; a wild beast has devoured him" (Gen. 37:33). Crazed with grief, the old man vowed to mourn his beloved son until his own death.

In Egypt, Joseph quickly gained the respect and trust of his new owner, **Potiphar**, captain of the royal guards. And because "the Lord caused all that he did to prosper in his hands" (Gen. 39:3), his master soon made Joseph overseer, with responsibility for all household matters. The admirable young Hebrew slave was also quite good-looking, a fact not lost upon Potiphar's wife. In an erotic episode that has fascinated artists and writers through the centuries, the besotted woman tried several times to seduce Joseph, who protested, "How can I do this great wickedness, and sin against God?" (Gen. 39:9). But one day, Potiphar's wife snatched at his clothing as he fled from her advances, leaving his garment behind. Mortified and enraged, she shouted for the servants. To them and to her husband later, she claimed that Joseph had forced himself upon her, then bolted when she shrieked for help. Surprisingly, the slave was not summarily executed for the supposed assault but was merely confined to the royal prison.

Joseph flees Potiphar's wife; a 16th-century Italian ceramic plate.

"The Lord was with Joseph" (Gen. 39:21), even in misfortune.

With God's help, Joseph once again rose to favor because of his outstanding abilities. The keeper of the prison soon gave him the responsibility of taking care of all the other prisoners, including two detainees of some importance—the Pharaoh's chief butler, who traditionally would have played a role as a royal adviser at the Egyptian court, and his baker. One morning, as Joseph was pursuing his daily rounds, he learned that both men were troubled by mysterious dreams. Acknowledging God's help, Joseph interpreted the butler's dream as meaning that he would be freed and restored to his office within three days; the baker's dream foretold his death by hanging.

A GIFT FROM GOD

Three days later, on the monarch's birthday, both prophecies came true. Beforehand, the enterprising Joseph had urged the butler to remember him to the Pharaoh and seek his release: "For I was indeed stolen out of the land of the Hebrews; and here also I have done nothing that they should put me into the dungeon" (Gen. 40:15). Once restored to power, however, the butler did not think of the gifted slave until two years later, when Egypt's ruler was tormented by two eerie dreams. In the first, seven horribly thin cows arose from the Nile River, the source of the nation's fertility, and devoured seven sleek, fat cattle, a principal food source in the country. In the second, seven thin, blighted ears of corn swallowed up seven plump and healthy ears. None of the wise men or magicians of Egypt could decipher these ominous visions, but the butler suddenly recalled the young man who had comforted him in prison.

Cleaned up and brought before the Pharaoh, Joseph once again stressed that his power to interpet dreams came from the Lord. "It is not in me," he said; "God will give Pharaoh a favorable answer" (Gen. 41:16). Indeed, each time Joseph's situation improved in Egypt, the Scriptures note that God was at work behind the scenes. Instantly, Joseph was able to reveal that the dreams predicted seven years of abundance in Egypt followed by seven years of dire famine; and that having two dreams with the same meaning proved that "the thing is fixed by God, and God will shortly bring it to pass" (Gen. 40:32). Therefore, Joseph continued, the Pharaoh should choose a wise, discreet individual to set up a nationwide program for stockpiling reserve grain

Summoned from prison, Joseph is asked to interpret Pharaoh's disturbing dreams.

during the fertile years. The ruler, astute enough to see that a very wise and discreet young man stood before him, appointed Joseph to the position, granting him enormous power.

The freed slave, now 30 years old after 13 years of servitude, was ritually adopted by the court and given an Egyptian name, Zaphenath-paneah (meaning "the god speaks; he lives"), and an Egyptian bride. This young woman, Asenath, is described as the daughter of **Potiphera**, a member of the elite priesthood at Heliopolis. Joseph was also given a chariot. Since horses and chariots were brought to Egypt by the people known to history as the Hyksos, some experts believe that Joseph lived during the regime of these mysterious, foreign-born rulers, or between about 1700 and 1550 B.C. Possibly, they would have been more likely than a native-born dynasty to accept a foreigner as a high government official.

In time, events came to pass precisely as Joseph had foreseen. For seven years, with his characteristic diligence, Joseph ensured that grain from his adopted country's famously rich harvest was gathered up and stored. During this period, he found not only prestige and wealth but personal happiness as well. Asenath gave birth to two sons, who were given the Hebrew names **Manasseh** and **Ephraim**, and Joseph could say with gratitude, "God has made me forget all my hard-

ship and . . . . has made me fruitful in the land of my affliction" (Gen. 41:51-52). When the seven years of famine came, Joseph as governor oversaw the distribution of grain to the stricken people. He had been so assiduous, in fact, that there was enough to be sold to people from other lands, for indeed "the famine was severe over all the earth" (Gen. 41:57).

This widespread disaster would again set in motion the domestic drama of Jacob's sons. Desperate to feed his household, the aged patriarch sent his ten oldest sons down into Egypt to buy grain. He kept behind only Benjamin, his youngest son and Rachel's second child, afraid that he would be harmed on the long journey. When the tired, hungry band of shepherds was brought before the luxuriously dressed Egyptian official wearing the Pharaoh's signet ring and the gold chain of office, they did not recognize the arrogant young boy they had nearly murdered. But Joseph instantly knew them and initiated a series of tests and ordeals that reads like an account of psychological torture. Or, as Reuben put it, "So now there comes a reckoning for his [Joseph's] blood" (Gen. 42:22).

First, the stern governor accused them of spying and threw them into prison for three days. Then he agreed to sell them grain, but only if they would leave one brother behind as hostage and promise to return with Benjamin, whose existence they had admitted under Joseph's intense questioning. **Simeon** was chosen to remain in custody.

Meanwhile, Joseph ordered his men to return his brothers' money secretly, slipping the coins into their full sacks of grain. When they discovered the money en route home, they began trembling with fear. They realized that they were somehow on the receiving end of divine punishment, for they asked themselves, "What is this that God has done to us?" (Gen. 42:28).

A FATHER IN DESPAIR

Once home, they told their father about the demands of the cruel Egyptian governor, and Jacob fell into despair. "You have bereaved me of my children," he cried; "Joseph is no more, and Simeon is no more, and now you would take Benjamin" (Gen. 42:36). He was determined that Benjamin not be taken down into Egypt. But the harsh reality of the prolonged famine eventually undermined the patriarch's resolve. When the Egyptian grain was exhausted, Jacob recognized that he must inevitably send Benjamin with his brothers to buy more food. Wisely, he told them to take double the money this time so that they could pay back the original amount.

The brothers were welcomed in Egypt with an invitation to the governor's house, but Joseph continued to disguise his identity even though the sight of Benjamin forced him to withdraw to an inner chamber to weep in yearning for his brother. Then he washed his face and proceeded with the complicated masquerade. It began with a bountiful, merry feast that astonished the rustic Israelites because they were treated with great honor, even though their hosts sat separately from them because of Egyptian laws of ritual purity. Afterward, Joseph again ensured that their money was secretly returned in the stuffed grain sacks. This time, he also had his personal silver cup hidden in young Benjamin's sack.

Scarcely beyond the city limits, the brothers were suddenly overtaken by the govenor's household steward, who accused them of stealing the cup with the question, "Why have you returned evil for good?" (Gen. 44:4). The Israelites were so certain of their innocence that they offered to become slaves if the cup was found, but the steward replied that the thief alone would be enslaved. The tense search began with Reuben's sack and came at last to Benjamin's. When the cup was pulled out, the astonished brothers tore their clothes in horror. Haled again before the Egyptian governor, they prostrated themselves in dread. Judah explained how painful it was

Jacob greets the long-lost Joseph; detail from a 16th-century tapestry design.

for their father to agree to let Benjamin come and offered himself as a slave instead of his youngest brother. "For how can I go back to my father if the lad is not with me?" he pleaded. "I fear to see the evil that would come upon my father" (Gen. 44:34).

Joseph could bear no more of this heart-wrenching drama. Dismissing his Egyptian servants, he at last revealed himself to his dumbfounded brothers and explained that, unwittingly, they had all been following the divine plan, "for God sent me before you to preserve life" (Gen. 45:5). Moreover, he said, since the famine was to last another five years, they were to return to Canaan and bring Jacob and the rest of his household down into Egypt. Hearing of this remarkable reunion, the Pharaoh joined in the celebration, sending rich presents to Jacob and promising his family "the best of the land of Egypt" (Gen. 45:18).

When the caravan of well-provisioned wagons reached Canaan and the brothers told their father that Joseph was still alive, "his heart fainted" (Gen. 45:26), but Jacob soon revived and immediately determined to visit his beloved Rachel's elder son. Significantly, this decision was affirmed afterward by the Lord's direct intervention at Beer-sheba, where Jacob paused to offer sacrifices on the journey away from the land of his fathers. In a promise that became central to the history of the Hebrews, the Lord said, "Do not be afraid to go down to Egypt; for I will there make of you a great nation. I will go down with you to Egypt, and I will also bring you up again" (Gen. 46:3-4). Soon the Israelites were settled with their flocks of sheep in the land of Goshen, the northeastern borderland of the fertile Nile delta. Farther upriver, the Egyptians traditionally bred cattle and loathed shepherds, since sheep leave nothing behind for cattle to eat after grazing a pasture.

DEATHBED BLESSINGS

Jacob survived another 17 years, to the age of 147. On his deathbed he made Joseph swear to have him buried in Canaan along with his patriarchal ancestors and, continuing a familiar theme, gave a stronger blessing to the second born of Joseph's sons, Ephraim, than to the firstborn Manasseh. When Joseph angrily protested, the old man explained, "[Manasseh] also shall be great; nevertheless his younger brother shall be greater than he, and his descendants shall become a multitude of nations" (Gen. 48:19). In fact, each of the sons sired a tribe of Israel, thus ensuring that the total number remained 12 when the tribe of Levi began functioning as the nation's priesthood. After Jacob's death, he was embalmed in the Egyptian fashion and given the equivalent of a royal funeral. His long-lost son, now so wealthy and powerful, accompanied the body back home to be entombed in Abraham's cave at Machpelah.

At first, Joseph's brothers feared that he would take revenge, now that Jacob was dead—an indication that the family's reconciliation was not flawless. "Do not fear," he promised them; "I will provide for you and your little ones." For his descendants, he made an even more important pledge just before his death: "God will visit you, and bring you up out of this land to the land which he swore to Abraham, to Isaac, and to Jacob" (Gen. 50:21, 24).

After years of service during which Joseph abolished private property and instituted a system of taxation and feudal obligations that became very profitable for the Pharaohs, the patriarch died at the age of 110. He was embalmed, probably placed in a wooden coffin with his portrait on the outside, and buried in his adopted land.

JOSEPH 2

The husband of **Mary**, Joseph plays an important role in the two Gospel narratives (Matthew and Luke) of the birth of **Jesus**. He is not named in Mark, and John mentions him only in references to Jesus as "the son of Joseph" (Jn. 1:45, 6:42). At the age of 12, according to Luke, Jesus made a Passover visit to Jerusalem with his parents;

this is Joseph's last appearance in the New Testament. Since Joseph was not involved in Jesus' ministry, many assume that he died sometime during Jesus' youth.

Both Matthew and Luke emphasize that Joseph was of the house of **David**, and through him Jesus also was counted as David's descendant. At the same time, both Gospels state that Mary and Joseph were betrothed but not yet married when "before they came together she was found to be with child." But Joseph was "a just man" (Mt. 1:18, 19) and, though he did not understand what had happened to Mary, he had no desire to bring charges of adultery against her. Since betrothal was as legally binding as marriage, he decided to divorce Mary quietly. At this point, however, Joseph had the first of a series of remarkable dreams that guided him through the dramatic events surrounding Jesus' birth.

In the first dream, an angel revealed that Mary's future son was "of the Holy Spirit . . . and you shall call his name Jesus, for he will save his people from their sins" (Mt. 1:20, 21). The second dream came perhaps

Joseph kindles a fire to prepare food for Mary and her newborn son.

two years later, after Jesus was born and wise men traveling from the East had come unexpectedly to his parents' home in Bethlehem. When they departed, an angel warned Joseph in a dream that King **Herod the Great** would try to kill the child. As instructed, Joseph took his family to Egypt for several months or, perhaps, years, until an angel in a third dream told him that it was safe to return. In a fourth dream, he was warned not to return to Bethlehem, where Herod's son and successor **Herod Archelaus** still posed a danger, but to withdraw to Galilee. Luke does not mention these dreams, but his Gospel recounts that the need to register for taxation in "the city of David" (Lk. 2:4) brought Joseph and Mary from Nazareth to Bethlehem in the first place.

Joseph, a village carpenter, evidently trained Jesus to follow in his footsteps, and Jesus himself apparently worked as a carpenter for some years before his ministry began. In later Christian tradition, as stories concerning Mary's miraculous birth and childhood developed, and as the doctrine of her perpetual virginity evolved, the accounts of Joseph also became much more specific. For example, a late-second-century tale called the Protoevangelium of James portrays Joseph as an elderly widower with grown sons who was chosen by a miraculous sign—a dove emerged from Joseph's walking staff and flew to his head—to be caretaker of Mary, the pure "virgin of the Lord," who had lived since infancy in the temple. Many other legends about Joseph developed through the centuries, raising him to a level of sanctity second only to that of Mary herself.

JOSEPH OF ARIMATHEA

The burial of **Jesus** is attributed in all four Gospels to Joseph, a wealthy man from the town of Arimathea in southern Samaria. Joseph was probably living in Jerusalem at the time of the crucifixion, and he was apparently a member—most likely a dissenting one—of the Sanhedrin, the Jewish council that had condemned Jesus. Described as one who was "looking for the kingdom of God" (Mk. 15:43; Lk. 23:51), Joseph is identified by both Matthew and John as a disciple of Jesus; but the relationship was kept secret according to John.

As a man of wealth and high social standing, Joseph was able to approach Pontius **Pilate** and ask that Jesus' body be removed from the cross and given to him. He did this at some risk. Not only was he associating himself in this way with a convicted criminal, he was also exposing himself to ritual uncleanliness by coming into contact with a dead body; this would have meant that he could not participate in the upcoming Passover ceremonies. (To avoid this, it is possible that he asked his servants to perform the actual burial.) Nonetheless, Joseph was performing a pious act by obeying the Jewish law that a corpse be buried before

The flight into Eygpt, from the 13th-century Ingeburg Psalter

Joseph of Arimathea, by Benedetto Gennari the Elder (1570-1610)

sundown on the day of death. In standard Roman practice, the body of an executed criminal was usually left on the cross for days until devoured by vultures.

In preparation for burial, Joseph anointed Jesus' body with myrrh and aloes and wrapped it in a linen shroud. According to John, **Nicodemus**, another member of the Sanhedrin, provided these spices and assisted with the burial. The body was placed in a new rock-hewn tomb, which may have been one that Joseph had recently obtained for his family's use, and a stone was rolled against the door. All this had to be done quickly, since nightfall and the beginning of the sabbath were approaching. Jesus' followers did not take part in the burial, but some of them watched from a distance.

Early Christian literature contains a number of stories relating to Joseph. He is said to have been imprisoned by angry Jews but rescued by the resurrected Jesus and is described as later caring for **Mary**, Jesus' mother, for the rest of her life. Medieval legends relate that Joseph was sent to establish Christianity in England and that he brought the Holy Grail there.

JOSEPH BARSABBAS
(bar sab' uhs) GREEK: BARSABBAS
possibly "son of the sabbath"

After the ascension of **Jesus, Peter** asked the remaining apostles to choose a replacement for **Judas Iscariot**. Two men were suggested: "Joseph called Barsabbas, who was surnamed Justus" (Acts 1:23) and

Matthias. Both were among the men who had traveled with Jesus from the time of his baptism. Lots were cast by those assembled to aid their decision, and Matthias was chosen over Joseph as the 12th apostle.

There is no other mention of this Joseph in the New Testament. Later legends claim that Joseph Barsabbas once drank a cup of poison without harm and that he was imprisoned by the emperor Nero, then released. The name Barsabbas is a patronymic; many meanings have been suggested, including "son of the sabbath." Justus was a Latin name meaning "the just," perhaps given to Joseph by his friends.

JOSHUA
(josh' oo ah) HEBREW: JEHOSHUA
"Yahweh saves"

Celebrated as "the successor of Moses in prophesying . . . [and] a great savior of God's elect" (Sir. 46:1), Joshua the son of Nun provides a model of faithful obedience to the Lord's Law. He is first mentioned in the Bible when, soon after the departure from Egypt, **Moses** designated him to defend Israel against the attack of Amalek at Rephidim. As Moses watched from a hilltop, **Aaron** and **Hur** steadying his arms raised for victory, Joshua "mowed down Amalek and his people with the edge of the

Aaron and Hur support Moses' arms to ensure Joshua's victory at Rephidim; a stone carving in the Israeli parliament garden in Jerusalem.

sword" (Ex. 17:13). Originally known as Hoshea (meaning "may Yahweh save"), the young man was renamed Joshua by Moses as an acknowledgment that all his victories in the future would depend on God's fighting the battle for him.

The next time Joshua is heard from is as Moses' "servant," the only person permitted to go with him "up into the mountain of God" (Ex. 24:13) to receive the Ten Commandments. Later, whenever Moses left the sacred tent where he communed with God to report the Lord's words to the people in the camp, Joshua stood guard at the entrance to the tent.

Joshua also represented Ephraim when Moses chose one man from each of the 12 tribes to "spy out the land of Canaan" (Num. 13:17). Upon their return, only he and **Caleb**, from the tribe of Judah, urged the people to trust that God would deliver the land to them; the other spies advised retreat because the inhabitants of Canaan appeared to be stronger than the Israelites. In fear, the people contemplated choosing a captain to take them back to Egypt and threatened to stone Joshua and Caleb. God angrily responded by declaring that none of the present generation would see "the land which I swore to give to their fathers" (Num. 14:23). Joshua and Caleb alone among all the people who left Egypt were destined to enter the Promised Land. The other spies died of a plague, while the Israelite nation was condemned to 40 years of wandering— a year for each day of the spies' mission.

Despite Joshua's obvious ability and faithfulness, Moses did not alone choose him as his successor, but rather asked God to appoint a new leader of Israel. Affirming that "the spirit" was in Joshua, the Lord told Moses to "invest him with some of your authority, that all the congregation of the people of Israel may obey" (Num. 27:18, 20). As Joshua stood before the priest **Eleazar**, Moses complied by ritually laying his hands on the designated heir. Eleazar confirmed the choice with the Urim, a device similar to dice that gave "yes" or "no" answers to questions posed by the priest. Thereafter, Joshua would serve as military commander in the conquest of Canaan

The bounty that Joshua, Caleb, and the other spies brought back from Canaan causes great excitement in the Israelite camp.

and as administrator over the division of the land—events recorded in the biblical book that bears his name.

After Moses' death, God assigned Joshua an additional role. "This book of the law [probably Deuteronomy] shall not depart out of your mouth," the Lord commanded, "but you shall meditate on it day and night, that you may be careful to do according to all that is written in it" (Jos. 1:8). Throughout Joshua's leadership of the Israelites, he often interpreted the Law to them and read it publicly to remind them of the terms of their relationship to God, both the Lord's promises to them and the demands he made of them. Concurrently, Joshua would speak the words of God that interpreted historical events in terms of the people's obedience or disobedience, occasionally accompanied by fresh words of judgment and guidance. "Just as we obeyed Moses in all things," the people responded to their new leader, "so we will obey you" (Jos. 1:17).

IN MOSES' FOOTSTEPS

Many of Joshua's activities echoed those of Moses. Thus, Joshua led the people across the Jordan River on dry land just as Moses had done at the Red Sea; interceded similarly for the people; and wrote the Law on stone tablets. And, as Moses had done in the wilderness, Joshua sent spies into Canaan, particularly to Jericho, a large, walled city set in an oasis in the desert immediately across the Jordan from where the Israelites were encamped on the plains of Moab. There the spies discovered that the people in

Jericho had become terrified ever since hearing how the Israelites' escaped from Egypt, crossed the Red Sea, and destroyed armies on the other side of the Jordan.

When Joshua learned the news from his spies, he instructed the priests to lead the Israelites across the river, carrying the ark of the covenant at the head of the procession. As soon as the feet of the priests touched the water, "the waters coming down from above stood and rose up in a heap" (Jos. 3:16) so everyone could walk across. While crossing the Jordan, elders of the 12 tribes took stones off the bottom of the riverbed, and with these stones Joshua built an altar in Gilgal to commemorate the miraculous passage. There Joshua also circumcised all the men born in the wilderness, and the people celebrated the Passover, eating produce from the land since the Lord no longer needed to provide manna.

Near Jericho, Joshua suddenly encountered a man with a drawn sword. "Are you for us, or for our adversaries?" Joshua asked. The man identified himself as "commander of the army of the Lord" and told Joshua to remove his shoes, as had Moses at the burning bush, for "the place where

you stand is holy" (Jos. 5:13-15). God's role in the fight against the Canaanites is evident in the capture of Jericho, where Joshua brought down the walls of the city with trumpet blasts, and in the subsequent failure at first to conquer the smaller city of Ai.

Despite the Lord's injunction not to take booty at Jericho, a man named **Achan** made off with a beautiful mantle, 200 shekels of silver, and a bar of gold—hiding the loot in a hole in the ground inside his tent. Subsequently, the 3,000 men sent to seize Ai were repulsed and 36 of them killed. In response to Joshua's bitter lament over the defeat, God told him that "Israel has sinned; they have transgressed my covenant which I commanded them" (Jos. 7:11). The man who took the illegal booty must be punished with death. By the casting of lots, Joshua finally identified Achan as the thief;

THE CONQUEST OF CANAAN

About the mid-13th century B.C., the diverse peoples of Canaan began hearing frightening stories about the lands destroyed by a nomadic band known as the Israelites as they moved northward east of the Dead Sea. Soon the group was poised at the Jordan River opposite Jericho, intent on claiming territory that they considered truly theirs—because God had promised it to their ancient ancestors. The biblical book named for Joshua, Israel's commander, recounts the numerous miracles by which the Lord aided the invasion and fought for his chosen people: drying up the Jordan so they could cross; bringing down the walls of Jericho; causing the sun to stand still at Gibeon.

The military campaign to capture Canaan is described in three phases. First, the Israelites established a foothold west of the river at Gilgal, where they paused for the rites of circumcision and Passover in preparation for a strenuous holy war. The war began with the miraculous conquest of Jericho, after which the invaders split Canaan in two, suffering a setback at Ai but defeating a five-city coalition at Gibeon.

The second phase began as the Israelites turned south to punish cities allied against them: Libnah, Lachish, Eglon, Hebron, and Debir. Finally, the Israelites headed north to confront the forces of Hazor, the largest Canaanite city. Though their enemy fought on horse-drawn chariots, the Israelite infantry succeeded with a surprise attack in a forested area where the chariots were useless. Many Canaanite towns and villages remained untouched—a thorn in Israel's side for centuries to come; but these three campaigns established Israelite hegemony in the land and began the people's history as a settled nation.

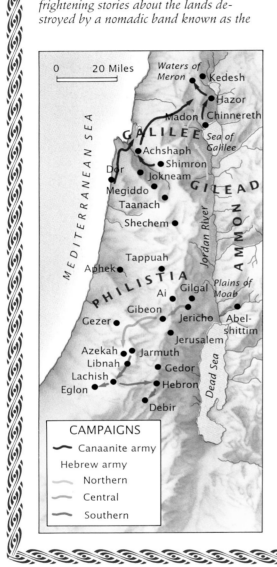

0   20 Miles

CAMPAIGNS
— Canaanite army
Hebrew army
～ Northern
— Central
— Southern

in the Valley of Achor, the people of Israel stoned him and his family and burned all of his belongings, including his tent, his animals, and all that he had stolen from Jericho. Released from the penalty of Achan's sin, Joshua and his army stormed Ai and set it on fire—after first drawing out the defenders by pretending to flee their counterattack. After this episode, Joshua summoned the priests to carry the ark to the top of Mount Ebal, which faced Mount Gerizim across a small valley. He offered burnt sacrifices on an altar he built on Mount Ebal,

then made a stone copy of Moses' Law and read it for all to hear.

Joshua had used a clever ruse to capture Ai; next he was to be the victim of one. Fearing defeat in battle, the men of Gibeon, a strategic highland city, dressed in ragged clothes and carrying only moldy bread and worn-out wine bags, set out to meet Joshua at Gilgal. They pretended to have traveled from a distant country, having heard stories about the Israelites' victories. Without consulting the Lord, Joshua made a covenant with them to let them live in peace. After

To prolong his victory over the five kings at Gibeon, Joshua asked the Lord to make the sun stand still; this is one of several Old Testament scenes painted by Raphael for the Vatican.

three days, he discovered that they came from nearby Gibeon. But having sworn by God's name in the covenant with them, Joshua could not go back on his word. For their trickery, however, the Gibeonites were forced into slavery among the Israelites.

VICTORIES FROM THE LORD

When the news of the Gibeonites' submission to Joshua spread, five kings joined together to wage war against the city. Because of the covenant, Joshua was obliged to defend it. God ensured an Israelite victory by throwing down great stones from heaven and, at Joshua's request, causing the sun and moon to stand still to give extra hours of daylight to pursue the enemy. The five kings sought refuge in a cave at Makkedah, only to be trapped inside when Joshua placed a stone over the entrance. After the battle subsided, he humiliated the kings by having his own commanders put their feet on the monarchs' necks, then hanged them and put their bodies in the same cave where they had tried to hide.

Joshua continued to capture other Canaanite cities, defeating one opponent after another. "And Joshua took all these kings and their land at one time, because the Lord God of Israel fought for Israel" (Jos. 10:42). At the end of these battles, Joshua distributed the land to the various tribes of Israel. But the Lord told Joshua that "there remains yet very much land to be possessed" (Jos. 13:1)—a statement that hints at a more complicated historical process underlying the biblical account, which presents the

conquest of Canaan as a unified event. In any case, Joshua admonished the people to be faithful if they wanted to inherit the rest of the land, and warned them of God's wrath if they disobeyed by sinful acts, including marriage with local women, which could bring compromising idolatry.

As his final official act, Joshua summoned all of Israel's leaders to meet at Shechem to make a covenant. When the people readily volunteered their consent, Joshua chided them, "You cannot serve the Lord; for he is a holy God; he is a jealous God; he will not forgive your transgressions or your sins" (Jos. 24:19). The people were not deterred, and Joshua therefore declared that they were that day witnesses against themselves if they ever disobeyed. Then, after adding his own statutes and ordinances to the book of the Law, he erected a huge stone monument by an oak tree within the sanctuary as a sign of the covenant renewed on that day. Soon thereafter, Joshua died at the age of 110—the lifespan also given **Joseph**, an indication in that period of a person's prominence—and was buried on his own land in the hill country of Ephraim.

JOSIAH

(joh si' ah) HEBREW: YOSIYYAHU
"Yahweh supports/brings forth/grants"

Preceded by two idolatrous and ruthless kings, Josiah came to the throne of Judah in 640 B.C. at the tender age of eight. In sharp contrast to his father, **Amon**, and his

Josiah; a 12th-century stained-glass window from Canterbury cathedral in England

grandfather, **Manasseh**, he matured into a ruler second only to **David** in the fame and praise he attained. Indeed, Josiah is remembered in the Bible as an unparalleled monarch: "Before him there was no king like him . . . nor did any like him arise after him" (2 Kg. 23:25). Though Josiah probably remained an Assyrian vassal during most of his 31-year reign, he took advantage of civil unrest and Babylonian incursions in Assyria to pursue extensive religious and political reforms within his domain and in parts of northern Israel as well.

Josiah's immediate forebears were notoriously evil. Manasseh, the son of the faithful King **Hezekiah**, had even offered a son as a burnt offering on one of many pagan altars he had built throughout Judah. Amon, who "walked in all the way in which his father walked, and served the idols that his father served" (2 Kg. 21:21), reigned only two years before his own servants murdered him. In retaliation, "the people of the land" (2 Kg. 21:24) killed the assassins and appointed Amon's young son Josiah to take his place.

Only gradually did Josiah come to affirm his faith in the Lord and his obedience to the Law of God given to **Moses**. He first "began to seek the God of David his father" (2 Chr. 34:3) at the age of 16. Later, when he was 20, Josiah condemned polytheistic religious practices in Judah and began to destroy the so-called high places (pagan shrines), with their idolatrous images and incense altars. Finally, at the age of 26, he financed the restoration of Jerusalem's temple with money collected from the people at

the entrance. It was then that the priest **Hilkiah** discovered the book of the Law in the long-neglected temple precincts.

When Josiah heard the words of the Law read by his secretary, **Shaphan**, he rent his garments in despair. The reason for his grief—he was probably reacting to the curses and the commentary on them in Deuteronomy 28:15-68—was that the book of the Law predicted the destruction of the entire nation of Judah. Josiah promptly sought out the prophetess **Huldah**, who confirmed that the nation would indeed suffer devastation owing to its history of disobedience to the Law. However, because of Josiah's humility before the Lord and his acceptance of the Law, the king himself would be spared from the judgment. Josiah then summoned all the priests, elders, and inhabitants of Jerusalem to the temple. Standing beside a pillar, he read the book of the Law out loud so that everyone could hear it. He thus convinced the people to join him in making "a covenant before the Lord, to walk after the Lord and to keep his commandments, and his testimonies, and his statutes" (2 Kg. 23:3).

TEMPLE WORSHIP RESTORED

Hilkiah's discovery of the book of the Law in the temple suggests that the few available copies had been neglected or misplaced during the reigns of Josiah's wicked predecessors. Perhaps a copy had been hidden someplace in the temple when Manasseh encouraged idol worship there. Throughout the history of the ancient Near East, books have occasionally been found during temple repairs, sometimes preserved in the cornerstone or elsewhere in the masonry of a building. Most modern scholars believe that the book of the Law referred to in the biblical account of Josiah's reign was some form of the present book of Deuteronomy, especially since the centralization of worship in Jerusalem became a major element in Josiah's reform and only Deuteronomy within the Pentateuch specifies that sacrifices ought to occur at "the place which the Lord your God will choose" (Dt. 12:5).

Immediately after the public reading of the book of the Law, Josiah launched his thorough religious reform. He destroyed all the altars outside of the temple, particularly the altar at Bethel that **Jeroboam** had built as an alternate to Jerusalem's temple soon after establishing the northern kingdom of Israel in 922 B.C. When Josiah finished these various cultic reforms, he prepared a Passover feast at the temple to symbolize the reconsecration of Judah. It was a celebration unlike any held "since the days of the judges . . . or during all the days of the kings of Israel or of the kings of Judah" (2 Kg. 23:22), a period of more than 400 years.

The stories about Josiah that are found in 2 Kings and 2 Chronicles differ on the order of some events, and the author of 2 Chronicles wrote that the temple reform had begun in part during the reign of Manasseh, even though pagan sacrifices continued to be made in the high places. However, the dating of Josiah's initial reforms to 628 B.C., the 12th year of his reign, coincides with an internal crisis in Assyria that would have allowed him freedom to pursue his own independent activities. These internal political troubles eventually led to the collapse of the Assyrian empire and the destruction of its capital, Nineveh, by the Medes and Babylonians in 612 B.C.—events that indirectly led to Josiah's death.

In 609 B.C., when Josiah was about 39 years old and at the height of his success, he was fatally wounded in battle with Pharaoh **Neco II** of Egypt at Megiddo. Whether Josiah died trying to prevent the Egyptians from passing through his kingdom to bring reinforcements to their beleaguered Assyrian allies, or whether Josiah had actually welcomed Neco only to be treacherously murdered, remains a mystery. The biblical narrative suggests that Josiah died for ignoring Neco's demands to "cease opposing God, who is with me" (2 Chr. 35:21).

The prophet **Jeremiah** was a contemporary of Josiah and evidently was a strong supporter of the king's religious reforms. Moreover, he once criticized **Jehoiakim**, a son and successor of Josiah, by asking, "Did not your father . . . do justice and righteousness?" (Jer. 22:15). In the preceding verses, the prophet observed that Josiah was better off dead than his other son and first successor, **Jehoahaz**, whom Neco had deposed and who was living in exile in Egypt. Finally, at the time of the king's death, the prophet "uttered a lament for Josiah" (2 Chr. 35:25) that was incorporated into the dirges still sung a hundred or more years later at the time his record and that of the other kings of Israel and Judah were incorporated into the Bible.

JOTHAM
(joh' thuhm) HEBREW: YOTAM
"Yahweh is perfect"

The youngest son of the judge **Gideon** (also known as Jerubbaal), Jotham was the only survivor of a massacre planned by his half brother **Abimelech**, Gideon's son by a concubine from Shechem. Upon Gideon's death, Abimelech convinced the people of Shechem, a center of Canaanite worship, to support him rather than any of Gideon's 70 other sons. Given 70 pieces of silver to hire "worthless and reckless fellows" (Jg. 9:4) as executioners, Abimelech went to his father's house at Ophrah, and there his paid assassins killed all the sons except for Jotham, who managed to hide.

Escaping to Mount Gerizim south of Shechem, Jotham climbed to a ledge and shouted out a story of how the trees selected a ruler. First they approached the valuable and useful olive tree, fig tree, and grape vine, but all declined as they were too busy pleasing the gods and men. Only the worthless bramble accepted, warning the trees that they would face destruction if their choice had not been made in good faith. Jotham then cursed the town's citizens for apparently not having acted in good faith by crowning Abimelech. The ill-fated king ruled only three years before the Schechemites rebelled against him, and he was killed at Thebez. Jotham's words against Shechem were fulfilled as God "made all the wickedness of the men of Shechem fall back upon their heads" (Jg. 9:57). After telling his fable, Jotham fled to Beer (an unknown location) and there vanished from the pages of the Bible.

JOTHAM 2

When King **Uzziah** of Judah was punished with leprosy for burning incense in the temple and forced to withdraw to "a separate house," his 25-year-old son Jotham became regent, "governing the people of the land" (2 Chr. 26:21) for 16 years. Historians date his regency to about 750-742 B.C. and his monarchy—following his father's death—to about 742-735.

Continuing his father's penchant for building, the young monarch constructed the upper, or northern, gate of the temple, fortified the wall south of the temple mount, and added many cities and forts to strengthen the frontier areas. Probably at the time of Uzziah's death, Jotham subjugated the Ammonites and demanded heavy tribute. For at least three years, the Ammonites paid tribute of "a hundred talents of silver, and ten thousand cors [six and a half bushels] of wheat and ten thousand of barley" (2 Chr. 27:5). During his rule, Jotham was greatly concerned about the growing Assyrian threat and the pressure exerted by King **Pekah** of Israel and King **Rezin** of Syria to form a triple alliance against the superpower to the north. Although Jotham managed to avoid any commitment, his son **Ahaz** would feel the heat of regional power politics. Jotham never rid Judah of the pagan shrines and tolerated sacrifice and incense burning there.

Jotham died when he was only in his early 40's and was buried in Jerusalem.

JUDAH
(joo' duh) HEBREW: YEHUDA
"praise"

Born in Paddam-aram in Mesopotamia, Judah was the fourth son of **Jacob** and **Leah**. His name was given to the tribe that came to occupy the hill country south of Jerusalem and west of the Dead Sea with Hebron at its center, territory that later became the kingdom of Judah. The patriarch Judah married the daughter of a Canaanite named Shua and they had three sons—Er, **Onan**, and Shelah. Only Shelah had descendants; Er and Onan died childless in Canaan, both cursed by God.

Jacob had many children, but he loved **Joseph**, his son by **Rachel**, most of all. Joseph's brothers were jealous of this favoritism and conspired to kill him. But Judah suggested that they instead sell the lad into slavery, protesting, "What profit is it if we slay our brother and conceal his blood?" (Gen. 37:26). Eventually, Joseph was taken to Egypt and sold to one of Pharaoh's officers, and he prospered greatly there.

Years later, during a famine in Canaan, Jacob sent ten of his sons to Egypt to purchase grain, keeping only Rachel's other son, **Benjamin**, with him. Joseph, by then "governor over the land" (Gen. 42:6) with control of the storehouses, tricked his brothers into bringing Benjamin to him on their next journey to Egypt. When Joseph tested Judah to see if he would also sell Benjamin into slavery, Judah offered himself, saying, "Let your servant . . . remain instead of the lad as a slave to my lord; and let the lad go back with his brothers. For how can I go back to my father if the lad is not with me? I fear to see the evil that would come upon my father" (Gen. 44:33-34). Joseph then wept openly, identified himself to his brothers, and invited Jacob and all his offspring to settle in Egypt, which they did. During the migration, Judah was sent ahead to Eygpt as spokesman for the family of Jacob.

An incident prior to the famine that brought the Israelites to Egypt reveals Judah in a most unpleasant light, however. For his wickedness, Judah's eldest son, Er, had been struck dead by the Lord, and the sec-

ond son, Onan, had refused to perform the traditional duty of taking his brother's wife, **Tamar**, as his own "and raise up offspring" (Gen. 38:8) for Er. Therefore, Judah sent his widowed daughter-in-law back to her father's house until his youngest son, Shelah, reached manhood and could marry her.

Seeing Shelah finally grown, Tamar suspected that Judah was stalling and devised a plan to beget children. She waited by a roadside, not in widow's clothes but covered by a veil. Judah, taking her for a prostitute, negotiated a price for her services: a kid from his flock of goats, offering as a pledge the signet he wore on a cord about his neck and his staff. Three months later, when told that Tamar was pregnant, Judah wanted to condemn her to death. However, after Judah learned that he was the father, he blamed himself for not giving Shelah to Tamar, saying, "She is more righteous than I" (Gen. 38:26). Tamar subsequently delivered twin sons named **Perez** and Zerah to Judah; and it was through Perez that the main line of Judah's descendants—including **David** and **Jesus**—was traced.

On his deathbed, Jacob blessed his sons and told them of the future. Of his fourth son he said, "Judah, your brothers shall praise you . . . your father's sons shall bow down before you" (Gen. 49:8)—the preeminence of the tribe of Judah over the other 11 tribes of Israel thus being foretold. Jacob also called Judah "a lion's whelp," and promised that "the scepter shall not depart from Judah" (Gen. 49:9,10)—a pledge of enduring kingship.

In rabbinical literature, Judah was known as a ferocious warrior who possessed great strength. He could chew pieces of iron until they became powder and his voice could carry from Egypt to Canaan. According to tradition, Judah died in Egypt at the age of 119.

When Tamar brings the signet, cord, and staff Judah had pledged for her services as a harlot, the patriarch is forced to acknowledge he had impregnated his own daugther-in-law.

JUDAS

(joo' duhs) GREEK: IOUDAS, form of
HEBREW: JUDAH

••••••••••

Judas, a Galilean Jew, led a sect of
Zealots in rebellion against Rome. Much
of what is known of Judas comes from the
first-century A.D. Jewish historian Josephus. The only biblical reference to him is
in the book of Acts in remarks made by the
rabbi **Gamaliel**.

In A.D. 6, the Roman governor of Syria,
Quirinius, initiated the first census of
Judea for tax enrollment purposes. Judas
and his followers fought against the census
as a secular infringement on God's divine
rights. They wanted to establish Judea as a
republic and recognize God as the sole ruler
but, according to Gamaliel, Judas "perished, and all who followed him were scattered" (Acts 5:37). The sons of Judas

followed in his footsteps. One, Menahem,
led a later rebellion; two others, James and
Simon, were crucified by the Romans.
Eleazar, possibly a grandson of Judas, was
the defender of Masada, the last fortress to
hold out against Rome.

JUDAS 2

••••••••••

A brother of **Jesus**, Judas's name appears
in the Gospels of Matthew and Mark on
the occasion of Jesus' visit "to his own country" (Mt. 13:54; Mk. 6:1), most likely
Nazareth, where he began teaching in the
synagogue. Skeptical of the "carpenter's son"
(Mt. 13:55), whose brothers and sisters were
well known to them, the townspeople were
punished by being denied the miracles that
Jesus had performed elsewhere.

While it is natural to assume that **Joseph**

and **Mary** are the parents of Judas and the others mentioned in these passages, some scholars have suggested that Judas may have been Joseph's son by a previous marriage. The church father Jerome held that the Greek word *adelphoi*, translated here as "brothers," could possibly mean "cousins." According to one early tradition, Judas was the author of the epistle of **Jude**. There is another tradition that the two grandsons of Judas became leaders of the church. Brought before the emperor Domitian, they were dismissed as harmless peasants when they showed their calloused hands.

Judas betrays Jesus with a kiss.

JUDAS 3

Although he was one of the 12 apostles, Judas "the son of James" (Lk. 6:16; Acts 1:13) is associated with only one event in the Gospels. In John 14:22, Judas asks **Jesus**, "Lord, how is it that you will manifest yourself to us, and not to the world?"—to which Jesus replies that love engenders obedience, which will be rewarded by divine favor. The identification of this Judas is much debated; he may be the **Thaddaeus** of Matthew 10:3 and Mark 3:18 since the first two Evangelists do not include this Judas in their lists of the apostles.

JUDAS BARSABBAS

(bahr sab' uhs) GREEK: BARSABBAS
possibly "son of the sabbath"

Along with **Silas**, Judas Barsabbas was chosen by the leaders of the Jerusalem church to deliver a letter to the Gentiles of Antioch, Syria, and Cilicia. These two "leading men among the brethren" (Acts 15:22) traveled with **Paul** and **Barnabas** to Antioch, where the letter was meant to ease the tension that existed between Jewish and Gentile Christians. All would be well, the letter said, as long as Gentiles remained chaste and abstained from eating meat offered to pagan idols and not ritually butchered. Judas and Silas, who are called prophets, spoke to the congregation at Antioch to supplement the letter. It is probable that Judas returned to Jerusalem while Paul and Silas continued the mission to Syria and Cilicia. Judas may have been the brother of **Joseph Barsabbas**.

JUDAS ISCARIOT

(is kair' ee uht) GREEK: ISKARIOTES
possibly "man of Kerioth"

Apart from being identified as the one who betrayed **Jesus**, Judas Iscariot plays no distinguishable role in the New Testament—though he appears in all three Synoptic Gospel lists of the 12 disciples, significantly mentioned last in each. The meaning of the name Iscariot is not entirely clear. Some have suggested that it derives from the Zealot sect known as the Sicarii, the dagger-bearing assassins who stalked Roman victims. Others argue that it comes from the Hebrew word *saqar*, the liar. But the most probable meaning is that it designates the town Judas came from, Kerioth, in Judea. This is evidently the interpretation of the Evangelist John, who twice refers to the traitor's father by the same designation, "Simon Iscariot" (Jn. 6:71, 13:26). Judas therefore seems to be the only one of the 12 who came from Judea.

Jesus clearly knew what kind of person Judas was. "Did not I choose you, the twelve," he said to his inner circle at a time when he was losing many followers, "and one of you is a devil?" (Jn. 6:70). Nonetheless, Judas was given a position of some importance, treasurer of the group, though he proved to be dishonest and took money for himself. At the Last Supper, Judas sat in a position of prominence, close enough for Jesus to hand him a morsel of bread dipped in a common dish as a sign that he was the traitor. Before he "turned aside, to go to his own place," however, Judas served the "ministry and apostleship" (Acts 1:25) of Jesus. He thus appears to have been an individual of promise when chosen and to have distinguished himself as something of a leader among the 12. But he obviously had a basic flaw that eventually led him to betray his master.

Judas did not make his fateful decision until late in Jesus' ministry. Why did he do it? The Gospel of Matthew suggests that his primary motivation was greed. He was paid 30 pieces of silver, an amount approximately equal to two or three months' wages for a laborer, a rather paltry sum for such a heinous act. But in biblical tradition it is the appropriate figure to pay an owner as compensation for accidentally killing his slave. In Matthew 27:9-10, the sum is connected with two Old Testament prophecies by combining the reference to 30 pieces of silver in Zechariah 11:12-13 with the purchase of a field in Jeremiah 32:6-15.

The forces of evil are also blamed for Judas's betrayal: "Satan entered into Judas" (Lk. 22:3); and "the devil had already put it into the heart of Judas . . . to betray him [Jesus]" (Jn. 13:2). Scholars have suggested yet another motivation: disillusionment. Jesus had failed to become the leader of an insurrection against Rome, as many—perhaps including Judas—expected. Therefore, he turned against Jesus, handing him over to those who considered him a dangerous person—probably without fully understanding that his treachery would lead to his master's death.

For whatever reasons, Judas "went to the chief priests in order to betray him [Jesus]" (Mk. 14:10). Apparently, he simply told them where they could find Jesus alone so that they could seize him away from the Passover crowds and avoid an ugly scene. Then, according to the Synoptic Gospels, Judas joined Jesus and the other 11 disciples for the Last Supper. The moment is a poignant one, for only Jesus and Judas knew what was about to happen. When Jesus remarked that someone with whom he had shared bread would betray him, Judas asked a lame question: "Is it I, Master?" Jesus replied, "You have said so" (Mt. 26:25). In the Gospel of John, the betrayal takes place after the supper. Having given the bread to Judas, Jesus says, "What you are going to do, do quickly" (Jn. 13:27). Some among the disciples thought Jesus was asking Judas, as treasurer, to buy more for the feast or to give alms to the poor and did not think it odd that Judas immediately left the room upon hearing Jesus' remark.

After the Last Supper, Jesus went to pray in the garden of Gethsemane, taking the 11 with him. It was a place Judas knew well, for Jesus had often gone there. Leading an armed crowd sent by the Jewish authorities to arrest Jesus, Judas entered the garden. He had previously arranged to identify Jesus with a kiss, and this he promptly did, greeting him as "Master!" (Mk. 14:45). The crowd seized Jesus and—after some scuffling, during which **Peter** cut off the ear of the high priest's slave **Malchus**—carried him away to be tried.

There are two different accounts of the fate of Judas; both involve a horrible death, as may seem appropriate for such a villain. According to Matthew, he repented of his deed, confessed his sin, tried to return the money, and then hanged himself in remorse. But in the book of Acts, Judas is said to have fallen headlong and "burst open in the middle and all his bowels gushed out" (Acts 1:18). In both accounts, however, his death came to be associated with a place near Jerusalem known as the Field of Blood. Tradition has identified the location of this field at the point where the Kidron, Tyropoeon, and Hinnom valleys converge.

The death of Judas, a 12th-century carved stone capital from Autun cathedral in France

JUDAS MACCABEUS

(mak uh bee' uhs) GREEK: MAKKABAIOS
"hammer"

At the death of his father, the priest **Mattathias**, in 166 B.C., Judas Maccabeus became the leader of the Jewish rebellion against the oppressive policies of **Antiochus IV Epiphanes**, the Seleucid king of Syria. Judas's second name—meaning "hammer"—was later collectively applied to all the sons of Mattathias, the Maccabees, and to the uprising they led, the Maccabean revolt or war.

Although he was an amateur fighting against professional soldiers, Judas enjoyed

Judas Maccabeus on horseback; a Limoges enamel dating to about 1540

viceable for Jewish worship, is described in the book of Daniel as "the abomination that makes desolate" (Dan. 11:31).

Judas chose "blameless priests devoted to the law" (1 Macc. 4:42) to cleanse the sanctuary. They decided to tear down the original altar, since it had been used for pagan sacrifices, and build a new one in its place. They also renovated the entire sanctuary complex and made new holy vessels with which to furnish it. When they were finished, "they burned incense on the altar and lighted the lamps on the lampstand, and these gave light in the temple" (1 Macc. 4:50). After placing bread on the table and hanging curtains, they rededicated the altar with an eight-day festival beginning on the 25th of the month Chislev (December) in 164 B.C., the third anniversary of the date the altar had been profaned by the Syrians. The reconsecration has been observed by Jews ever since as the Feast of Dedication, or Hanukkah, also called the Feast of Lights.

Because Syria was preoccupied with battles elsewhere, Judas was left virtually undisturbed for nearly two years and was thus able to consolidate his power and rule over Judea. After fortifying the temple mount and his base at Beth-zur, he launched a siege against the last remaining Syrian garrison in Jerusalem. News of this attack reached Syria, and Lysias, now serving as regent for Antiochus's minor son **Antiochus V Eupator**, was forced to react. Once more, the Syrians attacked from the south and besieged Beth-zur. Judas advanced against them with his main army, and the two forces met at Beth-zechariah, between Jerusalem and Beth-zur.

This time the Jewish forces were no match for the huge Syrian army, which included 100,000 infantry, 20,000 cavalry, and—for the first time—war elephants. In a valiant gesture, Judas's younger brother Eleazar darted beneath one of the beasts and sunk his sword in its belly—only to be crushed as the elephant fell dead. Badly beaten, Judas withdrew to the hills north of Jerusalem as Lysias advanced to the city and laid siege to the temple mount. Just as victory seemed assured, however, Lysias was forced to make a quick peace and return to Antioch where court intrigues had placed him in a precarious political position. He conceded to the Jews that for which they had fought for five years: the right to worship as they pleased. But political independence was withheld.

early success on the battlefield. Operating out of the hills of Judea, his guerrilla forces began to strike at the occupying armies of the Seleucids, whose home base was Antioch in Syria. In his first victory, an ambush of the Syrian commander Apollonius, Judas seized his slain enemy's sword "and used it in battle the rest of his life" (1 Macc. 3:12). He next defeated the Syrian general Seron at Beth-horon, northwest of Jerusalem. Meanwhile, preoccupied with a campaign against the Parthians, Antiochus charged his chief minister, **Lysias**, with the task of crushing the nettlesome rebels.

Lysias sent a large army commanded by three generals: Ptolemy, Nicanor, and **Gorgias**. Leaving the others camped at Emmaus, Gorgias took a 6,000-man force to search the hills for the insurgents. But Judas easily evaded Gorgias, made a surprise attack on Emmaus, and routed the Syrian main army. Gorgias and his detachment returned to the burning camp, only to flee in panic at the sight of destruction. Lysias himself led the next expedition against Judas, this time attacking him from the south. He was defeated at Beth-zur, 16 miles south of Jerusalem, and fled ignominiously back to Antioch.

Emboldened by these successes, Judas marched into Jerusalem and began the process of purifying the temple so that Jewish sacrifices could again be offered there. In one of his first oppressive acts, Antiochus had decreed that sacrifices be made to Zeus on a pagan altar set up in the temple. The desecration, which made the temple unser-

Conflicts continued over the future lead-

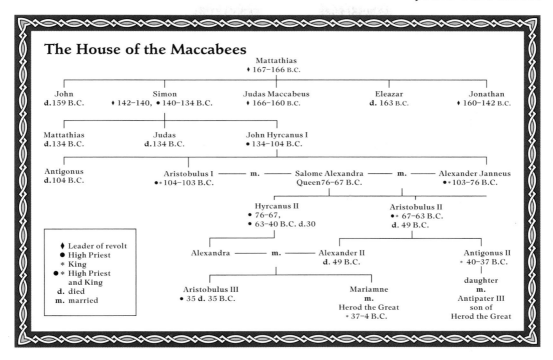

The House of the Maccabees

Mattathias
♦ 167–166 B.C.

John	Simon	Judas Maccabeus	Eleazar	Jonathan
d.159 B.C.	♦ 142–140, ● 140–134 B.C.	♦ 166–160 B.C.	d. 163 B.C.	♦ 160–142 B.C.

Mattathias	Judas	John Hyrcanus I
d.134 B.C.	d.134 B.C.	● 134–104 B.C.

Antigonus	Aristobulus I	m.	Salome Alexandra	m.	Alexander Janneus
d.104 B.C.	●* 104–103 B.C.		Queen 76–67 B.C.		●* 103–76 B.C.

Hyrcanus II	Aristobulus II
● 76–67,	●* 67–63 B.C.
● 63–40 B.C. d.30	d. 49 B.C.

Alexandra	m.	Alexander II	Antigonus II
		d. 49 B.C.	* 40–37 B.C.

daughter
m.

Aristobulus III	Mariamne	Antipater III
● 35 d. 35 B.C.	m.	son of
	Herod the Great	Herod the Great
	* 37–4 B.C.	

♦ Leader of revolt
● High Priest
* King
●* High Priest and King
d. died
m. married

A victorious Judas Maccabeus surveys the battlefield in this 15th-century manuscript illumination.

ership of the Jews. When the hellenized, or pro-Greek, Jews supported **Alcimus**, the Syrian candidate for the high priesthood, Judas objected. Alcimus appealed to the new Seleucid ruler, **Demetrius I Soter**, who sent Nicanor with a large army against Judas early in 161 B.C. Nicanor was decisively defeated at Adasa, a few miles north of Jerusalem, and killed on the battlefield. Now hoping for independence from the Seleucids, Judas sought an alliance with Rome. But it was too late, for Demetrius had already dispatched an army under the general Bacchides to avenge the defeat of Nicanor. It was far superior to any force Judas could muster, and many of his men deserted the cause. In the spring of 160 B.C., the small Jewish army was decisively defeated at Elasa and Judas was killed in action.

Although Judea remained subject to Syria, the legacy of Judas was nevertheless significant. It was he who had rededicated the temple and restored its sacrifices and he who secured for Judea a measure of political power that future generations would capitalize on. After his burial at the family tomb in Modein, leadership of the revolt passed to his brother **Jonathan**.

JUDE
(jood) short for JUDAS

T he letter of Jude was authored by "a servant of Jesus Christ and brother of James" (Jude 1). The last of the New Testament epistles, the letter appears to have been directed to a church or group of churches, probably in Asia Minor. The text, perhaps written about A.D. 80, warned the faithful that false teachers had infiltrated the church. Jude appealed to the readers to "build yourselves up on your most holy faith" (Jude 20). Jude's writing reveals a dependence on the Hebrew Bible and apocryphal literature, including a quotation from a book attributed to **Enoch,**

Traditionally, Jude has been identified with **Judas**, the brother of **Jesus**, since the James referred to at the beginning of the letter was probably Jesus' better known brother **James**, a major figure in the early church. Jude, or Judas, most likely had become a traveling missionary after the resurrection, spreading the gospel throughout Palestine and even beyond to Jews of the Diaspora. The letter was in keeping with such a mission. Some

scholars, however, suggest that a later writer attributed his work to Judas in order to give it the authority of coming from a blood relative of Jesus.

JUDITH
(joo' dith) HEBREW: YEHUDIT
"Jewess"

S avior of her city and people, Judith is the heroine of a great Jewish folktale: the apocryphal book of Judith. She is probably a composite character created to embody courage and patriotism and serve as a role model for later generations. Most likely written by a Palestinian Jew of the second century B.C., the powerful tale has survived in various Greek and Latin versions though the original Hebrew text has been lost. The work contains gross chronological, historical, and geographical errors, and was once dismissed as an inconsequential fable. However, some scholars contend that the mistakes are intentional, a device of the time to mark a book as fiction.

The story is set in the time when the Jews "had only recently returned from the captivity" (Jdt. 4:3)—that is, sometime after 538 B.C. Yet the adversary **Nebuchadnezzar**—incidentally, ruler of Babylon, not Assyria as the introduction claims—was the conqueror of Jerusalem five decades earlier and had died in 562. When introduced in the story, Judith is given an extensive genealogy—though most of the names are unidentifiable. She is said to have lived in the town of Bethulia, located at a pass in the hill country of Judea. An unknown place-name, Bethulia may be symbolic or a pseudonymn for the well-known Shechem.

As Judith enters the story, at the midpoint of the text, Bethulia is enduring a month-long siege by Nebuchadnezzar's army. Angered that the people of Persia, Syria, Lebanon, Palestine, and Egypt had refused his call for assistance in his recently concluded victorious war with the Medes, Nebuchadnezzar had dispatched his army commander **Holofernes** on a punitive mission to the west. The huge force was "like a swarm of locusts, like the dust of the earth—a multitude that could not be counted" (Jdt. 2:20) as it

Judith deposits Holofernes's head in her maid's food bag; the wooden figurines date to the 16th century.

marched forward, ravaging the countries through which it passed.

When Holofernes approached their lands, the Israelites prepared to resist him at the narrow passes leading to Judea. Seeking intelligence, Holofernes was told by Achior of the Ammonites that he should bypass the Jews because they had not sinned against their God and would be unbeatable. A proud Holofernes asked Achior, "Who is God except Nebuchadnezzar?" (Jdt. 6:2)— and banished the outspoken Ammonite to Bethulia, where he was warmly received. During reconnaissance outside Bethulia, Holofernes was advised to capture and control the water supply to the towns of the hill country rather than sacrifice his warriors in an effort to take fortified positions. After 34 days of suffering, the cisterns and vessels of Bethulia were dry and the streets were filled with the weak and helpless. The town leader, Uzziah, appealed to all residents to wait five more days for God's mercy before surrendering. In the midst of this crisis, Judith emerged to rebuke the town elders for so testing God.

Judith's husband Manasseh had died more than three years earlier from sunstroke while in the field supervising the barley harvest. He left Judith with gold, silver, slaves, cattle, and property, an extensive estate she was able to maintain. Known for her beauty, she was also respected for her devotion to God and was thus heeded when she informed the elders of her plan to leave the city with her maid that night. "The Lord will deliver Israel by my hand" (Jdt. 8:33), she told them.

She then returned home to remove her widow's garments, bathe, and prepare herself "to entice the eyes of all men who might see her" (Jdt. 10:4). With her maid carrying wine, oil, and food, Judith left Bethulia, soon to encounter an Assyrian patrol. She told them that she had a report for Holofernes. Won over by Judith's beauty, the enemy escorted the women to their camp, the arrival causing much excitement. As she was ushered into Holofernes's tent, Judith pretended to honor Nebuchadnezzar and told the general that the people of Bethulia were about to sin by eating and drinking what was forbidden. She offered to stay in the camp, only to pray every night at a spring in the valley to learn when the Jews had sinned and would be vulnerable to conquest. Judith would then lead the army through Bethulia and on to Jerusalem.

For three days Judith remained at the camp establishing her nightly pattern. On the fourth day, Holofernes sent his eunuch to invite her to a private party, to be filled with food, wine, and romance. Knowing that she would have the opportunity to fulfill her mission, Judith "arrayed herself in all her woman's finery" (Jdt. 12:15). When the night grew late, the servants were dismissed. The two were alone in the tent, but Holofernes was sprawled out on the bed in a drunken stupor. With her maid waiting outside, Judith reached for the sword over the commander's head, asking, "Give me strength this day, O Lord God of Israel!" (Jdt. 13:7). Grabbing his hair, she chopped off Holofernes's head, rolled the body from the bed, tore down the purple and gold canopy to take as proof of her action, and gave the bloody head to her maid to be placed inside their food bag. As customary, they left for their evening prayer near the spring only to return to Bethulia instead.

Gathered around a fire, the elders looked on as Judith displayed Holofernes's head and bed canopy and assured them that she had not been defiled. Judith instructed them to hang the head on the town wall at dawn for the Assyrian army to see and send soldiers to the passes. Seeing the Jews boldly approaching, the Assyrians went to wake up Holofernes, only to find his decapitated body. In turmoil, the army fled in every direction as the Israelites rushed to ravage the enemy's camps throughout the hill country. Meanwhile, Achior, seeing the power of Israel's God, was admitted to the faith.

During the 30 days of plundering that followed, the high priest Joakim came from Jerusalem to greet Judith. She was honored by the women of Israel, given the possessions of Holofernes, and—after singing a hymn of thanksgiving—taken to Jerusalem where she offered Holofernes's vessels and bed canopy to the Lord. Judith returned to Bethulia and never remarried. She freed her maid and lived to the ripe age of 105, all Israel mourning her death for a week.

JULIUS
(joo' li uhs) GREEK: IOULIOS

A centurion of the Augustan cohort, Julius was assigned to escort **Paul** on the voyage from Caesarea to Rome, where the apostle was to make an appeal to the emperor after his inconclusive hearings in Judea. The second day out, the ship put in at the port of Sidon, where "Julius treated Paul kindly, and gave him leave to go to his friends and be cared for" (Acts 27:3). When the merchant ship reached Myra in Lycia, Paul and the other prisoners were transferred to a ship bound for Italy. Approaching Crete, Paul warned the crew that continuing the voyage in winter would be dangerous. Behind schedule, they proceeded anyway, until a fierce storm pushed them toward North Africa. After 14 more days at sea, the 276 passengers and crew were shipwrecked as they hit a shoal off Malta.

In the confusion, Julius managed to dissuade the soldiers from killing the prisoners to prevent their escape. They all swam ashore or paddled to the beach on debris. Paul eventually made it to the Italian peninsula and on to Rome, but Julius is not mentioned again in the Bible. By placing so much emphasis on the Roman officer, **Luke** perhaps meant to show that Christians and pagans could enjoy friendly relationships beneficial to both groups.

JUNIAS
(joo' nee uhs) GREEK: IOUNIA (JUNIA)

In **Paul**'s letter to the Romans, the name Junias appears for the only time in the Bible. Near the end of the letter, Paul sends greetings to Andronicus and Junias, "my kinsmen and my fellow prisoners; they are men of note among the apostles, and they were in Christ before me" (Rom. 16:7). Since the name Junias is otherwise unknown, scholars have suggested that Junias is actually Junia, a Jewish woman and possibly the wife of Andronicus. If so, she would be the only female apostle named in the New Testament. The masculine name Junias may have been created by medieval copyists as a means of explaining this unimaginable occurrence.

KETURAH
(kuh too' ruh) HEBREW: QETURA
"incense"

After the death of **Sarah** and the marriage of Isaac, **Abraham** took Keturah as his wife. In 1 Chronicles 1:32, she is described as Abraham's concubine, making it clear that only Isaac is to be considered the patriarch's legitimate heir. Keturah's six sons—characterized by the Jewish historian Josephus as "men of courage and of sagacious minds"—were Zimran, Jokshan, Medan, **Midian**, Ishbak, and Shuah. Abraham gave Keturah's sons gifts but "sent them away from his son Isaac, eastward to the east country" (Gen. 25:6). Through them, Abraham is connected to those Arabian tribes not included among the descendants of **Hagar**. Midian's descendants are mentioned frequently in the Old Testament—as friends, in the story of **Moses**, but more often as enemies of the Israelites.

Korah challenged the leadership of Moses.

KISH
(kish) HEBREW: QIS
"bestow" or "gift"

The wealthy Benjaminite Kish sent his tall, handsome son **Saul** with a servant to search for some strayed asses; instead of the beasts, Saul found his destiny and was anointed the first king of Israel. The father was doubtless among the number of assembled tribesmen when Saul was chosen by lot to be ruler.

Kish is first mentioned in the Bible as "the son of Abiel" (1 Sam. 9:1), but in 1 Chronicles 8:32 he appears as the son of Ner. If the latter is true, Kish was the brother of Saul's famous commander **Abner**. Kish was buried in his own tomb in Zela, as Saul and his son **Jonathan** were later.

KOHATH
(koh' hath) HEBREW: QEHAT
possibly "obedience"

One of the three sons of **Levi**, Kohath was the grandfather of **Aaron** and **Moses**. As such, he was the ancestor of the chief Levitical family, the Kohathites. During the wilderness period, there were 8,600 male Kohathites "attending to the duties of the sanctuary"; they were charged with "the ark, the table, the lampstand, the altars, the vessels of the sanctuary with which the priests minister, and the screen" (Num. 3:28, 31). As the people traveled through the wilderness, the Kohathites carried the sanctuary and its holy fittings supported by poles on their shoulders—the burden was too sacred to be transported by oxcart, like the rest of the tabernacle furnishings. Through the centuries, Kohathites were closely associated with religious services. In **David**'s time they were among those who "ministered with song before the tabernacle of the tent of meeting" (1 Chr. 6:32). When the temple was rebuilt after the return from exile, Kohathites prepared the sabbath shewbread.

KORAH

(koh' ruh) HEBREW: QORAH
"bald"

A grandson of **Kohath**, Korah took advantage of the discontent of the Israelites after their flight from Egypt to lead a rebellion against **Moses** and **Aaron**. Korah accused the two of glorifying themselves above the people when "all the congregation are holy, every one of them, and the Lord is among them" (Num. 16:3). In reality, Korah was jealous of the perquisites belonging to Aaron's sons and was demanding a role in the priesthood for all Levites. An angered Moses answered the Korahites: "You have gone too far, sons of Levi!" (Num. 16:7). He instructed Korah and his 250 followers to appear the next morning before the tent of meeting with their censers prepared to burn incense to the Lord.

At the same time that Korah was seeking a larger religious role, the Reubenites **Dathan** and Abiram were protesting the hardships the people suffered in the wilderness compared with their comfortable life in Egypt, "a land flowing with milk and honey" (Num. 16:13). For these rebellious acts, the three men and their families were swallowed up by the earth, and fire from the Lord consumed the 250 Levites allied with Korah. The holocaust, however, only angered the people further. As they accused Moses and Aaron of the mass killings, a plague descended on them, slaying 14,700, before Aaron was able to intercede.

The bronze censers dropped by the guilty Levites were hammered into plates to cover the altar because of their inherent holiness and value, and also because they would serve to remind the people that none except descendants of Aaron "should draw near to burn incense before the Lord, lest he become as Korah and as his company" (Num. 16:40). In later times, Korahites were temple singers. They had other duties as well; they were "in charge of the gates of the house of the Lord" and, as chief gatekeepers, looked after "the chambers and the treasures of the house of God" (1 Chr. 9:23, 26)

For their defiance of Moses, Korah, Dathan, and Abiram werre swallowed by the earth, as shown at left in this painting by Sandro Botticelli (c. 1444-1510)

LABAN

(lay' buhn) HEBREW: LABAN
"white"

W hen **Abraham** left Haran for the land of Canaan, part of his family remained behind in upper Mesopotamia. Many years later, fearing that his son **Isaac** would take a Canaanite wife, Abraham sent his oldest servant—most likely **Eliezer**—to seek a bride for Isaac among his faraway kinsmen. Among those kinsmen was Laban, the son of **Bethuel** and the grandson of Abraham's brother **Nahor**. Laban and the aged Bethuel received Abraham's emissary graciously—perhaps, some suggest, because of greed for the rich presents Eliezer bore. Still, they recognized the will of God in Eliezer's request for the hand of Laban's sister **Rebekah**. "Take her and go," they said, "and let her be the wife of your master's son, as the Lord has spoken" (Gen. 24:51).

Many years later, when Rebekah sent her son **Jacob** to Mesopotamia for his own safety and to find a wife among his kinfolk, he met with seeming kindness from Laban. But, after promising Jacob the hand of his beautiful daughter **Rachel** in return for seven years of service, Laban substituted her plain older sister **Leah** on the wedding night. He thereby got an unmarriageable daughter off his hands and forced Jacob to agree to a further seven years of labor in return for being allowed also to marry his first choice, Rachel. Jacob had already proved his worth by causing Laban's flocks to increase and prosper.

Presumably, Laban undertook a form of adoption agreement with Jacob, a not uncommon Mesopotamian practice when a

Jacob disputes ownership of the flocks with his father-in-law, Laban; a painting by Jean Restout (1692-1768).

man had no sons of his own. Later, however, Laban did have his own sons, who grew jealous of Jacob, saying "from what was our father's he has gained all this wealth" (Gen. 31:1). Laban himself no longer favored Jacob and considered him an enemy after Jacob fled with his wives and children and with the flocks he had earned.

The furious Laban caught up with the fugitives in the hill country of Gilead east of the river Jordan and cried out, "What have you done, that you have cheated me, and carried away my daughters like captives of the sword? . . . And why did you not permit me to kiss my [grand]sons and my daughters farewell?" (Gen. 31:26, 28). He pressed Jacob for the return of his household gods, which Rachel had secretly taken and hidden in her camel's saddle, and searched for them through the tents without success.

Finally acknowledging himself defeated in every regard, Laban made a covenant with Jacob by gathering a heap of stones into a pillar of witness. Laban said, "If you ill-treat my daughters, or if you take wives besides my daughters . . . remember, God is witness between you and me" (Gen. 31:50). The two further swore not to pass the boundary established by the pillar of stones to harm each other and sealed the pact with a feast. The next morning, Laban kissed his daughters and grandchildren good-bye and returned to Haran.

LAMECH

(lay' meck) HEBREW: LEMEK
"vigorous/strong youth"

A fifth-generation descendant of **Cain**, Lamech was the first biblical figure to have two wives, Adah and Zillah. The women bore three sons: Jabal, whose descendants were "those who dwell in tents and have cattle"; Jubal, who "was the father of all those who play the lyre and pipe"; and

Tubal-cain, "the forger of all instruments of bronze and iron" (Gen. 4:20-22). These instruments were, in fact, weapons as well as tools. They marked another step in mankind's decline, illustrated by Lamech's boastful song: "I have slain a man for wounding me, a young man for striking me. If Cain is avenged sevenfold, truly Lamech [is avenged] seventy-sevenfold" (Gen. 4:23-24). The sins of pride and vengefulness and the glorification of killing were thus added to the list of human failings.

LAMECH 2

The biblical figures who lived before the Flood—"the generations of Adam" (Gen. 5:1)—were given remarkably long lives. A descendant of **Adam**'s son **Seth**, Lamech was the son of **Methuselah** and the father of **Noah**, who was born when Lamech was 182. Of Noah, Lamech said, "Out of the ground which the Lord has cursed this one shall bring us relief from our work and from the toil of our hands" (Gen. 5:29). This is a unique Old Testament reference to the lost paradise, which Noah was to restore.

Lamech, who subsequently fathered other children, died at the not unusual antediluvian age of 777.

Jesus raises Lazarus from the dead in this early-19th-century Greek icon.

LAZARUS

(laz' uh ruhs) GREEK: LAZAROS, an abbreviation of HEBREW: ELAZAR
"God has helped"

In only one parable did **Jesus** name a character: the beggar Lazarus at the entrance of a wealthy man's house, "who desired to be fed with what fell from the rich man's table" (Lk. 16:21). When the two men died, Lazarus went to dwell with **Abraham**, while the rich man went to Hades, a fiery place of torment. In Jesus' narrative, the wicked and the good could observe each other in the afterlife but were separated by a chasm.

Not wanting his family to end up where he did, the rich man asked Abraham to send Lazarus to warn them. In the story's climax, Abraham says that if the family does not listen to **Moses** and the prophets, they will not be convinced even by someone returning from the dead. Some scholars say this shows that Jesus told the story with **Lazarus** of Bethany in mind, since he, in fact, was raised from the dead. And Jewish leaders refused to believe Jesus was the Messiah the prophets had foretold.

The parable suggests that wealth is dangerous but also warns against a then current Sadducean belief that rewards and punishments are limited to this life, there being no hereafter. Medieval readers of the Latin Bible took the word *dives* ("rich") to be the wealthy man's name, and thus the parable came to be called Lazarus and Dives.

LAZARUS 2

When their brother Lazarus became deathly ill, the sisters **Mary** and **Martha** sent an urgent message to their friend **Jesus**, who had withdrawn across the Jordan to avoid arrest and possible execution for his supposed blasphemy. But Jesus, surprisingly, waited two days. "Our friend Lazarus has fallen asleep, but I go to awake him" (Jn. 11:11), he told his disciples before setting out for the sisters' home in Bethany, a village of Judea some two miles from Jerusalem.

To correct the disciples' misunderstanding of this remark, Jesus bluntly informed them that his friend was dead and that he was glad he had not been there. Clearly, he was determined to work a miracle, though he was taking a great risk by returning to Judea. By the time he got to Bethany, Lazarus had been dead four days. Devout Jews believed that the soul hovered near the body for three days, not finally departing

Rachel and Leah; an 1855 painting by Dante Gabriel Rossetti

until the fourth day. Martha may have believed this and objected when Jesus ordered her brother's tomb opened. But he insisted and called the dead man back to life.

The resurrection of Lazarus—recounted only in the Gospel of John—divided the Jews who had come to Bethany to mourn with the sisters. Some believed that Jesus was the promised Messiah who would restore Israel. Others apparently saw trouble brewing and reported it to the Jewish leaders, who decided to kill Jesus, as well as Lazarus. They were afraid the masses would rally around the miracle worker and precipitate a military intervention that would destroy the working relationship the high priest had with the Romans. However, the other three Gospels say the decision to kill Jesus came after he overturned the money changers' tables in the temple .

On the Saturday before his crucifixion, Jesus was once more in Bethany, the guest at a dinner in Lazarus's house. The following day he entered Jerusalem in triumph—many having come out to see the man who had raised Lazarus from the dead.

LEAH

(lee' uh) HEBREW: LEA
"wild cow"
∗∗∗∗∗∗∗∗∗∗

The elder of **Laban**'s two daughters, Leah did not share her sister **Rachel**'s beauty. Her eyes are described as weak, but any other undesirable features are not re-

vealed in the Bible. She became **Jacob**'s first wife only through Laban's deceitful stratagem of substituting her for Rachel on the wedding night, and she was always aware that her husband preferred his second wife, Rachel. At one point, when Rachel asked her for some mandrakes to induce fertility, Leah asked her bitterly, "Is it a small matter that you have taken away my husband?" (Gen. 30:15). But Leah was more fortunate than her younger sister in one important respect: "When the Lord saw that Leah was hated, he opened her womb" (Gen. 29:31). She bore Jacob six sons and a daughter, while her maid **Zilpah** bore two additional sons to Jacob (which also counted as hers) before Rachel was able to have sons of her own.

Leah's sons were **Reuben**, **Simeon**, **Levi**, **Judah**, **Issachar**, and **Zebulun**, ancestors of half the tribes of Israel. (Zilpah's sons were **Gad** and **Asher**.) Their rivalry with Rachel's son **Joseph**, Jacob's favorite among his sons, had extraordinary consequences for the history of Israel. And Levi and Judah, unremarkable save for an outburst of savagery on Levi's part, became the tribal ancestors, respectively, of the priesthood and the monarchy that was to come under **David**.

When Jacob resolved to leave after his 20 years of servitude to Laban, Leah and Rachel both encouraged him, saying, "Is there any portion or inheritance left to us in our father's house? Are we not regarded by him as foreigners? For he has sold us, and he has been using up the money given for us" (Gen. 31:14-15)—that is, the money gained by Jacob's services, which had enabled Laban to become rich. This bitterness against an unloving father doubtless made it easier for the sisters to leave their homeland forever.

When Leah died, some years after her sister, Jacob buried her in the cave at Machpelah that **Abraham** had bought for **Sarah** and where **Isaac** and **Rekekah** had also been placed. Rachel and Leah are praised as women "who together built up the house of Israel" (Ru. 4:11).

Lot's wife turned to a pillar of salt; a late-13th-century illuminated Hebrew manuscript

LEVI

(lee' vi) HEBREW: LEWI
"to be joined"

Levi, the third son of **Jacob** and **Leah**, gave his name to the tribe from which generations later the temple priests and attendants were drawn. For the most part, Levi's character is not clearly distinguished from that of his brothers until the rape of his sister **Dinah** by **Shechem**, son of the ruler of the city of Shechem. It was then Levi and his brother **Simeon** wrought a terrible vengeance on the city of Shechem—to Jacob's horror and dismay, killing all the men of the city. The bloody act is commemorated in Jacob's deathbed blessing; speaking of Simeon and Levi, he says, "weapons of violence are their swords. . . . Cursed be their anger, for it is fierce" (Gen. 49:5, 7). Nonetheless, Levi's descendant **Aaron** was to become the first priest of Israel, and Aaron's sons and their fellow Levites conducted the temple services.

At the conquest, when the territory of the Canaanites was being divided among the tribes, the Levites received no land of their own. The Lord said to Aaron: "You shall have no inheritance in their land . . . I am your portion and your inheritance among the people of Israel" (Num. 18:20). The Levites were to support themselves from the tithes offered by the people as a payment for their services. In addition, **Moses** granted the Levites 48 cities to live in, together with pasture for their flocks; in return for this they were enjoined to offer sacrifices and to teach the law of God.

After the monarchy was divided into the kingdoms of Israel and Judah, "the Levites left their common lands and their holdings and came to Judah and Jerusalem" (2 Chr. 11:14). This was a demonstration of their continued loyalty to the house of **David** and their devotion to the strict worship of the Lord, but their powers were gradually curtailed. As time went by, the priesthood was reserved to a particular family, and the Levites were assigned lesser roles as mere temple functionaries. Speaking through the prophet **Ezekiel**, the Lord explained his reasons: "The Levites who went far from me, going astray from me after their idols when Israel went astray, shall bear their punishment. . . . They shall not come near to me, to serve me as priest" (Ezek. 44:10, 13). Nonetheless, they retained their high status throughout the New Testament period.

LOIS

(loh' is) GREEK: LOIS

A devout Jewish woman living in Lystra, in Asia Minor, Lois had a daughter, Eunice, who had been married to a Greek. **Timothy**, the child of this marriage, was for some reason never circumcised despite the requirements of his mother's religion. Nonetheless, he was "acquainted with the sacred writings" (2 Tim. 3:15) from childhood, thanks to Lois and Eunice. Both his mother and grandmother became Christians and were praised by **Paul** for their "sincere faith" (2 Tim. 1:5), a faith they passed on to Timothy, who became an eager convert and an ardent missionary..

LOT

(laht) HEBREW: LOT

"covering"

Because his father, Haran, had died in Ur, Lot accompanied his grandfather, **Terah**, and his uncle, **Abraham,** on the migration to Canaan. The clan settled temporarily at a place called Haran (in Hebrew, the two names are spelled differently). After Terah's death, Lot continued toward the Promised Land with his 75-year-old uncle. Obviously, a bond had developed between them, and the childless Abraham may have wrongly supposed that Lot was the offspring from whom the great nation promised by God would be descended. The two men entered Canaan but, when famine struck, continued on to Egypt. The Genesis Apocryphon, a book discovered among the Dead Sea Scrolls, preserves an ancient Jewish tradition that says Lot found a wife in Egypt and served as Abraham's spokesman before Pharaoh.

By the time the two families returned to Canaan, their herds had grown so large they had to separate to find adequate grazing land. Abraham gave his nephew first choice of land, perhaps because he believed Lot was destined to inherit the land anyway. Lot chose the fertile valley that stretched north and south along the Jordan River. For his uncle, he left the dry hilly territory of central Canaan. It was in the doomed city of Sodom that Lot finally settled. While Lot was raising a family in Sodom, four kings from the north attacked the region and kidnapped him. Abraham mustered an army of 318 servants and chased the raiders 150 miles to Dan, a city north of the Sea of Galilee. There he routed the invaders and rescued his nephew.

Shortly before the fiery destruction of Sodom and Gomorrah, God sent angelic messengers to warn Lot to leave quickly. But a group of men, young and old alike, surrounded Lot's house and ordered him to bring the strangers out "that we may know them" (Gen. 19:5)—referring here to the townsmen's desire to have sexual relations with the visitors. Lot, some scholars say, showed supreme hospitality by offering his daughters to the mob; others say that he allowed his concern for social obligations to override his responsibility as a father. In any case, the messengers blinded the men, and Lot left the city with his wife and unharmed daughters. Lot's wife, however, ignored the Lord's injunction not to look back and was turned into a pillar of salt.

Because the Dead Sea area is rich with combustible minerals, including oil, tar, and sulfur, Sodom may have been destroyed after lightning, "fire from the Lord out of heaven" (Gen. 19:24), ignited gases released by an earthquake. A shift in the landscape caused by such an earthquake could have flooded the once fertile plain surrounding the cities. Salt pillars, eroded from a nearby salt hill, have been associated with Lot's wife for millennia. The apocryphal Wisdom of Solomon—attributed to King **Solomon** but probably composed by a hellenized Jew in Alexandria toward the end of the first century B.C.—says "a pillar of salt [is still] standing as a monument to an unbelieving soul" (Wis. 10:7).

Following his flight from the destruction,

Lot and his daughters; detail of a painting by Lucas Cranach (1472-1553)

Lot lived in a cave with his two daughters. The women—unnamed in the biblical account—believed that they were the last humans on earth, got their father drunk, and had sexual relations with him to "preserve offspring through our father" (Gen. 19:34). Two sons were born from these incestuous encounters: **Moab** and Ben-ammi, ancestors of two of Israel's enemies, the Moabites and the Ammonites.

*The evangelist Luke painting
Mary's portrait*

LUKE THE ARTIST

*I*n the church of Santa Maria Maggiore in Rome is an ancient painting that legend holds is from the hand of Luke. The Byzantine-style portrait is of Mary holding the infant Jesus. According to one story, Pope Gregory the Great had the painting carried in a procession to the basilica of Saint Peter in 590 to implore God to end a citywide pestilence. In response, an angel appeared, sheathing its bloody sword and halting the plague.

Legends about this and other paintings by Luke have persisted throughout the centuries. But scholars doubt Luke was a painter of anything but word pictures. Clearly, however, the vivid imagery of his prose has inspired countless artists through the ages.

LUKE
(louk) GREEK: LOUKAS
"light"

By tradition identified as the author of the third Gospel and the book of Acts, Luke is mentioned three times in the letters of **Paul**. While under house arrest in Rome between A.D. 61 and 63, Paul named Luke as a "fellow worker" (Philem. 24) and called him "the beloved physician" (Col. 4:14). "Luke alone is with me" (2 Tim. 4:11), the apostle wrote in the second of what are referred to as his three pastoral epistles.

Based on these references and certain facts in the two New Testament books attributed to him, it is possible to draw a composite picture of this early leader of the Christian church. He appears to have been a Gentile convert to Christianity who, according to one early source, came from Antioch in Syria. As a physician, he was a member of a highly skilled profession that was sometimes, but not always, connected with the Greek god of healing, Asclepius. He was clearly well educated and a native speaker of the Greek language, as evidenced by his literary output. He was also well-versed in the Greek Old Testament, which he seems to have studied intensely—an unusual accomplishment if Luke indeed was a Gentile. Since the evangelist did not number himself among those "who from the beginning were eyewitnesses and ministers of the word" (Lk. 1:2), Luke probably did not know **Jesus** personally. However, as Paul's fellow worker, he would have been a member of the apostle's traveling entourage, aiding him in his missionary activities across the Roman world and perhaps sharing imprisonment with him.

How long Luke traveled with Paul is unknown. The so-called "we-sections" of Acts, where the narrative shifts from the third to the first person, are thought by some scholars to be based on Luke's personal journals. If so, they suggest that Luke accompanied Paul on many of his journeys: from Troas to Philippi, Philippi to Miletus, Miletus to Caesarea, and finally from Caesarea to Rome. Thus, Luke was with Paul off and on during the latter half of his ministry and possibly during the final hours before the apostle's death in Rome about A.D. 64.

After the death of Paul, Luke evidently became a leader in the church of his home region. Sometime during the 80's he decided to write an ambitious two-volume work giving an historical and theological account of the life of Jesus and the origins of the Christian church. He began his work with a prologue similar to those employed by many

Greek authors, specifying that he would use only the best sources and organize them into an "orderly account" (Lk. 1:3). Luke noted that other such narratives had already been compiled, a statement many scholars take to be a reference to his use of the Gospel of Mark, a now lost collection of Jesus' sayings sometimes referred to as "Q" (from *quelle*, German for "source"), and other traditions about Jesus and the early church, as well as his own memoirs. Since his account of the birth of Jesus is partly written from the perspective of **Mary** the mother of Jesus, it has been suggested that he actually interviewed her or talked to those who had known her—though Luke himself gives no indication of such conversations. Both of Luke's books were dedicated to an unknown Christian named **Theophilus**. Perhaps Theophilus was a wealthy patron, or—because the name means "lover of God"—Luke could have been writing to any Christian reader.

Luke wrote not only as an historian but also as a theologian. His message emphasized the place of the Gentile Christian community in God's overall plan, demonstrating that Jesus himself had equated his own mission with the preaching of Old Testament prophets to Gentiles. "Truly, I say to you," Jesus told the congregation in the synagogue at Nazareth, "no prophet is acceptable in his own country" (Lk. 4:24). Furthermore, Luke showed in Acts that the expansion of the Christian message to the Gentile world took place consistently through the guidance of the **Holy Spirit**. Consequently, Theophilus and his companions were assured that, though members of a Gentile community, they had a firm claim to the legacy of Jesus.

Nothing is known of Luke following the compilation of his great two-volume work, which accounts for more than a quarter of the New Testament. But clearly the author is entitled to the distinction of being the first Christian historian.

LYDIA

(lid' ee uh) GREEK: LYDIA

In a dream the apostle **Paul** saw a man calling him to Macedonia, a region in northern Greece, and there the apostle made his first convert in Europe. At Philippi, on the sabbath, he "went outside the gate to the riverside, where we supposed there was a place of prayer" (Acts 16:13). There he met Lydia, a Gentile who worshiped as a Jew. Since Paul did not mention her in his letter to the Philippians, some suggest the name identified only the territory of Lydia in Asia Minor, which encompassed the woman's hometown of Thyatira, and that she was either Euodia or Syntyche, the converts the apostle urged to stop their disputations and "agree in the Lord" (Phil. 4:2).

Lydia apparently was a prosperous merchant who sold royal purple cloth to the rich. Inscriptions of the period show her hometown had a guild of dyers. And Homer's *Iliad* tells of two women in Lydia famous for their work in purple dyeing. Lydia had either moved to Philippi or had access to a large

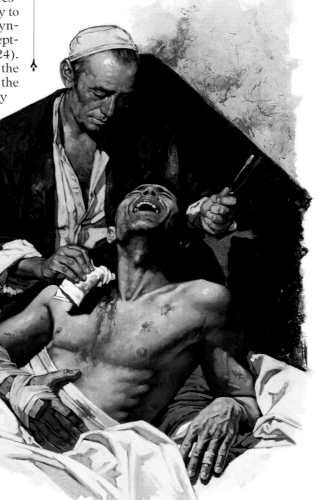

Luke, the compassionate physician, tends to a suffering patient.

house there. After she and her household were baptized, she invited Paul and **Silas** to use her home as a center for their ministry while they were in town. Macedonian women were known for their independence, and Lydia's prominence allowed her to overcome Jewish custom that would have prevented her from making such an offer. It may have been Lydia's hospitality that persuaded Paul to keep accepting help from this church though he refused it from others—for example, the one at Corinth.

LYSANIAS

(li say' nee uhs) GREEK: LYSANIAS

Biblical scholars point out that **Luke**, a conscientious and normally reliable historian, made an apparent error in compiling the Gospel that bears his name. He establishes the date of **John the Baptist**'s ministry by mentioning Lysanias, tetrarch of the small Roman territory of Abilene, north of Galilee, in a list of famous leaders such as **Tiberius**, **Pilate**, and **Herod An-**

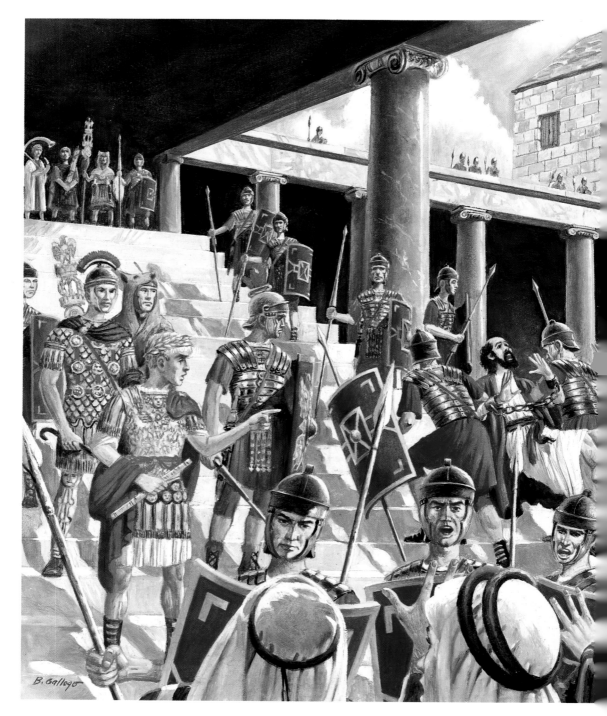

tipas. But he misses the date by some 65 years. The only other mention of a Lysanias who ruled Abilene is by the first-century A.D. Jewish historian Josephus, who says Mark Antony executed the man in 36 B.C. Luke, however, places Lysanias in office there about A.D. 28-29.

There may have been two rulers by the same name, and some of Josephus's references to Lysanias perhaps failed to distinguish between them. An inscription dating to about A.D. 14 suggests this; it was found near Abilene and claims to be the work of a former slave of Lysanias. Luke may have mentioned this second Lysanias because his readers would have known him well.

LYSIAS

(lis' ee uhs) GREEK: LYSIAS

At the time Jewish rebels led by **Judas Maccabeus** were fighting to preserve their religion and get back their temple, the Seleucid king of Syria, **Antiochus IV Epiphanes**, dominated much of the Middle East and was striving to consolidate his control. Antiochus grew angry over Jewish rebel victories about the same time that he noticed his treasury was getting low. And so, in 166 B.C., he took half his army east to Persia to collect taxes and left his chief minister Lysias in charge, ordering him to put down the Jewish rebels.

Lysias first sent an army under the generals Nicanor and **Gorgias**, but it was defeated near Emmaus. The next year he led the army himself, but he, too, was apparently defeated or managed no more than a standoff followed by a treaty. After the Syrian army withdrew, Judas Maccabeus ordered the Jerusalem temple rededicated. The eight days of celebration that followed became an annual observance: Hanukkah.

LYSIAS 2

A riot broke out at the Jerusalem temple when a group of Jews from Asia Minor recognized **Paul** and accused him of desecrating the temple by bringing Greeks inside. Claudius Lysias, commander of a 1,000-troop garrison, which was probably stationed in the nearby tower of Antonia, responded by sending troops to rescue and arrest Paul. The next day he called a meeting of the Sanhedrin, the Jewish governing council, to find out what Paul had done. But the meeting ended in an uproar and soldiers had to rescue Paul again. When Lysias heard that some 40 Jews had vowed to kill Paul, he ordered nearly half his command to escort Paul to Caesarea, where the apostle began a two-year imprisonment before being taken to Rome for trial.

Born a Greek, Lysias may have added his Roman first name when he purchased citizenship, possibly taking it in honor of **Claudius**, at that time Roman emperor.

The Roman commander Lysias rescues Paul from the Jerusalem mob.

MACHIR

(may' keer) HEBREW: MAKIR
"bought" or "hireling [of God]"

This grandson of **Joseph**—the firstborn son of **Manasseh** and an unnamed Aramaean concubine—gained a reputation for military prowess. Like King **David**, he was one of a select few described as a "man of war" (Jos. 17:1). Ironically, the first time he is mentioned in the Bible is before the Exodus, when his children are being placed on their great-grandfather's lap. By the time of the conquest his descendants had become the largest family in the tribe of Manasseh.

Machir's warlike clan received an allotment of land east of the Jordan River from **Moses** and fought alongside **Deborah** and **Barak** west of the river. The Machirites probably helped conquer much of central Canaan before moving to the eastern perimeter of the Israelite settlements to claim their inheritance of Gilead and Bashan, where they managed to displace the indigenous Amorites.

MAHER-SHALAL-HASH-BAZ

(may' uhr shal' uhl hash' bahz)
HEBREW: MAHER-SALAL-HAS-BAZ
"the spoil speeds, the prey hastes"

Faced with the threat of invasion by the combined forces of Israel and Syria, King **Ahaz** of Judah decided to make a treaty with Assyria. The prophet **Isaiah** objected and, in an unsuccessful attempt to convince Ahaz to trust God, gave the symbolic name Maher-shalal-hash-baz (incidentally, the longest name in the Bible) to

As Judas betrays Jesus with a kiss, Peter lunges at the high priest's slave, Malchus; the fresco by Barna da Siena dates to about 1350.

his own second or third son before the child's conception. The treaty would be unnecessary, the name indicated, because the threat would soon end; Israel and Syria would be defeated and plundered before the prophet's child learned to talk. And, indeed, Assyria crushed both of Judah's northern neighbors in the Syro-Ephraimite War of 734 to 732 B.C.

MALACHI

(mal' uh ki) HEBREW: MALAKI
"my messenger/angel"

The presumed author of the biblical book bearing his name, Malachi was one of the 12 Minor Prophets whose writings bring the Old Testament to a close. Nothing is known about the prophet himself, but scholars have been able to date his book with some accuracy, in part because in one verse Malachi mentions an invasion of Edom (**Esau**) that "laid waste his hill country and left his heritage to jackals of the desert" (Mal. 1:3). The ravaging of the Edomite kingdom is believed to have occurred toward the end of the sixth century B.C. and is referred to by other prophets, among them **Jeremiah** and **Ezekiel**. More important, Malachi reveals in his writings a devotion to temple worship that was only restored in 515 B.C., following the return of the Jews from exile in Babylon. Therefore, Malachi is thought to have prophesied in Jerusalem between that date and about 450 B.C., during the period when the city's populace was ruled by a Persian governor.

Though the temple had been rebuilt, services there were no longer being properly conducted. Malachi kept a watchful eye on the behavior of the temple priests and complained bitterly about those who dared to offer unsatisfactory animals as sacrifices, animals that had been "taken by violence or . . . [were] lame or sick" (Mal. 1:13), instead of the unblemished animals required by Mosaic Law. He also reproached the returned exiles for failing to tithe. "Will man rob God?" Micah asked in his characteristic question-and-answer format. "Yet you are robbing me. But you say, 'How are we robbing thee?'" Having asked the question, the prophet then provided the answer: "In your tithes and offerings." The results of such a lapse would be crop failure, drought, and a plague of locusts. Punctilious tithing, on the other hand, would be rewarded with "an overflowing blessing. . . [and] you will be a land of delight" (Mal. 3:8, 10, 12). Not long after Malachi's preaching, the temple service was reformed, just as he had proposed, when **Nehemiah** arrived in Jerusalem with a mandate from the Persian king to restore Jewish Law in the little province centered around the city. Along with these religious reforms came the restoration of proper tithing.

Malachi's name means "my messenger" and may be a title rather than a real name. Christians have always considered him to be a messenger of the new covenant that appears in the Gospels. Indeed, the placement of his book as the very last in the Old Testament, directly before the Gospels, reinforces this idea. "Behold, I send my messenger to prepare the way before me" (Mal. 3:1), Malachi proclaimed. And he concluded his oracle by saying the Lord had promised to send the prophet **Elijah** as forerunner of the Messiah. All three Synoptic Gospels contain references to these verses in Malachi as being fulfilled in the lives of **John the Baptist** and **Jesus**.

It has been suggested that the book of Malachi was originally written by **Ezra**. That, however, is disputed. Also disputed is the theory that the verses that make up the book originally formed part of **Zechariah**'s writings. Yet Malachi's concerns were those that also preoccupied Ezra and Zechariah: neglect of temple worship and payment of tithes to support it, the dangers of intermarriage with foreign women, and hope for the messianic age. Whatever the date or authorship of the book attributed to him, Malachi is considered a messenger of the future because of the universality of his preachings. "Have we not all one father?" he asked. "Has not one God created us?" (Mal. 2:10).

Crossing his arms, Jacob bestows the right-hand blessing on Ephraim rather than on the elder Manasseh; a 12th-century enamel plaque.

MALCHUS
(mal' kuhs) GREEK: MALCHOS
derived from a Semitic root for "king"

The night Roman soldiers and temple police arrested **Jesus**, **Peter** cut off the right ear of **Malchus**, the high priest **Caiaphas**'s slave. The slave was most likely only an observer representing Caiaphas; the first-century A.D. Jewish historian Josephus says servants of the high priest were known to represent their master at unpleasant functions. Judging from Malchus's name, he may have been a Nabatean Arab slave from the deserts east or south of Judea. Inscriptions show Malchus was a common Nabatean name.

The arrest, which took place on the Mount of Olives, several hundred yards beyond the temple grounds, is recorded in all four Gospels. Only John names the victim of Peter's attack; and only **Luke**, traditionally held to be **Paul**'s "beloved physician" (Col. 4:14), says that Jesus healed the slave's wound.

MANAEN
(man' ee uhn) HEBREW: MENAHEM
"comforter"

Together with **Simeon** called Niger and Lucius the Cyrenian, Manaen is named as one of the "prophets and teachers" (Acts 13:1) of the church in Antioch at the time when Saul (**Paul**) and **Barnabas** were called by the **Holy Spirit** to their missionary work. He is also described in this passage as a member of the court of the tetrarch **Herod Antipas**. In some translations, Manaen is said to have been "brought up" with Antipas as a foster brother. However, most scholars consider it more likely that Manaen was a close childhood friend who joined the court circle in adulthood.

MANASSEH

(muh na' suh) HEBREW: MENASSEH
"[God] has made [me] forget"
....

Virtually nothing is known about the eponymous ancestor of the tribe of Manasseh. The firstborn son of **Joseph** and his Egyptian wife Asenath was given his name, his father said, because "God has made me forget all my hardship and all my father's house" (Gen. 41:51). Some years later, Joseph took Manasseh and his younger son, **Ephraim**, for the deathbed blessing of their grandfather **Jacob**. Much as Jacob had gained the blessing of his father, **Isaac**, over his older brother, **Esau**, the old man switched hands at that moment, bestowing the primary, right-hand blessing on Ephraim: "He [Manasseh] also shall be great; nevertheless his younger brother shall be greater than he, and his descendants shall become a multitude of nations" (Gen. 48:19). Before he died at the age of 110, Joseph lived to see the grandchildren of both his sons—the expression "born upon Joseph's knees" (Gen. 50:23) indicating they were adopted as his descendants.

Despite the blessing of Jacob, the progeny of Manasseh greatly outnumbered those of Ephraim in the census taken on the plains of Moab before the entry into the Promised Land: 52,700 versus 32,500 as recorded in Numbers 26:28-37. Manasseh's descendants played a major role in the conquest of Canaan and, after the priestly tribe of **Levi** was omitted in the allocation of conquered territory, Manasseh—along with the other half-tribe of Ephraim—was elevated to full tribal status. "You are a numerous people, and have great power," **Joshua** told the descendants of Joseph's two sons; "you shall not have one lot only" (Jos. 17:17). Manasseh received considerable territory in the central highlands west of the Jordan and also land across the river in Gilead.

Among the prominent members of the tribe of Manasseh were the judges **Gideon** and **Jephthah**. Much later, some Manassites deserted the army of King **Saul** to support **David**'s bid for power. But when **Solomon**'s realm was divided, Manasseh formed an important component of the northern kingdom of Israel; the successive capitals of Shechem, Tirzah, and Samaria were all located within the territory of Manasseh. Nevertheless, a few Manassites, according to report, still undertook the traditional pilgrimage to Jerusalem in order to celebrate the Passover festival there, and some apparently defected to Judah in response to the religious reforms of King **Asa**, Solomon's great-grandson.

When the Assyrians conquered Israel in 721 B.C. and carried the northern tribes off into exile, the tribe of Manasseh disappeared from history. Yet, people of both Manasseh and Ephraim are listed with the Judahites and Benjaminites as living in Jerusalem following the return from captivity in Babylon two centuries later.

MANASSEH 2

....

The king of Judah from about 687 to 642 B.C., Manasseh came to the throne at the age of 12, possibly as coregent during the illness of his father, **Hezekiah**. If a ten-year coregency is included, his reign of 55 years was the longest in either Judah or the northern kingdom of Israel. But Manasseh

In this 13th-century Greco–Byzantine manuscript, King Manasseh of Judah is led off to Babylon in yoke and chains.

"did what was evil in the sight of the Lord" by reintroducing "the abominable practices" (2 Kg. 21:2) of the pagans who had inhabited the land of Canaan before it was conquered by the Israelites.

Whereas Hezekiah had rebelled against Assyria, Manasseh yielded to the expanding power of that enemy and, as a loyal vassal, provided the Assyrians with assistance in their war of conquest against Egypt. In the Assyrian records, Manasseh is listed as one of 22 subject kings who were required to transport material for King **Esarhaddon**'s building projects. Apparently to placate his Assyrian overlords and show his loyalty to them, Manasseh restored the pagan worship that his father had ousted from Jerusalem. He rebuilt the shrines to **Baal**, raised images of the goddess Asherah, erected altars to the sun, moon, and stars in the temple courts, and "practiced soothsaying and augury and sorcery, and dealt with mediums and with wizards" (2 Chr. 33:6). In accordance with pagan customs, he even offered up his own sons as sacrifices, burning them to death in the valley of Hinnom outside Jerusalem. Not surprisingly, he is considered the worst apostate king ever to occupy the throne of **David**. According to legend, one of the idols Manasseh erected in the temple had four faces, one for each direction. That way worshipers entering the temple from any direction would have to confront it.

Manasseh did not escape the humiliations imposed on an Assyrian subject king. He was put into chains and taken "with hooks" (2 Chr. 33:11) to Babylon, presumably to appear before the Assyrian king to reaffirm his loyalty. That may have been at a time when the Assyrians were punishing vassals who had joined a rebellion centered on Babylon. Upon his return, Manasseh built an outer wall for Jerusalem, perhaps permitted to do so by his Assyrian overlords to strengthen his capital against an attack from a resurgent Egypt or possibly in preparation for a rebellion of his own.

As if to justify such a lengthy and apparently successful reign, the author of 2 Chronicles preserved a tradition that Manasseh eventually repented of his evil ways. His original prayer of repentance has been lost but his supposed contrition was given voice much later in the apocryphal Prayer of Manasseh, written long after his reign, perhaps between 250 and 150 B.C. The prayer is a brief psalm in which Manasseh asks God to forgive his sins, "more in number than the sand of the sea" (Man. 9).

MANOAH

(muh noh' uh) HEBREW: MANOAH
"rest/resting place"

Samson's father, Manoah, was a member of the tribe of Dan who lived at Zorah. Manoah's unnamed wife—like such earlier Old Testament figures as **Sarah** and **Rachel** and like **Elizabeth** in the New Testament—was promised divine relief

A mosaic from the cathedral of San Marco in Venice celebrates the legend that Mark brought the gospel to that city.

from her barrenness. "Behold, you are barren," an angel of the Lord said to her, ". . . but you shall conceive and bear a son" (Jg. 13:3). The child, the angel revealed, would help deliver Israel from the Philistines.

As soon as Manoah heard his wife's good news, he prayed for the angel to return and instruct the couple on how to raise their son, but he was again absent when the heavenly messenger reappeared. Manoah finally encountered the angel and invited him to eat with them. The angel rejected the offer, urging Manoah to make the food into a burnt offering instead. Then the angel ascended in the flames from the sacrifice, proving his supernatural identity.

Samson's parents later criticized his resolve to marry a Philistine woman, unaware that the union was also a part of God's plan. Nonetheless, Manoah apparently arranged the wedding feast. Samson did not tell his parents about killing a lion and later finding its carcass swarming with bees—events that inspired the riddle he offered at the feast. When Samson died, he was buried beside Manoah in the family tomb at Zorah.

MARK

GREEK: MARKOS; LATIN: MARCUS
"large hammer"

In this 11th-century ivory carving from Italy, Peter dictates his memoirs to Mark—the basis for the second Gospel.

The second-century Christian writer Papias first recorded the tradition that one of the four Gospels was written by Mark. He evidently meant the "John whose other name was Mark" (Acts 12:12), to whose mother's house **Peter** went after being miraculously released from prison. Elsewhere in the book of Acts and in the letters of the New Testament, this individual is referred to as John called Mark, John, or Mark. Such dual names were commonly adopted by hellenized Jews of the period— John (Johanan) being a Hebrew name, Mark (Marcus) being a Latin one.

Mark accompanied his cousin **Barnabas** and **Paul** as they set out on their first missionary journey. The two had enlisted him at Jerusalem and taken him with them to Antioch before sailing for Cyprus from the port of Seleucia Pieria. But when the missionaries reached Perga on the south coast of what is now Turkey, Mark left them and returned to Jerusalem. Why he went home is not known, but it evidently displeased Paul; for when Barnabas asked that Mark accompany them on a second missionary journey, Paul refused. This led to the apostle's break with Barnabas after "a sharp contention" (Acts 15:39) between them over Mark. Barnabas and Mark then went to-

gether to Cyprus, presumably on a missionary tour of their own, while Paul took **Silas** to Cilicia. Yet Mark must have been reconciled with Paul, because he is mentioned later in Paul's letters as one of his "fellow workers" (Philem. 24), who was "very useful in serving me" (2 Tim. 4:11).

Mark was also associated with Peter, who referred to him as "my son" (1 Pet. 5:13), indicating a close spiritual relationship. And this connection led Papias to propose Mark as author of the Gospel that now bears his name. According to this theory, Mark joined Peter in Rome, where he recorded or interpreted Peter's reminiscences, which became the principal source for the second Gospel.

Modern scholars, however, regard the Gospel of Mark as an anonymous work, perhaps written in Rome sometime near the destruction of Jerusalem in A.D. 70. They also consider it to be the earliest of the Gospels, a model for the others and in particular a source for the Gospels of Matthew and Luke. In Mark's Gospel, **Jesus'** teaching and ministry are reinforced by his mighty deeds and by the endorsement of God himself at his baptism and the transfiguration. Nevertheless, his work is misunderstood by the people around him, including his own disciples, who cannot grasp the idea of a suffering Messiah or that, as Jesus said, "the Son of man must suffer

Jesus dining in the house of Martha and Mary; detail of a painting by Tintoretto (1518-1594)

many things" (Mk. 8:31). And thus anyone who would be with Jesus must "take up his cross and follow" (Mk. 8:34) in a discipleship willing to accept suffering. Before his death, Jesus' disciples one by one betray, deny, or forsake him. It is only through his death and resurrection that he is recognized as "the son of God" (Mk. 15:39).

The Evangelist Mark is also sometimes identified as the "young man" who followed Jesus on the night of his arrest clad in "nothing but a linen cloth about his body" (Mk. 14:51) and who escaped being captured by slipping out of the wrap and fleeing naked—an incident recorded only in the second Gospel. However, this tradition is inconsistent with Papias's statement that Mark "had neither heard the Lord nor been his personal follower."

MARTHA

GREEK: MARTHA; ARAMAIC: MARTA
"lady" or "mistress [of the house]"

Martha lived with her sister **Mary** and brother **Lazarus** in the village of Bethany just outside of Jerusalem; the three were beloved friends of **Jesus**. It was Martha, evidently the older of the two sisters and the head of the household, who "received him [Jesus] into her house" (Lk. 10:38). But

while Mary sat listening to Jesus' teaching, Martha was preoccupied with the duties of a hostess. Her complaint that her sister was not helping elicited a mild rebuke from Jesus: "Martha, Martha, you are anxious and troubled about many things; one thing is needful." Mary, he observed, had "chosen the good portion" (Lk. 10:41-42).

Yet, in the story of the raising of Lazarus, Martha emerges as a supreme example of the devoted follower. Running out to meet Jesus when he arrived at Bethany after Lazarus had been dead for four days and already placed in a tomb, she first expressed disappointment that Jesus had not arrived earlier, in time to prevent Lazarus's death. Nonetheless, she still exhibited faith that God would grant Jesus whatever he asked. Jesus then told her that Lazarus would rise again. "I know that he will rise again in the resurrection at the last day," Martha said. To which Jesus responded, "I am the resurrection and the life . . . . Do you believe this?" "Yes, Lord," she said; "I believe that you are the Christ, the Son of God, he who is coming into the world" (Jn. 11:24-27). Her words are the most profound confession of faith in the entire Gospel of John, comparable to the great confession of **Peter** in the Synoptic Gospels: "You are the Christ, the Son of the living God" (Mt. 16:16; *see also:* Mark 8:29 and Luke 9:20).

MARY

GREEK: MARIA/MARIAM derived from
HEBREW: MIRYAM
"bitterness"
. . . .

Mary is a central figure in the two Gospel accounts of the birth of **Jesus** and in later centuries became an important focus of Christian theology and piety. Given the prominence of Mary in the history of Christianity, it is perhaps surprising that she is seldom mentioned in the New Testament outside the birth narratives. She is never explicitly named in the New Testament letters and only once in the book of Acts. Although she figures in two important episodes, the Gospel of John never gives her name, and the Gospel of Mark mentions her name only once. Mary shines brilliantly, however, in the narratives of Jesus' birth in the opening chapters of the Gospels of Matthew and Luke—the latter, in particular, giving the reader a strong impression of the character and strength of Mary.

Mary was a virgin of Nazareth betrothed to a man named **Joseph**—that is, they were legally committed to marry but were not yet living together. The age of Mary is not given, though typically she would have been only a few years past puberty. Nothing is said of Mary's ancestry except that she was a relative of **Elizabeth**, the mother of **John the Baptist**, who was of the tribe of Levi. At some point during the betrothal period—usually a year long—the angel **Gabriel** appeared to Mary and announced that she would bear a son to be named Jesus, a royal successor to King **David**. When Mary objected that she had no husband, the angel told her that "the Holy Spirit will come upon you, and the power of the Most High will overshadow you"; the child would be called "holy, the Son of God." An enduring example of obedient faith, she replied, "I am the handmaid of the Lord; let it be to me according to your word" (Lk. 1:35, 38).

Mary soon visited the elderly Elizabeth, who was six months pregnant. As Mary greeted her kinswoman, the child in Elizabeth's womb leaped for joy. Mary responded to Elizabeth's salutation in the poem commonly known (from its first word in Latin) as the Magnificat. By including this poem, Luke reveals Mary, young as she was, as profoundly perceptive. She was deeply aware of her "low estate," which had been elevated by a blessing from God that "all generations" would recognize. She connected her own experience directly with her belief that God was now helping "his servant Israel," since he had "scattered the proud," and "put down the mighty," while he "exalt-

ed those of low degree" and "filled the hungry with good things" (Lk. 1:48, 51-53). As the events of Jesus' birth unfolded, Mary continued to meditate on them, or in Luke's words, "Mary kept all these things, pondering them in her heart" (Lk. 2:19).

And what a course of events it was, pushing Mary through emotional peaks and valleys! It began with a threat of divorce from Joseph, which was blocked by an angelic assurance to him that her conception was "of the Holy Spirit" (Mt. 1:20). It included the long trip to Bethlehem, giving birth in a stable, using a feeding trough for her newborn's bed, shepherds telling that angels had announced the birth of the Messiah, aged prophets in the temple exalting her month-old infant, wise men arriving from the distant East with wonderful gifts for her child, angelic warnings that King **Herod the Great** would try to slay the baby, a hurried escape into Egypt to await the death of the tyrant, and finally the return to Palestine and settling down in Nazareth. Mary had much to ponder.

From the next 30 years, the Gospels include but a single incident. Having gone to Jerusalem with his parents at Passover, the 12-year-old Jesus remained in the temple as his family started home. When the worried Mary and Joseph turned back to find him, Jesus seemed perfectly at ease,

*Mary gazes fondly at the infant Jesus;
a painting by Carlo Maratta (1625-1713).*

Mary given an embroidery lesson; detail of a painting by Dante Gabriel Rossetti (1828-1882)

MARY'S CHILDHOOD

According to the second-century Protoevangelium of James, Mary was miraculously born to a rich man named Joachim and his barren wife, Anne—a story obviously based on the Old Testament account of Samuel's birth to Hannah. From the age of six months, the child was kept pure in a ``sanctuary in her bedchamber,'' cared for by ``the undefiled daughters of the Hebrews.'' At three, Mary was taken to live in the temple at Jerusalem, there to be fed by ``the hand of an angel.'' As she approached puberty, when she would be forced to leave the sacred precincts, Mary was given over to the care of the aged widower Joseph.

Unlike the canonical Gospels of Matthew and Luke, the Protoevangelium makes Mary rather than Jesus the central character of its narrative. It is she who is the long anticipated child, her childhood that reflects Old Testament tales, she who is raised to serve the Lord, her name that is to be remembered by future generations.

"sitting among the teachers" in what he called "my Father's house" (Lk. 2:46, 49).

Gospel passages that refer to Jesus as Mary's "first-born son" (Lk. 2:7) or list "his brothers James and Joseph and Simon and Judas" and mention "all his sisters" (Mt. 13:55-56) apparently indicate that, after the birth of Jesus, Mary lived simply as the wife of Joseph and bore several more children. However, late in the second century, an important tradition developed in the church that Mary was not only a virgin when Jesus was conceived but remained one until her death. If the tradition is accepted, Mary's life appears quite different: She never consummated her marriage to Joseph and bore no other children. The biblical references to "brothers" and "sisters" cannot then be taken in their ordinary sense but as referring to some other relationship, perhaps that of cousins, as some suggest, or stepbrothers and stepsisters, children of Joseph by an earlier, unrecorded marriage.

PROMPTING HIS FIRST MIRACLE

Mary was probably in her late 40's when Jesus began his ministry. Some interpreters believe that she was a widow by that time, but the Gospels do not explicitly say so, and some passages seem to indicate that Joseph was alive and known to Jesus' acquaintances. Each time Mary is mentioned during Jesus' ministry, there is a hint of some separation between Jesus and his mother.

In the most colorful incident involving Mary, the marriage at Cana, it is Jesus' mother who informs him simply, "They have no wine." Jesus' response is surprising for its mysterious abruptness: "O woman, what have you to do with me? My hour has not yet come" (Jn. 2:4). The statement reveals not that Jesus was impolite to his mother but that his ministry had its own timetable, one that could not be rushed even by his own mother. But Mary was not put off by Jesus' words and told the servants to do whatever her son asked, indicating she already perceived Jesus' remarkable power. Jesus then worked his first miracle, turning water into wine to save his host from embarrassment.

Later, as controversy swirled around Jesus, "his family . . . went out to seize him, for people were saying, 'He is beside himself'" (Mk. 3:21). They may have been worried for Jesus' safety in the midst of charges of demonic possession, but Jesus refused to heed them. Although little more is said of Mary during this period, Jesus certainly held his mother in high esteem, since on more than one occasion he stressed the importance of the command to "honor your father and your mother" (Mt. 15:4).

Jesus' honor for his own mother was supremely manifested at his crucifixion. As he was dying, Jesus tenderly committed Mary, who was standing near the cross, to the care of "the disciple whom he loved" (Jn. 19:26). Henceforth, evidently, she considered this beloved disciple (see page 56) as her son and stayed for some time with him. After Jesus' resurrection, Mary remained in Jerusalem with the band of perhaps 120 disciples. During the following years she may have been present as **James**, whom **Paul** calls "the Lord's brother" (Gal. 1:19), rose to become the leader of the Jerusalem church. James was most likely her second son (or, if later tradition is correct, perhaps a stepson or Jesus' cousin). The New Testament says nothing of Mary's later life or of her death.

Many details about the life of Mary not provided by the Bible soon began to be filled in by ever expanding traditions. By the late second century, some Christian theologians had drawn the analogy that as Jesus was the second **Adam** so Mary was the second **Eve**. In about the same period, an elaborate narrative of Mary's life, known today as the Protoevangelium (or Infancy Gospel) of James, began to circulate. According to this work, the midwife who helped deliver Jesus saw, and proved to a disbeliever, that the physical signs of Mary's virginity continued unchanged even after she gave birth.

With its emphasis on Mary's purity, the Protoevangelium of James laid the groundwork for the doctrine of her perpetual virginity. In the pious work, Mary's virginity is far more than the physical state that showed that Jesus' birth was a miraculous act of God. Rather, in keeping with the growing ascetic piety of the times, her virginity was viewed as a special state of spiritual purity that would be spoiled by any sexual relations, even with her husband. By the fourth century, this sensibility was so dominant that leading Christian writers condemned as heretics those who said that Mary had married Joseph and had children by him. From that time on, "virgin" became a permanent part of her name, often in the reverent phrase "Blessed Virgin Mary."

Doctrines concerning Mary continued to develop through the fifth century, when the Nestorian controversy over the nature of Christ arose. Should Mary properly be called "Mother of Christ," as Nestorius, patriarch of Constantinople, said, or rather "Mother of God," as Cyril, patriarch of Alexandria, held? In the politically charged atmosphere of the Council of Ephesus in 431, Nestorius was deposed and Mary was officially affirmed as Mother of God.

The doctrine that Mary was uniquely conceived without original sin (the Immaculate Conception) was debated throughout the Middle Ages but officially defined for Roman Catholics in 1854. The doctrine that at her death Mary was bodily assumed into heaven (the Assumption of Mary) was widely accepted by the sixth century but officially defined as an article of faith for Catholics only in 1950.

The theological role of Mary has been a line of division between Protestant churches and Catholic and Eastern Orthodox churches. Veneration of Mary has remained strong among Catholics since the Middle Ages and

A sorrowing Mary cradles the body of her crucified son; a painting by Fra Angelico (1387-1455).

has found myriad forms of expression, including the use of the Rosary, major feasts of the Blessed Virgin Mary, countless churches dedicated to "Our Lady," and pilgrimages to Lourdes and Fatima, where Mary is said to have made miraculous appearances. The Protestant reformers, however, criticized the elaborate superstructure of legend, theological speculation, and glorification that the medieval church had erected around the simple figure of Mary the mother of Jesus. On both sides of that theological division, however, Mary continues to be a fascinating and beloved figure.

MARY 2

The mother of **James** and Joseph—and perhaps the same as "Mary the wife of Clopas" (Jn. 19:25)—this Mary was one of the women "who had followed Jesus from Galilee, ministering to him" (Mt. 27:55). Probably one of those who provided financial support for his ministry, she no doubt was among the group who accompanied Jesus on his last journey to Jerusalem, for she, along with **Mary Magdalene**, witnessed his death and burial. In order to ensure that his body would be properly anointed, the two women returned to the tomb on the day after the sabbath only to find it empty. "Do not be afraid," an angel sitting on the stone rolled back from the entrance told them. "Go quickly and tell his disciples that he has risen from the dead" (Mt. 28:5, 7). As they departed, according to Matthew, Jesus himself appeared to the two women, making them the first witnesses to the resurrection.

Mary of Bethany washing Jesus' feet; an illumination from the tenth-century Codex Egberti

MARY 3

Mary of Bethany and her sister **Martha** are featured in three stories in the Gospels. On the occasion when **Jesus** was invited to dinner at Martha's house, Mary seemed to shirk her duties in the kitchen, instead sitting at the feet of Jesus and listening in rapt attention to his teaching. When Martha complained about her sister not helping, Jesus gently chastised her, saying, "Mary has chosen the good portion, which shall not be taken away from her" (Lk. 10:42).

The raising from the dead of **Lazarus**, the brother of Mary and Martha, is recounted only in the Gospel of John, where the three are said to have been especially loved by Jesus. While he was across the Jordan, having fled the threat of stoning and arrest in Judea, Jesus received word from the sisters that Lazarus was ill. He first delayed going to the bedside of his friend, saying that it was not an illness "unto death" but was "for the glory of God, so that the Son of God may be glorified by means of it" (Jn. 11:4). But after two days, Jesus left for Bethany, telling his disciples that "our friend Lazarus has fallen asleep, but I go to awake him out of sleep." Misunderstanding their master, the disciples expressed confidence that Lazarus would recover. Jesus bluntly informed them that he had meant the sleep of death but that he would nonetheless go to Lazarus "so that you may believe" (Jn. 11:11,15). By the time Jesus arrived in Bethany, Lazarus had been dead four days and placed in a tomb.

Martha ran out to meet him, but Mary stayed in the house. Here, in contrast to the story in Luke's Gospel, it is Martha who follows Jesus' actions closely while Mary seems to be withdrawn. Yet in both stories Martha is presented as the more impulsive, while Mary is the more contemplative. Mary did not go out to meet Jesus until Martha returned to say that Jesus was calling for her. She then arose, went to him, and repeated the words said by Martha when she had encountered him: "Lord, if you had been here, my brother would not have died" (Jn. 11:32). Jesus responded to her weeping, and the weeping of those around her, by weeping himself. Then—despite Martha's fear of the odor of a man four days' dead—Jesus called forth Lazarus from the tomb.

Sometime later, Jesus was again being served a meal at the

home of Mary and Martha, the resurrected Lazarus sitting at table with them. As before, Martha did the serving, while Mary once more responded to Jesus in a special way. She "took a pound of costly ointment of pure nard," an extravagant amount of expensive perfume, "and anointed the feet of Jesus and wiped his feet with her hair" (Jn. 12:3). **Judas Iscariot** reacted to Mary's action by saying that the ointment should be sold and the proceeds given to the poor, but Jesus rebuked him: "Let her alone, let her keep it for the day of my burial. The poor you always have with you, but you do not always have me" (Jn. 12:7-8). Matthew and Mark also tell of Jesus' being anointed shortly before his triumphal entry into Jerusalem, but neither of them gives the name of the woman who anointed him.

MARY 4

The house of **Mark**'s mother, Mary, was used as a meeting place for the early Christians, one of the first examples of a home serving as a church. Since she is named as the owner of the house, Mary was likely a widow, and a wealthy one at that, for her dwelling contained an area large enough for the Christians to meet in and she had servants. It was to her house that **Peter** returned after his miraculous release from prison, being met at the door by the servant **Rhoda**. Mary's son "John, whose other name was Mark" (Acts 12:12) was a companion of **Paul** and her nephew **Barnabas** on their missionary journey to Cyprus and Asia Minor. According to tradition, he was also the author of the Gospel of Mark.

MARY MAGDALENE
(mag' da len)
"of Magdala"

The most prominent of the women who accompanied **Jesus** from Galilee to Jerusalem, Mary Magdalene is named in all four Gospels as a witness to his crucifixion, burial, and resurrection. She came from Magdala, a town located on the Sea of Galilee, just north of Tiberius. Along with **Joanna**, the wife of **Herod Antipas**'s steward Chuza, and **Susanna**, she "had been healed of evil spirits and infirmities"; Mary Magdalene was the one "from whom seven demons had gone out" (Lk. 8:2). Apparently all were women of some wealth, for they were able to provide for Jesus and the 12 apostles "out of their means" (Lk. 8:3).

Church tradition long identified Mary

*Mary Magdalene by Piero di Cosimo
(1462-1521)*

Magdalene as the "woman of the city" (Lk. 7:37), a sinner who came to Jesus while he was dining at the home of a Pharisee and anointed his feet with her tears and wiped them with her hair. However, since Luke does not give the name of the woman in that story and introduces Mary Magdalene almost immediately thereafter, it is not likely he considered them to be the same person. A more plausible conclusion is that Mary Magdalene, as a person of means and as a companion of the wife of Antipas's steward, was a woman of high social status and not the prostitute she was said to have been.

The story of Jesus' death is a tragedy, in part because he was betrayed, forsaken, or denied by all but one of his male followers. It was only the beloved disciple (see page 56) and the women—including Mary Magdalene—who stayed with Jesus to the bitter end. Mary Magdalene stood by Jesus as he was dying on the cross, saw him buried, and came to the empty tomb on the third day. Because the names of the other women with her vary, she is considered the primary witness to those momentous events. Moreover, according to the Gospel of Matthew, Mary Magdalene, along with **Mary** the mother of **James** and Joseph, heard the news of the resurrection from an angel and was also the first to whom the risen Jesus appeared. "Do not be afraid," he told them; "go and tell my brethren to go to Galilee, and there they will see me" (Mt. 28:10).

The most detailed version of Jesus' resurrection appearance to Mary Magdalene is in the Gospel of John. Arriving at the tomb alone and finding it empty, she ran to tell **Peter** and the beloved disciple that "they have taken the Lord out of the tomb, and we do not know where they have laid him" (Jn. 20:2). The two disciples raced to the tomb, saw that it was indeed empty, and noted that the grave clothes had been left neatly behind. Not yet realizing the full significance of what they observed, the two went back to the city; Mary Magdalene remained at the tomb weeping.

Suddenly two angels appeared to ask why she was weeping. "Because they have taken away my Lord, and I do not know where they have laid him," she answered. But turning, she saw Jesus, mistook him for the gardener, and replied to his query as to why she was weeping and whom she sought: "Sir, if you have carried him away, tell me where you have laid him, and I will take him away." Jesus had only to call her by name for Mary to recognize him and address him as "Rabboni" (Jn. 20:13, 15-16). She was responding in the manner earlier described by John: "He calls his own sheep by name and leads them out . . . and the sheep follow him, for they know his voice" (Jn. 10:3-4). Then, because she tried to embrace him, Jesus said, "Do not hold me, for I have not yet ascended to the Father; but go to my brethren and say to them, I am ascending to my Father and your Father, to my God and your God." And thus Mary Magdalene became the first to announce to the waiting disciples, "I have seen the Lord" (Jn. 20:17-18).

MATTATHIAS
(mat uh thi' uhs) HEBREW: MATTATHIAS
"gift of Yahweh"

Mattathias was a priest of the line of Joarib who lived in the Judean village of Modein, located some 20 miles northwest of Jerusalem. Together with his five sons— John, **Simon**, **Judas Maccabeus**, Eleazar, and **Jonathan** (collectively known as the Maccabees)—he initiated a rebellion against the Seleucid dynasty that had ruled Judea since 198 B.C.

The situation of the Jews had become intolerable during the reign of **Antiochus IV Epiphanes** (175-164 B.C.), who tried to abolish the Jewish religion by banning daily sacrifice in the temple, observance of the sabbath, adherence to dietary laws, and circumcision. To publicize the bans, his soldiers "put to death the women who had their children circumcised . . . and they hung the infants from their mothers' necks" (1 Macc.

As an angel reveals the empty tomb to the other women, Jesus cautions Mary Magdalene not to touch him; a 14th-century German painting on wood.

THE SAYINGS SOURCE

*I*n early Christian centuries, teachers recognized that the Gospels of Matthew, Mark, and Luke (the so-called Synoptic Gospels) are very similar to one another whereas the Gospel of John is largely different; some of these teachers even tabulated the parallel passages among the Gospels. In modern times, however, when the Gospels were first printed with parallel passages side by side, it became possible to analyze the relationships more closely.

Though some diversity of opinion exists, most students hold that the shortest Gospel, Mark, was the first to be written. It appears that both Matthew and Luke made use of Mark's text, but supplemented it with many additional traditions. An analysis of these traditions shows further that there was a collection of Jesus' sayings and teachings that Matthew and Luke shared but that were not used by Mark. Most scholars today are reasonably convinced that Matthew and Luke drew these common traditions from a single substantial source. Unfortunately, that source has not survived intact, but it is often called the Sayings Source or Q, from the German word *Quelle*, which means ``source.''

1:60-61). When a delegation from Antiochus appeared in Modein to force the populace to make a pagan sacrifice, Mattathias refused to participate. And when a fellow Jew came forward to obey the order, he slew the offender along with the king's officer and cried out, "Let every one who is zealous for the law and supports the covenant come out with me!" (1 Macc. 2:27).

Mattathias and his sons and followers fled to the hills to launch a guerrilla war against the Seleucids and their Jewish sympathizers. Though he was a priest, Mattathias quickly assumed the role of military leader, even deciding at one point that it was lawful to fight on the sabbath if necessary to defend oneself. The books of 1 and 2 Maccabees in the Apocrypha present the revolt as a holy war fought to protect the Law from pagan incursions. Consequently, the forces of Mattathias not only "struck down sinners in their anger" but also "tore down the altars . . . [and] forcibly circumcised all the uncircumcised boys that they found within the borders of Israel" (1 Macc. 2:44-46).

Mattathias did not live to see the revolt through to its conclusion, dying soon after it began. In his last testament he urged continued resistance under his son Judas Maccabeus. "Pay back the Gentiles in full, and heed what the law commands," he urged. Then he died, "and all Israel mourned for him with great lamentation" (1 Macc. 2:68, 70). His descendants ruled Judea as the Hasmonean dynasty until the time of **Herod the Great** (37-4 B.C.).

MATTHEW
GREEK: MATHTHAIOS; HEBREW or
ARAMAIC: MATTAI or MATTIYAH
"gift of God"

*A*ll four New Testament lists of the 12 apostles (Matthew 10:2-4, Mark 3:16-19, Luke 6:14-16, Acts 1:13) include the name Matthew. His call is described in the Gospel of Matthew: "Jesus . . . saw a man called Matthew sitting at the tax office; and he said to him, 'Follow me.' And he rose and followed him" (Mt. 9:9). This same story appears in the Gospels of Mark and Luke, but the tax collector is called "Levi the son of Alphaeus" (Mk. 2:14) or simply "Levi" (Lk. 5:27). Consequently, most scholars assume that Matthew and Levi were the same person and suggest that **Jesus** may have renamed Levi, just as he had given Simon the new name **Peter**. If so, Matthew may also have been a brother of **James** the son of Alphaeus, who was also one of the 12 apostles—though nowhere in the Scriptures are the two identified as brothers.

As a tax collector, Matthew could have been one of the local inhabitants who bid for the office, agreeing to pay **Herod Antipas**, the ruler of Galilee, a certain sum in advance; any money collected over that amount went into his own pocket. His tax office would have been located at a border to collect tolls on goods being brought from one district to another. Understandably, tax collectors were widely despised, not only because they at least indirectly served the oppressors of the Jews, the Romans, but also because they made a profit by adding their own charges to the established levies. They were classified as unclean individuals with whom pious Jews could not associate. When Jesus ate at Matthew's home in a company of "tax collectors and sinners," he scandalized the Pharisees. Yet to Jesus, this action was a symbol that his kingdom included all people no matter how the world viewed them, "for I came not to call the righteous, but sinners" (Mt. 9:10, 13).

By a tradition recorded in the second century, the apostle Matthew was the author of the Gospel that now bears his name. About the actual writer of the first Gospel, whether Matthew or not, we know very little. He was probably a Jewish Christian with some rabbinic training who evidently lived in Antioch of Syria. His narrative emphasizes Jesus as one who taught with such authority that his listeners were astounded. Although Jesus was increasingly in conflict with the Pharisees over his interpretation of the Law, he nevertheless affirmed that he had come not "to abolish the law and the prophets . . . but to fulfil them" (Mt. 5:17). This emphasis seemed well tailored for Matthew's presumed audience, a group of Jewish Christians who were involved in tense debate with members of the local synagogue and who needed an affirmation of their new identity as a people of God separate from the Jews and with a mission to all nations.

Other than his calling, there are no independent stories about Matthew in the New Testament. According to tradition, he later preached as far afield as Ethiopia, Persia, and Macedonia and died a martyr.

MATTHIAS
(muh thai' uhs) GREEK: MATTHIAS or MATHTHIAS, short for MATTATHIAS
"gift of God"

After the death, resurrection, and ascension of **Jesus**, a group of his followers were gathered in Jerusalem, where **Peter** preached to them, "in all about a hundred

Matthew pauses in counting tax money to heed the call of Jesus.

and twenty" (Acts 1:15). He said that just as the Scriptures had prophesied **Judas Iscariot**'s betrayal of Jesus, so they prophesied that another must be chosen in his place: "His office let another take" (Acts 1:20). The new 12th apostle, however, must have been with Jesus from his baptism to the time of his resurrection and ascension. Two individuals so qualified were put forward: **Joseph Barsabbas** and Matthias.

To determine the Lord's choice, the disciples cast lots, probably by some procedure such as putting stones with the two names on them in a vessel and shaking it until one fell out. The lot fell on Matthias. Nothing more is said about him in the Bible, but church tradition identifies Matthias as one of the 70 whom Jesus had previously sent out "two by two, into every town and place where he himself was about to come" (Lk. 10:1). He is also said to have preached in Judea and died as a martyr.

The priest Melchizedek; a 13th-century stone carving from Chartres cathedral in France

MELCHIZEDEK

(mel kiz' uh dek) HEBREW: MALKISEDEQ
"king of righteousness"

A puzzling biblical figure, Melchizedek is mentioned twice in the Old Testament. Called the "king of Salem [Jerusalem]" and "priest of God Most High" (Gen. 14:18), he first appears bringing bread and wine to welcome **Abraham** back from his victory over the four kings who had captured his nephew **Lot**. Abraham, in turn, gives this dignitary of pre-Israelite Canaan a tenth of the bounty he has won in battle. In the book of Psalms, Melchizedek is named as the representative priest in whose succession the Davidic king is ordained—"priest for ever after the order of Melchizedek" (Ps. 110:4). In the New Testament, Melchizedek becomes the sacral king whose royal holiness transcends all human orders. He seems to be a supernatural figure whose origins and eternal life—"without father or mother or genealogy . . . [who] has neither beginning of days nor end of life" (Heb. 7:3)— foreshadow the divinity of **Jesus**.

Melchizedek is the focus of much speculation. Some interpreters of the Old Testament have proposed that the story of Abraham's paying the tithe to Melchizedek and being blessed by him means that Melchizedek was even more important

than the patriarch himself. To explain such an anomaly, rabbinical scholars sometimes identify Melchizedek with **Shem**, the son of **Noah**, who was thought to have lived until Abraham's time. Other scholars believe that Melchizedek's priesthood was taken away because he blessed Abraham before blessing God. Some maintain that the Melchizedeks mentioned in Genesis and in Psalms are the same person; others say the reference in Psalms is merely symbolic.

Fragments of first-century A.D. scrolls found in the Qumran caves near the Dead Sea in 1956 also refer to Melchizedek. Some historians view the Qumran Melchizedek as an earthly person who met Abraham; others think of him as the archangel **Michael**. The Qumran sources may have been the basis for the New Testament use of Melchizedek to presage Jesus' coming.

The 15th-century Italian artist Masolino included a contemporary pope (left) in his portrait of Judas's replacement, Matthias.

In successive panels from an illuminated manuscript, Saul offers his daughter Merab first to David (left), then to Adriel.

MENAHEM

(muh nah' hem) HEBREW: MENAHEM
"comforter"

The 16th king of Israel, Menahem ruled the northern kingdom for ten years, from about 745 to 738 B.C. Menahem, whose father's name, Gadi, suggests that he came from the tribe of Gad, was not in line for succession to the throne. But after the death of the powerful king **Jeroboam II**, a struggle for control of Israel ensued. **Shallum** ascended to the throne by assassinating Jeroboam's son **Zechariah**, who ruled six months after his father's death. Menahem, in turn, wrested power from Shallum by murdering him a month later.

In Hebrew, the name Menahem means "comforter" and is frequently used in the sense of one who consoles another for the death of a relative; for instance, the name was often given to a child who would comfort his or her parents by taking the place of a sibling who had died. There was, however, very little that was comforting about Menahem's reign. His assassination of Shallum was followed by an attack on the community of Tappuah (in some translations, Tipsah), which resisted his rule: "He sacked it [Tappuah], and he ripped up all the women in it who were with child" (2 Kg. 15:16).

During Menahem's reign, Assyria came to dominate the region. Pul, the name taken by **Tiglath-pileser III** when he conquered Babylon and assumed its throne, demanded 1,000 talents of silver from Menahem as tribute. In order to stabilize his holdings against possible rebels within his domain and rivals beyond his borders, including Judah, Menahem complied. He collected 50 shekels from each of the wealthy men in his kingdom, that amount being about the cost of one slave at the time. It has been calculated that some 60,000 men were thus taxed—

an indication that Israel had a relatively prosperous population. Sending the tribute to Assyria kept the peace in Menahem's kingdom in the short run, but the payment marked the beginning of submission to a foreign power that eventually led to the destruction of Israel.

MENELAUS

(men' uh lay uhs) GREEK: MENELAOS;
from HEBREW: MENAHEM
"comforter"

A duplicitous, self-serving high priest during the reign of the Seleucid king **Antiochus IV Epiphanes**, Menelaus advanced his career through bribery and unscrupulous behavior. He was a Benjaminite or perhaps a Levite from the territory of Benjamin; his brother Simon was chief administrator of the temple. But Menelaus did not come into the priesthood through his family connections.

In 171 B.C., the high priest **Jason** sent Menelaus to Antioch to pay tribute to the Seleucid monarch. But rather than act as Jason's messenger, Menelaus purchased the high priest's position for himself by offering to pay Antiochus 300 talents of silver more than Jason's tribute. And so he returned to Jerusalem, "possessing no qualification for the high priesthood, but having the hot temper of a cruel tyrant and the rage of a savage wild beast" (2 Macc. 4:25). Jason fled to Ammon while Menelaus, by continuing his intrigues, held onto his position as high priest for a decade.

Not long after his return, Menelaus was summoned back to Antioch to make good on his promised payment. Leaving his brother Lysimachus in charge of the temple, the high priest arrived in Antioch during the king's absence and proceeded to bribe

Andronicus, Antiochus's deputy, with several gold vessels that belonged to the temple. Accepting the bribe, Andronicus agreed to kill the former high priest **Onias III**, who was threatening to undermine Menelaus.

Meanwhile, back in Jerusalem, the people were up in arms against Lysimachus, who was plundering the temple. Lysimachus was killed and a delegation was sent to Antiochus to bring Menelaus to justice. With another bribe—this time to a powerful friend of the king—Menelaus got himself acquitted and arranged for his enemies' execution. At this point, Jason reappeared and attempted to seize the high priesthood back from Menelaus. Antiochus interpreted Jason's actions as a challenge to his authority and responded by sacking Jerusalem, murdering many people, and plundering the temple with the help of Menelaus. Eventually, during the reign of **Antiochus V Eupator**, Menelaus lost favor; he was killed about 162 B.C.

MEPHIBOSHETH

(muh fib' uh sheth) HEBREW: MEPIBOSET

"from the mouth of shame"

Mephibosheth was a boy of five when his grandfather, **Saul**, and his father, **Jonathan**, both died in battle with the Philistines on Mount Gilboa. Upon hearing news of the disaster, Mephibosheth's nurse grabbed the child and fled. But in the hasty departure the boy fell, apparently breaking both his legs or feet. Evidently, the injuries were not properly cared for, and Mephibosheth grew up lame.

After **David** gained the kingdom, he wanted to honor his close friendship with Jonathan and sought out a servant of the house of Saul named **Ziba** to learn whether any heirs survived. Brought forward, Mephibosheth approached the king with dread—for new rulers customarily had all members of the previous dynasty executed. "Do not fear," David said; ". . . I will restore to you all the land of Saul your [grand]father; and you shall eat at my table always" (2 Sam. 9:7). While Mephibosheth remained at court, Ziba and his sons worked the restored lands. Later, during **Absalom**'s rebellion, Ziba charged that Mephibosheth was trying to regain the throne for Saul's dynasty, but Mephibosheth was able to convince the king that the charge was untrue. Perhaps believing that both were lying, David separated Ziba from Mephibosheth's service and divided the land between them.

Like his uncle **Ish-bosheth**, Mephibosheth originally had a name that recalled the Canaanite god **Baal**. And thus that name, Meribaal, meaning "from the mouth of the lord," was changed to Mephibosheth, "from the mouth of shame."

MERAB

(mee' rab) HEBREW: MERAB

"increase"

The elder daughter of King **Saul**, Merab found herself a pawn in her father's conflict with **David**. First, Saul offered to give Merab as wife to any man who killed **Goliath**. But though David slew the giant, he was not awarded a royal bride. Later, as David became a famous warrior and a threat to Saul, the king offered Merab to David if he would lead the fight against the Philistines, while secretly hoping that the Philistines would kill David. Shortly before the marriage, however, Saul reneged and gave Merab to a man named Adriel. With him Merab was apparently content and she bore him five sons. Years later, disaster struck when the Gibeonites demanded blood vengeance for a wrong Saul had done them. David, by then king, gave them all five of Merab's sons, whom the Gibeonites slaughtered and left unburied on a mountain.

MERODACH-BALADAN

(mair' oh dahk buh lah' duhn) from AKKADIAN: MARDUK-APLA-IDDINA

"Marduk has given an heir"

An ambitious, tenacious strategist, the Chaldean chieftain Merodach-baladan first appears in the inscriptions of Assyria's King **Tiglath-pileser III** as a ruler of Bit-Yakin in southern Babylonia, along the Persian Gulf. Tiglath-pileser's records show that Merodach-baladan paid tribute to him and, in return, was allowed to maintain tribal authority. But after **Sargon II** assumed the Assyrian throne in 722 B.C., Merodach-baladan began seeking greater power. Allying himself with other southern tribes and the Elamites, he seized control of Babylon and reigned for the next 12 years. In 720, when Sargon staged a battle at the city of Der, Merodach-baladan and his troops arrived late, leaving his Elamite allies to represent his interests but taking advantage of the stalemate there to cling to his throne. Merodach-baladan continued to rule until 710, when Sargon marched into Babylonia and forced him to retreat into his native marshes.

After Sargon's death, Merodach-baladan began to reassert himself, and it was probably during this period that he managed to send an envoy to Judah's King **Hezekiah**, ostensibly to inquire about the king's health but perhaps also to ask for support in his battles against Assyria. Despite such maneuvering, Sargon's son and successor **Sennacherib** vanquished Merodach-baladan, who fled along the Persian Gulf to Elam, where he died, probably in 694 B.C.

MESHA

(mee' shah) HEBREW: MESA
"salvation" or "savior"

Mesha, the sheep-breeding king of Moab, inherited from his father a land subjugated by Israel and a requirement that he pay annual tribute in the form of 100,000 lambs and the wool from 100,000 rams to the ruler of the northern kingdom. But after King **Ahab** of Israel died, Mesha rebelled. Joined by King **Jehoshaphat** of Judah and the king of Edom, King **Jehoram** of Israel attacked Moab from the south—having received the prediction of adequate water for their campaign and an oracle of victory from the prophet **Elisha**. At first they were successful, destroying cities, slaughtering people, felling trees, ruining land, and blocking springs of water.

Faced with seemingly certain defeat, Mesha took drastic action, which both sides believed saved his land: "He took his eldest son who was to reign in his stead, and offered him for a burnt offering upon the wall. And there came great wrath upon Israel; and they withdrew from him and returned to their own land" (2 Kg. 3:27).

The prophet Micah by French miniaturist André Beauneveu (c. 1360-1403)

Mesha sacrifices his son; detail from a 13th-century German manuscript

METHUSELAH

(muh thoo' zuh luh) HEBREW: METUSELAH
"javelin man" or "worshiper of the deity"

Most often recalled for his extraordinary longevity and fertility, Methuselah was the son of **Enoch** and the grandfather of **Noah**. Becoming the father of **Lamech** at the age of 187, Methuselah lived another 782 years and had other sons and daughters. "Thus all the days of Methuselah were nine hundred and sixty-nine years" (Gen. 5:27), making him the longest-lived person in the Bible.

However, when his lifespan is considered in the context of the prevailing Babylonian tradition in which ancestors were said to have lived for tens of thousands of years, Methuselah spent a comparatively short time on earth. He did not live even the thousand years that, according to Psalms 90:4, were but a single day in the life of the Lord. Methuselah died in the year of the Flood.

MICAH

(mi' kuh) HEBREW: MIKA, abbreviated form of MIKAYAHU
"[one] who is like Yahweh"

An Ephraimite who lived in the tribal hill country, Micah is the central figure in the first of two episodes that appear as appendices to the book of Judges. When Micah confessed to stealing 1,100 silver pieces from his mother and returned them to her, she rewarded his repentance by giving 200 pieces to a silversmith, who crafted for Micah's home shrine "a graven image and a molten image" (Jg. 17:4). Micah then hired a young Levite to serve as its priest.

Sometime later, five spies from the migrating tribe of **Dan** came to Micah's home and obtained from the Levite an oracle promising success in their journey. After the spies had found a new tribal homeland, a Danite army returned to Micah's house, seized the young priest, and took him, the images, and other elements of Micah's shrine with them. The story explains the origins of the cult of Dan, linking its lineage to **Moses**, and dramatically portrays the political and religious anarchy of the period during which the Israelite tribes conquered and settled Canaan.

MICAH 2

At the outset of the biblical book that bears his name, Micah is identified as coming from Moresheth, a small village on the border of Philistia, 20 miles southwest of Jerusalem. The designation indicates that he prophesied outside his hometown—probably in Jerusalem—and that his place of origin would have been more recognizable to his audience than the name of his family. But the small number of surviving oracles attributed to him lack any explicit historical references beyond dating his ministry to the last half of the eighth century B.C. and the beginning of the seventh, or during the reigns of three kings of Judah: **Jotham**, **Ahaz**, and **Hezekiah**, who reigned between 742 and 687 B.C.

Each of these kings faced the enormous challenge of either protecting Judah's borders from an Assyrian threat or, in the case of Hezekiah, subjugating himself as a vassal. In both circumstances, heavy taxes had to be levied to maintain an army or pay tribute to Assyria. Owing to these political pressures and economic hardships, most citizens of Jerusalem lived on the edge of survival and became easy prey to their corrupt leaders. On behalf of the majority of impoverished people who lived in Jerusalem and the provincial villages, Micah excoriated the wealthy landowners who oppressed the poor, the judges who were cannibals in the way they consumed people, and the opportunistic prophets who offered only false hopes of peace.

Although no information about Micah himself is preserved, his reputation as a prophetic challenger to kings was well enough known to be cited more than seven decades later, during the reign of King **Jehoiakim**. Defending the prophet **Jeremiah**, certain elders recalled that, when Micah

THE MOABITE STONE

Remarkably, King Mesha's own account of the ninth-century B.C. war of Israel and Judah against Moab has been preserved in a black basalt stele discovered east of the Jordan in 1868. Before it could be purchased, local Arabs smashed the stone—but only after a French scholar had copied the inscription. The reassembled fragments are now in the Louvre museum in Paris.

The 34 lines on the Moabite Stone (also called the Mesha Inscription) commemorate the king's building activities as well as his military accomplishments; his achievements are attributed to the favor of the Moabite god Chemosh. The inscription confirms Israel's oppression of Moab under the house of Omri, Mesha's revolt against Omri's son (actually his grandson, Jehoram), and a brutal slaughter to appease Chemosh—in this instance, the Gadites living at Ataroth rather than Mesha's own son, as reported in 2 Kings. The Moabite Stone bears the oldest known reference to Israel's God, Yahweh, outside the Bible. It records Mesha's capture of Israel's sacred vessels and his presentation of them to Chemosh.

The Moabite Stone dates to c. 840-820 B.C.

had once pronounced dire judgments against Judah, King Hezekiah had wisely spared his life. They cited Micah's very words: "Zion shall be plowed as a field; Jerusalem shall become a heap of ruins, and the mountain of the house a wooded height" (Mic. 3:12; Jer. 26:18). Noting that Micah's harsh criticisms caused Hezekiah to repent, the elders pointed out how God in response had withdrawn the punishment he had planned and promised instead peace from foreign aggression throughout the king's lifetime.

As were most other Old Testament prophets, including his older contemporary **Isaiah**, Micah was an agent of God and not simply a political analyst. When people reacted to Micah's words, they were actually responding to God himself rather than to the personal opinions of the prophet. Micah's provocative eloquence often gave a sharp poetic bite to his words of judgment. Once he issued a dirge for the nation of Judah in which he lamented the destruction of cities leading to the very gates of Jerusalem itself. Despite the obscurity of some of these cities and the forgotten subtleties of the original Hebrew text, scholars can detect a series of sophisticated, satirical puns. His advice to the city of Beth-le-aphrah ("house of dust") is a play on the last part of that name: "Roll yourselves [from the verb 'aphar] in the dust" (Mic. 1:10); rolling in dust was the way people of that time demonstrated grief or mourning.

Though his oracles often sound like final judgments, the pronouncements recollected in the book of Jeremiah confirm that Micah's stringent words served more as threats to evoke change than as condemnation. He offered the kings and others he addressed the possibility of confessing their sins in the hope of God's pardon and blessing.

The organization of the prophecies in his book reveal Micah's intent. Though many scholars now think that only the first three chapters contain oracles from the historical Micah, the arrangement of those chapters, as well as the additional traditions found in the remaining four chapters, conforms to a pattern of judgments followed immediately by promises of restoration and comfort. This horizon of hope in God's mercy, which always accompanies the harshest words of criticism, comes into clear view at the end of his book: "Who is a God like thee, pardoning iniquity and passing over transgression?" (Mic. 7:18). The authors of two Gospels, Matthew and John, found in one of Micah's messages of hope a messianic promise that from Bethlehem, "little to be among the clans of Judah" would come forth "one who is to be ruler in Israel" (Mic. 5:2).

While Micah and Isaiah prophesied in the same period, neither mentioned the other in their oracles preserved in the Bible. However, Micah's promise that **David**'s kingdom would be restored—best known for the phrase "they shall beat their swords into plowshares, and their spears into pruning hooks" (Mic. 4:3)—is the same as that assigned to Isaiah in Isaiah 2:2-5. The attributions were made at a time later than either of the two prophets, suggesting that the

The archangel Michael; a 13th-century enamel from the treasury of San Marco in Venice

scribes of a subsequent generation may have been divided over who actually spoke the words. Nor is this the only example in which Isaiah employs some expressions remarkably similar to those of Micah. Whatever their relationship, Micah seems more provincially oriented than the prophet Isaiah, for he lacks Isaiah's breadth in addressing international issues and larger issues of reform. Micah is remembered, instead, for his concentrated but equally pungent focus on purity of worship and matters of social injustice, best exemplified by the admonition, "What does the Lord require of you but to do justice, and to love kindness, and to walk humbly with your God?" (Mic. 6:8).

MICAIAH

(mi kai' yuh) HEBREW: MIKAYAHU
"who is like Yahweh?"

The story of Micaiah the son of Imlah illustrates the conflict over prophecy in ancient Israel. When King **Ahab** of Israel and King **Jehoshaphat** of Judah wanted to attack the city of Ramoth-Gilead together, they consulted the hundreds of prophets of Yahweh that served the royal courts. Led by **Zedekiah**, these prophets unanimously predicted victory. Jehoshaphat, however, was suspicious of the court prophets and insisted on seeking an independent oracle. Ahab summoned Micaiah, warning that his prophecies were always of evils to come.

At first Micaiah too predicted triumph. But when Ahab urged him to speak the truth, he recounted a vision of Israel's leaderless forces, "as sheep that have no shepherd" (1 Kg. 22:17). He further told of a vision of the Lord enthroned with the host of heaven, in which God sent an untruthful spirit into the mouths of the court prophets to entice Ahab to death in battle. Incensed by the charge, Zedekiah struck Micaiah on the cheek. Ahab chose to believe Zedekiah's predictions of victory and imprisoned Micaiah. In the battle that followed, however, Ahab was killed. There is no other mention of the prophet Micaiah in the Bible.

MICHAEL

(mai' kuhl) HEBREW: MIKAEL
"who is like God?"

Although the archangel Michael is mentioned only a few times in the Bible, he is given several distinctive roles in Jewish and Christian apocalyptic tradition: He is said to be one of the four archangels chosen to stand beside God's throne, the others being **Gabriel**, **Raphael**, and **Uriel**; the angel who records the names of persons who merit everlasting life and is the gatekeeper of paradise; the intermediary who brought God's law to **Moses** and revelations of the future to **Elijah**; and the patron and defender of Israel against its enemies. However, only the last of these traditions can be substantiated by biblical evidence.

Michael's name first appears in the Bible after the prophet **Daniel** has completed a three-week purification in preparation for revelations. An awesome figure, possibly Gabriel, "his face like the appearance of lightning, his eyes like flaming torches . . . and the sound of his words like the noise of a multitude," comes to deliver the message that Michael is "your prince" (Dan. 10:5-6, 21). This powerful guardian will protect Israel from its earthly enemies and ultimately lead the host of angels in the final battle against the forces of evil.

Michael appears twice in the New Testament. In the letter of Jude, he is recollected as one who fought with the devil over the disposal of Moses' body, and in Revelation, he appears as the leader of the righteous angels in a battle that ends with Satan's fall from heaven.

MICHAL

(mai' kuhl) HEBREW: MICHAL
"who is like God?"

The daughter of King **Saul** and wife of **David**, Michal was a woman of strong will caught between the two warrior antagonists. As Saul grew to hate David, Michal fell in love with him. Saul thought to put David in peril by offering Michal as a bride—but at the price of killing 100 Philistines. David accepted the challenge, killed 200 Philistines, and claimed Michal as his own.

When Saul decided to get rid of David, Michal sided with her husband and helped David escape by putting a dummy in his bed and pretending that he was sick. Saul soon annulled the marriage and gave Michal as wife to a man named **Palti**.

About ten years later, when David was king, he demanded to have Michal back. Taken from Palti, Michal was led to the king—her husband "weeping after her all the way" (2 Sam. 3:16) to the outskirts of Jerusalem. By this time, however, Michal's ardor for David had turned to contempt. After she scorned the king's enthusiastic dancing as he brought the ark of the covenant into Jerusalem, David refused to treat her any longer as his wife, and she died childless.

MIDIAN

(mid' ee uhn) HEBREW: MIDYAN

Midian was one of the six sons of **Abraham**'s second wife **Keturah**. Before his death, Abraham bestowed the bulk of his estate on his son **Isaac** and sent "the sons of his concubines . . . eastward to the east country" (Gen. 25: 6).

Little more is known of Midian himself, but his descendants, the nomadic Midianites, wandered far and wide—from Moab east of the Dead Sea to the Arabian and Sinai deserts and into Egypt. They first appear in the Bible as the traders who rescued **Joseph** from the pit into which his brothers had cast him. The Midianites sold Joseph to the Ishmaelites, who took him to Egypt. Later, **Moses** married the daughter of the Midianite priest **Jethro**. The arid geographical territory the Midianites occupied as compared with that of the Israelites, their distant relatives, reflected the inferiority of their legacy.

MIRIAM

(mir' ee uhm) HEBREW: MIRYAM

"bitterness" or "plump"

Unnamed in her first dramatic appearance in the book of Exodus and rarely mentioned at all in the Scriptures thereafter, Miriam is nevertheless an important figure in the history of Israel. She was the first woman to be given the title of prophetess and was also a political leader along with her brothers **Moses** and **Aaron**. Whether as God's instrument, a charismatic heroine of her wandering people, or a rebel against divine authority, she is always seen in the context of climactic events.

When three-month-old Moses was left floating in a rush basket among reeds at the riverbank, his sister stood guard at a distance. Her feelings are not described, but her self-possession and quick wit are soon revealed. The moment Pharaoh's daughter saw the crying infant, Miriam approached with the offer to find a Hebrew nurse. Her ruse disguised the reunion of the baby with his mother, **Jochebed**. Thus, it was Miriam who helped change the course of history by protecting the baby who would become Israel's greatest spiritual leader.

She is next mentioned, this time by name, leading the ecstatic victory dance of the Israelite women to celebrate the salvation of Israel from the Egyptians and the drowning of Pharaoh's charioteers in the sea of reeds. This merry festival, accompanied by the striking and rattling of tambourines, was a venerable Hebrew custom. The famous

Miriam, a stained-glass panel by Edward Burne-Jones (1833-1898)

words of the Song of Miriam are among the oldest poetic couplets in the Scriptures: "Sing to the Lord, for he has triumphed gloriously; the horse and his rider he has thrown into the sea" (Ex. 15:21). At this point, she is called a prophetess, perhaps because her music and dancing kindled a spiritual euphoria that was a form of worship.

The third mention of Miriam suggests, unfortunately, that pride in her status as a spiritual guide led to disaster. Claiming that they were the equals of Moses as prophets, she and Aaron rebelled against their brother. "Has the Lord indeed spoken only through Moses?" they asked. "Has he not spoken through us also?" (Num. 12:2). Scholars believe that the wording of the original Hebrew implies that Miriam was actually the instigator and that Aaron merely followed her lead.

Ironically, Moses had been more than eager to share the burdens of leadership and the gift of prophecy, but this was not God's plan. Furious, the Lord confronted the rebels in a pillar of cloud and defined their brother's unique status: "With him I speak mouth to mouth, clearly, and not in dark speech; and he beholds the form of the Lord" (Num. 12:8). As punishment, Miriam was struck with leprosy (likely some disfiguring skin disease). Although Aaron was untouched, he implored that she be spared. Moses too interceded for his mutinous sister. But the Lord was adamant that she endure the ailment for seven days and be kept outside the camp for that period.

One confusing element in the story is the additional explanation that Miriam revolted because Moses had married a Cushite woman, perhaps a Nubian or an Arab. Some experts have suggested that she was punished with the whiteness of leprosy because she objected to the woman's black skin. But most scholars believe that the essential theme of Miriam's insurgency was to gain the right to prophesy in the Lord's name. When Miriam died during the years of wandering, she was buried at Kadesh; her tomb was venerated in later generations.

Founder of the female prophetic tradition and first of many musical women in the Bible, Miriam is recalled in the Scriptures as the equal of her brothers, as when the Lord reminds the Hebrews, "I sent before you Moses, Aaron, and Miriam" (Mic. 6:4). According to nonbiblical tradition, she, like her brothers, died only when God kissed her, because the angel of death was powerless before her. By the time of **Herod the Great**, her name, which is the Hebrew form of Mary, was commonly given to Jewish girls, including **Jesus'** mother and several other women in the New Testament. Herod's second and third wives were named Mariamne, a Greek form of the name.

MNASON

(nay' suhn) GREEK form of HEBREW: MANASSEH
"[God] has made [me] forget"

A Cypriot Christian living in or near Jerusalem, Mnason merits a brief mention in the New Testament for playing host to the apostle **Paul** and his Gentile companions at the end of their third missionary journey, as they returned from Caesarea to Jerusalem about A.D. 57. He is referred to as "an early disciple" (Acts 21:16), which probably means that he was one of the founding members of the church at Jerusalem. Some students interpret the word "early" to mean that Mnason was one of the original disciples—perhaps among the 120 who are mentioned in Acts 1:15—personally recruited by **Jesus**. It is more likely, however, that he was an early convert to the church.

MOAB

(moh' ab) HEBREW: MOAB
"from my father"

A fter **Lot** was spared from the destruction of Sodom and Gomorrah, he went up into the hills above Zoar with his two daughters. Lot's wife had been turned into a pillar of salt for looking back toward Sodom in disobedience to God's command. So, to preserve their line, Lot's two daughters conspired to conceive children by their father. Moab was the son born to Lot and his elder daughter, while the incestuous union between Lot and his younger daughter produced Moab's half brother, Ben-ammi.

The descendants of Moab, the Moabites, were closely related to the descendants of Ben-ammi, the Ammonites; through Lot, both tribes were connected to the Israelites, but they were often at war with them. Once Moab's birth is recorded, he is not mentioned again in the Bible. Further references to Moab mean the land east of the Dead Sea between the rivers Arnon and Zered or the Moabite people.

MORDECAI

(mohr' duh kai) HEBREW: MORDEKAY;
derived from MARDUK, the Babylonian god
"most excellent man" or "belonging to Marduk"

T he hero of the book of Esther, Mordecai foiled a plot to kill all his fellow Jews living in exile in the Persian empire. Mordecai had adopted his younger cousin **Esther** when she was orphaned, and she grew into a

Haman forced to lead Mordecai in triumph; a third-century A.D. wall painting from a synagogue in Dura-Europos, Iraq

devout and beautiful young woman. When King **Ahasuerus** chose Esther to succeed **Vashti** as his queen, Mordecai saw a chance to improve the plight of his captive people. Stationing himself near the palace, he happened to overhear two of the king's eunuchs scheming to assassinate Ahasuerus. He told Esther, who warned the king, and the plotters were hanged.

Soon, however, Mordecai antagonized the grand vizier, **Haman**, by refusing to bow as the self-important official made his daily rounds. Haman learned that Mordecai was a Jew, launched a plan to annihilate the Jews, and ordered the erection of a tall gallows on which to hang Mordecai. Again Mordecai used Esther as an intermediary, asking her to intercede with the king. As Esther carefully developed her plan to help save the Jews, Ahasuerus belatedly learned that it was Mordecai who had saved him from the assassination attempt. The king was surprised that Mordecai had not been rewarded for the deed and asked Haman's advice on how to honor a hero. Thinking that the king meant the tribute for him, Haman suggested a grand procession. To the vizier's great shock

and humiliation, the king put him in charge of the parade for his enemy Mordecai.

Ultimately, Esther told Ahasuerus of her people's peril. Enraged, the king had Haman hanged from the gallows intended for Mordecai's execution. He also gave Mordecai Haman's signet ring and named him the new grand vizier. Mordecai led his fellow Jews in taking vengeance on their opponents, after which they held a grand celebration. The accomplishments of Esther and Mordecai are celebrated in the two-day Jewish Feast of Purim—the first day of which, by the time of **Judas Maccabeus**, was known as Mordecai's day.

MOSES

(moh' ziz, -zes) HEBREW: MOSHEH
"drawn out"

The preeminent figure in the Old Testament, Moses was a shy, humble man who sought obscurity. But when the Lord goaded him into rescuing the Israelites from their harsh bondage in Egypt, this reluctant hero revealed the courage, tenacity, and moral fervor required to forge a nation out of an undisciplined horde of mutually suspicious slaves who had forgotten their patriarchal past and lacked all sense of shared community. Although he would demonstrate his own flawed humanity more than once, Moses was the great spiritual leader of his people who received from God on Mount Sinai the Law that guided Israel throughout the centuries.

All that is known about the man himself is in the Torah, or Pentateuch, the first five books of the Bible, and in a few scattered references elsewhere in the Old Testament. He is not mentioned in any primary sources outside the Scriptures; neither is the Exodus, the Hebrew migration that he led. Yet it is the personality of Moses that unites Israel throughout its history, for he plays a unique variety of roles in the national consciousness: lawgiver, military and political leader, prophet, and founder of the state religion.

Moses was born to a Levite named Amram and his wife **Jochebed** sometime after the rise to power of an Egyptian Pharaoh who was concerned by the number of descendants of **Joseph** and his 11 brothers within the kingdom. "Come, let us deal shrewdly with them," he said, "lest they multiply, and, if war befall us, they join our enemies and fight against us and escape from the land" (Ex. 1:10). First, Pharaoh increased the workload of the Israelites, but they still prospered. Next, he ordered two Hebrew midwives to kill all male infants at

FEAST OF PURIM

Both Jews and Christians of antiquity argued against including the book of Esther in the biblical canon—in part because the original text contained no reference to God and in part because the festival of Purim mentioned therein was thought to be pagan in origin. The first objection was countered by the apocryphal additions to Esther, six extended passages totaling 107 verses that usually appear as chapters 11 through 16 of Catholic Bibles, though they can also be integrated into the text.

Scholars have attempted to link the Jewish festival to both Babylonian (*puhru*) and Persian (*purdighan*) New Year festivals. Indeed, Purim is celebrated on the 14th and 15th days of Adar, last month of the biblical year, corresponding to February–March.

The discovery of Moses becomes a triumphal procession in this painting by Lawrence Alma-Tadema (1836-1912).

birth, but the women outwitted him. Finally, not long before Moses' birth, the Egyptian king issued his infamous edict: "Every son that is born to the Hebrews you shall cast into the Nile" (Ex. 1:22).

DESTINED FOR GREATNESS

Moses' mother was able to keep him hidden until he was three months old, but was then forced to abandon him in a basket of bulrushes among the reeds beside the banks of the Nile. Keeping watch, his sister **Miriam** saw that he was rescued and adopted into the Egyptian royal family by a daughter of Pharaoh himself. Miriam ensured that Jochebed was hired to nurse the infant. Perhaps significantly, other great national heroes in the ancient Middle East, such as Sargon of Akkad and **Cyrus II** of Persia, were said to have been saved in infancy by being set afloat in a crude basket. Most probably, the folktale quality of these stories, of which more than 30 survive today, is meant to foreshadow the career of an extraordinary individual who will someday have to deal with ominous events. In Moses' case, God's hand is evident, directing the future of Israel. Indeed, the very name Moses, pop-

ularly interpreted in its Hebrew form to mean drawn out of the water, might more precisely indicate that the day would come when Moses would draw his people out of their slavery in Egypt.

Of his childhood and adolescence the Scriptures divulge nothing. One might reasonably assume that Moses would have been given the best possible education in reading, writing, weaponry, and horsemanship, making him to all outward appearances an Egyptian noble. Such schooling would have prepared him well for his face-to-face confrontations with his Egyptian adversaries. Yet, the adult Moses did not forget his origins. One day, when he was about 40 years old, he happened to see an Egyptian beating a Hebrew. Enraged, he killed his adopted countryman and buried the corpse in the sand. The very next day, he intervened in a fight between two Israelites, one of whom blurted out, "Do you mean to kill me as you killed the Egyptian?" (Ex. 2:14). Moses was horrified, realizing that his crime had been discovered, and fled to the land of Midian in the Sinai desert east of the Gulf of Suez just as Pharaoh determined to punish him with death.

*Moses and the daughters of Jethro at the well; detail of a painting
by Sandro Botticelli (c. 1444-1510)*

Characteristically, Moses once again defended the helpless as soon as he reached Midian, driving away some shepherds who were bullying the seven daughters of a local priest named **Jethro**. In gratitude, Jethro gave the brave fugitive his daughter **Zipporah** in marriage. And thus Moses, presumably reared in the lap of luxury, became an unassuming shepherd. As descendants of **Abraham** and his second wife, **Keturah**, the Midianites were distantly related to the Israelites. And the Lord in time chose a Midianite sacred place, "the mountain of God" (Ex. 3:1), known as either Sinai or Horeb, to reveal himself and his plan for the deliverance of the Israelites.

After Moses' flight, Pharaoh died, but the new ruler, possibly history's Ramses II, drove his Hebrew slaves even harder in an ambitious program of public building. Moved by their oppression, the Lord manifested himself to Moses in the wilderness as a fire burning within a bush but not consuming it. Intrigued by this phenomenon, the solitary shepherd edged closer and was startled to hear his name called out. But the speaker, God, warned him to take off his sandals, following an ancient custom practiced whenever one entered a holy place. Moses, who had not previously demonstrat-

ed unusual piety or interest in religious matters, became terrified and hid his face when the Lord explained that he was "the God of your father, the God of Abraham, the God of Isaac, and the God of Jacob" (Ex. 3:6). According to traditional belief, it was fatal to look directly at divinity.

SIGNS FROM GOD

His awe did not prevent Moses from stubbornly resisting God's command that he liberate the Israelites and lead them out of Egypt and across the harsh Sinai desert peninsula into Canaan. Frankly humble and lacking in ambition, Moses argued that he was not worthy of such responsibility, did not know the Lord's true name, and could not persuade the Hebrews to follow him. God replied that Moses should explain that he had been sent by "I AM WHO I AM" (Ex. 3:14), a phrase with similarities in Hebrew to the sacred Israelite name for God, Yahweh. Moreover, the Lord provided Moses with signs of divine power: He would be able to turn his shepherd's rod into a snake and back again; show a hand appearing leprous, then cleansed; and, if necessary, turn water from the Nile into blood.

Still, the exile held back, quibbling that he lacked the required eloquence, being "slow of speech and of tongue" (Ex. 4:10). Exasperated, the Lord agreed to allow **Aaron**, Moses' elder brother still living in Egypt, to act as his spokesman. And so Moses gave in and began the journey westward to Egypt with his family, carrying the shepherd's rod with which he would perform signs before Pharaoh. Aaron, alerted by the Lord, came out to meet his brother in the desert. Their mission began.

The initial outcome was disastrous. After convincing the Hebrew elders that he truly was God's envoy, Moses went before Pharaoh. "The God of the Hebrews has met with us," he said; "let us go, we pray, a three days' journey into the wilderness, and sacrifice to the Lord" (Ex. 5:3). The Egyptian ruler, himself considered a deity in an official state religion with numerous gods, sneered that he had never heard of the Lord. Suspecting that Moses' request was a ruse for permanent escape, he ordered the Hebrews back to work. Worse, he added to their burdens by increasing their work quotas and decreeing that they would henceforth have to gather their own straw for

As instructed by God from the burning bush, Moses removes his shoes before entering the sacred place; a painting by Domenico Fetti (1589-1624).

making bricks rather than have access to government supplies. When the Israelites understandably turned against Moses, he cried out to God in despair: "O Lord, why hast thou done evil to this people? Why didst thou ever send me?" (Ex. 5:22). In an unprecedented affirmation, God repeated his promise of redemption, and Moses reported this to the Hebrews. But they turned a deaf ear, "because of their broken spirit and their cruel bondage" (Ex. 6:9).

PLAGUES UPON THE EGYPTIANS

Nonetheless, inspired by God, the two elderly but still vigorous men, Moses, 80, and Aaron, 83, defied Pharaoh in his own court by demanding that their people be released. The Lord had already disclosed that the king would not yield. "I will harden Pharaoh's heart," he had explained, making it necessary to perform "great acts of judgment" (Ex. 7:3, 4). Even after a contest in which Aaron used supernatural power to defeat the facile tricks of the Egyptian magicians, Pharaoh was still unmoved. Next God called down a series of plagues, ten in all. The first, which turned all the waters of Egypt to blood, struck at the very heart of the nation, for the Nile was the source of all life and fertility. Though the Bible is recording the work of God, this plague and the next eight—frogs, gnats, flies, cattle disease, boils, hail, locusts, daytime darkness—all reflect natural phenomena of the Middle East. For example, the Nile in high midsummer flood often looks reddish, either because of minute organisms or dirt particles. The cattle disease could have been anthrax spread by the flies of the previous plague. In spring in the Nile valley, a powerful hot wind known as *khamsin* can literally blacken the air with blowing sand and dust.

Gradually, these accumulating horrors—which never afflicted the Hebrews but drove the Egyptians to desperation—wore down Pharaoh's intransigence. He agreed to release the Israelites but not their flocks. The Lord was not satisfied.

As foreordained in order to reveal his invincible might, God prepared the final and most horrifying plague: at midnight on the 14th of Nisan, the first month in the Hebrew calendar, the firstborn of all human and animal families were to die. The Hebrews were instructed to save their children and flocks by sacrificing an unblemished young lamb in the evening and daubing its blood on the two doorposts and the lintel at the front of each house, so that the Lord would pass over it on his mission of vengeance. Their compliance would be commemorated in the Passover feast of the new nation. God's

ROUTE OF THE EXODUS

When Moses and the Israelites made their escape from Egypt's Pharaoh, they entered on a long journey through the Sinai Peninsula, a largely barren and sparsely occupied triangle of land about 230 miles long from north to south and some 150 miles wide at its northern end. Forty years later the Israelites emerged to invade Canaan from the east, crossing the Jordan near Jericho. Though the Bible names many places where they camped, few can be identified with certainty.

The Exodus falls into three sections. First was the journey from Egypt to Mount Sinai, where the Law was given, and on to Kadesh-barnea, located at the far southern end of Canaan. It began

with the miraculous crossing of the Red Sea, more properly translated ``sea of reeds,'' from the Hebrew, yam suph. Some scholars identify this as Lake Sirbonis on the Mediterranean coast, though it is very close to the forbidden Way to the Land of the Philistines. Others hold to its traditional identification with the Gulf of Suez, though most today believe that it refers to a body of water such as the shallow, reed-fringed Bitter Lakes, which perhaps had an outlet into the gulf and thus to the Red Sea itself.

Once free of the Egyptians, the Israelites headed toward Mount Sinai, traditionally identified with a 7,500-foot peak at the southern end of the peninsula

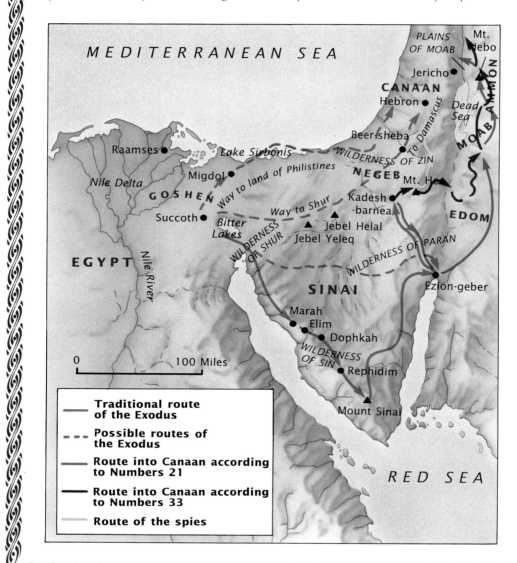

known in Arabic as Jebel
Musa, the Mountain of
Moses. This identification,
however, can be document-
ed no earlier than the fourth
century A.D., more than
1,500 years after the
event, and numerous
scholars have chal-
lenged its validity.
They have proposed
that the Israelites trav-
eled more directly
across the Sinai,
perhaps following
the Way to Shur or
another of the
desert trails. In this
case, Mount
Sinai may well
have been the
shorter but still
prominent
mountain today
called Jebel

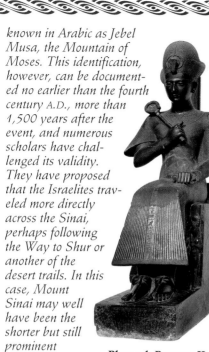

Pharaoh Ramses II

Yeleq (3,566 feet) or perhaps Jebel Helal
(2,920 feet). After the epochal events at
Mount Sinai over the course of nearly a
year, the people traveled toward Kadesh-
barnea, stopping at more than 20 sites
listed in Numbers 33. None can be identified except Ezion-geber at the northern
tip of the Gulf of Aqabah.

At Kadesh, the people were frightened
by their spies, refused to invade Canaan,
and were condemned to 40 years in the
wilderness. Most of that long second section of the journey was evidently spent in
the region around Kadesh and in the area
north of Ezion-Geber, but the Bible passes
over it almost in silence. The narrative
resumes with the death of Aaron, less
than a year before Moses' death.
Numbers 21:4 suggests that on their way
to Moab the Israelites made another
detour south to the Gulf of Aqabah (called
the Red Sea) to avoid passing through
Edom. The itinerary in Numbers 33, however, suggests that they traveled across
Edom before turning north toward Moab.

The final months of Israel's journey—
the third section of the trek—were filled
with conflict, as the Israelites swept up
the eastern side of the Dead Sea and
conquered the territory north of Moab.
Only then was the long passage ended,
as the tribes reached the Jordan and prepared to enter the Promised Land.

command to Moses and Aaron was explicit:
"This day shall be for you a memorial day,
and you shall keep it as a feast to the Lord;
throughout your generations you shall observe it as an ordinance for ever" (Ex. 12:14).

Precisely at midnight, God struck dead
all of Egypt's firstborn, including Pharaoh's
child. Terrified, the monarch summoned
Moses and Aaron before sunrise and urged
them to leave immediately with all of their
people and their flocks and herds. Consequently, the departure was so hurried that
the Hebrews were not able to leaven that
day's bread. According to the biblical narrative, this incident was the origin of the Jewish seven-day feast of unleavened bread that
begins with Passover.

TOWARD THE PROMISED LAND

After 430 years in a foreign land, the Israelites trekked northeastward toward their
spiritual home in Canaan. The book of Exodus gives their number as 600,000 men on
foot in addition to women and children.
Since this figure would imply a total of perhaps 2.5 million, some suggest that it is exaggerated. According to linguistic scholars,
the term translated in this passage as "thousand" can also mean "clan"; 600 clans, or
tribal units, may have totaled only 15,000 to
20,000 people making the flight. Whatever
their numbers, the marchers faced dangers,
first from Egyptian troops manning border
forts who were likely to try to prevent their
escape, and later from hostile people en
route to Canaan. God led his chosen people
around these obstacles by assuming the
form of a pillar of cloud during daylight
hours, a pillar of fire at night.

Eventually, however, the Israelites were
trapped between the pursuing Egyptian
army and a body of water called the sea of
reeds in Hebrew. This was most likely one
of several shallow bodies of water north of
the Gulf of Suez, an extension of the Red
Sea, the designation given in the English
translation of the Bible. Meanwhile, the
Egyptians had come to regret the loss of
their slaves and wanted them brought back.
Summoning an army with all his charioteers, Pharaoh set off in hot pursuit. Characteristically, when the Hebrews spied the
advance of the royal forces, they became
frightened, lost their faith, and blamed
Moses for their plight: "For it would have
been better for us to serve the Egyptians
than to die in the wilderness" (Ex. 14:12).

At this point, the Lord instructed Moses
to raise his shepherd's rod over the sea. As
the pillar of cloud intervened, hiding the
Hebrews from their pursuers in a false
night, a powerful wind from the east drove

*As Moses and Aaron (center) watch, the Israelites gather manna;
an early-17th-century stained-glass panel from the church of
St. Etienne du Mont in Paris.*

back the waters, forming a pathway of dry land between two walls of water. The Israelites strode quickly to safety, but the heavy chariots of their pursuers became mired in the bottom mud. Toward sunrise, Moses followed the divine command to stretch his hand over the sea and release the waters. The charioteers, horses, and foot soldiers of the king were drowned beneath the surging waves.

Exhilarated, Moses and the Israelites sang one of the most magnificent psalms recorded in the Scriptures, beginning with the famed couplet, "I will sing to the Lord, for he has triumphed gloriously; the horse and his rider he has thrown into the sea" (Ex. 15:1). Although phrased in the first person, the verses nowhere mention Moses' name. Moses was making certain that God alone was given the credit for Israel's victories and good fortune. He steadfastly refused to let himself become idolized as the center of a cult of personality.

MANNA FROM HEAVEN

Even so, Moses continued to act as the single mortal instrument of God's grace and power, especially when the faith of the Hebrews wavered. When they complained that water in the desert was bitter, the Lord told Moses to throw a tree into the water, which became fresh. When they argued that they should have remained in Egypt where the food was delicious, Moses transmitted God's promise that quail would soon flock round for them to eat and a honey-tasting food, manna, would be found in abundance on the ground after the morning dew each day ex-

cept the sabbath. Yet again, as the band continued its march through the wilderness, the water supplies were completely exhausted. The usual grumbling began, but God instructed Moses to strike a rock with his rod and sweet water flowed forth from it.

In the third month of their journey, the Israelites reached Mount Sinai, the site divinely chosen for the ultimate goal of their liberation from Egypt, sealing the covenant that formed the religious and ethical foundation of the nation of Israel. Ever afterward, the people would be held to belief in one God, and they would be bound to follow his commandments. Descending to the mountain from heaven, God appeared in fire and smoke, accompanied by the rumbling of thunder, earth tremors, and the blast of a very loud trumpet. The Hebrews were frightened, but Moses climbed to the top of the shrouded desert peak and received the summary of ethical conduct known as the Ten Commandments. The first dictate is the foundation of all that follow: "You shall have no other gods before me" (Ex. 20:3). This and the next two commandments deal with humanity's relationship to the Lord; the other seven concern relations between human beings.

After he had descended to tell the people of the Lord's ordinances, Moses returned to the mountaintop and remained secluded in communion with the Lord for 40 days and 40 nights. He was given scores of meticulous religious and ethical laws along with instructions for correctly building a tabernacle with all of its furnishings, including the sacred ark of the covenant. He also received detailed descriptions of the duties and rituals to be performed by priests in proper worship of the Lord, for Aaron and his sons would be the first generation of the priestly caste of Levites.

DEFYING GOD'S COVENANT

Meanwhile, the Israelites had lost faith once again in their leader and their God. Assuming that Moses had disappeared, they importuned Aaron to make a visible god to lead them, a calf fashioned from gold melted down from their earrings. Although Moses' brother seems to have considered this image as a symbol of the Lord's earthly throne, it nonetheless explicitly defied the second commandment: "You shall not make for yourself a graven image" (Ex. 20:4). On Mount Sinai, God told Moses what was going on and furiously decided to destroy the ingrates, but their leader interceded, reminding the Lord of his promise to make a great nation from the seed of Abraham, Isaac, and Israel. God relented.

Carrying two stone tablets covered on both sides with laws "written with the finger of God" (Ex. 31:18), Moses descended to the Hebrew encampment. There he found his faithless people singing and dancing around the golden calf, exuberantly flaunting their breaking of the covenant with the Lord. Irate, Moses dashed the tablets to bits, symbolizing the broken covenant. He burned the calf to powder, which he forced the Israelites to drink with water. Then he sent his loyal Levite brethren through the camp to kill about 3,000 of the men among the sinners. After this terrible punishment, the Lord sent a plague to afflict his people. In addition, he withdrew his presence from the camp, sending down an angel to guide them toward Canaan in his place. Significantly, God had patiently dealt with the complaints of the Israelites before his appearance to them at Mount Sinai. Afterward, in recognition that they were then bound to him by the covenant established there, the Lord became angry with their murmurings and promptly punished any rebellions against his Law or Moses' authority.

On this occasion, in response to Moses' intercession yet again, God agreed to forgive his people for their idolatry. He ordered his emissary to bring two blank stone tablets to the heights of Sinai and again dictated the terms of the covenant, including the Ten Commandments, for Moses to write down. This time,

when their leader returned to the valley, the people were astonished to see that his face glowed; he was so transfigured by the radiance of God's glory that he had to veil his features to allay their fear of coming near enough to hear his message.

Then, in accord with the divine instructions, Moses oversaw construction of the tabernacle, the first shrine of the covenant nation of Israel. Carefully built and appointed with rich furnishings, the sanctuary housed the ark and the tablets with the commandments. This structure was to be the symbol of the Lord's ongoing presence, "for throughout all their journeys the cloud of the Lord was upon the tabernacle by day, and fire was in it by night, in the sight of all the house of Israel" (Ex. 40:38). In certain passages, it seems that the tabernacle is synonymous with the so-called tent of meeting, which was pitched outside the encampment. There the Lord appeared to Moses in order to give advice or hear prayers. At other times, the tent and tabernacle are treated as separate structures.

Shortly after leaving Egypt, the Lord's

Furious at the Israelites for worshiping a golden calf (top), Moses smashes the tablets of the Law (bottom); two panels from the 13th-century Ingeburg Psalter.

might had been dramatically demonstrated when the people were attacked by a fierce desert tribe, the Amalekites. Most probably, this seminomadic people saw the Hebrews as interlopers who would compete for the scarce resources of food, water, and grazing areas. Under the leadership of Moses' aide-de-camp **Joshua**, the Hebrews fought back bravely. Miraculously, they dominated the battle so long as Moses, observing from the crest of a hill nearby, held his hands aloft. But whenever his energy flagged and he dropped his arms, the tide of battle turned. Finally, Moses sat down on a large rock and others supported his outstretched arms until sunset, by which time Joshua had at last achieved victory.

DOUBTS AND FEARS

The Israelites tended to forget such divine intervention with remarkable dispatch. For the next four decades, as the tribe wandered through the harsh, implacable Sinai desert, Moses continually faced new challenges to his leadership and to the national religion. Again and again, the Hebrews grew weary of their journey and tried to replace him. Their weakness and mistrust became graphically, even tragically, apparent when Moses sent 12 spies to reconnoiter the land

of Canaan. As the Israelites paused at the very doorstep of the land promised them by God for generations, ten of the spies returned with a mixed message: "[The land] flows with milk and honey . . . . Yet the people who dwell in the land are strong, and the cities are fortified and very large" (Num. 13:27, 28). Instantly, the people lost hope and began wailing that it would be better to return to servitude in Egypt than to be slaughtered there. However, the other two spies, Joshua and **Caleb**, urged them onward, protesting that the Lord was on their side. Just as these two steadfast young men were about to be stoned for their advice, the Lord appeared, enraged and determined at last to wipe out the faithless Israelites with disease. After Moses interceded, the Lord agreed to pardon his recalcitrant people yet one more time—but there would be a grim price to pay: None over the age of 20, save Joshua and Caleb, would live to enter the Promised Land.

Throughout all the trials Moses never hesitated to intercede, even when his own position was at risk. In one case, Moses' cousin **Korah** demanded an equal share in religious leadership for himself and his kin. The rebellious challenge was emphatically, horribly punished by the Lord, who caused

The Israelites punished for their lack of faith with a plague of poisonous snakes; detail from a painting by Simon Vouet (1590-1649)

At a blow from Moses' rod, God sends water gushing from a rock to quench the Israelites' thirst; a painting by Raphael.

the earth to swallow up the rebels and their families alive. But beforehand God had threatened to destroy the entire encampment except for Moses and Aaron. He was dissuaded by the plea, "O God, the God of the spirits of all flesh, shall one man sin, and wilt thou be angry with all the congregation?" (Num. 16:22). On another occasion, weary from a particularly exhausting detour around the land of Edom, the Hebrews whined so churlishly that God punished them with a plague of fatally poisonous snakes. When Moses stepped in, the Lord softened his anger and devised a cure: "Make a fiery serpent, and set it on a pole; and every one who is bitten, when he sees it, shall live" (Num. 21:8). According to 2 Kings 18:4, the image survived in the temple at Jerusalem until the eighth century B.C., when King **Hezekiah** had it destroyed because the people were committing sins by offering sacrifices to it.

Meanwhile, despite all the backsliding and quarrels, the years of exile gradually strengthened the Israelites, molding a nation from a motley band of former slaves tested harshly by adversity and by their own human failings. Through it all, of course, God was directly involved in the endeavor, alternately chastising and protecting his people. Centuries later, some of the Old Testament prophets looked back longingly on this period as a time of national unity, unparalleled intimacy with the Lord, devotion to religion and the Law, and firm belief in a

shared destiny. Not least in importance, Moses took advantage of these decades to teach his people how to take care of themselves when he was gone. Never greedy for power himself, he prepared the nation for its destiny by appointing 70 elders. He also asked the Lord to appoint a successor; the choice, Joshua, implied that ability, not heredity, would be the criterion for the leadership post, even though the priesthood was to be inherited through Aaron's line.

DENIED THE PROMISED LAND

For all of his ethical and secular accomplishments, however, Moses himself never forded the Jordan River and entered into the land of promise. The generally accepted explanation involves a cryptic story that may show Moses in an uncharacteristic display of impiety. On yet another of the occasions when the Israelites bewailed their fate in the desert, especially the lack of water, the Lord ordered Moses to take his shepherd's rod in hand and tell a rock to yield forth water. Perhaps in a fit of temper, the lawgiver approached this rock, turned on his people as Aaron stood beside him, and said, "Hear now, you rebels; shall we bring forth water for you out of this rock?" (Num. 20:10). He struck the rock twice with the rod, and water gushed out. Immediately, the Lord declared, "Because you did not believe in me, to sanctify me in the eyes of the people of Israel, therefore you shall not bring this assembly into the land which I have given

*The head of Michelangelo's famous statue
of Moses, from the church of San Pietro
in Vincoli in Rome*

them" (Num. 20:12). Apparently, Moses was being punished for speaking so angrily, for not stating that God was responsible for the miracle, and for striking the rock as if he himself wielded the supernatural power to bring forth water.

Nearing death at the age of 120 but with his eyesight and physical strength unimpaired, Moses implored God to relent and allow him to enter Canaan. But the leader who had so often interceded to save his people could not successfully press his own case. The Lord was adamant: "Speak no more to me of this matter. Go up to the top of Pisgah, and lift up your eyes westward and northward and southward and eastward, and behold it with your eyes; for you shall not go over this Jordan" (Dt. 3:26-27). Before Moses enjoyed his tantalizing glimpse of Canaan, he delivered three long exhortations to the Israelites, recalling the four decades of their travails and triumphs in the desert since leaving Egypt and repeating the basic tenets of the Law handed down to them on Mount Sinai.

At last, Moses ascended the peak of either Pisgah or Nebo, both of which are in a mountain range in Moab across the Jordan from Jericho. With God beside him, he scanned the sweeping panorama of earthly bounty that awaited his long-suffering people. Today's geographers would describe the scene as stretching from the Sea of Galilee in the north to the southern end of the Judean wilderness, from the Mediterranean in the west toward the southeastern Jordan valley and the Dead Sea.

Miriam and Aaron having preceded him in death, Israel's great lawgiver died and was buried by the Lord in a hidden grave somewhere in a valley of Moab. God kept the location secret so that the Israelites would not make the religious error of turning the site into a shrine of worship. In effect, the epitaph for Moses, and indeed the summation of traditional Jewish reverence for him and his accomplishments, appears at the very end of the Pentateuch: "And there has not arisen a prophet since in Israel like Moses, whom the Lord knew face to face, none like him for all the signs and the wonders which the Lord sent him to do" (Dt. 34:10-11).

AT JESUS' SIDE

For Christians, Moses—mentioned in the New Testament more often than any other Old Testament figure—is often a symbol of the contrast between traditional Judaism and the teachings of **Jesus**. Occasionally, the New Testament writers make a comparison with Moses in order to explain Jesus' mission. In the book of Acts, for example, the rejection of Moses by the Jews when they worshiped the golden calf is likened to their later rejection of Jesus. The author of the Gospel of John argues that anyone who accepts the writings of Moses must logically accept the ministry of Jesus. He also relates a conversation in which Jesus points out to his disciples that it was God, not Moses, who sent down manna in the wilderness. By contrast, Jesus proclaims, "I am the bread of life" (Jn. 6:35).

Among the most memorable events of Jesus' ministry is the occasion—recorded in all three Synoptic Gospels—when Jesus took his three closest disciples "up a high mountain apart" (Mt. 17:1). There he was transformed into a figure of dazzling brightness, and his awestruck disciples saw him conversing with Moses and the prophet **Elijah**. When the vision dissolved, Jesus cautioned the three disciples "to tell no one what they had seen, until the Son of man should have risen from the dead" (Mk. 9:9).

For the most part, however, references to Moses in the New Testament emphasize his historical role as national leader or lawgiver, often as the source of specific restrictions or commandments. He is shown as the precursor of Jesus in the seamless, unified story of God's relationship to and interaction with humankind throughout the ages. And Jesus is portrayed as the long-awaited fulfillment of the divine promise made to Moses in the covenant on Mount Sinai.

*From a mountaintop opposite Jericho,
Moses surveys the Promised Land;
for his single display of doubt, the
Lord prevented him from leading the
Israelites across the Jordan.*

NAAMAN

(nay uh' muhn) HEBREW: NAAMAN
"pleasantness"

Naaman was a commander of the Syrian army made victorious by Israel's God, but he had leprosy. From a captive Israelite maid he learned about a prophet in Samaria who could heal the ailment; he set off for Israel with money and a letter from the king of Syria demanding a cure. When Naaman arrived in Samaria, the king—unnamed in the Bible but most likely **Jehoram**—thought the letter a pretext for war. However, the prophet **Elisha** heard about Naaman and offered to heal him.

Naaman came to Elisha expecting an elaborate healing ritual. But Elisha did not even come out to meet him; instead he sent word by a messenger for Naaman to wash seven times in the Jordan to be cured. At first Naaman was outraged at this apparent dismissal, but his servants convinced him to wash in the river, and he was healed. Naaman returned to Elisha full of gratitude and faith in Yahweh. When the prophet refused his proffered gifts, he begged to take "two mules' burden of earth" (2 Kg. 5:17) back to Damascus so that he could always worship the Lord on Israelite soil.

NABAL

(nay' bahl) HEBREW: NABAL
"fool"

A descendant of **Caleb** and a wealthy sheepherder from Maon in the tribal lands of Judah, Nabal was a man who acted out the meaning of his name. During the

In this detail from a painting by Jacob Savery II (1593-1627), all creation's animals gather to board Noah's ark.

years when **David** led his own band of soldiers in Judah—often pursued by King **Saul**—the renegades protected Nabal's shepherds and other herders of Judah from enemy raids. But at shearing time, when David sent Nabal a request for food for his men, the "churlish and ill-behaved" (1 Sam. 25:3) man responded with contempt, calling David a runaway servant and refusing to help him.

David would have attacked and destroyed Nabal had not the latter's beautiful and diplomatic wife **Abigail** heard of the incident and intervened, bringing David provisions and soothing words that calmed his rage. Meanwhile, Nabal lay in a drunken stupor at a lavish banquet. In the morning Abigail informed him of what had happened, and he was so angry or frightened that "his heart died within him, and he became as a stone" (2 Sam. 25:37)—perhaps having suffered a stroke or heart attack. Within ten days he was dead. Shortly thereafter, David claimed the widow Abigail as his second wife.

NABOTH

(nay' buhht) HEBREW: NABOT
possibly "sprouts" or "elevation"

In his hometown of Jezreel, Naboth owned a vineyard next to the palace of King **Ahab**. Wanting the land for a vegetable garden, the king offered to give Naboth a better vineyard in exchange. But since the vineyard had belonged to his clan for generations, Naboth felt obligated to maintain it as part of his ancestral patrimony and refused the exchange.

Though "vexed and sullen" (1 Kg. 21:4), Ahab recognized Naboth's right and accepted this rebuff, but his queen, **Jezebel**, was determined to get the vineyard for her husband. She sent letters in Ahab's name to the elders and nobles of Jezreel, instructing them to suborn two false witnesses to charge

Declining to help the renegade David, Nabal was punished with death.

Naboth publicly with blasphemy and treason. "Then take him out," she instructed in the letter, "and stone him to death" (1 Kg. 21:10). The officials bowed to the king's power and executed Naboth—a demonstration of how easily Israel's judicial system could be corrupted. When Ahab went to confiscate Naboth's property, the prophet **Elijah** met him with a dire prediction: "Where dogs licked up the blood of Naboth shall dogs lick your own blood" (1 Kg. 21:19). And so it came to pass, when Ahab's corpse was returned from the battlefield at Ramoth-gilead. In final fulfillment of the prophecy, **Jehu**, the assassin of Ahab's son and successor **Jehoram**, ordered the body of his royal victim dumped in Naboth's field, quoting the Lord, "As surely as I saw yesterday the blood of Naboth . . . I will requite you on this plot of ground" (2 Kg. 9:26).

NADAB

(nay' dab) HEBREW: NADAB
"generous" or "noble"

The eldest son of **Aaron** and Elisheba, Nadab is always paired with his brother Abihu in the Bible. Along with their father and the 70 elders of Israel, the two accompanied **Moses** up Mount Sinai to ratify the covenant with the Lord. There God chose Aaron and his sons to serve as priests at the tabernacle altar. After a week-long ordina-

tion ceremony, Nadab and Abihu were punished for a sin of unclear nature. As they offered "unholy fire" (Lev. 10:1) to the Lord in their censers, flames from heaven devoured them. The Jewish historian Josephus believed that they failed to bring sacrifices specifically ordered by Moses. Other authorities suggest that they were intoxicated, citing the Lord's words to Aaron shortly thereafter: "Drink no wine nor strong drink . . . when you go into the tent of meeting, lest you die" (Lev. 10:9). Rabbinical literature reports that the souls of Nadab and Abihu were burned by streams of fire entering their nostrils. The brothers left no children to continue their line.

NADAB 2

Succeeding to the throne of his father **Jeroboam**, Nadab ruled Israel for less than two years at the end of the tenth century B.C. The only notable event associated with his reign was the siege of Gibbethon, a Levitical city in Dan held by the Philistines. Nadab's siege was possibly aimed at disrupting the economic position of Judah and consolidating the power of the fledgling northern kingdom. In the midst of the struggle, Nadab was killed in a revolt led by **Baasha**, who also "left to the house of Jeroboam not one that breathed" (1 Kg. 15:29). **Ahijah** the Shilonite had prophesied that, for its sins, the Lord would destroy Jeroboam's dynasty, "as a man burns up dung until it is all gone" (1 Kg. 14:10).

NAHOR

(nay' hohr) HEBREW: NAHOR
meaning uncertain

The brother of **Abraham** and Haran, Nahor is thought to be the progenitor of 12 Aramean tribes. He had eight sons by Haran's daughter Milcah and four sons by his concubine Reumah. Milcah's sons were Uz, Buz, Kemuel, Chesed, Hazo, Pildash, Jidlaph, and **Bethuel**, the father of **Laban** and **Rebekah**; Reumah's sons were Tebah, Gaham, Tahash, and Maacah. The sons of the wife and the concubine symbolize the geographical distribution of the tribes throughout Syria and Palestine. Swearing to a covenant made with his fugitive son-in-law **Jacob** in the hill country of Gilead, Laban asked that "the God of Abraham and the God of Nahor, the God of their father, judge between us" (Gen. 31:53). Some scholars view this distinction as evidence that Nahor harbored pagan beliefs.

NAHUM

(nay' huhm) HEBREW: NAHEM

"comfort"

Allll that is known about the seventh of the so-called Minor Prophets is his name: Nahum of Elkosh. Elkosh has not been identified with certainty, but it may have been a town in southwestern Judah. Precise dating of the book of Nahum is also impossible, but it was probably completed shortly before the destruction of Nineveh in 612 B.C. by the Medes and Chaldeans, or Babylonians, and the fall of the Assyrian empire.

The book is called "an oracle concerning Nineveh" (Nah. 1:1) and begins with a psalm telling of an avenging Lord: "The Lord is slow to anger and of great might . . . . His wrath is poured out like fire, and the rocks are broken asunder by him" (Nah. 1:3, 6). But Nahum also speaks of a good Lord, "a stronghold in the day of trouble; he knows those who take refuge in him" (Nah. 1:7). Through Nahum, the Lord informs the people of Judah that they will soon be free of their Assyrian bondage and that the wicked empire will never again molest them.

Nahum then shifts to a graphic description of the violent demise of Nineveh. While the Assyrians prepared for the onslaught, the enemy opened the river floodgates and were thus able to breach the defenses of the inundated city. The Medes and Babylonians began their plunder of the city, taking silver and gold; "there is no end of treasure, or wealth of every precious thing" (Nah. 2:9). Since the Lord was against Nineveh, the city paid for its misdeeds. Cavalry charged through the streets with "flashing sword and glittering spear," leaving behind "heaps of corpses, dead bodies without end" (Nah. 3:3).

The Assyrian empire was never to recover. Its far-flung forts were "like fig trees with first-ripe figs—if shaken they fall into the mouth of the eater" (Nah. 3:12). The Lord taunted the Assyrians, saying that they would end as the Egyptian capital Thebes had ended, defeated and enslaved. Ironically, it was the Assyrians who had captured Thebes in 663 B.C.

NAOMI

(nay oh' mee) HEBREW: NOOMI

"pleasant"

Innn the period of the judges, Naomi lived in Bethlehem with her husband **Elimelech** and their two sons, Mahlon and Chilion. But a famine forced the family to leave Judah and migrate to Moab, east of the Dead Sea. During the next ten years, Elimelech

died and both sons married local women, **Ruth** and **Orpah**. When the sons died too, Naomi decided to return to Judah—having heard that the famine in her homeland had finally ended.

Told by Naomi to remain in Moab with their families and find new husbands, "Orpah kissed her mother-in-law, but Ruth clung to her." Mahlon's widow, Ruth, was determined to accompany Naomi, saying, "where you go I will go . . . your people shall be my people, and your God my God." Not even death, Ruth vowed, would part them: "where you die I will die, and there will I be buried" (Ru. 1:14, 16-17).

The two women reached Bethlehem during the barley harvest. While gleaning the fields for remnants, Ruth met a wealthy kinsman of her husband's named **Boaz**. Following Naomi's advice, Ruth charmed Boaz into taking her as a wife so that Elimelech's property, which neither of the two widows could claim for her own, would remain in the family. Ruth gave birth to Obed, but the neighbors proclaimed, "a son has been born to Naomi" (Ru. 4:17); Boaz, in this instance, was a proxy not only for Ruth's deceased husband but for Naomi's as well. Obed was the grandfather of King **David**.

Widowed in a strange land, Naomi returned to Judah; at harvest time, her daughter-in-law Ruth found a new husband.

NAPHTALI

(naf' tuh lee) HEBREW: NAPTALI
"wrestling"

Naphtali was the second son born to **Jacob** by **Rachel**'s maid **Bilhah**. Rachel named him for the struggles she had endured with her older sister **Leah**, Jacob's first wife. All that is known of Naphtali is that he had four sons and died in Egypt, by tradition at the age of 130. But since in his deathbed blessing Jacob compared Naphtali to "a hind let loose, that bears comely fawns" (Gen. 49:21), a quick, vital character is suggested for this son.

Naphtali and his older brother **Dan** gave their names to two tribes of Israel. The tribe of Naphtali numbered 53,400 adult males at the first census in the wilderness. Following the conquest, the tribe settled in the areas west and northwest of the Sea of Galilee. Within its borders were three Levitical cities and the important fortress of Hazor. The people "dwelt among the Canaanites" (Jg.

1:33) and maintained commercial contacts with the Phoenician coastal cities. While **Pekah** ruled Israel, **Tiglath-pileser III** of Assyria conquered "all the land of Naphtali; and he carried the people captive to Assyria" (2 Kg. 15:29).

NATHAN

(nay' thuhn) HEBREW: NATAN
"gift [of God]"

As a court prophet for **David**, Nathan played a prominent role in three significant events of the king's career. When David had consolidated his kingdom and wished to build a temple to God, Nathan at first approved. Later, however, he received a revelation that not David but his son would build the temple. Through Nathan, God also promised David an everlasting dynasty whose "throne shall be established for ever" (2 Sam. 7:16).

After David arranged to have the warrior

Accused by the prophet Nathan (center), King David (lower right) repents his sin against Uriah; two scenes from a tenth-century manuscript illumination.

Uriah killed, he married Uriah's widow **Bathsheba** and had a child by her. Nathan confronted the king with a story about a rich man who selfishly slaughtered a poor man's pet lamb to feed a visitor. David was outraged, saying that the rich man deserved to die. "You are the man" (2 Sam. 12:7), Nathan said, predicting that trouble would plague David's house and that Bathsheba's child would soon die.

Ironically, when Nathan last appears, about 20 years later, he is the ally of Bathsheba and her second son, **Solomon**, in the struggle over succession as David nears death. The king had treated his eldest living son, **Adonijah**, as crown prince, but Nathan urged Bathsheba to remind the invalid king that he had sworn to give the throne to Solomon. After she had done so, Nathan came in and warned that Adonijah was already seizing the kingdom without David's permission. Together, they convinced David to install Solomon as king even before his death, and Nathan joined the priest **Zadok** in anointing the new king. Nathan also wrote a history, now lost, of David and his times.

NATHANAEL

(nuh than' ee uhl) HEBREW: NETANEL
"God has given"

A disciple of **Jesus** mentioned only in the Gospel of John, Nathanael was an Israelite from the Galilean town of Cana. Both Nathanael and **Philip** of Bethsaida met Jesus on the same day as he was journeying to Galilee. After Jesus had found him, Philip carried the news to a dubious Nathanael, who asked, "Can anything good come out of Nazareth?" (Jn. 1:46). When Jesus saw Nathanael, he revealed a premonition he had had of him under a fig tree, an appropriate place for rabbis to study and meditate. Quickly convinced of Jesus' power, Nathanael responded, "Rabbi, you are the Son of God! You are the King of Israel!" (Jn. 1:49). Jesus promised that he would see even greater wonders in the future. And, indeed, Nathanael was among those disciples to whom the resurrected Jesus appeared on the shore of the Sea of Galilee.

Nathanael has often been identified with the apostle **Bartholomew**, since the Synoptic Gospels—which do not mention him—always pair Philip with Bartholomew.

For refusing to worship his golden image, Nebuchadnezzar condemned Daniel's three friends to a fiery furnace; a 12th-century manuscript illumination.

NEBUCHADNEZZAR

(neb uh kuhd nez' uhr) HEBREW: NEBUKADNESSAR; also NEBUCHADREZZAR
"may Nabu protect my boundary"

For 43 years (605-562 B.C.) Nebuchadnezzar dominated the Middle East as king of the Neo-Babylonian, or Chaldean, empire; he was the eldest son of Nabopolassar, founder of the empire. Early in 605, while still crown prince, Nebuchadnezzar led the Babylonian army to a victory over Egypt at Carchemish on the Euphrates River; this victory established Babylonian power throughout Syria and Palestine. But when his father died on August 15, 605, Nebuchadnezzar hurried home to Babylon to lay claim to the throne. He was crowned on September 7, though officially his reign did not start until the beginning of the next Babylonian year, April 2, 604, when he formally "took the hands" of the god Bel.

Almost immediately, Nebuchadnezzar returned to war. From June to December of 604, he marched into Palestine, reduced King **Jehoiakim** of Judah to vassal status, attacked Philistia, and totally destroyed Ashkelon. Over the course of the next 20 years, Nebuchadnezzar was repeatedly involved in campaigns to solidify the Babylonian expansion into Syria and Palestine and to keep Egypt at bay.

In December 601, Nebuchadnezzar tried to conquer Egypt itself but was blocked at the border by the army of Pharaoh **Neco**—both sides suffering heavy losses in a major

SEVEN WONDERS OF THE ANCIENT WORLD

A number of biblical stories intersect with the spectacular monuments classified as wonders of the world by the Greeks in the second century B.C. The pyramids at Giza—oldest, largest, and the only intact of those wonders—were already more than a thousand years old when Pharaoh used the Israelites as forced labor. The conqueror of Judah, Nebuchadnezzar, is credited with building the hanging gardens of Babylon. Having passed through Palestine late in the fourth century, Alexander the Great founded the Egyptian city of Alexandria, later the site of the Pharos, an enormous lighthouse. When Paul visited Ephesus in Asia Minor, he came into conflict with worshipers of the fertility goddess Artemis, whose temple there was said to rival the Parthenon of Athens.

The three other ancient wonders were the 40-foot statue of Zeus at Olympia; the Colossus of Rhodes, an even larger statue commissioned by the citizens of that island to commemorate a victory over Macedonia; and the tomb of Prince Mausolus at Halicarnassus in Asia Minor—so famed that monumental tombs are still known as mausoleums.

battle. Nebuchadnezzar next spent two years rebuilding his army and expanding into Arabia. Jehoiakim foolishly took this opportunity to rebel against Babylon, hoping for support from Egypt. Nebuchadnezzar waited a year to put down the rebels but, during the interval, had his vassals around Judah send raiding parties to harass them.

In December 598, Nebuchadnezzar marched against Jerusalem; that same month Jehoiakim died, possibly by assassination. His 18-year-old heir **Jehoiachin** reigned only three months before surrendering to Nebuchadnezzar on March 16, 597. The book of Jeremiah records that Nebuchadnezzar deported 3,023 Jews to Babylon; it was the beginning of the so-called Babylonian exile. The captives included Jehoiachin and most of the aristocracy of Jerusalem. Babylonian chronicles record that Nebuchadnezzar, after capturing Jerusalem, "appointed in it a new king of his liking." The new king of Judah was **Zedekiah**, Jehoiachin's uncle.

During the following years Nebuchadnezzar was engaged in other parts of his empire: a rebellion in Elam in the east, a long siege of the island city of Tyre, campaigns in northern Syria. Meanwhile, Jerusalem again became a hotbed of rebellion, fanned by optimistic prophets who claimed God was about to break the yoke of Babylon. The prophet **Jeremiah**, who predicted that rebellion against Nebuchadnezzar would bring disaster, was considered a traitor. When Zedekiah led Judah into open rebellion, Nebuchadnezzar again blockaded

Jerusalem, this time for a two-year siege. At the end of this bitter war in July 587, the Babylonian forces flattened Jerusalem's walls, stripped the temple of all its valuables and burnt it to the ground, set the city afire, and deported 832 more prominent citizens.

In his own land Nebuchadnezzar was famous as a builder. He constructed and beautified dozens of temples across southern Mesopotamia. He expanded Babylon's fortifications, paved streets, dug canals, and repaired the great ziggurat of Marduk. Nebuchadnezzar is said to have built the

A cuneiform tablet dating to the reign of Nebuchadnezzar

famous hanging gardens of Babylon, one of the seven wonders of the ancient world, to remind a princess from Media to whom he was married of her mountainous homeland.

Though Nebuchadnezzar destroyed the temple, in Jewish tradition he is usually remembered as an instrument God used to punish Judah's apostasy, and thus he is often treated positively in the Bible. In the book of Daniel, for example, he is portrayed as a wise pagan king who was sometimes deceived by evil counselors but was ready to recognize the superiority of Israel's God.

NEBUZARADAN

(neb oo zah rad' uhn) HEBREW: NEBUZARADAN
"Nabu has given offspring"

As captain of the guard to Babylon's King **Nebuchadnezzar**, Nebuzaradan entered Jerusalem after its final capture in July 587 B.C. A Chaldean, or Neo-Babylonian, army had taken Judah's rebellious king **Zedekiah** to Riblah, where he was blinded after seeing his sons put to death before him. Nebuzaradan then led a punitive force that burned and ransacked Jerusalem, destroying the temple and royal palace. Most of the populace was sent into exile, leaving only "the poorest of the land to be vinedressers and plowmen" (2 Kg. 25:12; Jer. 52:16). Nebuzaradan also confiscated the bronze, gold, and silver of the temple and brought Jerusalem's leading men to Riblah, where the Babylonian king had them all executed. Riding with the portrait of his master Nebuchadnezzar attached to his chariot, Nebuzaradan returned to Jerusalem a few years later and rounded up 745 more Jews to take into exile.

NECO

(nee' koh) HEBREW: NEKOH

The second king of Egypt's 26th dynasty, Neco II ruled from his capital at Sais from 610 to 595 B.C. At Megiddo, near a pass in the Carmel Range, Neco defeated and killed King **Josiah** of Judah in 609. Josiah had sought to delay Neco as the Pharaoh marched north to aid the crumbling Assyrian empire against an attack from the Chaldeans, or Neo-Babylonians. With Josiah dead, the people put his younger son, **Jehoahaz,** on the throne, but Neco had him seized, imprisoned, and later deported to Egypt. The Egyptian ruler then installed Josiah's older son, Eliakim, as king of Judah, changing his name to **Jehoiakim**

Nehemiah, an 11th-century stone carving from the church of St. Lazare in Avallon, France

and demanding heavy tribute in silver and gold from him.

Neco controlled Syria and Palestine until Egypt's defeat at Carchemish on the Euphrates River in 605 at the hands of the Babylonians. He withdrew homeward and in 601 stopped a Babylonian army on Egypt's frontier in a battle with heavy losses to both sides. From then until his death six years later, Neco focused on domestic policies, including the granting of favorable trade terms to Greek merchants. According to the Greek historian Herodotus, Neco sent a Phoenician crew on a three-year voyage around Africa and began construction of a canal from the Nile to the Red Sea that cost the lives of 120,000 Egyptians.

NEHEMIAH

(nee uh mai' uh) HEBREW: NEHEMEYAH
"Yahweh comforts"

Celebrated as the close colleague of **Ezra** among the exiles who returned from Babylon to reestablish a Jewish state in Judah, Nehemiah rebuilt Jerusalem's walls so that the abandoned city could be repopulated. But he confronted opposition from the

Judeans who had remained behind. He probably first arrived in Jerusalem with a commission as governor shortly after the 20th year of Persian King **Artaxerxes I**, in 445 B.C., remained for 12 years, and—after a year-long visit to Persia—returned to Judah about 433. Although the date and place of his death are unrecorded, it is known from sources outside the Bible that Nehemiah was no longer governor in 407.

Though the order of the biblical books bearing their names implies that Ezra preceded Nehemiah, some scholars think that Nehemiah originally came to Jerusalem more than a decade before Ezra. The ancient editors of the two books were clearly less concerned with certain historical details than with making the point that all of Nehemiah's reforms, whenever they occurred, stood fully within the shadow of the Torah, which Ezra read in public and established as the formal constitution of the Jewish state. For in addition to Nehemiah's repairing the walls of the city, he is presented in the Bible as one of the primary architects of the Jewish faith as it is practiced today.

Most of what is known about Nehemiah is derived from his own autobiographical account, which describes his success in a mixture of pious prayers and grand, self-confident accounts. Some scholars believe that his words betray vanity—as when, for example, he boldly contrasts his own virtue with the wrongdoing of all the other leaders in Judah: "I did not do so, because of the fear of God" (Neh. 5:15). Still, the point of his autobiography was not to offer a balanced view, but to testify to his role as a national hero owing to God's remembrance and blessing of him.

As did **Esther** and **Daniel**, this remarkable man rose from the ranks of exiles to gain recognition at the highest level of the foreigners among whom he lived. Dwelling in the Persian capital of Susa, Nehemiah was Artaxerxes's cupbearer, a trusted official who guaranteed that the king's wine was not poisoned. But when he heard from fellow exiles that the walls of Jerusalem had been destroyed, Nehemiah "sat down and wept, and mourned for days" (Neh. 1:4). In a prayer, he blamed this disaster on the failure of the exiles to obey the commandments God had given to **Moses**. Later, as he served wine to Artaxerxes, his sad countenance caused the king to ask what was wrong. "Why should not my face be sad," he answered, "when the city, the place of my fathers' sepulchres, lies waste" (Neh. 2:3). At Nehemiah's request, the king agreed to send him to Jerusalem for the purpose of rebuilding the city, with the understanding

that he would someday return to resume serving in the palace.

Operating as an independent authority under the aegis of Artaxerxes, Nehemiah traveled westward with a royal guard. But he "told no one what my God had put into my heart to do for Jerusalem" (Neh. 2:12). Three days after his arrival, he made a nocturnal tour of the city's gates and walls. The next day, he publicly confronted the people with his estimate of what needed to be done. Only then did he announce that God's hand would guide him in this task and, no less significantly, that the Persian king supported his mission. Since Judah belonged to the Persian empire, Nehemiah's claim to authority could not be taken lightly. And when the nearby governors **Sanballat**, **Tobiah**, and the Arab **Geshem** voiced opposition, Nehemiah retorted that as non-Jews they had "no portion or right or memorial in Jerusalem" (Neh. 2:20).

The high priests and most of the other Jewish leaders decided to join with Nehemiah and, after repairing and consecrating the gates, they set to work on the walls. Sanballat, Tobiah, and their comrades harassed the workers. They made fun of the "feeble Jews" who worked on the walls and claimed that the construction was so poor that, "if a fox goes up on it he will break down their stone wall!" (Neh. 4:2, 3).

Learning that his critics were plotting an attack, Nehemiah stationed armed men at various places around the walls to protect the workers. When all the breaches in the walls had been repaired—though the doors to the gates had not yet been installed—Sanballat and Geshem asked Nehemiah to meet with them to negotiate an agreement. Nehemiah interpreted the invitation as a trap and declined their offer. After three other appeals were ignored, Sanballat finally sent an open letter falsely accusing Nehemiah of planning a rebellion to make himself king and appointing prophets to support his claim—actions that would have brought the

Seeing his saddened cupbearer Nehemiah, Persian King Artaxerxes I learns of the exile's desire to rebuild Jerusalem.

full weight of Persian power against him.

A Judean prophet named Shemaiah urged Nehemiah to hide behind the closed doors of the temple and pray, since his enemies would soon come to kill him. Nehemiah refused to listen, discerning that the prophet had been hired by Sanballat. And so, by maintaining his defense of the city, Nehemiah finished restoring the walls and gates in 52 days, ending on the 25th day of the month of Elul (August/September). Surrounding nations were frightened by the speed and daring of the accomplishment, and many Judeans within the city were still of divided loyalty, pretending to support Nehemiah while secretly reporting his words to Tobiah.

At this point, Nehemiah's account is interrupted by a description of a census made according to "the book of the genealogy of those who came up at the first" (Neh. 7:5)— that is, the list of the exiles who returned with **Zerubbabel** as reported in Ezra 2:1-

70. Following his census, Nehemiah stood by as Ezra read the book of the Law to the people, who publicly accepted it as a religious constitution for the new Jewish state. In response to Ezra's reading, Nehemiah directed a public confession of sin, supervised a dedication of the walls of Jerusalem, and—as had Ezra—sought to cleanse the people from foreign influences. Later Jewish tradition also credited Nehemiah with collecting the rest of the Scriptures, beside the Pentateuch, for use in the temple.

NICODEMUS
(nik oh dee' muhs) GREEK: NIKODEMOS
"conqueror of the people"

M entioned only in the Gospel of John, Nicodemus was a devout Jew and a member of the Sanhedrin. As a Pharisee, he struggled to understand **Jesus** and gradually revealed his faith more openly—though

it is not recorded by John that he became a disciple.

Whether he was hoping for a secret meeting or trying to avoid crowds, Nicodemus first sought out Jesus at night. "Rabbi, we know that you are a teacher come from God," he said; "for no one can do these signs that you do, unless God is with him" (Jn. 3:2). But when Jesus told him that only those "born anew" could enter the kingdom of God, a dumbfounded Nicodemus asked, "How can a man be born when he is old? Can he enter a second time into his mother's womb and be born?" (Jn. 3:3, 4). Jesus revealed his frustration that such a teacher and spiritual guide could not understand the testimony he was giving and went on to speak of the light brought to the world by God. According to some scholars, this nocturnal meeting serves as an analogy not only of the spiritual darkness in which many of Jesus' contemporaries lived but also of their sincere if often unsuccessful effort to understand the gospel he preached.

Later, when Jesus attempted to visit Jerusalem incognito at the Feast of Tabernacles, Nicodemus defended Jesus against those chief priests and Pharisees who sought to arrest him. "Does our law judge a man without first giving him a hearing and learning what he does?" (Jn. 7:51) he asked. The leaders replied, "Are you from Galilee too? Search and you will see that no prophet is to rise from Galilee" (Jn. 7:52).

Finally, after the crucifixion, Nicodemus came forward to help **Joseph of Arimathea** prepare Jesus' body for burial. Bringing "a mixture of myrrh and aloes, about a hundred pounds' weight" (Jn. 19:39), the Pharisee joined Joseph in anointing the body and wrapping it in linen before placing it in the garden tomb.

Did the cautious Nicodemus become a true disciple? Yes, according to the non-canonical Acts of Pilate, a fourth-century work later known as the Gospel of Nicodemus. In its pages, Jesus is accused before Pilate of performing cures on the sabbath. Nicodemus stands up before the assembly and defends Jesus, stating, "He is a man who has wrought many useful and glorious miracles, such as no man on earth ever wrought before, nor will ever work."

Joseph of Arimathea and Nicodemus, by Michel Wohlgemuth (1434-1519)

NICOLAUS

(nik' uh lay' uhs) GREEK: NIKOLAOS
"conqueror of the people"

Nicolaus was one of "seven men of good repute, full of the Spirit and of wisdom" (Acts 6:3), who were chosen by the Jerusalem congregation to help the twelve apostles. The seven, all Hellenists, or Greek-speaking Jewish Christians, as opposed to the more conservative Hebrews who spoke Aramaic, were appointed to serve the poor and widows in the daily distribution of relief. This allowed the twelve to focus on preaching and prayer. Nicolaus is called "a proselyte of Antioch" (Acts 6:5)—that is, he was a Gentile who had converted to Judaism prior to becoming a Christian. Nothing more is known about him, nor is he ever mentioned again in the New Testament.

Though much debated, Nicolaus is probably not connected to the Nicolaitans, a short-lived heretical sect in the early church of Asia Minor denounced by **John of Patmos** in the book of Revelation. While little is known of the sect, its members seem to have advocated "that they might eat food sacrificed to idols and practice immorality" (Rev. 2:14). The followers of this sect, evidently Christians seeking compromise with paganism, may have misinterpreted Nicolaus's teachings, or merely borrowed his name to describe themselves, or had a leader of the same name. John commended the church at Ephesus for rejecting the Nicolaitans.

NIMROD

(nim' rod) HEBREW: NIMROD

••••••••••

The grandson of **Noah**'s son **Ham**, Nimrod ruled in Mesopotamia after the Flood, "the first on earth to be a mighty man" (Gen. 10:8). His kingdom was said to have stretched across what would later be Babylonia and Assyria. Renowned as a hunter, he is also by tradition the first to eat meat and to make war. Nimrod was also said to have founded the cities of Babel, Erech, and Accad in Shinar (Babylonia), and then the cities of Nineveh, Rehoboth-Ir, Calah, and Resen in Assyria, a country later referred to in the Bible as "the land of Nimrod" (Mic. 5:6).

Scholars have made numerous efforts to identify Nimrod, but there is no consensus. In traditional literature, Nimrod conceived the tower of Babel that rabbis would later call "the house of Nimrod." According to Josephus, Nimrod was "a bold man, and of great strength in hand," who thought to outsmart God by building a tower too high for rising waters in case God "should have a mind to drown the world again."

TOWER OF BABEL

Scholars have long sought an historical precedent for the well-known story in Genesis 11 of the tower of Babel. Most of them propose the second-millennium B.C. ziggurat pyramids of Mesopotomia as an inspiration. Indeed, the land of Shinar, where the tower was built, has been identified as the Tigris-Euphrates basin, site of the ancient city of Babylon. In the biblical account, the name Babel is given the tower because the Lord—displeased with humanity's presumption that it could reach the heavens with the structure—confused their language. The word *balal* in Hebrew means confuse.

Jesus taken down from the cross; a 14th-century Italian painting

*Noah's family entering the ark;
a 13th-century carved cameo*

NOAH

(no' uh) HEBREW: NOAH
possibly "to rest"
::::::::::

Revered along with **Daniel** and **Job** as one of ancient Israel's three righteous men, Noah plays two important roles in history. First, he is virtually the second father of humankind, because all of **Adam**'s other descendants were destroyed in the great Flood that covered the world more than 1,600 years after creation. In that role, he acts as a link between the fragmentary accounts of humanity's first generations and the more detailed biographies of Israel's patriarchs that follow in the book of Genesis. Second, he is the discoverer of viniculture, or the growing of grapes, and the first person known to make wine.

Born to the tenth generation to follow Adam, 126 years after his death, Noah was marked for greatness from birth. According to his father, **Lamech**, the very name Noah implies that "out of the ground which the Lord has cursed this one shall bring us relief from our work and from the toil of our hands" (Gen. 5:29). The next thing the Scriptures tell us about Noah is that, after he was 500 years old, he sired three sons: **Shem**, **Ham**, and **Japheth**.

During these centuries, humanity evidently grew so wicked that the Lord decided to cleanse the earth of evil with a tremendous flood that would annihilate virtually all life: "I will blot out man whom I have created from the face of the ground, man and beast and creeping things and birds of the air, for I am sorry that I have made them" (Gen. 6:7). But because Noah, who was by then 600 years old, had remained steadfast in faith, indeed "a righteous man, blameless in his generation" (Gen. 6:9), God was moved to save him and his family from the worldwide devastation.

A VESSEL DESIGNED BY GOD

Following divine instructions, Noah constructed a huge ark out of gopher wood, which may have been cypress (the word "gopher" is nowhere else used in the Bible). Inside and out the three-deck vessel, no doubt honeycombed with partitions to make many separate compartments, was caulked with bitumen, a mineral pitch used for waterproofing in the ancient Near East. The dimensions of the rectangular craft are given in Genesis in cubits, a standard of measurement that was perhaps the equivalent of about 18 inches. The ark, therefore, was 450 feet long, 75 feet wide, and 45 feet high, better designed for stability in floating than for cruising. Into this strange vessel—little more than a buoyant box—the sole human being who had "found favor in the eyes of the Lord" (Gen. 6:8) led his family along with seven pairs of ritually clean animals, a pair of each unclean animal, and seven pairs of each type of bird.

Seven days later, as God had warned, great torrents of rain began falling from the skies and did not cease for a total of 40 days and nights. The landscape was obliterated, and every one of the sinful progeny of Adam and **Eve** was drowned. But as the waters inexorably rose and covered even the highest mountains, Noah and his family remained safe, protected within the mammoth ark.

The Flood remained at full strength for 150 days, then "God made a wind blow over the earth, and the waters subsided; the fountains of the deep and the windows of the heavens were closed, the rain from the heavens was restrained, and the waters receded from the earth continually" (Gen. 8:1-3). It took another 150 days for the water level to drop low enough to let the ark come to rest upon a mountain in the region of Armenia known as Ararat. Yet 40 more days passed before Noah tested the situation by releasing a raven, which did not return. A week later, he sent out a dove, which came back because it could not find a dry spot to rest upon. Released again the following week, the dove returned with a fresh olive leaf in its beak, an indication that the floodwaters had subsided. When Noah sent out the dove a third time, seven days later, the bird did not return. At last, "the face of the ground was dry" (Gen. 8:13).

The human and animal survivors left the ark, and Noah built an altar. After he had made a prodigious blood sacrifice that included every ritually clean animal and bird, God was pleased and promised that he would never again annihilate all living things, nor would the natural order of the seasons ever again be disrupted in such a catastrophic fashion. As token of his universal covenant with all human beings to come and all other living creatures as well, God placed a rainbow in the heavens. Interestingly, there is no specific word for "rainbow" in ancient Hebrew. Some biblical experts believe that the scriptural reference is a poetic use of the word "bow," the weapon. In that case, God can be seen as laying down his bow as a highly visible sign of his truce with humankind. To accent Noah's role as ancestor of the renewed human race, God repeated the edict he had given Adam so many centuries before: "Be fruitful and multiply, and fill the earth" (Gen. 9:1).

There is one significant contrast: Adam and his immediate descendants were vegetari-

As humanity drowns in the Flood below, Noah—safely aboard his ark—reaches for the dove's olive leaf; a tenth-century Spanish manuscript illumination.

ans, but after the Flood, God said, "every moving thing that lives shall be food for you; and as I gave you the green plants, I give you everything" (Gen. 9:3).

The commands then given to Noah, supported by the implied connection with Adam, led to the development in Jewish tradition of the seven so-called Noachide laws. Briefly stated, these include six proscriptions—against idolatry, bloodshed, blasphemy, theft, sexual sins, and eating the flesh of a living animal—and the charge to set up a legal system. Because these seven concepts reflect divine commands to Noah and Adam, the ancestors of all humankind, Jewish thinkers believed that they define moral obligations laid by God upon everyone, Jew and Gentile alike. Therefore, Noah is seen in traditional rabbinical thought as a symbol of the unity of human beings throughout all generations. Indeed, the Scriptures stress that from Noah and his sons "the whole earth was peopled" (Gen. 9:19).

SEEING HIS FATHER'S SHAME

Yet the new beginning for the human race would not be without conflict and error. In his second major historical role, Noah discovered not only the process of making wine but also the hazards of overindulgence.

Noah releasing the dove; a 14th-century mosaic from the cathedral of San Marco in Venice

When he drank to excess and passed out in his tent, his son Ham discovered him naked and unconscious. No doubt smirking, Ham ran off to share the jest with his brothers. More respectful, Shem and Japheth walked backward into their father's tent, so that they would not add to his shame, and tossed a garment over him. As punishment for his gross insult to a parent, Ham—in this biblical passage referred to as **Canaan**, the name later given to Ham's fourth son—was cursed: "A slave of slaves shall he be to his brothers" (Gen. 9:25).

Biblical scholars caution today's reader about the proper interpretation of this incident. From the ancient point of view, viniculture was considered fundamental to civilized living, and wine making was thought to be an appropriate use of the grape. Nor does the account in Genesis criticize Noah for becoming intoxicated. In other words, the intent of the story is not to warn against drunkenness but to offer an explanation for the traditional Hebrew contempt for the Canaanites, their longstanding adversaries in the Promised Land. According to the Scriptures, Ham's descendants also included several other tribes that were later under the control of Egypt. In the Islamic tradition, Ham is considered the ancestor of the Copts of Egypt, the Berbers of North Africa, and unidentified black people.

Noah's sacrifice; a Byzantine ivory carving from the cathedral of San Matteo in Salerno, Italy

Although archeologists have not yet uncovered evidence for an extraordinarily devastating deluge in ancient times, the historicity of the Flood is supported by a number of even older traditions from the cultures to the north and east of Palestine in Mesopotamia. But while the similarities between the Mesopotamian legends and the Old Testament story are striking, there is an essential difference: Noah, unlike the heroes of those flood myths, does not win immortality but dies. His fate is linked with that of his descendants, the whole of humanity that follows him. Similarly, the parallel flood tales in ancient Persian and Indian mythology do not have the ethical and religious resonance of the saga in Genesis.

God's covenant with Noah, for example, is recalled by the prophet **Isaiah** in order to remind his dejected people that divine compassion is great and everlasting. "As I swore that the waters of Noah should no more go over the earth," the Lord speaks through Isaiah, "so I have sworn that I will not be angry with you and will not rebuke you" (Is. 54:9). However, if he determined to vent his wrath upon the land, the Lord declared on another occasion, "even if Noah, Daniel, and Job were in it," they could not save others and "would deliver but their own lives by their righteousness" (Ezek. 14:20).

DELIVERANCE, OLD AND NEW

For many Christians, the story of Noah is profoundly symbolic. When **Jesus** was baptized in the Jordan, his emergence from the water of salvation can be said to recall Noah's deliverance from the Flood. Just as the hero of the Flood avoided death, the son of God and his followers would be able to triumph over death and Satan in the ritual of baptism. The dove that appeared to Jesus, symbolizing the **Holy Spirit**, was anticipated by the dove that eventually revealed to Noah that he and his family had been saved. Peter made the comparison explicit: "Baptism, which corresponds to this [that is, being saved from the deluge], now saves you" (1 Pet. 3:21). Finally, Jesus' mission on earth marked the beginning of a new epoch in human history, just as the story of Noah divided the generations of Adam from a new age for humankind.

Several times in the New Testament, the comparatively smaller ordeal of the Flood is compared with the forthcoming last judgment of God. Jesus said, "For as in those days before the flood they were eating and drinking, marrying and giving in marriage, until the day when Noah entered the ark, and they did not know until the flood came and swept them all away, so will be the com-

THE BABLONIAN NOAH

Flood stories were common among the literary traditions of Israel's neighbors, but the most famous ancient parallel to the biblical story of Noah occurs in the Babylonian epic of Gilgamesh. When the hero Gilgamesh goes on a journey to discover the secret of eternal life, he encounters a man named Utnapishtim, who had been warned that the god Enlil intended to drown humankind because the people gave him insomnia.

As in Genesis, a chosen mortal is given specific instructions for building the boat that will provide an escape for him and his family. During the deluge, which lasts seven days, the vessel carries the seeds of all life, along with Utnapishtim and his family. When Gilgamesh meets him, Utnapishtim has become immortal.

A seventh-century B.C. stone carving of Gilgamesh

327

Obadiah hiding the prophets of Yahweh; an illumination
from the 12th-century Winchester Bible

ing of the Son of man" (Mt. 24:38-39). The anonymous author of the book of Hebrews saw Noah as a shining example of trust in God: "He condemned the world and became an heir of the righteousness which comes by faith" (Heb. 11:7).

Noah has been a popular figure outside of the Bible as well. In nonscriptural Jewish writing, he is so distressed by the fate that awaits others that he delays building the ark by planting cedars and waiting for them to grow large enough to be used to build his vessel. He feverishly warns his neighbors of the impending doom, but they refuse to repent. During the deluge, Noah reveals another aspect of his characteristic righteousness by devoting himself assiduously to the care of the animals aboard the ark, literally going without sleep for the entire 40 days and nights.

The prophet Muhammad felt that his own life mirrored Noah's, since both brought a message of repentance that was ignored by their contemporaries. In the Koran, Noah has a fourth son who is drowned when he refuses to enter the ark, and it is suggested that Noah's wife also perished. One Islamic writer claims that the total number of survivors in the ark was exactly 80: Noah himself, his three sons and their wives, and 73 believers. But from the biblical point of view, the crucial aspect of the story of Noah is that one man's righteousness made possible the continuation of humankind.

THE GENERATIONS OF ADAM

*H*umanity's history from creation to the Flood, Adam to Noah, is abridged in Genesis 5. The recitation of names covers 1,656 years—that is, from the beginning of Adam's 930-year lifespan to the great deluge that occurred when Noah was 600 years old.

Like Genesis, Babylonian tradition records ten heroes before the Flood, the seventh of which—like Enoch in the Bible—was spared death, called to walk with God in heaven. Although the ages assigned the descendants of Adam range from Enoch's 365 years to Methuselah's record longevity of 969 years, they are brief in comparison with ages Babylonians assigned their heroic ancestors. The ten biblical names are repeated with two variations, in Luke 3:36-38

OBADIAH

(oh buh dai' uh) HEBREW: OBADYAHU
"servant/worshiper of Yahweh"

Although he served as steward to the apostate king **Ahab**, Obadiah was faithful to the Lord, hiding 100 of Yahweh's prophets in a cave and bringing them bread and water. In the third year of the drought predicted by **Elijah**, Obadiah and the king went out in different directions on a search for fodder for the horses and mules in the royal stables. When Elijah met the pious Obadiah and asked to see Ahab, the steward expressed fear that the prophet would merely disappear—as he had done before—and that he would have to face the wrath of the king. With Elijah's assurances, however, the meeting was arranged, the king and his nemesis at last facing one another. "Is it you, you troubler of Israel?" (1 Kg. 18:17) Ahab shouted. The prophet answered that it was the king, by his support for the worship of **Baal**, who was troubling Israel.

Later traditions identified the steward with the author of the book of Obadiah. The nearly 300-year discrepancy between the time of Ahab's reign and the destruction of Jerusalem, about which the prophet **Obadiah** wrote, makes this unlikely.

OBADIAH 2

Nothing is known about the author of the book of Obadiah, the shortest in the Old Testament. The content of the book, however, reveals that Obadiah lived in the harsh and bitter times following the capture and destruction of Jerusalem by the Babylonians that brought the kingdom of Judah to an end in 587 B.C. Some of Obadiah's words are almost exact parallels of verses ascribed to **Jeremiah**, a witness to those events. It is possible that the name Obadiah, meaning "servant of Yahweh," is only a pen name—as the name **Malachi** also may be—for a prophet who wished to speak anonymously.

Obadiah's vision comes in the form of poetic oracles that indict the people of Edom, south of Judah, for gloating over Judah's defeat and for plundering the land. He also foretells a day of retribution for Edom and one of restoration for Judah. The work is one of several Old Testament prophetic books that are concerned with the fate of nations other than Israel and Judah.

The Jews of that period considered the neighboring Edomites as hostile relatives; the uneasy relationship can be traced all the way back to the antagonism between **Jacob** and **Esau**, the biblical ancestors of the two nations. Across the centuries, the Edomites, who inhabited the arid region south of the Dead Sea, were regularly at odds with Israel. The Edomites had obstinately opposed the Israelites under **Moses** as they approached the Promised Land. Later, **David** conquered Edom, and his ruthless commander **Joab** set out to kill every male in the country, slaughtering 18,000 and establishing military garrisons throughout the land. Edom was so weakened by the massacre that a century and a half passed before it could regain sufficient strength to break fully free of Israelite domination, in about

The prophet Elijah meets Obadiah searching for fodder; a marble inlay from the cathedral of Siena, Italy.

845 B.C., only to be invaded again and punished with great slaughter 50 years later.

Like Judah, Edom was conquered first by Assyria and then by Babylon, but the centuries-old hostility between them kept the two neighbors from uniting against their common enemies. When Judah under King **Zedekiah** rebelled against Babylon, the Edomites evidently remained faithful vassals, just as Jeremiah had advised them to be. Their land served as a resource and occasional staging area for the Babylonian attack on Judah during the final, two-year siege of Jerusalem, and at least some Edomite troops joined in the sack and plunder of the city. In the aftermath, Edomites also took the opportunity to seize broad areas of southern Judah, later known as Idumea. The hostility so vividly expressed by Obadiah continued as long as the two lands existed; centuries later, it lay behind the Jewish antagonism toward King **Herod the Great**, an Idumean.

Obadiah, author of the Bible's shortest book; an English stained-glass window

OBED-EDOM

(oh' bed ee' duhm) HEBREW: OBED-EDOM
"worshiper of Edom"

While the ark of the covenant was being transported from Kiriath-jearim to Jerusalem, **Uzzah**, one of two oxcart drivers, touched the ark and was immediately struck dead. As a result, **David** was afraid to continue moving the ark and left it in the care of Obed-edom, a Philistine from Gath. He had taken up residence in Judah, perhaps as a convert to the religion of David, who had many followers among the Gittites, as those from Gath were called. This could explain David's willingness to entrust a foreigner with care of the ark of the covenant. Whatever the reason, three months later—learning that Obed-edom and his entire household had been blessed "because of the ark of God" (2 Sam. 6:12)—David decided to continue his journey and bring the ark to Jerusalem with great rejoicing.

OG

(ahg) HEBREW: OG
meaning unknown

One of the Bible's most curious figures, Og, the ruler of Bashan, a kingdom east of the Jordan River, is described as the last remnant of a race of giants called the Rephaim; his huge iron bedstead was exhibited in Rabbath-ammon long after his death. The bedstead, the dimensions of which were supposed to be six by thirteen and a half feet, may have been a sarcophagus of the ancient megalithic culture that legend magnified into a race of giants.

Og was defeated by the Israelites on their way to the land of Canaan. Winning this fertile, grain-producing kingdom, which is said to have contained many fortified towns, was a major victory for the Israelites, commemorated repeatedly in the Bible. Og's territory was assigned mainly to the tribe of Manasseh.

OMRI

(ohm' ree) HEBREW: OMRI
possibly "the life Yahweh has given"

The reign of Omri as king of Israel (c. 876-869 B.C.) was marked by brilliant political accomplishments and fateful religious developments. In the Bible he appears as a monarch irreparably stained by allowing the worship of **Baal** to flourish. Only six verses are devoted to his reign, concluding with the charge that he "did more evil than

Paul sending Onesimus with a letter to his owner Philemon; a medieval manuscript illumination

all who were before him" (1 Kg. 16:25). Omri's accomplishments outside the sphere of religion, however, have caused many historians to describe him as one of Israel's most effective rulers.

When Omri came to power, Israel was on the verge of self-destruction—without a stable royal dynasty and subject to intrigue and seizure of power by assassination. After King **Elah** was murdered by the chariot commander **Zimri**, civil war broke out. Omri, the commander of the army, decided to punish the assassin and besieged Zimri in the capital of Tirzah. Seeing that his situation was hopeless, Zimri ended his seven-day-old reign by burning the palace down around himself. Omri had to overcome **Tibni**, another powerful rival for the throne, before he was able to consolidate his power and end civil strife. Historians argue about the dates for his reign, twelve years if the period of civil war is included, six to eight years of undisputed rule.

Once firmly in power, Omri set about pacifying his borders. First, he ended 50 years of war with Judah and began collaborating with his southern neighbor to promote trade. Next, he subdued the bothersome Moabites and kept both Moab and Syria from causing trouble. Finally, he developed a close alliance with the flourishing Canaanite kingdom of Phoenicia, solidifying the connection by arranging the marriage of his son **Ahab** to **Jezebel**, daughter of the king of Sidon. Omri also built a new capital at Samaria, a city that became a center for the prosperity that followed peace and expanded trade.

Omri's social and religious policy was ✦

cosmopolitan and tolerant rather than distinctly Israelite. He himself was evidently a worshiper of Yahweh, but accepted and even encouraged the worship of Baal, the god of the large Canaanite population in Israel. This policy led to a dissolution of Israel's distinct religious identity and brought intense opposition from prophets like **Elijah**. Omri's impact on Israelite society was so great that three decades later, even after his own dynasty had ended with the death of his grandson **Jehoram**, Israel was still known to other nations of the area as the house of Omri.

ONAN
(oh' nuhn) HEBREW: ONAN
"power" or "wealth"

Onan, the second of three sons of **Judah** and a daughter of the Canaanite Shua, refused to accept the obligations of a levirate marriage—that is, to marry **Tamar**, the childless widow of his elder brother, Er. According to the requirement in Deuteronomy 25:5-10, Onan was supposed to ensure that Er's line was continued by impregnating Tamar. But when Judah specifically asked Onan to perform "the duty of a brother-in-law to her," Onan declined and instead "spilled the semen on the ground" (Gen. 38:8-9), apparently by an act of coitus interruptus. For his shocking act of defiance, Onan was slain by the Lord.

ONESIMUS
(oh nes' i muhs) GREEK: ONESIMUS
"useful"

The slave on whose behalf **Paul** wrote the letter to **Philemon**, Onesimus was also "the faithful and beloved brother" (Col. 4:9) who accompanied **Tychicus** in delivering the letter to the Colossians. Both letters were written while Paul was a prisoner, perhaps during the period of his house arrest in Rome, A.D. 61-63.

Onesimus was apparently a runaway slave from Philemon's household who may have financed his escape by robbing his master. Amazingly, the fugitive met Paul, was converted by him, and became the apostle's valued helper and companion. A common name for a slave, Onesimus means "useful," and Paul played on this word when he beseeched Philemon to release Onesimus: "Formerly he was useless to you, but now he is indeed useful to you and to me" (Philem. 11). Paul sent Onesimus back to Philemon in the hope that he would bless his slave with freedom and perhaps return him, for by then Paul regarded Onesimus as "my child" and "beloved brother" (Philem. 10, 16). Paul implied that, by his apostolic authority, he could simply order Philemon, a devoted member of the early church congregation at Colossae, to release Onesimus. But he preferred the gentler approach outlined in the letter.

ONESIPHORUS

(ohn uh sif' uh ruhs) GREEK: ONESIPHOROS
"profit-bringer"

In his second letter to **Timothy**, **Paul** asked the Lord to bless the household of Onesiphorus, praising this man for his contributions to the church at Ephesus and thanking him for his devotion to the apostle himself as a prisoner in Rome: "He often refreshed me; he was not ashamed of my chains" (2 Tim. 1:16). Because Paul began by praying for the household and not specifically for the man, scholars speculate that Onesiphorus was dead or away from his home at the time Paul sent this letter. The passages in which Paul exhorted Timothy to "be strong" and "share in suffering as a good soldier of Christ Jesus" (2 Tim. 2:1, 3) suggest to some that Timothy was grieving. If Onesiphorus was dead, Paul's words "may the Lord grant him to find mercy from the Lord on that Day" (2 Tim. 1:18) constitute the earliest prayer for the dead in Christian literature. Of course, there were Jewish precedents for such prayers and praying for the dead was a common practice among early Christians. Therefore, Paul's prayer does not provide a scriptural foundation for a doctrine of praying for the dead.

ONIAS III

(oh ni' uhs) GREEK: ONIAS; HEBREW:
HONEYU or HONI

Onias was the name of several members of a priestly family in the pre-Maccabean period. Onias I, Judean high priest from about 320 to 290 B.C., traced his lineage to **Solomon**'s high priest **Zadok**. Onias II, grandson of the first Onias, was challenged by his nephew Joseph, the head of the Tobiad family, who had maneuvered himself into a position of temporal power. Decades of rivalry between Oniads and Tobiads ensued.

In about 190 B.C., Onias III, the grandson of Onias II, became high priest. In contrast to his predecessors, he aligned himself with the Ptolemaic dynasty of Eygpt rather than with the Seleucid kings of Syria who then ruled Palestine. His cousins, the descendants of Joseph, maintained financial control of the state and sided with the Seleucids. One of them, the temple captain Simon, told King Seleucus IV of Syria that there were large amounts of money hidden in the temple. When Seleucus sent his minister Heliodorus to investigate, the people were aroused by the threat of desecration, and Onias attempted to stop the Syrian official from entering the sacred precincts by saying that the treasure was far less than reported. Heliodorus entered anyway and was so shocked by a vivid, disturbing vision that he would have died had not Onias been entreated to pray for his recovery.

Afterward, Onias struggled unsuccessfully to maintain control of the high priesthood, eventually traveling to Antioch to plead his case before the Syrian king. But before he could do so, Seleucus was assassinated and succeeded by his brother **Antiochus IV Epiphanes**, whereupon Onias's own brother **Jason** bought the office of high priest from the new king. Jason was later outbid by **Menelaus**, Simon's brother. When Onias protested Menelaus's pilfering from the temple, he was murdered, according to some accounts, by order of Menelaus.

SLAVERY

Paul's entreaty on behalf of Onesimus in the letter to Philemon sheds some light on early Christian attitudes toward slavery. Although the implications of Paul's elevating Onesimus from indentured servitude to fellowship in the church seem clear to readers today, freeing slaves was not a matter of course for early Christians. Roman law gave a master absolute authortity over the life of his slave and was not lightly or easily challenged.

Rather than dispute the institution of slavery, Paul asked his friend in Colossae to release Onesimus to him, implying a Christian obligation to treat all brothers in faith equally.

OREB

(aw' reb) HEBREW: OREB
"raven"
•••••••••

After his victory over the Midianites, **Gideon** called on the Ephraimites to seize the fords of the Jordan River in order to prevent his fleeing enemies from reaching their homeland to the east. Though offended because Gideon had not enlisted their aid earlier, the men of Ephraim obliged him and captured two Midianite princes, Oreb and Zeeb. Decapitating their prisoners, the Ephraimites presented the heads to Gideon as war trophies. "What have I been able to do in comparison with you?" (Jg. 8:3), Gideon said in further mollification of the Ephraimites, who were at last vindicated for the slight. The places where Oreb and Zeeb were slain—the rock of Oreb and the winepress of Zeeb—became emblematic of Israel's victories over its enemies.

ORPAH

(or' puh) HEBREW: ORPA
possibly "neck" or "cloud"
•••••••••

Driven by famine, **Elimelech** and **Naomi** fled from Bethlehem in Judah to Moab. After Elimelech died, their two sons, Mahlon and Chilion, married the Moabite women **Ruth** and Orpah. Within ten years, the sons also died; and Naomi, hearing that the famine in Judah was over, decided to go home. Her daughters-in-law would have accompanied her, but she told them to stay in Moab, where they would stand a better chance at remarriage. After some persuasion, Orpah submitted to Naomi's wishes, but Ruth returned to Judah with Naomi. Though Orpah is not criticized for remaining in her homeland in the book of Ruth, where the story appears, Jewish tradition says that her name—one possible meaning of which is "neck"—was given because she turned the back of her neck on Naomi.

OTHNIEL

(ahth' nee el) HEBREW: OTNIEL
•••••••••

When **Joshua** died at the age of 110, Israel was left without a leader. And so "the Lord raised up judges, who saved them out of the power of those who plundered them" (Jg. 2:16). Othniel was the first of these judges, or deliverers, of the nation. His great achievement—rescuing the Israelites from the oppression of King **Cushan-rishathaim** of Mesapotamia and ushering in a generation of peace—set a pattern: Is-

Orpah remained in Moab, while Ruth insisted on accompanying their mother-in-law, Naomi, back to Judah.

rael sins; God sends an enemy to punish the nation for its sins; Israel repents; God delivers his chosen people from the enemy; a grace period ensues.

Othniel's tale presents the major elements that characterize those of all the judges. God himself selects the judge, imbuing him with "the Spirit of the Lord" (Jg. 3:10)—that is, the wisdom and courage he needs to deliver Israel. And thus, the judge is the Lord's instrument for working out his plan of history. The 40 years of rest that follow Othniel's deliverance is a characteristic round number for a generation in the Bible.

Although Othniel's deliverance of Israel from Cushan-rishathaim is the highlight of his story, it begins with another military victory. Responding to a challenge from his uncle **Caleb**, Othniel restored the city of Debir to the Israelites—Debir having initially been captured by Joshua but apparently lost during the process of allocating territory among the 12 tribes. As a reward for taking Debir, Caleb bestowed his daughter Achsah's hand in marriage on Othniel—just as **Saul** later gave his daughter **Michal** to **David** for a victory over the Philistines. When Achsah and Othniel wed, she asked her father for land watered by springs as a wedding gift. This dowry provided Othniel's descendants with fertile fields in the otherwise arid Negeb.

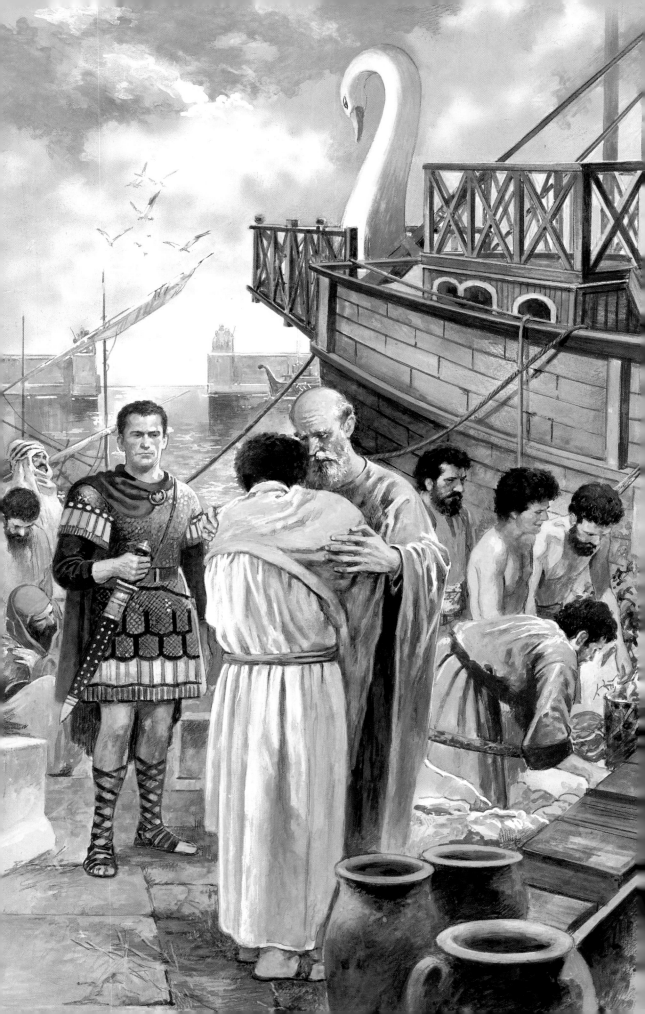

PALTI

(pal' tai) HEBREW: PALTI
"my deliverance"

David was too popular to suit his father-in-law, King **Saul**. So the king "sent messengers to David's house to watch him, that he might kill him in the morning" (1 Sam. 19:11). But with the aid of his wife, Saul's daughter **Michal**, David escaped being murdered and fled. The king retaliated by giving Michal to another man, Palti, of the tribe of Benjamin. After Saul died, the commander of his army, **Abner**, sought a reconciliation with David, who agreed to peace on the condition that Michal be returned to him. She was taken from Palti (in this passage called Paltiel), who followed behind, "weeping after her all the way to Bahurim" (2 Sam. 3:16) on the eastern outskirts of Jerusalem; he stopped only when the commander ordered him to go home.

PASHHUR

(pash' uhr) HEBREW: PASHUR
"destruction all around"

As priest and chief officer of the temple, Pashhur was responsible for keeping order, and thus he responded swiftly to an unsettling prophecy about the coming fall of Jerusalem. "Pashhur beat Jeremiah the prophet, and put him in the stocks" (Jer. 20:2). When **Jeremiah** was released the next day, he had a new name for the priest, and a description of his destiny: "Terror on every side," an obvious play on the word *pashur*. The priest would see his friends fall in battle, the prophet said; Jerusalem would be plundered; and the populace of Judah,

A prisoner bound for Rome, Paul bids a coworker good-bye on the quay at Caesarea.

including Pashhur and his family, would be carried off into exile. The terrible prophecy was likely fulfilled in 597 B.C., when Babylon punished Judah's rebellion by exiling its leading citizens. Another rebellion led to the fall of Jerusalem and exile of more people a decade later, in 587 B.C.

PAUL

GREEK: PAULOS

Although he was the leading persecutor of Christians in the first years of the new faith, Paul became a believer in **Jesus** and the most influential voice—after Jesus himself—in the history of the church. Paul's conversion placed him on the borderline between two worlds. He had been raised in a strict Jewish home that led him to devote his life to the defense of Mosaic Law against a "sect" that not only questioned that Law and worship in the temple but also claimed a crucified Galilean teacher was the Messiah. Paul's transformation convinced him that indeed the crucified Galilean was the Messiah and son of God and that the Messiah's message was not only for Jews but also for Gentiles. The experience could not have been more traumatic or ultimately more joyful for Paul. Although he continued to devote his life to the same God he had always worshiped, Paul came to see God's will as pointing in another direction.

Paul was born in the Greek city of Tarsus, a prosperous and renowned center of education and philosophy in the region of Cilicia in southern Asia Minor. Paul's family thus lived in the two worlds of Greek and Jewish culture. As Paul told an assembly of Pharisees and Sadducees, "I am a Pharisee, a son of Pharisees" (Acts 23:6). His parents gave him the Hebrew name Saul, in honor of King **Saul**, who was of their tribe of Benjamin. He also bore the Latin name Paulus and was proud to assert that he was both a citizen of the Greek city of Tarsus and a citizen of Rome. Relatively few Jewish families of the Diaspora enjoyed such privileges of citizenship, which often required compromise with pagan culture and having sons educated in Greek culture in the city school, called a *gymnasion*. Paul's father, it would seem, had enough wealth to attain citizen status while remaining a strict Pharisee; life in the Diaspora, besieged by Greek political and cultural influences, evidently made him more devoted to his own religion.

Apparently, while Paul was still a youth, the family moved to Jerusalem, where Paul was educated and where his only known sibling, a married sister with a son, still lived many years later. Paul's Pharisaic roots led him to study with one of the leading teachers of the time, **Gamaliel** the elder, known in tradition as the grandson of the great Hillel, the leading Jewish teacher of the first century B.C. Through this training, Paul said, "I advanced in Judaism beyond many of my own age among my people, so extremely zealous was I for the traditions of my fathers" (Gal. 1:14). At the same time, Paul learned the craft of tent making in order to support himself for his study of the Law.

A cosmopolitan city, Jerusalem had numerous synagogues where Jews from Greek-speaking regions gathered for study and mutual support. The book of Acts mentions synagogues for Jews from Cyrene, Alexandria, Cilicia, and Asia (the region around Ephesus). Since he was from Tarsus, Paul most likely made the synagogue of the Cilicians his base, and there he began to dispute with Christians such as **Stephen**, one of the leaders of the Greek-speaking church in Jerusalem. To Paul such people seemed determined to undermine the Law and worship at the holy temple, all in the name of Jesus of Nazareth. Though Paul was probably in Jerusalem during the final period of Jesus' life, he never gives any hint in his writings that he saw or heard of Jesus during his ministry. It was only in later debates with Jesus' followers that Paul became alarmed at the rapid development of the movement.

Paul (still known as Saul) first appears in the New Testament as a consenting witness at the execution of Stephen, the first Christian martyr. Stephen was brought before a council to be charged with speaking "against this holy place and the law" and with arguing that Jesus would "destroy this place and change the customs which Moses delivered to us" (Acts 6:13, 14). Stephen confirmed the worst fears of people like Paul by attacking his countrymen for always opposing God, for believing that God could ever dwell in a man-made house like the temple, and for betraying and killing the Messiah. For Paul, these were words of war. Everything that he held dear, the Law, the temple, the traditions of his people, seemed at risk if a sect like Stephen's was allowed to survive. What is more, the sect was proclaiming as the Messiah a man who had been hanged on

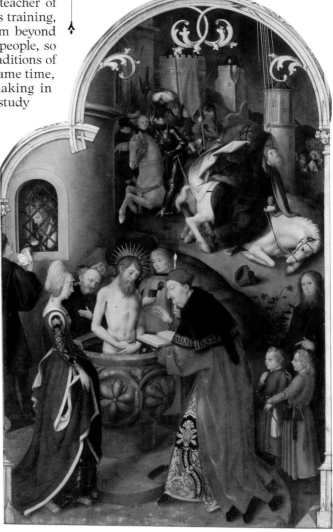

Following his vision on the road to Damascus (rear), Paul is baptized; the scenes are the work of Hans Holbein the Elder (c. 1465-1524).

a cross, whereas the Scriptures taught, "a hanged man is accursed by God" (Dt. 21:23). A broken Law, a destroyed temple, and an accursed Messiah—to Paul these heresies summarized the dangerous new sect. Thus, as he later wrote, "I persecuted the church of God violently and tried to destroy it" (Gal. 1:13).

The first target of Paul's attacks were evidently the Christians of Jerusalem, who were Jews from the Greek Diaspora, like Stephen and Paul himself. Many, including the evangelist **Philip**, another of the seven leaders of the Greek-speaking Christians, fled to Samaria, Damascus, Phoenicia, Cyprus, or Antioch of Syria. Paul even used his influence with the high priest in Jerusalem to reach beyond the city to attack Christians in regions outside Judea, obtaining from him letters to the synagogues at Damascus. Though the high priest had no legal authority outside Judea, his word could certainly affect how synagogues would cooperate with Paul in his opposition to the new faith.

A TRANSFORMING VISION

About A.D. 35, some five years after Jesus' crucifixion, Paul—perhaps about 30 years old—was on his way to Damascus with the letters from the high priest in hand. God chose that moment to reverse his life. In later years Paul described the event calmly, saying simply that God "was pleased to reveal his Son to me, in order that I might preach him among the Gentiles" (Gal. 1:16). In Acts, the event is recounted three times in considerable detail.

Paul was nearing Damascus when a brilliant light from heaven surrounded him. A voice addressed Paul by his Hebrew name: "Saul, Saul, why do you persecute me?" Paul might have hoped for such a vision to approve his work for God, but he was dumbfounded when the voice accused him of persecution. He could only ask, "Who are you, Lord?" The next words Paul heard crushed his world and transformed his future. The voice answered, "I am Jesus, whom you are persecuting" (Acts 9:4, 5).

Impossible! Jesus had been crucified—accursed. He could not be the Messiah, much less be speaking to him in a vision from heaven. But Paul was himself experiencing that vision, and he could not deny it. The experience was such that Paul simply knew with profound assurance that this was indeed a "heavenly vision" (Acts 26:19) from the very God whom he had been serving but whom he had radically misunderstood. For Paul the impossible had become real.

The dazzling light had blinded Paul, per-

Paul (rear) guards the cloaks of the men stoning Stephen, the first Christian martyr.

haps to teach him the blindness of the violent persecution he had instigated. But with his companions Paul continued to Damascus, where he spent three days praying in that unaccustomed darkness—fasting, cut off from his past, not knowing what the future held. Finally, he was approached by a man named **Ananias**, a devout Jew who was also an adherent of the new faith. Through Ananias, Paul's blindness was healed; he was baptized and experienced the power of the **Holy Spirit** that had emboldened Stephen.

Immediately, Paul began to proclaim his new faith in Jesus with some of the same vigor he had used before to defend the Law. He startled Jews and Christians in Damascus by entering their debates on the opposite side from the one they had expected. When the situation became dangerous, Paul did not return directly to Jerusalem but traveled south into Arabia, then a part of the kingdom of Nabatea, and remained there two or three years, preaching and teaching. By the time he went back to Damascus, he had evidently become the object of such antagonism that King **Aretas** of Nabatea had the city guarded to prevent Paul's escape.

Paul escapes Damascus in a basket; a 12th-century enamel.

But aided by Christian friends, Paul "was let down in a basket through a window in the wall, and escaped his hands" (2 Cor. 11:33).

In about A.D. 38, Paul finally returned to Jerusalem, where many Christians had formerly suffered persecution at his hands. At that time he met only two of the church's leaders, **Peter** (whom he calls Cephas) and **James**, "the Lord's brother" (Gal. 1:19), who was becoming the major voice of the Jerusalem community. **Barnabas**, a Levite from Cyprus who was one of the original members of the Christian community in Jerusalem, vouched for Paul and helped overcome the suspicion about him. Paul's very presence in Jerusalem was such a catalyst for conflict, however, that he soon departed for Tarsus and spent the next several years working in Cilicia and Syria.

A MESSAGE FOR GENTILES?

Few details are known of Paul's work in those first 10 to 12 years after his dramatic conversion. It was doubtless a time of much activity but also profound reflection for Paul. He knew that God had called him not simply to repeat the words of others but to delve deeply into the revelation that he himself had received. What did it mean to trust that one who had been crucified was indeed God's Messiah? What did it mean that the message was for Gentiles not as proselytes to Judaism but as Gentiles? Paul was a highly trained Jew, and his understanding of the Law, tradition, Israel's history, and God's grace and love had to be completely rethought. The message of the cross, which had once seemed so scandalously foolish, he now saw as the very embodiment of God's wisdom and power. During those years, his preaching and reflection crystallized into the powerful theological message that is apparent in the letters Paul later wrote.

In practical terms, the problem of the relevancy of the gospel to Gentiles as well as Jews was becoming the thorniest theological dilemma for the early Christian communities. Peter was pushed by a dramatic vision to overcome his strong personal aversion and preached the gospel to a pious Gentile named **Cornelius**. His action sparked a sharp controversy within the church in Jerusalem. The entire first generation of believers was Jewish, and to many of them faith in the Messiah was intimately linked to observance of Mosaic Law. It seemed impossible to them that a community of believers in the Messiah would not faithfully keep the Law.

It was evidently in Antioch of Syria that the new faith was first actively taught among Gentiles, who were then accepted into the community without having to be circumcised or without being required to observe the dietary laws and regulations of purity that distinguish Judaism. Barnabas came from Jerusalem and strongly approved of these new developments. Needing additional help, he went to Tarsus, found Paul, and brought him to Antioch. Together these two functioned as the leading teachers in Antioch for a year. And there, outsiders began to call the disciples "Christians," meaning "followers of Christ," to distinguish them from other Jewish groups. Though the ethnic mix of this community made it very different from the Jerusalem church, the Christians in Antioch were careful to maintain close ties with that community by sending aid in times of famine. On one occasion, perhaps about A.D. 46, Barnabas and Paul took the aid to Jerusalem and returned with Barnabas's cousin, John **Mark**.

Soon after their return to Antioch, Paul and Barnabas realized that the Spirit was calling them to new areas of work. With fasting and prayer, the two set out for Cyprus, taking John Mark as their assistant on what has traditionally been called the first missionary journey (*see next page*).

With Barnabas's knowledge of his home island, the company began work in Salamis on the east coast, preaching in synagogues there before traveling west across the island to Paphos. At Paphos they encountered one of the many strange religious characters that could be found in cities throughout the Roman empire: a Jew named **Bar-Jesus** who claimed to be a prophet and a magician and who had become a spiritual adviser to the Roman proconsul Sergius **Paulus**. When the magician tried to keep the proconsul from listening to the Christian message, Paul struck Bar-Jesus blind, and Paulus believed, "astounded at the teaching of the Lord" (Acts 13:12). In Acts, this event marks the point at which Paul becomes the leader of the missionary enterprise and, coincidentally, begins to be called by his

Latin name; whereas **Luke** had earlier written of "Barnabas and Saul," he now speaks of "Paul and his company" (Acts 13:7, 13).

Next, the group of missionaries crossed over to Asia Minor and traveled inland through the region of Pisidia to another of the towns named Antioch, where Paul preached in the synagogue. "We bring you the good news," Paul proclaimed, "that what God promised to the fathers, this he has fulfilled to us their children by raising Jesus" (Acts 13:32-33). Many responded enthusiastically, but others in the synagogue were outraged. The message split the Jewish community and soon stirred up the whole town. But an exuberant Christian community, made up primarily of Gentiles, was formed apart from the synagogue. After a few weeks, however, the opposition to Paul and Barnabas became so intense that they traveled on to other cities: Iconium, Lystra, and Derbe, all in the region called Lycaonia.

HAILED AS GODS

In each of these cities, the missionaries met with a combination of positive response and intense opposition. Pagan crowds in Lystra first thought that Paul and Barnabas were gods for having healed a lame man but later turned on them and stoned Paul till they thought he was dead. The severe injuries from such a stoning might well have weakened Paul's health permanently, for he was later to complain of physical frailty. Yet communities of believers were established in each of these cities, drawing people from both Jewish and pagan backgrounds into the new faith. After Derbe, Paul and Barnabas retraced their steps to each city, "strengthening the souls of the disciples, exhorting them to continue in the faith, and saying that through many tribulations we must enter the kingdom of God" (Acts 14:22). At some point on this trip Paul and Barnabas were joined by **Titus**, a young Greek convert who later became one of Paul's most important coworkers. Together they traveled back to Antioch in Syria and reported to the church there how God "had opened a door of faith to the Gentiles" (Acts 14:27).

The simmering tensions between Jews and Gentiles within the church, however, were coming to a boil. Christian teachers from Judea came to Antioch with a warning for all the Gentile converts: "Unless you are circumcised according to the custom of Moses, you cannot be

Paul preaching in the synagogue at Damascus; a 12th-century mosaic from the cathedral of Monreale, Sicily

saved" (Acts 15:1). These were Christians who, like Paul, had been Pharisees before they came to believe in Jesus and who vigorously challenged Paul's understanding of the gospel. In the face of this pressure, in about A.D. 49, Paul and Barnabas took Titus—refusing to allow him to be circumcised—and went to Jerusalem to confront the issue with the leaders of the church. Thus, by taking Titus as an example of the power of the gospel among Gentiles, Paul kept the issue from becoming too abstract. For Paul and others like him, the very heart of his message—what he calls "the truth of the gospel" (Gal. 2:5)—was at stake. If the grace of God in Jesus that he had preached was to be only for Jews and for Gentiles who became proselytes to Judaism, then Paul had profoundly misunderstood the gospel, and indeed, as he expressed it, he "had run in vain" (Gal. 2:2).

The results of this crucial meeting were positive from Paul's point of view. Two accounts of the event highlight very different aspects, but both report the same basic results. In Acts, written a generation later,

Luke describes a general assembly of the apostles and elders with speeches by Peter and James the brother of Jesus and a report of their work by Barnabas and Paul. From this meeting the church issued a letter that refused to require Gentiles to be circumcised in order to become Christians but required them to avoid meat from animals sacrificed to pagan gods or from which the blood was not properly removed and to shun unchastity. Paul himself describes the meeting in his letter to the Galatians. He and Barnabas met with the so-called pillars of the church in Jerusalem—Peter, James, and **John** the son of **Zebedee**. They agreed that just as Peter had been chosen by God to lead the mission to the Jews (at that time the great majority of all Christians), so Paul had been chosen to lead the mission to the Gentiles. According to Paul, the Jerusalem leaders gave him and Barnabas "the right hand of fellowship, that we should go to the Gentiles and they to the circumcised." They also asked that the Gentile Christians remember to help the poor, "which very thing," Paul says, "I was eager to do" (Gal. 2:9, 10).

PAUL'S MISSIONARY JOURNEYS

The apostle Paul was impelled by his faith to spread the gospel of Jesus as widely as he was physically able to do so—always working on the spreading frontier of Christianity, never preaching where others had been. As the apostle to the Gentiles, he left a permanent stamp on Christianity by transforming it from a movement within Judaism to a faith for all nations. Moreover, the fact that he centered his efforts in major cities of the

Roman empire helped shape Christianity as an urban religion—so much so that the word "pagan" comes from the Latin word for country dweller.

Paul's travels are usually divided into three missionary journeys plus his voyage to Rome as a prisoner. When the first missionary journey began, however, Paul had already been traveling and preaching for more than a decade in the area of his hometown of Tarsus and throughout Syr-

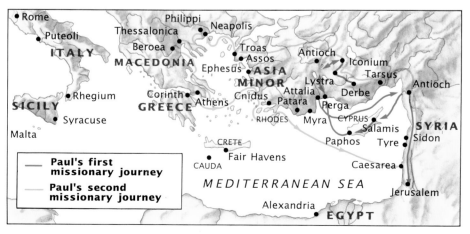

The stand of Paul and Barnabas at the conference in Jerusalem by no means ended all controversy over the volatile issue of Jews and Gentiles, but it tipped the balance. Christianity was to be a universal religion; the church could spread freely in the broad world of the Roman empire and beyond but would not be limited to the domain of Jews and proselytes. Questions of dietary laws and table fellowship between Jewish and Gentile Christians remained in dispute, leading to sharp differences between Paul and Peter and even between Paul and Barnabas. But Paul never wavered in his conviction that God had called the Gentiles to faith as Gentiles, entirely apart from the distinctive requirements of the Law of Moses, and he was confident enough to defend that conviction even in opposition to a pillar of the church like Peter.

Paul's disagreements with Barnabas led them to continue their ministries separately. Barnabas took John Mark and sailed to Cyprus to preach, while Paul chose **Silas** (short for Silvanus) and traveled by land to Asia Minor on what is known as the second

In this stained-glass panel, an angel leads Paul from the jail at Philippi.

ia and Arabia. To the Corinthians Paul wrote that he had been "on frequent journeys" (2 Cor. 11:26), and he mentioned numerous beatings and shipwrecks not recorded in the book of Acts.

The apostle's first documented journey began from Antioch of Syria in partnership with Barnabas. They passed through Cyprus, crossed to Asia Minor, traveled into the mountainous interior of Pisidia, and turned eastward to the cities of Lycaonia. Then they retraced their steps to Antioch, a journey of more than 1,200 miles.

That trek seemed short, however, compared with Paul's second journey, begun some months later with Silas. The pair traveled widely in Asia Minor, crossed into Europe, and worked in cities down the Greek peninsula before returning to Asia Minor, Palestine, and Antioch. On his third journey Paul returned to Asia Minor, Macedonia, and Greece to consolidate his work there. He later intended to travel to Spain by way of Rome, but was arrested by Roman authorities in the temple at Jerusalem and sent on an ill-fated voyage to Rome for trial.

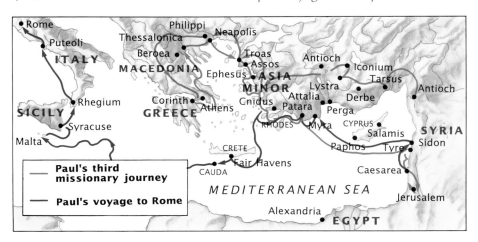

*Paul addressing the philosophers of Athens; a tapestry after a design
by Raphael (1483-1520)*

missionary journey. They passed through Lystra where **Timothy**—a young man like Titus who was to become one of Paul's principal aides—joined them. The three traveled north into the interior cities of Galatia, then west into Phrygia, founding small communities of disciples all along the way. Paul perhaps spent extra time in Galatia "because of a bodily ailment," which he does not identify. But the joy of the new converts was such that they cared for Paul "as an angel of God" (Gal. 4:13, 14).

BEATEN, IMPRISONED, FREED

Eventually, Paul and Silas came to Troas (ancient Troy), and sailed from there to Macedonia, taking the Christian message for the first time to Europe. Every city offered its particular challenges, dangers, and opportunities. In Philippi, Paul and Silas converted **Lydia**, a Gentile woman sympathetic to Judaism. Her home became the first center in Philippi of the church; the community there developed a particularly affectionate relationship with Paul. But when Paul and Silas healed a slave girl whose owners touted her as a soothsayer with a spirit of divination, they found themselves dragged before the town magistrates

in the forum, stripped, beaten with rods, and locked in stocks in prison. Undaunted, they were singing hymns for the other prisoners at midnight when a terrifying earthquake shook the prison—miraculously throwing open the doors and loosening their fetters. After converting their jailer to the faith, they were set free.

Leaving Philippi, Paul's company traveled along the main Roman road, the Via Egnatia, to Amphipolis, Apollonia, and finally to Thessalonica, the Roman capital of Macedonia. As was Paul's practice, the apostle first began to teach in the synagogue, where he would find people who knew the Scriptures and what it meant to say, "This Jesus, whom I proclaim to you, is the Christ" (Acts 17:3). As the radical meaning of Paul's proclamation of Jesus as the Messiah became clear, however, the Jewish community split. From the synagogue Paul drew off a few of the Jews, many "devout Greeks," and "leading women" (Acts 17:4) who had been attracted to the synagogue. These joined with a number of pagans who, as Paul wrote, "turned to God from idols, to serve a living and true God" (1 Th. 1:9). This diverse group formed the new Christian community at Thessalonica.

It is not hard to understand the bitterness of the many Jews who rejected Paul's teaching and saw their synagogue communities torn asunder by this religious earthquake. In Thessalonica they failed to arrest Paul but brought his host, a Jewish believer named Jason, before the magistrates, accusing him of harboring "these men who have turned the world upside down" (Acts 17:6). Paul and Silas were often pushed or pulled from town to town both by grateful believers, who desired to protect those who had brought them new life, and by those who were outraged at the effect they had on the community.

Leaving Macedonia, Paul preached briefly in Athens, where he made a memorable speech concerning the unknown God to Greek philosophers before the council known as the Areopagus. His message elicited little positive response among the literati of Athens, however, and he soon moved on to Corinth, the Roman capital of the region of Achaia.

Paul was becoming ever more aware of how vulnerable were the small communities of believers that he had founded. The church in Thessalonica had faced strong opposition, and Paul was afraid that in the weeks since he had left it the community might have been overwhelmed. When Paul "could bear it no longer" (1 Th. 3:1), he sent Timothy back north to Thessalonica to learn what had happened. In the glow of relief and gratitude that Paul felt when Timothy returned with good news, Paul began a new enterprise that was to affect the entire history of Christianity. He began to write letters.

Paul's first letter, to the Thessalonians in about A.D. 51, represents the earliest writing in the New Testament. The letter was a genuine outpouring of affection for the Christians in Thessalonica. It is colored with memories of the struggles they had faced combined with instruction in their new faith and exhortations to grow spiritually, love each other, live quietly, and "rejoice always, pray constantly, give thanks in all circumstances" (1 Th. 5:16-18). It was not a private letter but a public document to be "read to all the brethren" (1 Th. 5:27). In the years that followed Paul's letters became an effective tool for dealing with the needs of his far-flung congregations; the documents substituted for the presence of the apostle himself in an era when travel was slow and often dangerous.

Meanwhile, Corinth had proved to be a place of both conflict and profitable work for Paul. He preached in the synagogue and won over **Crispus**, the ruler of the synagogue, as well as Titius Justus, a devout

Gentile who lent Paul his house next door to the synagogue for his teaching. Many other Gentiles were also converted to Christianity. Paul was aided in his work not only by Silas and Timothy but also by **Aquila** and his wife, Priscilla (**Prisca**), Jewish Christians who had been forced to leave Rome and who shared with Paul the craft of tent making. Though the Jews once tried to have Paul condemned as a criminal before the Roman proconsul **Gallio**, the official refused to hear a dispute "about words and names and your own law" (Acts 18:15).

RICH WITH SPIRITUAL GIFTS

As in other places, the community Paul founded at Corinth was a diverse assortment of Jews and Gentiles, mostly from the lower classes, but with a few who had some personal wealth. They responded to the message of Jesus and the power of the Holy Spirit with particular enthusiasm. Both Jews and Gentiles had broken with their own religious traditions and communities to become part of the new fellowship, and they delighted in experiences of spiritual fulfillment, wisdom, freedom, and intimacy with God. The tendency of the Corinthian Christians was always to push their individual spiritual experiences to the furthest extent. They felt like kings, sated with a wealth of spiritual gifts. In spite of strong opposition, Paul was able to remain with them a year and a half, longer than he had stayed at any place since leaving Antioch.

When he left Corinth, Paul took Priscilla and Aquila with him to Ephesus and soon booked passage alone to Caesarea. From there he went on to Jerusalem. After stopping at the temple and calling on the Christian community, Paul headed north to revisit the churches in Antioch and the regions of Galatia and Phrygia before returning to Ephesus, where he rejoined Priscilla and Aquila. But part of what Paul found on his third missionary journey deeply disturbed him.

Among the largely Gentile churches of Galatia, other Christian missionaries had followed in his own footsteps and had tried with some success to convince these Gentile Christians that they must be circumcised and follow the Law of Moses. Paul wrote an urgent letter to all the churches of the region warning against such revisions of the gospel: "Even if we, or an angel from heaven, should preach to you a gospel contrary to that which we preached to you, let him be accursed." "For freedom Christ has set us free," he urged them; "stand fast therefore, and do not submit again to a yoke of slavery." Those who depend on obedience to the Law for salvation "are severed from Christ," he warned, and "have fallen away from grace" (Gal. 1:8; 5:1, 4).

Back in Ephesus, the Roman capital of the province of Asia, Paul began a more than two-year period of work, using the city as a base from which he sent his coworkers out into the surrounding regions to establish churches. Paul himself taught daily in a hired lecture room called "the hall of Tyrannus" (Acts 19:9), and the church thrived. But all was not well elsewhere.

Paul received reports of growing problems in the church at Corinth, and a letter from the Christian community there posed a series of questions about such topics as spiritual gifts, the resurrection of the dead, and eating food that had been offered to idols. The Corinthians were still very enthusiastic in their faith, but their delight in their individual spiritual experiences was straining the fabric of mutual love that held the congregation together. They were competing with each other in displaying such gifts as speaking in tongues; they were dividing up in their allegiance to various teachers; they were showing such indifference to taboos surrounding food sacrificed to idols that the faith of some Christians was being destroyed.

Paul wrote to the Corinthians, calling on them to refocus their faith not on their spiritual accomplishments but on the self-giving love shown in Christ on the cross, the true "power of God and the wisdom of God" (1 Cor. 1:24). The highest spiritual gift, one that would last beyond this world, he told them, is simple love. They must put love for each other and the good of the whole community above personal desires. Without that love, no amount of faith or religious insight could have any more meaning than "a noisy gong or a clanging cymbal" (1 Cor. 13:1). By keeping the cross of Christ and the love that it expressed as their central vision, the Corinthians could handle all the diverse questions troubling them.

In Ephesus the impact of Paul's preaching, as always, won converts and roused opposition. Paul told the Corinthians how he "fought with beasts at Ephesus" (1 Cor. 15:32)—perhaps a metaphor for strong opposition. It may have been while he was

The tireless missionary Paul holds a book of his writings; a fifth-century ivory carving.

imprisoned there that he wrote to the church at Philippi to encourage the congregation and thank its members for sending one of their own, **Epaphroditus**, to help him in his work. "Rejoice in the Lord always," he urged them, "again I will say, Rejoice." "I have learned," he confided, "in whatever state I am, to be content. . . . I can do all things in him who strengthens me" (Phil. 4:4, 11, 13).

Paul's "anxiety for all the churches" (2 Cor. 11:28), however, could never be fully relieved. He had to deal with rival missionaries in both Corinth and Philippi, men who denigrated his work and tried to alienate the churches from him. With sharp irony, Paul termed these men "superlative apostles" (2 Cor. 11:5) because of the extravagant claims they made for their own spiritual power. For a time it appeared that the church at Corinth would renounce its association with Paul and abandon his teaching. But by using Titus as an emissary, Paul finally reestablished his close relationship with the Corinthians, to his great relief.

The situation at Ephesus finally exploded. Devotees of Ephesus's famous goddess, the many-breasted **Artemis**, felt the impact of Paul's work on their religion and their livelihood. Led by a silversmith named **Demetrius**, they rioted against Paul, shouting "Great is Artemis of the Ephesians!" (Acts 19:28). As the object of this uproar, Paul—who had been wanting to revisit the churches—decided that it was best to leave Ephesus, and he traveled around the Aegean coast to Macedonia and ultimately returned to Corinth.

SUMMARIZING HIS PREACHING

Through many difficulties and struggles and in the face of harsh persecution, Paul felt that he had finally brought the churches around the Aegean and in the interior of Asia Minor to a level of maturity and stability that they could maintain on their own. He believed it was time to move on. When he arrived in Corinth for a final three-month visit, he had decided to travel west to Spain, a region as yet untouched by the message of Jesus.

From Corinth, in the winter of A.D. 55-56, Paul wrote a letter to the church in Rome, requesting its members' hospitality and aid as he traveled through the imperial city on his way to Spain. Paul used this letter to a distant church—his longest and most important—as an opportunity to lay out in summary fashion the foundations of the gospel he preached.

That gospel, he asserted, "is the power of God for salvation to every one who has faith, to the Jew first and also to the Greek" (Rom. 1:16). In response to the violence and corruption that enslave humanity, God had sent his son to break the enslaving power of sin through his redemptive death on the cross. Though humanity is weak and unworthy, Paul announced, "God shows his love for us in that while we were yet sinners Christ died for us" (Rom. 5:8). No human being can break the power of sin and stand righteous before God, but God in his grace chooses to pronounce over the guilty person who trusts in Jesus the verdict of innocent. What is more, as the believer is "baptized into Christ Jesus" and experiences "the Spirit of life in Christ Jesus," the power of sin and death is broken, and God makes the believer his own child. "When we cry, 'Abba! Father!'" Paul said, "It is the Spirit himself bearing witness with our spirit that we are children of God." The power of this vision gave Paul the basis for profound peace, joy, and confidence in God: "If God is for us, who is against us?" Nothing, Paul concluded, "in all creation, will be able to separate us from the love of God in Christ Jesus our Lord" (Rom. 6:3; 8:2, 15-16, 31, 39).

Before leaving for Spain, Paul decided to make a final visit to Jerusalem to deliver to the church there gifts for the poor that he had gathered from all the churches he had founded—thereby fulfilling his promise to Peter, James, and John. He bade farewell to the churches around the Aegean, expecting "that they should see his face no more" (Acts 20:38), and he traveled with considerable trepidation toward Jerusalem, where he was welcomed by James and the elders. But unfortunately his notoriety among other Jews had preceded him. When he entered the temple, Jews from the region of Ephesus accused him of desecrating the temple by bringing Greeks inside, and they started a riot. The tribune Claudius **Lysias** sent Roman soldiers from the garrison that overlooked the temple court to intervene, saving Paul from being beaten to death but also putting him under arrest. From that moment on, Paul was never again free, so far as Acts recounts, and all his plans were foiled.

The antipathy against this Pharisee who had become a Christian and devoted himself to the Gentiles was so great that Lysias

THE EPISTLES OF PAUL

How did Paul's letters, written to widely scattered churches and addressing specific needs of those communities, come to be gathered in a group and made part of the New Testament? Unfortunately, no one knows the exact process, but Paul's words show that there were early exchanges (and perhaps collections) of his letters. But some letters also were clearly lost, since Paul's letter from Laodicea, mentioned in Colossians 4:16, does not survive. Similarly, in 1 Corinthians 5:9-11, Paul mentions a no longer extant earlier letter to them.

During the 30 to 40 years after Paul, a period of church history about which little is known, his letters were collected as a small book. Some historians think Onesimus, the slave mentioned in the letter to Philemon, may well have been the first to gather them. There is a tradition that he became bishop of Ephesus during that period, and he would have had particular knowledge of the brief letter that Paul had sent to Philemon concerning himself.

By the middle of the second century a book including 10 or 11 of Paul's letters (sometimes including the anonymous letter to the Hebrews but not including 1 and 2 Timothy and Titus) was in wide circulation. The earliest surviving copy dates to about A.D. 200 and arranges the letters in general order of length from the longest to the shortest: Romans, Hebrews, 1 and 2 Corinthians, Ephesians, Galatians, Philippians, Colossians, 1 and 2 Thessalonians, and perhaps Philemon. Over time, Galatians and Ephesians were switched, Hebrews was moved to the end of the collection because its authorship was questionable, and the letters to Timothy and Titus were added to the collection and placed before the shorter letter to Philemon.

had to send his prisoner to Caesarea, seat of the governor, for protection. The governor, **Felix**, was acquainted with Christianity and evidently discounted all the charges against Paul but nevertheless held him in custody in Caesarea for two years.

In A.D. 59, Felix was replaced by a new governor, **Festus**, who suggested that Paul be returned to Jerusalem, but Paul refused to go and appealed for a hearing before the emperor in Rome—his right as a Roman citizen. When the well-educated but dissolute **Herod Agrippa II** and his sister **Bernice** visited Caesarea, Paul recounted his story and his faith at length before them. Agrippa was amazed at Paul's audacity in trying to convert him, but all recognized that Paul did not deserve to be imprisoned. Because of his appeal, however, they agreed that he must be sent to Rome.

HIS FINAL DESTINATION

Soon Paul was put aboard ship with several companions in the care of a kindly centurion named **Julius**, who was transporting several prisoners to Rome. The voyage started late in the year, nearing the time when the Mediterranean became too tempestuous for ship travel. At first the trip went well, but as the ship left Crete it was caught in a major storm; for 14 days it was driven by the wind until it broke apart on a shoal off the island of Malta. Miraculously, all on board escaped with their lives.

When spring of A.D. 60 arrived, Paul was transported to Rome. He and his compan-

ions were welcomed by leaders of the church, and Paul also met with leaders of the Jewish community. Though he received some positive response from them, the lines between Christians and Jews were already drawn in Rome. The book of Acts concludes with a description of Paul living in Rome for two years under a loose house arrest but able to preach and teach freely to all who came to him. Paul's coworkers, including John Mark and Luke "the beloved physician" (Col. 4:14), helped him continue his missionary work even under arrest. It was evidently during this period that he wrote letters to the churches in Colossae and Ephesus as well as a short letter to a Christian in Colossae named **Philemon** about his slave **Onesimus**, who had become one of Paul's coworkers. He sent these letters back to Asia Minor by **Tychicus** and Onesimus.

By this time, Paul had evidently given up on his plans to go to Spain. He wrote to Philemon to "prepare a guest room for me" (Philem. 22) because he hoped to visit Colossae soon. Without the aid of Acts, it is difficult to reconstruct the course of Paul's last years. Many scholars argue that the so-called pastoral letters (1 and 2 Timothy and Titus) were not written by Paul himself but by one of his followers, because their Greek style is so different from that of Paul's other letters. In that case, Paul may well have been executed in A.D. 62 or later, perhaps during Nero's persecution of Christians after the fire that destroyed Rome in 64. If the pastoral letters were written by Paul, however, they show that the apostle was released from house arrest in Rome and traveled back to the Aegean area, visiting Crete, Ephesus, Miletus, Troas, Macedonia, Corinth, and Nicopolis in Epirus. Eventually, he was arrested and taken to Rome for trial. Though apparently alone at this time, he defended himself successfully and was released.

Soon, however, Paul was rearrested and accused of a capital offense, perhaps simply the charge of being a Christian leader. When he wrote 2 Timothy, Paul was awaiting trial but did not expect a successful result. His coworkers were scattered far and wide; only Luke remained with him. But Paul was undaunted. "I am already on the point of being sacrificed," he wrote to Timothy; "the time of my departure has come. I have fought the good fight, I have finished the race, I have kept the faith" (2 Tim. 4:6-7).

According to tradition, Paul

In this 16th-century ceramic, Paul and a companion meet martyrs' deaths in Rome.

*A*t first, the Roman government treated Christianity as a sect within Judaism. By the year A.D. 64, however, the emperor Nero clearly recognized Christians as a separate, unpopular group and falsely arrested and executed many for setting the disastrous fire at Rome. Recounting the fire, the historian Tacitus condemned Christians for their "detestable superstition" but nevertheless felt that Nero's tortures were excessive: Covered with the skins of beasts, they were torn by dogs and perished, or were nailed to crosses, or were doomed to the flames.

This imperial action apparently established a precedent of official condemnation. From a letter of Pliny the Younger, the Roman governor of Bithynia in Asia Minor, it is clear that simply being a Christian was considered a capital offense. He wrote to the emperor Trajan in A.D. 112 that he had tried numerous people accused of being Christians: "I asked them whether they were Christians, and if they confessed, I ordered them executed."

was beheaded in Rome, though no one recorded the exact circumstances of his death. He was probably less than 60 years old. Though he was a highly controversial figure throughout his life, Paul was recognized as a genuine hero of the faith in the generation after his death, when, for example, Acts of the Apostles was written. Throughout the history of Christianity, Paul's powerful formulation of the gospel—his emphasis on salvation by the grace of God through faith in Jesus and his focus on love as the central value of Christian life—has served as a beacon for the church's greatest theologians. Men such as Saint Augustine, Martin Luther, or, in modern times, Karl Barth, have seen their own theological work as an attempt to recapture the insight and spirit of Paul the apostle, a man who truly kept the faith.

PAULUS
(paw' luhs) GREEK: PAULOS

The first Roman official thought to have been converted to Christianity, Sergius Paulus was proconsul of Cyprus. He summoned the missionaries **Barnabas** and Saul (**Paul**) so that he could "hear the word of God" (Acts 13:7). But a Jewish magician named **Bar-Jesus** tried to persuade the proconsul not to believe the two. In response, Saul struck the magician temporarily blind, further convincing Paulus that their words were from God. Although **Luke** does not say that Paulus was baptized, the inclusion of this story in Acts indicated an acceptance of Christianity by one of high standing and thus gave encouragement to converts from all ranks of society. A tradition reported by the Christian teacher Origen, about A.D. 250, held that Saul changed his name to Paul in honor of the Roman proconsul. It was only after Paulus's apparent conversion that Luke in Acts began referring to the apostle as Paul.

PEKAH
(pee' kuh) HEBREW: PEQAH, abbreviated form of PEKAHIAH

The military officer who led a coup against King **Pekahiah** of Israel stole the ruler's throne and perhaps even his name. Pekah is so similar to Pekahiah that scholars speculate the assassin took the name to give the impression that he was the rightful successor. As Israel's next-to-last king, Pekah "reigned 20 years" (2 Kg. 15:27). Assyrian annals, however, disagree with the biblical record. They indicate that Pekahiah's father, King **Menahem**, paid tribute to the empire as late as 738 B.C. and that **Hoshea**, Israel's last king, began his reign in 732. That leaves only six years for the combined reigns of Pekahiah, who "reigned two years" (2 Kg. 15:23), and Pekah. Perhaps the biblical author was counting the time Pekah may have commanded Gilead, east of the Jordan. It was "fifty men of the Gileadites" (2 Kg. 15:25) who assisted him in the coup.

Whatever the length of his reign, Pekah decided not to pay tribute to Assyria, as the two kings before him had done. Instead, he joined Syria in heading an anti-Assyrian coalition. **Tiglath-pileser III** responded swiftly, subduing the coalition and leading many Israelites into exile. Pekah lost his throne as he had gained it; for his incredible miscalculation, he was himself assassinated and replaced by Hoshea.

Jesus summons the fishermen Peter and Andrew; a sixth-century mosaic from Ravenna, Italy.

PEKAHIAH

(pee kuh hai' uh) HEBREW: PEQAHYAH
"Yahweh opened [the eyes]" or "Yahweh is open-eyed/alert"

Like his father and predecessor on the throne of Israel, **Menahem**, King Pekahiah "did what was evil in the sight of the Lord" (2 Kg. 15:23) by following in the footsteps of **Jeroboam**, the idolatrous founder of the northern kingdom. But it was apparently Pekahiah's lack of patriotism that got him killed, for he continued his father's pro-Assyrian policy of collecting taxes from the wealthy in order to pay tribute to Assyria as a vassal of that powerful empire. Patriots considered this a sign of weakness and a threat to the sovereignty of the nation; they had assassinated five earlier kings of Israel for such failings. Pekahiah became the sixth when a band of Israelites from Gilead, south of Syria, supported a military officer in a coup that ended the king's two-year reign (c. 738-737 B.C.). The officer, **Pekah**, took the throne, stopped paying tribute to Assyria, then led the nation to defeat in a war against the empire. Shortly thereafter he, too, was assassinated.

PELEG

(pe' leg) HEBREW: PELEG
"to divide"

Peleg was notable enough to show up as an ancestor in the family tree of both **Abraham** and **Jesus**, but what little the Bible says of the man leaves scholars perplexed. A descendant of **Noah** through his son **Shem**, Peleg lived to be 239, and "in his days the earth was divided" (Gen. 10:25).

Some biblical commentators speculate that this important event refers to the division of humanity at the tower of Babel, when God decided to "confuse their language, that they may not understand one another's speech" (Gen. 11:7). Yet others theorize that the division may refer to the separation of Peleg's family—who were perhaps builders of canals for irrigation (his name is similar to the Akkadian word for "canal")—from those people who continued to roam the land as nomadic animal herders instead of settling down as farmers.

PEREZ

(pay' rez) HEBREW: PERES
"bursting forth" or "breach"

Among the ancestors of both **David** and **Jesus** was the child of an illicit liaison between a man and his widowed daughter-in-law. When **Tamar**'s husband died, her father-in-law, **Judah**, ordered his second son to obey the custom of marrying his brother's widow. But this son also died, and Judah's third son was too young to marry. Judah told Tamar to return to her father, "till Shelah my son grows up" (Gen. 38:11). But the marriage never took place. So Tamar, wanting an heir to take care of her when she grew old, disguised herself, pretended to be a prostitute, and lured Judah into having intercourse with her. Perez was the first of the twin boys born from that encounter. Though Perez's brother put out a hand during delivery and the midwife tied a scarlet thread to it to mark the firstborn, the hand was withdrawn and Perez came out first, earning the name "bursting forth." Hebrew elders later invoked Perez's name to bless **Boaz** when he fulfilled the duty of marrying his widowed relative, **Ruth**.

PETER

GREEK: PETROS
"rock"

He was an unlikely candidate to lead a religious revolution, but at the moment **Jesus** called him as a disciple, the life of Peter the fisherman changed dramatically and irrevocably. He became not only the most prominent of Jesus' disciples but also, later, the leader and principal spokesman of a fledgling Christian church.

Little is known of Peter's life before he met Jesus. His name was Simeon (often shortened to Simon) bar Jona, Aramaic for "son of Jonah." He was evidently born in Bethsaida-Julias on the north coast of the

Sea of Galilee. The town, whose name means "house of the fisherman," lay just east of the Jordan River and was thus outside the province of Galilee proper and under the rule of **Herod Philip**, a son and one of the successors of the notorious **Herod the Great**. Philip had built the Jewish village Beth-saida into a wealthy town with a mixed population of Greeks and Jews, adding Julias to its name in honor of the emperor **Augustus**'s daughter. Peter and his brother **Andrew**, who had been given a Greek name, grew up in a fishing family that no doubt traded with both Jews and Greeks. Peter most probaly spoke Aramaic with a Galilean accent as well as some Greek. Although he probably received a basic synagogue education, it is highly unlikely that Peter was given a scholar's advanced training in the Torah.

By the time he met Jesus, Peter had married and moved a few miles west to the Galilean town of Capernaum. There, he and Andrew went into partnership with **James** and **John** the sons of **Zebedee**. Even before they encountered Jesus, Peter and Andrew were filled with messianic expectations for they had traveled down the Jordan valley to hear the prophet **John the Baptist** preach God's coming judgment and call all Israel to repentance. They both not only were baptized by John but also became his disciples, remaining with him to learn from his teaching.

The crucial moment when Peter began to follow Jesus is described in three different ways in the New Testament. According to the Gospel of John, Andrew met Jesus through the Baptist and brought his brother to Jesus. Immediately recognizing Simon, as if he already knew him, Jesus said, "You shall be called Cephas" (Jn. 1:42). The Aramaic name Cephas means "rock" just as the Greek name Petros does. The Gospels of Matthew and Mark tell of Jesus first encountering Peter by the Sea of Galilee. Peter and Andrew were casting a net into the sea, and Jesus simply said, "Follow me, and I will make you fishers of men" (Mt. 4:19). The power of Jesus' words was such that "imme-

Peter with the keys of heaven; a late-15th-century painting

diately they left their nets and followed him" (Mk. 1:18).

It is the Gospel of Luke, however, that provides the most dramatic account of Peter's call. Jesus was teaching by the lake alongside boats where men were washing nets after a night of luckless fishing. Stepping into Peter's boat, Jesus asked him to put out a little from shore, and there he sat and taught. When he finished, Jesus told Peter and his coworkers to go into deep water and let down their nets. At first Peter protested but then yielded: "Master, we toiled all night and took nothing! But at your word, I will let down the nets" (Lk. 5:5). The nets immediately began pulling violently with the weight of a huge catch. Peter instantly perceived that he was not simply having good fortune in fishing; rather, he was in the presence of a power he could not understand in the person of Jesus.

Peter's immediate response was one of unworthiness and fear: "He fell down at Jesus' knees, saying, 'Depart from me, for I am a sinful man, O Lord'" (Lk. 5:8). But Jesus would not depart. It was precisely such a person, a man who knew his own weakness and sinfulness but could recognize and acknowledge the presence of God's power, that Jesus wanted. "Do not be afraid," Jesus said tenderly to the prostrate fisherman, "henceforth you will be catching men" (Lk. 5:10). Peter then left everything to follow Jesus.

From the beginning, Peter was a dominant personality among Jesus' disciples and developed a close relationship with his master. When Jesus chose 12 to form an inner circle, Peter was first among them. Peter regularly acted as their spokesman but often spoke impetuously, not fully understanding what he was saying. When in Capernaum, Jesus seems to have made Peter's house his home and center for his teaching. When Jesus first went to Peter's home, he healed his disciple's mother-in-law of a fever with a mere touch of his hand.

The Gospels often present Peter as a paradigm of

both vigorous faith and human uncertainty and doubt. There is, for example, the story of Jesus walking through the darkness on the wind-tossed waters of the Sea of Galilee toward his disciples, who were rowing their boat against the wind. When they spotted him, the disciples cried out in terror. But as soon as Jesus reassured them, "It is I; have no fear," Peter immediately shouted, "Lord, if it is you, bid me come to you on the water." Jesus told him to come. Confident in his faith, Peter leaped overboard and walked toward Jesus—doing the impossible with ease. But the power of the wind and the towering waves diverted his eyes. "When he saw the wind, he was afraid, and beginning to sink he cried out, 'Lord, save me.'" Jesus lifted him from the waves and said, "O man of little faith, why did you doubt?" (Mt. 14:27, 28, 30, 31). Peter's uncertain faith epitomized the struggle of the disciples to understand the great mystery of Jesus' coming in a turbulent world.

On another occasion Peter again combined insight and misunderstanding as he sought to grasp the meaning of Jesus' mission. While traveling to the source of the Jordan River, Jesus asked his disciples who people thought he was. The popular speculation was remarkable: John the Baptist,

As Jesus is arrested, Peter strikes the high priest's slave; a painting dated c. 1450.

Elijah, perhaps some other prophet. Then Jesus asked pointedly, "But who do you say that I am?" Peter answered for them all, saying simply, "You are the Christ" (Mk. 8:29).

The word Christ, or Messiah, embodied so many hopes and expectations that Peter could hardly have uttered more powerful words of faith. Matthew stresses the greatness of Peter's confession by adding Jesus' effusive praise: "Blessed are you, Simon Bar-Jona! For flesh and blood has not revealed this to you, but my Father who is in heaven. And I tell you, you are Peter [Greek, *Petros*], and on this rock [*petra*] I will build my church" (Mt. 16:17-18). Jesus not only blessed Peter but also used a play on his name to link him to the very foundation of the church.

STRENGTH AND WEAKNESS

Yet with sharp irony Mark and Matthew reveal that Peter did not realize the meaning of Jesus' words. When Jesus began to tell them that he must suffer and be killed—ideas that did not fit with the disciples' concept of the Messiah—Peter promptly rebuked Jesus. Realizing that Peter was expressing the misperception of all the disciples, Jesus turned on Peter in the strongest possible terms, "Get behind me, Satan! You are a hindrance to me" (Mt. 16:23). In showing both the strength and weakness of Peter, the Gospels by no means undermine his importance. Rather, he becomes an example of the struggle of faith and understanding that every disciple faces.

Peter was also part of the select group of three disciples (along with James and John, the sons of Zebedee) that Jesus took with him at times of special revelation. The three went with Jesus "up a high mountain apart" (Mk. 9:2), where they saw him transfigured in glory with **Moses** and Elijah. And on the last night before his crucifixion, Jesus took Peter, James, and John with him deep into the garden of Gethsemane. There they could have witnessed what in some ways was the most compelling and heartrending of Jesus' revelations of his unique relationship to God, as he prayed, "Abba, Father, all things are possible to thee; remove this cup from me; yet not what I will, but what thou wilt" (Mk. 14:36). The three, however, were overwhelmed with sleep.

Imprisoned for preaching after Pentecost, Peter is freed by an angel; a fresco by Filippino Lippi (c. 1457-1504).

calmly and said, "This very night, before the cock crows, you will deny me three times." No, Peter vowed for them all, "Even if I must die with you, I will not deny you" (Mt. 26:31, 33, 34, 35).

No one will ever know the turmoil within Peter as that night wore on. After his sleepy stupor in the garden of Gethsemane, his startled awakening as a mob came to arrest Jesus, his futile lashing out at the high priest's slave **Malchus** with a sword, and his panic and flight as Jesus was taken into custody, he finally found the courage to follow the arresting party and even enter the courtyard of the high priest **Caiaphas**, where Jesus had been detained. But as Jesus was being interrogated and condemned, Peter felt his panic rising. When bystanders pointed him out as a follower of Jesus, he denied and denied and denied. The cock crowed, "and Peter remembered the saying of Jesus . . . . and he went out and wept bitterly" (Mt. 26:75). But after Jesus' crucifixion, Peter came to himself, helped to reassemble the disciples, and waited.

After **Mary Magdalene** and some of the other women announced Jesus' resurrection, Peter was the first of the inner 12 (now 11, after **Judas Iscariot**'s betrayal) to whom Jesus chose to appear, though the Gospels do not describe the appearance in detail. Peter was indeed present at several resurrection appearances, including a remarkable one on the shore of the Sea of Galilee, where he and some other disciples were again fishing. Just as at Peter's initial call, Jesus revealed himself by rewarding the luckless fishermen with a great catch of fish. He then offered a breakfast of fish and bread to the disciples and turned to Peter.

As Peter had denied him three times, so Jesus asked three times, "Simon, son of John, do you love me?" And thrice Peter responded—no longer with impetuous confidence in himself, but emphasizing Jesus' knowledge—"Yes, Lord; you know that I love you." Jesus commissioned Peter to "feed my sheep" (Jn. 21:15, 17), but he also mysteriously foretold Peter's death: He would eventually, as he had vowed, die for his master. Peter had finally come through the crucible. He had been burned by the fire of his own weakness and cowardice; he had been held fast by the scorching vision of Jesus' death; he had been restored to love and service by the mystery of Jesus' resurrection.

THE GIFT OF TONGUES

Seven weeks after Jesus' crucifixion, on the day of Pentecost, the beginning of the great Feast of Weeks, Peter and the other disciples received the new power Jesus had foretold—

Jesus had clearly seen this combination of strength and weakness in Peter but never wavered in his affirmation of the apostle. And Peter's difficulty with the lessons Jesus had to teach him continued to the end of Jesus' life. By the time of the Last Supper, Peter had steeled himself to the dangers Jesus had predicted. He was devoted to his teacher and sure that he would endure with him to death. But at that meal, when Jesus knelt with a basin of water to wash the disciples' feet, Peter could not accept his master doing a slave's work. He vehemently refused to be washed, until Jesus said, "If I do not wash you, you have no part in me"; then Peter insisted, "Lord, not my feet only but also my hands and my head!" (Jn. 13:8, 9).

Later that evening Jesus warned the disciples of the grim trials that lay ahead: "You will all fall away because of me this night." Just as surely as Peter earlier had known that the Messiah could not suffer, so then he knew that this was impossible. "I will never fall away," he pledged. Jesus looked at him the coming of the **Holy Spirit**. Gathered in Jerusalem, the disciples heard a sound like a tremendous wind and saw what looked like tongues of fire dividing and alighting on each of them. They rushed forth into the festival crowds and began to proclaim "the mighty works of God" (Acts 2:11) as the Spirit filled them with its power. Amazingly, the crowds of Jews from all over the Roman and Parthian empires and beyond recognized that they were hearing this mighty message in the native languages of their home regions. Peter stepped forward as spokesman and calmly proclaimed the meaning of what was happening.

Speaking through the prophet **Joel**, as Peter reminded his audience, God had foretold what was then taking place: "In the last days . . . I will pour out my Spirit upon all flesh, and your sons and your daughters shall prophesy, and your young men shall see visions, and your old men shall dream dreams" (Acts 2:17). This long-awaited return of the prophetic Spirit, Peter said, was sent by the very Jesus in whom

they had witnessed God's mighty power but whom "lawless men" had crucified. God reversed that human condemnation, however, by raising Jesus from the dead and exalting him to "the right hand of God" (Acts 2:23, 33). About 3,000 people were convinced by this remarkable message and were baptized that day, joining Peter and the disciples to form the strong core of a new community of faith.

The following months were times of excitement and struggle, as recorded in the book of Acts. Once Peter, accompanied by John, healed a lame beggar in the temple court and with that event proclaimed Jesus and his resurrection to a great crowd of astounded temple worshipers. Such preaching, however, incensed the aristocratic temple priests, who were largely Sadducees and did not believe in the resurrection of the dead. Peter and other disciples were repeatedly arrested and severely threatened but refused to stop their work. "We must obey God," Peter asserted, "rather than men" (Acts 5:29). Such confident boldness in "uneducated, common men" caused wonder even in their antagonists, who "recognized that they had been with Jesus" (Acts 4:13). It even won a cautious tolerance from the Pharisee **Gamaliel**, who urged the authorities to let these men alone, lest they "be found opposing God" (Acts 5:39).

During this period, Peter and the other apostles were regular worshipers in the temple—using a large colonnade called

Solomon's Portico as their regular meeting place—and "the people held them in high honor" (Acts 5:13). Remarkably, when intense persecution against Greek-speaking believers, such as **Stephen** and the evangelist **Philip**, forced many to flee Judea, Peter and the rest of the 12 remained untouched in Jerusalem. But the Jerusalem leaders remained in close contact with the scattered believers. Peter and John traveled to Samaria to aid and confirm the work of Philip there and lay hands on the converts so that "they might receive the Holy Spirit" (Acts 8:15). There Peter encountered a popular magician named **Simon**, who had deluded many Samaritans but now was a believer. When Simon saw the power of the Holy Spirit given by Peter and John, he offered Peter money if he also could be made to transmit the Spirit by his touch. "Your silver perish with you," Peter retorted, "because you thought you could obtain the gift of God with money!" (Acts 8:20).

ACCEPTING GENTILES

Soon afterward, Peter found that that same Spirit forced him into the most explosive issue of the first generation of Christians—whether Gentiles could be accepted into the new faith. One noontime in the town of Joppa, Peter was praying on the flat roof of the house of **Simon**, a leather tanner, when he found himself witnessing a strange vision. A great linen sheet descended to earth, carrying all sorts of animals that were forbidden as food under the Law of Moses. Unexpectedly, a voice said, "Rise, Peter; kill and eat." Peter emphatically refused to eat such things that were "common or unclean." But the voice was equally emphatic: "What God has cleansed, you must not call com-

mon" (Acts 10:13, 14, 15). Twice more the vision was repeated before the Spirit told Peter that men had come seeking him. He must "accompany them without hesitation" (Acts 10:20).

The men took Peter and a group of Jewish companions north to Caesarea to the home of **Cornelius**, a Gentile soldier who had come to believe in the God of the Jews. Peter now realized that his vision had meant that he "should not call any man common or unclean." He told Cornelius and his household the story of Jesus, but before he could finish, "the Holy Spirit fell on all who heard the word." The message of the Holy Spirit was unmistakable to Peter; the Gentiles were to be received as Christians. "Can any one forbid water for baptizing these people who have received the Holy Spirit just as we have?" (Acts 10:28, 44, 47) Peter asked. The example of Peter—which he had to defend vigorously when he returned to Jerusalem—opened the future of Christianity to a far wider horizon than any of the disciples had ever imagined.

Later, many Jewish Christians continued to insist that all Gentile converts be circumcised and observe dietary regulations. About A.D. 49, **Paul** and **Barnabas** came to

Seeking safety after his miraculous release from prison, Peter knocks at a friend's gate; the servant Rhoda is astonished to hear his voice.

Jerusalem for a conference to resolve the issue, and Peter's example guided the settlement in favor of the Gentiles. At the same time, Paul records that the church leaders agreed that Peter would continue to lead the mission to the Jews, while he would lead the one to the Gentiles. By that time, however, Jerusalem had become a dangerous place to preach the gospel. **Herod Agrippa I** had executed James, the son of Zebedee, and arrested Peter. As Peter awaited death, he was miraculously freed from prison by an angel and soon left Jerusalem "and went to another place" (Acts 12:17).

In fact, Peter went to many other places, often Gentile regions. Paul indicates that Peter (or Cephas, as Paul usually calls him) became an important figure in the churches in both Antioch and Corinth. It was at Antioch that Peter and Paul came to a major disagreement over how far Gentile Christians should yield to Jewish Christians in the practice of dietary laws. Peter also traveled widely and taught among the churches at "Pontus, Galatia, Cappadocia, Asia, and Bithynia" (1 Pet. 1:1).

By the time Peter wrote his first letter to those churches, he was near the end of his career and had gone to Rome, which he disparagingly referred to as "Babylon" (1 Pet. 5:13). Because those churches were facing a "fiery ordeal" (1 Pet. 4:12) of persecution, Peter asked the faithful to understand the sufferings of Jesus. The believers were "aliens and exiles" in a pagan world, but they could remain courageous in their sufferings since they knew that "Christ also suffered for you, leaving you an example, that you should follow in his steps" (1 Pet. 2:11, 21). "After you have suffered a little while," Peter assured them, "the God of all grace, who has called you to his eternal glory in Christ, will himself restore, establish, and strengthen you" (1 Pet. 5:10). Peter's second letter was perhaps written soon after the first, though its authenticity was widely disputed among early Christian writers, and many historians argue that it was likely written by a follower of Peter after his death and given his name for authority.

Nothing certain is known about how Peter came to Rome or how long he stayed there. He was accompanied by Silvanus (**Silas**) and **Mark**, both of whom also worked with Paul. A second-century Christian named Papias recorded a tradition that Mark served as Peter's translator and wrote the Gospel of Mark based on Peter's recollections of Jesus. Another writer told that Paul and Peter worked together in Italy, and still others even counted Peter and Paul as joint founders of the church in Rome.

Peter is said to have died in Rome during the horrific persecution under Nero beginning in A.D. 64. By the late second century, an elaborate web of legends surrounding Peter's death was available in a work of

Rembrandt's portrait of an aged Peter with the keys of heaven but not those of his prison is dated 1631.

pious fantasy called the Acts of Peter, the earliest of many noncanonical works centering on the apostle. In this work, Peter was sent by Jesus from Jerusalem to Rome, where he converted many prominent women, including the beautiful wife of a friend of Caesar, to a life of celibacy. In rage, the frustrated husband plotted Peter's death. Peter was warned of the plot and was leaving Rome in disguise when he met Jesus entering the city. *Domine quo vadis?* ("Lord, where are you going?") Peter asked. "I am coming to Rome to be crucified," Jesus replied. Peter understood his meaning and turned back to face arrest and his own crucifixion. When the apostle went to the cross, according to the Acts of Peter, he asked to be crucified head downward.

Tradition places Peter's crucifixion on Vatican hill, where the Circus of Nero stood; archeological excavations have uncovered there an early shrine to the memory of Peter. Legends about Peter's work and martyrdom in Rome continued to multiply and contributed greatly to the development of the papacy and the central authority of Rome in the western church. From Galilean fisherman to confessor, denier, proclaimer, missionary, bishop, and martyr, Peter had made an astonishing journey with Jesus.

Peter's crucifixion in an inverted position; a painting by Hans Holbein the Elder

PHILEMON

(fai lee' muhn) GREEK: PHILEMON

An apparently wealthy, slave-owning Christian in whose house the Colossian church assembled, Philemon was the recipient of a letter from the apostle **Paul**, who had converted him but was then "a prisoner for Christ Jesus" (Philem. 1). Although one of the shortest books in the New Testament, the letter offers a valuable glimpse of the early Christian attitudes toward slavery. It was occasioned by a delicate situation: Philemon's slave **Onesimus** had left his home at Colossae in Asia Minor and gone to either Ephesus or Rome, where he gained Paul's protection. The letter is the apostle's attempt to effect a reconciliation between slave and master.

The traditional view of the crisis is that Onesimus escaped to Rome, where Paul was under house arrest, and there happened to encounter the apostle, perhaps as a result of his own capture and imprisonment. However, recent research into ancient slavery practices suggests that, after causing some serious loss to Philemon, Onesimus might have been permitted to leave home to seek out a respected intermediary. Less plausibly, it has been suggested that

Philemon sent Onesimus, who was soon due for emancipation, to serve the imprisoned apostle, and that Paul was urging the master not to delay granting his slave's freedom. Further, it has been proposed that Onesimus met Paul not in distant Rome but in Ephesus, some 120 miles west of Colossae, or even in Caesarea in Judea. Paul is known to have been imprisoned at Caesarea before being sent to Rome; however, no incarceration at Ephesus has been firmly documented. Whatever the occasion or the place, Onesimus found Paul under arrest and during his stay with the apostle was converted to Christianity.

The letter to Philemon is often praised as a masterpiece of gentle persuasion. Intended to be read to the congregation at Colossae, the letter praises Philemon as Paul's "beloved fellow worker" (Philem. 1), whose faith, love, and ministry were widely known and who was an encouragement to Paul. The apostle then refers to Onesimus as "my child" and "my very heart," and says that he is only reluctantly sending the slave back to his master because Onesimus has been so "useful" (Philem. 10, 12, 11)—this being a play on the Greek name Onesimus, which means "useful."

If Philemon had done all Paul asked, he would have put aside his anger, forgiven Onesimus (including waiving any financial debt), smoothed out any remaining difficulties within the household, and prepared a room for Paul's visit. Above all, Philemon would have freed Onesimus, treating him "no longer as a slave but more than a slave, as a beloved brother" (Philem. 16).

PHILIP II
(fil' ip) GREEK: PHILIPPOS

King Philip II of Macedonia started what his son, **Alexander the Great**, finished: conquering the Middle East. Philip began by usurping the throne of Macedonia from his deceased brother's infant son. During his reign (359-336 B.C.), Philip founded cities and built a formidable military force, investing heavily in weaponry. Then he attacked the Greek city-states, eventually becoming the king "who first reigned over the Greeks" (1 Macc. 6:2). An ambitious conqueror, he next prepared for war with Persia, the dominant power in the Middle East. But he did not live to execute that plan, for one of his officers assassinated him at his daughter's wedding. Two years later, however, his son and successor Alexander invaded Persia.

PHILIP

One of the twelve apostles, Philip is depicted in the Gospel of John as a loyal, earnest, but at times overly literal-minded follower of **Jesus**. According to John, Philip was the third to join Jesus' entourage, after **Andrew** and his brother Simon **Peter**; but he was the first whom Jesus directly invited into discipleship, with a simple command, "Follow me" (Jn. 1:43). At the time he may have been a disciple of **John the Baptist**, as was Andrew and perhaps Peter. All three were from Beth-saida, a fishing village located on the northeastern shore of the Sea of Galilee, and may have known each other before becoming followers of Jesus.

Philip played an important role in bringing **Nathanael** into the circle of the twelve. Apparently well versed in the Scriptures, Philip believed the mission of Jesus was foreshadowed in the Old Testament: "We have found him of whom Moses in the law and also the prophets wrote, Jesus of Nazareth, the son of Joseph," he told Nathanael. When Nathanael asked skeptically how anything good could come from the obscure village of Nazareth, Philip replied, "Come and see" (Jn. 1:45, 46).

After teaching a crowd of 5,000 who had flocked to hear him near Beth-saida, Jesus tested Philip's understanding of his power

The evangelist Philip baptizes the Ethiopian eunuch; a stained-glass panel.

by asking him how to feed the people. Philip's answer shows that he did not anticipate the miracle Jesus was about to perform to feed the people, but saw only a practical problem: "Two hundred denarii would not buy enough bread for each of them to get a little" (Jn. 6:7).

During the week before Jesus' death, some Greek-speaking Gentile visitors to Jerusalem sought an audience with Jesus, and it was Philip and Andrew who tried to accommodate them. The names Philip and Andrew are Greek, and Beth-saida was predominately Greek-speaking, so it is possible Philip spoke Greek and ministered at other times to the many non-Hebrew-speaking Jews who were drawn to Jesus.

At the Last Supper, Philip became an example once more of those who did not fully understand the mission of Jesus. Following the withdrawal of **Judas Iscariot** and Peter's assertion that he would never betray Jesus, Philip asked for a personal experience to bolster his faith: "Lord, show us the Father and we shall be satisfied." Jesus' answer revealed some exasperation: "Have I been with you so long, and yet you do not know me, Philip? He who has seen me has seen the Father; how can you say, 'Show us the Father'?" (Jn. 14:8, 9).

The only references to Philip in the three Synoptic Gospels appear in lists of the 12. He is also named as one of the 11 disciples gathered in an upper room after the crucifixion, just before the coming of the **Holy Spirit** at Pentecost. In later centuries, legends concerning Philip were compiled in a work called the Acts of Philip, which often confused him with **Philip** the evangelist—a mistake made by a number of early writers.

PHILIP 2

A leader of the Jerusalem church in its early days, the evangelist Philip helped resolve a major controversy, and then became a successful missionary. After Greek-speaking Christians protested that their widows were being neglected in the daily distribution of food to the needy, the apostles chose seven of their leaders, including Philip, to take over this duty so that they could devote themselves completely to preaching and prayer.

With the help of these seven, "the number of the disciples multiplied greatly in Jerusalem" (Acts 6:7). But the growth of the church was halted when one of the seven, **Stephen**, was stoned to death by a mob. In the wake of further persecution, Philip, along with other adherents of the new faith, left Jerusalem for safer regions.

Several episodes from Philip's ministry show how the persecution resulted not in the weakening of the gospel but in its expansion. Philip first went to Samaria, where he healed the sick, exorcised unclean spirits, and converted many of the people who were being scorned by the Jews. One notable Samaritan convert was a former magician named **Simon**—though in view of **Peter**'s later encounter with him, the sincerity of Simon's conversion might well be questioned. As Philip was journeying south from Samaria, he was offered a ride by an official of the Candace, queen of Ethiopia. Evidently a student of prophecy, the Ethiopian official, described as a eunuch, asked about a passage in Isaiah concerning a figure who was suffering humiliation and injustice. After Philip applied the prophecy to the life and death of **Jesus**, the Ethiopian eunuch asked to be baptized. Philip next appeared in Azotus, or Ashdod, an ancient Philistine city, "and passing on he preached the gospel to all the towns till he came to Caesarea" (Acts 8:40).

Some years later Philip apparently settled in Caesarea, for he

The apostles James the Less, Philip, and Barnabas; a late-15th- or early-16th-century altar panel

is said to have provided lodgings there for **Paul** and **Luke**, who noted that Philip "had four unmarried daughters, who prophesied" (Acts 21:9). In Philip's home a prophet named **Agabus** predicted that Paul's arrival in Jerusalem would lead to his arrest; undeterred, the apostle departed for the city.

PHINEHAS
(fin' ee uhs) HEBREW: PINEHAS
"southerner," possibly referring to the Nubians of southern Egypt

A aron's grandson Phinehas was a zealous priest whose first notable act was to run a spear through an Israelite man and the foreign woman with him. The Israelites were camped in Moab, east of the Jordan River, where the local women enticed many of the men to join them in sexual rituals in worship of the Canaanite god **Baal**. At the Lord's command, **Moses** ordered the execution of the leaders of those people who had taken part in the rites. But in blatant defiance, the head of a Simeonite household named **Zimri** walked a Midianite woman right past Moses and the weeping masses that had assembled at the tent of meeting and took her into his dwelling. Phinehas followed. With a single spear thrust he ran them both through. In recognition of this act of zeal God lifted a plague he had sent, which had taken 24,000 lives. Phinehas and his descendants were rewarded with "a perpetual priesthood" (Num. 25:13).

The Bible records three more events about the priest, who became a hero described in some Jewish wisdom literature as "third in glory" (Sir. 45:23) after Moses and **Aaron**. Each story involves military action or threats. In the first, Phinehas accompanied an army of 12,000 in a holy war against Midian. The Israelites killed all the males among their enemy, "took all the spoil and all the booty" (Num. 31:11), and then—at Moses' command—slew the captive boys and women, sparing only virgin girls.

After the Israelites began conquering Canaan, the ten tribes west of the Jordan heard that the tribes east of the river had built an altar. Believing this an act of idolatry, they mustered an army for a punitive attack. But Phinehas led a delegation to the east and averted the war when he learned that the altar was only a reminder "that the Lord is God" (Jos. 22:34).

In the third story about Phinehas, he conveyed the Lord's order to the Israelites to attack the tribe of Benjamin in retaliation for the rape and murder of a woman traveling through the land with her master. In the assault, 25,100 Benjamite warriors died, and their towns were set on fire. For Phinehas's strong defense of the Lord's Law, he became a model to zealots of later generations. His descendants were named among those returning from the exile in Babylon.

PHOEBE

(fee' bee) GREEK: PHOIBE
"pure," "bright," or "radiant"
·········

Though her name appears only once in the New Testament, Phoebe offers evidence that women played important roles in the early Christian church. In the final chapter of **Paul**'s letter to the church at Rome, her name precedes a list of greetings: "I commend to you our sister Phoebe, a deaconess of the church at Cenchreae, that you may receive her in the Lord as befits the saints, and help her in whatever she may require from you, for she has been a helper of many and of myself as well" (Rom. 16:1-2).

Phoebe evidently was the one entrusted

Paul hands Phoebe his letter to the Romans; a 12th-century manuscript illumination.

Phinehas slays Zimri and the Midianite woman; a manuscript dating to about 1200.

with the mission of delivering Paul's letter, written at Corinth, a city near Cenchreae, to Rome. In referring to her as a "deaconess" and a "helper," Paul used terms that may have indicated offices or ministries by which Phoebe served the larger church. The Greek translated in this passage as "deaconess" is actually masculine, *diakonos*, or "deacon." Others in the New Testament who were given that title include **Paul**, **Apollos**, **Timothy**, **Epaphras**, and **Jesus** himself. Paul often described as deacons those who helped him plant new churches. Whether Phoebe was one of those traveling missionaries or a local leader is not known.

The term translated as "helper" is the feminine form of a word that is found nowhere else in the New Testament. Its secular form referred to a financial or legal patron and may have been applied to women as well as men. In Paul's usage, "helper" may imply that, as his patroness, Phoebe assisted Paul financially; thus, when Paul asked the Romans to "help her in whatever she may require," she may have been raising financial support for Paul, perhaps for the long-planned mission of which the apostle had written just before introducing Phoebe: "I shall go on by way of you to Spain" (Rom. 15:28).

PILATE

(pai' luht) GREEK: PILATOS; LATIN: PILATUS
"armed with a javelin"
·········

The Roman governor of Judea from about A.D. 26 to 37, Pontius Pilate presided over the trial of **Jesus** and ordered his execution. He is thus featured prominently in all four Gospels and is also mentioned in the book of Acts and in **Paul**'s first letter to

Timothy. Outside the New Testament, his administration of the province is documented by references in the works of the Jewish historians Josephus and Philo and the Roman historian Tacitus.

As governor of Judea, Pilate was responsible for collecting tributes and taxes, which were either used to meet local governmental needs or were forwarded to Rome with appropriate reports. To keep the peace he could call on auxiliary units of infantry and cavalry stationed in Judea; any major disorders, however, would be taken care of by his administrative superior, the legate of Syria, who had four legions at his disposal. Pilate's headquarters and residence were in Caesarea, on the Mediterranean coast, rather than in Jerusalem.

Although nothing is known of Pilate's career before his appointment to the post in Judea, it is assumed that he had some influential friends in Rome and that he had likely served previously in the Roman army. But Pilate earned lasting notoriety by presiding at Jesus' trial, the only record of his performing a judicial function in Judea—though Josephus confirms that Pilate's authority included "power even to execute." **Herod Agrippa I** described Pilate in extremely harsh terms in a letter to the emperor Caligula, speaking of him as "naturally inflexible, a blend of self-will and relentlessness."

The Gospel of John offers the most detailed account of the trial of Jesus, with seven scenes that alternate between events outside and inside the praetorium, an unidentified location in Jerusalem that served as the governor's headquarters in the city. In John, Pilate is depicted as one whose sole allegiance is to the powers of this world. All four Gospels declare that the charge against Jesus was one of rebellion, an offense the Roman governor was bound to stop and punish. But the Gospels picture Pilate as firmly convinced of Jesus' innocence, yet who is inexorably driven against his better judgment to sentence his hapless prisoner to death.

While the trial has been popularly condemned as illegal, most of the normal judicial procedures for that time and place were followed: A charge was independently brought before the governor in his judicial role by the high priest **Caiaphas** and his colleagues; an investigation was initiated by the judge since the charge was one he was required to evaluate; proceedings were conducted by prosecutors before the judge; an interrogation was conducted by the judge in a case in which the accused refused to enter a plea. John portrays Pilate as yielding to the explicit threat of the accusers: "If you release this man, you are not Caesar's friend" (Jn. 19:12). This may have implied that the accusers were prepared to appeal to Rome to have Pilate investigated for neglecting his duty to ensure the integrity of the state he ruled.

This is precisely what happened a few years later. According to Josephus, Pilate suppressed an armed uprising by a group of Samaritans who had gathered at their shrine on Mount Gerizim to search for and excavate holy vessels of **Moses** that were sup-

Jesus before Pilate; from Duccio's altarpiece for the cathedral of Siena, Italy, 1308-1311

posedly buried there. In the ambush Pilate ordered, many were killed and others were later executed. A delegation from Samaria protested to the legate of Syria, who suspended Pilate from his office and sent him to Rome to face an imperial investigation.

While Pilate was en route to Rome for the investigation of the Samaritan massacre, the emperor **Tiberius** died, in March 37. According to a later tradition, Pilate was found guilty by Tiberius's successor, Caligula, and, following a brief exile in Vienne-on-Rhone, committed suicide—as was customary among Roman aristocrats convicted of a crime. Later tradition produced the fictitious Acts of Pilate, which contains fanciful accounts of the trial of Jesus and Jesus' descent into hell after his death to rescue captive souls. Other post-biblical Christian popular literature portrays Pilate as recognizing not only Jesus' innocence but even his divinity. The Coptic Christians of Eygpt go so far as to count Pilate among the saints they venerate.

Nothing is known of Pilate's personal life, other than that he was married. During the trial, his wife sent word that she was greatly disturbed by a dream about the prisoner. "Have nothing to do with that righteous man" (Mt. 27:19), she begged. But he ignored her plea, called for water in which to wash his hands as a gesture of his innocence, and "having scourged Jesus, delivered him to be crucified" (Mt. 27:26).

POTIPHAR

(pah' tuh fuhr) HEBREW: POTIPAR
"he whom Re [the sun god] has given"

The Egyptian captain of the guard in Pharaoh's court, Potiphar is remembered as the husband of the woman who tried to seduce **Joseph**, one of the couple's household slaves. Potiphar bought the young Hebrew, who was "handsome and good-looking" (Gen. 39:6), from the Ishmaelite

Heeding his wife's warning, Pilate washes his hands of the guilt for Jesus' death; a 15th-century painting.

traders who had brought him down from Canaan. They had purchased Joseph, for about eight ounces of silver, from his brothers, who had endured all they could take of his bragging and had thrown him into a cistern while plotting to kill him. Fortunately, the caravan of slave traders came along, and Joseph was sent on his way to Egypt.

The young Hebrew slave, perhaps still in his late teens, eventually worked himself into the job of managing Potiphar's household; "his master saw that the Lord was with him, and that the Lord caused all that he did to prosper" (Gen. 39:3). Potiphar's wife took notice of him too, and she began trying to seduce him. One day when they were alone in the house, she grabbed him and repeated her invitation, "Lie with me" (Gen. 39:12). Joseph ran out of the house, leaving his cloak in her hands. The woman told her husband that Joseph had tried to rape her. The infuriated Potiphar immediately had Joseph thrown in prison. Yet he stopped short of having him executed, the fit punishment for a slave who tried to rape the wife of a royal official—an indication that the Lord remained with Joseph even in adversity.

POTIPHERA

(pah tif' uh ruh) HEBREW: POTIPERA,
a variant of POTIPHAR

The daughter of Potiphera, a priest of the sun god Re, became part of **Joseph**'s reward for interpreting Pharaoh's perplexing dreams. The Egyptian ruler appointed Joseph second in command of Egypt and "gave him in marriage Asenath, the daughter of Potiphera priest of On" (Gen. 41:45). The city of On, later known as Heliopolis, was near modern Cairo and served as headquarters for worship of the sun. Since Joseph was Pharaoh's top officer, scholars speculate that Potiphera was On's high priest—one of the most influential people in the nation. His grandchildren, through Joseph and his daughter, were **Manasseh** and **Ephraim**.

PRISCA

(pris' kuh) GREEK: PRISKA

In the book of Acts, **Luke** calls the early Christian missionary Prisca by the more familiar Priscilla. By twice placing Prisca's name before that of her husband, the Jewish tent maker **Aquila**, Luke may have been implying that she was a more active minister than he or of a higher social position.

JOSEPHUS

What we know of the chaotic power politics in Palestine around the time of Jesus is largely due to a Jewish historian called Flavius Josephus. Joseph ben Mattathias—his Hebrew name—was born in Jerusalem about seven years after Jesus' death and grew up in a prominent priestly family. In his 20's, Josephus traveled to Rome to plead a court case before Nero, became acquainted with the imperial family, and formed a strong sense of Roman power.

Returning to Judea, he at first opposed the growing revolt against Rome but ultimately accepted command of Jewish forces in Galilee. When a Roman army led by Vespasian crushed his position, he surrendered. Brought before Vespasian, Josephus boldly predicted that the general would soon be emperor. After his prediction came true in A.D. 69, Josephus enjoyed imperial patronage and took the name Flavius, the emperor's family name.

During the siege of Jerusalem, a city held by zealot factions intensely opposed to the Jewish priestly families like Josephus's, he served the Romans as interpreter. After the city and temple were devastated in 70, Josephus moved to Rome and devoted himself to writing. His first work, completed in 79, was a detailed narrative of the Jewish war in which he sought both to defend the Jewish nation and condemn the zealot factions whom he blamed for the calamity.

Over the next decade Josephus worked on a more ambitious project, to present to the Greco-Roman world the entire course of biblical and Jewish history from the creation to his own time. This vast historical defense of Judaism, called Jewish Antiquities, appeared in A.D. 94.

*The legendary martyrdoms of Prisca and Aquila; an
11th-century Byzantine manuscript illumination*

Prisca and Aquila were perhaps among the first Christian converts in Rome. When the two spoke of **Jesus** in the synagogues, the ensuing controversy grew so inflammatory that in about A.D. 49 the emperor **Claudius** expelled all Jews from Rome, including Prisca and Aquila.

The couple then moved to Corinth, where **Paul** met them and, because he too was a tent maker, lodged with them and worked at his trade alongside Aquila. After a year and a half, all three moved to Ephesus, where Prisca and Aquila offered their home as a meeting place for the Christian congregation. There they met **Apollos**, a former disciple of **John the Baptist** who professed ignorance of Christian baptism. But Prisca and Aquila took Apollos aside "and expounded to him the way of God more accurately" (Acts 18:26).

After the death of Claudius in A.D. 55, the couple apparently returned to Rome, again hosting a church in their home. When Paul sent greetings to the church at Rome, they headed his list: "Greet Prisca and Aquila, my fellow workers in Christ Jesus, who risked their necks for my life, to whom not only I but all the churches of the Gentiles give thanks" (Rom. 16:3-4). The peril from which the couple appears to have saved Paul is not known, though the apostle wrote that he "fought with beasts at Ephesus" (1 Cor. 15:32). According to some biblical commentators, the last chapter of Romans is actually an addition to a copy of the letter

Paul sent to Ephesus; if so, Prisca and Aquila never returned to Rome but continued to provide a meeting place for the Ephesus congregation in their home there.

PUBLIUS
(poob' lee uhs) GREEK: POPLIOS
"popular" or "of the people"

Publius, the leading Roman official of Malta, extended hospitality to **Paul** and **Luke** following a shipwreck that landed them near his estates. After identifying Publius by his official title, "chief man of the island" (Acts 28:7), Luke calls him by his first name, suggesting that the governor established a friendly relationship with his shipwrecked guests. Though Publius would have been responsible for any visitors to the island, Luke writes that he went beyond minimum custody and "entertained us hospitably for three days" (Acts 28:7). Paul rewarded the courtesies by healing Publius's father of fever and dysentery.

PUDENS
(poo' denz) GREEK: POUDES
"modest" or "humble"

The single mention of Pudens in the New Testament links him with a man named Linus and a woman named Claudia; they are said to have joined the apostle **Paul** in sending greetings to the missionary **Timothy**. According to one church tradition, Pudens was an early Christian martyr, a Roman senator whose son Linus succeeded **Peter** as bishop of Rome. This Pudens was canonized in the sixth century, and his feast day is celebrated on April 14 in the East and May 19 in the West.

QUIRINIUS

(kwi rin' ee uhs) GREEK: KYRENIOS
··········

Publius Sulpicius Quirinius held important posts under two Roman emperors, **Augustus** and **Tiberius**, but he is best remembered from being mentioned in the birth narrative of **Jesus** in the Gospel of Luke: "In those days a decree went out from Caesar Augustus that all the world should be enrolled. This was the first enrollment, when Quirinius was governor of Syria" (Lk. 2:1-2). Since **Luke** earlier dated the events surrounding Jesus' birth to the reign of **Herod the Great**, modern historians have puzzled over this statement. Ancient sources, including the historians Tacitus, Josephus, and Strabo, agree that Herod died in 4 B.C., some ten years before Quirinius became governor of Syria. However, a census early in his term in office is confirmed by Josephus.

Quirinius was born about 51 B.C. and spent his early career in the Roman army, perhaps taking part in the campaign that ended with Augustus's victory at Actium in 31 B.C. and possibly serving in Spain for the

next decade. In 14 B.C. he was named governor of Crete and Cyrene, where he defeated a tribe of desert raiders known as the Marmarici. Two years later he was named a consul in Rome, evidence that he was a favorite of the emperor. In 6 B.C. Quirinius was sent to govern Pamphylia-Galatia, a trouble spot in the eastern empire. A successful campaign in that area earned him triumphal honors in Rome. In A.D. 2 he was appointed chief adviser to Augustus's grandson Gaius Caesar, but when the emperor's stepson Tiberius began to emerge as the heir apparent, Quirinius moved into his circle. In A.D. 6 Quirinius was named governor of Syria, with authority over Judea, which had become restless following the emperor's removal of **Herod Archelaus** as ruler of that client kingdom. By A.D. 12 Quirinius was back in Rome as a close associate of Tiberius, who had become emperor two years earlier, following Augustus's death. When Quirinius died in A.D. 21, he was given a public funeral, an indication that he retained Tiberius's favor to the end.

As for the census mentioned in Luke, if it was not the one documented to about A.D. 6 or 7, early in Quirinius's governorship of Syria, it could have been the one taken between 9 and 6 B.C. under a previous governor named Sentius Saturninus. An alternate theory, to avoid the suggestion that Luke got the name of the governor wrong, proposes a prior governorship of Syria for Quirinius, since there are gaps in the historical record. A much disputed inscription gives some support to this hypothesis.

In this medieval manuscript illumination, Quirinius presides over the census that brought Joseph and Mary to Bethlehem.

RACHEL

(ray' chuhl) HEBREW: RAHEL
"ewe"

In all of the Bible there is only one scene of a man kissing a woman. It took place at Haran in Paddan-Aram, or upper Mesopotamia, when **Isaac**'s son **Jacob** first met his cousin Rachel, a shepherdess. After he removed the stone covering her well and helped her water her flock, "Jacob kissed Rachel, and wept aloud" (Gen. 29:11). A month later he asked her father, his uncle **Laban**, if he could marry her. But Jacob was a fugitive from Canaan and lacked money for the customary payment. So he made Laban an offer: "I will serve you seven years for your younger daughter Rachel" (Gen. 29:18).

Jacob had fled to the kinfolk of his mother, **Rebekah**, because he had cheated his older brother, **Esau**, out of their father's blessing, and Esau had vowed to kill him. Moreover, his parents did not want Jacob to marry a Canaanite woman, as had Esau, and had sent him to Paddan-Aram with the charge to "take as wife from there one of the daughters of Laban" (Gen. 28:2).

It seems no coincidence that Jacob ended up getting cheated out of the seven years of hard work. For in Canaan he had dressed in his brother's clothes and convinced his blind father that he was Esau. Now Laban dressed Rachel's older and apparently less attractive sister, **Leah**, in Rachel's wedding veil and convinced Jacob he was marrying the woman he loved. Only the next morning, after the marriage had been legally consummated, did Jacob realize he had married Leah. Furious, he demanded Rachel, yet he had no alternative but to pay the price:

seven more years of labor. After finishing the week of celebrating his marriage to Leah, Jacob was allowed to wed Rachel as well.

The two sisters became intense competitors in their struggle for their husband's affection, though Jacob "loved Rachel more than Leah" (Gen. 29:30). Each sought to do what was expected of a woman in those days: give birth to children, preferably males. Leah quickly produced **Reuben**, **Simeon**, **Levi**, and **Judah**. But Rachel remained infertile and finally resorted to having two sons, **Dan** and **Naphtali**, through a surrogate, her maid **Bilhah**.

Still, Rachel wanted sons of her own. She even offered Leah a night with Jacob in exchange for "some of your son's mandrakes" (Gen. 30:14). The root of this wild plant resembles a human and was thought to promote conception; and, indeed, Leah conceived her fifth son, **Issachar**, that night—though Rachel remained barren. Only after Leah had given birth to a sixth son, **Zebulun**, and a daughter, **Dinah**, did Rachel conceive her first child. She named the boy **Joseph**, saying, "God has taken away my reproach" (Gen. 30:23).

Later, when Jacob moved his family back to Canaan, Rachel stole her father's household gods, apparently because she felt that Laban had cheated her by not giving her a dowry equal to Jacob's seven years of labor. Ironically, this woman who so desperately wanted children died in childbirth on the trip south. Rachel lived long enough to name her second son Ben-oni, "son of my sorrow." But Jacob renamed the infant **Benjamin**, "son of the right hand," and loved him dearly.

Rachel was buried on the way to Bethlehem, her grave marked by a pillar. She was the only one among the first three patriarchal generations not interred in the cave at Machpelah, which **Abraham** had purchased from **Ephron** the Hittite as a last resting place for his wife, **Sarah**.

Laban searches for the idols stolen by Rachel; detail of a 17th-century painting.

Jacob meets his cousin and future wife Rachel; a painting by William Dyce (1806-1864).

RAHAB

(ray' hab) HEBREW: RAHAB; from REHABIAH
"wide" or "broad"

Israel's 40 years of wandering in the wilderness were over, and the conquest of Canaan was about to begin. Led by **Joshua**, the Israelites were camped at Shittim on the Plains of Moab east of the Jordan River and opposite Canaan's fortified border town of Jericho. Before launching his attack, Joshua sent two spies, telling them, "Go, view the land, especially Jericho" (Jos. 2:1). When they reached this largest settlement in the lower Jordan valley, they found lodging with a harlot named Rahab.

Perhaps the spies felt that Rahab's house would serve as an inconspicuous location, since it was frequented by strangers. But someone leaked word to the king of Jericho that Israelites were there, and he sent a message demanding that Rahab bring the men out. Instead, she risked her life by hiding the spies on her roof, under stalks of flax she had laid out to dry. She told the king, "True, men came to me, but I did not know where they came from; and when the gate was to be closed, at dark, the men went out; where the men went I do not know; pursue them quickly, for you will overtake them" (Jos. 2:4-5). The king's men left, searching the roads that led to the Jordan.

Rahab helps Joshua's spies flee Jericho by lowering them from her window.

Rahab then went to the spies and pleaded for her life and for the lives of her parents, brothers, sisters, and their families. She had heard stories of how the Lord helped the Israelites by parting the Red Sea and by destroying Israel's enemies. And she expressed faith in God by saying, "I know that the Lord has given you the land" (Jos. 2:9). The spies agreed to spare her and her family, but only if she promised to keep silent about their mission. They told Rahab to gather her family in the house and mark it with a scarlet cord hung from her window.

Since Rahab's house was attached to the city wall, she was able to use a rope to lower the men out of the city. On her advice, the spies hid in the hills three days before returning to their camp in Moab. As the men promised, "Rahab the harlot, and her father's household, and all who belonged to her, Joshua saved alive; and she dwelt in Israel to this day" (Jos. 6:25).

Some Jewish legends hold that Rahab later married Joshua and was an ancestor of

the prophet **Jeremiah**. But the New Testament seems to place her in the family tree of **Jesus**: "Salmon the father of Boaz by Rahab" (Mt. 1:5). Scholars are uncertain if the mother of **Boaz**—the man who married **Ruth**—is the Rahab of Jericho. But the possibility seems strengthened because Jesus' genealogy includes two other women with questionable backgrounds: **Tamar**, who seduced her father-in-law, **Judah**; and **Bathsheba**, who committed adultery with **David**.

RAHAB 2

(ray' hab) HEBREW: RAHAB
"proud/boisterous/arrogant one" or "strength"

Rahab is the name given in the Old Testament to a powerful enemy of God. In some passages it signifies an awesome monster, while in others it denotes one of Israel's historical enemies.

Rahab the monster was a sea serpent of demonic strength that God overcame in battle so that an orderly creation could take place. Although Rahab was no ordinary animal, neither was it a match for God, a fact **Job** emphasized: "By his power he [God] stilled the sea; by his understanding he smote Rahab" (Job 26:12). Some scholars say Rahab is another name for Leviathan, mentioned in Job 3:8 and Job 41:1; others say they are separate creatures.

In the Old Testament, Rahab is also a pejorative name for Egypt, a traditional enemy of Israel. Characterizing that country's help as "worthless and empty," God calls Egypt "Rahab who sits still" (Is. 30:7).

RAPHAEL

(raf' i el or ray' fi el) HEBREW: REPAEL
"God heals" or "God is fearsome"

In the book of Tobit in the Apocrypha, God sends the archangel Raphael to help **Tobit**, who is blind, and Sarah, who is haunted by the demon Asmodeus, who has

killed each of her seven husbands before the marriage could be consummated.

Disguised as Azarias, a relative of Tobit, Raphael accompanies Tobit's son **Tobias** on a journey. Along the way they catch a fish, and Raphael tells Tobias how to use the gall to restore Tobit's sight and the heart and liver to free Sarah from the demon in order that he might marry her. This illustrates one meaning of Raphael's name: "God heals." The other meaning, "God is fearsome," may reflect the fact that, following God's orders, Raphael bound the demon Azazel and threw him into a dark pit. This story, in which Raphael is elevated to the second rank in the hierarchy of angels, appears in the pseudepigraphical 1 Enoch, one of a number of Jewish writings dating to the period between 250 B.C. and A.D. 200 that are not included in any biblical canon.

In other traditional Jewish literature, Raphael governs the sun, commands the west, and represents the color green. His name appears often in magical papyri, on amulets, in incantations, and on a number of ancient tombstones.

The angel Raphael guiding Tobias; a painting by Benozzo Gozzoli (1420-1498)

REBEKAH

(ruh bek' uh) HEBREW: RIBQA
meaning uncertain, possibly "to bind" or "cattle"

When a stranger came to town seeking a wife for his master's 40-year-old son, Rebekah accepted the proposal by proxy and agreed to leave immediately. At the time she was a young maiden, perhaps still in her early teens, and "very fair to look upon, a virgin" (Gen. 24:16).

Abraham had sent his most trusted servant, possibly **Eliezer**, on the trip several hundred miles north of Canaan to find a bride for **Isaac** among his kin in Mesopotamia; he was determined that his son not marry a Canaanite. The servant, accompanied by ten camels loaded with bridal gifts of gold, silver, and fine clothing, stopped at a well outside the city of Nahor. There he asked God for a sign: The future bride should not only agree to give him a drink but volunteer to water his camels as well. Rebekah did both. If the servant had any doubt that Rebekah was God's choice, it was likely dispelled when she identified herself as the daughter of Abraham's nephew **Bethuel**. Rebekah's father and her brother **Laban** quickly agreed to the match, saying to the servant, "Take her and go, and let her be the wife of your master's son, as the Lord has spoken" (Gen. 24:51). The family wanted Rebekah to have ten days for good-byes and preparations, but the servant insisted on departing the next morning.

When the party reached the Negeb, where Isaac was then living, Rebekah alighted from her camel and—as a maiden should— covered her face with a veil. But Isaac took her into his tent, "and she became his wife; and he loved her" (Gen. 24:67).

During a famine in the region, the couple temporarily moved to Philistine territory in western Canaan, perhaps no more than 20 miles from the Mediterranean Sea. Rebekah was so "fair to look upon" (Gen. 26:7) that Isaac thought someone there might kill him to marry her. So he told the people that he was her brother. The king, however, caught him caressing her one day and scolded him for lying, but then gave orders that no one should hurt them.

Through 20 years of marriage, Rebekah remained infertile. In this regard she was like other presumably barren women of the Bible who late in life gave birth to sons destined for greatness: Isaac's own mother, **Sarah**; **Joseph**'s mother, **Rachel**; **Samuel**'s mother, **Hannah**; and **John the Baptist's** mother, **Elizabeth.** Only after 60-year-old Isaac prayed that she would conceive did Rebekah give birth to

Abraham's servant encounters Rebekah at the well in this painting by Bartolemé Estéban Murillo (1617-1682).

twins: **Esau** and **Jacob**. Isaac favored Esau, the hunter, and Rebekah favored Jacob, the quiet one. When Isaac grew old, Rebekah masterminded a plot to fool him into giving his blessing to Jacob instead of Esau, the older son. (The blessing, which conveys clan leadership, could not be withdrawn once spoken.) Then, to spare Jacob from his brother's revenge, she convinced Isaac to send Jacob north to look for a wife from within the circle of her own family.

There is no record that Rebekah ever saw her son again. They were, however, reunited in burial near Hebron, "in the cave that is in the field at Machpelah" (Gen. 49:30).

RECHAB
(ree' kab) HEBREW: REKAB

Rechab was the father or ancestor of **Jonadab** (also called Jehonadab), an ardent supporter of **Jehu**'s bloody revolt against the house of **Omri**. As the patriarch of a group of nomadic shepherds or itinerant chariot makers called the Rechabites, Jonadab fled to Jerusalem during **Nebuchadnezzar**'s invasion of Judah.

The Rechabites zealously worshiped God and maintained a disciplined life-style. When the prophet **Jeremiah** offered them

wine to test their obedience, they refused, saying, "Jonadab the son of Rechab, our father, commanded us, 'You shall not drink wine, neither you nor your sons for ever; you shall not build a house; you shall not sow seed; you shall not plant or have a vineyard; but you shall live in tents all your days, that you may live many days in the land where you sojourn'" (Jer. 35:6-7).

Jeremiah commended the Rechabites for remaining true to their principles, in contrast to the people of Judah, who were faithless to God. As a reward, the Lord promised that "Jonadab the son of Rechab shall never lack a man to stand before me" (Jer. 35:19). This prophecy turned out to be accurate, since the Rechabites are known to have thrived from at least the ninth to the sixth century B.C.

REHOBOAM
(ree huh boh' uhm) HEBREW: REHABAM
"may the people increase"

King **Solomon**'s son and successor, Rehoboam presided over the collapse of the Israelite empire. His reign has been dated as starting in 931 or 922 B.C.; according to two passages in the Bible, it lasted 17 years. Some scholars suggest that those years included a coregency with his father during Solomon's final years and propose the dates 922 to 915 B.C. for Rehoboam's sole rule of the kingdom of Judah.

Whatever the dates, Rehoboam's reign began in crisis. In his reorganization of **David**'s kingdom, Solomon had repressed tribal loyalties—except for those due his own tribe of Judah—and had neglected the priestly tribe of Levi. Long pent-up resentment erupted shortly after Solomon's death, and tribal leaders insisted that Rehoboam be crowned in the ancient northern city of Shechem rather than in Jerusalem, whose grandiose structures could only remind them of the forced labor that had built them. At Shechem, the leaders demanded to know Rehoboam's intentions. He consulted his father's advisers, who urged restraint: "If you will be a servant to this people today and serve them, and speak good words to them when you answer them, then they will be your servants for ever" (1 Kg. 12:7). His younger counselors, however, called for a reign of terror. Rehoboam agreed with them, giving a defiant reply to the leaders: "My father made your yoke heavy, but I will add to your yoke; my father chastised you with whips, but I will chastise you with scorpions" (1 Kg. 12:14). Furious, the lead-

ers left Shechem and prepared to secede. The unified Israelite empire of David and Solomon was no more.

Hoping to impose order, Rehoboam sent his father's head of forced labor, Adoram; the northerners promptly stoned him to death. Rehoboam then formed a new army drawn from the tribes of Judah and Benjamin. By this time the northern tribes had crowned **Jeroboam** son of Nebat as ruler of the secessionist kingdom of Israel, and he, too, began building an army. Pharaoh **Shishak**, Jeroboam's protector and possibly his brother-in-law as well, warned Rehoboam that if Judah—Rehoboam's rump kingdom in the south—attacked Israel, Egypt would intervene. Still worse, a prophet named **Shemaiah** declared that God opposed an army levied to fight Rehoboam's northern kinsmen. However, Rehoboam received support from priests and Levites shut out by Jeroboam's religious innovations.

For years a border war raged between Judah and Israel, mainly over control of the territory of Benjamin, a border tribe that had failed to support Rehoboam. The king built 15 defensive sites, circling Jerusalem except in the north, where, perhaps, even building fortresses was unsafe.

Rehoboam tells leaders of the northern tribes he will deal with them even more harshly than had Solomon.

In the fifth year of Rehoboam's reign, Pharaoh Shishak of Egypt invaded. The Bible tells little about the attack, except that the Egyptians took treasures from the temple and royal palace, and Rehoboam was forced to replace his guards' golden shields with ones of bronze. Wall carvings at the temple at Karnak vividly portray Shishak's victories, each of some 150 captives depicted in stone representing a conquered city. Archeology verifies that the invasion covered not only Judah, but Philistia, Transjordan, parts of Edom, and even Israel, despite the Pharaoh's former friendship with Jeroboam. Shishak may have put off an earlier invasion of Solomon's united kingdom; his success this time shows how quickly division led to weakness.

It is unclear whether the defenses around Jerusalem were built before or after the invasion. Excavations at Lachish and Azekah show no signs of destruction during Shishak's time. At any rate, Shishak died shortly after the invasion, and his successor seems not to have renewed the war or exacted tribute from Jerusalem.

Rehoboam continued Solomon's practice of intermarriage and the sanctioning of each wife's culture and religion. By his 18 wives and 60 concubines, he had 60 daughters and 28 sons, some of whom he appointed to rule various parts of his territory. He chose **Abijah**, his son by a woman named Micaiah, as successor some years before he died.

REUBEN

(roo' ben) HEBREW: REUBEN
"behold a son"

The name Reuben, meaning "behold a son," is a natural reaction to the birth of a boy and also refers to the circumstances of the birth of **Jacob**'s eldest son by his first wife **Leah**. Although Jacob loved Leah's younger sister **Rachel**, he had been tricked into marrying the less attractive Leah, whom he grew to hate. After Leah gave birth to Reuben, she said, "The Lord has looked upon my affliction; surely now my husband will love me" (Gen. 29:32).

As a boy, Reuben gathered some mandrakes (considered an aphrodisiac) for his mother. But when the barren Rachel asked for some, Leah gave them to her in return for a night with Jacob, which led to the birth of **Issachar**. Later Reuben had sexual relations with **Bilhah**, Rachel's maid by whom Jacob had had two other sons, **Dan** and **Naphtali**. His action may have been an attempt to get his father to return to Leah or an effort to usurp his father's authority. As a

Joseph's brothers lift him from the well to sell him into slavery; a painting by Raphael.

result, Reuben forfeited his birthright to be the leader of his father's sons, and the rights that should have gone to the tribe of the Reubenites went instead to the descendants of **Joseph**. Reuben did, however, assume the role of the eldest when he intervened on Joseph's behalf as the other brothers were plotting his death. Reuben had four sons and, according to tradition, died in Egypt at the age of 125.

In return for their help in the conquest of Canaan, **Moses** gave Reuben's descendants land in Gilead so they could raise cattle and sheep. Although the Reubenites were "valiant men, who carried shield and sword, and drew the bow, expert in war" (1 Chr. 5:18), the tribe sank into obscurity after the time of King **David**. They probably were absorbed by the tribe of Gad and by the neighboring Moabites.

REZIN

(ree' zin) HEBREW: RESIN
"pleasant/agreeable"

After paying tribute to the Assyrian king **Tiglath-pileser III** in 738 B.C., King Rezin of Aram-Damascus, or Syria, joined an alliance against Assyria with Israel, Tyre, Damascus, Philistia, and some Arab tribes. When King **Ahaz** of Judah refused to join the alliance, Rezin and King **Pekah** of Israel attacked Judah and laid siege to

Jerusalem in an attempt to install a ruler who would support them. Although the prophet **Isaiah** advised Ahaz not to fear "these two smoldering stumps of firebrands" (Is. 7:4), Ahaz asked Tiglath-pileser for help, sending a bribe of gold and silver. In response, Assyria dispatched forces that defeated the alliance. Tiglath-pileser successfully besieged Damascus in 732 B.C., and the Assyrians executed Rezin. Assyria annexed Aram-Damascus and much of Israel and deported many of the residents.

RHODA

(roh' duh) GREEK: RHODE

"little rose"

After **Peter** was miraculously released from prison, he came to the home of **Mary** the mother of John **Mark** and knocked at the gate. Rhoda, a family servant and probably a Christian attending a prayer meeting there, answered the knock. But when she recognized Peter's voice, Rhoda was so excited that she ran to tell the others without letting him in. At first no one believed her, saying "You are mad" (Acts 12:15). However, at the continued knocking, the others went to see for themselves and were astonished to find Peter.

RIZPAH

(riz' puh) HEBREW: RISPA

"live coal"

The concubine of King **Saul**, Rizpah bore him two sons, Mephibosheth and Armoni. After Saul's death, his son and would-be successor **Ish-bosheth** confronted the military commander **Abner** with the accusation that he had made Rizpah his own concubine—an act that could be taken as laying claim to the throne. "I keep showing loyalty to the house of Saul your father," Abner angrily responded; ". . . and yet you charge me today with a fault concerning a woman" (2 Sam. 3:8). Immediately thereafter, Abner defected to **David**.

During David's reign there was a three-year famine. Seeking relief, David ordered Rizpah's sons and the five sons of **Merab**, Saul's oldest daughter, to be ritually executed and left unburied. The devoted Rizpah watched over the seven bodies, "and she did not allow the birds of the air to come upon them by day, or the beasts of the field by night" (2 Sam. 21:10) from April until rain fell in October. David then gave the remains an honorable burial with the exhumed bones of Saul and his son **Jonathan**.

RUTH

HEBREW: RUT

"companion/friend" or "satisfied"

This great grandmother of King **David** is remembered as a gentle heroine in spite of the fact that she boldly approached the man she wanted to marry. Her story, recorded in the biblical book bearing her name, is one of an indigent widow who eventually remarried and gave birth to a family of kings. The four-chapter book is one of the most masterfully crafted works of Hebrew literature, moving from suspense to suspense before reaching a surprise conclusion. Interestingly, Ruth was not a Hebrew. In a nation that prided itself on being chosen by God and spiritually distinct from others, she was a foreigner from Moab, Judah's neighbor just east of the Dead Sea.

The story, which most biblical scholars say was passed on by word of mouth for generations before being written down, took place "in the days when the judges ruled" (Ru. 1:1). A famine throughout Judah led a resident of Bethlehem named **Elimelech** to move to Moab in search of food. With him he took his wife, **Naomi**, and their sons, Mahlon and Chilion. After the family settled in Moab, the sons took local women as wives; Mahlon married Ruth and Chilion married **Orpah**. But within ten years all three men died, leaving behind widows without children. In this male-dominated society, women without a father, husband, or son to care for them could quickly become destitute; they had few rights.

Naomi, hearing that the famine in Judah had ended, decided to return to her homeland. Perhaps she thought relatives would take pity on her and give her a place to live. But they would certainly not take in all three women. Moreover, Naomi pointed out, she was too old to bear other sons, even if the women were willing to wait until they were grown to marry them. So Naomi urged Ruth and Orpah each to return to her mother and begin looking for another husband. Both initially rejected the idea; but after Naomi reasoned with them further, Orpah agreed and left with a tearful good-bye. Ruth, however, absolutely refused to leave Naomi alone. "Where you go," Ruth insisted, "I will go, and where you lodge I will lodge; your people shall be my people, and your God my God" (Ru. 1:16).

When the two women reached Bethlehem, the entire town was moved with sympathy for Naomi and, no doubt, with admiration for Ruth's unfailing loyalty toward her aging mother-in-law. Yet no one offered to take them in. However, according to Mosaic Law, the poor are allowed to collect any crops that were missed during the first pass of the reapers.

The barley harvest had just started, so Ruth decided to go gleaning behind the reapers. Fortunately, she chose the field of **Boaz**. This man had heard how Ruth refused to abandon Naomi, and he took an immediate liking to her. He even ordered that the workers leave extra grain for her and that the young men not bother her. When Ruth returned to Naomi with more than half a bushel of grain and reported what happened, Naomi was elated. Boaz was not just a friendly neighbor, Naomi explained, "the man is a relative of ours, one of our nearest kin" (Ru. 2:20). The Law obliged a man to marry his brother's widow, to produce children to carry on the dead brother's family name and—incidentally—

As Orpah turns homeward, Ruth follows Naomi; a contemporary British painting.

to claim the deceased man's property. Apparently, the rule could be extended to include relatives other than brothers.

Having observed the spark of interest Boaz had shown in the young widow, Naomi advised Ruth to act quickly. Ruth was to wash, anoint herself, and dress in her best clothes. Then she was to go down to the threshing floor, where Boaz and the workers were separating the grain from the chaff. "Do not make yourself known to the man until he has finished eating and drinking," Naomi instructed. "But when he lies down, observe the place where he lies; then, go and uncover his feet and lie down; and he will tell you what to do" (Ru. 3:3-4).

However bold and out of character Ruth's action may appear, Boaz seemed to feel no pressure. When he awakened in the middle of the night and Ruth proposed by asking, "spread your skirt over your maidservant, for you are next of kin" (Ru. 3:9), Boaz responded with compassion. He assured her that he would do as she asked, then told her to lie at his feet the rest of the night but to leave before dawn so that no one would see where she had been. But in their clandestine conversation Boaz added a new element of suspense. He told Ruth he was not her closest relative and said he could marry her only if the other relative chose not to. Though the unnamed man had first choice, he waived his right.

Boaz married Ruth and together they had a son: Obed, the father of **Jesse** and grandfather of David. In one of the final scenes of the book Naomi holds her grandson on her lap and cares for him. And the women of the village praise Ruth as showing more love toward Naomi than would seven sons—a number symbolic of perfection. These same women call the child Naomi's "restorer of life" (Ru. 4:15). A thousand years later **Jesus**, a descendant of Obed, was born in Bethlehem; he is described as one who gives "life for all men" (Rom. 5:18). The genealogy of Jesus, recorded in Matthew 1, lists but four women—and Ruth is one of them.

Biblical scholars are uncertain who wrote the book of Ruth. Nor do they know when or why it was written. A popular hypothesis is that the book was compiled sometime between the tenth and eighth centuries B.C., shortly after the time of David, and was written to trace the lineage of David. Likely, however, the story was preserved for many reasons. One may have been to allow future generations to learn from Ruth's inspiring example of love for Naomi. Jews today still honor Ruth by rereading her story during the annual Feast of Weeks that marks the end of the grain harvest.

SALOME

(suh loh' mee, sal oh may') GREEK: SALOME

Called upon to dance at the birthday banquet of her stepfather, **Herod Antipas**, the daughter of **Herodias** pleased him so much that he said, "Ask me for whatever you wish, and I will grant it" (Mk. 6:22). At the prompting of her mother, she requested and received the head of **John the Baptist**, whom Antipas had imprisoned for having condemned his marriage to Herodias, previously the wife of one of his half brothers. The young woman then presented John's head to her mother.

The daughter of Herodias is unnamed in the New Testament. But the first-century A.D. Jewish historian Josephus says her name was Salome and that she later married **Herod Philip**.

SALOME 2

According to the Gospel of Mark, Salome was among **Jesus'** women disciples who had followed him from Galilee to Jerusalem and who observed his crucifixion, "looking on from afar" (Mk. 15:40). Then, at sunrise on Sunday, she went with **Mary Magdalene** and **Mary** the mother of **James** and Joseph to the tomb where Jesus had been laid to rest to anoint his body for proper burial—only to find it empty. Confronted by an angel with the news of Jesus' resurrection, the three women fled in fear and amazement.

All four of the Gospels place women at the crucifixion and at the empty tomb, but differ in identifying them. The third woman in

Salome's dance for her stepfather, Herod Antipas, is given an exotic setting in this painting by Armand Point (1860-1932).

Matthew's Gospel is called not Salome but only "the mother of the sons of Zebedee" (Mt. 27:56). Earlier this woman had sought special favor for **James** and **John**: "Command that these sons of mine may sit, one at your right and one at your left, in your kingdom." Jesus said that the honor was not his to bestow, "but it is for those whom it has been prepared by my Father" (Mt. 20:21, 23). The request for preference was greeted with indignation by the other disciples.

SAMSON

(sam' suhn) HEBREW: SHIMSHON, possibly derived from SHEMESH
"sun"

For a national hero chosen by God, Samson was surprisingly unrighteous and earthy. He was the last of the charismatic heroes of the book of Judges, a man endowed with incredible physical strength; but he had a weakness for immoral women, a temper that provoked him to kill 30 innocent bystanders, and a vengeance that drove him to hunt down 300 foxes, set their tails on fire, and turn them loose in the grain fields of a people who had done him wrong.

Like such other prominent biblical figures as **Isaac**, **Joseph**, **Samuel**, and **John the Baptist**, Samson was born to a woman previously considered infertile. His father was **Manoah**, from the tribe of Dan, who lived with his wife (unnamed in the Bible) in Zorah, about 15 miles west of Jerusalem, on the border with Philistia. One day an angel appeared to the childless woman to say she would at last have a son. "The boy shall be a Nazirite to God from birth," the heavenly messenger announced; "and he shall begin to deliver Israel from the hand of the Philistines" (Jg. 13:5). Nazirites stood out from other Hebrews because of the vows they had taken. Like other Hebrews, they were to avoid anything ritually unclean, such as corpses. In addition, they were not to cut their hair, and they were to refrain from drinking wine or even from eating grapes. But Samson eventually broke each of these vows. He ate honey from the carcass of a lion he had killed earlier; wine flowed freely at his wedding feast; and he let himself be tricked into a haircut.

When he became old enough, Samson asked his parents to arrange a marriage with a Philistine woman from Timnah, five miles to the west. They refused with a sarcastic question: "Is there not a woman among the daughters of your kinsmen, or among all our people, that you must go to take a wife from the uncircumcised Philistines?" (Jg. 14:3). But Samson persisted, and a marriage was contracted with the woman of Timnah. However, God used Samson's lust for erotic encounters with Philistine women to drive a wedge between Philistia and Israel. Prior to Samson's run-ins with the Philistines—all of which started over women—the two nations had been on relatively friendly terms, with Philistia the dominant nation. Intermarriage was permitted, as was commerce. But Samson made coexistence much less comfortable and helped keep Israel from being absorbed into Philistine culture.

AN INTERRUPTED WEDDING

The fighting between Samson and the Philistines began almost immediately after Samson's wedding. Guests were starting the traditional week-long festivities when Samson challenged the 30 Philistine men there to a friendly wager. Solve his riddle, he explained, and he would give each of them a set of clothes. Fail, and they would each give him an outfit. The riddle involved a lion Samson had killed earlier and told no one about. He later saw that bees had swarmed onto the carcass and ate honey from their hive. So his riddle was, "Out of the eater came something to eat. Out of the strong came something sweet" (Jg. 14:14).

The guests managed to solve the riddle, but only by threatening the bride into badgering the secret out of Samson. She then told the guests, who promptly asked Samson, "What is sweeter than honey? What is stronger than a lion?" (Jg. 14:18). Furious that his wife had betrayed him, Samson stormed off to Ashkelon, a Philistine city 25 miles away on the Mediterranean coast. There he killed 30 men, stripped them, and took their clothes back to the wedding guests. Instead of living with his wife, he went back to his parents. By the time he calmed down enough to return to his wife, she had been given to the best man.

Samson immediately took revenge on the Philistine people, who had caused him so much grief. He caught 300 foxes, lit their tails with torches, and turned them loose in fields and orchards. The Philistines responded by burning to death Samson's former wife and her father. Then Samson retaliated by killing more Philistines before retreating to a cave in Judah, away from the Philistine border. Their soldiers, however, came after him. Rather than cause his fellow Israelites to suffer for his actions, Samson agreed to let his own people tie him up and turn him over to the Philistines. But once in Philistine hands, Samson broke his ropes, picked up the jawbone of an ass, and killed 1,000 Philistine soldiers.

Sometime later, Samson showed

Samson killing the lion; a 16th-century gilded and painted statue

Succumbing to Delilah's persistence, Samson reveals the secret of his strength: his uncut hair; a painting by Guercino (1591-1666).

up in another Philistine town, Gaza, near the coast. While there, he visited a prostitute. News of his arrival quickly spread through the town, and the citizens surrounded the house. They decided to capture him at dawn, after he was worn out from a night of lovemaking. Samson, however, surprised them by leaving in the middle of the night. He took with him the huge doors of the city gate—posts and all—and carried them nearly 40 miles before depositing them on a hilltop near Hebron.

HIS SECRET REVEALED

The best-known story about Samson, of course, concerns his love for **Delilah**. It was a fatal attraction because the Philistine leaders bribed her into nagging out of Samson the secret of his supernatural strength. "A razor has never come upon my head; for I have been a Nazirite to God from my mother's womb," he eventually confided. "If I be shaved, then my strength will leave me" (Jg. 16:17). As his wife had done before, Delilah reported the secret. Then, after he had fallen asleep on her lap, she called a man to cut his locks and delivered him to the Philistines. They promptly gouged out his eyes and put him to work grinding meal at the prison mill in Gaza, the city whose gate he had earlier stolen and carried away.

After Samson's shaved hair started growing back, the nation's rulers gathered in the city temple for a festival to honor their god, **Dagon**. As part of the celebration they put on display the once mighty enemy whom, they said, their god had delivered to them. In that temple, between two pillars likely built of stone or wooden blocks mounted on top of each other, Samson prayed. Although Samson's recorded prayers are selfish rather than pious, they show he had faith that God would answer. And for that faith, he was later commended by the anonymous author of the letter to the Hebrews, who listed Samson along with **Gideon**, **Barak**, **Jephthah**, **David**, and Samuel as a man who "won strength out of weakness, became mighty for war, [and] put armies to flight" (Heb. 11:34). Samson's last prayer also showed he had not lost his appetite for revenge. "Strengthen me, I pray thee, only this once, O God, that I may be avenged upon the Philistines for one of my two eyes" (Jg. 16:28). God heard his plea, Samson strained against the pillars, and the temple collapsed. Samson died amid the rubble but took with him more Philistines than he had killed in his 20 years as a judge in Israel; about 3,000 were on the temple roof alone.

Samson was an individualistic rabble-rouser seeking to satisfy his appetites. But God was able to use him to move Israel in the direction it needed to go. About 50 years later King David finished the job Samson started; sometime after 1000 B.C. he crushed the Philistines and ended their dominance of the region once and for all.

SAMUEL

(sam' yoo uhl) HEBREW: SHEMUEL
"his divine name is El"
···········

Overseeing a major social and political transition at the end of the period of the judges (the last three-quarters of the 11th century B.C.), Samuel anointed the first two kings of ancient Israel, **Saul** and **David**. Samuel himself was the last of the judges and the first of the classical prophets. During most of his career, he judged Israel from his home in Ramah, a few miles north of Jerusalem, where he built an altar for sacrifices and where he began his yearly tour of the cities of Bethel, Gilgal, and Mizpah to adjudicate cases brought to him. Though never called a priest, Samuel offered sacrifices and conducted worship at the shrine in Shiloh where the ark of the covenant was kept before it was captured by the Philistines in battle at Ebenezer. He appears in the Bible as a man renowned for his extraordinary faith and for his ability to intercede with the Lord.

Born in answer to the tearful prayers of his barren mother, **Hannah**, Samuel became a Nazirite to fulfill her vow. For Hannah had sworn that if God gave her a son, "no razor shall touch his head" (1 Sam. 1:11); she had also promised to bring her son, as soon as he was weaned, to live at the Shiloh shrine and to be dedicated forever to the Lord. Although 1 Samuel indicates that Samuel was an Ephraimite, in 1 Chronicles 6:28 it is implied that Samuel was a Levite, probably owing to his early attachment to the tabernacle as well as his inheritance (he was a descendant of **Levi**'s son **Kohath**). Wearing a linen ephod, the young boy Samuel routinely assisted the priest **Eli** at the Shiloh shrine. Whenever Hannah visited Shiloh for her family's annual sacrifice, she brought a new robe she had made for her son.

Eli would normally have been succeeded by his priestly sons, **Hophni** and Phinehas. However, they violated their sacred offices by demanding from worshipers the best meat, which ought to have been offered as sacrifices. Though Eli warned them that sins directly against the Lord have no hope of intercession, the two continued to abuse

---

NAZIRITES

The **biblical** *figures known as Nazirites took their name from a Hebrew word meaning "consecrated one"; regulations governing their behavior appear in Numbers 6:1-21. Samson and Samuel were dedicated to the Lord's service for life before birth—the first by the angel announcing his birth, the second by his mother. But when the apostle Paul shaved his head (Acts 18:18), he took a temporary Nazirite vow that he later terminated at Jerusalem.*

---

their privileges. At length, an unnamed prophet announced to Eli an end to his family's right to inherit the priesthood; God had decided to "raise up for myself a faithful priest, who shall do according to what is in my heart and in my mind" (1 Sam. 2:35). A new priestly clan would serve in place of Eli's family.

Later, as the boy Samuel slept in the main room of the shrine that housed the ark, and Eli slept in a nearby room of his own, God called to the boy in a vision. Visions from God were rare in Samuel's days, so he presumed that Eli must have summoned him and ran to the priest. Eli assured him he had not called out. The same misunderstanding occurred twice more before Eli instructed the boy, who "did not yet know the Lord," to respond the next time with the words, "Speak, Lord, for thy servant hears" (1 Sam. 3:7, 9). When Samuel answered the fourth call, God revealed to him news so shocking that the "ears of every one that hears it will tingle" (1 Sam. 3:11). The priestly dynasty of Eli, once believed to be established forever, would be completely destroyed. The next morning, Eli insisted that the frightened boy share the message with him. Calmly accepting this word of God, Eli let all Israel know about Samuel's vision in the shrine and that the boy had been appointed to be a prophet of the Lord. Sometime later, Eli's sons were killed in a battle with the Philistines. When Eli heard the news, he fell backward off his chair, broke his neck, and died.

After Eli's death, Samuel—by then a man—summoned all Israel to abandon idolatry and join him at the city of Mizpah to offer sacrifices on behalf of the nation. At the end of these ceremonies, God's thunderous voice frightened away the Philistines who had encamped nearby. Samuel commemorated this deliverance by erecting a stone he called Ebenezer, meaning, "Hitherto the Lord has helped us" (1 Sam. 7:12).

ASKING FOR A KING

Samuel and his unnamed wife had two sons, Joel and Abijah, who proved to be as corrupt as Eli's sons had been. Some elders of Israel took advantage of this family problem by pressuring Samuel to appoint a king who would eliminate the need for any future judges. The initial argument would have seemed reasonable to Samuel, but their final point betrayed their real rationale: "Behold, you are old and your sons do not walk in your ways; now appoint for us a king to govern us like all the nations" (1 Sam. 8:5). The elders wanted a king because they preferred the security of a royal standing army to reliance on God's miraculous intervention through judges, like Samuel, who needed to assemble a makeshift fighting force for each new crisis. Feeling rejected, Samuel sent the elders away and prayed. But God commanded his prophet to honor the request, "for they have not rejected you, but they have rejected me from being king over them" (1 Sam. 8:7).

Samuel agreed to anoint a king but, following God's orders, spelled out the consequences of a monarchy: Kings would take the best land, co-opt the best animals, make soldiers or servants of the most able young people, and tax the populace heavily. Under these burdens, citizens would be little better than slaves of the king. Using language reminiscent of the Hebrews who had sought God to alleviate their slavery in Egypt, Samuel described how the people in Israel would "cry out because of your king" (1 Sam. 8:18). But this time God would not answer their pleas by setting them free. When the elders persisted in their demand for a king, Samuel sent them back to their homes with his warning still ringing in their ears.

The biblical account of Samuel's anointing Saul as the first king of Israel seems to preserve older, conflicting traditions that have been carefully edited together. Some parts of the narrative put in a negative light the people's unfaithful demand for a human king as a replacement for God, while other parts describe God's own plan to find an ideal prince as a positive response to their prayers for national defense. In these latter traditions, Saul appears as the handsomest and tallest young man in Israel.

Saul was totally unprepared for his selection as Israel's first king. At the end of an unsuccessful three-day search for his father's lost donkeys, the young man sought out the prophet Samuel to ask God where the animals were. The previous day the Lord had told Samuel that he would "send to you a man from the land of Benjamin, and you shall anoint him to be prince over my people Israel" (1 Sam. 9:16). When Saul met Samuel, the prophet told him his donkeys were safe and insisted that Saul and his servant join him at the shrine for a special meal. Saul humbly expressed surprise, reminding the prophet that his tribe was the least significant in Israel and his family the most humble in the tribe. Nonetheless, Samuel put Saul at the head of the table, among 30 invited guests, and arranged for him to be served the best portion of meat. Walking with Saul outside the city the next morning, Samuel asked Saul to send his servant ahead, then privately anointed Saul as God's chosen prince and told him of various future confirming signs. These included an experience of Saul's prophesying with a band of prophets, so that people wondered, "Is Saul also among the prophets?" (1 Sam. 10:11).

Hannah offers her son, Samuel, to the priest Eli; from a 15th-century illuminated manuscript.

This positive portrait of God's using Samuel to anoint Saul is interwoven in the Bible with testimonies about the poor judgment of those who asked for a king. In the 11th hour of the inauguration of Saul as king, at a massive public gathering Samuel had called at the city of Mizpah, Saul could not be found. God revealed that Saul had shyly hidden himself "among the baggage" of those traveling to the meeting. Still, Samuel seemed impressed with Saul, for when he stood up in front of everyone, he was "taller than any of the people from the shoulders upward" (1 Sam. 10:22, 23). Most people cheered, "Long live the king!" but a few "worthless fellows" wondered out loud, "How can this man save us?" (1 Sam. 10:24, 27) and declined to offer tribute.

After Saul vindicated his leadership by repelling an attack on Israel by the Ammonites, Samuel called all the people to meet in Gilgal to reaffirm their loyalty to the king. There Samuel, as an old man, gave a farewell speech in which he publicly defended his own integrity. Recalling the people's foolish demand for a king "when the Lord your God was your king," he still promised things would go well if they would "fear the Lord" (1 Sam. 12:12, 14) and obey his commandments. As a threatening sign, God brought thunder and rain, though it was harvest time in late May, when rains usually no longer occurred. After interceding for the people, Samuel warned them bluntly, "if you still do wickedly, you shall be swept away, both you and your king" (1 Sam. 12:25).

Despite a promising start in about 1025 B.C., King Saul shattered his relationship with Samuel by desperately offering a sacrifice before a battle without waiting for the prophet to arrive. Samuel condemned Saul for disobeying a commandment of God and, as punishment, announced that the Lord would take the kingdom from him and give it to another, "a man after his own heart" (1 Sam. 13:14). In a similar story in 1 Samuel 15, Saul achieved victory over the Amalekites, then violated a religious ban by sparing the life of the enemy leader, **Agag**, and allowing his men to bring home cattle as spoils of war. When confronted by Samuel, Saul gave the unconvincing excuse that he wanted to save the best animals for a

Samuel; a stone carving from Chartres cathedral in France

grand sacrifice of thanksgiving to God. In a short but eloquent speech that is echoed in the words of later prophets, Samuel drove home an enduring truth: "To obey is better than sacrifice" (1 Sam. 15:22).

THE LORD'S FAVOR LOST

Though Saul responded with a sincere confession of his sin, Samuel was adamant, announcing God's unequivocal rejection of his kingship. As Samuel tried to leave, Saul desperately grabbed hold of the end of the prophet's robe, accidentally tearing off a small piece of cloth. Using a pun, Samuel declared, "The Lord has torn the kingdom of Israel from you this day" (1 Sam. 15:28). Saul confessed his sin and begged Samuel at least to lead him, the elders, and the people of Israel in worship. After doing so, Samuel commanded Saul to bring the captive Agag before him. Although Agag thought he was by then safe, Samuel recited Agag's deeds of killing innocent children and in righteous rage cut him into pieces with his sword.

From that moment on, Samuel never spoke to Saul again, though he began to grieve over Saul's plight.

Growing impatient with Samuel's misplaced sentiments, God chided him, "How long will you grieve over Saul, seeing I have rejected him from being king over Israel?" (1 Sam. 16:1), and commanded Samuel to fill his horn with oil and travel to Bethlehem, south of Jerusalem, to anoint one of the sons of a farmer named **Jesse** as king in Saul's place.

As Samuel traveled to Bethlehem from Ramah, he had to pass through Gibeah, Saul's home city. Samuel expressed to God his fear that Saul, who ruled there as king, might try to kill him. For Samuel's own protection, God instructed him to take a heifer and send word ahead that he was going to offer a sacrifice and wished Jesse to join him. When Samuel arrived safely at Bethlehem, the elders of the city nervously asked him if he had come in peace. Samuel reiterated only his earlier aim to worship with Jesse, saying nothing of his secret intent to anoint another king.

At the house of Jesse, Samuel examined each of Jesse's seven oldest sons in turn. But God instructed Samuel not to judge on the basis of physical attributes, stating, "Do not look on his appearance or on the height of his stature . . . for the Lord sees not as a man sees; man looks on the outward

Samuel anoints David king of Israel as the young shepherd's father and older brothers look on; a painting by Raphael.

appearance, but the Lord looks on the heart" (1 Sam. 16:7). To everyone's astonishment, God chose David, the youngest son in the family, who was brought in from tending sheep. As Samuel anointed him in the presence of his brothers, "the Spirit of the Lord came mightily upon David" (1 Sam. 16:13) and stayed with him throughout his life.

David, who was forced into hiding by King Saul, once visited Samuel in Ramah, and they both escaped by traveling to Naioth, a few miles north of Jerusalem. In Ramah, Saul demanded to know, "Where are Samuel and David?" (1 Sam. 19:22). When Saul tried to approach Samuel among a band of prophets in Naioth, the king fell suddenly into an involuntary ecstasy under the power of God, stripping off his clothes before Samuel and lying naked all night. Samuel left without speaking to him and soon died of old age.

We hear of Samuel one last time in a bizarre account of Saul's desperate search for advice on the eve of battle with the Philistines at Gilboa. Because the priestly Urim, dice used to provide answers, no longer worked and no prophet could be found, the king disguised himself and went to a medium at Endor, who conjured up the dead prophet's spirit. The spirit responded with complaints about being disturbed and announced the impending death of Saul and his sons: "Tomorrow you and your sons shall be with me; the Lord will give the army of Israel also into the hands of the Philistines (1 Sam. 28:19). The next day, the king and his sons died in battle. Samuel was, at last, allowed to rest in peace.

SANBALLAT

(san ba' lat) HEBREW: SANBALLAT; AKKADIAN: SIN-UBALLIT

"[the moon god] Sin gives life"

After several decades of exile in Babylon, the Jews began returning to Judah, where they started rebuilding Jerusalem. In charge of the construction was **Nehemiah**, cupbearer to King **Artaxerxes I** of Persia, ruler of the empire that had defeated Babylon. Nehemiah had received the king's permission to return to the city, "the place of my fathers' sepulchres" (Neh. 2:3), in order to restore its destroyed walls and gates. Sanballat, governor of Samaria, vigorously opposed the project.

Biblical scholars are uncertain why Sanballat objected. But as ruler of what had once been part of the northern kingdom of Israel, he may have feared that the rebirth of the southern kingdom would threaten the security of his own domain.

Sanballat tried several ways to stop the work, starting with ridicule. "What are these feeble Jews doing?" he mocked. "Will they revive the stones out of the heaps of rubbish, and burned ones at that?" (Neh.

4:2). He next plotted an attack he never carried out, then repeatedly tried to lure Nehemiah into a meeting in an apparent effort to assassinate him. All Sanballat's attempts to stop Nehemiah's work failed, and the walls were repaired in 52 days. Sometime later, Nehemiah banished a grandson of the high priest for having married Sanballat's daughter.

An Aramaic letter on papyrus from a community of Jews in Egypt, written in 407 B.C., confirms Sanballat's governorship of Samaria. Historians believe that Sanballat's descendants to at least the fifth generation continued to hold the post. Sanballat III, who served between 335 and 330 B.C., gave his daughter in marriage to the brother of the high priest **Jaddua**—indicating that the forbidden intermarriages between Jews and Samaritans continued to take place.

SAPPHIRA

(suh fai' ruh) GREEK: SAPPHIRA from
ARAMAIC: SAPPIRA
"good" or "beautiful"

Members of the Jerusalem church, Sapphira and her husband **Ananias** committed the first recorded sin in the community of believers. It was over money, and both received swift punishment for their transgression.

Early Christians were expected to share their wealth with the needy, but the couple withheld some money from the proceeds of a land sale and "brought only a part and laid it at the apostles' feet." Confronted individually by **Peter**, first Ananias, then Sapphira three hours later, lied about the sale and were miraculously struck dead. As a result, a "great fear came upon the whole church" (Acts 5:2, 11).

SARAH

(sehr' uh) HEBREW: SARA
"princess"

Her name means "princess," and indeed Sarah was the first matriarch of what became the Jewish nation, which produced such highly esteemed royalty as **David** and **Solomon**. But her behavior, at times, seemed less than regal. Twice she acquiesced in a deception about her identity; for this she ended up first in the harem of the Pharaoh and later in the household of a local chieftain.

Sarah is introduced in the Bible as Sarai, the infertile wife of Abram (**Abraham**), whom she married in Ur, in what is now

BARREN WOMEN

In ancient Israel children, and especially sons, were regarded as gifts of God, often as the reward for a righteous life. A woman who could not bear children seemed marked with divine disapproval and might well be divorced or pushed aside in disdain by a rival wife. It is striking that so many important mothers in early Hebrew history are described as originally barren. In each case, however, God intervened miraculously to give a son who was destined to preserve or aid his people.

In addition to Sarah, who had to wait till she was 91 years old to bear Isaac, other initially barren women in the Old Testament were Isaac's wife, Rebekah, infertile until God answered her husband's prayer to grant her twins; Rachel, the wife of Jacob, one of those twins, who eventually gave birth to Joseph, the boy destined to preserve his family and all Egypt from famine; the unnamed mother of Samson; and Hannah, the mother of Samuel.

In the New Testament, an angel told the priest Zechariah that his elderly wife, Elizabeth, would miraculously conceive a son. That child, who was to herald a new age, was John the Baptist.

southern Iraq. In the course of the narrative Abram identifies her as his half sister, "the daughter of my father but not the daughter of my mother" (Gen. 20:12). Born about 4,000 years ago, Sarai predated by several hundred years the Mosaic Law that prohibited sexual relations between close relatives: "You shall not uncover the nakedness of your sister, the daughter of your father or the daughter of your mother" (Lev. 18:9).

When Abram's father, **Terah**, decided to move to Canaan, Abram and Sarai accompanied him, as did **Lot**, the couple's nephew. Instead of completing the journey, however, they stopped several hundred miles north of their destination, at Haran in what is now southeastern Turkey. Only after Terah died did the three resume their journey to Canaan. By then, Abram was 75 years old and Sarai was 66. Though they still had no children, God promised to make them into "a great nation" (Gen. 12:2).

Once they reached Canaan, however, a famine forced them to seek refuge in Egypt. There, Abram first deceived people into believing that he and Sarai were only brother and sister. Even at her age, Sarai was so beautiful that Abram feared that some powerful Egyptian would kill him to get her. Sarai indeed was taken into the Egyptian Pharaoh's harem, and Abram received lavish gifts of livestock and servants. Before Sarai had to confront the issue of adultery, God plagued Pharaoh's household with disease and revealed to him that Sarai was Abram's wife. Pharaoh sent the couple away, with all the gifts he had given them.

The couple used the same ploy sometime later when they moved to Gerar, a town on the northern edge of the Negeb desert. King **Abimelech** brought Sarai into his household but discovered the truth in a dream. Again Sarai was spared the sin of adultery, and again the couple was showered with gifts, perhaps because God had revealed to the king that Abram was "a prophet" (Gen. 20:7) who would pray for him.

By the time Sarai reached her mid-70's, she concluded she would never have a child and instructed Abram to use her servant, **Hagar**, as a surrogate mother—an accepted practice of the day. Hagar gave birth to **Ishmael**, by tradition the ancestor of the Arab people. Yet a decade and a half later, when Sarai was 90 and her husband was 99, the Lord promised them that within a year they would have a son. It was then that God marked the pledge by giving Abram the name Abraham and Sarai the name Sarah.

A short time later heavenly messengers on their way to investigate Sodom and Gomorrah repeated this promise to Abraham.

The aged Sarah offers her Egyptian servant, Hagar, to Abraham as a surrogate mother; the painting is by Adriaen van der Werff (1659-1722).

Overhearing heavenly visitors say she will bear a son, Sarah laughs.

When Sarah overheard it, she "laughed to herself" (Gen. 18:12). But her laughter of disbelief became the laughter of astonishment and delight when at the age of 91 she gave birth to a son. Appropriately, she named him **Isaac**, from a Hebrew word meaning "laughter." She also guaranteed his inheritance by having her husband drive away Hagar and Ishmael.

Sarah lived to be 127 and was buried in the cave of Machpelah near Hebron, which Abraham had purchased from the Hittite **Ephron** for her final resting place. She was cited by the apostle **Peter** as a model wife because she "obeyed Abraham, calling him lord" (1 Pet. 3:6).

SARGON II

(sahr' gahn) HEBREW: SARGON;
AKKADIAN: SARRU-KIN
"legitimate king"

••••••••••

Mentioned only once in the Bible, King Sargon II of Assyria claimed to have defeated the northern kingdom of Israel in 722 B.C. But he likely ascended to power only in time for the mopping-up action, which included sending the northern tribes into an exile from which they never returned.

The king's name, meaning "legitimate king," is perhaps one he took after he seized the throne in a coup that ousted **Shalmaneser V**. During the struggle, smaller nations in the region formed alliances to rebel against Assyria. It was for this reason that "the commander in chief, who was sent by Sargon the king of Assyria, came to Ashdod," (Is. 20:1), a major Philistine city that was besieged and conquered.

Sargon reigned from 721 to 705 B.C., and spent much of that time putting down rebellions. He died on such a campaign in southeastern Turkey and was succeeded by his son **Sennacherib**, who crushed a rebellion led by King **Hezekiah** of Judah.

SATAN

(say' tuhn) HEBREW: SATAN
"adversary," "accuser," or "slanderer"

••••••••••

The figure of Satan, or the devil, is one of the most mysterious in the Bible, especially in the Old Testament, for the perception of the devil among ancient peoples changed over time. The name is Hebrew, but Satan rarely appears as a distinct figure in the Hebrew Bible. His name is much more common in the New Testament, written in Greek, where it occurs more than 30 times and denotes a being of great power and wickedness, the ruler of a demonic realm. The Hebrew word *satan* and the Greek word *diabolos*, from which the English word "devil" is derived, are both common nouns that mean "adversary," "accuser," or "slanderer." These basic meanings are important in many references to the devil in the Bible, though they are often lost in the English translation.

Among the ancient Israelites there was no conception of a personal supernatural force of absolute evil standing in opposition to God. The word *satan* is used both in the ordinary sense of a human adversary and in the sense of a supernatural adversary or accuser. On the human level, for example, **David** was described as a potential "adversary [*satan*]" (1 Sam. 29:4) to the Philistines, and **Solomon** proclaimed that he faced "neither adversary [*satan*] nor misfortune" (1 Kg. 5:4). One psalmist asked that "an accuser [*satan*]" (Ps. 109:6) might charge his enemy with some crime.

On the supernatural level, the word *satan* is first applied to an angel sent by God to withstand the Mesopotamian prophet **Bal-**

An Assyrian nobleman appears before Sargon II (right) in this eighth-century B.C. *marble relief.*

aam, who was hired by the king of Moab to curse the people of Israel. As Balaam was traveling to Moab, "the angel of the Lord took his stand in his way as his adversary [*satan*]" (Num. 22:22). In three other passages, however, the supernatural adversary or accuser stands in opposition to good individuals, and thus is more like descriptions of Satan in the New Testament.

The prophet **Zechariah**, for example, described a vision in which he saw the high priest Joshua, who returned to Jerusalem with **Zerubbabel** in 522 B.C. Joshua was standing trial before God for the sins of himself and the people, and Satan stood "at his right hand to accuse him" (Zech. 3:1) like a prosecutor. In mercy, however, God acquitted Joshua and rebuked the accuser: "The Lord said to Satan, 'The Lord rebuke you, O Satan! The Lord who has chosen Jerusalem rebuke you!'" (Zech. 3:2). Satan (evidently a proper name here) had apparently played the role of bringing unjustified accusations against Joshua or of urging God not to be merciful to him.

INCITING DAVID TO SIN

A more incendiary role for Satan is described in 1 Chronicles 21:1, which states that "Satan stood up against Israel, and incited David to number Israel"—taking a census being an act that was considered rebellion against God's sovereignty and for which Israel suffered severe punishment. Perhaps the most remarkable thing about this passage is how it compares with the parallel description of the same event in 2 Samuel, written perhaps a century earlier. There the text states, "The anger of the Lord was kindled against Israel, and he incited David against them, saying, 'Go, number Israel and Judah'" (2 Sam. 24:1). The author of Chronicles evidently felt uneasy with saying that God incited David to sin and then punished Israel for his sin. Instead, Chronicles attributed the temptation to Satan, the adversary of Israel and David.

By far the best known description of Satan in the Old Testament, however, is from the first two chapters of the book of Job, where Satan was the instrument of **Job**'s suffering. The narrative describes "a day when the sons of God came to present themselves before the Lord, and Satan also came among them" (Job 1:6). Thus, Satan (always in Hebrew with the article—*the* accuser) stood in the heavenly court, and God interrogated him about a wealthy man of perfect piety and rectitude named Job. The accuser, true to his character, interpreted Job's piety cynically, arguing that Job worshiped God because he was blessed with

Satan in stained glass

OTHER DEVILS

*I*n the New Testament, Satan is also called Beelzebul (Beelzebub in some versions). Scholars dispute the origin of the name, suggesting that it means, among other things, "master of the heights" or "lord of the flies." It is possibly derived from Baalzebub, the Canaanite god of Ekron. Jesus' opponents accused him of casting out demons in Beelzebul's name. Paul used yet another name for the devil, asking, "What accord has Christ with Belial?" (2 Cor. 6:15). In intertestamental literature, the devil is called Beliar, Mastema, Sammael, and Semyaz.

good and bad to God: "Shall we receive good at the hand of God and shall we not receive evil?" (Job 2:10). Once the dialogue between Job and his friends begins, the book never again mentions Satan, and no attempt is ever made to blame Job's plight on Satan rather than God. Thus, in the book of Job, Satan appears as an angelic being who views the motives and actions of the pious with a jaundiced and accusatory eye, but who acts within the limits permitted by God.

RULER OF AN EVIL EMPIRE

Near the beginning of the Christian era, however, Jewish writings began to contain descriptions of Satan that were much more diabolical and varied. Israel had lived for centuries under foreign domination, and as the pious found themselves oppressed generation after generation, the people came to understand Satan as a far more dominant and ferocious figure, indeed, as the ruler of a vast demonic empire encompassing this world. Many came to see that though God was the creator of the world and would ultimately reclaim it completely for himself, the world in their time had come primarily under the power of Satan and was a continual battleground between good and evil.

In this literature there is extensive elaboration of traditions about angelic wars and conspiracies against God and the fall of Satan from heaven. The evil ruler is always understood to be a creature of God, never a second deity, though he became the controlling force for many people. One document from the famous Dead Sea Scrolls called the Community Rule describes the power of evil in stark terms: "The Angel of Darkness leads all the children of righteousness astray, and until his end, all their sin, iniquities, wickedness, and all their unlawful deeds are caused by his dominion in accordance with the mysteries of God."

The New Testament expresses the same understanding of Satan's power. At the beginning of his ministry, **Jesus** had to confront the temptations of Satan directly through 40 days of fasting in the wilderness. Oozing skepticism, Satan challenged Jesus' identity as the son of God and urged him to prove it by turning stones into bread for his own satisfaction or by leaping from the pinnacle of the temple and asking angels to bear him up. Satan even touted his claim to be prince of this world by promising Jesus "all the kingdoms of the world and the glory of them" (Mt. 4:8) if Jesus would worship him. Each time Jesus turned aside the tempter with a simple quotation from the Scriptures that revealed his confidence in God and in his own identity, and "when the

such wealth. "But put forth thy hand now, and touch all that he has," Satan argued, "and he will curse thee to thy face" (Job 1:11). God gave Satan permission, and he destroyed all that Job possessed or loved. Job recognized that these disasters came from God but did not sin by cursing God.

When again Satan came with the sons of God before the Lord, he once more cynically attributed Job's integrity to the fact that he had not suffered personal, physical pain. God gave Satan permission, and he covered Job "with loathsome sores from the sole of his foot to the crown of his head" (Job 2:7). Still Job did not sin. Although the narrative takes the reader into the heavenly court to see the argument between God and Satan about Job, the suffering Job knew nothing of Satan's role. Rather, he attributed both devil had ended every temptation, he departed from him" (Lk. 4:13).

Jesus' ministry of proclaiming the kingdom of God was perceived by some in his time as a frontal attack on the pervasive rule of Satan in the world, as manifested in demonic spirits that possessed many people. Jesus' opponents, however, argued that Jesus himself was an instrument of the prince of demons, who empowered him to cast out the evil spirits. "If Satan casts out Satan," Jesus responded, "he is divided against himself; how then will his kingdom stand? . . . But if it is by the Spirit of God that I cast

out demons, then the kingdom of God has come upon you" (Mt. 12:26, 28). When Jesus sent out 70 disciples into the villages to preach the kingdom of God, they returned with joy, saying, "even the demons are subject to us in your name!" In response, Jesus exulted: "I saw Satan fall like lightning from heaven" (Lk. 10:17, 18).

Throughout the New Testament, there is an awareness of the continual warfare of Satan against the message of the gospel of Jesus. Christians were sometimes called to join the battle "against the wiles of the devil . . . against the world rulers of this present

Adam and Eve's serpentine tempter assumes human attributes in this scene by Hugo van der Goes (c. 1440-1482).

Jesus overcomes Satan to release souls from hell; a 12th-century enamel and gilded copper plaque.

darkness, against the spiritual hosts of wickedness in the heavenly places" (Eph. 6:11-12). Though the believers were confident that Satan's ultimate doom had been sealed by Jesus' crucifixion and resurrection, they were ever on guard, knowing that their "adversary the devil prowls around like a roaring lion, seeking some one to devour" (1 Pet. 5:8).

The book of Revelation gives the ultimate dramatic and symbolic expression to the ongoing battle between good and evil. At one point, a great war in heaven is described in which the archangel **Michael** led angelic armies against Satan: "And the great dragon was thrown down, that ancient serpent, who is called the Devil and Satan, the deceiver of the whole world—he was thrown down to earth, and his angels were thrown down with him" (Rev. 12:9). Through many twists and turns the battle continues as Satan marshals all his forces against God, but the outcome of the titanic struggle is never in doubt. Ultimately, Satan, the great dragon and deceiver, is "thrown into the lake of fire and sulphur . . . [to be] tormented day and night for ever and ever" (Rev. 20:10).

Thus, throughout the New Testament, understanding the figure of Satan helped believers to grasp the tremendous power of evil, violence, and corruption in the world, and at the same time to have confidence that the forces of goodness and grace represented by Jesus would ultimately prevail.

SAUL

(sawl) HEBREW: SHAUL
"the one asked for" or "the one asking"

Few stories in the Bible are more tragic than that of Saul, the first king of Israel. A shy and apparently unambitious man, Saul was drawn into the role of king but soon lost God's favor and, despite many successes, lapsed into a profound sense of failure and loss. His initial renown is easily overshadowed in the biblical narrative by the fame of his protégé, rival, and eventual successor, **David**.

Saul was born in the 11th century B.C. (probably in the 1060's) to a wealthy farmer of the tribe of Benjamin named Kish. He grew up on the land, plowing with oxen, growing wheat, keeping a herd of donkeys— all on his father's extensive lands near Gibeah, a hill town three miles north of Jerusalem. When first introduced in the Bible, he is already married to a woman named Ahinoam, and has a son named **Jonathan**. He was most likely still in his mid-30's. Saul stood out in any crowd of Israelites: He was head and shoulders taller than most men and remarkably good-looking. In spite of these physical characteristics and his family's wealth, Saul was self-effacing and retiring, "little" (1 Sam. 15:17) in his own eyes. He harbored no desire for power, having grown up in the period of the judges, when the political structure of Israel was very loose. The tribes and clans were unified only by a common tradition and by respect for such charismatic figures as **Samuel**, who combined the roles of priest, prophet, and judge. But this structure was militarily weak and vulnerable to corrupt officials like Samuel's sons, who were apparently destined to succeed him. Thus, Israel's elders urged Samuel to "appoint for us a king to govern us like all the nations" (1 Sam. 8:5).

The book of 1 Samuel allows Saul to emerge as king in three steps, each of which many historians believe represents a distinct tradition. The first recounts his seem-

Hoping to avoid the crown, Saul hides among the baggage train at Mizpah.

ingly chance introduction to Samuel as he was hiking with a servant through the hill country of Ephraim in search of his father's lost donkeys. Frustrated with the futile quest, Saul wanted to return home, but the servant knew of a nearby seer who might be able to locate the donkeys. And God, the text reveals, had already instructed Samuel to meet Saul and "anoint him to be prince over my people Israel" (1 Sam. 9:16). When the two met, Samuel immediately invited the astonished Saul to a sacrificial banquet, informed him that the donkeys had been found, and hinted broadly that he should have "all that is desirable in Israel" (1 Sam. 9:20). Saul was flabbergasted, since he regarded himself as belonging to a humble family in a small tribe.

The next morning Samuel poured a vial of oil on Saul's head with the words, "Has not the Lord anointed you to be prince over his people Israel?" Samuel promised Saul that soon "the spirit of the Lord will come mightily upon you and you shall . . . be

turned into another man." Then Samuel instructed him to "do whatever your hand finds to do, for God is with you" (1 Sam. 10:1, 6, 7). Turning for home, Saul found himself filled with the spirit of God and joined the ecstatic dance of an itinerant band of prophets so that people asked, "Is Saul also among the prophets?" (1 Sam. 10:11). But he told no one of the anointing.

THE RELUCTANT MONARCH

The second step in Saul's accession emphasizes Samuel's negative attitude toward the idea of a king. Samuel summoned the people to Mizpah, a fortified city on the ridge route north of Jerusalem, to answer their cry for a king. He fiercely upbraided them because, as he said, "you have this day rejected your God, who saves you" (1 Sam. 10:19). Nevertheless, God would select a king for them through the casting of lots. Thus, Samuel narrowed the selection down from tribes to families to an individual— Saul. But Saul could not be found; he was hiding among the pack animals, doubtless hoping the Lord would select someone else. Some agreed with him. Though many

Unaware of his father's ban on eating during battle with the Philistines, Jonathan takes honey with his staff; behind him, Saul follows the ark.

shouted, "Long live the king!" (1 Sam. 10:24), others—likely leaders of powerful tribes such as Judah or Ephraim—held this unknown candidate-king in contempt.

The third step of Saul's accession solidified popular support. While Saul returned to farming, King Nahash of the Ammonites besieged Jabesh-gilead east of the Jordan. The town was ready to surrender, but Nahash threatened to gouge out the right eye of each inhabitant. The elders sent an urgent plea for help, which reached Saul as he was bringing oxen in from a field. Again filled with the spirit of God and blazing with wrath, he cut the oxen in pieces and sent them to all parts of the country as a sign of what would happen to any who did not send aid against the Ammonites.

The tactic worked. Thousands of Israelite militia mustered to his call, saved the people of Jabesh-gilead, and drove back the Ammonites. Saul was everyone's hero, and even Samuel, who despised the idea of kingship, summoned the people to the shrine at Gilgal, and "all the people . . . made Saul king before the Lord" (1 Sam. 11:15). Samuel promptly retired as a political leader but remained influential as a priest and prophet.

Israel's military situation was precarious. The gravest threat came from the Philistines, who had invaded Canaan from the west as Israel arrived from the east and who had numerous military garrisons throughout the land. Having brought iron weapons with them, the Philistines had a powerful advantage over the Canaanites and Israelites, who were armed only with bronze. Indeed, the Philistines rigidly controlled iron smelting that not only kept the superior weapons out of their rivals' hands but also forced Canaanite and Israelite farmers to come to them to have their plowshares, axes, and sickles sharpened.

However, Saul began organizing Israel's tribal militias by establishing two Israelite garrisons—one under Jonathan in Gibeah; the other under his own command at Michmash, five miles farther north. When Jonathan prematurely sparked a conflict by capturing a Philistine garrison at nearby Geba, Saul proclaimed the victory throughout the land but soon found himself faced with an overwhelming Philistine army bent on punishing the Israelites. With his ragtag soldiers deserting in droves, Saul tried to rally his troops at Gilgal, site of an ancient shrine due east of Michmash, so that Samuel could offer a sacrifice to ensure God's favor in the coming battle. Samuel had told Saul to wait for him seven days, and Saul did so. But when the prophet did not appear within that time, Saul—seeing his men scattering and fearing an imminent Philistine attack—made the burnt offerings himself to entreat "the favor of the Lord" (1 Sam. 13:12).

The effect was just the reverse. At the moment he finished, Samuel arrived like a thunderstorm. Saul had waited the seven days, but he had not waited for Samuel to tell him what to do. Samuel's verdict was immediate and devastating: "Your kingdom shall not continue; the Lord has sought out a man after his own heart; and the Lord has appointed him to be prince over his people" (1 Sam. 13:14). From that moment, Saul always had reason to be looking over his shoulder in fear of the man who was to replace him as king of Israel.

Saul continued his preparation for battle, but it was Jonathan's bold attack on a Philistine garrison that panicked the enemy and turned sure defeat into victory. Saul's poor judgment, however, spoiled the celebration. He had sworn death to any of his soldiers who ate before the Philistines were totally defeated. Unaware of the oath, Jonathan ate some wild honey; when his act was discovered, Saul—trapped by his own foolish oath—nearly executed his son before the people stopped him.

Despite his successes, Saul always found himself unable to meet Samuel's religious expectations. The prophet demanded that Saul make war against the Amalekites, a nomadic tribe of the Negeb, because their ancestors had opposed the Israelites when they escaped from Egypt. Saul carried out the expedition but did not fulfill the absolute rigors of holy war that demanded that every man, woman, child, and domesticated animal be slaughtered. When Samuel learned that Saul had brought the Amalekite king back alive as well as many sheep and oxen for sacrifice, he condemned him: "To obey is better than sacrifice . . . . Because you have rejected the word of the Lord, he has also rejected you from being king" (1 Sam. 15:22, 23). From that day on, Samuel refused to see Saul. But more important, "the Spirit of the Lord departed from Saul, and an evil spirit from the Lord tormented him" (1 Sam. 16:14). With every success turned to ashes, bereft of the spiritual support that gave him legitimacy, and distraught in mind, Saul became despondent to the brink of madness.

At that point, Saul's servants advised that a man be summoned to play the lyre for the king in order to soothe his spirit. One of them suggested the young son of a farmer named **Jesse**: David, whom Samuel had already secretly anointed as Saul's successor. With no suspicion of treason, Saul wel-comed David into his service, "loved him greatly" (1 Sam. 16:21), and made the valiant young man his armor-bearer. After David's feat of killing the giant **Goliath**, Saul made David an army commander, and his heroic deeds soon came to be celebrated even above Saul's. From that point on, the biblical narrative becomes the story of David, and Saul's activities are told of only in relation to David's exploits.

ADMIRATION TURNED TO JEALOUSY

With Samuel's denunciations haunting his mind, Saul soon began to suspect that the young hero from Judah whom he had welcomed was indeed the man whom Samuel had threatened would overthrow him. Love and admiration alternated with blinding fear, jealousy of David's spectacular successes, and hatred. Saul tried to murder David with the throw of a spear but then promoted him to a higher command. Jonathan became David's closest confidant, and David was given Saul's daughter **Michal** in marriage. The lives of the old king and the young warrior were inextricably entwined, but Saul could not escape the sense of loss and destruction that David represented for him.

The king began systematic attempts to capture and execute David, and he thereby alienated both Jonathan and Michal and found his efforts blocked even by divine power. His fear and hatred led him into atrocities such as the execution of all the priests of the sanctuary at Nob, whom he suspected of supporting David. After David formed a private army in the hills of Judah, Saul squandered much of his strength by relentlessly pursuing his ever elusive foe. Though David protested his loyalty and even spared Saul's life when he could have taken it, Saul could never escape the echo of Samuel's dire predictions, especially after Samuel died and David joined forces with the Philistines.

Saul had made great gains against the Philistines, but they eventually made ready for an assault on Israel to recoup their losses. David even agreed to join in the attack, though so many of the Philistine commanders distrusted him that he was excluded from the battle. When Saul recognized the strength of the Philistine forces, he knew he could not face it without an assurance of divine favor, and he was terrified. He sought the

King Saul; detail of a painting by Rembrandt

blessing of God, but "the Lord did not answer him" (1 Sam. 28:6) by any of the normal means: dreams, a response to the casting of lots, or the oracles of a prophet.

The desperate monarch's last hope was the dead Samuel, whom he thought he might reach through a medium or necromancer—though he himself had banned mediums from Israel. In disguise, Saul went to such a medium in the village of Endor, where Samuel rose like "a god coming up out of the earth." But not a syllable of comfort did Samuel bring: "The Lord has turned from you and become your enemy.... and tomorrow you and your sons shall be with me; the Lord will give the army of Israel also into the hand of the Philistines" (1 Sam. 28:13, 16, 19). Saul had fasted with fear and trembling before this encounter, but now the certainty of death seemed to restore his equilibrium. He ate a large meal to strengthen himself for the coming battle.

The next day—it was about 1004 B.C.—the army of Israel tried to hold Mount Gilboa, a peak overlooking the Jezreel valley southwest of the Sea of Galilee, as the Philistines attacked. Jonathan and his brothers Abinadab and Malchishua fell in battle. Philistine archers spotted Saul and rained arrows on him, badly wounding the king. In order to avoid capture, Saul fell on his own sword and died, his tragedy ended.

The Philistines beheaded Saul's corpse, hung his armor in one of their temples, and strung up his body and those of his sons on the walls of the captured city of Beth-shan—food for vultures, the ultimate indignity. When the people of Jabesh-gilead heard what was done, they traveled all night to rescue the bodies, just as Saul had rescued them in earlier, more hopeful times.

The length of Saul's reign is uncertain, perhaps about 20 years. Writing long after Saul's death, the biblical authors were concerned primarily with highlighting Saul's failures that led to the rise of King David. But they did include one summary statement stressing Saul's accomplishments: "He fought against all his enemies on every side. . . . And he did valiantly . . . and delivered Israel out of the hands of those who plundered them" (1 Sam. 14:47-48).

SCEVA

(see' vuh) GREEK: SKEYAS
possibly "left-handed" or "favorable omen"

Sceva is identified in the book of Acts as a Jewish high priest, although his name does not appear on surviving lists of Jewish religious officials. It is likely that his seven

Saul falls on his sword; from a 12th-century English Bible.

sons, who were itinerant exorcists in Ephesus during the two years the apostle **Paul** spent there, simply claimed that title for him to lend authority to their own work.

Because Paul's miracles had achieved such widespread fame, Jewish exorcists took to using the name of **Jesus** in the hope of getting similarly dramatic results. But when Sceva's seven sons (possibly his disciples) invoked Jesus' name during an exorcism, the evil spirit reacted so violently that the sons "fled out of that house naked and wounded" (Acts 19:16). This had a profound effect in Ephesus, which was famous for its practitioners of the magical arts. Many magicians burned their magic scrolls and gave up their trade. Thus, God's superior power working through Paul was emphasized, as was the fact that Jesus' name should not be used in magic incantations.

SENNACHERIB

(suh na' kuh rib) HEBREW: SANHERIB;
ASSYRIAN: SIN-AHHE-ERIBA
"[the god] Sin has substituted the dead brothers"

The king of Assyria from 704 to 681 B.C., Sennacherib was so named because he was the first son of his father, **Sargon II**, to survive childhood. Sennacherib was both a great statesman and a fierce warrior who received tribute from a vast number of states and cities. He left voluminous records of his reign, which tell of eight campaigns, the spoils of one he tallied as 200,000 prisoners plus numerous livestock.

In that campaign, about 701 B.C., Sennacherib invaded Judah. When his troops besieged the frontier fortress of Lachish, King **Hezekiah** of Judah sent Sennacherib "all the silver that was found in the house of the Lord, and in the treasuries of the king's house" (2 Kg. 18:15) in an effort to buy him off. Despite the bribe, Assyrian troops advanced on Jerusalem. After they reached its walls, the Rabshakeh (an Assyrian official) delivered an eloquent speech to a delegation sent out by Hezekiah, asking for surrender of the city without a fight. Hezekiah consulted the prophet **Isaiah**, who confidently predicted that the Assyrians would withdraw on their own.

A second time Sennacherib sent the same message to the people of Jerusalem, and again Isaiah advised that they not submit, saying that Sennacherib "shall not come into this city or shoot an arrow there, or come before it with a shield or cast up a siege mound against it" (2 Kg. 19:32). That night, an angel of the Lord killed 185,000 Assyrian warriors as they slept, and in the morning the survivors quickly withdrew.

At home, Sennacherib rebuilt Nineveh, turning it into a garden city with 18 canals, wide roads, and a lavish palace. He was assassinated in 681 B.C. by two of his sons, jealous of their brother **Esarhaddon**, who had been named his father's heir.

SERAIAH

(se ray' ya) HEBREW: SERAYAH
"Yah[weh] is prince/has persevered"

Seraiah, a grandson of the **Hilkiah** who discovered the lost book of the Law during the reign of King **Josiah**, was the chief priest of Jerusalem when it fell to the Babylonians in 587 B.C. He and other royal officials of Judah were brought to the headquarters of King **Nebuchadnezzar** at Riblah in Syria and executed. But his son Jehozadak was led into exile in Babylon. Seraiah's grandson Joshua was high priest after the exile, when **Zerubbabel** led a group of Jews back to their homeland.

SETH

HEBREW: SHET

After **Cain** killed his brother **Abel** and was banished, **Eve** bore another son to her husband, **Adam**. She called him Seth, saying, "God has appointed for me another child instead of Abel, for Cain slew him" (Gen. 4:25). At the age of 105, Seth sired a son, Enosh, and lived another 807

years. The image of God that was conferred upon the human race in Genesis 1:26-27 was transmitted through the line of Seth; his descendant **Noah** was the ancestor of all humanity after the Flood. During the lifetime of Seth and Enosh, "men began to call upon the name of the Lord" (Gen. 4:26).

SHADRACH

(shad' rak) HEBREW: SHADRAK

In 597 B.C., King **Nebuchadnezzar** of Babylon captured Jerusalem and carried off into exile most of its leading citizens. From Judah's royal and noble families a number of "youths without blemish, handsome and skilful in all wisdom" (Dan. 1:4) were selected to serve in the royal palace at Babylon. Among them were the prophet **Daniel** and three companions, Hananiah, Mishael, and Azariah, who were given new Babylonian names by the king's chief eunuch: Shadrach, Meshach, and Abednego.

The four soon proved that their vegetarian diet was superior to the rich food served at the king's table, and the monarch found them "ten times better than all the magicians and enchanters that were in all his kingdom" (Dan. 1:20). After Daniel further proved his worth by interpreting Neb-

In working miracles at Ephesus, Paul provoked the sons of Sceva; detail of a painting by Jean Restout the Elder (1663-1702).

uchadnezzar's troubling dream, the grateful king awarded his three friends important provincial posts.

Shadrach, Meshach, and Abednego later roused Nebuchadnezzar to fury, however, when they refused to abjure their faith by worshiping a golden image he had set up. At the king's order, they were "cast into the burning fiery furnace" (Dan. 3:21) prepared for those who defied the royal will. But when the king came to gloat over their deaths, he discovered four men walking amid the flames, the fourth being "like a son of the gods"—that is, an angel of the Lord. Astonished, Nebuchadnezzar released and promoted the three men, decreeing mortal punishment for any who spoke against their God, "for there is no other god who is able to deliver in this way" (Dan. 3: 25, 29).

SHALLUM
(sha' luhm) HEBREW: SHALLUM
"payment" or "recompense"
••••••••••

About the year 745 B.C., Shallum seized the throne of Israel by assassinating **Zechariah**, who had reigned in Samaria for only six months. He thus put an end to the dynasty of **Jehu**, which had ruled Israel for nearly a century. Shallum's coup also marked the end of the prosperity Israel had

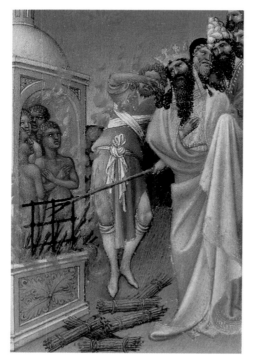

King Nebuchadnezzar amazed that Shadrach and his companions have survived the fiery furnace; a 15th-century manuscript illumination

enjoyed under the 40-year reign of Zechariah's father, **Jeroboam II**.

Shallum lasted only a month on the throne before he, too, was assassinated and succeeded by his killer, **Menahem**. The two royal slayings set a pattern for Israel as the nation sunk into near anarchy before it was finally conquered by Assyria in 722 B.C. and its citizens taken off into a captivity from which they never returned.

SHALMANESER V
(shal' muh nee' zuhr) HEBREW: SHALMANESER; ASSYRIAN: SHULMANU-ASARED
"[the god] Sulmanu is foremost"
••••••••••

The son and successor of **Tiglath-pileser III**, Shalmaneser was the last of five Assyrian kings of that name but the only one mentioned in the Bible. He reigned from 727 to 722 B.C.

Among Shalmaneser's tributaries was the king of Israel, **Hoshea**. When Hoshea stopped sending treasure to Assyria and turned to the Egyptian Pharaoh for help, Shalmaneser seized and imprisoned the king and besieged his capital, Samaria. After three years, the city fell, and the people of Israel were taken captive to Assyria—just punishment, according to the biblical narrator, because they "had sinned against the Lord their God" (2 Kg. 17:7). The Assyrians repopulated the land with subjects brought from Syria and Babylon. When the new inhabitants introduced their own religions, the Lord "sent lions among them, which killed some of them." Consequently, the king of Assyria ordered one of the deported priests of Israel sent back to Samaria to teach the new residents "how they should fear the Lord" (2 Kg. 17: 25, 28).

Shalmaneser died in the month of Tebetu (December/January) of 722/21 B.C. He was succeeded by **Sargon II**, who claimed that it was he who conquered Samaria—a claim that has prompted much debate among historians. Some biblical scholars believe that, based on the date of Shalmaneser's death and the date that Sargon assumed the throne, Shalmaneser was the actual conqueror but that the deportation of the Israelites took place under Sargon.

SHAMGAR
(sham' gar) HEBREW: SHAMGAR
••••••••••

Shamgar was one of the so-called minor judges (*see* **Tola**), or deliverers, of Israel in the period before the rise of the monarchy. According to the Song of Deborah, in

Shamgar's time "caravans ceased and travelers kept to the byways" (Jg. 5:6) because neighboring marauders made regular travel too dangerous. Shamgar was praised for killing "six hundred of the Philistines with an oxgoad" (Jg. 3:31). The number of his victims need not be taken literally since 600 was the standard number of a military unit in ancient times. Rather, the passage suggests that Shamgar single-handedly destroyed an entire Philistine brigade with his weapon—an eight-foot-long metal-tipped pole—a feat comparable to **Samson**'s slaying of 1,000 Philistines with the jawbone of an ass and therefore certainly deserving mention in the Bible.

SHAPHAN

(shay' fan) HEBREW: SHAPAN

In the 18th year of his reign, about 621 B.C., King **Josiah** of Judah instructed his scribe Shaphan to take money collected from the people for repairing the temple in Jerusalem and distribute it among the workmen. Soon afterward, with the work under way, the high priest **Hilkiah** presented him with the book of the Law (most likely an earliest form of the book of Deuteronomy), which had been found among the rubble of the temple.

When Shaphan read the document to the king, Josiah "rent his clothes" with alarm "because our fathers have not obeyed the words of this book" (2 Kg. 22:11, 13); he sent Shaphan to the prophetess **Huldah** to learn God's will. She replied that the Lord was indeed wrathful against the people but would spare Josiah for being penitent. Her oracle prompted Josiah's religious reforms.

SHEAR-JASHUB

(shee ar ya' shub) HEBREW: SHEAR YASHUB
"a remnant shall return"

When king **Ahaz** of Judah refused to join an anti-Assyrian coalition, Syria and Israel attacked Judah about 735 B.C. and captured all its cities except for Jerusalem. At that point God sent the prophet **Isaiah** with his elder son Shear-jashub to tell the king to trust in the Lord and not to fear the invaders. The significance of Shear-jashub's name and his presence at this meeting can be interpreted in several ways. It may indicate a threat that only a remnant will return, that is, only a few from Judah will survive the war with Syria and Israel, or, conversely, only a few of the attackers will survive. On the other hand, it may express

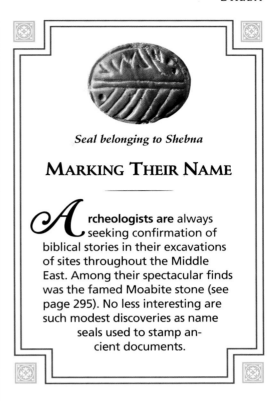

Seal belonging to Shebna

MARKING THEIR NAME

*A*rcheologists are always seeking confirmation of biblical stories in their excavations of sites throughout the Middle East. Among their spectacular finds was the famed Moabite stone (see page 295). No less interesting are such modest discoveries as name seals used to stamp ancient documents.

Isaiah's hope that what remains of Judah will return to God. As it happened, Syria and Israel were defeated by Assyria, but Ahaz's turning to Assyria for protection proved to be a serious miscalculation with adverse consequences for his kingdom.

SHEBA

(shee' buh) HEBREW: SHEBA
"seven"

Introduced in the Bible as "a worthless fellow" (2 Sam. 20:1), Sheba died in an unsuccessful attempt to usurp King **David**'s dominion over Israel. When David returned from suppressing the revolt of his son **Absalom**, he asked the men of Judah to greet him first. His action aroused the jealousy of the northern tribes and gave Sheba, a Benjaminite from the hill country of Ephraim, the pretext for launching his own rebellion.

David took the new threat to his kingdom quite seriously, sending first **Amasa**, then **Abishai** and **Joab**, to squelch the uprising. Joab seized the opportunity provided by the assignment to slay his rival, Amasa; he then marched on to Abel of Bethmaacah, a fortified city north of the Sea of Galilee to which Sheba had fled. As Joab was about to attack, "a wise woman" (2 Sam. 20:16) interceded with him, negotiating for the safety of the city in return for Sheba's head, which the obliging townspeople tossed over the wall to David's commander.

SHEBNA

(sheb' nah) HEBREW: SHEBNAH; possibly an
abbreviation of SHEBANIAH
"youthfulness" or "return now, O Yahu"

An important official during the reign of
King **Hezekiah** of Judah (c. 715-687
B.C.), Shebna bears the dubious distinction
of being the only individual against whom
the prophet **Isaiah** issued an oracle of
doom. He is also the subject of scholarly
controversy centering on the titles that are
used to describe him in two different books
of the Bible.

Some historians question whether the
Shebnah who is called a secretary to
Hezekiah in 2 Kings 18:18 and the Shebna
who is Hezekiah's steward, or overseer, in
Isaiah 22:15 can be the same person. Most
scholars agree that it would be unlikely for
two men with essentially the same name to
hold high office in the same court. While the
position of secretary had more prestige than
the title implies, it was not as distinguished
a position as the stewardship referred to in
Isaiah. Shebna seems to have been involved
in some sort of scandal, but scholars still
puzzle over the reasons for Shebna's apparent demotion—some suggesting that it was
for his advice that Hezekiah seek Egyptian
support for resistance to Assyria rather than
rely solely on the Lord's support.

Shebna's name first appears in the Bible
in the context of the siege of Jerusalem by
King **Sennacherib** of Assyria. Hezekiah
sent Shebna and two other emissaries, Eliakim and Joah, to negotiate with the Assyrian attackers. After an unsuccessful
interview with Sennacherib's representatives, the emissaries were sent to Isaiah to
seek the prophet's advice. At first the
prophet was reassuring: "Behold, I will put
a spirit in him [Sennacherib], so that he
shall . . . return to his own land" (2 Kg.
19:7). But later Isaiah predicted dire consequences for Jerusalem if Hezekiah involved
the city in international power struggles.
The prophet then singled out Shebna as a
specific example of Jerusalem's materialis-
tic tendencies, denouncing him for building
a fancy tomb and predicting that he would
never be buried there.

SHECHEM

(sheh' kuhm) HEBREW: SHEKEM
"shoulder" or "slope"

Most of the times Shechem is mentioned
in the Bible, the reference is to the ancient city in a pass between central Palestine's two highest peaks, Mount Gerizim

and Mount Ebal, some 30 miles north of
Jerusalem. In 13 instances, however, the
name Shechem denotes the son of Hamor,
king of Shechem. Prince Shechem brought
about the downfall of his city when he raped
Jacob's daughter, **Dinah**, and then fell in
love with her.

As the story unfolds in Genesis 33:18-
34:31, Hamor—in response to Shechem's
desire to have Dinah for a wife—suggests to
Jacob that their tribes intermarry. Jacob's
sons, however, still incensed at the rape of
their sister, demand that all the men of
Hamor's tribe be circumcised before they
are allowed to marry Israelite women. Then,
on the third day after the circumcisions,
when the Shechemites "were sore" (Gen.

*Noah's sons covering his nakedness; a stone
carving from Venice's ducal palace*

396

34:25), Jacob's sons **Simeon** and **Levi** attack and kill them all. This story may reflect an early justification for the Israelite occupation of the prosperous city of Shechem.

SHEM

(shem) HEBREW: SHEM
"son," "name," or "renown"
··········

The eponymous ancestor of the Semites, Shem was the eldest of **Noah**'s three sons; the other two were **Ham** and **Japheth**. In 1 Chronicles 1:24, Shem's lineage is recorded down to the tenth generation, which included **Abraham**.

Noah's three sons and their wives accompanied their father and mother on the ark, riding out the storm that inundated the world and sharing in Noah's covenant with God after the Flood. Thus, biblical tradition credits Noah's sons with repopulating the earth, dividing the human race into three groups, each of which is descended from one of the sons.

Those who descended from Shem inherited the Promised Land, displacing the Canaanites, who were descendants of Ham. The book of Genesis foreshadows this change of fortune with a story in which Ham behaved disrespectfully toward his father, gazing at Noah when he "became drunk, and lay uncovered in his tent" (Gen. 9:21). Shem and Japheth responded by walking backward into the tent and covering their father without looking at him. When he awakened and learned of Ham's disrespect, Noah cursed **Canaan**, the son of Ham, and blessed Shem and Japheth.

SHEMAIAH

(shuh may' uh) HEBREW: SHEMAYAH, SHEMAYAHU
"Yahweh has heard"
··········

The late-10th-century B.C. prophet Shemaiah warned King **Solomon**'s son and successor, **Rehoboam**, not to resist the insurgency of the northern tribes of Israel because the revolt was God's will. Thereupon, the force Rehoboam had mustered was released, while Rehoboam's rival, **Jeroboam,** consolidated his power over the breakaway northern kingdom. Shemaiah's warning seems to have stopped the fighting temporarily but not for long because "there was war between Rehoboam and Jeroboam continually" (1 Kg. 14:30).

Some interpreters equate Shemaiah's action with that of the prophet **Ahijah**, who earlier had encouraged the secession by tearing his garment into pieces, giving ten

shreds to Jeroboam to symbolize his future rule over the ten northern tribes. Later in the biblical narrative, Shemaiah tells the apostate Rehoboam that Pharaoh **Shishak** of Egypt will destroy Jerusalem: "You abandoned me, so I have abandoned you to the hand of Shishak" (2 Chr. 12:5). But he soon amends his message to say that God will not allow Shishak to destroy Jerusalem because Rehoboam has repented. Shemaiah compiled a record of Rehoboam's reign, now lost, but evidently a source for the author of Chronicles.

SHEMAIAH 2
··········

A false prophet among the Jewish captives taken to Babylon by King **Nebuchadnezzar** in 597 B.C., Shemaiah contradicted the prophet **Jeremiah** by predicting a speedy end to their exile. In letters to the people of Jerusalem and particularly in one to the high priest **Zephaniah**, Shemaiah called for Jeremiah's imprisonment because he had foretold a lengthy exile. By opposing Jeremiah, Shemaiah provoked the Lord's anger, and the prophet denounced Shemaiah as one who made the people "trust in a lie" (Jer. 29:31). Speaking through Jeremiah, God issued a warning to Shemaiah that neither he nor his family would live to see the return from exile. It was the Lord's will that the Jews remain in captivity for some time; predicting otherwise, Shemaiah was fomenting rebellion against God.

SHESHBAZZAR

(shesh baz' uhr) HEBREW: SHESHBASSAR, perhaps from AKKADIAN: SIN-ABA-USUR
"O, Sin [the moon god] protect the father"
··········

An elusive character who appears only briefly in the book of Ezra (and in the parallel passages found in 1 Esdras in the Apocrypha), Sheshbazzar is perhaps most notable for the historical problems he represents. Sheshbazzar is introduced as "the prince of Judah" (Ezra 1:8) to whom the Persian king **Cyrus II** entrusted the return of temple vessels to Jerusalem after the Babylonian exile. He is also described as the first post-exilic Judean governor who "laid the foundations of the house of God which is in Jerusalem" (Ezra 5:16).

Until recently, some biblical scholars maintained that Sheshbazzar was the same person as Shenazzar, who appears in 1 Chronicles 3:18, arguing that a transcription error accounts for the minor difference in the two names. This idea was appealing because it established a lineage to King **David** for Sheshbazzar and enhanced the continuity between accounts in Chronicles and Ezra–Nehemiah. But in recent years, linguistic advances have made it possible to discredit the identification.

Attempts to identify Sheshbazzar with **Zerubbabel**, whose name appears in the books of Ezra and Nehemiah, have also fallen out of favor. Like Sheshbazzar, Zerubbabel is called a prince of Judah and a governor after the exile, and both men are credited with restoring the temple's foundations. However, scholars now believe that Sheshbazzar preceded Zerubbabel, was probably his uncle, and that during the reign of **Darius**, Zerubbabel continued the restoration of the temple begun by Sheshbazzar at the command of Cyrus.

SHIMEI

(shim' ee ai) HEBREW: SHIMI, short for
SHEMAIAH or ELISHAMA
"God has heard"

When the revolt of **Absalom** forced King **David** to abandon Jerusalem, Shimei, a Benjaminite from the family of **Saul**, cursed the king, throwing stones and dirt at him. "Begone, you man of blood, you worthless fellow!" Shimei shouted. "The Lord has avenged upon you all the blood of the house of Saul" (2 Sam. 16:7-8). Shimei's anger reflected the general hostility Benjaminites felt toward David for Saul's downfall and death. The commander **Abishai** wished to kill Shimei on the spot, but David restrained him, seeing Shimei's curse as a message from God.

After Absalom's revolt failed, Shimei gathered a thousand Benjaminites to welcome David back to Jerusalem and begged to be forgiven for his curse. Although David absolved the man of guilt, the king on his deathbed urged his son **Solomon** to destroy Shimei, among his other enemies—and Solomon eventually did so. This brief story is a revealing example of David's public clemency and private vengeance.

SHISHAK

(shi' shak) HEBREW: SHISHAQ

Upon the death of Pharaoh Psusennes II in about 945 B.C., the Libyan commander in chief of the Egyptian army assumed power—presumably because Psusennes left no male heir and because the marriage of the general's son to the Pharaoh's daughter

gave him some claim to the throne. As Sheshonk I, the general founded Egypt's 22nd dynasty, inaugurating more than two centuries of Libyan rule. Sheshonk's 21-year reign (c. 945-924 B.C.) was most notable for restoring Egypt's political and military clout, at least temporarily. He was a shrewd ruler who overthrew the power of the high priests of Amon at Thebes to bring political unity to Egypt, built extensively in the Delta region, and took an active role in the political affairs of the Middle East. His court became a haven for dissidents, including **Jeroboam**, who were fleeing the oppression of Sheshonk's contemporary King **Solomon**. In the Bible, Sheshonk is called Shishak.

After Solomon's death, Jeroboam returned to his homeland, where he was proclaimed ruler of the northern kingdom of Israel. Solomon's son **Rehoboam** governed the rump kingdom of Judah from his capital of Jerusalem.

For reasons that remain unclear, Shishak assembled a huge army of Egyptians, Libyans, and Ethiopians and launched a full-scale attack on Palestine in the fifth year of Rehoboam's reign. Shishak's forces conquered the fortified cities of Judah. Jerusalem, however, was spared after Rehoboam paid Shishak a large ransom. The prophet **Shemaiah** had revealed that Shishak's invasion was God's punishment of an erring nation, and his oracle caused Rehoboam to repent his apostasy and pay the tribute that saved his capital from destruction. It is doubtful that the campaign was motivated by any alliance between Shishak and Jeroboam. Indeed, Israel was not spared in the Egyptian attack, which may have been launched because Jeroboam showed insufficient gratitude for Shishak's earlier protection when he was a fugitive and was not proving to be a loyal vassal of the Egyptian monarch.

SIHON

(si' hahn) HEBREW: SIHON

The Amorite king of Heshbon, Sihon was defeated by **Moses** and the Israelites in battle when he refused to let the Israelites pass through his territory east of the Jordan on their way from the wilderness to the Promised Land. Sihon's defeat was a monumental victory for the Israelites and an important confirmation of Yahweh's covenant with his chosen people. This victory is sometimes paired with the Israelites' defeat of **Og**, king of Bashan, and is frequently invoked in the Old Testament. The destruc-

Shishak holding prisoners taken on his invasion of Palestine by their hair; a temple bas-relief at Karnak

tion of Heshbon, Sihon's capital city, is described in an ancient song: "For fire went forth from Heshbon, flame from the city of Sihon" (Num. 21:28).

SILAS

(si' luhs) GREEK: SILAS; LATIN: SILVANUS
"from the forest"

As a leading member of the Jerusalem church, Silas took part in the ministries of both **Paul** and **Peter**. About A.D. 50, he and **Timothy** joined Paul in sending the two letters to the Thessalonians, in the first of which Paul called him one of the "apostles of Christ" (1 Th. 2:6). Some 14 years later, Peter entrusted him with the letter he sent to persecuted Christians in Asia Minor. Scholars agree that the Silvanus named by Paul and Peter in their letters is the same person **Luke** refers to as Silas in Acts of the Apostles. Silas was a Greek name; Silvanus was the Latin form more familiar in Greek and Roman cities. Like Paul, Silas is identified in Acts as claiming the privileges of Roman citizenship.

To accompany Paul and **Barnabas** to Antioch, the church elders at Jerusalem chose Silas and **Judas Barsabbas**, "leading men among the brethren" (Acts 15:22).

The four were to present a letter intended to heal a breach over the necessity of requiring converts to observe Jewish practices, specifically circumcision. The letter introduced Silas as one of those "who have risked their lives for the sake of our Lord Jesus Christ"; its message—that Christians need only abstain from eating ritually unclean meat and remain chaste—was well received in Antioch, for the church there "rejoiced at the exhortation" (Acts 15:26, 31).

Silas may have kept the letter in order to make its contents known in the other provinces he visited with Paul, namely Syria and Cilicia. Luke reports that Timothy joined Paul and Silas in Lystra, and that together they preached in Phrygia, Galatia, Neapolis, and Philippi, where they stayed in the home of **Lydia**. In Philippi, Paul and Silas were beaten and imprisoned. When an earthquake shook the foundations of the prison and burst open its doors, they refused the chance to escape. In gratitude, the jailer asked them what he should do to be saved. That night Paul and Silas baptized him, and he took them into his house, washed their wounds, and fed them. After Paul identified himself and Silas as Roman citizens, the magistrates arranged for their release with an apology, but asked them to leave the city at once.

Symbols of their tribes, Simeon and five of his brothers stand on Mount Gerizim for Moses' blessing; from a 14th-century manuscript illumination.

Silas next accompanied Paul and Timothy to Thessalonica, where Paul preached in the synagogue. The conversion of a number of synagogue members provoked an uprising, and the three missionaries escaped by night to nearby Beroea. When word of their success in Beroea brought angry Thessalonians to the city, Paul had to flee once more. He left Silas and Timothy in charge of the mission, urging them to join him soon.

Sometime later the three were reunited at Corinth, as Silas and Timothy arrived from Macedonia with financial support for Paul. As a result, Paul was able to give up tent making to devote himself full-time to the church. It was from Corinth that Paul wrote two letters to the church at Thessalonica, his earliest known writings. Both letters to the Thessalonians open with greetings from Paul, Silvanus, and Timothy, and the frequent use of "we" suggests that Silas—though apparently not Timothy—had a hand in the compositions. At the very least, he probably took dictation from Paul.

Silas later joined the apostle Peter in Rome. Peter concluded his first letter with the words, "By Silvanus, a faithful brother as I regard him, I have written briefly to you" (1 Pet. 5:12). Some scholars believe Silas was more than an amanuensis for Paul and Peter. Having worked longer in Thessalonica than Paul, Silas would have been more familiar with the problems addressed in the two letters to the Thessalonians and possibly supplied Paul with ideas for those epistles. And in style, vocabulary, and thought,

1 Peter is highly characteristic of Paul's writings, leading some to propose that Silas actually wrote it or at the very least polished an outline drafted or dictated by Peter.

SIMEON

(sim' ee uhn) HEBREW: SHIMON
"hearing"

After **Jacob** took **Leah**'s younger sister, **Rachel**, as his second wife, Leah keenly felt her husband's disdain. Taking pity, the Lord "opened her womb" (Gen. 29:31), and Leah soon gave birth to **Reuben**, Simeon, **Levi**, and **Judah**. The name Simeon, from a Hebrew word meaning "hearing," came from Leah's exclamation at the birth of her second son: "Because the Lord has heard that I am hated, he has given me this son also" (Gen. 29:33).

Simeon and Levi are linked in Israel's tribal history. It began with the rape of their sister **Dinah** by **Shechem**, a Canaanite prince. After his attack, Shechem asked permission to marry Dinah. Her brothers consented on condition that Shechem and his fellow townsmen agree to be circumcised. While the men were healing, Simeon and Levi murdered Shechem and all the other males of his town.

In his deathbed blessing, Jacob lamented their vengeance and predicted punishment: "Simeon and Levi are brothers; weapons of violence are their swords. . . . I will divide them in Jacob and scatter them in Israel" (Gen. 49:5, 7). And, indeed, the tribes of Simeon and Levi did lack their own permanent territories in the Promised Land. As the priestly tribe, the Levites received no lands, while the Simeonites were given only towns in the midst of Judah and seem to have been absorbed by that powerful tribe.

Apart from his role in the brutal act against Shechem, the patriarchal Simeon is mentioned only one other time in the biblical narrative. When he sent his brothers back to Canaan for **Benjamin**, **Joseph** held Simeon for ransom in Egypt.

SIMEON 2

According to Mosaic Law, a woman was required to offer two turtledoves or pigeons in a purification ceremony at the temple 40 days after the birth of a son and at that time present her child to the Lord. When **Joseph** and **Mary** brought **Jesus** to the temple for his presentation, an elderly prophet named Simeon took the infant in his arms and offered a blessing and a prophecy. Described as "righteous and devout, looking for the consolation of Israel" (Lk. 2:25), Simeon was the first to recognize Jesus as Israel's Messiah and the savior of the Gentiles as well.

The **Holy Spirit** had promised Simeon that he would not die without seeing "the Lord's Christ" (Lk. 2:26). So, in thanksgiving, he recited a prayer that has come to be called the *Nunc Dimittis* (for the first two words in Latin): "Lord, now lettest thou thy servant depart in peace, according to thy word; for mine eyes have seen thy salvation which thou hast prepared in the presence of

all peoples, a light for revelation to the Gentiles, and for glory to thy people Israel" (Lk. 2:29-32). Then Simeon uttered a prophecy that not only anticipated salvation but also forecast pain and trouble for Mary and her infant son: "Behold, this child is set for the fall and rising of many in Israel" (Lk. 2:34).

SIMEON 3

As a prophet and teacher in the church at Antioch, Simeon was known both by his Hebrew name and by his Latin name, Niger, meaning "dark" or "black." Simeon may indeed have been African; in the early years of the church, Antioch was second only to Jerusalem in prominence, and actively supported missions to the Gentiles. Ethnic diversity is suggested in **Luke**'s list of names and backgrounds for Antioch's leaders: "Now in the church at Antioch there were prophets and teachers, Barnabas, Simeon who was called Niger, Lucius of Cyrene, Manaen a member of the court of Herod the tetrarch, and Saul" (Acts 13:1).

SIMON

(sai' muhn) GREEK and HEBREW: SHIMON

There is some scholarly debate about the identity of the high priest Simon, who is credited by **Jesus Ben Sira** as the one "who in his life repaired the house [of the Lord], and in his time fortified the temple" (Sir. 50:1). Some suggest the reference is to the high priest who died about 270 B.C.; most scholars, however, favor his grandson, the Simon who served as high priest from about 210 to 196 B.C. Called Simon the Just, he was a member of the Great Synagogue, the assembly that regulated Jewish life in the centuries following **Ezra**. Through him were passed certain traditions still observed by teachers of the Law in the time of **Jesus**.

As a reward for supporting Antiochus III of Syria in a victorious war against the Ptolemies of Egypt, Simon was permitted to restore the temple. He is credited with the saying, "On three things the world stands: on the Torah, on the [temple] service, and on deeds of loving kindness."

Simeon and the elderly prophetess Anna attend Jesus' presentation in the temple; a painting by Rogier van der Weyden (c. 1399-1464).

SIMON 2

Simon, or Simeon, was the third son of the priest **Mattathias** to lead the Jewish revolt that succeeded in overthrowing Syrian rule of Judea in the second century B.C. The older brother of **Judas Maccabeus** and **Jonathan**, Simon restored religious practices that had been forbidden on pain of death and, in 142 B.C., established nearly a century of independence under the Hasmonean dynasty. (The dynastic title, according to Josephus, was derived from an ancestor named Hashman.)

On his deathbed in 166 B.C., Mattathias commended the wisdom of Simon: "Always listen to him; he shall be your father" (1 Macc. 2:65). However, he designated the younger Judas Maccabeus as commander of the rebel army. For some unknown reason, Simon was again passed over for military leadership when the youngest son of Mattathias, Jonathan, succeeded Judas as commander in 160 B.C. The years of apparent apprenticeship to his brothers seem to have made Simon both an accomplished general and a clever politician. For in 142 B.C., after the Syrian general **Trypho** lured Jonathan into captivity, Simon took over as the Jewish commander and forced Trypho to negotiate. When the Syrian reneged on his agreements and tried to invade Judea, Simon's army repulsed him. But before withdrawing, Trypho killed Jonathan.

To combat Trypho, who was claiming the Syrian throne for himself, Simon skillfully began to strengthen relations with the new king of Syria, **Demetrius II Nicator**. Demetrius freed Judea from taxes in 142 B.C., a date that marks the birth of Judean independence. Two years later, Simon was named high priest by the grateful Jewish populace; the office was to be handed down to his descendants "until a trustworthy prophet should arise" (1 Macc. 14:41).

Simon ruled for about six years (140-134 B.C.) before being challenged by **Antiochus VII Sidetes**, who made a final effort to restore Syrian control of Judea. Simon defiantly refused Antiochus's demand for territory, insisting that the lands held by the Jews were their ancestral heritage. His sons Judas and **John Hyrcanus** enforced the claim by defeating the Syrian governor Cendebeus in battle on the western slopes of the Judean hills. But shortly thereafter, Antiochus bribed Simon's son-in-law Ptolemy, governor of Jericho, to murder Simon and his sons during a visit. One son, John Hyrcanus, survived the assassin's attack and took over the Judean government before Antiochus could invade the country.

Jesus dining in the house of Simon; a stained-glass window from Strasbourg cathedral, France

SIMON 3

All four New Testament references to **Jesus**' disciple Simon, one of the inner 12, identify him as a Zealot: "Simon who was called the Zealot" (Lk. 6:15); "Simon the Zealot" (Acts 1:13); and "Simon the Cananaean" (Mt. 10:4; Mk. 3:18). The word "Cananaean" does not mean that Simon was a Canaanite or that he came from the city of Cana; rather, it is a Greek transliteration of *qan'an*, an Aramaic word meaning "zealous one."

Scholars disagree as to whether the designation is merely descriptive of Simon's religious fervor or marks him as a member of a revolutionary group opposed to Roman occupation of Palestine, a group willing to oppose the foreigners by force. They also disagree on the nature and dates for such a movement or whether there even was a Zealot party. Some years before the ministry of Jesus, in A.D. 6, a group led by **Judas** the Galilean unsuccessfully resisted the Roman incorporation of Judea as a province. It was then, perhaps, that the Zealot movement had its beginning, although the tradition of religious zeal can be traced back at least to **Aaron**'s grandson **Phinehas**.

Jewish allegiance to Rome was a burning issue for both followers and opponents of Jesus. But his ministry was broad enough to include within the innermost circle two of apparently opposite backgrounds: Simon, perhaps an advocate of armed resistance to foreign rule, and **Matthew**, a tax collector for Judea's rulers. Unfortunately, the Gospels offer no additional information about these two or how their attitudes might have changed after they became disciples.

SIMON 4

Hosting a dinner for **Jesus**, the Pharisee Simon was scandalized by an uninvited guest. "A woman of the city, who was a sinner" (Lk. 7:37) wet Jesus' feet with her tears, dried them with her hair, kissed them, and anointed them. Simon decided that Jesus was no true prophet, saying to himself that his guest should have known what sort of woman was ministering to him. Jesus read Simon's mind and told about a man who forgave two debtors, one who owed much and one who owed little. Which of the two should be more grateful, he asked the Pharisee. "The one, I suppose, to whom he forgave more" (Lk. 7:43), Simon replied. In a gentle rebuke, Jesus pointed out that his host had not greeted him with a kiss, washed his feet, or anointed him. But for her act of pious humility, Jesus said, the woman's "sins, which are many, are forgiven, for she loved much" (Lk. 7:47).

SIMON 5

All four Gospels contain stories of Jesus being approached at dinner by a woman who washed his feet in an act of humble devotion. **Luke** places the event early in the ministry at the home of **Simon** the Pharisee. In the Gospels of Matthew, Mark, and John, the incident takes place in Bethany shortly before the Passover that was to be Jesus' last on earth. John identifies **Mary** of Bethany as the woman who anoints Jesus during a supper at the home she shared with her brother, **Lazarus**, and her sister, **Martha**. Matthew and Mark, however, record that Jesus was in the house of one Simon the leper when an unnamed woman approached and anointed him. It has been proposed that this Simon was the father of Jesus' three close friends, Lazarus, Martha, and Mary. If so, he must have been cured, or perhaps even healed by Jesus himself, since lepers were not permitted to mingle with unafflicted people.

SIMON 6

As **Jesus** was being led to his crucifixion, Roman soldiers "came upon a man of Cyrene, Simon by name; this man they compelled to carry his cross" (Mt. 27:32). The incident is confirmed in the Gospels of Mark and Luke, in both of which Simon is said to have been "coming in from the country" (Mk. 15:21; Lk. 23:26)—likely a Jew coming to Jerusalem for Passover. Mark further identifies Simon as "the father of Alexander and Rufus" (Mk. 15:21). Mention of Simon's sons perhaps indicates they were well-known Christian converts at the time the Gospel was written. One son may have been known to **Paul**, who wrote: "Greet Rufus, eminent in the Lord, also his mother and mine" (Rom. 16:13)—suggesting that the apostle felt particularly close to both. By identifying Simon of Cyrene with **Simeon** called Niger, tradition often portrays the one who bore the cross as a black man.

Simon of Cyrene carrying Jesus' cross; from Duccio's altarpiece for Siena cathedral, Italy

SIMON 7

A practitioner of magic and the occult, Simon drew a large following in Samaria before his conversion by **Philip** the evangelist, but his impact was even greater in the centuries after his death. In introducing Simon in the book of Acts, **Luke** attests to his local fame: "They all gave heed to him, from the least to the greatest, saying, 'This man is that power of God which is called Great'" (Acts 8:10). But when Philip brought the gospel to Samaria, many among Simon's followers were converted. Eventually, Simon himself was baptized, being especially impressed with Philip's "signs and great miracles" (Acts 8:13).

Shortly thereafter, **Peter** and **John** the son of **Zebedee** came to Samaria to confer the gift of the **Holy Spirit** on the new believers by the laying on of hands. Simon was even more impressed, offering the disciples money and saying, "Give me also this power, that any one on whom I lay my hands may receive the Holy Spirit." Peter's rebuke was swift: "Your silver perish with you, because you thought you could obtain the gift of God with money!" (Acts 8:19, 20). When Peter entreated Simon to repent, the magician begged for prayers that would ensure forgiveness for his blasphemy.

Though nothing more is said about Simon in the New Testament, later history makes clear that a group who called themselves Simonians considered him their founder. The Simonians, who preached a sexual libertinism based on ultimate freedom from physical and spiritual limitations, were influential for several centuries, drawing the fire of leading Chrisitan theologians such as Justin Martyr and Irenaeus, both of whom wrote in the second century. Although there is much disagreement, some scholars regard Simon as a founder of a sect within the movement known as Christian gnosticism—the term "gnostic" referring to a belief that salvation is to be won through *gnosis*, or knowledge, usually through a revelation.

Besides his disputed relationship to gnosticism, Simon lives on in two other ways. His name is at the root of the word "simony," the act of buying or selling a church office

A furious Peter rejects the magician Simon's attempt to buy the Holy Spirit's power.

or ecclesiastical preferment. In addition, his story is one source of the Faust legends about the man who sold his soul in exchange for earthly power.

SIMON 8

By making a living as a tanner, the Simon with whom **Peter** lodged at Joppa would have been viewed as somewhat of an outcast in Jewish society. This perhaps explains why his house was "by the seaside" (Acts 10:6, 32)—that is, outside the town. However, Peter apparently had no qualms about staying there, an indication that all were welcome in the new faith whose gospel the apostle was so intent on spreading. Indeed, it was on the roof top of Simon's home that Peter dreamed of a sheet filled with "all kinds of animals and reptiles and birds of the air" (Acts 10:12) and heard a voice telling him to kill and eat them. When Peter objected on the grounds that they were unclean, the voice answered, "What God has

the voice answered, "What God has cleansed, you must not call common" (Acts 10:15). Peter interpreted the vision to mean that "God shows no partiality, but in every nation any one who fears him and does what is right is acceptable" (Acts 10:34–35). Almost immediately thereafter, the apostle was summoned to Caesarea by the Roman centurion **Cornelius**, who became Peter's first Gentile convert.

SISERA
(si' se ruh) HEBREW: SISERA

Hearing that **Deborah** and **Barak** had mustered Hebrew forces on Mount Tabor, Sisera, commander of a coalition army of Canaanites, led 900 chariots onto a nearby plain for what became the last full-scale Canaanite battle against Israel. After a sudden rainstorm had turned the plain into a bog that immobilized the chariots, the Hebrews swarmed down from the hilltop "and all the army of Sisera fell by the edge of the sword" (Jg. 4:16).

Sisera, however, managed to escape, fleeing on foot. He stopped, exhausted, at the tent of a nomadic metalsmith named Heber. The man's wife, **Jael**, invited him inside to rest and covered him with a rug. When Sisera asked for water, Jael gave him something better: milk, implying sympathy for him. It also acted as a sedative.

Once Sisera fell asleep, Jael gathered the tools she had likely used many times to set up camp. She "took a tent peg, and took a hammer in her hand, and went softly to him and drove the peg into his temple" (Jg. 4:21). Deborah's prophecy that the Lord would "sell Sisera into the hand of a woman" (Jg. 4:9) had been fulfilled.

SOLOMON
(sah' luh muhn) from HEBREW: SHALOM
"peace" or "prosperity"

Israel's third king, Solomon, was also known as Jedidiah, "beloved of the Lord," a name divinely revealed to the prophet **Nathan**, and his life story indicates that God, indeed, favored him. Even during his lifetime, King Solomon was internationally revered as being exceptionally wise and just. Today, his four-decade reign in the tenth century B.C. is considered Israel's golden age, one of unprecedented stability, prosperity, and national unity. Yet, in the long run, his rule proved disastrous because of its oppression of the people and tolerance of pagan worship, which fatally

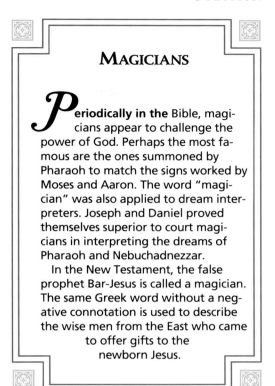

MAGICIANS

*P*eriodically in the Bible, magicians appear to challenge the power of God. Perhaps the most famous are the ones summoned by Pharaoh to match the signs worked by Moses and Aaron. The word "magician" was also applied to dream interpreters. Joseph and Daniel proved themselves superior to court magicians in interpreting the dreams of Pharaoh and Nebuchadnezzar.

In the New Testament, the false prophet Bar-Jesus is called a magician. The same Greek word without a negative connotation is used to describe the wise men from the East who came to offer gifts to the newborn Jesus.

undermined Israel's hope for continued national unity.

Second son of **David** and his wife **Bathsheba**, the tenth of his father's 17 or 19 sons, Solomon achieved power only through the court intrigues of his mother, Nathan, and their fellow conspirators, who took advantage of the dying old king in his dotage. Even after David's surviving eldest son and expected heir, **Adonijah**, was acclaimed in a formal ceremony, Nathan urged Bathsheba to persuade David to keep a previous vow to grant the succession to Solomon. Apparently, there was no strict law of inheritance at the time. David, reminded of his promise and deceived into believing that Adonijah was mounting a rebellion, proclaimed Solomon as "ruler over Israel and over Judah" (1 Kg. 1:35).

Hastily, the crafty Nathan arranged an investiture at the spring of Gihon, a significant site because it was Jerusalem's main water source. There the priest **Zadok** anointed Solomon as David's coregent with the indispensable backing of the palace bodyguard. When the prince appeared on the king's mule to the blare of the symbolic ram's horn, the people were enthusiastic, "rejoicing with great joy, so that the earth was split by their noise" (1 Kg. 1:40).

The manner of Solomon's selection was a departure from Israelite tradition. Unlike **Saul** or David, he had won no military victories nor become a charismatic national hero. He gained the throne only because he was the son of his father's favorite wife, who set a precedent for memorable queen mothers in Judah. But Solomon swiftly, ruthlessly established his authority as soon as his father died, about 961 B.C. When Adonijah made the mistake of requesting one of the late king's handmaidens for himself, a move that could be interpreted as undermining royal authority over the palace harem, Solomon ordered Adonijah executed and his chief supporters banished or killed.

In the case of the murder of one of them, David's widely feared army commander **Joab**, the repercussions lasted throughout Solomon's reign. Emboldened by the elimination of such a formidable leader, the Edomite prince **Hadad** returned from Egyptian exile to reclaim a portion of Edom from the empire David had forged in battle. And in the Aramean states near Damascus, an outlaw chief arose to become a persistent annoyance, nibbling at the northeastern boundaries of Israel. Even so, Solomon never waged a serious military campaign against these or any other adversaries, although his army of 12,000 horsemen and 1,400 charioteers was an extremely powerful one for the time.

AN EXTRAVAGANT BUILDER

Instead, Solomon focused his attention on domestic issues, building on his father's policies and organizational structure to gain greater central control in Jerusalem. Echoing systems developed in Egypt and in Mesopotamia, Solomon divided his kingdom into 12 administrative districts, intentionally cutting across traditional tribal boundaries in order to enhance the power of the central government. The prefect of each district was responsible for providing one month's worth of the immense royal needs in kind: food for the palace tables and fodder for the extensive royal stables, substantial offerings for official daily worship, and workers for local construction projects. Each day, the palace received "ten fat oxen, and twenty pasture-fed cattle, a hundred sheep, besides harts, gazelles, roebucks, and fatted fowl" (1 Kg. 4:23). In addition to retaining many of his father's officials, Solomon created two important new posts, a royal chamberlain and a governor in charge of the administrative districts.

Even more rigorous organization was necessary for Solomon's famously ambitious national projects, which ranged from a series of impressive defensive fortifications throughout the land to the citadel of Zion in the capital, a complex that included a grand new royal palace and the remarkable temple

of Solomon. These extravagant undertakings weakened the national economy, for they required burdensome taxes and drained great numbers of workers from other enterprises. By one account, the king's 3,300 chief officers supervised 70,000 burden-bearers and 80,000 hewers of stone. Moreover, popular resentment simmered when Solomon extended the system of forced labor, imposed by his father only on enemy captives and foreigners living within the kingdom, and drafted Israelites themselves, perhaps to the number of 30,000. They were sent in relay teams of 10,000 to gather construction materials in Lebanon, working one month there and coming home for two months.

The magnificent temple in Jerusalem, begun in the fourth year of Solomon's reign, or 480 years "after the people of Israel came out of the land of Egypt" (1 Kg. 6:1), was erected on the threshing floor atop a hill where David had set up an altar to the Lord. Modeled somewhat on the plan of the typical Syrian temple and ornamented with features revealing Assyrian and Egyptian influence, it faced east. Perhaps 45 feet high with a rectangular floor plan of some 90 by 30 feet, the temple was divided into three rooms. A 10-foot-long vestibule led into the main room, a nave perhaps 60 feet in length. The sacred inner sanctuary, known as the holy of holies, was a perfect cube, 30 by 30 by 30 feet, entirely covered in gold.

Into this holy of holies, when the temple was completed after seven years of pain-staking construction, the hallowed ark of the covenant was brought from the city of David. Cherubim carved from olive wood and covered in gold, perhaps 15 feet tall, stood guard with outstretched wings. The five-sided entrance to the sanctuary had olive wood doors carved with cherubim, palms, and blossoms in full flower, also overlaid with gold.

King Solomon overseeing the construction of his temple, grandest of his works for Jerusalem

Another of Solomon's famous structures was the 150-foot-long House of the Forest of Lebanon, perhaps a weapons storehouse, built with cedar beams, columns, and paneling. Adjacent was a portico known as the Hall of Pillars and the king's cedar-paneled audience room, the Hall of Judgment, with its royal ivory throne. Solomon's private quarters and a house for Pharaoh's daughter, whom he married in an important political alliance with Egypt early in his reign, were separate buildings. There were also shrines built for the religious practices of the king's many foreign wives. The construction of the entire royal complex, which utilized huge, well-dressed blocks of stone and was lavishly decorated, took 13 years.

To obtain the materials for such extensive and often luxurious architectural achievements, Solomon became a prominent trader as well as a skilled diplomat. He owned copper and iron mines and refining operations in southern Palestine between the Dead Sea and his seaport at Aqabah. His treaty with King **Hiram** of Tyre provided that the Phoenician monarch

would cut and ship Lebanon's cypress and cedar, along with gold, in exchange for Israel's wheat and oil. As part of the special relationship that developed between the two countries, Hiram and Solomon also agreed to cooperate in trade on the Red Sea; the famously skilled Phoenician shipbuilders probably provided a fleet financed by Israel and manned by mixed crews. Venturing as far as the African coast near Somaliland, they traded iron and copper for ivory, precious gems, silver, gold, peacocks, and two kinds of monkeys. At one point, Solomon transferred 20 Galilean cities to Tyre, an event often but perhaps inaccurately interpreted as proof that Israel was bankrupted by her monarch's construction projects.

Since he controlled the caravan routes connecting Egypt with Syria, Solomon's

407

highly profitable trade in horseflesh from the Anatolian region of today's Turkey and chariots from Egypt was virtually a monopoly in the ancient Middle East. In addition, he collected tolls on caravan traffic, which had become possible only a couple of centuries before when the camel was domesticated. Any merchant using the Via Maris (Way of the Sea) through Philistine territory or the King's Highway east of the Jordan was required to pay tribute in spices and precious metals, horses, and fine clothing.

But it was Solomon's increasing control of land routes and sea trade farther south in the Arabian region that apparently inspired one of the Old Testament's most popular stories, the visit to Jerusalem of the legendary queen of Sheba. Although tradition emphasizes her curiosity about the Jewish king's wisdom and adds an element of romantic dalliance, the South Arabian queen was actually on a trade mission, keen to take the measure of an increasingly powerful competitor in the spice trade. She arrived "with a very great retinue, with camels bearing spices, and very much gold, and precious stones" (1 Kg. 10:2).

Solomon's wisdom and his court's splendor took her breath away. "Your wisdom and prosperity surpass the report which I heard" (1 Kg. 10:7), she said and gave him, among other treasures, gold talents worth perhaps $3.6 million in modern terms. Before she returned to her kingdom, the two monarchs concluded a mutually beneficial trade treaty. According to Christian belief in Ethiopia, they also conceived a child who gained the Ethiopian throne, thus founding

Solomon threatening to divide a child between two women claiming to be the mother; a medieval Hebrew manuscript illumination

a branch of the house of David in Africa.

The story draws upon two aspects of Solomon's image in tradition: his supposed sexual prowess as a lover of many women and his reputation as the wisest ruler of his day. The biblical figures of 700 wives and 300 concubines may be exaggerated, but his royal harem was undoubtedly large, in part because of the many marriages he made with foreign women for reasons of diplomacy. His wives included Hittites, Moabites, Edomites, Sidonians, and Ammonites.

Solomon's renown for wisdom has more basis in fact, although the total of 3,000 proverbs and 1,005 songs given in 1 Kings 4:32 is likely to be traditional exaggeration. He is also credited with writing the books of Proverbs, Ecclesiastes, and the Song of Solomon, as well as the Wisdom of Solomon in the Apocrypha.

A GIFT OF UNDERSTANDING

Not long after he ascended the throne, the young king, perhaps about 20 years old, received his first divine vision at the ancient altar at Gibeon, where he often made 1,000 burnt offerings at a time. In a dream, God said, "Ask what I shall give you." Solomon requested an "understanding mind to govern thy people, that I may discern between good and evil" (1 Kg. 3:5, 9). The Lord was so pleased that he not only granted the wish but also promised riches and honor that would be unsurpassed among all the other rulers of the day.

Solomon's reply was key to one category of his fabled wisdom: the model Oriental ruler's gift for rendering judicious decisions. As if to prove the point, the biblical writer tells the famous story of the two harlots immediately after the dream sequence. These women gave birth to male infants at the same time; when one boy died, each claimed the living child as her own. Solomon listened to their stories, then asked for a sword. "Divide the living child in two," he said, "and give half to the one, and half to the other" (1 Kg. 3:25). One woman agreed to this decision, but the other offered to give up the baby rather than see it slaughtered. It was the latter, of course, who was the real mother, and she was awarded the child.

A second type of Solomonic wisdom, as evidenced in his deft use of appropriate proverbs, drew upon the lore of many civilizations in the ancient world, including those of Egypt, Canaan, and Mesopotamia. It seems that Israel's king became internationally recognized for his perspicacity: "Solomon's wisdom surpassed the wisdom of all the people of the east, and all the wisdom of Egypt" (1 Kg. 4:30). This type of

The queen of Sheba's arrival at Solomon's palace is opulently re-created in this 17th-century French painting.

wisdom often used examples from the natural world, and Solomon in popular legend and in Islam's Koran was credited with the ability to converse with birds and beasts.

Solomon was also supremely clever in answering riddles. It was this talent that first attracted the interest of the queen of Sheba, although she recognized on meeting him that his wisdom was much more profound, making him a just and righteous leader. The sum of all Solomon's wisdom, according to the Scriptures, was responsible for the peace and prosperity of the kingdom during his lengthy reign.

Historically, it is clear that Solomon changed the definition of kingship in ancient Israel. Unlike his father, he offered sacrifices and blessed his people, thus taking over certain priestly functions. Rather than rely on prophets for divine messages, as David had, Solomon was able to communicate directly with the Lord. Uniquely in the ancient Middle East, he built the temple close to the royal palace, physically linking the state religion and the house of David, which owned the site.

In another innovative move, Solomon's determination to weaken tribal society and affirm central control led to the growth of a new bureaucracy, from soldiers to administrative officials, that was dependent on him. Priests and village elders, too, became integrated into the government. Towns became more populous with an increase in the number of luxury craftsmen serving a sophisticated urban population.

Yet another defining characteristic of Solomon's reign was the unprecedented toleration of pagan religions and the acceptance of foreign elements within traditional Israelite society. Some Canaanite towns were incorporated into the kingdom; stylistic and ritualistic borrowings from other cults were introduced into services at the temple; and, perhaps because of the vigorous trading activities with other countries, there was increased marriage with foreigners among the common people. Such changes were resisted by many people, however, and the 12 tribes did not forget their tradition of self-government. Nor did the common people fail to note the disparity between their tax-burdened lives and the opulence enjoyed by Solomon's retinue.

According to some interpreters, Solomon's toleration of other religions, often spurred by the request of his pagan wives, was responsible for the collapse of the kingdom immediately after his death and internal problems while he was still alive. "For when Solomon was old his wives turned away his heart after other gods," the biblical author summarizes, "and his heart was not wholly true to the Lord his God, as was the heart of David his father" (1 Kg. 11:4). Earlier in Solomon's reign, after the dedication of the temple, God had appeared a second time to him and warned that if he or his descendants turned to other gods, "Israel will become a proverb and a byword among all peoples. And this house will become a heap of ruins" (1 Kg. 9:7-8). Indeed, when Solomon died and the throne passed to his son **Rehoboam**, the kingdom split in two, shattering the legacy of King David. Eventu-

ally, both fragments, the northern kingdom of Israel and the rump kingdom of Judah in the south, fell to foreign invaders.

Solomon's legacy to the ages, therefore, was not his highly organized, wealthy, and architecturally magnificent nation-state, but rather the wisdom with which he meted out justice to his subjects. Whether or not his actual words are captured in Proverbs, Ecclesiastes, and the Song of Solomon, his influence as enlightened ruler and gifted thinker has deeply enriched both Judaism and Christianity.

MARTYRDOM

The **English word** martyr is derived from the Greek term *martys*, meaning "witness." It was applied to early Christians—like Stephen—who bore witness to their faith by giving their lives. In the church of the second century A.D., accounts of Christian martyrs became a popular and powerful form of literature. As the church faced deadly persecution, the martyrs helped transform the horror and degradation of the present into hope for triumph in the future. "The blood of the martyrs," observed the early theologian Tertullian, "is the seed of the church."

Stephen's martyrdom, shown on a 12th-century French reliquary

SOSTHENES

(sahs' thuh neez) GREEK: SOSTHENES

Sosthenes was the leader of the Corinthian synagogue at the time the apostle **Paul** arrived in the Greek city. When the Jews brought Paul before the Roman consul **Gallio** because he was "persuading men to worship God contrary to the Law" (Acts 18:13), Gallio threw the case out of court. He judged the dispute a religious matter to be settled among the Jews. The crowd then seized Sosthenes "and beat him in front of the tribunal" (Acts 18:17). **Luke**, the author of Acts, does not say whether Sosthenes was for or against Paul; nor does he identify who did the beating or why. The attack may have been by Jews venting their frustration over Sosthenes's failure to win the case before Gallio, by Greeks exhibiting anti-Semitism, or by a combination of both.

Some biblical scholars speculate that Sosthenes eventually became a Christian since Paul referred to "our brother Sosthenes" (1 Cor. 1:1) in one of his letters. If Sosthenes did convert, he would not have been the first Jewish leader to do so. **Crispus**, another "ruler of the synagogue" (Acts 18:8) at Corinth, also converted.

STEPHANAS

(stef' uh nuhs) GREEK: STEPHANAS
"crown"

One of **Paul**'s first converts, and among the few Corinthians the apostle personally baptized, Stephanas was a devoted churchman who likely helped Paul decide what to write in his first letter to the Corinthians. Stephanas was part of a delegation of three men who sailed more than 200 miles to Ephesus to consult with Paul when trouble broke out in their church.

It was probably in response to this news that Paul wrote 1 Corinthians. The apostle's advice to the Christians of Corinth, "I urge you to be subject to such men" (1 Cor. 16:16), has led scholars to suggest that Stephanas and his companions delivered the letter and that Paul wanted the three to help the people understand its message.

STEPHEN

(stee' vuhn) GREEK: STEPHANOS
"crown"

The story of the first Christian martyr, Stephen, stands at a turning point in the development of the early church. The conflicts that swirled around him helped to push the new faith outside the orbit of Palestinian Judaism and into the wider Roman empire and eventually into the entire Gentile world. Since the name Stephen is Greek, he was evidently one of the many Greek-speaking Jews from the Diaspora, who are described in the book of Acts as "Hellenists" to distinguish them from the Aramaic-speaking Palestinian Jews, who are called "Hebrews" (Acts 6:1).

First-century Jerusalem was a cosmopolitan city, populated by Jews who had immigrated from many lands. The attitudes and beliefs of such Jews were diverse. Some wanted to find points of unity between Judaism and the best of Greek culture. Others emphasized the distinctiveness of Mosaic Law and temple worship. Whatever their attitude, however, Hellenistic Jews from the Diaspora could not hide their cultural difference from the Aramaic-speaking Jews of

The martyr Stephen, by Ghirlandaio (1449-1494)

Palestine. Jews from both the Hebrews and the Hellenists joined the disciples of **Jesus**, and Stephen was evidently one of the early converts among the Hellenists. He may even have known Jesus and have been among the 120 disciples who were present at Pentecost, for he is introduced in Acts as "a man full of faith and of the Holy Spirit" (Acts 6:5).

The catalyst that brought Stephen forward as a leader of the Jerusalem church was the first substantial conflict among Christians recorded in Acts. From the beginning, the rapidly growing church cared for its poor, including widows and orphans, through a daily distribution of food and other goods. In some manner not described

in Acts, the split between Diaspora Jews and Palestinian Jews led to Hellenist widows being neglected in the distribution.

When the Hellenists began to complain about this situation, "the twelve," who were all Hebrews from Galilee, saw the need to face the situation squarely. Through an assembly of the church, seven men were chosen, "men of good repute, full of the Spirit and of wisdom" (Acts 6:2, 3), who were to make sure the distribution was fair to all. All seven had distinctly Greek names, which probably indicates that the church chose to put seven leaders of the Hellenists in charge of the matter so that there could be no doubt about fairness. These leaders came to be called simply "the seven" (Acts 21:8), corresponding to the twelve. Although they are popularly referred to as the first deacons of the church, Acts does not refer to them as such. The work of only two of them, Stephen and the evangelist **Philip**, is described in Acts, revealing that they were primarily active in preaching and teaching.

Stephen was immediately embroiled in a debate concerning the new faith with Jews from the Greek-speaking synagogues of Jerusalem. He was one of the first to see that Jesus' message could be a direct challenge to many of the most distinctive characteristics of Judaism that separated it from Gentile culture. The debates are not recorded in Acts, but the impact of Stephen's arguments can be seen in the charges that were eventually made against him. Stephen evidently argued that the gospel of Jesus removed the need for the temple and all the sacrifices and other rites commanded by Mosaic Law. To his opponents who, like Saul (**Paul**) of Tarsus, were zealous for the Law, Stephen seemed to "speak blasphemous words against Moses and God" (Acts 6:11). His power as a preacher and debater led Stephen's opponents to try silencing him.

The Jews brought Stephen before a judicial council on the charge of speaking "words against this holy place and the law" and of saying that "Jesus of Nazareth will destroy this place, and will change the customs which Moses delivered to us" (Acts

6:13, 14). Stephen's opponents saw the very existence of their faith endangered.

Stephen was given an opportunity to answer the charges, but he made no attempt to assuage his opponents or to defend himself by convincing the council that their charges were untrue. Rather, he used the occasion to make a forceful attack on his opponents. Following an ancient scriptural tradition, he reviewed the history of his people, highlighting their repeated rebellions against Moses and other prophets sent by God. He challenged the very idea that God should have a fixed temple built for him. Finally, he used the phraseology of the Scriptures to mount a blistering denunciation of his hearers: "You stiff-necked people, uncircumcised in heart and ears, you always resist the Holy Spirit. As your fathers did, so do you. Which of the prophets did not your fathers persecute?" (Acts 7:51-52). This ancient attitude, now realized in the present, Stephen charged, had led to the betrayal and murder of "the Righteous One" (Acts 7:52), whose coming the prophets had foretold.

The speech turned the judicial council into an enraged mob, while Stephen, realizing what was about to happen, saw a vision of heaven with "the Son of man [Jesus] standing at the right hand of God" (Acts 7:56). The throng rushed at Stephen, took him outside Jerusalem, and stoned him to death. Just as Jesus had prayed "Father, forgive them" and "Father, into thy hands I commit my spirit" (Lk. 23:34, 46), so Stephen prayed, "Lord Jesus, receive my spirit" and "Lord, do not hold this sin against them" (Acts 7:59, 60).

The death of Stephen marked the beginning of an onslaught of persecution directed primarily against Hellenist believers. It was led by Saul, who was a consenting witness to Stephen's execution. With supreme irony, a few years later, God called that same Saul to become an apostle of the new faith and bring the work of Stephen to fulfillment.

SUSANNA

(soo zan' uh) GREEK: SOUSANNA;
HEBREW: SHOSHANNA
"lily"
••••••••••

A beautiful and rich young woman named Susanna can be said to have launched the career of the prophet **Daniel**. According to the book of Susanna in the Apocrypha, she and Daniel were among the Jewish exiles living in Babylon. Susanna and her husband, Joakim, owned a large house with an attached garden.

Among those who assembled in Susan-

Susanna and the elders; from a 14th-century Italian manuscript

na's home each day to hear lawsuits were two lecherous elders who had recently been appointed judges. Spending so much time there, the two became obsessed with Susanna and plotted to seduce her. They hid in the garden one hot afternoon, when Susanna was preparing to bathe. She asked her maids to close the gates, then sent them away. Immediately, the two elders ran to her and said, "Look, the garden doors are shut, no one sees us, and we are in love with you; so give your consent, and lie with us" (Sus. 20). If she refused, they threatened to testify that she had sent her maids away in order to meet a young man in the secluded spot.

Susanna knew that the elders would be believed and that the penalty for adultery was death, but she refused to consent to their demands and sin against the Lord. Instead, she gave a loud shout, which provoked the elders to begin yelling accusations at her. During her trial the next day, in her own home and before the assembled community, the elders testified they had caught her with a man who was so strong he got away when they tried to seize him. Without questioning the elders, the community condemned Susanna to death.

She immediately prayed to God for help, and as she was being led to her execution, the Lord inspired Daniel, then merely a lad, to come to her defense. He ordered the elders separated, then asked them each under which tree they had witnessed Susanna's sin. "Under a mastic tree," the first one said. "Under an evergreen oak" (Sus. 54, 58), the other said. Convinced of Susanna's innocence, the community condemned the elders to the very death they had planned for Susanna, presumably stoning. This was in accordance with Mosaic Law: "If the witness is a false witness and has accused his brother falsely, then you shall do to him as he had meant to do to his brother; so you shall purge the evil from the midst of you" (Dt. 19:18-19).

Everyone rejoiced for Susanna "because nothing shameful was found in her" and from then on "Daniel had a great reputation among the people" (Sus. 63, 64).

SUSANNA 2

Apparently a wealthy woman, Susanna became a member of the group traveling with Jesus after he healed her of an illness or of demonic possession. She is mentioned only once in the Bible, where she is identified as one of several women—including **Mary Magdalene** and **Joanna**, the wife of **Herod Antipas**'s steward, Chuza—who joined with Jesus and his disciples in Galilee and "provided for them out of their means" (Lk. 8:3). Likely, these women supported the disciples by giving money as well as their time in cooking and cleaning. Jewish rabbis of the day would have criticized as scandalous Susanna's decision to travel with a mixed group. But Jesus welcomed women as disciples, several of whom remained faithful to the end as witnesses to his crucifixion and were among the first to hear of his resurrection.

Surprised at her bath, Susanna fends off the lustful judges;
a painting by Anthony Van Dyck (1599-1641).

TAMAR

(tay' mahr) HEBREW: TAMAR
"date palm"

Widowed when **Judah**'s oldest son died, Tamar was, according to custom, supposed to wed his second son, **Onan**. Any child she then bore would be considered the offspring of her first husband. But Onan refused to cooperate, and as a result God struck him dead. There was a third son next in line, but Judah put off his marriage to Tamar, fearing that he too would die.

Husbandless and childless (and thus in her culture worthless), Tamar veiled her face and doffed her widow's garments, pretending to be a harlot; she was then hired by Judah himself. Tamar demanded his seal and staff as a pledge of payment for her services. Later, after it became evident that she was pregnant, Tamar was brought before Judah to be punished. But when Judah was shown his pledge and learned that he was the father of her child, he repented, saying, "She is more righteous than I" (Gen. 38:26). Tamar bore twin sons, the elder of whom, **Perez**, was an ancestor of **Jesus**.

TAMAR 2

David's oldest son, **Amnon**, was so enamored of his half sister Tamar that he pretended to be sick and convinced the king to send her into his bedroom to prepare food for him. Then he raped her. Tamar urged him to wed her and erase her shame, there being no law against marriage between siblings at that time. But by then Amnon's hatred for her "was greater than the love with

With tent makers of his trade in the background, Paul dictates a letter to Tertius, his only identified scribe.

which he had loved her" (2 Sam. 13:15), and he drove her away. David was saddened but did nothing about the disgraceful incident. Desolate, Tamar sought the protection of her full brother, **Absalom**, who avenged the rape by arranging for Amnon to be killed when he was drunk.

TERAH

(tair' uh) HEBREW: TERAH
possibly "ibex/mountain goat"

Adescendant of **Noah**'s eldest son, **Shem**, Terah lived in the Mesopotamian city of Ur, on the banks of the Euphrates River, some 25 miles northwest of the Persian Gulf. He left to lead his family—his son **Abraham**, Abraham's wife, **Sarah**, and his grandson **Lot**—toward the land of Canaan. Heading there, they traveled only as far as the town of Haran, where they stopped and settled; Terah died there at the age of 205.

"Your fathers lived of old beyond the Euphrates," **Joshua** reminded the Israelites, "Terah, the father of Abraham and of Nahor; and they served other gods" (Jos. 24:2). According to Jewish legend, Terah was an idol maker. He fashioned 12 idols, one for each month, and worshiped each one of them in turn. Scoffing at idol worship, Abraham revolutionized the history of religion by smashing his father's idols with an ax. Then he put the ax in the hand of the largest idol and said that it had destroyed the others.

TERTIUS

(tuhr' shi uhs) GREEK: TERTIOS;
LATIN: TERTIUS
"third"

The apostle **Paul** most likely dictated his letters, for when he did not, he called attention to the fact: "I, Paul, write this greeting with my own hand" (1 Cor. 16:21; Col.

4:18; 2 Th. 3:17); and "See with what large letters I am writing to you with my own hand" (Gal. 6:11). But the only secretary named in any of Paul's epistles is Tertius, to whom Paul dictated the letter to the Romans in about A.D. 56, while the two were in Corinth. Tertius inserted his own words in the closing greetings, "I Tertius, the writer of this letter, greet you in the Lord" (Rom. 16:22). This unusual note has led some scholars to suggest Tertius was a Roman Christian taking the opportunity to say hello to friends back home. As "the writer," Tertius would have done little more than record the words of Paul, though he may have had the freedom to do some rewriting that was later approved by the apostle.

Apart from this unique insertion, nothing is known of Paul's amanuensis.

THADDAEUS

(thad' ee uhs) GREEK: THADDAIOS

Within the New Testament, Thaddaeus is hardly more than a name—one of the 12 whom **Jesus** chose as his inner circle of disciples, as listed in the Gospels of Matthew and Mark. **Luke** does not mention Thaddaeus among the 12, but in his place twice lists "Judas the son of James" (Lk. 6:16; Acts 1:13).

Some manuscripts have Lebbaeus in place of Thaddaeus in Matthew 10:3, or "Lebbaeus, whose surname was Thaddaeus," as the King James Version of the Bible reads. The uncertainty about Thaddaeus's name left his identity and status ambiguous in later tradition, where he was often identified as one of the 70 disciples whom Jesus sent out rather than as one of the 12.

THEOPHILUS

(thee ahf' uh luhs) GREEK: THEOPHILOS
"friend/beloved of God"

By tradition as well as scholarly consensus, the Gospel of Luke and Acts of the Apostles are attributed to a fellow missionary of the apostle **Paul**, "Luke, the beloved physician" (Col. 4:14). Far less certain is the identity of Theophilus, to whom both works were dedicated. Some biblical scholars suggest he never existed, speculating that when **Luke** said the books were "for you, most excellent Theophilus" (Lk. 1:3), he was referring to anyone who could be described as a "friend of God," one meaning of the name Theophilus. Yet the name was a common one in Roman times, showing up on many inscriptions and papyruses, and the title "most excellent" suggests a real person—perhaps a Roman

So that he may believe in the resurrection, Thomas touches Jesus' wound; from Duccio's early-14th-century altarpiece for Siena cathedral.

official. Paul used the same phrase to describe the Roman procurator **Felix** and his successor, **Festus**.

Luke said he wrote his life of **Jesus** and the history of the early Christian church for Theophilus "so that you may know the truth concerning the things of which you have been informed" (Lk. 1:4). This phrase has led some commentators to propose that Theophilus was a Roman official who had heard about the Christian movement, including some distorted facts that had been circulating. If Theophilus had been such an official, Luke's intention was to give him an accurate account of what Jesus and his followers taught, perhaps not only to show that the movement was no threat to Rome but to convert Theophilus as well.

There is, however, an alternate translation of the phrase describing Luke's motive, reading, "so that you may learn how well founded the teaching is that you have received." In this case, Theophilus may have been a Christian in need of further instruction in the faith.

THEUDAS
(thyoo' duhs) GREEK: THEUDAS

A self-proclaimed messiah of Roman-occupied Palestine, Theudas promised to part the waters of the Jordan River and lead his followers into the Promised Land—just as **Joshua** had done 1,200 years before. The Roman army caught him, however, and all that got parted was Theudas, at the neck. The soldiers sent his head to Jerusalem, quickly ending the Jewish uprising. **Luke**, in the book of Acts, implies this happened about the time of **Jesus'** birth—that is, "in the days of the census" (Acts 5:37). But the first-century Jewish historian Josephus dates the event to A.D. 44 to 46. Although it is possible that there were two rebels named Theudas, it is more likely that the two authors reached different conclusions in reading the sources for their historical works. Efforts to link Theudas to other millennial leaders of the time have proved unconvincing.

In the biblical account, a respected rabbi named **Gamaliel** reminded the Jewish elders in Jerusalem of Theudas's story when they called for the execution of the apostles, who refused to stop teaching that the Messiah had come, died, and risen from the dead. "Let them alone," Gamaliel argued, "for if this plan or this undertaking is of men, it will fail; but if it is of God, you will not be able to overthrow them" (Acts 5:38-39). Taking his advice, the leaders released the men—but only after beating them and charging them to preach no more.

THOMAS
(tah' muhs) GREEK: THOMAS

In the Gospels of Matthew, Mark, and Luke, Thomas appears only in the lists of **Jesus'** innermost circle of disciples, the 12 apostles. He is always in the middle third of those listed, along with **Philip**, **Bartholomew**, and **Matthew**. The Gospel of John, however, includes several incidents late in Jesus' ministry in which Thomas played a leading role.

Thomas is first mentioned in the Gospel of John at a point when Jesus' life was in danger. He had preached in the temple at the Feast of Dedication (Hanukkah), but his words had led to threats of stoning for blasphemy. When the authorities had attempted to arrest him, Jesus fled Jerusalem and crossed the Jordan. Then word came that Jesus' friend **Lazarus** was on the point of death in Bethany, a village just outside Jerusalem. At first, Jesus delayed two days in returning to the dangerous territory. Only when he knew that Lazarus was dead did he summon his disciples to say, "Let us go to him" (Jn. 11:15). Many of the disciples likely thought it was foolhardy to risk the very real threats of arrest and execution for the sake of visiting the tomb of a dead friend. But when Thomas realized that Jesus was serious about returning to Jerusalem despite the death threats, he urged his fellow disciples, "Let us also go, that we may die with him" (Jn. 11:16). Although he apparently expected the worst, Thomas was committed to his master—willing to stand by him in the face of threats and if necessary to die with him.

LEARNING WHO JESUS WAS

The plot to arrest and execute Jesus took longer to come to fruition than Thomas had feared, but as Passover approached, Jesus knew that he had reached his last opportunity to teach the disciples. During his final discourses, Jesus taught them that he was going to his father's house to prepare a place for them and would come again to take them to be with him. "And you," Jesus assured them, "know the way where I am going." The disciples, however, were puzzled by Jesus' mysterious way of speaking. Thomas expressed the group's confusion when he said, "Lord, we do not know where you are going; how can we know the way?" (Jn. 14:4, 5). Thomas's question evoked Jesus' revelation that he was speaking not about knowing directions or a location but about knowing a person: "Jesus said to him, 'I am the way, and the truth, and the life; no one comes to the Father, but by me'" (Jn. 14:6).

THE NAG HAMMADI FIND

Digging for nitrate soil to use as fertilizer at a location some 300 miles up the Nile from Cairo, a group of Arab peasants made one of the most important biblical finds of all time in 1945: the Nag Hammadi codices. The papyrus documents contain a number of fourth-century treatises used by Coptic-speaking Christians, including the Gospel of Thomas, previously known only by fragments in its original Greek language, and the Gospel of Philip, another Greek work that survives only in the Nag Hammadi find.

According to one tradition, Jesus' sayings were recorded by three of the 12 apostles: Matthew, Thomas, and Philip; only the work of the first is included in the biblical canon. Of the 114 sayings attributed to Jesus in Thomas's Gospel, 40 are unique. The Gospel also contains a remark that indicates the division of mankind into sexes would be eliminated in heaven.

A third Nag Hammadi document is the so-called Book of Thomas the Contender, a conversation between the resurrected Jesus and Thomas, identified as Jesus' twin brother. The tradition that the two were so related is perhaps based on the Gospel of John, which three times calls Thomas didymos, Greek for "twin."

Thomas is best known, of course, for his response to the resurrection of Jesus, a response that gave him the epithet "doubting Thomas." On the day of his resurrection, Jesus appeared suddenly to his disciples within a closed room, showed all of them the wounds of his crucifixion, and commissioned them with the words, "Peace be with you. As the Father has sent me, even so I send you." He also gave them authority by breathing on them and saying, "Receive the Holy Spirit. If you forgive the sins of any, they are forgiven; if you retain the sins of any, they are retained" (Jn. 20:21, 22-23).

Somehow, Thomas was not present for this supremely important moment. When he arrived and the others told him what had happened, he could not overcome his sense of loss and doubt. He had had the courage to face death with Jesus, but to believe in his resurrection required even more: "Unless I see in his hands the print of the nails," Thomas said, "and place my finger in the mark of the nails, and place my hand in his side, I will not believe." The tension of a doubter in the midst of the believing disciples continued for a week until Jesus resolved it by appearing again to the group with Thomas present. He showed himself specifically for Thomas's sake and said to him, "Put your finger here, and see my hands; and put out your hand and place it in my side; do not be faithless, but believing (Jn. 20:25, 27).

In many ways the Gospel of John comes to its climax as all the fears and doubts of Thomas are swept away in that moment of revelation, and he responds to Jesus, "My Lord and my God!" Jesus, in turn, draws the readers of the Gospel into Thomas's faith by adding, "Have you believed because you have seen me? Blessed are those who have not seen and yet believe" (Jn. 20:28, 29). Six centuries later, Pope Gregory the Great expressed the impact of this narrative when he wrote, "Thomas's lack of faith did more for our faith than did the faith of the disciples who believed."

Sometime later, Thomas was among those disciples at the Sea of Galilee to whom Jesus revealed himself, rewarding them with a miraculous draft of fish and serving breakfast to them on the shore. The last reference to Thomas in the New Testament — Acts 1:13—simply lists him among other disciples in the period prior to Pentecost.

It is only in extrabiblical Christian writings that extensive traditions flourished about Thomas's missionary work. These traditions are especially associated with Edessa in eastern Syria, where memories of Thomas—usually called Judas Thomas—were long treasured. According to legend, the apostles cast lots to divide the world among them for their missions. The portion allotted to Thomas is variously given as Parthia, Persia, or India. The legend of King Abgar, recorded by the early church historian Eusebius, indicates that Thomas sent **Thaddaeus** to evangelize Edessa.

It was perhaps also in Edessa that the Gospel of Thomas was composed around the end of the first century. It claims to record "the secret sayings which the living Jesus spoke and which Didymus Judas Thomas wrote down." This important early document had been lost and was rediscovered in 1945 at Nag Hammadi in upper Egypt in a cache of hidden manuscripts. The same group of manuscripts also contained another work, the Book of Thomas the Contender, dating to around the end of the second century. It purports to be a secret conversation between Jesus and Judas Thomas recorded by **Matthias**, the apostle chosen to suceed **Judas Iscariot**.

The most extensive and colorful of the writings associated with Thomas, however, is the Acts of Thomas, a novelistic work written early in the third century. It tells of Thomas's miracle-filled mission to India and his martyrdom. The tradition that Thomas preached in India is particularly upheld today by a group of Syrian Christians in Malabar on the southwestern coast of India; they claim a direct lineage from those converted by the apostle and call themselves Christians of St. Thomas. The sect contends that Thomas was buried near Madras, though other traditions place his burial in Edessa. All of these extrabiblical writings emphasize Thomas's asceticism and celibacy and some have a substantial element of Gnostic teaching.

TIBERIUS

(tai beer' ee uhs) GREEK: TIBERIOS

In response to a question about taxes, **Jesus** held up a Roman coin, saying, "Render to Caesar the things that are Caesar's, and to God the things that are God's" (Mk. 12:17). He was referring to Tiberius, the emperor whose profile was stamped into the silver denarius. Tiberius's 23-year reign (A.D. 14-37) spanned the entire ministry of Jesus as well as the early years of the Christian church. Mentioned by name only once in the New Testament, the second emperor of Rome—officially Tiberius Julius Caesar Augustus—was nonetheless the Caesar often referred to in the Gospels. (The Caesar mentioned in Acts 25, 26, 27, and 28 was Nero.) The one exception is in Luke 2:1, a reference to the census decreed by Tiberius's stepfather and predecessor, the first emperor, **Augustus**.

Four years after Tiberius's

birth in 42 B.C., his parents divorced so that his mother could marry Augustus, who was then heir to Julius Caesar. Tiberius spent much of his adult life as a military man, from age 22 to 54. During that time, however, he took an eight-year voluntary exile on the island of Rhodes, after he had apparently fallen out of favor with Augustus.

Tiberius married, but in 12 B.C. his mother and Augustus talked him into divorcing his wife and marrying Augustus's daughter, Julia, to produce an heir to the throne. They had no children, and subsequently Augustus banished his daughter for adultery. Without a suitable heir, the aging Augustus reluctantly adopted Tiberius and named him successor in A.D. 4. It was ten more years before Augustus died and the senate confirmed Tiberius, at age 56, as the new emperor.

Tiberius's rule has fixed the date that **John the Baptist** began his ministry: "in the fifteenth year of the reign of Tiberius Caesar" (Lk. 3:1), or A.D. 29. During that reign, Tiberius appointed Pontius **Pilate**

Thomas and Jesus, by Andrea del Verrocchio (1435-1488)

as governor of Judea, and ten years later removed him. Midway through that decade, Pilate ordered the crucifixion of Jesus. Early Christian sources claim that Pilate sent the emperor a report of Jesus' trial and execution, but there is no evidence that Tiberius ever heard about the new religion burgeoning in a remote corner of his empire.

Tiberius eventually withdrew to the island of Capri to escape the burdens of administering so vast an empire and, historians say, indulge his vices. He died of natural causes in A.D. 37, at age 78, and was succeeded by his brother's grandson, Caligula.

Roman emperor Tiberius

centralized Assyrian empire through a combination of outstanding generalship and astute, if fearsome, civilian policies. As elsewhere, his aim in Syria and Palestine (which earns him mention in the Bible) was not merely tribute but conquest. To this end, he resettled native populations in remote parts of his empire and reorganized the captive lands as Assyrian provinces.

King **Menahem** of Israel managed to buy off the Assyrian monarch in 738 B.C. at an enormous cost and was forced to become his vassal. Five years later, his successor, **Pekah**, in alliance with King **Rezin** of Damascus, attacked Judah, whose people and ruler, King **Ahaz**, "shook as the trees of the forest shake before the wind" (Is. 7:2). Against the advice of the prophet **Isaiah**, Ahaz sought an alliance with Tiglath-pileser, surrendering treasures of the temple and the palace in return for the Assyrian's protection. Tiglath-pileser destroyed Damascus and reduced Israel to a pitiful remnant, but Judah's independence was seriously compromised.

In the Bible he is called both Tiglath-pileser and Tilgath-pilneser, as well as Pul, the name he assumed after conquering Babylon. He died in 727 B.C. and was succeeded by **Shalmaneser V**, who ably pursued his father's objectives.

TIBNI

(tib' nee) HEBREW: TIBNI
possibly a parody of Tabni, "man of straw"

The assassination of King **Elah** of Israel in 876 B.C. left three rivals for the throne of the northern kingdom. The assassin, **Zimri**, reigned but seven days before he was besieged in the capital at Tirzah by the army commander **Omri** and died in the flames of a fire he set in his own palace. However, Omri had to contend with another would-be usurper, for "half of the people followed Tibni the son of Ginath to make him king, and half followed Omri" (1 Kg. 16:21). Apparently, it took the commander four years to establish undivided control of the kingdom. But when Omri's forces overcame those supporting Tibni, his rival died—by what means is unrecorded.

Nothing more is known about Tibni. The name Ginath is nowhere else mentioned in the Bible and may refer to Tibni's father or to his hometown. The historian Josephus gives his name as Tabni, which can be translated as "man of straw"—making the unsuccessful claimant literally a scarecrow.

TIGLATH-PILESER III

(tig' lath pai lee' zuhr) HEBREW: TIGLAT
PILESER; ASSYRIAN: TUKULTI-APIL-ESARRA
"my trust is in the heir of [the shrine] E-sharra [of the god Ashur]"

One of the greatest conquerors of the ancient world, Tiglath-pileser III came to the throne of Assyria in 745 B.C. At once, he revitalized a failing nation, establishing a

TIMOTHY

(ti' muh thee) GREEK: TIMOTHEOS

None of the coworkers of the apostle **Paul** was closer to him than Timothy, a young man from Lystra in southern Asia Minor. As one of Paul's most responsible associates, Timothy helped Paul nurture the small far-flung congregations of believers around the Greek world.

Timothy was born in a religiously divided household, with a Jewish mother and a Greek father. This parentage probably caused Timothy to be considered a Gentile rather than a Jew. In any case, Timothy was not circumcised as a Jewish boy would have been, but was nevertheless strongly influenced by the deep faith in God of both his mother, Eunice, and his grandmother, **Lois**. Timothy, along with his mother and grandmother, were converted to Christianity, possibly during the first turbulent visit of Paul and **Barnabas** to Lystra.

About A.D. 47 Paul and Barnabas had encountered dangerous opposition to their message in Iconium of Phrygia and traveled 20 miles south to Lystra in Lycaonia. They preached for some time with considerable success, but their situation changed one day when they healed a man who had been crippled from birth. News of the healing struck the city like lightning, convincing the majority who worshiped Greek gods that they were being blessed by a divine visitation. With great difficulty, the missionaries halted pagan sacrifices to themselves.

This incident left Paul and Barnabas in an ambiguous and vulnerable position: Were they good men because of the healing or charlatans who had fooled the people by impersonating deities? When some of their opponents from Iconium came to Lystra, they were able to turn opinion against Paul. Finally, crowds threw Paul outside the city gates and stoned him till they thought he was dead. It was in this highly charged and dangerous atmosphere that Timothy joined his mother and grandmother in pledging their faith in **Jesus**.

After the stoning, Paul and Barnabas departed for the nearby town of Derbe; they returned briefly a few weeks or months later to encourage the fledgling church at Lystra and appoint elders to lead its members, and then departed for Palestine. The Christians in Lystra and nearby Iconium and Derbe did not see an apostle for more than a year, but were able to encourage one another and thrive in spite of "many tribulations" (Acts 14:22). During that period, Timothy was ordained for the work of preaching.

About A.D. 49 Paul returned to Lystra accompanied by **Silas** and other coworkers. He recognized Timothy's abilities and invit-

Assyrian king Tiglath-pileser III; a bas-relief from his capital, Nimrud, the biblical Calah

ed him to join his group as they traveled through Asia Minor and later Macedonia and Greece. They resolved Timothy's ambiguous status as half-Jewish by having him circumcised. Evidently, this was done to forestall prejudice against Timothy and not as a matter of Christian faith, since Paul was also accompanied by **Titus**, a Greek whom he had resolutely refused to have circumcised. As the company traveled and preached, a close bond of faith and affection developed between Paul and Timothy, so that Paul came to speak of Timothy as his "beloved and faithful child" (1 Cor. 4:17).

Paul was soon using Timothy as an emissary to nurture congregations when he could not himself visit them. When, for example, a public uproar forced Paul to leave Thessalonica, he feared that persecution would destroy the fragile Christian community he left behind. "When we could bear it no longer," Paul later wrote to the Thessalonians, "we sent Timothy, our brother and God's servant in the gospel of Christ, to establish you in your faith and to exhort you, that no one be moved by these afflictions." Timothy's mission was successful, and he returned to Paul with "good news of your faith and love" (1 Th. 3:1-3, 6).

Similarly, when Paul was in prison and the church in Philippi was in distress, he wrote the Philippians that he planned to send Timothy to them. "I have no one like him," Paul said, "who will be genuinely anxious for your welfare. . . . Timothy's worth you know, how as a son with a father he has served with me in the gospel" (Phil. 2:20, 22). It was perhaps after Timothy visited Philippi that Paul had him visit Corinth, writing to the Corinthians that Timothy would "remind you of my ways in Christ, as I teach them everywhere" (1 Cor. 4:17).

Timothy continued to work directly with Paul until the apostle was imprisoned on a trip to Jerusalem and taken to Rome. Then, as Paul's letters to Timothy indicate, Timothy worked as Paul's emissary in dealing with major difficulties in the church at Ephesus. Those two letters were meant to give guidance for the practical tasks of leading a community of faith under pressure.

By the time of his second letter to Timothy, Paul was again in prison and facing death. He wrote in warm personal terms reminding him of their shared experiences and sufferings and also in weighty cadences charging him before God and Christ to "preach the word . . . convince, rebuke, and exhort, be unfailing in patience and in teaching" (2 Tim. 4:2). Paul also urged Timothy to come to Rome: "Do your best to come before winter" (2 Tim. 4:21).

Timothy evidently came to Rome and at some point was imprisoned and released. Later tradition says he returned to Ephesus and, after becoming the first bishop there, was martyred in A.D. 97.

TITUS
(tai' tuhs) GREEK: TITOS

As a Greek, Titus was perhaps the first Gentile to become one of the apostle **Paul**'s coworkers in spreading the gospel of **Jesus**. He became, like **Timothy**, an important emissary in dealing with congregations that the apostle could not visit.

No details of Titus's background are known. He was evidently converted by Paul and **Barnabas** on their first missionary journey, or perhaps he was a Gentile convert in the church at Antioch. Titus first comes into view in A.D. 49, when Paul and Barnabas took him with them to Jerusalem for a conference with the leaders of the church there. A sharp dispute had developed over whether the law of circumcision had to be observed by all Christians, including Gentiles. The church at Antioch had been accepting Gentiles without requiring them to be circumcised. Many Jewish Christians, however, insisted that unless Gentiles were circumcised, they could not be saved.

Titus was evidently the only Gentile at the Jerusalem meeting where the issue was to be decided, and he represented the great number of Gentile converts whose faith was at risk. The situation could not have been pleasant for Titus. Paul later wrote of "false brethren secretly brought in, who slipped in to spy out our freedom which we have in Christ Jesus, that they might bring us into bondage." The focus of their efforts was to force Titus to be circumcised, but Paul and Titus "did not yield submission even for a moment" (Gal. 2:4, 5). As a result, the Jerusalem conference ended with the affirmation that Gentile Christians were not required to be circumcised.

Titus apparently traveled and worked with Paul on his second and third missionary journeys, and Paul described him as "my partner and fellow worker" (2 Cor. 8:23) and "my true child in a common faith" (Tit. 1:4). The most difficult assignment Paul gave to Titus was to deal with the church at Corinth. Little is known of what Titus did, but he was successful in combating false teaching and in repairing the relationship between Paul and the Corinthians. When he returned to Paul with good news, he brought the apostle palpable relief. Paul later wrote to the Corinthians, "Our bodies had no rest but we were afflicted at every turn—fighting without and fear within. But God, who comforts the downcast, comforted us by the coming of Titus" (2 Cor. 7:5-6).

Titus eventually traveled with Paul to Jerusalem, where the apostle was arrested and sent to Rome. The letter to Titus indicates that Paul must have been released and then traveled back to the Aegean area, where he left Titus in Crete to "amend what was defective" in the churches and "appoint elders in every town as I directed you" (Tit. 1:5). After finishing his work in Crete, Titus evidently met Paul at Nicopolis in western Greece and was sent to the region of Dalmatia on the eastern Adriatic coast at about the time that Paul was arrested for the last time.

TOBIAH
(toh bai' uh) HEBREW: TOBIYAH
"Yah[weh] is my good/God"

When King **Artaxerxes I** of Persia gave permission for his royal cupbearer **Nehemiah** to return to his homeland and rebuild the walls of Jerusalem in about 445 B.C., Judah was severed from Samaria and made a separate province with Nehemiah as governor. This outraged **Sanballat**, the governor of Samaria, and his ally Tobiah, called the Ammonite, governor of the neighboring province across the Jordan where the Ammonites had once lived. "It displeased them greatly that some one had come to seek the welfare of the children of Israel" (Neh. 2:10), Nehemiah wrote.

Both governors tried to impede Nehemiah's efforts to rebuild Jerusalem's walls, and their threats were so dangerous that Nehemiah had to carry out his work in secret. Despite their plotting, the city's walls were rebuilt in only 52 days, ensuring that the newly autonomous province would be defensible. After Nehemiah went back to Persia, the high priest Eliashib gave Tobiah a room in the Jerusalem temple though there was a law against Ammonites entering the sacred precincts. As soon as Nehemiah returned to Jerusalem, he ousted Tobiah and had the defiled chambers cleansed.

TOBIAS
(toh bai' uhs) GREEK: TOBIAS
"My good is Yah[weh]" or "Yah[weh] is good"

As the son of **Tobit**, the narrator of the apocryphal book bearing his name, Tobias plays a major role in his father's unfolding story. He readily accepts the assignment of the blind and impoverished

Top to bottom in this 18th-century German textile: Tobit, his wife, and son burying the Jewish dead; Tobias catching the fish; and Tobias restoring his father's sight

---

Tobit to travel from his home in the Assyrian capital of Nineveh to Media to retrieve money from a friend and picks a supposed relative named Azarias as his guide. Camping on the banks of the river Tigris, the young man is attacked by a huge fish. But Azarias orders him to seize the fish and save its heart, liver, and gall.

As the travelers approach Ecbatana, the capital of Media, Azarias tells Tobias about a distant relative named Sarah whose seven husbands have been killed by the demon Asmodeus before her marriages were consummated. Now, Azarias says, it is Tobias's duty to marry Sarah, but he assures the young man that no harm will come to him.

After the wedding, Tobias exorcises the demon by burning the fish's heart and liver. Much relieved, Sarah's father gives Tobias half of his estate. Azarias leaves the celebration and obtains the money for Tobit, after which the wedding party travels back to

Nineveh. There Tobias heals his father's blindness with the fish gall. In gratitude to Azarias, Tobias offers him half his fortune. At this point Azarias reveals himself to be the angel **Raphael**.

TOBIT
(toh' bit) GREEK: TOBEIT
"Yahweh is my God"

The hero of the book in the Apocrypha bearing his name, Tobit serves as a model for living a faithful life in a foreign land—one who could claim to have "walked in the ways of truth and righteousness all the days of my life" (Tob. 1:3). According to the moralizing tale, which was probably written in Hebrew or Aramaic between 225 and 175 B.C., Tobit was a Jewish exile in the Assyrian capital of Nineveh during the reign of King **Shalmaneser V** five centuries earlier. Tobit was named by the king as his purchasing agent, an honor the first person narrator attributes to divine reward for his observance of dietary laws.

After Shalmaneser's death, his successor **Sennacherib** forbade private burial of those executed by the state. Tobit continued to observe Jewish burial laws, however, and when his defiance was discovered, he was forced to flee, along with his wife, Anna, and his son, **Tobias**, and his property was confiscated. Soon after, Sennacherib was assassinated, and his son and successor **Esarhaddon** permitted Tobit to return.

One day word came to Tobit of the murder of a fellow Jew whose body had been unceremoniously dumped in the marketplace. Tobit retrieved the corpse and gave it a proper burial. Following ritual procedure, Tobit slept outdoors that night. There a calamity befell him: Droppings from sparrows in the trees overhead fell on his eyes and blinded him. Severely tested in his faith in a God who rewards the righteous, Tobit began to pray that the Lord would take his life.

Coincidentally, at the very same time, another Jewish exile was praying for death—a woman named Sarah, who lived in Ecbatana, the capital of Media. Sarah had been married seven times, but before the marriages could be consummated, each of her seven husbands had been killed by an evil spirit, the Persian demon Asmodeus. To help both Tobit and Sarah, God sent the angel **Raphael** disguised as Tobit's relative Azarias. Raphael's efforts resulted in the exorcism of Sarah's evil spirit; her marriage to Tobias; the retrieval of money Tobit had left with a relative; and finally the healing of Tobit's blindness.

TOLA

(toh' luh) HEBREW: TOLA
"crimson worm" or "cochineal" (source of a red dye)

The book of Judges tells very little about Tola. It provides the names of his father and grandfather and identifies him as a member of the tribe of Issachar. It gives the length of his rule, 23 years, and mentions the place, Shamir, in the hill country of Ephraim, from which he judged Israel and where he was buried.

Tola was the first of the five so-called minor judges listed in Judges, the others being **Jair**, **Ibzan**, Elon, and **Abdon**. Biblical scholars argue over whether their names were included to fill chronological gaps or to round out the number of judges at 12; whether only these brief fragments of their stories survived; or whether they served locally during times of peace and were thus not associated with any military exploits as were the other judges.

Although the Bible states that Tola "arose to deliver Israel" (Jg. 10:1), many scholars believe that he was not a warrior but rather a magistrate, a position he may have attained because his family was prominent in the tribe of Issachar. The fact that Tola lived in the hill country of Ephraim is adduced as proof that families of his tribe lived there before their final migration northward to settle in the plain of Jezreel.

TROPHIMUS

(trohf' uh muhs) GREEK: TROPHIMOS
possibly "foster child" or "nourishment"

Through no fault of his own, Trophimus was the reason **Paul** was arrested in Jerusalem and shipped off to Rome to stand trial before Caesar. Trophimus, a Gentile Christian from Ephesus in what is now western Turkey, had accompanied Paul on his third missionary journey and joined him on the return to Palestine to deliver relief money collected for Jerusalem's Christians. Some Jews from Trophimus's home region in Asia Minor spotted Paul at the temple. They knew the apostle had been traveling with Trophimus and "supposed that Paul had brought him into the temple" (Acts 21:29). If Paul had been guilty, which biblical scholars say is unlikely, he could have been executed.

The Jews seized Paul at the temple, and their accusations incited a riot. The Roman commander Claudius **Lysias** quickly sent soldiers stationed nearby to arrest Paul, rescuing him from the crowd and probably saving his life. Paul was later transferred to Caesarea, then to Rome, where he was probably tried and released, though some speculate he was then executed. That Paul wrote "Trophimus I left ill at Miletus" (2 Tim. 4:20) suggests that the apostle was freed and that the two traveled together again before Paul was once more arrested, then executed.

TRYPHO

(trai' foh) GREEK: TRYPHON
"magnificent" or "luxurious"

The cunning and murderous Syrian general Diodotus changed his name to Trypho, meaning "magnificent" or "luxurious," and stole the throne out from under a new king. **Alexander Balas**, the Seleucid monarch he had served from 150 to 145 B.C., died and was replaced by **Demetrius II Nicator**, who foolishly disbanded the army and kept only foreign mercenaries. At that point Diodotus changed his name, then mustered the former army and proclaimed Balas's son, **Antiochus VI Epiphanes Dionysus**, as king and himself as regent.

With the help of the Maccabean leader **Jonathan**, Trypho defeated Demetrius, then "dealt treacherously with the young king Antiochus; he killed him and became king in his place" (1 Macc. 13:31-32). Having seen that his Jewish allies were powerful enough to threaten him, Trypho lured Jonathan into a meeting, held him hostage, and—after accepting a ransom of nearly four tons of silver—murdered him. **Simon**, Jonathan's brother and successor as Maccabean leader, united with Demetrius's brother, **Antiochus VII Sidetes**, to defeat Trypho, who apparently committed suicide.

TYCHICUS

(tik' uh kuhs) GREEK: TYCHIKOS
"chance" or "child of fortune"

Along with a fellow Ephesian named **Trophimus**, Tychicus was a trusted associate and traveling companion of **Paul** on a portion of his third missionary journey. He also served as a substitute pastor and as a courier who delivered at least two of Paul's letters: Ephesians and Colossians. Paul's letter to the Christians at Colossae introduced his messenger by saying, "Tychicus will tell you all about my affairs; he is a beloved brother and faithful minister and fellow servant in the Lord. I have sent him to you for this very purpose, that you may know how we are and that he may encourage your hearts" (Col. 4:7-8). A similar message appears in Ephesians 6:21-22.

UV

URIAH

(yoo rai' uh) HEBREW: URIYA, URIYAHU
"Yahweh is light"

While Uriah the Hittite was serving in King **David**'s army during a siege of the Ammonite capital, Rabbah, the king spied on the warrior's wife, **Bathsheba**, as she was bathing, ordered her brought to him, and "lay with her" (2 Sam. 11:4). After he learned that Bathsheba was pregnant, David brought Uriah back from battle and urged him to spend the night at home, even sending food and wine from the royal table. Uriah, however, kept his oath to abstain from intercourse during a war, and "slept at the door of the king's house" (2 Sam. 11:9).

David's next ploy was to invite Uriah to the palace and see that he became drunk. Uriah still did not go home. Finally, David returned Uriah to the battlefield with a note to his commander, **Joab**, instructing that Uriah be placed in the thick of the battle, then isolated from his comrades so the enemy would be sure to kill him. No novice in palace intrigue, Joab obeyed David's order, then sent a messenger to the king with news of Uriah's death.

After Bathsheba's public mourning for her husband, David married her before their child, a son unnamed in the Bible, was born. Although David may have hoped to cover up his adultery, he was soon confronted by the prophet **Nathan**, who told him Uriah's murder would be punished by the death of the child.

Elsewhere it is recorded that Uriah was one of the "thirty" (2 Sam. 23:39), David's elite force, which—according to a list of the men and their heroic deeds—actually totaled 37, including their chief, Joab.

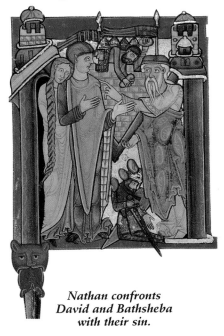

Nathan confronts David and Bathsheba with their sin.

URIAH 2

Having gone to Damascus to make obeisance to his overlord, King **Tiglath-pileser III** of Assyria, Judah's King **Ahaz** saw a pagan altar and sent "a model of the altar, and its pattern, exact in all its details" (2 Kg. 16:10) to Uriah, chief priest of the Jerusalem temple. By the time Ahaz returned to his capital, Uriah had built a replica in the temple. The king so admired it that he authorized its use as a replacement for the bronze altar built by **Solomon**, which was moved aside though still used for divinations. On his new altar, Ahaz began offering sacrifices to the Syrian gods "but they were the ruin of him, and of all Israel" (2 Chr. 28:23).

The Uriah who built Ahaz's altar is almost certainly the same priest employed by the prophet **Isaiah** to confirm his oracle that Ahaz's enemies would be defeated by Assyria.

URIAH 3

For having preached "in words like those of Jeremiah" (Jer. 26:20), the prophet Uriah received a death warrant from King **Jehoiakim** of Judah. Uriah's unpopular message no doubt was that Jerusalem would fall to the might of Babylon. But the prophet's flight to Egypt proved no safe haven, since Jehoiakim was in effect a vassal of Pharaoh **Neco**. Brought back to Jerusalem, Uriah was executed in the king's presence and thrown into a pauper's grave. The scribe **Baruch** added Uriah's story to the book of Jeremiah to show the courage it took to be a prophet and the importance of those friends in high places who were able to protect **Jeremiah** from a similar fate.

URIEL

(yoo' ree uhl) HEBREW: URIEL
"God is my light/fire"
··········

In the apocryphal book of 2 Esdras, the archangel Uriel instructs **Ezra** in the inscrutable ways of God, orders him to fast and mourn, and interprets his vision of the heavenly Jerusalem. Uriel also appears in 1 Enoch, a pseudepigraphical work—that is, one of those generally anonymous Jewish writings dated between 200 B.C. and A.D. 200 not included in any biblical canon.

The archangel Uriel; an English stained-glass window

In the former work, Ezra asks why wicked nations prosper while Israel suffers. Uriel responds, "Weigh for me the weight of fire, or measure for me a measure of wind, or call back for me the day that is past." When Ezra admits his inability to do so, Uriel replies, "You cannot understand the things with which you have grown up; how then can your mind comprehend the way of the Most High?" (2 Esd. 4:5, 10).

In the latter work, Uriel has charge of the celestial lights and the fiery region where rebellious angels are imprisoned. His dual role can perhaps be explained by the ambiguity of his name, which can be translated as "God is my light" or "God is my fire."

UZZAH

(uhz' uh) HEBREW: UZZA
"God is my strength"
··········

When King **David** attempted to take the ark of the covenant by oxcart to Jerusalem some 20 years after it had been captured by the Philistines, Uzzah and his brother Ahio were enlisted as drivers. They were sons of **Abinadab**, who had taken custody of the ark when the Philistines returned it to Kireath-jearim.

En route to Jerusalem, the oxen stumbled, Uzzah reached out to steady the ark, "and the anger of the Lord was kindled against Uzzah; and God smote him there" (2 Sam. 6:7). Uzzah's mysterious death so frightened David that he left the ark at the house of **Obed-edom** for three months before permitting the procession to resume.

UZZIAH

(uh zai' uh) HEBREW: UZZIYAH
"my strength is Yahweh"
··········

Only 16 at the time he ascended the throne of Judah, Uzziah enjoyed a lengthy reign, from about 783 to 742 B.C., and was, all things considered, one of the southern kingdom's most able rulers. He succeeded his father, **Amaziah**, perhaps when Amaziah was held captive in Samaria after his disastrous war with Israel. Uzziah was succeeded in turn by his son **Jotham** when he was stricken with leprosy and apparently forced to live in seclusion for the last years of his life. He is called both Uzziah, possibly a throne name, and Azariah, perhaps the personal name he resumed upon retiring to private life.

Uzziah came to power at a particularly troubled time. His father's war had left Judah weakened, the walls of Jerusalem

Persian queen Vashti is sent from court in this detail from a painting by Filippino Lippi (c. 1457-1504).

breached, and the temple treasures removed to Samaria. But Uzziah seems to have made peace with King **Jeroboam II** of Israel, and the two kingdoms enjoyed a rare time of mutual prosperity. Uzziah is remembered for strengthening the military defenses around Jerusalem, reorganizing the army of Judah, and gaining control over numerous caravan routes to the south. He also extended Judah's frontiers into neighboring Philistia and Edom and opened Judah to widespread trade by building the port of Elath on the Gulf of Aqabah.

The religious assessment of Uzziah's reign is also favorable: "He did what was right in the eyes of the Lord." But there was a reservation: "The high places were not taken away; the people still sacrificed and burned incense on the high places" (2 Kg. 15:3, 4). His neglect is given as a reason for the king's being struck with leprosy. During his early years, Uzziah relied on a certain Zechariah, "who instructed him in the fear of God" (2 Chr. 26:5). But Uzziah's pride in his own considerable accomplishments led to his undoing. When Uzziah entered the Jerusalem temple and usurped the priestly role by burning incense, he was reprimanded by a priest named Azariah and 80 of his colleagues. The king became so angry at their lack of respect that "leprosy broke out on his forehead" (2 Chr. 26:19).

VASHTI

(vash' tai) HEBREW: WASTI; PERSIAN: VAHISTA
"the beloved/desired one"

In the third year of his reign, King **Ahasuerus** of Persia gave a banquet "for all his princes and servants, the army chiefs of Persia and Media and the nobles and governors of the provinces" (Est. 1:3). The resulting festivities lasted 180 days, followed by a seven-day feast for all the people of his capital, Susa. After these long nights of drinking with his guests, Ahasuerus sent for Queen Vashti to show off her beauty "for she was fair to behold" (Est. 1:11).

When the queen refused to obey his command to appear, the guests urged Ahasuerus to depose Vashti, lest their own wives be incited by this display of independence, "and there will be contempt and wrath in plenty" (Est. 1:18). Consulting his legal experts, the king stripped Vashti of her title and issued a decree that "every man be lord in his own house" (Est. 1:22). Vashti's removal led to the king's search for a new queen, resulting in the selection of the Jewish beauty Hadassah, better known as **Esther**.

There are no people in the Bible whose names begin with the letters W, X, or Y.

ZACCHAEUS

(zuh kee' uhs) GREEK: ZAKCHAIOS;
HEBREW: ZAKKAY
"pure" or "righteous"

Known from a single incident in the Gospel of Luke in which he became a follower of **Jesus**, Zacchaeus was a rich tax collector under the Romans. He lived in Jericho, a customs station on a major trade route. Because of the way he had gained his wealth, townspeople viewed him as "a man who is a sinner" (Lk. 19:7).

When Jesus traveled through Jericho, Zacchaeus wanted to see him badly enough to climb a tree to get a better view. Jesus noticed him, called to him, and invited himself to Zacchaeus's house. While they were together, Zacchaeus said, "Behold, Lord, the half of my goods I give to the poor; and if I have defrauded any one of anything, I restore it fourfold." His repayment was the Old Testament restitution for theft. Jesus responded, "Today salvation has come to this house" (Lk. 19:8, 9). The story illustrates **Luke**'s theme that sinners who display a penitent attitude are more worthy than self-professing pious persons.

ZADOK

(zay' dahk) HEBREW: SADOQ
"righteous"

A priest with unwavering loyalty to King **David**, Zadok stayed behind in Jerusalem after a palace coup ousted David, then served as a spy to keep the king informed while he was mustering support east of the Jordan. **Absalom**, the king's ambitious son, had plotted the short-lived upris-

Jesus bids Zacchaeus to come down from his perch in a tree.

ing to get revenge on David for banishing him for three years. (Absalom's punishment was for murdering his half brother **Amnon**, who had raped Absalom's sister **Tamar**.)

As David led the procession of his family and servants out of the capital and into the wilderness, Zadok and his fellow priest **Abiathar** came with Levites, "bearing the ark of the covenant of God; and they set down the ark of God, until the people had all passed out of the city" (2 Sam. 15:24). David then instructed Zadok to remain in Jerusalem and serve as his informer. The rebellion ended when David's army defeated Absalom's militia. Despite David's order to spare Absalom, the prince was killed.

Years later, when David had grown old, it was Zadok along with the prophet **Nathan** whom the king called to anoint **Solomon** as heir to the throne. And when David's oldest surviving son, **Adonijah**, tried to seize control without David knowing it, Zadok refused to cooperate. However, Zadok's colleague Abiathar, who was descended from the priest **Eli**, had the misfortune of siding with Adonijah. Solomon banished Abiathar from Jerusalem, leaving Zadok as the sole priest. Zadok's takeover of the office, at the expense of Eli's descendants, fulfilled God's prophecy: "I will raise up for myself a faithful priest, who shall do according to what is in my heart and in my mind." (1 Sam. 2:35). Zadok's descendants served Israel as high priests until the reign of **Antiochus IV Epiphanes** (175-164 B.C.).

ZEBEDEE

(zeb' uh dee) GREEK: ZEBEDAIOS;
HEBREW: ZEBADYA
"gift of Yah[weh]"

The father of the apostles **James** and **John** and the husband of **Salome**, Zebedee indirectly supported the ministry of Jesus, though the Gospels do not say he himself became a disciple. He and his sons were fishermen in Capernaum, working alongside **Peter** and **Andrew**. Zebedee was with James and John when Jesus called them to leave their work to follow him and was left "in the boat with the hired servants" (Mk. 1:20). He seems not to have protested the departure of his sons or later that of his wife, who was among the women who traveled with Jesus from Galilee to Jerusalem and "ministered to him" (Mk. 15:41).

The fact that Zebedee had men working for him and that Salome was able to provide help for Jesus suggests that he was a man of some means. And since James and John are so often identified as the sons of Zebedee, it would appear that he was a fairly well-known person in his locale.

ZEBULUN

(zeb' yoo luhn) HEBREW: ZEBULUN
"honor," "exalt," or "dwell"

W hen Zebulun was born, his mother **Leah**, the less attractive and less loved wife of **Jacob**, thought her husband would finally begin treating her with the devotion he had bestowed on her sister **Rachel**.

The prophet Zechariah, as painted by Michelangelo (1475-1564) for the Vatican's Sistine Chapel

"Now my husband will honor me, because I have borne him six sons" (Gen. 30:20), she said. Unfortunately, the Bible gives no clue that this happened. Nothing further is known of Zebulun except that he and his three sons joined the migration to Egypt at the invitation of the Pharaoh so ably served by his half brother **Joseph**.

Like each of Jacob's 12 sons, Zebulun was the ancestor of one of the 12 tribes of Israel. Usually listed sixth, Zebulun's tribe settled in the forested hills of southern Galilee around Nazareth, later the hometown of **Jesus**. Though the people were landlocked most of the time, they may have managed temporarily to extend their borders to the Mediterranean Sea, as Jacob had promised in his deathbed blessing: "Zebulun shall dwell at the shore of the sea; he shall become a haven for ships, and his border shall be at Sidon" (Gen. 49:13). Sidon was a seaport 50 miles northwest of the Sea of Galilee, in what is now Lebanon.

Though the tribe was not able to hold all this territory, its members did manage to distinguish themselves on the battlefield. In **Deborah** and **Barak**'s battle with **Sisera** at Mount Tabor, the Zebulunites fought so well that they were the only ones praised twice in the Song of Deborah. They also helped **Gideon** fight the Midianites, produced the minor judge Elon, and mustered the single largest army to fight for **David**'s installation as king. The people of Zebulun were later taken captive when **Tiglath-pileser III** of Assyria conquered Galilee in 733-732 B.C. A few remaining members of the tribe heeded King **Hezekiah**'s plea that the northern tribes return to Jerusalem for the celebration of Passover.

ZECHARIAH

(zek uh rai' uh) HEBREW: ZEKARYAH
"Yah[weh] remembers"

I n ordering the priest Zechariah stoned to death in the temple courtyard, King **Joash** of Judah ignored his obligation to the victim, for he owed his very life to Zechariah's parents. When Joash's father, King **Ahaziah**, was killed in a rebellion, the queen mother, **Athaliah**, had the royal family exterminated so that she could seize power. The infant Joash was spared, however, because his aunt Jehosheba rescued the boy and gave him to her husband, the priest **Jehoiada**, who raised him secretly in the temple. Six years later, Jehoiada led an uprising that ended with seven-year-old Joash being crowned king and his usurping grandmother put to death.

Joash served the Lord until Jehoiada died; then he began worshiping idols. That is when "the Spirit of God took possession of Zechariah the son of Jehoiada the priest." Because he condemned the people for breaking God's laws, Zechariah was executed. As he lay dying, he cried out, "May the Lord see and avenge!" (2 Chr. 24:20, 22). By the end of the year, Joash was bedridden with a severe battle wound. Two of his officials assassinated him to avenge the killing of Zechariah.

ZECHARIAH 2

The son and successor of **Jeroboam II**, Zechariah lasted only six months as king of Israel, about 746-745 B.C. Then, in front of witnesses, **Shallum** "killed him, and reigned in his stead" (2 Kg. 15:10). Although the Bible does not give the assassin's motive, it does say Zechariah "did what was evil in the sight of the Lord" (2 Kg. 15:9), continuing his father's practice of worshiping idols. And it places the event in politically unstable days. Assyria, a growing empire feeding on conquest, was only a few years away from ravaging Israel in 733-732 B.C. and then destroying the northern kingdom in 722–721.

Zechariah was the fourth and last ruler descended from **Jehu**. Ironically, it was because Jehu eliminated idol worship that God promised that his descendants through "the fourth generation shall sit on the throne of Israel" (2 Kg. 10:30).

ZECHARIAH 3

The 11th of the 12 Minor Prophets whose works conclude the Old Testament, Zechariah wanted to motivate the Jews to rebuild the temple after their return from exile in Babylon. But he used a different approach from that of his contemporary **Haggai**. Prophesying between August and December of 520 B.C., Haggai promised the Jews an end to their crop failures and economic misery. "From this day on," the prophet said, quoting God, "I will bless you" (Hag. 2:19). Zechariah, prophesying from October of 520 B.C. to December of 518 B.C., promised them a Messiah and a return to the glorious days of King **David**.

The messianic theme in the book that bears Zechariah's name is so powerful that

New Testament writers used excerpts from it to show **Jesus** as the fulfillment of the prophecies. Jesus' acclaimed ride into Jerusalem before Passover bears a striking similarity to one of Zechariah's oracles: "Lo, your king comes to you; triumphant and victorious is he, humble and riding on an ass, on a colt the foal of an ass" (Zech. 9:9). In the Gospel of Matthew it is said Jesus made his entry on a colt "to fulfil what was spoken by the prophet" (Mt. 21:4)—though the evangelist apparently misread the original to give Jesus two mounts—an ass and a colt. And Zechariah's vision about a man receiving money for releasing a flock of sheep to be slaughtered has parallels with the story of **Judas Iscariot** being paid for betraying Jesus into his executioners' hands. Both men received 30 pieces of silver, and both returned the money to the temple.

Zechariah was likely not only a prophet but a priest as well. He is identified as a descendant of Iddo, who was probably the same Iddo as was listed among the priests who returned to Jerusalem with **Zerubbabel** in 538 B.C.

The book of Zechariah is divided into two sections. Chapters 1 to 8 contain eight visions that came to the prophet during the night, shortly after the Jews began rebuilding their temple. Most of the visions symbolize an idyllic life, with the Jewish community living in peace after the temple is completed. The Lord returns to dwell in Jerusalem, secures the land for the Jews, and establishes peace among the nations. "Many peoples and strong nations shall come to seek the Lord of hosts in Jerusalem" (Zech. 8:22), God says, speaking through his prophet Zechariah.

Chapters 9 to 14, which many historians argue were added later, contain two sets of prophetic warnings, each with the title "An Oracle," meaning an authoritative pronouncement from God. The first oracle speaks of the restoration of Israel and the humiliation of its enemies. The second describes the day of the Lord, when nations that attack Jerusalem are destroyed. Afterward, "the Lord will become king over all the earth" (Zech. 14:9).

ZECHARIAH 4

The first witness to the dawning age of the Messiah was the elderly priest Zechariah, who became the father of **John the Baptist**. Zechariah's priestly division, one of 24, was serving at the Jerusalem temple. Each division served a one-week rotation every six months. There were thou-

The angel Gabriel appearing to Zechariah in the temple; a 15th-century Italian painting

sands of priests involved, so it was a rare privilege for Zechariah to be chosen by lot to burn the twice daily incense offering in the sanctuary. As Zechariah stood there alone in the dim light, the angel **Gabriel** appeared. "Do not be afraid, Zechariah," the heavenly messenger said, "for your prayer is heard, and your wife Elizabeth will bear you a son, and you shall call his name John" (Lk. 1:13).

The priest found it hard to believe that **Elizabeth** would join the ranks of **Sarah** and **Hannah**, two other infertile women who miraculously gave birth in their old age. So he asked for a sign: "How shall I know this?" (Lk. 1:18). As punishment for his doubt, Gabriel said, the priest would remain mute until the child was born. And indeed, Zechariah's first words came at the child's circumcision, eight days after his birth. Elizabeth broke with custom by naming the boy John, instead of after his father. When the family protested, Zechariah

asked for a tablet and wrote, "His name is John" (Lk. 1:63). His speech restored, Zechariah gave praise to the Lord and prophesied his son's ministry: "You, child, will be called the prophet of the Most High; for you will go before the Lord to prepare his ways" (Lk. 1:76).

Nothing further is recorded of Zechariah, though in Luke 1:80 it is implied that he and his wife sent their son to be raised by some religious group—perhaps the Essenes—away from Jerusalem.

ZEDEKIAH
(zeh duh kai' uh) HEBREW: SIDQIYAH, SIDQIYAHU
"Yahweh is righteousness"
··········

There were 400 prophets who assured King **Ahab** of Israel that if he went to war with Syria he would win. Zedekiah was the most vocal of them all; he put on iron horns to symbolize the bull-like strength of an army he claimed would "push the Syrians until they are destroyed" (1 Kg. 22:11). A lone prophet named **Micaiah** predicted that Israel would not only lose the fight, but its leader as well. After Micaiah spoke, Zedekiah slapped his face and asked, "How did the Spirit of the Lord go from me to speak to you?" (1 Kg. 22:24).

Ahab and his ally, King **Jehoshaphat** of Judah, prepared a joint attack to capture Ramoth-gilead, in what is now northern Jordan near the border with Syria. In the ensuing battle, Ahab was mortally wounded, and Jehoshaphat was forced to flee to Jerusalem. The Bible is silent on the fate of Zedekiah after his prophecy proved false.

ZEDEKIAH 2
··········

King Zedekiah of Judah caused perhaps the most memorable disaster in ancient Jewish history. For his actions, he was forced to watch the execution of his young sons; then he was blinded and led in chains to Babylon, where he died in exile. His crime, both in the eyes of God and of King **Nebuchadnezzar** of Babylon, was to break his sacred oath of loyalty to Babylon—an oath likely taken in the Lord's name. His legacy was the defeat of his nation in 587 B.C., the destruction of Jerusalem and its temple, and the exile of Jewish survivors.

Eleven years earlier, Zedekiah—the third and youngest son of King **Josiah**—had been installed on the throne by Nebuchadnezzar. It was then that Nebuchadnezzar changed his vassal's name from Mattaniah to Zedekiah, for to rename someone was to claim control over that person. So, though Zedekiah ruled Judah, Nebuchadnezzar ruled him. All this took place just after the Babylonians invaded Judah and captured the previous king, Zedekiah's 18-year-old nephew, **Jehoiachin**.

Nebuchadnezzar took as his spoils the treasures of the palace and the temple. In addition, he took Jehoiachin and his family, along with "all the princes, and all the mighty men of valor, ten thousand captives, and all the craftsmen and the smiths; none remained, except the poorest people of the land" (2 Kg. 24:14). This left 21-year-old Zedekiah with inexperienced officials to help him run his puppet kingdom. The prophet **Jeremiah** described those left be-

hind as "vile figs which are so bad they cannot be eaten" (Jer. 29:17).

About three years later a rebellion broke out in Babylon, according to clay tablets known as the Babylonian Chronicle. This fueled hopes in Judah that Babylon would crumble. A false prophet named **Hananiah** added to the anticipation by claiming that the God of Israel had "broken the yoke of the king of Babylon" (Jer. 28:2) and within two years would bring back the treasures Nebuchadnezzar had plundered from the temple and restore Jehoiachin and all the other exiles to their homeland. About this time, Zedekiah considered joining a coalition of five neighboring nations in rebellion against Babylon, but this never materialized.

By 589 B.C., under mounting public pres-

EXILE TO BABYLON

In three stages between 597 and 582 B.C., King Nebuchadnezzar of Babylon reduced the rebellious little kingdom of Judah to ruins, destroyed the temple of Solomon, and deported thousands of political and economic leaders and productive craftsmen to Babylon. For more than four centuries the Jews lost their independence, their land becoming a provincial backwater of powerful empires.

When Cyrus II of Persia conquered Babylon in 539, 47 years after the destruction of Jerusalem, he allowed the exiled Jews to begin returning to their homeland. During the next century, many did so, but a large number stayed in Babylon, maintaining a thriving Jewish community. The harsh experience of exile helped the Jews to develop institutions and attitudes that strengthened their identity in the face of a dominating pagan environment. The Jewish Scriptures began to be canonized and systematically copied, while synagogues were established as centers of community study.

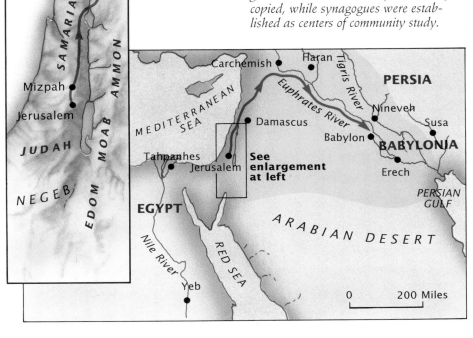

sure but against the advice of Jeremiah, Zedekiah had joined forces with Egypt. Nebuchadnezzar invaded again, destroying Judean fortresses and laying siege to Jerusalem. Jeremiah told his king to give up. He said God had promised that if Zedekiah surrendered, "your life shall be spared and this city shall not be burned with fire, and you and your house shall live" (Jer. 38:17). Zedekiah said he was afraid to do as the prophet advised, but he did, apparently, try to appease the Lord by ordering the citizens to release all their Hebrew slaves. As soon as the besieging army left to deal with the advancing Egyptians, however, Zedekiah allowed the people to take back their slaves. The Babylonians promptly returned, after chasing off the Egyptians.

Two years into the siege, "the famine was so severe in the city that there was no food for the people" (2 Kg. 25:3). In what may have been an eyewitness account, the author of Lamentations describes the horrors: "The hands of compassionate women have boiled their own children; they became their food" (Lam. 4:10).

Babylonian soldiers broke through part of the wall in the eleventh year of Zedekiah's reign, on the ninth day of the fourth month (which some historians make July 18, 587 B.C.). That evening, Zedekiah tried to escape with his army. But they were overcome near Jericho, about 15 miles away, and led to Nebuchadnezzar's military base in what is now western Syria. There the Babylonians killed Zedekiah's sons and officials, put

out his eyes, bound him in bronze shackles, "took him to Babylon, and put him in prison till the day of his death" (Jer. 52:11). In August Jerusalem was burned, its walls and temple razed and left in ruins for several decades—until the first of the exiles returned and began the rebuilding.

ZELOPHEHAD

(zuh loh' fuh had) HEBREW: SELOPEHAD
possibly "shadow" or "terror"

When he died in the wilderness following the Exodus, Zelophehad stranded his five daughters. Since he had no male heirs, his name would disappear from the tribe; his daughters would have no legal right to inherit his estate, including his share of the Promised Land. The women took their case to **Moses**, arguing, "Why should the name of our father be taken away from his family, because he had no son? Give to us a possession among our father's brethren" (Num. 27:4). Moses consulted the Lord, who ruled in the women's favor and told him to institute a law recognizing the rights of female heirs when a man died without a son. One restriction placed on the five was that they had to "marry within the family of the tribe of their father" (Num. 36:6). This was to make certain the land remained in the possession of Manasseh, the tribe to which it was given. Had any married outside the tribe, the land would have passed to her husband's tribe, since he would be legal head of the household.

His sons' bodies at his feet, the blinded and shackled Zedekiah howls in despair.

ZEPHANIAH

(zeh fuh nai' uh) HEBREW: SEPANYA,
SEPANYAHU
possibly "God hides" or "God treasures"

::::::::::

The prophet Zephaniah's warning of a global disaster may have been the catalyst for the spiritual reform movement launched by King **Josiah** of Judah in 622 B.C. Last of the nine Minor Prophets before the exile to Babylon, Zephaniah said God was going to "utterly sweep away everything from the face of the earth" (Zeph. 1:2). To those familiar with the story of how God created the earth, the prophet's words revealed a reverse order of destruction. For God had brought forth fish, birds, beasts, and humanity, in that order. But Zephaniah said God would "sweep away man and beast . . . the birds of the air and the fish of the sea" (Zeph. 1:3).

Zephaniah's words were accepted into the Hebrew canon almost immediately, likely first by those who supported Josiah's reform movement. Unfortunately, the reform did not last, and, about 35 years later, Babylonian soldiers destroyed Jerusalem, tearing down the temple and much of the walls. The devastation was so great that many Judeans saw in it at least the partial fulfillment of Zephaniah's prophecy: "I will stretch out my hand against Judah, and against all the inhabitants of Jerusalem" (Zeph. 1:4).

Although it can be inferred that Zephaniah prophesied in Jerusulem, all that is known about the prophet himself is in the first verse of the book bearing his name. There he is given an exceptional genealogy—distinguishing him as the only prophet whose ancestry is traced back four generations, starting with his great-great-grandfather Hezekiah. Usually, only the prophet's father is named. Because of Zephaniah's association with the reform movement, some scholars suggest the family tree is given to show his link with Judah's renowned reformer king, **Hezekiah**, who died in 687 B.C. But others point out that the genealogy does not identify Zephaniah's progenitor as a king, that the name was not uncommon, and that there is no record of the king having a son named Amariah, identified as the prophet's great-grandfather.

Zephaniah lived at a time when the power of the Assyrian empire was giving way to new Mesopotamian states. This made Zephaniah a contemporary of a perhaps younger **Jeremiah**, who lived to witness the fiery end of Jerusalem. Not surprisingly, their writings share similar styles and concerns. Both use the vivid imagery and symbolism that are characteristic of apocalyptic

The prophet Zephaniah; a 15th-century German stained-glass roundel

literature and that speak of imminent judgment at the end of the world.

In a last-ditch effort to convince Judah to repent, Zephaniah announced the coming destruction of all humanity, beginning with Judah and the capital city of Jerusalem. He then told how God's wrath would spread over the entire earth. He did this by using neighboring nations to symbolize the four points of the compass: Philistia to the west, Moab and Ammon to the east, Egypt to the south, and Assyria to the north.

Though many people apparently took the prophet's message seriously, the reform died with King Josiah, who was mortally wounded in battle with Egypt's Pharaoh **Neco** in 609 B.C. The king's son and successor, **Jehoahaz**, led the nation back to idol worship. This only added authority to Zephaniah's words, for in the final chapter of his book he said of Jerusalem, "She listens to no voice, she accepts no correction. She does not trust in the Lord, she does not draw near to her God" (Zeph. 3:2). But like the earlier prophet **Isaiah**, Zephaniah concluded his prophecy with a message of hope. "I will bring you home. . . " the Lord, speaking through Zephaniah, said. "I will make you renowned and praised among all the peoples of the earth, when I restore your fortunes" (Zeph. 3:20).

ZEPHANIAH 2

::::::::::

Perhaps a cousin of the prophet **Jeremiah**, Zephaniah was second in rank only to the high priest in Jerusalem. He was one of those officials who urged resistance to

Babylon in the final decade of the kingdom of Judah. Twice King **Zedekiah** sent Zephaniah to consult with the prophet about their rebellion against Babylon. And though Jeremiah advised the king to surrender, Zedekiah was not among those who called for his arrest for such defeatism. When the prophet **Shemaiah**, who had been exiled to Babylon, sent a letter urging the priest to punish Jeremiah and every other "madman who prophesies" (Jer. 29:26), Zephaniah refused, read the letter to Jeremiah, and allowed him to prophesy that no one in Shemaiah's family would live to see the return to Judah. Zephaniah himself was among the officials executed after Jerusalem fell to Babylon in 587 B.C.

ZERAH

(zee' rah) HEBREW: ZERAH
"dawn"
∷∷∷∷∷∷∷

The Ethiopian commander Zerah invaded Judah with a vast army, including 300 chariots, and marched to within 25 miles of Jerusalem. King **Asa**, the fifth ruler of **David**'s dynasty, called on God for help. The Hebrews then routed the enemy, chasing them 20 miles southwest to Gerar, where the invaders "fell until none remained alive" (2 Chr. 14:13). Biblical scholars are uncertain where Zerah came from or for whom he was fighting. There is no ruler of the Ethiopian or Cushite dynasty of Egypt by that name, and no sound in Egyptian that could be translated "z" in Hebrew. Since the name does show up among Arabs, some suggest Zerah was an Arab or Ethiopian mercenary of the Pharaoh.

ZERUBBABEL

(zuh roo' buh buhl) HEBREW: ZERUBBABEL; probably derived from AKKADIAN: ZER-BABILI
"seed of Babylon"
∷∷∷∷∷∷∷

The temple that Zerubbabel built in Jerusalem in the sixth century B.C. lasted longer than the temples of **Solomon** and **Herod the Great** combined, but Zerubbabel disappears from the biblical narrative even before his temple is dedicated. This has fueled speculation that he was executed for leading a messianic movement that would have crowned him king of an independent Jewish nation.

The prophets of his day certainly seemed to have messianic expectations of Zerubbabel as a descendant of King **David**. **Haggai** said the Jew who helped lead the first wave of his people home from exile in Babylon

would be used by God to destroy other nations: "On that day, says the Lord of hosts, I will take you, O Zerubbabel my servant, the son of Shealtiel, says the Lord, and make you like a signet ring; for I have chosen you, says the Lord of hosts" (Hag. 2:23). The words "servant," "signet ring," and "chosen" all imply kingship.

Zerubbabel was most likely born during Judah's five-decade exile in Babylon. Though many leading citizens of Judah were exiled in 597 B.C., most were not taken until Babylon leveled Jerusalem in 587 B.C. Forty-seven years later, the Persians captured Babylon, and, within a year, the Persian king **Cyrus II** issued a decree allowing the Jews to return home to "rebuild the house of the Lord, the God of Israel" (Ezra 1:3). Cyrus also restored the temple treasures the Babylonians had stolen and agreed to help finance the building project.

The decree of 538 B.C. was not unique. Cyrus, like Persian kings after him, had a policy of allowing captured people to return home and encouraging native religions. Ancient nonbiblical sources show that Cyrus gave money to rebuild temples in Ur and Uruk. Cambyses II, his son and successor, helped finance restoration of the temple at Sais, Egypt. And **Darius I**, who succeeded Cambyses, won over the priests of Egypt by rebuilding their temples and restoring their incomes.

Zerubbabel was placed in charge of the returning Jews and given the title "governor of Judah." He allowed the people about 14 months to get settled, probably to build their homes and plant crops. Then, about 536, the Jews began in earnest the rebuilding of the temple. Sometime after they laid the foundation over what had been Solomon's temple, opposition arose that slowed the work, then finally put a 15-year halt to it. The opposition came from non-Jews in the region, perhaps descendants of settlers the Assyrians had brought in after they crushed the northern kingdom of Israel in 721 B.C. Some of those people apparently worshiped Yahweh, at least as one of many gods, and asked to help build the temple.

The response of Zerubbabel and the other leaders was blunt: "You have nothing to do with us in building a house to our God; but we alone will build to the Lord, the God of Israel, as King Cyrus the king of Persia has commanded us" (Ezra 4:3). In retaliation, the neighbors harassed the builders to the point of bringing the work to a standstill, where it remained throughout the reign of Cyrus as well as that of his son Cambyses. (According to another school of thought, one **Sheshbazzar**—possibly Zerubbabel's uncle—led the first returnees and initiated the temple construction. Zerubbabel himself did not arrive until about 521 B.C., in time to oversee the second phase of building.)

A year and a half into the reign of the next Persian king, Darius, the prophets Haggai and **Zechariah** convinced Zerubbabel it was time to finish the job. And they began again "on the twenty-fourth day of the month, in the sixth month" (Hag. 1:15)—that is, mid-September 520. Again, neighboring communities took notice of the project and raised objections, this time expressed by the governor of Syria. He asked who authorized the work. When Zerubbabel and the other Jewish leaders told him the Persians, the Syrian governor wrote to Darius asking him to confirm it by checking the royal archives.

Darius ordered the search and found the decree of Cyrus. Then he not only confirmed what the Jews had said, he ordered the non-Jews to leave the Jews alone and to give them any money from the royal revenues or supplies that they needed to complete the temple. If anyone did not comply, Darius said, "a beam is to be pulled out of his house, and he shall be impaled upon it" (Ezra 6:11).

The temple was completed in March 516, about three and a half years after the second effort began. Zerubbabel, presumably the leader of the project, is nowhere mentioned in the details of the temple's completion and dedication. He disappears from the Bible except for three New Testament verses that include him in the genealogy of **Jesus**. Yet this may mean nothing other than that his most memorable contribution to Jewish history had been recorded, and there was nothing significant left to say.

Zerubbabel supervising the returnees in rebuilding Jerusalem's temple

ZERUIAH
(zuh roo' yah) HEBREW: SERUYAH
"the balsam of Yahweh"

King **David**'s sister Zeruiah raised three sons who became his fiercely loyal commanders: **Joab**, **Asahel**, and **Abishai**. They were also headstrong, vindictive, and sometimes overzealous. Indeed, they were so violently impetuous that David once lamented, "These men the sons of Zeruiah

are too hard for me" (2 Sam. 3:39). Joab, for example, killed the king's rebel son in spite of David's order, "Deal gently for my sake with the young man Absalom" (2 Sam. 18:5). The three are always identified as sons of Zeruiah; their father is unnamed.

ZEUS

(zoos) GREEK: ZEUS

The people of Lystra, in what is now Turkey, were astonished at having seen **Paul** heal a crippled man and exclaimed, "The gods have come down to us in the likeness of men" (Acts 14:11). Because of Paul's skill at oratory, they assumed he was Hermes, the messenger god in the Greek pantheon. Paul's companion, **Barnabas**, they supposed to be the supreme god of the universe, Zeus. Scarcely able to restrain the crowd from worshiping them, the two angrily ripped their garments (the common reaction to blasphemy), proclaimed their humanity, and asked the citizenry to heed the gospel of **Jesus**.

The Christian missionaries from Palestine may have been upset partly because they remembered stories of the atrocities committed some 200 years earlier in the name of Greek religion. **Antiochus IV Epiphanes** tried to replace Judaism with the Greek way of life. He slaughtered Jews who resisted and went so far as to "pollute the temple of Jerusalem and call it the temple of Olympian Zeus" (2 Macc. 6:2).

Also known among the Romans as Jupiter, Zeus was considered ruler of the other gods. Greeks referred to the chief god of any non-Greek religion as Zeus.

ZIBA

(zai' buh) HEBREW: SIBA
"planting" or "branch"

Ziba may have been a lying opportunist who stole a crippled man's only means out of town just before an invasion. Or he may have been unselfishly devoted to King **David**. From the record, it is hard to tell.

When David asked whether there was anyone left of **Saul**'s family to whom he could show kindness "for Jonathan's sake" (2 Sam. 9:1), Ziba directed the king to **Mephibosheth**, the lame son of **Jonathan** and a grandson of Saul. David then gave Mephibosheth all of Saul's property and ordered Ziba, Saul's former servant, to manage the land and have his family work it.

Near the end of David's reign, when the king's son **Absalom** staged a coup and

Zeus transformed the maiden Io into a cow to avoid his wife's jealousy; a fifth-century B.C. Greek vase.

marched on Jerusalem, Ziba brought food and a string of donkeys so the king and his officials could flee to safety. When David asked why Mephibosheth was not joining them, Ziba replied, "He remains in Jerusalem; for he said, 'Today the house of Israel will give me back the kingdom of my father'" (2 Sam. 16:3). Furious, David gave all of Mephibosheth's property to Ziba.

After the coup failed, Ziba and his family rushed to meet the king. Close behind was Mephibosheth. To express his sorrow over David's flight, Mephibosheth had not put on shoes, washed his clothes, or trimmed his beard since the king left Jerusalem. When David asked why he had stayed behind, Mephibosheth said, "My servant deceived me" (2 Sam. 19:26). He further charged that Ziba had not only refused to saddle a donkey for him so he could escape with David, but had rushed to slander him before the king. David, either unable to decide whom to believe or regretting his earlier award but still appreciative of Ziba's help in the crisis, divided the property between the two.

ZILPAH

(zil' puh) HEBREW: ZILPA
"short-nosed"

Caught in the feud of two women competing for the attention of their shared husband, Zilpah became **Jacob**'s concubine and the surrogate mother of two of his 12 sons: **Gad** and **Asher**. "When Leah saw that she had ceased bearing children, she took her maid Zilpah and gave her to Jacob as a wife" (Gen. 30:9). In a culture that lauded women who produced children, especially sons, **Leah** had already given birth to four boys. But she apparently offered her maid to Jacob in response to the infertile **Rachel**'s having given him her maid, **Bilhah**. Rachel's maid had produced two sons, **Dan** and **Naphtali**, who, like Zilpah's sons, gave their names to two of Israel's 12 tribes.

ZIMRI

(zim' rai) HEBREW: ZIMRI
possibly "my song" or "mountain sheep"

Zimri's death ended a plague among the Israelites of the Exodus and made a hero of **Aaron**'s grandson, a priest named **Phinehas**. God had sent the plague because the Israelites allowed the women of Moab to lure them into fertility rites and into eating meals associated with the worship of **Baal**. **Moses** ordered the offending Israelites executed. But in blatant defiance, Zimri, the head of an extended family in the tribe of Simeon, walked a Moabite princess right past Moses and into the tent of meeting. Phinehas picked up a spear and followed. With a single thrust, he "pierced both of them, the man of Israel and the woman, through her body" (Num. 25:8). This ended a plague that had killed 24,000.

ZIMRI 2

No king of Israel served a shorter term than did Zimri. The commander of half the nation's chariot forces lasted only seven days on the throne before burning himself to death in the palace.

Most of the army was laying siege to Gibbethon, a Philistine border town some 40 miles away from Tirzah, where King **Elah** was laying siege to the wine supply in the home of a palace official. Zimri came into the house, murdered the drunken king, then proceeded to kill every male heir of Elah. This fulfilled an oracle of the prophet **Jehu** against the family of **Baasha**, Elah's father: "I will utterly sweep away Baasha and his house" (1 Kg. 16:3). When the army heard what had happened, the troops appointed their commander, **Omri**, as king. Omri immediately marched his forces to Tirzah. After the city fell, Zimri "went into the citadel of the king's house, and burned the king's house over him with fire, and died" (1 Kg. 16:18).

Zimri's name became an expression of contempt. Ironically, it was used by **Jezebel**, Omri's daughter-in-law, to revile the man who had assassinated her son **Jehoram**. "You Zimri, murderer of your master" (2 Kg. 9:31), she cried out from her palace window when the usurper **Jehu** rode into the city of Jezreel.

ZIPPORAH

(zip poh' ruh) HEBREW: SIPPORA
"sparrow" or "swallow"

The wife of **Moses**, Zipporah is also the heroine who wards off a divine attack in perhaps the most obscure and bizarre episode in the book of Exodus. Three short verses tell about Moses and his family going to Egypt when "the Lord met him and sought to kill him" (Ex. 4:24). Biblical scholars speculate that God was angry because Moses, or possibly one of his sons, had not been circumcised. Zipporah immediately circumcised her son and touched the foreskin to the genitals of Moses, implying a substitutionary circumcision. Had Moses himself undergone the surgical procedure, his mission to Egypt no doubt would have been delayed.

Zipporah met and married Moses when he fled to Midian after having killed an Egyptian. She bore him two sons, **Gershom** and Eliezer. The mother and sons did not accompany Moses all the way to Egypt, but returned to Zipporah's father, the Midianite priest **Jethro**. Moses and his family were reunited during the Exodus.

Moses, Zipporah, and their two sons set out for Egypt; from a 14-century manuscript.

ZOPHAR

(zoh' far) HEBREW: SOPAR

possibly "bird"

One of three friends of **Job** who came "to condole with him and comfort him" (Job 2:11), Zophar was the first to condemn him. Job had just lost his 11,500 head of livestock, his ten children, and his health. Yet, in an insensitive attack, Zophar said, "God exacts of you less than your guilt deserves" (Job 11:6). Because Zophar was always the last of the three to speak, and because of his lack of compassion, some scholars suggest he was the youngest.

Unlike his colleagues, **Eliphaz** and **Bildad**, Zophar made no attempt to empathize with Job's pain. Instead, he callously declared, "a stupid man will get understanding, when a wild ass's colt is born a man" (Job 11:12). Zophar believed that tragedy in life came as God's judgment for sin, and that prosperity was a sign of righteousness. So in Zophar's second and final speech, he harshly charged that any person as wicked as Job "will perish for ever like his own dung" (Job 20:7).

God eventually came to Job's defense and told Eliphaz, "My wrath is kindled against you and against your two friends; for you have not spoken of me what is right, as my servant Job has" (Job 42:7). God ordered the three to offer a sacrifice for their sins and to have Job pray for them.

Job's friends confront the hapless man seated in an ash heap; from the duc de Berry's early-15th-century book of hours.

A

AARON, Moses' brother, *Ex. 4:14*

ABADDON, angel of destruction, *Rev. 9:11*

ABAGTHA, eunuch, chamberlain of Ahasuerus, *Est. 1:10*

ABDA, father of Adoniram, *1 Kg. 4:6*

2, Levite in Jerusalem after exile, *Neh. 11:17*

ABDEEL, father of Shelemiah, Jehoiakim's servant, *Jer. 36:26*

ABDI, grandfather of Ethan the musician, *1 Chr. 6:44*

2, Levite, father of Kish, *2 Chr. 29:12*

3, left foreign wife, *Ezra 10:26*

ABDIEL, clan leader in Gad, *1 Chr. 5:15*

ABDON, judge in Ephraim, *Jg. 12:13*

2, uncle of Saul, *1 Chr. 8:30*

3, Benjaminite of Jerusalem, *1 Chr. 8:23*

4, *2 Chr. 34:20, see* Achbor 2

ABEDNEGO, Daniel's companion, *Dan. 1:7*

ABEL, second son of Adam and Eve, *Gen. 4:2*

ABI, mother of Hezekiah, *2 Kg. 18:2*

ABI-ALBON, one of David's 30 warriors, *2 Sam. 23:31*

ABIASAPH, Levite clan leader, *Ex. 6:24*

ABIATHAR, high priest under David, *1 Sam. 22:20*

ABIDA, grandson of Abraham, son of Midian, *Gen. 25:4*

ABIDAN, leader of Benjamin under Moses, *Num. 1:11*

ABIEL, grandfather of Saul, *1 Sam. 9:1*

2, *1 Chr. 11:32, see* Abi-albon

ABIEZER, head of clan in Manasseh, *Jos. 17:2*

2, one of David's 30 warriors, *2 Sam. 23:27*

ABIGAIL, wife of Nabal and David, *1 Sam. 25:3*

ABIGAL, sister of David, *2 Sam. 17:25*

ABIHAIL, Levite, father of clan leader, *Num. 3:35*

2, wife of clan leader in Judah, *1 Chr. 2:29*

3, clan leader in Gad, father of seven sons, *1 Chr. 5:14*

4, niece of David, *2 Chr. 11:18*

5, father of Esther, *Est. 2:15*

ABIHU, son of Aaron, destroyed by fire, *Ex. 6:23*

ABIHUD, grandson of Benjamin, *1 Chr. 8:3*

ABIJAH, grandson of Benjamin, *1 Chr. 7:8*

2, son of Samuel, corrupt judge, *1 Sam. 8:2*

3, head of division of priests, *1 Chr. 24:10*

4, son of Jeroboam, *1 Kg. 14:1*

ABIJAH 5, king of Judah, *1 Chr. 3:10*

6, *2 Chr. 29:1, see* Abi

7, head of clan of priests under Zerubbabel, *Neh. 12:4*

8, priest, sealed Nehemiah's covenant, *Neh. 10:7*

ABIJAM, *1 Kg. 15:2, see* Abijah 5

ABIMAEL, great-grandson of Shem, *Gen. 10:28*

ABIMELECH, king of Gerar, ally of Abraham, *Gen. 20:2*

ABIMELECH 2, king of Gerar, ally of Isaac, *Gen. 26:1*

KEY TO THE LIST

*S*tarting on this page is a list of the people named in the Old Testament, New Testament, and Apocrypha. Each entry includes a brief description and the first passage in which the name appears. Names in **bold** type indicate articles in the main body of Who's Who in the Bible (pages 7–440). When two or more people bear a single name, they are listed in chronological order insofar as that order can be established. The second and following persons are indicated simply by number unless they are the subject of an article, in which case the name is repeated in **bold** type. When a person is mentioned by two or more names, a cross reference gives the main listing.

ABIMELECH 3, son of Gideon, usurper king, *Jg. 8:31*

4, *see* Achish, *Ps. 34:0*

ABINADAB, keeper of ark, *1 Sam. 7:1*

2, brother of David, *1 Sam. 16:8*

3, son of King Saul, *1 Sam. 31:2*

ABINOAM, father of Barak, *Jg. 4:6*

ABIRAM, rebel against Moses, *Num. 16:1*

2, son of Hiel, builder of Jericho, *1 Kg. 16:34*

ABISHAG, David's nurse, *1 Kg. 1:3*

ABISHAI, David's nephew, warrior, *1 Sam. 26:6*

ABISHALOM, *1 Kg. 15:2, see* Absalom 1

ABISHUA, grandson of Benjamin, *1 Chr. 8:4*

2, great-grandson of Aaron, *1 Chr. 6:4*

ABISHUR, clan leader in Judah, *1 Chr. 2:28*

ABITAL, wife of David, *2 Sam. 3:4*

ABITUB, clan leader in Benjamin, *1 Chr. 8:11*

ABIUD, son of Zerubbabel, *Mt. 1:13*

ABNER, commander of Saul's army, *1 Sam. 14:50*

2, father of an officer for David, *1 Chr. 27:21*

ABRAHAM, patriarch of Israel, *Gen. 11:26*

ABRAM, *Gen. 11:26, see* Abraham

ABSALOM, son of David, rebel, *2 Sam. 3:3*

2, father of general under Jonathan 16, *1 Macc. 11:70*

3, Jewish envoy to Syrians, *2 Macc. 11:17*

ABUBUS, father of Jewish governor of Jericho, *1 Macc. 16:11*

ACHAICUS, Corinthian Christian, *1 Cor. 16:17*

ACHAN, thief killed for taking booty from Jericho, *Jos. 7:1*

ACHAR, *1 Chr. 2:7, see* Achan

ACHBOR, father of king of Edom, *Gen. 36:38*

2, officer of Josiah, *2 Kg. 22:12*

ACHIM, ancestor of Jesus, *Mt. 1:14*

ACHIOR, Ammonite ally of Israel, *Jdt. 5:5*

ACHISH, king of Gath, ally of David, *1 Sam. 21:10*

ACHSAH, daughter of Caleb, *Jos. 15:16*

ADAH, wife of Lamech, *Gen. 4:19*

2, wife of Esau, *Gen. 36:2*

ADAIAH, ancestor of Asaph, *1 Chr. 6:41*

2, Benjaminite clan leader, *1 Chr. 8:21*

3, father of army commander, *2 Chr. 23:1*

4, grandfather of Josiah, *2 Kg. 22:1*

5, clan leader in Judah, *Neh. 11:5*

6, left foreign wife, *Ezra 10:29*

7, left foreign wife, *Ezra 10:39*

8, priest under Nehemiah, *1 Chr. 9:12*

ADALIA, son of Haman, *Est. 9:8*

ADAM, first man, *Gen. 3:17*

ADBEEL, son of Ishmael, *Gen. 25:13*

ADDAR, grandson of Benjamin, *1 Chr. 8:3*

ADDI, ancestor of Jesus, *Lk. 3:28*

ADIEL, father of David's treasurer, *1 Chr. 27:25*

2, clan leader in Simeon, *1 Chr. 4:36*

3, father of priest Maasai, *1 Chr. 9:12*

ADIN, ancestor of returned exiles, *Ezra 2:15*

2, sealed Nehemiah's covenant, *Neh. 10:16*

ADINA, Reubenite warrior for David, *1 Chr. 11:42*

ADLAI, father of Shaphat, David's herder, *1 Chr. 27:29*

ADMATHA, Persian noble, adviser of Ahasuerus, *Est. 1:14*

ADNA, head of priestly house of Harim, *Neh. 12:15*

2, left foreign wife, *Ezra 10:30*

ADNAH, warrior for David from Manasseh, *1 Chr. 12:20*

2, commander for Jehoshaphat, *2 Chr. 17:14*

ADONI-BEZEK, king of Canaanites and Perizzites, *Jg. 1:5*

ADONI-ZEDEK, king of Jerusalem, opposed Joshua, *Jos. 10:1*

ADONIJAH, son of David, 2 Sam. 3:4

2, Levite under Jehoshaphat, *2 Chr. 17:8*

3, sealed Nehemiah's covenant, *Neh. 10:16*

ADONIKAM, ancestor of returned exiles, *Ezra 2:13*

ADONIRAM, head of forced labor, *1 Kg. 4:6*

ADORAM, *2 Sam. 20:24*, see Adoniram

ADRAMMELECH, deity of Sepharvites in Samaria, *2 Kg. 17:31*

2, son of Sennacherib of Assyria, *2 Kg. 19:37*

ADRIEL, husband of Merab, Saul's daughter, *1 Sam. 18:19*

Abimelech, not Saul, was Israel's first king; he ruled three years.

ADUEL, ancestor of Tobit, *Tob. 1:1*

AENEAS, man of Lydda healed by Peter, *Acts 9:33*

AGABUS, Christian prophet, *Acts 11:28*

AGAG, king of Amalek in Balaam's prophecy, *Num. 24:7*

AGAG 2, king of Amalek, killed by Samuel, *1 Sam. 15:8*

AGEE, father of Shammah, David's soldier, *2 Sam. 23:11*

AGIA, wife of Jaddus, *1 Esd. 5:38*

AGRIPPA, *Acts 25:13*, see Herod Agrippa II

AGUR, author of Proverbs 30, *Pr. 30:1*

AHAB, king of Israel, married Jezebel, *1 Kg. 16:28*

2, prophet condemned by Jeremiah, *Jer. 29:21*

AHARAH, *1 Chr. 8:1*, see Ahiram

AHARHEL, clan leader in Judah, *1 Chr. 4:8*

AHASBAI, father of one of David's 30 warriors, *2 Sam. 23:34*

AHASUERUS, king of Persia, married Esther, *Ezra 4:6*

2, father of Darius the Mede, *Dan. 9:1*

AHAZ, great-grandson of Saul, *1 Chr. 8:35*

AHAZ 2, king of Judah, sacrificed son, *2 Kg. 15:38*

AHAZIAH, son of Ahab, king of Israel, *1 Kg. 22:40*

AHAZIAH 2, son of Jehoram, king of Judah, *2 Kg. 8:24*

AHBAN, clan leader of Judah, *1 Chr. 2:29*

AHER, Benjaminite, short for Ahiram, *1 Chr. 7:12*

AHI, clan leader in Gad, *1 Chr. 5:15*

AHIAH, sealed Nehemiah's covenant, *Neh. 10:26*

AHIAM, one of David's 30 warriors, *2 Sam. 23:33*

AHIAN, clan leader in Manasseh, *1 Chr. 7:19*

AHIEZER, leader of Dan under Moses, *Num. 1:12*

2, warrior of Benjamin joined David, *1 Chr. 12:3*

AHIHUD, clan leader in Benjamin, *1 Chr. 8:7*

2, leader of Asher, helped divide land, *Num. 34:27*

AHIJAH, clan leader in Judah, *1 Chr. 2:25*

2, clan leader in Benjamin, *1 Chr. 8:7*

3, priest for Saul, son of Ahitub, *1 Sam. 14:3*

4, one of David's 30 warriors, *1 Chr. 11:36*

5, Levite in charge of temple treasury, *1 Chr. 26:20*

6, secretary for Solomon, *1 Kg. 4:3*

AHIJAH 7, prophet from Shiloh, *1 Kg. 11:29*

8, father of Baasha, *1 Kg. 15:27*

AHIKAM, officer of Josiah, *2 Kg. 22:12*

AHIKAR, nephew of Tobit, *Tob. 1:21*

AHILUD, father of Jehoshaphat, recorder, *2 Sam. 8:16*

AHIMAAZ, father of Saul's wife, Ahinoam, *1 Sam. 14:50*

2, son of Zadok, loyal to David, *2 Sam. 15:27*

3, district governor under Solomon, *1 Kg. 4:15*

AHIMAN, descendant of Anak, Canaanite, *Num. 13:22*

2, Levite, gatekeeper of temple, *1 Chr. 9:17*

AHIMELECH, high priest at Nob, *1 Sam. 21:1*

2, Hittite with David as outlaw, *1 Sam. 26:6*

3, chief priest under David, *1 Chr. 24:3*

AHIMOTH, Levite ancestor of Samuel, *1 Chr. 6:25*

AHINADAB, district governor under Solomon, *1 Kg. 4:14*

AHINOAM, wife of Saul, *1 Sam. 14:50*

AHINOAM 2, wife of David, *1 Sam. 25:43*

AHIO, clan leader in Benjamin, *1 Chr. 8:14*

2, Benjaminite, kinsman of Saul, *1 Chr. 8:31*

3, helped David move ark to Jerusalem, *2 Sam. 6:3*

AHIRA, leader of Naphtali under Moses, *Num. 1:15*

AHIRAM, son of Benjamin, *Num. 26:38*

AHISAMACH, Danite, helped build tabernacle, *Ex. 31:6*

AHISHAHAR, clan leader in Benjamin, *1 Chr. 7:10*

AHISHAR, steward of Solomon's palace, *1 Kg. 4:6*

AHITHOPHEL, adviser to David and Absalom, *2 Sam. 15:12*

AHITUB, priest, grandson of Eli, *1 Sam. 14:3*

2, Levite, grandfather or father of Zadok 1, *2 Sam. 8:17*

3, priest, descendant of Ahitub 2, *1 Chr. 6:11*

AHLAI, daughter of Sheshan of Judah, *1 Chr. 2:31*

2, father of warrior for David, *1 Chr. 11:41*

AHOAH, grandson of Benjamin, *1 Chr. 8:4*

AHOHI, grandfather of warrior for David, *2 Sam. 23:9*

AHUMAI, clan leader in Judah, *1 Chr. 4:2*

AHUZZAM, clan leader in Judah, *1 Chr. 4:6*

AHUZZATH, adviser of Abimelech of Gerar, *Gen. 26:26*

AHZAI, priest in Jerusalem, *Neh. 11:13*

AIAH, Horite, uncle of Esau's wife, *Gen. 36:24*

2, father of Rizpah, Saul's concubine, *2 Sam. 3:7*

AKAN, Horite chief in Esau's time, *Gen. 36:27*

AKKUB, ancestor of Levite gatekeepers, *Ezra 2:42*

2, ancestor of Levite temple servants, *Ezra 2:45*

3, Levite, temple gatekeeper, *1 Chr. 9:17*

4, Levite, assisted Ezra reading Law, *Neh. 8:7*

5, descendant of Zerubbabel, *1 Chr. 3:24*

ALCIMUS, high priest, opposed Maccabees, *1 Macc. 7:5*

ALEMETH, grandson of Benjamin, *1 Chr. 7:8*

2, descendant of Saul and Jonathan, *1 Chr. 8:36*

ALEXANDER THE GREAT, king of Macedon, *1 Macc. 1:1*

ALEXANDER, son of Simon of Cyrene, *Mk. 15:21*

2, member of Sanhedrin with Annas, *Acts 4:6*

3, spokesman for Jews in Ephesus, *Acts 19:33*

4, heretical teacher opposed by Paul, *1 Tim. 1:20*

5, coppersmith who opposed Paul, *2 Tim. 4:14*

Alexander Balas is called Alexander Epiphanes in the Bible.

ALEXANDER BALAS, king of Syria, *1 Macc. 10:1*

ALIAH, *1 Chr. 1:51*, see Alvah

ALIAN, *1 Chr. 1:40*, see Alvan

ALLON, clan leader in Simeon, *1 Chr. 4:37*

ALMODAD, descendant of Shem and of Eber, *Gen. 10:26*

ALPHAEUS, father of Levi the tax collector, *Mk. 2:14*

2, father of James 2, apostle, *Mt. 10:3*

ALVAH, clan chief in Edom, *Gen. 36:40*

ALVAN, ancestor of Horites, *Gen. 36:23*

AMAL, clan leader in Asher, *1 Chr. 7:35*

AMALEK, grandson of Esau, ancestor of Amalekites, *Gen. 36:12*

AMARIAH, Levite, grandson of Kohath, *1 Chr. 23:19*

2, grandfather of Zadok the priest, *1 Chr. 6:7*

3, priest, descendant of Amariah 2, *1 Chr. 6:11*

4, chief priest under Jehoshaphat, *2 Chr. 19:11*

5, Levite, distributed contributions to priests, *2 Chr. 31:15*

Rivals David and Saul each had a wife named Ahinoam; David's was the mother of his first-born son, the lecherous Amnon.

6, ancestor of Zephaniah, *Zeph. 1:1*

7, clan leader in Judah, *Neh. 11:4*

8, left foreign wife, *Ezra 10:42*

9, priest, sealed Nehemiah's covenant, *Neh. 10:3*

AMASA, nephew of David, army commander, *2 Sam. 17:25*

2, opposed enslaving Judahites, *2 Chr. 28:12*

AMASAI, Levite clan leader, Kohathite, *1 Chr. 6:25*

2, chief of David's 30 warriors, *1 Chr. 12:18*

3, priest, trumpeter before ark, *1 Chr. 15:24*

AMASHSAI, priest in Jerusalem under Nehemiah, *Neh. 11:13*

AMASIAH, army commander for Jehoshaphat, *2 Chr. 17:16*

AMAZIAH, Levite, temple musician, *1 Chr. 6:45*

AMAZIAH 2, king of Judah, son of Joash 7, *2 Kg. 12:21*

3, priest at Bethel, opposed Amos, *Am. 7:10*

4, clan leader in Simeon, *1 Chr. 4:34*

AMI, servant of Solomon, *Ezra 2:57*

AMITTAI, father of Jonah the prophet, *2 Kg. 14:25*

AMMIEL, leader of Dan, spy sent into Canaan, *Num. 13:12*

2, father of Machir, ally of David, *2 Sam. 9:4*

3, *1 Chr. 3:5,* see Eliam

4, temple gatekeeper under David, *1 Chr. 26:5*

AMMIHUD, father of Elishama, leader of Ephraim under Moses, *Num. 1:10*

2, father of leader of Simeon under Moses, *Num. 34:20*

3, father of leader of Naphtali under Moses, *Num. 34:28*

4, father of king of Geshur, *2 Sam. 13:37*

5, clan leader in Judah after exile, *1 Chr. 9:4*

AMMINADAB, grandson of Levi, *1 Chr. 6:22*

2, Aaron's father-in-law, *Ex. 6:23*

3, Levite, carried ark for David, *1 Chr. 15:10*

AMMISHADDAI, father of leader of Dan under Moses, *Num. 1:12*

AMMIZABAD, captain in David's bodyguard, *1 Chr. 27:6*

AMNON, clan leader in Judah, *1 Chr. 4:20*

AMNON 2, son of David, raped Tamar, *2 Sam. 3:2*

AMOK, priest under Zerubbabel, *Neh. 12:7*

AMON, *Neh. 7:59,* see Ami

2, governor of Samaria for Ahab, *1 Kg. 22:26*

AMON 3, king of Judah, son of Manasseh, *2 Kg. 21:18*

4, Egyptian deity of Thebes, *Jer. 46:25*

AMOS, prophet from Tekoa, *Am. 1:1*

2, ancestor of Jesus, *Lk. 3:25*

3, *Mt. 1:10,* see Amon 3

AMOZ, father of Isaiah, *2 Kg. 19:2*

AMPLIATUS, Christian at Rome, greeted by Paul, *Rom. 16:8*

AMRAN, father of Moses, Aaron, Miriam, *Ex. 6:18*

2, left foreign wife, *Ezra 10:34*

AMRAPHEL, king of Shinar, fought Abraham, *Gen. 14:1*

AMZI, Levite, clan leader, *1 Chr. 6:46*

2, priest, clan leader in Levi, *Neh. 11:12*

ANAEL, brother of Tobit, *Tob. 1:21*

ANAH, Esau's father-in-law, *Gen. 36:2*

2, Horite chief, son of Seir, *Gen. 36:20*

ANAIAH, Levite, assisted Ezra reading Law, *Neh. 8:4*

ANAK, father of the giant Anakim, *Num. 13:22*

ANAMMELECH, deity of Sepharvites in Samaria, *2 Kg. 17:31*

ANAN, sealed Nehemiah's covenant, *Neh. 10:26*

ANANI, descendant of Zerubbabel, *1 Chr. 3:24*

ANANIAH, ancestor of returned exiles, *Neh. 3:23*

ANANIAS, relative of Tobit, *Tob. 5:12*

2, ancestor of Judith, *Jdt. 8:1*

ANANIAS 3, Damascus Christian, baptized Paul, *Acts 9:10; see Ananias,* page 42

ANANIAS 4, high priest, *Acts 23:2; see* Ananias 2, page 42

ANANIAS 5, Christian, husband of Sapphira, *Acts 5:1; see Ananias 3,* page 42

ANANIEL, ancestor of Tobit, *Tob. 1:1*

ANATH, father of the judge Shamgar, *Jg. 3:31*

ANATHOTH, grandson of Benjamin, *1 Chr. 7:8*

2, sealed Nehemiah's covenant, *Neh. 10:19*

ANDREW, apostle, brother of Peter, *Mt. 4:18*

ANDRONICUS, Syrian governor, executed Onias III, *2 Macc. 4:31*

2, Syrian governor of Gerizim, *2 Macc. 5:23*

3, Paul's kinsman and fellow prisoner, *Rom. 16:7*

ANER, Amorite ally of Abraham, *Gen. 14:13*

ANIAM, clan leader in Manasseh, *1 Chr. 7:19*

ANNA, wife of Tobit, *Tob. 1:9*

ANNA 2, temple prophet, saw infant Jesus, *Lk. 2:36*

ANNAN, *1 Esd. 9:32,* see Harim 4

ANNAS, high priest, father-in-law of Caiaphas, *Lk. 3:2*

ANNIAS, ancestor of returned exiles, *1 Esd. 5:16*

ANNIUTH, *1 Esd. 9:48,* see Bani 9

ANNUNUS, priest under Ezra, *1 Esd. 8:48*

ANTHOTHIJAH, clan leader in Benjamin, *1 Chr. 8:24*

ANTIOCHUS, father of Numenius, Jewish envoy, *1 Macc. 12:16*

2, III, the Great, king of Syria, *1 Macc. 1:10*

ANTIOCHUS IV EPIPHANES, king of Syria, *1 Macc. 1:10*

ANTIOCHUS V EUPATOR, king of Syria, *1 Macc. 3:33*

ANTIOCHUS VI EPIPHANES DIONYSUS, king of Syria, *1 Macc. 11:54*

ANTIOCHUS VII SIDETES, king of Syria, *1 Macc. 15:1*

ANTIPAS, Christian martyr in Pergamum, *Rev. 2:13*

ANTIPATER, Jewish envoy to Rome, *1 Macc. 12:16*

ANUB, clan leader in Judah, *1 Chr. 4:8*

APAME, concubine of Darius I, *1 Esd. 4:29*

APELLES, Roman Christian greeted by Paul, *Rom. 16:10*

APHERRA, servant of Solomon, *1 Esd. 5:34*

APHIAH, Benjaminite ancestor of Saul, *1 Sam. 9:1*

APOLLONIUS, Syrian governor of Coelesyria, *2 Macc. 3:5*

2, chief minister of Antiochus IV, *2 Macc. 4:4*

3, Syrian governor of Samaria, *1 Macc. 3:10*

4, Syrian governor in Palestine, *2 Macc. 12:2*

5, son of Apollonius 1, *1 Macc. 10:69*

APOLLOPHANES, Syrian soldier killed by Jews, *2 Macc. 10:37*

APOLLOS, Christian teacher, ally of Paul, *Acts 18:24*

APOLLYON, angel of the bottomless pit, *Rev. 9:11*

APPAIRM, clan leader in Judah, *1 Chr. 2:30*

APPHIA, Christian in Colossae, greeted by Paul, *Philem. 1:2*

APPHUS, *1 Macc. 2:5,* see Jonathan 16

Christian converts Apollos and Artemas bore names of Greek gods.

AQUILA, Christian, husband of Prisca, *Acts 18:2*

ARA, clan leader in Asher, *1 Chr. 7:38*

ARAD, clan leader in Benjamin, *1 Chr. 8:15*

ARAH, clan leader in Asher, *1 Chr. 7:39*

2, clan leader in exile, *Ezra 2:5*

ARAM, son of Shem, *Gen. 10:22*

2, son of Abraham's nephew Kemuel, *Gen. 22:21*

3, clan leader in Asher, *1 Chr. 7:34*

ARAN, Horite clan leader in Edom, *Gen. 36:28*

ARAUNAH, sold threshing floor to David, *2 Sam. 24:16*

ARBA, ancestor of Anakim, *Jos. 14:15*

ARCHELAUS, *Mt. 2:22, see* Herod Archelaus

Only one woman served
as sole ruler of Israel or Judah:
Athaliah, widow of Jehoram
and mother of Ahaziah.

ARCHIPPUS, Christian at Colossae, cited by Paul, *Col. 4:17*

ARD, son or grandson of Benjamin, *Gen. 46:21*

ARDON, clan leader in Judah, *1 Chr. 2:18*

ARELI, son of Gad, *Gen. 46:16*

ARETAS, king of Nabatean Arabia, *2 Macc. 5:8*

ARETAS 2, king of Nabatean Arabia, *2 Cor. 11:32*

ARIARATHES, king of Cappadocia, *1 Macc. 15:22*

ARIDAI, son of Haman, *Est. 9:9*

ARIDATHA, son of Haman, *Est. 9:8*

ARIEL, envoy of Ezra to get temple servants, *Ezra 8:16*

ARIOCH, king of Ellasar, fought Abraham, *Gen. 14:1*

2, captain of Nebuchadnezzar's guard, *Dan. 2:14*

ARISAI, son of Haman, *Est. 9:9*

ARISTARCHUS, coworker of Paul, from Thessalonica, *Acts 19:29*

ARISTOBULUS, priest, adviser to Ptolemy VII, *2 Macc. 1:10*

2, Christian in Rome, greeted by Paul, *Rom. 16:10*

ARIUS, king of Sparta, *1 Macc. 12:7*

ARMONI, son of Saul and Rizpah, *2 Sam. 21:8*

ARNA, *2 Esd. 1:2, see* Zerahiah

ARNAN, descendant of Zerubbabel, *1 Chr. 3:21*

ARNI, ancestor of Jesus, great-grandson of Judah, *Lk. 3:33*

AROD, son of Gad, *Num. 26:17*

AROM, ancestor of clan under Zerubbabel, *1 Esd. 5:16*

ARPACHSHAD, son of Shem, grandson of Noah, *Gen. 10:22*

ARPHAXAD, *Lk. 3:36, see* Arpachshad

2, king of the Medes, *Jdt. 1:1*

ARSACES IV, king of Parthia, *1 Macc. 14:2*

ARSINOE III, sister and wife of Ptolemy IV, *3 Macc. 1:1*

ARTAXERXES I, son of Xerxes I, king of Persia, *Ezra 4:7*

ARTEMAS, Christian coworker of Paul, *Tit. 3:12*

ARTEMIS, Greek goddess, *Acts 19:24*

ARZA, steward of Elah, *1 Kg. 16:9*

ASA, king of Judah, son of Abijah 5, *1 Kg. 15:8*

2, Levite, ancestor of Berechiah, *1 Chr. 9:16*

ASAHEL, David's nephew, brother of Joab, *2 Sam. 2:18*

2, Levite under Jehoshaphat, *2 Chr. 17:8*

3, Levite, overseer of tithes under King Hezekiah, *2 Chr. 31:13*

4, father of Jonathan, Ezra's opponent, *Ezra 10:15*

ASAIAH, Levite, helped David bring ark, *1 Chr. 6:30*

2, prince in Simeon, *1 Chr. 4:36*

3, Josiah's servant, sent to Huldah, *2 Kg. 22:12*

4, *1 Chr. 9:5, see* Maaseiah 16

ASAIAS, *1 Esd. 9:32, see* Isshijah

ASAPH, ancestor of Levite gatekeepers, *1 Chr. 26:1*

ASAPH 2, Levite, chief musician for David, *1 Chr. 6:39*

3, father of Joah, King Hezekiah's recorder, *2 Kg. 18:18*

4, ancestor of Levites, *1 Chr. 9:15*

5, royal forest keeper in Judah, *Neh. 2:8*

ASAREL, clan leader in Judah, *1 Chr. 4:16*

ASENATH, Egyptian wife of Joseph, *Gen. 41:45*

ASHARELAH, son of Asaph 2, temple musician, *1 Chr. 25:2*

ASHBEL, son of Benjamin, *Gen. 46:21*

ASHER, son of Jacob and Zilpah, *Gen. 30:13*

ASHERAH, Canaanite goddess, *Dt. 16:21*

ASHHUR, son of Caleb, founder of Tekoa, *1 Chr. 2:24*

ASHIMA, deity of Hamathites in Samaria, *2 Kg. 17:30*

ASHKENAZ, great-grandson of Noah, *Gen. 10:3*

ASHPENAZ, Babylonian official in charge of Daniel, *Dan. 1:3*

ASHTORETH, Canaanite goddess of fertility, *1 Kg. 11:5*

ASHURBANIPAL, king of Assyria, *see* Osnapper

ASHVATH, clan leader in Asher, *1 Chr. 7:33*

ASIBIAS, left foreign wife, *1 Esd. 9:26*

ASIEL, clan leader in Simeon, *1 Chr. 4:35*

2, scribe for Ezra, copied Scriptures, *2 Esd. 14:24*

ASMODEUS, evil demon in book of Tobit, *Tob. 3:8*

ASNAH, Levite ancestor of temple servants, *Ezra 2:50*

ASPATHA, son of Haman, *Est. 9:7*

ASRIEL, son of Manasseh, *Num. 26:31*

ASSHUR, son of Shem, ancestor of Assyrians, *Gen. 10:22*

ASSIR, Levite, son of Korah, *Ex. 6:24*

2, Levite, great-grandson of Assir 1, *1 Chr. 6:23*

ASTYAGES, last king of Media, *Bel 1:1*

ASUR, Levite ancestor of temple servants, *1 Esd. 5:31*

ASYNCRITUS, Christian in Rome, greeted by Paul, *Rom. 16:14*

ATARAH, wife of Jerahmeel of Judah, *1 Chr. 2:25*

ATER, ancestor of temple gatekeepers, *Ezra 2:16*

2, sealed Nehemiah's covenant, *Neh. 10:17*

ATHAIAH, Judahite under Nehemiah, *Neh. 11:4*

ATHALIAH, clan leader in Benjamin, *1 Chr. 8:26*

ATHALIAH 2, daughter of Ahab, queen of Judah, *2 Kg. 8:26*

3, clan leader of Elamites after exile, *Ezra 8:7*

ATHENOBIUS, envoy of Antiochus VII, *1 Macc. 15:28*

ATHLAI, left foreign wife, *Ezra 10:28*

ATTAI, clan leader in Judah, *1 Chr. 2:35*

2, warrior of Gad, joined David, *1 Chr. 12:11*

3, son of Rehoboam, *2 Chr. 11:20*

ATTALUS II, king of Pergamum, *1 Macc. 15:22*

ATTHARATES, Persian governor, *1 Esd. 9:49*

ATTHARIAS, Persian governor, *1 Esd. 5:40*

AUGUSTUS, first emperor of Rome, *Lk. 2:1*

AURANUS, leader of foolish revolt against Syria, *2 Macc. 4:40*

AVARAN, *1 Macc. 2:5, see* Eleazar 10

AZAL, left foreign wife, *1 Esd. 9:34*

AZALIAH, father of Josiah's secretary, *2 Kg. 22:3*

AZANIAH, father of one who sealed Nehemiah's covenant, *Neh. 10:9*

AZAREL, Korahite warrior, joined David, *1 Chr. 12:6*

2, David's officer over Dan, *1 Chr. 27:22*

3, Levite, son of Heman the musician, *1 Chr. 25:18*

4, father of priest after exile, *Neh. 11:13*

5, left foreign wife, *Ezra 10:41*

6, priest, trumpeter when Jerusalem's walls dedicated, *Neh. 12:36*

AZARIAH, clan leader in Judah, *1 Chr. 2:8*

2, Levite, ancestor of Samuel, *1 Chr. 6:36*

3, priest, ancestor of Zadok 2 and Ezra, *1 Chr. 6:11*

4, chief priest, son of Zadok 1, *1 Kg. 4:2*

5, Solomon's chief officer, *1 Kg. 4:5*

6, priest, grandson of Zadok 1, *1 Chr. 6:9*

7, clan leader in Judah, *1 Chr. 2:38*

8, prophet under King Asa of Judah, *2 Chr. 15:1*

9, chief priest, son of Johanan 3, *1 Chr. 6:10*

10, son of Jehoshaphat 4, *2 Chr. 21:2*

11, son of Jehoshaphat 4, *2 Chr. 21:2*

12, son of Jeroham 5, helped overthrow Queen Athaliah, *2 Chr. 23:1*

13, son of Obed 5, helped overthrow Queen Athaliah, *2 Chr. 23:1*

14, *2 Kg. 14:21, see* Uzziah 3

15, chief priest, opposed King Uzziah, *2 Chr. 26:17*

16, Levite, father of Joel 11 under Hezekiah, *2 Chr. 29:12*

17, opposed enslaving Judahites, *2 Chr. 28:12*

18, Levite, helped purify temple for King Hezekiah, *2 Chr. 29:12*

19, chief priest under King Hezekiah, *2 Chr. 31:10*

20, priest, grandfather of Ezra, *Ezra 7:3*

21, *Dan. 1:7, see* Abednego

22, enemy of Jeremiah, *Jer. 42:1*

23, Jew who returned with Zerubbabel, *Neh. 7:7*

24, Levite, assisted Ezra reading Law, *Neh. 8:7*

25, stood with Ezra reading Law, *1 Esd. 9:43*

26, *1 Esd. 9:21, see* Uzziah 6

27, helped Nehemiah repair Jerusalem, *Neh. 3:23*

28, priest, clan leader in Jerusalem, *1 Chr. 9:11*

29, priest, sealed Nehemiah's covenant, *Neh. 10:2*

30, prince of Judah under Nehemiah, *Neh. 12:33*

31, commander under Judas Maccabeus, *1 Macc. 5:18*

AZARIAS, name taken by angel Raphael, *Tob. 5:12*

AZARU, ancestor of returned exiles, *1 Esd. 5:15*

AZAZ, clan leader in Reuben, *1 Chr. 5:8*

AZAZEL, symbolic demon who receives scapegoat, *Lev. 16:8*

AZAZIAH, father of an officer for David, *1 Chr. 27:20*

2, played lyre for ark, *1 Chr. 15:21*

3, Levite over tithes under King Hezekiah, *2 Chr. 31:13*

AZBUK, father of Nehemiah 3, *Neh. 3:16*

AZEL, descendant of King Saul, *1 Chr. 8:37*

AZETAS, clan leader with Zerubbabel, *1 Esd. 5:15*

AZGAD, ancestor of clan with Zerubbabel, *Ezra 2:12*

2, sealed Nehemiah's covenant, *Neh. 10:15*

AZIEL, played lyre for ark, *1 Chr. 15:20*

AZIZA, left foreign wife, *Ezra 10:27*

The second most common name in the Bible is Azariah.

AZMAVETH, father of two warriors for David, *1 Chr. 12:3*

2, one of David's 30 warriors, *2 Sam. 23:31*

3, David's chief of treasuries, *1 Chr. 27:25*

4, descendant of King Saul, *1 Chr. 9:42*

AZOR, ancestor of Jesus, *Mt. 1:13*

AZRIEL, father of David's officer over Naphtali, *1 Chr. 27:19*

2, clan leader in Manasseh, *1 Chr. 5:24*

3, father of officer sent to seize Jeremiah, *Jer. 36:26*

AZRIKAM, commander of Ahaz' palace, *2 Chr. 28:7*

2, son of Azel, *1 Chr. 8:38*

3, Levite in Jerusalem after exile, *1 Chr. 9:14*

4, descendant of Zerubbabel, *1 Chr. 3:23*

AZUBAH, wife of Caleb, *1 Chr. 2:18*

2, mother of King Jehoshaphat, *1 Kg. 22:42*

AZZAN, father of leader of Issachar under Moses, *Num. 34:26*

AZZUR, father of Hananiah 6, false prophet, *Jer. 28:1*

2, father of Jaazariah, seen by Ezekiel in vision, *Ezek. 11:1*

3, sealed Nehemiah's covenant, *Neh. 10:17*

B

BAAL, Canaanite god, *Num. 25:3*

2, uncle of King Saul, *1 Chr. 8:30*

3, descendant of Reuben, *1 Chr. 5:5*

BAAL-BERITH, deity Israel worshiped after Gideon, *Jg. 8:33*

BAAL-HANAN, king of Edom, *Gen. 36:38*

2, David's overseer of olive trees, *1 Chr. 27:28*

BAALIS, king of Ammonites, *Jer. 40:14*

BAALSAMUS, stood with Ezra reading Law, *1 Esd. 9:43*

BAAL-ZEBUB, god of Ekron in time of Elijah, *2 Kg. 1:2*

BAANA, district governor under Solomon, *1 Kg. 4:12*

2, district governor under Solomon, *1 Kg. 4:16*

3, father of Zadok 6, *Neh. 3:4*

BAANAH, father of one of David's 30 warriors, *2 Sam. 23:29*

2, assassin of Ish-bosheth, *2 Sam. 4:2*

3, leader who returned with Zerubbabel, *Ezra 2:2*

4, sealed Nehemiah's covenant, *Neh. 10:27*

BAARA, wife of Shaharaim of Benjamin, *1 Chr. 8:8*

BAASEIAH, Levite ancestor of Asaph the musician, *1 Chr. 6:40*

BAASHA, son of Ahijah 8, king of Israel, *1 Kg. 15:16*

BACCHIDES, Syrian official, *1 Macc. 7:8*

BACENOR, officer for Judas Maccabeus, *2 Macc. 12:35*

BAEAN, ancestor of hostile tribe, *1 Macc. 5:4*

BAGOAS, aide to Holofernes, *Jdt. 12:11*

BAITERUS, ancestor of clan under Zerubbabel, *1 Esd. 5:17*

BAKBAKKAR, Levite in Jerusalem after exile, *1 Chr. 9:15*

BAKBUK, ancestor of temple servants, *Ezra 2:51*

BAKBUKIAH, Levite, returned with Zerubbabel, *Neh. 12:9*

2, Levite, guarded temple storehouses, *Neh. 12:25*

3, Levite in Jerusalem after exile, *Neh. 11:17*

BALAAM, Mesopotamian prophet, blessed Israel, *Num. 22:5*

BALADAN, father of Merodach-Baladan of Babylon, *2 Kg. 20:12*

BALAK, king of Moab, hired Balaam, *Num. 22:2*

BANI, ancestor of Ethan, David's musician, *1 Chr. 6:46*

2, one of David's 30 warriors, *2 Sam. 23:36*

3, ancestor of clan with Zerubbabel, *Ezra 2:10*

4, ancestor of clan that returned with Ezra, *1 Esd. 8:36*

5, ancestor of clan that left foreign wives, *Ezra 10:34*

6, ancestor of Uthai 1, *1 Chr. 9:4*

7, Levite, present when Ezra read Law, *Neh. 9:4*

8, Levite, present when Ezra read Law, *Neh. 9:4*

9, Levite, assisted Ezra reading Law, *Neh. 8:7*

10, father of Rehum, Levite builder, *Neh. 3:17*

11, sealed Nehemiah's covenant, *Neh. 10:14*

12, father of overseer of Levites, *Neh. 11:22*

13, Levite, sealed Nehemiah's covenant, *Neh. 10:13*

BANNAS, ancestor of Levite clan, *1 Esd. 5:26*

BARABBAS, insurrectionist, released instead of Jesus, *Mt. 27:16*

BARACHEL, father of Elihu, who argued with Job, *Job 32:2*

BARACHIAH, father of Zechariah, mentioned by Jesus, *Mt. 23:35*

BARAK, general for Deborah, *Jg. 4:6*

BARIAH, descendant of Zerubbabel, *1 Chr. 3:22*

BAR-JESUS, Jewish prophet, opposed Paul, *Acts 13:6*

BARKOS, ancestor of Levite temple servants, *Ezra 2:53*

BARNABAS, Christian leader, coworker of Paul, *Acts 4:36*

BARODIS, ancestor of clan with Zerubbabel, *1 Esd. 5:34*

BARSABBAS, *Acts 1:23, see* Joseph Barsabbas

2, *Acts 15:22, see* Judas Barsabbas

BARTACUS, father of Apame, Darius' concubine, *1 Esd. 4:29*

BARTHOLOMEW, apostle of Jesus, *Mt. 10:3*

BARTIMAEUS, blind man of Jericho, *Mk. 10:46*

BARUCH, son of Neriah, aide to Jeremiah, *Jer. 32:12*

2, clan leader in Judah after exile, *Neh. 11:5*

3, helped Nehemiah build Jerusalem's walls, *Neh. 3:20*

4, priest, sealed Nehemiah's covenant, *Neh. 10:6*

BARZILLAI, father of Adriel, Saul's son-in-law, *2 Sam. 21:8*

2, elderly Gileadite, aided David, *2 Sam. 17:27*

3, ancestor of a priestly clan, *Ezra 2:61*

BASEMATH, wife of Esau, daughter of Ishmael, *Gen. 36:3*

2, *Gen. 26:34, see* Adah 2

3, daughter of Solomon, *1 Kg. 4:15*

BATHSHEBA, wife of Uriah and David, mother of Solomon, *2 Sam. 11:3*

BATHSHUA, Canaanite wife of Judah, *1 Chr. 2:3*

2, *1 Chr. 3:5, see* Bathsheba

BAVVAI, Levite, repaired Jerusalem wall, *Neh. 3:18*

BAZLITH, *Neh. 7:54, see* Bazluth

BAZLUTH, ancestor of Levite temple servants, *Ezra 2:52*

BEALIAH, kinsman of Saul, joined David, *1 Chr. 12:5*

BEBAI, ancestor of clan with Zerubbabel, *Ezra 2:11*

2, sealed Nehemiah's covenant, *Neh. 10:15*

BECHER, son of Benjamin, *Gen. 46:21*

2, son of Ephraim, *Num. 26:35*

BECORATH, ancestor of King Saul, *1 Sam. 9:1*

BEDAD, father of Hadad, king of Edom, *Gen. 36:35*

BEDAN, clan leader in Manasseh, *1 Chr. 7:17*

BEDEIAH, left foreign wife, *Ezra 10:35*

BEELIADA, son of David, *1 Chr. 14:7*

BEELZEBUL, prince of demons, *Mt. 10:25*

BEERA, clan leader in Asher, *1 Chr. 7:37*

BEERAH, chief in Reuben, exiled by Tiglath-Pileser, *1 Chr. 5:6*

About 1,000 names appear for the first time in 1 Chronicles.

BEERI, Hittite, father of Esau's wife Judith, *Gen. 26:34*

2, father of Hosea the prophet, *Hos. 1:1*

BEL, name of Marduk, god of Babylon, *Is. 46:1*

BELA, son of Benjamin, *Gen. 46:21*

2, king of Edom, *Gen. 36:32*

3, clan leader in Reuben, *1 Chr. 5:8*

BELIAL, name for Satan, *2 Cor. 6:15*

BELNUUS, left foreign wife, *1 Esd. 9:31*

BELSHAZZAR, king of Babylon, *Dan. 5:1*

BELTESHAZZAR, Babylonian name of Daniel, *Dan. 1:7*

BELTETHMUS, Persian official in Samaria, *1 Esd. 2:16*

BEN-ABINADAB, district governor under Solomon, *1 Kg. 4:11*

BENAIAH, father of Jehoiada, David's counselor, *1 Chr. 27:34*

BENAIAH 2, captain of David's bodyguard, Solomon's commander, *2 Sam. 8:18*

3, one of David's 30 warriors, *2 Sam. 23:30*

4, Levite, musician on the harp, *1 Chr. 15:18*

5, priest, blew trumpet before the ark, *1 Chr. 15:24*

6, Levite, descendant of Asaph 2, *2 Chr. 20:14*

7, clan leader in Simeon, *1 Chr. 4:36*

8, Levite over tithes under King Hezekiah, *2 Chr. 31:13*

9, father of Pelatiah 2, *Ezek. 11:1*

10, left foreign wife, *Ezra 10:25*

11, left foreign wife, *Ezra 10:30*

12, left foreign wife, *Ezra 10:35*

13, left foreign wife, *Ezra 10:43*

BEN-AMMI, son of Lot, ancestor of Ammonites, *Gen. 19:38*

BEN-DEKER, district governor under Solomon, *1 Kg. 4:9*

BEN-GEBER, district governor under Solomon, *1 Kg. 4:13*

BEN-HADAD, king of Syria, son of Tabrimmon, *1 Kg. 15:18*

2, king of Syria, opponent of Ahab, *1 Kg. 20:1*

3, king of Syria, opponent of Jehoahaz 2, *2 Kg. 13:3*

BEN-HAIL, prince under King Jehoshaphat, *2 Chr. 17:7*

BEN-HANAN, clan leader in Judah, *1 Chr. 4:20*

BEN-HESED, district governor under Solomon, *1 Kg. 4:10*

BEN-HUR, district govenor under Solomon, *1 Kg. 4:8*

BENINU, Levite, sealed Nehemiah's covenant, *Neh. 10:13*

BENJAMIN, youngest son of Jacob, *Gen. 35:18*

2, great-grandson of Benjamin 1, *1 Chr. 7:10*

3, left foreign wife, *Ezra 10:32*

4, helped repair Jerusalem's wall, *Neh. 3:23*

BENO, Levite, of the sons of Jaaziah, *1 Chr. 24:26*

BEN-ONI, *Gen. 35:18*, see Benjamin 1

BEN-ZOHETH, clan leader in Judah, *1 Chr. 4:20*

BEOR, father of Bela, first king of Edom, *Gen. 36:32*

2, father of Balaam, Mesopotamian prophet, *Num. 22:5*

BERA, king of Sodom, aided by Abraham, *Gen. 14:2*

BERACAH, Benjaminite who joined David, *1 Chr. 12:3*

BERAIAH, clan leader in Benjamin, *1 Chr. 8:21*

BERECHIAH, father of Asaph, David's musician, *1 Chr. 6:39*

2, Levite, gatekeeper for the ark, *1 Chr. 15:23*

3, Ephraimite, opposed enslaving Judahites, *2 Chr. 28:12*

4, father of Zechariah the prophet, *Zech. 1:1*

5, son of Zerubbabel, *1 Chr. 3:20*

6, father of Meshullam 16, *Neh. 3:4*

7, Levite in Jerusalem after exile, *1 Chr. 9:16*

BERED, grandson or descendant of Ephraim, *1 Chr. 7:20*

BERI, clan leader in Asher, *1 Chr. 7:36*

BERIAH, son of Asher, *Gen. 46:17*

2, son of Ephraim, *1 Chr. 7:23*

3, Benjaminite clan leader in Aijalon, *1 Chr. 8:13*

4, Levite descendant of Gershom, *1 Chr. 23:10*

BERNICE, daughter of Herod Agrippa I, *Acts 25:13*

BESAI, ancestor of Levite temple servants, *Ezra 2:49*

BESODEIAH, father of Meshullam, who repaired Jerusalem, *Neh. 3:6*

BETHUEL, father of Rebekah, nephew of Abraham, *Gen. 22:22*

BEZAI, ancestor of clan with Zerubbabel, *Ezra 2:17*

2, sealed Nehemiah's covenant, *Neh. 10:18*

BEZALEL, craftsman, designer of the tabernacle, *Ex. 31:2*

2, left foreign wife, *Ezra 10:30*

BEZER, clan leader in Asher, *1 Chr. 7:37*

BICHRI, father of Sheba, rebel against David, *2 Sam. 20:1*

BIDKAR, aide of King Jehu, *2 Kg. 9:25*

BIGTHA, eunuch, chamberlain for King Ahasuerus, *Est. 1:10*

BIGTHAN, eunuch, conspired against King Ahasuerus, *Est. 2:21*

BIGTHANA, *Est. 6:2*, see Bigthan

BIGVAI, clan leader with Zerubbabel, *Ezra 2:2*

2, sealed Nehemiah's covenant, *Neh. 10:16*

BILDAD, the Shuhite, friend of Job, *Job 2:11*

BILGAH, head of a division of priests, *1 Chr. 24:14*

2, priest with Zerubbabel, *Neh. 12:5*

BILGAI, priest, sealed Nehemiah's covenant, *Neh. 10:8*

BILHAH, concubine of Jacob, mother of Dan and Naphtali, *Gen. 29:29*

BILHAN, clan chief of Horites in Seir, *Gen. 36:27*

2, son of Jediael 1, grandson of Benjamin, *1 Chr. 7:10*

BILSHAN, clan leader with Zerubbabel, *Ezra 2:2*

BIMHAL, clan leader in Asher, *1 Chr. 7:33*

BINEA, descendant of King Saul and Jonathan 3, *1 Chr. 8:37*

BINNUI, *Neh. 7:15*, see Bani 3

2, Levite with Zerubbabel, *Neh. 12:8*

3, father of Levite Noadiah, *Ezra 8:33*

4, father of Jews with foreign wives, *Ezra 10:38*

5, left foreign wife, *Ezra 10:30*

6, left foreign wife, *1 Esd. 9:34*

7, helped repair Jerusalem's walls, *Neh. 3:24*

BIRSHA, king of Gomorrah, aided by Abraham, *Gen. 14:2*

BIRZAITH, great-grandson of Asher, *1 Chr. 7:31*

BISHLAM, wrote letter to Artaxerxes against Jews, *Ezra 4:7*

BITHIAH, Egyptian woman married to Mered of Judah, *1 Chr. 4:17*

BIZTHA, eunuch, chamberlain for King Ahasuerus, *Est. 1:10*

BLASTUS, chamberlain for Herod Agrippa I, *Acts 12:20*

BOANERGES, sons of thunder, nickname of James 1 and John 6, *Mk. 3:17*

Boaz may have been the son of a harlot, Rahab.

BOAZ, Ruth's husband, great-grandfather of David, *Ru. 2:1*

BOCHERU, descendant of King Saul and Jonathan 3, *1 Chr. 8:38*

BOHAN, son of Reuben, *Jos. 15:6*

BORITH, see Bukki 2, *2 Esd. 1:2*

BUKKI, leader of Dan, helped divide land, *Num. 34:22*

2, descendant of Aaron, *1 Chr. 6:5*

BUKKIAH, Levite, son of Heman the musician, *1 Chr. 25:4*

BUNAH, descendant of Judah, *1 Chr. 2:25*

BUNNI, ancestor of Levites after exile, *Neh. 11:15*

2, Levite, present when Ezra read Law, *Neh. 9:4*

3, sealed Nehemiah's covenant, *Neh. 10:15*

BUZ, son of Nahor 2 and nephew of Abraham, *Gen. 22:21*

2, clan leader in Gad, *1 Chr. 5:14*

BUZI, father of the prophet Ezekiel, *Ezek. 1:3*

C

CAESAR, surname of Roman emperors, *Mt. 22:17*

CAIAPHAS, high priest, son-in-law of Annas, *Mt. 26:3*

CAIN, son of Adam, murderer of Abel, *Gen. 4:1*

CAINAN, *Lk. 3:37*, see Kenan

2, great-grandson of Noah, ancestor of Jesus, *Lk. 3:36*

CALCOL, wise man surpassed by Solomon, *1 Kg. 4:31*

CALEB, great-grandson of Judah, *1 Chr. 2:18*

CALEB 2, leader of Judah, spy sent into Canaan, *Num. 13:6*

CALLISTHENES, Syrian officer, burned temple gates, *2 Macc. 8:33*

CANAAN, grandson of Noah, son of Ham, *Gen. 9:18*

CANDACE, title of the queen of Ethiopia, *Acts 8:27*

CARABASION, left foreign wife, *1 Esd. 9:34*

CARKAS, eunuch, chamberlain for King Ahasuerus, *Est. 1:10*

CARMI, son of Reuben, *Gen. 46:9*

2, father of Achan, who stole Jericho booty, *Jos. 7:1*

3, son of Judah, *1 Chr. 4:1*

CARPUS, Christian in Troas, coworker of Paul, *2 Tim. 4:13*

CARSHENA, Persian noble, adviser of Ahasuerus, *Est. 1:14*

CATHUA, ancestor of Levite temple servants, *1 Esd. 5:30*

CENDEBEUS, Syrian army commander in chief, *1 Macc. 15:38*

CEPHAS, *Jn. 1:42*, see Peter

CHABRIS, city magistrate in time of Judith, *Jdt. 6:15*

CHAEREAS, Ammonite opponent of Judas Maccabeus, *2 Macc. 10:32*

CHALPI, father of Judas, a supporter of Jonathan, *1 Macc. 11:70*

CHAREA, ancestor of Levite temple servants, *1 Esd. 5:32*

CHARMIS, city magistrate in time of Judith, *Jdt. 6:15*

CHEDORLAOMER, king of Elam, fought Abraham, *Gen. 14:1*

CHELAL, left foreign wife, *Ezra 10:30*

CHELUB, clan leader in Judah, *1 Chr. 4:11*

2, father of Ezri, an officer of David, *1 Chr. 27:26*

CHELUBAI, *1 Chr. 2:9*, see Caleb 1,

CHELUHI, left foreign wife, *Ezra 10:35*

CHEMOSH, god of the Moabites, *Num. 21:29*

CHENAANAH, great-grandson of Benjamin, *1 Chr. 7:10*

2, father of Ahab's prophet Zedekiah, *1 Kg. 22:11*

CHENANI, Levite, present when Ezra read Law, *Neh. 9:4*

CHENANIAH, Levite, leader of musicians, *1 Chr. 15:22*

2, Levite, officer for David, *1 Chr. 26:29*

CHERAN, Horite chief, son of Dishon, *Gen. 36:26*

CHESED, nephew of Abraham, *Gen. 22:22*

CHEZIB, ancestor of Levite temple servants, *1 Esd. 5:31*

CHILEAB, son of David and Abigail, *2 Sam. 3:3*

CHILION, son of Naomi and Elimelech, *Ru. 1:2*

CHIMHAM, relative of Barzillai, ally of David, *2 Sam. 19:37*

CHISLON, father of leader of Benjamin under Moses, *Num. 34:21*

CHLOE, Christian woman, *1 Cor. 1:11*

CHORBE, ancestor of clan with Zerubbabel, *1 Esd. 5:12*

CHOSAMAEUS, *1 Esd. 9:32*, see Simon 1

CHRIST, *Mt. 1:1*, see Jesus Christ

CHUZA, steward of Herod Antipas, husband of Joanna, *Lk. 8:3*

CLAUDIA, Christian in Rome, greets Timothy, *2 Tim. 4:21*

CLAUDIUS, emperor of Rome, *Acts 11:28*

CLAUDIUS LYSIAS, *Acts 23:26*, see Lysias 2

CLEMENT, Christian at Philippi, coworker of Paul, *Phil. 4:3*

CLEOPAS, disciple, saw resurrected Jesus, *Lk. 24:18*

CLEOPATRA II, sister and wife of Ptolemy VI, *Ad. Est. 11:1*

CLEOPATRA III, daughter of Ptolemy VI, *1 Macc. 10:57*

CLOPAS, husband of Mary, disciple of Jesus, *Jn. 19:25*

Some 3,424 people are listed in the Bible; they bear 2,087 names.

COLHOZEH, ancestor of clan in Judah, *Neh. 11:5*

2, father of Shallum, who repaired Jerusalem, *Neh. 3:15*

CONANIAH, Levite over tithes under King Hezekiah, *2 Chr. 31:12*

2, Levite chief under Josiah 1, *2 Chr. 35:9*

CONIAH, *Jer. 22:24*, see Jehoiachin

CORNELIUS, centurion, first Gentile Christian, *Acts 10:1*

COSAM, ancestor of Jesus, *Lk. 3:28*

COZBI, Midianite woman killed by Phinehas, *Num. 25:15*

CRATES, commander of Cyprian troops, *2 Macc. 4:29*

CRESCENS, coworker of Paul, went to Galatia, *2 Tim. 4:10*

CRISPUS, Corinth synagogue official, baptized by Paul, *Acts 18:8*

CUSH, grandson of Noah, son of Ham, *Gen. 10:6*

2, Benjaminite, enemy of David, *Ps. 7:0*

CUSHAN-RISHATHAIM, king of Mesopotamia, *Jg. 3:8*

CUSHI, ancestor of Jehudi, who took Jeremiah's scroll, *Jer. 36:14*

2, father of Zephaniah the prophet, *Zeph. 1:1*

CUTHA, ancestor of Levite temple servants, *1 Esd. 5:32*

CYRUS II, king of Persia, *2 Chr. 36:22*

D

DABRIA, scribe, wrote books for Ezra, *2 Esd. 14:24*

DAGON, Philistine god of grain, *Jg. 16:23*

DALPHON, son of Haman, *Est. 9:7*

DAMARIS, Athenian woman converted by Paul, *Acts 17:34*

DAN, son of Jacob and Bilhah, *Gen. 30:6*

DANIEL, ancient wise man, *Ezek. 14:14*

2, *1 Chr. 3:1*, see Chileab

DANIEL 3, exiled Jewish wise man and prophet, *Dan. 1:6*

4, priest, clan leader under Ezra, *Ezra 8:2*

DARA, *1 Chr. 2:6*, see Darda

DARDA, wise man surpassed by Solomon, *1 Kg. 4:31*

DARIUS I, king of Persia, *Ezra 4:5*

DARIUS THE MEDE, succeeded Belshazzar, *Dan. 5:31*

2, II Nothus, king of Persia, *Neh. 12:22*

DARKON, ancestor of clan of Solomon's servants, *Ezra 2:56*

DATHAN, Reubenite, rebel against Moses, *Num. 16:1*

DAVID, son of Jesse, king of Israel, *Ru. 4:17*

DEBIR, king of Eglon, defeated by Joshua, *Jos. 10:3*

DEBORAH, nurse of Rebekah, *Gen. 35:8*

DEBORAH 2, prophet and judge of Israel, *Jg. 4:4*

3, grandmother of Tobit, *Tob. 1:8*

DEDAN, great-grandson of Noah, *Gen. 10:7*

2, grandson of Abraham and Keturah, *Gen. 25:3*

DELAIAH, head of a division of priests, *1 Chr. 24:18*

2, prince under Jehoiakim 1, *Jer. 36:12*

3, ancestor of Levitical clan, *Ezra 2:60*

4, father of Shemaiah, under Nehemiah, *Neh. 6:10*

5, descendant of David and Zerubbabel, *1 Chr. 3:24*

DELILAH, Philistine wife of Samson, *Jg. 16:4*

DEMAS, coworker of Paul, later deserted him, *Col. 4:14*

DEMETRIUS, a silversmith in Ephesus, *Acts 19:24*

DEMETRIUS I SOTER, king of Syria, *1 Macc. 7:1*

DEMETRIUS II NICATOR, king of Syria, *1 Macc. 10:67*

2, Christian praised by John, *3 Jn. 1:12*

DEMOPHON, Syrian general, harassed Jews, *2 Macc. 12:2*

DEUEL, father of Eliasaph of Gad, also called Reuel, *Num. 1:14*

DIBLAIM, father of Gomer, wife of Hosea, *Hos. 1:3*

DIBRI, father of Shelomith, whose son blasphemed, *Lev. 24:11*

DIKLAH, son of Joktan, descendant of Noah, *Gen. 10:27*

DINAH, daughter of Jacob and Leah, *Gen. 30:21*

DIONYSIUS, the Areopagite, converted by Paul in Athens, *Acts 17:34*

DIONYSUS, Greek god of wine, *2 Macc. 6:7*

DIOTREPHES, church leader, opponent of John, *3 Jn. 1:9*

DIPHATH, *1 Chr. 1:6, see Riphath*

DISHAN, Horite chief, son of Seir, *Gen. 36:21*

DISHON, Horite chief, son of Seir, *Gen. 36:21*

2, Horite chief, Esau's brother-in-law, *Gen. 36:25*

DODAI, *1 Chr. 27:4, see Dodo 2*

DODANIM, grandson of Japheth, *Gen. 10:4*

DODAVAHU, father of Eliezer 6, *2 Chr. 20:37*

DODO, grandfather of Tola the judge, *Jg. 10:1*

2, father of Eleazar 3, *2 Sam. 23:9*

3, father of Elhanan, David's warrior, *2 Sam. 23:24*

DOEG, Edomite, Saul's agent against priests at Nob, *1 Sam. 21:7*

DORCAS, Christian of Joppa, healed by Peter, *Acts 9:36*

DORYMENES, father of Ptolemy Macron, Syrian general, *1 Macc. 3:38*

DOSITHEUS, apostate Jew who saved Ptolemy IV, *3 Macc. 1:3*

2, captain under Judas Maccabeus, *2 Macc. 12:19*

3, soldier under Judas Maccabeus, *2 Macc. 12:35*

4, Levite who brought book of Esther to Egypt, *Ad. Est. 11:1*

DRIMYLUS, father of Dositheus 1, *3 Macc. 1:3*

DRUSILLA, daughter of Herod Agrippa I, wife of Felix, *Acts 24:24*

DUMAH, son of Ishmael, *Gen. 25:14*

E/F

EBAL, 1 Chr. 1:22, see Obal

2, Horite chief, son of Shobal, *Gen. 36:23*

EBED, father of Gaal of Shechem, *Jg. 9:26*

2, clan leader who returned with Ezra, *Ezra 8:6*

EBED-MELECH, Ethiopian eunuch who rescued Jeremiah, *Jer. 38:7*

EBER, ancestor of Hebrews, son of Shelah, *Gen. 10:21*

2, clan leader in Gad, *1 Chr. 5:13*

3, clan chief in Benjamin, *1 Chr. 8:12*

4, clan chief in Benjamin, *1 Chr. 8:22*

5, head of priestly family, *Neh. 12:20*

EBIASAPH, *1 Chr. 6:23, see Abiasaph*

EDEN, Levite who aided King Hezekiah's reform, *2 Chr. 29:12*

EDER, clan chief in Benjamin, *1 Chr. 8:15*

2, Levite in time of David, *1 Chr. 23:23*

EDNA, mother-in-law of Tobias, *Tob. 7:2*

EDOM, *Gen. 25:30, see Esau*

EGLAH, wife of David, mother of Ithream, *2 Sam. 3:5*

EGLON, king of Moab, enemy of Israel, *Jg. 3:12*

EHI, *Gen. 46:21, see Ahiram*

EHUD, descendant of Benjamin, *1 Chr. 7:10*

EHUD 2, judge, slew Eglon of Moab, *Jg. 3:15*

EKER, clan leader in Judah, *1 Chr. 2:27*

ELA, father of Shimei 12, *1 Kg. 4:18*

ELAH, clan chief in Edom, *Gen. 36:41*

2, son of Caleb the spy, *1 Chr. 4:15*

ELAH 3, king of Israel, son of Baasha, *1 Kg. 16:6*

4, father of King Hoshea of Israel, *2 Kg. 15:30*

5, Benjaminite in Jerusalem, *1 Chr. 9:8*

ELAM, son of Shem, *Gen. 10:22*

2, temple gatekeeper, *1 Chr. 26:3*

3, clan leader in Benjamin, *1 Chr. 8:24*

4, ancestor of clan with Zerubbabel, *Ezra 2:7*

5, ancestor of clan with Zerubbabel, *Ezra 2:31*

6, sealed Nehemiah's covenant, *Neh. 10:14*

7, priest under Nehemiah, *Neh. 12:42*

ELASAH, took Jeremiah's letter to Babylon, *Jer. 29:3*

2, priest, left foreign wife, *Ezra 10:22*

ELBERITH, *see Baal-berith, Jg. 9:46*

ELDAAH, son of Midian, grandson of Abraham, *Gen. 25:4*

ELDAD, elder in wilderness, prophesied with Medad, *Num. 11:26*

ELEAD, Ephraimite, killed by men of Gath, *1 Chr. 7:21*

ELEADAH, clan leader in Ephraim, *1 Chr. 7:20*

ELEASAH, clan leader in Judah, *1 Chr. 2:39*

2, clan leader in Benjamin, *1 Chr. 8:37*

ELEAZAR, clan leader in Levi, *1 Chr. 23:21*

ELEAZAR 2, son of Aaron, high priest, *Ex. 6:23*

3, one of David's three mighty men, *2 Sam. 23:9*

4, son of Abinadab, in charge of ark, *1 Sam. 7:1*

5, priest, received temple gold from Ezra, *Ezra 8:33*

6, left foreign wife, *Ezra 10:25*

7, priest under Nehemiah, *Neh. 12:42*

8, ancestor of Jesus, great-grandfather of Joseph, *Mt. 1:15*

9, scribe, Jewish martyr, *2 Macc. 6:18*

10, brother of Judas Maccabeus, *1 Macc. 2:5*

11, father of Jason, emmisary to Rome, *1 Macc. 8:17*

ELHANAN, warrior for David, slew Philistine giant, *2 Sam. 21:19*

2, one of David's 30 warriors, *2 Sam. 23:24*

ELI, priest at Shiloh, reared Samuel, *1 Sam. 1:3*

Only in post-biblical times did Jews name their children for Bible heroes and heroines.

ELIAB, father of rebels against Moses, *Num. 16:1*

2, leader of Zebulun under Moses, *Num. 1:9*

3, great-grandfather of Samuel, *1 Chr. 6:27*

4, eldest brother of David, *1 Sam. 16:6*

5, Gadite warrior with David, *1 Chr. 12:9*

6, Levite temple musician, *1 Chr. 15:18*

7, ancestor of Judith, *Jdt. 8:1*

ELIADA, *2 Sam. 5:16, see Beeliada*

2, father of Rezon, king of Syria, *1 Kg. 11:23*

3, commander under King Jehoshaphat, *2 Chr. 17:17*

ELIAHBA, one of David's 30 warriors, *2 Sam. 23:32*

ELIAKIM, ancestor of Jesus, *Lk. 3:30*

2, palace governor for King Hezekiah, *2 Kg. 18:18*

3, *2 Kg. 23:34, see King Jehoiakim*

4, priest under Nehemiah, *Neh. 12:41*

5, grandson of Zerubbabel, ancestor of Jesus, *Mt. 1:13*

ELIALIS, left foreign wife, *1 Esd. 9:34*

ELIAM, warrior for David, father of Bathsheba, *2 Sam. 11:3*

ELIASAPH, leader of Gad under Moses, *Num. 1:14*

2, Levite leader of Gershonites under Moses, *Num. 3:24*

ELIASHIB, head of a division of priests, *1 Chr. 24:12*

2, priest in the time of Ezra, *Ezra 10:6*

3, Levite, left foreign wife, *Ezra 10:24*

4, left foreign wife, *Ezra 10:27*

5, left foreign wife, *Ezra 10:36*

6, high priest under Nehemiah, *Neh. 3:1*

7, clan leader in Judah, *1 Chr. 3:24*

ELIASIS, left foreign wife, *1 Esd. 9:34*

ELIATHAH, Levite, son of Heman the musician, *1 Chr. 25:4*

ELIDAD, leader of Benjamin, helped divide land, *Num. 34:21*

ELIEHOENAI, Levite gatekeeper, *1 Chr. 26:3*

2, clan leader, with Ezra, *Ezra 8:4*

ELIEL, clan leader in Manasseh, *1 Chr. 5:24*

2, *1 Chr. 6:34, see Eliab 3*

3, clan leader in Benjamin, *1 Chr. 8:20*

4, clan leader in Benjamin, *1 Chr. 8:22*

5, warrior for David, *1 Chr. 11:46*

6, warrior for David, *1 Chr. 11:47*

7, Gadite warrior for David, *1 Chr. 12:11*

8, Levite, helped bring ark to Jerusalem, *1 Chr. 15:9*

9, Levite under Hezekiah, *2 Chr. 31:13*

ELIENAI, clan leader in Benjamin, *1 Chr. 8:20*

ELIEZER, servant of Abraham, *Gen. 15:2*

2, grandson of Benjamin, *1 Chr. 7:8*

3, second son of Moses, *Ex. 18:4*

4, priest, blew trumpet before ark, *1 Chr. 15:24*

5, David's officer over Reuben, *1 Chr. 27:16*

6, prophet against King Jehoshaphat, *2 Chr. 20:37*

7, ancestor of Jesus, *Lk. 3:29*

8, sent by Ezra to find Levites, *Ezra 8:16*

9, priest, left foreign wife, *Ezra 10:18*

10, Levite, left foreign wife, *Ezra 10:23*

11, left foreign wife, *Ezra 10:31*

ELIHOREPH, secretary for Solomon, *1 Kg. 4:3*

ELIHU, the Buzite, conversed with Job, *Job 32:2*

2, *1 Sam. 1:1*, see Eliab 3

3, *1 Chr. 27:18*, see Eliab 4

4, warrior for David, *1 Chr. 12:20*

5, Levite gatekeeper, *1 Chr. 26:7*

ELIJAH, the Tishbite, prophet, *1 Kg. 17:1*

2, clan leader in Benjamin, *1 Chr. 8:27*

3, ancestor of Judith, *Jdt. 8:1*

4, priest, left foreign wife, *Ezra 10:21*

5, left foreign wife, *Ezra 10:26*

ELIKA, one of David's 30 warriors, *2 Sam. 23:25*

ELIMELECH, husband of Naomi, *Ru. 1:2*

ELIOENAI, grandson of Benjamin, *1 Chr. 7:8*

2, clan leader in Simeon, *1 Chr. 4:36*

3, priest, left foreign wife, *Ezra 10:22*

4, left foreign wife, *Ezra 10:27*

5, priest under Nehemiah, *Neh. 12:41*

6, clan leader in Judah, *1 Chr. 3:23*

ELIPHAL, *1 Chr. 11:35*, see Eliphelet 1

ELIPHAZ, the Temanite, friend of Job, *Job 2:11*

2, son of Esau and Adah, *Gen. 36:4*

ELIPHELEHU, Levite, played lyre before ark, *1 Chr. 15:18*

ELIPHELET, one of David's 30 warriors, *2 Sam. 23:34*

2, son of David, *1 Chr. 3:6*

3, son of David, *2 Sam. 5:16*

4, descendant of Saul and Jonathan, *1 Chr. 8:39*

5, returned to Jerusalem with Ezra, *Ezra 8:13*

6, left foreign wife, *Ezra 10:33*

ELISHA, prophet, follower of Elijah, *1 Kg. 19:16*

ELISHAH, great-grandson of Noah through Japheth, *Gen. 10:4*

ELISHAMA, leader of Ephraim under Moses, *Num. 1:10*

2, *1 Chr. 3:8*, see Elishua

3, son of David, *2 Sam. 5:16*

4, priest under King Jehoshaphat, *2 Chr. 17:8*

5, clan leader in Judah, *1 Chr. 2:41*

6, noble of Judah, grandfather of assassin of Gedaliah, *2 Kg. 25:25*

7, secretary for King Jehoiakim, *Jer. 36:12*

ELISHAPHAT, helped overthrow Queen Athaliah, *2 Chr. 23:1*

ELISHEBA, wife of Aaron, *Ex. 6:23*

ELISHUA, son of David, *2 Sam. 5:15*

ELIUD, ancestor of Jesus, *Mt. 1:14*

ELIZABETH, wife of Zechariah, mother of John the Baptist, *Lk. 1:5*

ELIZAPHAN, *Num. 3:30*, see Elzaphan

2, leader of Zebulun, helped divide land, *Num. 34:25*

ELIZUR, leader of Reuben under Moses, *Num. 1:5*

ELKANAH, Levite, grandson of Korah, *Ex. 6:24*

2, Levite, ancestor of Samuel, *1 Chr. 6:26*

3, father of Samuel, *1 Sam. 1:1*

4, warrior for David, *1 Chr. 12:6*

5, Levite, gatekeeper for ark, *1 Chr. 15:23*

6, minister for King Ahaz, *2 Chr. 28:7*

7, Levite, grandfather of Berechiah 7, *1 Chr. 9:16*

ELKIAH, ancestor of Judith, *Jdt. 8:1*

ELMADAM, ancestor of Jesus, *Lk. 3:28*

ELNAAM, father of two of David's warriors, *1 Chr. 11:46*

ELNATHAN, aide to King Jehoiakim, grandfather of King Jehoiachin, *2 Kg. 24:8*

2, sent by Ezra to find Levites, *Ezra 8:16*

3, sent by Ezra to find Levites, *Ezra 8:16*

4, sent by Ezra to find Levites, *Ezra 8:16*

ELON the Hittite, father-in-law of Esau, *Gen. 26:34*

2, son of Zebulun, *Gen. 46:14*

3, judge in Zebulun, *Jg. 12:11*

ELPAAL, clan leader in Benjamin, *1 Chr. 8:11*

ELPELET, *1 Chr. 14:5*, see Eliphelet 2

ELUZAI, warrior for David from Benjamin, *1 Chr. 12:5*

ELYMAS, *Acts 13:6*, see Bar-Jesus

ELZABAD, warrior for David from Gad, *1 Chr. 12:12*

2, Levite gatekeeper in temple, *1 Chr. 26:7*

ELZAPHAN, Levite clan leader under Moses, *Ex. 6:22*

EMADABUN, Levite clan leader under Ezra, *1 Esd. 5:58*

EMATHIS, *1 Esd. 9:29*, see Athlai

EMMANUEL, *Mt. 1:23*, see Immanuel

ENAN, leader of Naphtali under Moses, *Num. 1:15*

ENOCH, son of Cain, *Gen. 4:17*

ENOCH 2, son of Jared, father of Methuselah, *Gen. 5:18*

ENOS, *Lk. 3:38*, see Enosh

ENOSH, grandson of Adam through Seth, *Gen. 4:26*

EPAENETUS, Christian in Rome, greeted by Paul, *Rom. 16:5*

EPAPHRAS, coworker of Paul, *Col. 1:7*

EPAPHRODITUS, coworker of Paul from Philippi, *Phil. 2:25*

EPHAH, son of Midian, grandson of Abraham, *Gen. 25:4*

2, concubine of Caleb, *1 Chr. 2:46*

3, clan leader in Judah, *1 Chr. 2:47*

EPHAI, father of military leaders after Exile, *Jer. 40:8*

EPHER, son of Midian, grandson of Abraham, *Gen. 25:4*

2, clan leader in Judah, *1 Chr. 4:17*

3, clan leader in Manasseh, *1 Chr. 5:24*

EPHLAL, clan leader in Judah, *1 Chr. 2:37*

EPHOD, father of leader of Manasseh under Moses, *Num. 34:23*

EPHRAIM, son of Joseph and Asenath, *Gen. 41:52*

EPHRATH, *1 Chr. 2:19*, see Ephrathah

EPHRATHAH, wife of Hezron and Caleb, *1 Chr. 2:24*

EPHRON, a Hittite, sold land to Abraham, *Gen. 23:8*

EPIPHANES, *1 Macc. 1:10*, see Antiochus IV Epiphanes

ER, eldest son of Judah, *Gen. 38:3*

2, grandson of Judah, *1 Chr. 4:21*

3, ancestor of Jesus, *Lk. 3:28*

The Bible's shortest names—Er and Ox—also have two letters in their original Hebrew or Greek.

ERAN, grandson of Ephraim, *Num. 26:36*

ERASTUS, coworker of Paul, sent to Macedonia, *Acts 19:22*

2, Christian, city treasurer of Corinth, *Rom. 16:23*

3, coworker of Paul, possibly the same as Erastus 1, *2 Tim. 4:20*

ERI, son of Gad, *Gen. 46:16*

ESARHADDON, king of Assyria, *2 Kg. 19:37*

ESAU, son of Isaac, brother of Jacob, *Gen. 25:25*

ESDRIS, commander under Judas Maccabeus, *2 Macc. 12:36*

ESHBAAL, *1 Chr. 8:33*, see Ish-bosheth

ESHBAN, Horite chief, son of Dishon, *Gen. 36:26*

ESHCOL, Amorite, aided Abraham in battle, *Gen. 14:13*

ESHEK, descendant of Saul, *1 Chr. 8:39*

ESHTEMOA, clan leader in Judah, *1 Chr. 4:17*

2, clan leader in Judah, *1 Chr. 4:19*

ESHTON, clan leader in Judah, *1 Chr. 4:11*

ESLI, ancestor of Jesus, *Lk. 3:25*

ESTHER, Jewish wife of King Ahasuerus, *Est. 2:7*

ETAM, clan leader in Judah, *1 Chr. 4:3*

ETHAN, grandson of Judah, *1 Chr. 2:6*

2, Levite, ancestor of Asaph, *1 Chr. 6:42*

3, sage and psalmist, surpassed by Solomon, *1 Kg. 4:31*

4, Levite, temple musician, *1 Chr. 6:44*

ETHANUS, scribe for Ezra, *2 Esd. 14:24*

ETHBAAL, king of Sidon, father of Jezebel, *1 Kg. 16:31*

ETHNAN, clan leader in Judah, *1 Chr. 4:7*

ETHNI, Levite, ancestor of Asaph, *1 Chr. 6:41*

EUBULUS, Christian in Rome, *2 Tim. 4:21*

EUERGETES, *Sir. Prologue*, see Ptolemy 4

EUMENES, king of Pergamum, *1 Macc. 8:8*

EUNICE, mother of Timothy, *2 Tim. 1:5*

EUODIA, leading Christian woman at Philippi, *Phil. 4:2*

EUPATOR, *1 Macc. 6:17*, see Antiochus V Eupator

EUPOLEMUS, emissary to Rome from Judas Maccabeus, *1 Macc. 8:17*

EUTYCHUS, Christian youth, healed by Paul, *Acts 20:9*

EVE, first woman, wife of Adam, *Gen. 3:20*

EVI, king of Midian killed by Israelites, *Num. 31:8*

EVIL-MERODACH, king of Babylon, *2 Kg. 25:27*

EZBAI, father of soldier for David, *1 Chr. 11:37*

EZBON, son of Gad, *Gen. 46:16*

2, grandson of Benjamin, *1 Chr. 7:7*

EZEKIEL, prophet during Babylonian exile, *Ezek. 1:3*

EZER, Horite chief, son of Seir, *Gen. 36:21*

2, son of Ephraim, killed by men of Gath, *1 Chr. 7:21*

3, clan leader in Judah, *1 Chr. 4:4*

4, warrior for David from Gad, *1 Chr. 12:9*

5, Levite, repaired Jerusalem, *Neh. 3:19*

6, priest under Nehemiah, *Neh. 12:42*

EZORA, father of men who left foreign wives, *1 Esd. 9:34*

EZRA, priest, returned with Zerubbabel, *Neh. 12:1*

EZRA 2, priest and scribe, *Ezra 7:1*

EZRAH, clan leader in Judah, *1 Chr. 4:17*

EZRI, overseer of farm labor for David, *1 Chr. 27:26*

FELIX, Roman procurator of Judea, *Acts 23:24*

FESTUS, Roman procurator of Judea, *Acts 24:27*

FORTUNATUS, Corinthian Christian, emissary to Paul, *1 Cor. 16:17*

G

GAAL, led rebellion against Abimelech in Shechem, *Jg. 9:26*

GABAEL, ancestor of Tobit, *Tob. 1:1*

2, poor Jew helped by Tobit, *Tob. 1:14*

GABATHA, eunuch of King Artaxerxes, *Ad. Est. 12:1*

GABBAI, Benjaminite in Jerusalem, *Neh. 11:8*

GABRIAS, brother or father of Gabael, *Tob. 1:14*

GABRIEL, angel, *Dan. 8:16*

GAD, son of Jacob and Zilpah, *Gen. 30:11*

GAD 2, prophet who advised David, *1 Sam. 22:5*

GADDI, leader of Manasseh, spy sent into Canaan, *Num. 13:11*

2, *1 Macc. 2:2*, see John 3

GADDIEL, leader of Zebulun, spy sent into Canaan, *Num. 13:10*

GADI, father of King Menahem of Israel, *2 Kg. 15:14*

GAHAM, nephew of Abraham, *Gen. 22:24*

GAHAR, ancestor of temple servants, *Ezra 2:47*

GAIUS, coworker of Paul from Macedonia, *Acts 19:29*

2, coworker of Paul from Derbe, *Acts 20:4*

3, Corinthian Christian, host to Paul, *Rom. 16:23*

4, Christian addressed in 3 John, *3 Jn. 1:1*

GALAL, Levite clan leader, *1 Chr. 9:16*

2, Levite in Jerusalem after exile, *1 Chr. 9:15*

One of five biblical names contains part of the word Yahweh.

GALLIO, Roman proconsul of Achaia, *Acts 18:12*

GAMAEL, *1 Esd. 8:29*, see Daniel 4

GAMALIEL, leader of Manasseh under Moses, *Num. 1:10*

GAMALIEL 2, leading Jewish teacher of the Law, *Acts 5:34*

GAMUL, head of a division of priests, *1 Chr. 24:17*

GAREB, one of David's 30 warriors, *2 Sam. 23:38*

GAS, ancestor of temple servants, *1 Esd. 5:34*

GATAM, grandson of Esau, *Gen. 36:11*

GAZEZ, son of Caleb, *1 Chr. 2:46*

2, grandson of Caleb, *1 Chr. 2:46*

GAZZAM, ancestor of temple servants, *Ezra 2:48*

GEBER, district governor under Solomon, *1 Kg. 4:19*

GEDALIAH, Levite, son of Heman the musician, *1 Chr. 25:3*

2, grandfather of the prophet Zephaniah, *Zeph. 1:1*

3, official, imprisoned Jeremiah in cistern, *Jer. 38:1*

GEDALIAH 4, governor of Judea for Babylon, *2 Kg. 25:22*

5, priest, left foreign wife, *Ezra 10:18*

GEDOR, clan leader in Judah, *1 Chr. 4:4*

2, clan leader in Judah, *1 Chr. 4:18*

3, clan leader in Benjamin, *1 Chr. 8:31*

GEHAZI, servant of Elisha, *2 Kg. 4:12*

GEMALLI, father of spy for Moses, *Num. 13:12*

GEMARIAH, official of King Jehoiakim, helped Baruch, *Jer. 36:10*

2, emissary of King Zedekiah to Babylon, *Jer. 29:3*

GENUBATH, son of Hadad the Edomite, *1 Kg. 11:20*

GERA, son of Benjamin, *Gen. 46:21*

2, grandson of Benjamin, *1 Chr. 8:3*

3, clan leader in Benjamin, *1 Chr. 8:7*

4, father of Ehud the judge, *Jg. 3:15*

5, father of Shimei, who cursed David, *2 Sam. 16:5*

GERSHOM, son of Moses and Zipporah, *Ex. 2:22*

2, Levite, returned with Ezra, *Ezra 8:2*

GERSHON, son of Levi, *Gen. 46:11*

GESHAN, clan leader in Judah, *1 Chr. 2:47*

GESHEM, Arab opponent of Nehemiah, *Neh. 2:19*

GETHER, grandson of Shem, *Gen. 10:23*

GEUEL, leader of Gad, spy sent into Canaan, *Num. 13:15*

GIBBAR, ancestor of Jews with Zerubbabel, *Ezra 2:20*

GIBEA, grandson of Caleb in Judah, *1 Chr. 2:49*

GIDDALTI, Levite, son of Heman the musician, *1 Chr. 25:4*

GIDDEL, ancestor of temple servants, *Ezra 2:56*

2, ancestor of temple servants, *Ezra 2:47*

GIDEON, judge, *Jg. 6:11*

GIDEONI, father of Abidan, leader of Benjamin, *Num. 1:11*

GILALAI, priest, musician under Nehemiah, *Neh. 12:36*

GILEAD, grandson of Manasseh, *Num. 26:29*

2, father of Jephthah the judge, *Jg. 11:1*

3, clan leader in Gad, *1 Chr. 5:14*

GINATH, father of Tibni, opponent of Omri, *1 Kg. 16:21*

GINNETHOI, *Neh. 12:4*, see Ginnethon

GINNETHON, priest, returned with Zerubbabel, *Neh. 12:16*

2, priest, sealed Nehemiah's covenant, *Neh. 10:6*

GISHPA, Levite over temple servants, *Neh. 11:21*

GOD, *Gen. 1:1*

GOG, clan leader in Reuben, *1 Chr. 5:4*

GOG 2, prince of Meshech and Tubal, *Ezek. 38:2*

GOLIATH, Philistine giant killed by David, *1 Sam. 17:4*

GOMER, son of Japheth, grandson of Noah, *Gen. 10:2*

GOMER 2, wife of the prophet Hosea, *Hos. 1:3*

GORGIAS, Syrian general, *1 Macc. 3:38*

GOTHOLIAH, father of Jeshaiah, who returned with Ezra, *1 Esd. 8:33*

GOTHONIEL, father of Bethulia magistrate, *Jdt. 6:15*

GUNI, son of Naphtali, *Gen. 46:24*

2, clan leader in Gad, *1 Chr. 5:15*

H

HAAHASHTARI, clan leader in Judah, *1 Chr. 4:6*

HABAIAH, ancestor of priests under Ezra, *Ezra 2:61*

HABAKKUK, prophet in Judea, *Hab. 1:1*

HABAZZINIAH, grandfather of Jaazaniah the Rechabite, *Jer. 35:3*

HACALIAH, father of Nehemiah, *Neh. 1:1*

HACHMONI, father of Jehiel, attendant of David, *1 Chr. 27:32*

HADAD, grandson of Abraham through Ishmael, *Gen. 25:15*

2, king of Edom, *Gen. 36:35*

3, king of Edom, *1 Chr. 1:50*

HADAD 4, Edomite, escaped slaughter of Edomites, *1 Kg. 11:14*

HADADEZER, Aramean king of Zobah, defeated by David, *2 Sam. 8:3*

HADADRIMMON, thunder deity worshiped at Megiddo, *Zech. 12:11*

HADAR, *Gen. 36:39, see Hadad 3*

HADASSAH, *Est. 2:7, see Esther*

HADLAI, clan leader in Ephraim, *2 Chr. 28:12*

HADORAM, son of Joktan, descendant of Noah, *Gen. 10:27*

2, son of King Tou of Hamath, *1 Chr. 18:10*

3, *2 Chr. 10:18, see Adoniram*

HAGAB, ancestor of temple servants with Zerubbabel, *Ezra 2:46*

HAGABA, *Neh. 7:48, see Hagabah*

HAGABAH, ancestor of temple servants, *Ezra 2:45*

HAGAR, Sarah's Egyptian maid, mother of Abraham's son Ishmael, *Gen. 16:1*

HAGGAI, prophet in Judea, *Ezra 5:1*

HAGGEDOLIM, father of Zabdiel the priest, *Neh. 11:14*

HAGGI, son of Gad, *Gen. 46:16*

HAGGIAH, Levite, clan leader, *1 Chr. 6:30*

HAGGITH, wife of David, mother of Adonijah, *2 Sam. 3:4*

HAGRI, father of one of David's 30 warriors, *1 Chr. 11:38*

HAKKATAN, father of one who returned with Ezra, *Ezra 8:12*

HAKKOZ, head of a division of priests, *1 Chr. 24:10*

2, ancestor of clan of priests, *Ezra 2:61*

3, ancestor of one who worked under Nehemiah, *Neh. 3:4*

HAKUPHA, ancestor of temple servants, *Ezra 2:51*

HALLOHESH, official in Jerusalem under Nehemiah, *Neh. 3:12*

HAM, son of Noah, *Gen. 5:32*

HAMAN, Persian noble, enemy of Jews, *Est. 3:1*

HAMMATH, ancestor of Rechabites, *1 Chr. 2:55*

HAMMEDATHA, father of Haman, *Est. 3:1*

HAMMOLECHETH, sister of Gilead, *1 Chr. 7:18*

HAMMUEL, clan leader in Simeon, *1 Chr. 4:26*

HAMMURABI, king of Babylon, *see Amraphel*

HAMOR, ruler of Shechem in the time of Jacob, *Gen. 33:19*

HAMRAN, *1 Chr. 1:41, see Hemdan*

HAMUL, grandson of Judah through Perez, *Gen. 46:12*

HAMUTAL, wife of King Josiah, mother of Jehoahaz and Zedekiah, *2 Kg. 23:31*

HANA, *1 Esd. 5:30, see Hanan 4*

HANAMEL, Jeremiah's cousin, sold field to the prophet, *Jer. 32:7*

HANAN, one of David's 30 warriors, *1 Chr. 11:43*

2, clan leader in Benjamin, *1 Chr. 8:23*

3, priest, son of Igdaliah, *Jer. 35:4*

4, ancestor of temple servants, *Ezra 2:46*

5, clan leader in Benjamin, *1 Chr. 8:38*

6, Levite, helped Ezra read the Law, *Neh. 8:7*

7, Levite, sealed Nehemiah's covenant, *Neh. 10:10*

8, sealed Nehemiah's covenant, *Neh. 10:22*

9, sealed Nehemiah's covenant, *Neh. 10:26*

10, Levite, assistant temple treasurer, *Neh. 13:13*

HANANI, Levite, son of Heman the musician, *1 Chr. 25:4*

2, prophet, imprisoned by Asa, *1 Kg. 16:1*

3, priest, left foreign wife, *Ezra 10:20*

4, brother of Nehemiah, *Neh. 1:2*

5, priest, temple musician, *Neh. 12:36*

HANANIAH, Levite, son of Heman the musician, *1 Chr. 25:4*

2, clan leader in Benjamin, *1 Chr. 8:24*

3, commander under King Uzziah, *2 Chr. 26:11*

4, grandfather of soldier who arrested Jeremiah, *Jer. 37:13*

5, father of an official for Jehoiakim, *Jer. 36:12*

HANANIAH 6, prophet from Gibeon, opponent of Jeremiah, *Jer. 28:1*

7, *Dan. 1:6, see Shadrach*

8, son of Zerubbabel, *1 Chr. 3:19*

9, priest, head of clan, *Neh. 12:12*

10, priest, returned with Ezra, *1 Esd. 8:48*

11, Levite, left foreign wife, *Ezra 10:28*

12, perfumer, helped rebuild Jerusalem, *Neh. 3:8*

13, helped rebuild Jerusalem, *Neh. 3:30*

14, governor of Jerusalem under Nehemiah, *Neh. 7:2*

15, sealed Nehemiah's covenant, *Neh. 10:23*

16, priest under Nehemiah, *Neh. 12:41*

HANNAH, wife of Elkanah 3, mother of Samuel, *1 Sam. 1:2*

HANNIEL, leader of Manasseh, helped divide land, *Num. 34:23*

2, chief in Asher, *1 Chr. 7:39*

HANOCH, grandson of Abraham through Midian, *Gen. 25:4*

2, eldest son of Reuben, *Gen. 46:9*

HANUN, king of Ammon, foe of David, *2 Sam. 10:1*

2, repaired gate of Jerusalem, *Neh. 3:13*

3, repaired Jerusalem's wall *Neh. 3:30*

HAPPIZZEZ, head of a division of priests, *1 Chr. 24:15*

HARAN, brother of Abraham, father of Lot, *Gen. 11:26*

2, great-grandson of Levi, *1 Chr. 23:9*

3, son of Caleb, *1 Chr. 2:46*

HARBONA, eunuch, chamberlain for Ahasuerus, *Est. 1:10*

HAREPH, clan leader in Judah, *1 Chr. 2:51*

HARHAIAH, father of Jerusalem repairer, *Neh. 3:8*

HARHAS, grandfather of husband of Huldah the prophetess, *2 Kg. 22:14*

HARHUR, ancestor of temple servants, *Ezra 2:51*

HARIM, head of a division of priests, *1 Chr. 24:8*

2, ancestor of family with Zerubbabel, *Ezra 2:32*

3, father of Jerusalem repairer, *Neh. 3:11*

4, sealed Nehemiah's covenant, *Neh. 10:27*

HARIPH, ancestor of family with Zerubbabel, *Neh. 7:24*

2, sealed Nehemiah's covenant, *Neh. 10:19*

HARNEPHER, clan leader in Asher, *1 Chr. 7:36*

HAROEH, clan leader in Judah, *1 Chr. 2:52*

HARSHA, ancestor of temple servants, *Ezra 2:52*

HARUM, clan leader in Judah, *1 Chr. 4:8*

HARUMAPH, father of Jerusalem repairer, *Neh. 3:10*

HARUZ, grandfather of King Amon, *2 Kg. 21:19*

HASADIAH, son of Zerubbabel, *1 Chr. 3:20*

HASHABIAH, Levite, ancestor of Ethan the musician, *1 Chr. 6:45*

2, official for David, *1 Chr. 26:30*

3, David's officer over Levi, *1 Chr. 27:17*

4, son of Jeduthun (Ethan), *1 Chr. 25:3*

5, Levite official for Josiah, *2 Chr. 35:9*

6, Levite clan leader, *1 Chr. 9:14*

7, grandfather of Levite under Nehemiah, *Neh. 11:22*

8, head of priestly division after exile, *Neh. 12:21*

9, Levite, returned with Ezra, *Ezra 8:19*

10, left foreign wife, *Ezra 10:25*

11, Levite, helped repair Jerusalem, *Neh. 3:17*

12, Levite, sealed Nehemiah's covenant, *Neh. 10:11*

HASHABNAH, sealed Nehemiah's covenant, *Neh. 10:25*

HASHABNEIAH, father of wall repairer, *Neh. 3:10*

2, Levite at Ezra's great confession, *Neh. 9:5*

HASHBADDANAH, Levite, aided Ezra in reading Law, *Neh. 8:4*

HASHEM, one of David's 30 warriors, *1 Chr. 11:34*

HASHUBAH, son of Zerubbabel, *1 Chr. 3:20*

HASHUM, ancestor of family with Zerubbabel, *Ezra 2:19*

2, Levite, aided Ezra in reading Law, *Neh. 8:4*

3, sealed Nehemiah's covenant, *Neh. 10:18*

HASRAH, *2 Chr. 34:22, see Harhas*

2, ancestor of family with Zerubbabel, *1 Esd. 5:31*

HASSENAAH, ancestor of wall repairers, *Neh. 3:3*

HASSENUAH, ancestor of Jerusalemite after exile, *1 Chr. 9:7*

HASSHUB, father of Levite in Jerusalem, *1 Chr. 9:14*

2, repaired Jerusalem's wall, *Neh. 3:11*

3, repaired Jerusalem's wall, *Neh. 3:23*

4, sealed Nehemiah's covenant, *Neh. 10:23*

HASSOPHERETH, ancestor of temple servants, *Ezra 2:55*

HASUPHA, ancestor of temple servants, *Ezra 2:43*

HATHACH, eunuch of King Ahasuerus, attended on Esther, *Est. 4:5*

HATHATH, son of Othniel the judge, *1 Chr. 4:13*

HATIPHA, ancestor of temple servants, *Ezra 2:54*

HATITA, ancestor of temple gatekeepers, *Ezra 2:42*

HATTIL, ancestor of families after exile, *Ezra 2:57*

HATTUSH, priest, returned with Zerubbabel, *Neh. 12:2*

2, descendant of Zerubbabel, *1 Chr. 3:22*

3, from Judah, returned with Ezra, *Ezra 8:2*

4, helped repair Jerusalem, *Neh. 3:10*

5, priest, sealed Nehemiah's covenant, *Neh. 10:4*

HAVILAH, great-grandson of Noah through Ham, *Gen. 10:7*

2, son of Joktan, descendant of Shem, *Gen. 10:29*

HAZAEL, assassin of Ben-hadad 2 and king of Syria, *1 Kg. 19:15*

HAZAIAH, ancestor of leader in Judah after exile, *Neh. 11:5*

HAZARMAVETH, son of Joktan, descendant of Shem, *Gen. 10:26*

HAZIEL, priest, head of priestly order, *1 Chr. 23:9*

HAZO, nephew of Abraham, *Gen. 22:22*

HAZZELELPONI, sister of clan leaders in Judah, *1 Chr. 4:3*

HEBER, grandson of Asher, *Gen. 46:17*

HEBER 2, husband of Jael, *Jg. 4:11*

3, clan leader in Benjamin, *1 Chr. 8:17*

4, clan leader in Judah, *1 Chr. 4:18*

HEBRON, grandson of Levi, cousin of Moses, *Ex. 6:18*

2, grandson of Caleb, *1 Chr. 3:42*

HEGAI, eunuch of Ahasuerus, in charge of harem, *Est. 2:3*

HEGLAM, *1 Chr. 8:7, see Gera 3*

HELAH, wife of Ashhur, clan leader in Judah, *1 Chr. 4:5*

HELDAI, *1 Chr. 27:15, see Heleb*

2, Jew who brought gold and silver from Babylon, *Zech. 6:10*

HELEB, one of David's 30 warriors, a commander, *2 Sam. 23:29*

HELED, *1 Chr. 11:30, see Heleb*

HELEK, clan leader in Manasseh, *Num. 26:30*

HELEM, clan leader in Asher, *1 Chr. 7:35*

HELEZ, one of David's 30 warriors, *2 Sam. 23:26*

2, clan leader in Judah, *1 Chr. 2:39*

HELI, father of Joseph, husband of Mary, *Lk. 3:23*

HELIODORUS, Syrian treasurer, tried to raid temple, *2 Macc. 3:7*

Many people have animal names: Huldah ("weasel"), Leah ("wild cow"), Caleb ("dog").

HELKAI, head of priestly house, *Neh. 12:15*

HELON, clan leader in Zebulun before Exodus, *Num. 1:9*

HEMAN, Horite clan chief, *Gen. 36:22*

2, sage and psalmist, surpassed by Solomon, *1 Kg. 4:31*

3, Levite musician, grandson of Samuel, *1 Chr. 6:33*

HEMDAN, Horite clan chief, *Gen. 36:26*

HENADAD, ancestor of Levites after exile, *Ezra 3:9*

HEPHER, clan leader in Manasseh, *Num. 26:32*

2, clan leader in Judah, *1 Chr. 4:6*

3, one of David's 30 warriors, *1 Chr. 11:36*

HEPHZIBAH, wife of King Hezekiah, mother of Manasseh, *2 Kg. 21:1*

HERCULES, Greek god, honored in Tyre, *2 Macc. 4:19*

HERESH, Levite, returned after exile, *1 Chr. 9:15*

HERMAS, Christian in Rome, greeted by Paul, *Rom. 16:14*

HERMES, Greek god, *Acts 14:12*

2, Christian in Rome, greeted by Paul, *Rom. 16:14*

HERMOGENES, Christian in Asia Minor, forsook Paul, *2 Tim. 1:15*

HEROD THE GREAT, king of Judea, *Mt. 2:1*

HEROD AGRIPPA I, king of Jews, grandson of Herod the Great, *Acts 12:1*

HEROD AGRIPPA II, king of Jews, son of Herod Agrippa I, *Acts 25:13*

HEROD ANTIPAS, ruler of Galilee, son of Herod the Great, *Mt. 14:1*

HEROD ARCHELAUS, ruler of Judea, son of Herod the Great, *Mt. 2:22*

HERODIAS, wife of Herod Antipas, *Mt. 14:3*

HEROD PHILIP, tetrarch of Gaulanitis, etc., son of Herod the Great, *Mt. 14:3*

HERODION, Christian in Rome, kinsman of Paul, *Rom. 16:11*

HETH, great-grandson of Noah, *Gen. 10:15*

HEZEKIAH, king of Judah, son of Ahaz, *2 Kg. 16:20*

2, ancestor of Zephaniah, possibly same as Hezekiah 1, *Zeph. 1:1*

3, head of family with Zerubbabel, *Ezra 2:16*

4, sealed Nehemiah's covenant, *Neh. 10:17*

5, *1 Esd. 9:43, see Hilkiah 11*

HEZION, grandfather of Ben-hadad of Syria, *1 Kg. 15:18*

HEZIR, head of a division of priests, *1 Chr. 24:15*

2, sealed Nehemiah's covenant, *Neh. 10:20*

HEZRO, one of David's 30 warriors, *2 Sam. 23:35*

HEZRON, son of Reuben, *Gen. 46:9*

2, grandson of Judah through Perez, *Gen. 46:12*

HIDDAI, one of David's 30 warriors, *2 Sam. 23:30*

HIEL, rebuilt Jericho, *1 Kg. 16:34*

HIERONYMUS, Syrian governor in Palestine, *2 Macc. 12:2*

HILKIAH, Levite, ancestor of Ethan 4 the musician, *1 Chr. 6:45*

2, Levite, temple gatekeeper, *1 Chr. 26:11*

3, ancestor of Baruch 1, *Bar. 1:1*

4, father of King Hezekiah's palace administrator, *2 Kg. 18:18*

5, priest, father of Jeremiah, *Jer. 1:1*

6, father of King Zedekiah's emissary to Babylon, *Jer. 29:3*

HILKIAH 7, high priest, found book of Law in temple, *2 Kg. 22:4*

8, father of Susanna, *Sus. 1:2*

9, priest, clan leader with Zerubbabel, *Neh. 12:7*

10, father of priest with Zerubbabel, *1 Chr. 9:11*

11, aided Ezra in reading Law, *Neh. 8:4*

HILLEL, father of Abdon the judge, *Jg. 12:13*

HINNOM, ancestor of owners of valley by Jerusalem, *Jos. 15:8*

HIRAH, friend of Judah, from Adullam, *Gen. 38:1*

HIRAM, king of Tyre, ally of David and Solomon, *2 Sam. 5:11*

HIRAM 2, architect of Solomon's temple, *1 Kg. 7:13*

HIZKI, clan leader in Benjamin, *1 Chr. 8:17*

HIZKIAH, clan leader in Judah, *1 Chr. 3:23*

HOBAB, brother-in-law of Moses; perhaps the same as Hobab 2, *Num. 10:29*

2, *Jg. 4:11, see Jethro*

HOBAIAH, *Neh. 7:63, see Habaiah*

HOD, clan leader in Asher, *1 Chr. 7:37*

HODAVIAH, clan leader in Manasseh, *1 Chr. 5:24*

2, ancestor of Levites with Zerubbabel, *Ezra 2:40*

3, ancestor of Benjaminite in Jerusalem, *1 Chr. 9:7*

4, clan leader in Judah, *1 Chr. 3:24*

HODESH, wife of chief Benjamin, *1 Chr. 8:9*

HODIAH, clan leader in Judah, *1 Chr. 4:19*

2, aided Ezra in reading Law, *Neh. 8:7*

3, Levite, sealed Nehemiah's covenant, *Neh. 10:13*

4, sealed Nehemiah's covenant, *Neh. 10:18*

HOGLAH, daughter of Zelophehad, *Num. 26:33*

HOHAM, Amorite king, attacked Gibeon, *Jos. 10:3*

HOLOFERNES, general of Nebuchadnezzar, *Jdt. 2:4*

HOLY SPIRIT, Spirit of God, *Ps. 51:11*

HOMAM, *1 Chr. 1:39, see Heman*

HOPHNI, son of Eli, *1 Sam. 1:3*

HOPHRA, king of Egypt, *Jer. 44:30*

HORAM, king of Gezer, defeated by Joshua, *Jos. 10:33*

HORI, brother of Heman, Horite clan chief, *Gen. 36:22*

2, father of Simeonite spy for Moses, *Num. 13:5*

HOSAH, temple gatekeeper for David, *1 Chr. 16:38*

HOSEA, prophet in Israel, husband of Gomer, *Hos. 1:1*

HOSHAIAH, father of Azariah, opponent of Jeremiah, *Jer. 42:1*

2, leader of Judah under Nehemiah, *Neh. 12:32*

HOSHAMA, son of Jehoiachin in exile, *1 Chr. 3:18*

HOSHEA, *Num. 13:8, see* Joshua 1

2, David's officer over Ephraim, *1 Chr. 27:20*

HOSHEA 3, last king of Israel, *2 Kg. 15:30*

4, sealed Nehemiah's covenant, *Neh. 10:23*

HOTHAM, clan leader in Asher, *1 Chr. 7:32*

2, father of two of David's warriors, *1 Chr. 11:44*

HOTHIR, Levite, son of Heman the musician, *1 Chr. 25:4*

HUL, son of Aram, grandson of Shem, *Gen. 10:23*

HULDAH, prophet consulted about Law, wife of Shallum 8, *2 Kg. 22:14*

HUPHAM, *Num. 26:39, see* Huppim

A few people have plant names: Elon ("oak"), Tamar ("date palm"), Susanna ("lily").

HUPPAH, head of a division of priests, *1 Chr. 24:13*

HUPPIM, son of Benjamin, *Gen. 46:21*

HUR, grandfather of the craftsman Bezalel, *Ex. 31:2*

HUR 2, helped support Moses' arms in battle, *Ex. 17:10*

3, king of Midian killed by Israel, *Num. 31:8*

4, official in Jerusalem under Nehemiah, *Neh. 3:9*

HURAI, *1 Chr. 11:32, see* Hiddai

HURAM, grandson of Benjamin, *1 Chr. 8:5*

2, *2 Chr. 2:3, see* Hiram 1

3, *2 Chr. 4:11, see* Hiram 2,

HURAM-ABI, *2 Chr. 2:13, see* Hiram 2

HURI, clan leader in Gad, *1 Chr. 5:14*

HUSHAH, clan leader in Judah, *1 Chr. 4:4*

HUSHAI, counselor of David, *2 Sam. 15:32*

HUSHAM, the Termanite, king of Edom, *Gen. 36:34*

HUSHIM, only named son of Dan, *Gen. 46:23*

2, clan leader in Benjamin, *1 Chr. 7:12*

3, wife divorced by Benjaminite leader, *1 Chr. 8:8*

HYMENAEUS, Christian, opponent of Paul, *1 Tim. 1:20*

HYRCANUS, *see* John Hyrcanus

2, wealthy man with money deposited in temple, *2 Macc. 3:11*

I

IBHAR, son of David, *2 Sam. 5:15*

IBNEIAH, clan leader in Benjamin after exile, *1 Chr. 9:8*

IBNIJAH, clan leader in Benjamin, *1 Chr. 9:8*

IBRI, Levite, of the sons of Jaaziah, *1 Chr. 24:27*

IBSAM, grandson of Issachar, *1 Chr. 7:2*

IBZAN, judge from Bethlehem, *Jg. 12:8*

ICHABOD, grandson of Eli through Phinehas, *1 Sam. 4:21*

IDBASH, clan leader in Judah, son of Etam, *1 Chr. 4:3*

IDDO, Levite clan leader, Gershomite, *1 Chr. 6:20*

2, David's officer over eastern Manasseh, *1 Chr. 27:21*

3, father of one of Solomon's governors, *1 Kg. 4:14*

4, seer and chronicler, source for Chronicles, *2 Chr. 9:29*

5, father or grandfather of the prophet Zechariah, *Ezra 5:10*

6, priest, returned with Zerubbabel, *Neh. 12:4*

7, Levite leader in Casiphia, aided Ezra, *Ezra 8:17*

IDUEL, *1 Esd. 8:43, see* Ariel

IEZER, clan leader in Manasseh, *Num. 26:30*

IGAL, leader of Issachar, spy sent into Canaan, *Num. 13:7*

2, one of David's 30 warriors, *2 Sam. 23:36*

3, clan leader in Judah, *1 Chr. 3:22*

IGDALIAH, father of Hanan 3, priest, *Jer. 35:4*

IKKESH, father of one of David's 30 warriors, *2 Sam. 23:26*

ILAI, *1 Chr. 11:29, see* Zalmon

ILIADUN, Levite, ancestor of Jerusalem repairers, *1 Esd. 5:58*

IMALKUE, Arabian prince, *1 Macc. 11:39*

IMLAH, father of Micaiah the prophet, *1 Kg. 22:8*

IMMANUEL, son of maiden mentioned by Isaiah, *Is. 7:14*

IMMER, head of a division of priests, *1 Chr. 24:14*

2, ancestor of priests with Zerubbabel, *1 Chr. 9:12*

3, priest, father of Pashhur, who punished Jeremiah, *Jer. 20:1*

4, father of one who repaired Jerusalem's wall, *Neh. 3:29*

IMNA, clan leader in Asher, *1 Chr. 7:35*

IMNAH, son of Asher, *Gen. 46:17*

2, Levite, gatekeeper under Hezekiah, *2 Chr. 31:14*

IMRAH, clan leader in Asher, *1 Chr. 7:36*

IMRI, clan leader in Judah, *1 Chr. 9:4*

2, father of one who repaired Jerusalem wall, *Neh. 3:2*

IOB, son of Issachar, *Gen. 46:13*

IPHDEIAH, clan leader in Benjamin, *1 Chr. 8:25*

IR, clan leader in Benjamin, *1 Chr. 7:12*

IRA, one of David's 30 warriors, *2 Sam. 23:26*

2, one of David's 30 warriors, *2 Sam. 23:38*

3, non-levitical priest for David, *2 Sam. 20:26*

IRAD, grandson of Cain, *Gen. 4:18*

IRAM, clan chief in Edom, *Gen. 36:43*

IRI, grandson of Benjamin, *1 Chr. 7:7*

IRIJAH, captain of guard, arrested Jeremiah, *Jer. 37:13*

IRNAHASH, clan leader in Judah, *1 Chr. 4:12*

IRU, son of Caleb the spy, *1 Chr. 4:15*

ISAAC, son of Abraham, *Gen. 17:19*

ISAIAH, prophet in Judah, *2 Kg. 19:2*

ISCAH, daughter of Haran, *Gen. 11:29*

ISCARIOT, *Mt. 10:4, see* Judas Iscariot

2, *Jn. 6:71, see* Simon 5

ISHBAH, clan leader in Judah, *1 Chr. 4:17*

ISHBAK, son of Abraham and Keturah, *Gen. 25:2*

ISHBIBENOB, Philistine warrior killed by Abishai, *2 Sam. 21:16*

ISH-BOSHETH, son of King Saul, *2 Sam. 2:8*

ISHHOD, clan leader in Manasseh, *1 Chr. 7:18*

ISHI, clan leader in Judah, *1 Chr. 2:31*

2, clan leader in Judah, descendant of Caleb, *1 Chr. 4:20*

3, clan leader in Manasseh, warrior, *1 Chr. 5:24*

4, clan leader in Simeon, *1 Chr. 4:42*

ISHMA, clan leader in Judah, son of Etam, *1 Chr. 4:3*

ISHMAEL, son of Abraham and Hagar, *Gen. 16:11*

2, father of a judge under King Jehoshaphat, *2 Chr. 19:11*

3, commander, aided overthrow of Queen Athaliah, *2 Chr. 23:1*

4, descendant of King Saul, clan leader in Benjamin, *1 Chr. 8:38*

5, assassin of Gedaliah 4, *2 Kg. 25:23*

6, priest, left foreign wife, *Ezra 10:22*

ISHMAIAH, Gibeonite warrior, joined David, *1 Chr. 12:4*

2, David's officer over Zebulun, *1 Chr. 27:19*

ISHMERAI, clan leader in Benjamin, *1 Chr. 8:18*

ISHPAH, clan leader in Benjamin, *1 Chr. 8:16*

ISHPAN, Benjaminite in Jerusalem, *1 Chr. 8:22*

ISHVAH, son of Asher, *Gen. 46:17*

ISHVI, son of Asher, *Gen. 46:17*

2, son of King Saul, *1 Sam. 14:49*

ISMACHIAH, Levite, temple official under King Hezekiah, *2 Chr. 31:13*

ISRAEL, *Gen. 32:28, see* Jacob

Jacob had 12 sons but only one named daughter, Dinah.

ISSACHAR, son of Jacob and Leah, *Gen. 30:18*

2, Levite gatekeeper, *1 Chr. 26:5*

ISSHIAH, clan leader in Issachar, *1 Chr. 7:3*

2, Levite clan leader, descendant of Moses, *1 Chr. 23:20*

3, one of David's 30 warriors, *1 Chr. 12:6*

4, Levite clan leader, *1 Chr. 24:21*

ISSHIJAH, left foreign wife, *Ezra 10:31*

ISTALCURUS, *1 Esd. 8:40,* see Zaccur

ITHAI, *1 Chr. 11:31,* see Ittai 1

ITHAMAR, son of Aaron, *Ex. 6:23*

ITHIEL, symbolic name, subject of proverb, *Pr. 30:1*

2, Benjaminite in Jerusalem after exile, *Neh. 11:7*

ITHMAH, one of David's 30 warriors, *1 Chr. 11:46*

ITHRA, father of Amasa, Absalom's commander, *2 Sam. 17:25*

ITHRAN, Horite clan chief, *Gen. 36:26*

2, clan leader in Asher, *1 Chr. 7:37*

ITHREAM, son of David and Eglah, *2 Sam. 3:5*

ITTAI, one of David's 30 warriors, *2 Sam. 23:29*

ITTAI 2, from Gath, supporter of David, *2 Sam. 15:19*

IZHAR, grandson of Levi, *Ex. 6:18*

2, clan leader in Judah, *1 Chr. 4:7*

IZLIAH, clan leader in Benjamin, *1 Chr. 8:18*

IZRAHIAH, clan leader in Issachar, *1 Chr. 7:3*

IZRI, Levite, leader of musicians, *1 Chr. 25:11*

IZZIAH, left foreign wife, *Ezra 10:25*

J

JAAKAN, son of Ezer, a Horite, *1 Chr. 1:42*

JAAKOBAH, Simeonite prince under King Hezekiah, *1 Chr. 4:36*

JAALAH, servant of Solomon, ancestor of exiles, *Ezra 2:56*

JAAREOREGIM, father of Elhanan the warrior, *2 Sam. 21:19*

JAARESHIAH, clan leader in Benjamin, *1 Chr. 8:27*

JAASIEL, one of David's 30 warriors, *1 Chr. 11:47*

2, David's officer over Benjamin, *1 Chr. 27:21*

JAASU, left foreign wife, *Ezra 10:37*

JAAZANIAH, Israelite whom Ezekiel saw in vision, *Ezek. 8:11*

2, Israelite whom Ezekiel saw in vision, *Ezek. 11:1*

3, Judean captain who joined Gedaliah, *2 Kg. 25:23*

4, leader of Rechabites brought to the temple, *Jer. 35:3*

JAAZIAH, Levite ancestor of clan in David's time, *1 Chr. 24:26*

JAAZIEL, Levite who played the lyre for David, *1 Chr. 15:18*

JABAL, descendent of Cain, ancestor of herders, *Gen. 4:20*

JABESH, father of Shallum, assassin and king of Israel, *2 Kg. 15:10*

JABEZ, clan leader in Judah, *1 Chr. 4:9*

JABIN, king of Hazor, opposed Joshua, *Jos. 11:1*

2, king of Canaan at Hazor in the time of Deborah, *Jg. 4:2*

JACAN, clan leader in Gad, *1 Chr. 5:13*

JACHIN, son of Simeon, *Gen. 46:10*

2, head of a division of priests, *1 Chr. 24:17*

JACOB, son of Isaac, *Gen. 25:26*

2, father of Joseph, ancestor of Jesus, *Mt. 1:15*

The Old Testament name Jacob became James in New Testament times.

JADA, clan leader in Judah, *1 Chr. 2:28*

JADDAI, left foreign wife, *Ezra 10:43*

JADDUA, sealed Nehemiah's covenant, *Neh. 10:21*

JADDUA 2, last high priest in Old Testament, *Neh. 12:11*

JADDUS, priest, head of clan questioned under Zerubbabel, *1 Esd. 5:38*

JADON, helped repair Jerusalem's walls, *Neh. 3:7*

JAEL, wife of Heber the Kenite, killed Sisera, *Jg. 4:17*

JAHATH, clan leader in Judah, *1 Chr. 4:2*

2, grandson of Gershom, Levite clan leader, *1 Chr. 6:20*

3, Levite, descendant of Gershom, *1 Chr. 23:10*

4, Levite, descendant of Kohath, *1 Chr. 24:22*

5, Levite, supervised temple construction, *2 Chr. 34:12*

JAHAZIEL, Benjaminite, joined David, *1 Chr. 12:4*

2, priest, blew trumpet before ark, *1 Chr. 16:6*

3, Levite clan leader, son of Hebron, *1 Chr. 23:19*

4, priest and prophet who advised King Jehoshaphat, *2 Chr. 20:14*

5, ancestor of Jews under Ezra, *Ezra 8:5*

JAHDAI, clan leader in Judah, *1 Chr. 2:47*

JAHDIEL, clan leader in Manasseh, *1 Chr. 5:24*

JAHDO, clan leader in Gad, *1 Chr. 5:14*

JAHLEEL, son of Zebulun, *Gen. 46:14*

JAHMAI, grandson of Issachar, *1 Chr. 7:2*

JAHZEEL, son of Naphtali, *Gen. 46:24*

JAHZEIAH, opponent of Ezra's reforms, *Ezra 10:15*

JAHZERAH, priest, ancestor of priest under Ezra, *1 Chr. 9:12*

JAHZIEL, *1 Chr. 7:13,* see Jahzeel

JAIR, clan leader in Manasseh, *Num. 32:41*

JAIR 2, minor judge from Gilead, *Jg. 10:3*

3, father of Elhanan the giant-slayer, *1 Chr. 20:5*

4, father of Mordecai, *Est. 2:5*

JAIRUS, father of girl raised from dead by Jesus, *Mk. 5:22*

JAKEH, father of Agur, author of Proverbs 30, *Pr. 30:1*

JAKIM, clan leader in Benjamin, *1 Chr. 8:19*

2, head of a division of priests, *1 Chr. 24:12*

JALAM, son of Esau, *Gen. 36:5*

JALON, clan leader in Judah, *1 Chr. 4:17*

JAMBRES, *2 Tim. 3:8,* see Jannes and Jambres

JAMES, son of Zebedee, apostle, *Mt. 4:21*

JAMES 2, son of Alphaeus, apostle, *Mt. 10:3*

JAMES 3, brother of Jesus, *Mt. 13:55*

JAMES 4, son of Mary, brother of Joseph, *Mt. 27:56*

5, father of Judas, *Lk. 6:16*

JAMIN, son of Simeon, *Gen. 46:10*

2, clan leader in Judah, *1 Chr. 2:27*

3, Levite who aided Ezra, *Neh. 8:7*

JAMLECH, clan chief in Simeon, *1 Chr. 4:34*

JANAI, clan leader in Gad, *1 Chr. 5:12*

JANNAI, ancestor of Jesus, *Lk. 3:24*

JANNES and JAMBRES, Egyptian magicians, *2 Tim. 3:8*

JAPHETH, son of Noah, *Gen. 5:32*

JAPHIA, Amorite king of Lachish killed by Joshua, *Jos. 10:3*

2, son of David, *2 Sam. 5:15*

JAPHLET, clan leader in Asher, *1 Chr. 7:32*

JARAH, *1 Chr. 9:42,* see Jehoaddah

JARED, father of Enoch, *Gen. 5:15*

JARHA, Egyptian slave married into tribe of Judah, *1 Chr. 2:34*

JARIB, *1 Chr. 4:24,* see Jachin

2, Jewish leader aided Ezra, *Ezra 8:16*

3, priest, left foreign wife, *Ezra 10:18*

JAROAH, clan leader in Gad, *1 Chr. 5:14*

JASHAR, author of the book of Jashar, *Jos. 10:13*

JASHEN, father of several in David's guard, *2 Sam. 23:32*

JASHOBEAM, Benjaminite who joined David, *1 Chr. 12:6*

2, *1 Chr. 11:11,* see Josheb-basshebeth

3, commander in David's army, *1 Chr. 27:2*

JASHUB, son of Issachar, *Num. 26:24*

2, left foreign wife, *Ezra 10:29*

JASON, author of history of Maccabees, *2 Macc. 2:23*

JASON 2, brother of Onias III, high priest, *2 Macc. 1:7*

3, Jewish ambassador for Judas Maccabeus, *1 Macc. 8:17*

4, father of an ambassador for Jonathan, *1 Macc. 12:16*

5, host of Paul in Thessalonica, *Acts 17:5*

6, companion of Paul, *Rom. 16:21*

JATHAN, brother of Ananias, *Tob. 5:13*

JATHNIEL, chief sanctuary gatekeeper, *1 Chr. 26:2*

JAVAN, son of Japheth, grandson of Noah, *Gen. 10:2*

JAZIZ, keeper of David's flocks, *1 Chr. 27:31*

JEATHERAI, Levite clan leader, *1 Chr. 6:21*

JEBERECHIAH, father of Zechariah 16, *Is. 8:2*

JECHONIAH, *Mt. 1:11, see* Jehoiachin

JECOLIAH, mother of King Uzziah, *2 Kg. 15:2*

JECONIAH, *1 Esd. 1:9, see* Conaniah 2

2, *1 Esd. 1:34, see* Jehoahaz 2

3, *1 Chr. 3:16, see* Jehoiachin

JEDAIAH, head of a division of priests, *1 Chr. 24:7*

2, priest, clan leader in Levi, *Ezra 2:36*

3, clan leader in Simeon, *1 Chr. 4:37*

More people are named in the book of Nehemiah than in Genesis.

4, priest, returned with Zerubbabel, *Neh. 12:6*

5, priest, returned with Zerubbabel, *Neh. 12:7*

6, brought gold from Babylon to Jerusalem, *Zech. 6:10*

7, helped repair Jerusalem's walls, *Neh. 3:10*

8, priest in Jerusalem after exile, *1 Chr. 9:10*

JEDIAEL, son of Benjamin 1, *1 Chr. 7:6*

2, man of Manasseh who joined David, *1 Chr. 12:20*

3, one of David's 30 warriors, *1 Chr. 11:45*

4, sanctuary gatekeeper, *1 Chr. 26:2*

JEDIDAH, mother of King Josiah, *2 Kg. 22:1*

JEDIDIAH, *2 Sam. 12:25, see* Solomon

JEDUTHUN, father of Obed-edom, *1 Chr. 16:38*

2, *1 Chr. 25:1, see* Ethan 4

JEHALLELEL, clan leader in Judah, *1 Chr. 4:16*

2, Levite under King Hezekiah, *2 Chr. 29:12*

JEHDEIAH, David's officer in charge of donkeys, *1 Chr. 27:30*

2, Levite clan leader under David, *1 Chr. 24:20*

JEHEZKEL, head of a division of priests, *1 Chr. 24:16*

JEHIAH, gatekeeper for the ark with Obed-edom, *1 Chr. 15:24*

JEHIEL, Levite, played lyre before ark, *1 Chr. 15:18*

2, Levite, oversaw treasury, *1 Chr. 23:8*

3, tutor of David's sons, *1 Chr. 27:32*

4, brother of King Jehoram of Judah, *2 Chr. 21:2*

5, Levite under King Hezekiah, *2 Chr. 29:14*

6, temple administrator under King Josiah, *2 Chr. 35:8*

7, father of Obadiah 9, *Ezra 8:9*

8, father of Shecaniah, who aided Ezra, *Ezra 10:2*

9, priest, left foreign wife, *Ezra 10:21*

10, left foreign wife, *Ezra 10:26*

JEHIELI, Levite over sanctuary treasury, *1 Chr. 26:21*

JEHIZKIAH, Ephraimite, opposed enslaving Judahites, *2 Chr. 28:12*

JEHOADDAH, clan leader in Benjamin, *1 Chr. 8:36*

JEHOADDAN, mother of King Amaziah, *2 Chr. 25:1*

JEHOADDIN, *2 Kg. 14:2, see* Jehoaddan

JEHOAHAZ, son of Jehu, king of Israel, *2 Kg. 10:35*

JEHOAHAZ 2, son of Josiah, king of Judah, *2 Kg. 23:30*

3, *see* Ahaziah, *2 Chr. 21:17*

JEHOASH, *2 Kg. 11.21, see* Joash 7

2, *2 Kg. 13:10, see* Joash 8

JEHOHANAN, sanctuary gatekeeper, *1 Chr. 26:3*

2, commander under King Jehoshaphat, *2 Chr. 17:15*

3, father of Ishmael, a commander, *2 Chr. 23:1*

4, father of one who opposed enslaving Judahites, *2 Chr. 28:12*

5, head of priestly family under Joiakim, *Neh. 12:13*

6, left foreign wife, *Ezra 10:28*

7, son of Tobiah, opponent of Nehemiah, *Neh. 6:18*

8, priest who helped dedicate Jerusalem's walls, *Neh. 12:42*

9, *Ezra 10:6, see* Johanan 7

JEHOIACHIN, son of Jehoiakim, king of Judah, *2 Kg. 24:6*

JEHOIADA, father of Benaiah, David's officer, *2 Sam. 8:18*

2, Levite who joined David, *1 Chr. 12:27*

3, son of Benaiah, adviser of David, *1 Chr. 27:34*

JEHOIADA 4, high priest, *2 Kg. 11:4*

5, chief priest in Jerusalem, *Jer. 29:26*

JEHOIAKIM, son of Josiah, king of Judah, *2 Kg. 23:34*

2, high priest, *Bar. 1:7*

JEHOIARIB, head of a division of priests, *1 Chr. 24:7*

2, priest after the exile, *1 Chr. 9:10*

JEHONADAB, *2 Kg. 10:15, see* Jonadab 2

JEHONATHAN, Levite under King Jehoshaphat, *2 Chr. 17:8*

2, head of priestly family under Joiakim, *Neh. 12:18*

JEHORAM, son of Ahab, king of Israel, *2 Kg. 1:17*

JEHORAM 2, son of Jehoshaphat, king of Judah, *1 Kg. 22:50*

3, priest under King Jehoshaphat, *2 Chr. 17:8*

JEHOSHABEATH, *2 Chr. 22:11, see* Jehosheba

JEHOSHAPHAT, recorder for David and Solomon, *2 Sam. 8:16*

2, district governor for Solomon, *1 Kg. 4:17*

3, father of King Jehu, *2 Kg. 9:2*

JEHOSHAPHAT 4, son of Asa, king of Judah, *1 Kg. 15:24*

JEHOSHEBA, daughter of King Jehoram of Judah, *2 Kg. 11:2*

JEHOZABAD, son of Obed-edom, sanctuary gatekeeper, *1 Chr. 26:4*

2, commander under King Jehoshaphat, *2 Chr. 17:18*

3, assassin of King Joash of Judah, *2 Kg. 12:21*

JEHOZADAK, father of Jeshua the high priest, *1 Chr. 6:14*

JEHU, Benjaminite who joined David, *1 Chr. 12:3*

2, clan leader in Judah, *1 Chr. 2:38*

JEHU 3, king of Israel, *1 Kg. 19:16; see* Jehu, page 191

JEHU 4, son of Hanani, prophet, *1 Kg. 16:1; see* Jehu 2, page 193

5, clan leader in Simeon, *1 Chr. 4:35*

JEHUBBAH, clan leader in Asher, *1 Chr. 7:34*

JEHUCAL, courtier for King Zedekiah, *Jer. 37:3*

JEHUDI, official for King Jehoiakim, *Jer. 36:14*

JEHUEL, Levite under King Hezekiah, *2 Chr. 29:14*

JEIEL, clan leader in Reuben, *1 Chr. 5:7*

2, great-grandfather of King Saul, *1 Chr. 8:29*

3, one of David's 30 warriors, *1 Chr. 11:44*

4, Levite, keeper of the ark, *1 Chr. 15:18*

5, Levite, played music before ark, *1 Chr. 16:5*

6, Levite, prophesied before King Jehoshaphat, *2 Chr. 20:14*

7, secretary of King Uzziah, *2 Chr. 26:11*

8, chief Levite under King Josiah, *2 Chr. 35:9*

9, left foreign wife, *Ezra 10:43*

God gave Solomon a second name: Jedidiah, "beloved of the Lord."

JEKAMEAM, Levite clan leader, *1 Chr. 23:19*

JEKAMIAH, clan leader in Judah, *1 Chr. 2:41*

2, son of King Jehoiachin, *1 Chr. 3:18*

JEKUTHIEL, clan leader in Judah, *1 Chr. 4:18*

JEMIMAH, daughter of Job, *Job 42:14*

JEMUEL, son of Simeon, *Gen. 46:10*

JEPHTHAH, judge from Gilead, *Jg. 11:1*

JEPHUNNEH, father of Caleb, *Num. 13:6*

2, clan leader in Asher, *1 Chr. 7:38*

JERAH, descendant of Noah through Shem, *Gen. 10:26*

JERAHMEEL, grandson of Judah, *1 Chr. 2:9*

2, Levite, sanctuary official, *1 Chr. 24:29*

3, courtier for King Jehoiakim, *Jer. 36:26*

JERED, clan leader in Judah, *1 Chr. 4:18*

JEREMAI, left foreign wife, *Ezra 10:33*

JEREMIAH, Benjaminite who joined David, *1 Chr. 12:4*

2, Gadite who joined David, *1 Chr. 12:10*

3, Gadite who joined David, *1 Chr. 12:13*

4, clan leader in Manasseh, *1 Chr. 5:24*

5, father of Hamutal, King Jehoahaz's mother, *2 Kg. 23:31*

JEREMIAH 6, prophet, *2 Chr. 35:25*

7, Rechabite, father of Jaazaniah, *Jer. 35:3*

8, priest with Zerubbabel, *Neh. 12:1*

9, helped dedicate Jerusalem's walls, *Neh. 12:34*

10, priest, sealed Nehemiah's covenant, *Neh. 10:2*

JEREMOTH, grandson of Benjamin, *1 Chr. 7:8*

2, clan leader in Benjamin, *1 Chr. 8:14*

3, David's officer over Naphtali, *1 Chr. 27:19*

4, Levite musician and clan leader, *1 Chr. 25:22*

5, Levite in the time of David, *1 Chr. 23:23*

6, left foreign wife, *Ezra 10:26*

7, left foreign wife, *Ezra 10:27*

8, left foreign wife, *Ezra 10:29*

JERIAH, Levite clan leader, *1 Chr. 23:19*

JERIBAL, one of David's 30 warriors, *1 Chr. 11:46*

JERIEL, grandson of Issachar, *1 Chr. 7:2*

JERIMOTH, grandson of Benjamin, *1 Chr. 7:7*

2, Benjaminite who joined David, *1 Chr. 12:5*

3, *1 Chr. 24:30, see Jeremoth 5*

4, Levite, son of Heman the musician, *1 Chr. 25:4*

5, son of David, father-in-law of Rehoboam, *2 Chr. 11:18*

6, Levite overseer under King Hezekiah, *2 Chr. 31:13*

JERIOTH, wife of Caleb, *1 Chr. 2:18*

JEROBOAM, first king of northern Israel, *1 Kg. 11:26*

JEROBOAM II, son of Joash, king of Israel, *2 Kg. 13:13*

JEROHAM, grandfather of Samuel, *1 Sam. 1:1*

2, clan leader in Benjamin, *1 Chr. 8:27*

3, father of two of David's warriors, *1 Chr. 12:7*

4, father of Azarel, David's officer for Dan, *1 Chr. 27:22*

5, father of Azariah 12, *2 Chr. 23:1*

6, ancestor of Benjamites in Jerusalem, *1 Chr. 9:8*

7, father of Adaiah, priest after exile, *1 Chr. 9:12*

JERUBBAAL, *Jg. 6:32, see Gideon*

JERUBBESHETH, *2 Sam. 11:21, see Gideon*

JERUSHA, wife of King Uzziah, mother of Jotham 2, *2 Kg. 15:33*

JESHAIAH, ancestor of an official for David, *1 Chr. 26:25*

2, Levite, sanctuary musician, *1 Chr. 25:3*

3, clan leader in Benjamin, *Neh. 11:7*

4, exile who returned with Ezra, *Ezra 8:7*

5, Levite who returned with Ezra, *Ezra 8:19*

6, grandson of Zerubbabel, *1 Chr. 3:21*

JESHAREIAH, sanctuary musician for David, *1 Chr. 25:14*

JESHEBEAB, head of a division of priests, *1 Chr. 24:13*

JESHER, son of Caleb, *1 Chr. 2:18*

JESHISHAI, clan leader in Gad, *1 Chr. 5:14*

JESHOHAIAH, clan leader in Simeon under King Hezekiah, *1 Chr. 4:36*

JESHUA, *Neh. 8:17, see Joshua 1*

2, head of a division of priests, *1 Chr. 24:11*

3, priest in King Hezekiah's time, *2 Chr. 31:15*

4, ancestor of exiles returning with Zerubbabel, *Ezra 2:6*

5, ancestor of Levites with Zerubbabel, *Ezra 2:40*

JESHUA 6, high priest, returned with Zerubbabel, *Ezra 2:2*

7, father of Levite under Ezra, *Ezra 8:33*

8, father of Ezer, who helped repair Jerusalem, *Neh. 3:19*

Jesus is mentioned 990 times, second only to David at 1,100; Moses is third with 870 citations.

9, Levite, when Ezra read Law, *Neh. 8:7*

10, Levite, sealed Nehemiah's covenant, *Neh. 10:9*

JESHURUN, personification of Israel, *Deut. 32:15*

JESIMIEL, clan leader in Simeon, *1 Chr. 4:36*

JESSE, son of Obed, father of David, *Ru. 4:17*

JESUS BEN SIRA, author of Ecclesiasticus, *Sir. 0:1*

JESUS CHRIST, *Mt. 1:1*

JESUS JUSTUS, coworker of Paul, *Col. 4:11*

JETHER, clan leader in Asher, *1 Chr. 7:38*

2, son of Gideon, *Jg. 8:20*

3, clan leader in Judah, *1 Chr. 4:17*

4, clan leader in Judah, *1 Chr. 2:32*

5, husband of Abigail, David's sister, *2 Sam. 17:25*

JETHETH, clan chief in Edom, *Gen. 36:40*

JETHRO, father-in-law of Moses, *Ex. 3:1*

JETUR, son of Ishmael, grandson of Abraham, *Gen. 25:15*

JEUEL, Levite under King Hezekiah, *2 Chr. 29:13*

2, returned to Jerusalem with Ezra, *Ezra 8:13*

3, Judahite who returned to Jerusalem, *1 Chr. 9:6*

4, Levite under King Hezekiah, *2 Chr. 29:13*

JEUSH, son of Esau, *Gen. 36:5*

2, clan leader in Benjamin, *1 Chr. 7:10*

3, clan leader in Levi, *1 Chr. 23:10*

4, son of King Rehoboam, *2 Chr. 11:19*

5, descendant of Saul, *1 Chr. 8:39*

JEUZ, clan leader in Benjamin, *1 Chr. 8:10*

JEZANIAH, *Jer. 40:8, see Jaazaniah 3*

JEZEBEL, wife of Ahab, queen of Israel, *1 Kg. 16:31*

2, false prophetess in church at Thyatira, *Rev. 2:20*

JEZER, son of Naphtali, *Gen. 46:24*

JEZIEL, Benjaminite who joined David, *1 Chr. 12:3*

JEZRAHIAH, choir leader for Nehemiah, *Neh. 12:42*

JEZREEL, clan leader in Judah, son of Etam, *1 Chr. 4:3*

JEZREEL 2, son of Hosea, *Hos. 1:4*

JIDLAPH, nephew of Abraham, *Gen. 22:22*

JOAB, son of Zeruiah, David's nephew and commander, *1 Sam. 26:6*

2, craftsman, clan leader in Judah, *1 Chr. 4:14*

3, ancestor of exiles under Zerubbabel, *Ezra 2:6*

JOAH, Levite clan leader, *1 Chr. 6:21*

2, son of Obed-edom, keeper of the ark, *1 Chr. 26:4*

3, Levite under King Hezekiah, *2 Chr. 29:12*

4, recorder under King Hezekiah, *2 Kg. 18:18*

5, recorder under Josiah, *2 Chr. 34:8*

JOAHAZ, *see Jehoahaz 2, 2 Kg. 14:1*

2, father of Joah, King Josiah's recorder, *2 Chr. 34:8*

JOAKIM, high priest who welcomed Judith, *Jdt. 4:6*

2, husband of Susanna in Babylon, *Sus. 1:1*

3, son of Zerubbabel, *1 Esd. 5:5*

JOANAN, grandson of Zerubbabel, ancestor of Jesus, *Lk. 3:27*

JOANNA, wife of Chuza, disciple of Jesus, *Lk. 8:3*

JOASH, grandson of Benjamin, *1 Chr. 7:8*

2, father of the judge Gideon, *Jg. 6:11*

3, clan leader in Judah, *1 Chr. 4:22*

4, Benjaminite who joined David, *1 Chr. 12:3*

5, David's official for olive oil, *1 Chr. 27:28*

6, son of King Ahab, *1 Kg. 22:26*

JOASH 7, son of Ahaziah, king of Judah, *2 Kg. 11:2; see Joash, page 226*

JOASH 8, son of Jehoahaz, king of Israel, *2 Kg. 13:9; see Joash 2, page 227*

JOB, wealthy man from Uz, *Job 1:1*

JOBAB, son of Joktan, *Gen. 10:29*

2, king of Edom, *Gen. 36:33*

3, king of Madon, opposed Joshua, *Jos. 11:1*

4, clan leader in Benjamin, *1 Chr. 8:9*

5, clan leader in Benjamin, *1 Chr. 8:18*

JOCHEBED, daughter of Levi, mother of Moses, *Ex. 6:20*

JODA, Levite, returned with Zerubbabel, *1 Esd. 5:58*

2, ancestor of Jesus, *Lk. 3:26*

JODAN, left foreign wife, *1 Esd. 9:19*

JOED, clan leader in Benjamin, *Neh. 11:7*

JOEL, clan leader in Issachar, *1 Chr. 7:3*

2, ancestor of Samuel, *1 Chr. 6:36*

3, son of Samuel, *1 Sam. 8:2*

4, clan leader in Reuben, *1 Chr. 5:4*

5, clan leader in Gad, *1 Chr. 5:12*

6, clan leader in Simeon, *1 Chr. 4:35*

7, one of David's 30 warriors, *1 Chr. 11:38*

8, Levite in David's time, *1 Chr. 15:7*

9, David's officer over western Manasseh, *1 Chr. 27:20*

10, Levite sanctuary treasurer, *1 Chr. 23:8*

11, Levite in King Hezekiah's time, *2 Chr. 29:12*

12, left foreign wife, *Ezra 10:43*

13, leader of Benjaminites in Jerusalem, *Neh. 11:9*

JOEL 14, prophet, *Jl. 1:1*

JOELAH, Benjaminite who joined David, *1 Chr. 12:7*

JOEZER, Benjaminite who joined David, *1 Chr. 12:6*

JOGLI, father of leader of Dan under Moses, *Num. 34:22*

JOHA, clan leader in Benjamin, *1 Chr. 8:16*

2, one of David's 30 warriors, *1 Chr. 11:45*

JOHANAN, Benjaminite who joined David, *1 Chr. 12:4*

2, Gadite who joined David, *1 Chr. 12:12*

3, great-grandson of the priest Zadok, *1 Chr. 6:9*

4, son of King Josiah, *1 Chr. 3:15*

JOHANAN 5, commander, supported Gedaliah 4, *2 Kg. 25:23; see Johanan, page 231*

6, Jew who returned with Ezra, *Ezra 8:12*

JOHANAN 7, high priest under Ezra, *Neh. 12:22; see Johanan 2, page 232*

8, descendant of Zerubbabel, *1 Chr. 3:24*

JOHN, grandfather of Judas Maccabeus, *1 Macc. 2:1*

2, father of Eupolemus, Jewish envoy, *1 Macc. 8:17*

3, brother of Judas Maccabeus, *1 Macc. 2:2*

4, Jewish envoy to Lysias, *2 Macc. 11:17*

5, father of Simon Peter, *Jn. 1:42*

JOHN 6, son of Zebedee, apostle, *Mt. 4:21; see John, page 232*

7, *Acts 12:12, see Mark*

JOHN THE BAPTIST, son of Zechariah, *Mt. 3:1*

JOHN OF PATMOS, author of Revelation, *Rev. 1:1*

JOHN HYRCANUS, son of Simon 4, high priest, *1 Macc. 13:53*

JOIADA, helped repair Jerusalem's walls, *Neh. 3:6*

2, son of the high priest Eliashib, *Neh. 12:10*

JOIAKIM, high priest, son of the high priest Jeshua, *Neh. 12:10*

JOIARIB, ancestor of returning exiles, *Neh. 11:5*

2, priest with Zerubbabel, *Neh. 12:6*

3, emissary for Ezra, *Ezra 8:16*

4, father of priest who returned to Jerusalem, *Neh. 11:10*

JOKIM, clan leader in Judah, *1 Chr. 4:22*

JOKSHAN, son of Abraham and Keturah, *Gen. 25:2*

JOKTAN, descendant of Shem, *Gen. 10:25*

JONADAB, son of Shimeah 2, David's nephew, *2 Sam. 13:3*

JONADAB 2, son of Rechab, Rechabite, *Jer. 35:6*

JONAH, prophet under Jeroboam II, *2 Kg. 14:25*

2, Levite in Ezra's time, *1 Esd. 9:23*

JONAM, ancestor of Jesus, *Lk. 3:30*

JONATHAN, young Levite, priest for Danites, *Jg. 18:30*

2, clan leader in Judah, *1 Chr. 2:32*

JONATHAN 3, son of Saul, *1 Sam. 13:2; see Jonathan 2, page 242*

4, uncle and counselor of David, *1 Chr. 27:32*

5, one of David's 30 warriors, *2 Sam. 23:32*

6, son of Abiathar, the high priest, *2 Sam. 15:27*

7, *2 Sam. 21:21, see Jonadab 1*

8, one of David's treasurers, *1 Chr. 27:25*

9, scribe for Zedekiah, *Jer. 37:15*

10, head of priestly family under Joiakim, *Neh. 12:14*

11, father of returning exile, *Ezra 8:6*

12, father of Zechariah, *Neh. 12:35*

13, opposed Ezra's reforms, *Ezra 10:15*

14, priest under Nehemiah, *2 Macc. 1:23*

15, priest, descendant of high priest Jeshua, *Neh. 12:11*

JONATHAN 16, brother of Judas Maccabeus, *1 Macc. 2:5; see Jonathan 3, page 241*

17, commander for Simon 4, *1 Macc. 13:11*

JORAH, ancestor of exiles with Zerubbabel, *Ezra 2:18*

JORAI, clan leader in Gad, *1 Chr. 5:13*

JORAM, ancestor of Levite under David, *1 Chr. 26:25*

2, *2 Sam. 8:10, see Hadoram 2*

3, *2 Kg. 8:16, see Jehoram 2*

4, *2 Kg. 11:2, see Jehoram 3*

JORIM, ancestor of Jesus, *Lk. 3:29*

JORKEAM, clan leader in Judah, *1 Chr. 2:44*

JOSECH, ancestor of Jesus, *Lk. 3:26*

JOSEPH, son of Jacob and Rachel, *Gen. 30:24*

2, father of spy for Moses, *Num. 13:7*

3, ancestor of Jesus, *Lk. 3:30*

4, musician for David, *1 Chr. 25:2*

5, ancestor of Judith, *Jdt. 8:1*

6, head of priestly family under Joiakim, *Neh. 12:14*

7, left foreign wife, *Ezra 10:42*

8, ancestor of Jesus, *Lk. 3:24*

9, commander for Judas Maccabeus, *1 Macc. 5:18*

10, *2 Macc. 8:22, see John 3*

JOSEPH 11, husband of Mary, the mother of Jesus, *Mt. 1:16; see Joseph 2, page 247*

12, brother of Jesus, *Mt. 13:55*

13, brother of James 4, son of Mary, *Mt. 27:56*

14, *Acts 4:36, see Barnabas*

JOSEPH OF ARIMATHEA, buried Jesus, *Mt. 27:57*

JOSEPH BARSABBAS, unsuccessful candidate to succeed Judas Iscariot, *Acts 1:23*

JOSES, *Mk. 6:3, see Joseph 12*

2, *Mk. 15:40, see Joseph 13*

JOSHAH, clan leader in Simeon, *1 Chr. 4:34*

JOSHAPHAT, one of David's 30 warriors, *1 Chr. 11:43*

2, priest, trumpeter before the ark, *1 Chr. 15:24*

JOSHAVIAH, one of David's 30 warriors, *1 Chr. 11:46*

JOSHBEKASHAH, Levite, son of Heman the musician, *1 Chr. 25:4*

JOSHEB-BASSHEBETH, David's chief warrior, *2 Sam. 23:8*

JOSHIBIAH, clan leader in Simeon, *1 Chr. 4:35*

JOSHUA, son of Nun, aide of Moses, *Ex. 17:9*

2, man of Beth-shemesh where ark stopped, *1 Sam. 6:14*

3, ancestor of Jesus, *Lk. 3:29*

4, governor of Jerusalem under King Josiah, *2 Kg. 23:8*

5, *Hag. 1:1, see Jeshua 6*

JOSIAH, son of Amon, king of Judah, *1 Kg. 13:2*

2, son of Zephaniah, *Zech. 6:10*

David's 30 "mighty men" actually numbered more than 30, which was merely a convenient round number.

JOSIPHIAH, father of leader under Ezra, *Ezra 8:10*

JOTHAM, son of Gideon, *Jg. 9:5*

JOTHAM 2, son of Uzziah 3, king of Judah, *2 Kg. 15:5*

3, clan leader in Judah, *1 Chr. 2:47*

JOZABAD, Benjaminite who joined David, *1 Chr. 12:4*

2, Manassite who joined David, *1 Chr. 12:20*

3, Manassite who joined David, *1 Chr. 12:20*

4, Levite under King Hezekiah, *2 Chr. 31:13*

5, chief Levite under Josiah, *2 Chr. 35:9*

6, priest, left foreign wife, *Ezra 10:22*

7, left foreign wife, *Ezra 10:23*

8, Levite under Ezra, *Ezra 8:33*

9, Levite who taught the Law, *Neh. 8:7*

JOZACAR, assassin of King Joash of Judah, *2 Kg. 12:21*

JOZADAK, *Ezra 3:2, see Jehozadak*

JUBAL, son of Lamech, descendant of Cain, *Gen. 4:21*

JUDAH, son of Jacob and Leah, *Gen. 29:35*

2, ancestor of Jesus, *Lk. 3:30*

3, Levite with Zerubbabel, *Neh. 12:8*

4, left foreign wife, *Ezra 10:23*

5, Benjaminite in Jerusalem, *Neh. 11:9*

6, helped dedicate Jerusalem's walls, *Neh. 12:34*

7, priest, musician in Jerusalem, *Neh. 12:36*

JUDAS, Jewish soldier, son of Chalphi, *1 Macc. 11:70*

2, son of Simon 4, *1 Macc. 16:2*

JUDAS 3, of Galilee, led insurrection, *Acts 5:37; see Judas, page 257*

JUDAS 4, brother of Jesus, *Mt. 13:55; see Judas 2, page 257*

JUDAS 5, son of James, apostle, *Lk. 6:16; see Judas 3, page 258*

6, owner of house in Damascus, *Acts 9:11*

JUDAS BARSABBAS, sent with Silas to deliver letter to Antioch, *Acts 15:22*

JUDAS ISCARIOT, apostle who betrayed Jesus, *Mt. 10:4*

JUDAS MACCABEUS, son of Mattathias, rebel leader, *1 Macc. 2:4*

JUDE, brother of James, author of epistle, *Jude 1:1*

JUDITH, wife of Esau, *Gen. 26:34*

JUDITH 2, daughter of Merari, pious widow, *Jdt. 8:1*

JULIA, Christian at Rome, *Rom. 16:15*

JULIUS, Roman centurion, *Acts 27:1*

JUNIAS (or Junia), coworker of Paul, *Rom. 16:7*

JUSHAB-HESED, son of Zerubbabel, *1 Chr. 3:20*

JUSTUS, *Acts 1:23, see Joseph Barsabbas*

2, *Acts 18:7, see Titius Justus*

3, *Col. 4:11, see Jesus Justus*

K

KADMIEL, Levite under Zerubbabel, *Ezra 2:40*

2, Levite under Nehemiah, *Neh. 9:4*

3, Levite, sealed Nehemiah's covenant, *Neh. 10:9*

KAIWAN, Babylonian deity, *Am. 5:26*

KALLAI, head of priestly family under Joiakim, *Neh. 12:20*

KAREAH, father of allies of Gedaliah, *2 Kg. 25:23*

KEDAR, son of Ishmael, *Gen. 25:13*

KEDEMAH, son of Ishmael, *Gen. 25:15*

KEILAH, clan leader in Judah, *1 Chr. 4:19*

KELAIAH, left foreign wife, *Ezra 10:23*

KELITA, *Ezra 10:23, see Kelaiah*

KEMUEL, nephew of Abraham, *Gen. 22:21*

2, leader of Ephraim, helped divide land, *Num. 34:24*

3, father of an officer for David, *1 Chr. 27:17*

KENAN, patriarch, grandson of Seth, *Gen. 5:9*

KENAZ, grandson of Esau, *Gen. 36:11*

2, brother of Caleb, father of Othniel, *Jos. 15:17*

3, grandson of Caleb, *1 Chr. 4:15*

KEREN-HAPPUCH, daughter of Job, *Job 42:14*

KEROS, ancestor of temple servants, *Ezra 2:44*

KETAB, ancestor of temple servants, *1 Esd. 5:30*

KETURAH, wife of Abraham, *Gen. 25:1*

KEZIAH, daughter of Job, *Job 42:14*

KISH, son of Jeiel of Benjamin, *1 Chr. 8:30*

KISH 2, father of King Saul, *1 Sam. 9:1*

3, clan leader in Levi, *1 Chr. 23:21*

4, Levite under Hezekiah, *2 Chr. 29:12*

5, great-grandfather of Mordecai, *Est. 2:5*

KISHI, *1 Chr. 6:44, see Kushaiah*

KITTIM, grandson of Japheth, *Gen. 10:4*

KOHATH, son of Levi, ancestor of Moses, *Gen. 46:11*

KOLAIAH, father of the prophet Ahab, *Jer. 29:21*

2, ancestor of returning exile, *Neh. 11:7*

KORAH, son of Esau, *Gen. 36:5*

2, grandson of Esau, Edomite chief, *Gen. 36:16*

Scholars agree that Luke wrote the Gospel named for him; they are uncertain about the identities of the other three Evangelists.

KORAH 3, rebel against Moses, ancestor of Korahites, *Ex. 6:21*

4, clan leader in Judah, *1 Chr. 2:43*

KORE, Levite gatekeeper, *1 Chr. 9:19*

2, Levite under Hezekiah, *2 Chr. 31:14*

KOZ, clan leader in Judah, *1 Chr. 4:8*

KUSHAIAH, father of Ethan, *1 Chr. 15:17*

L

LAADAH, clan leader in Judah, *1 Chr. 4:21*

LABAN, son of Bethuel, brother of Rebekah, *Gen. 24:29*

LACCUNUS, left foreign wife, *1 Esd. 9:31*

LADAN, Ephraimite, ancestor of Joshua, *1 Chr. 7:26*

2, *1 Chr. 23:7, see Libni*

LAEL, clan leader in Levi, *Num. 3:24*

LAHAD, clan leader in Judah, *1 Chr. 4:2*

LAHMI, brother of Goliath, Philistine giant, *1 Chr. 20:5*

LAISH, father of Palti, *1 Sam. 25:44*

LAMECH, son of Methushael, descendant of Cain, *Gen. 4:18*

LAMECH 2, son of Methuselah, father of Noah, *Gen. 5:25*

LAPPIDOTH, husband of the judge Deborah, *Jg. 4:4*

LASTHENES, Syrian royal official, *1 Macc. 11:31*

LAZARUS, beggar in Jesus' parable, *Lk. 16:20*

LAZARUS 2, raised from the dead by Jesus, *Jn. 11:1*

LEAH, daughter of Laban, wife of Jacob, *Gen. 29:16*

LEBANA, *Neh. 7:48, see Lebanah*

LEBANAH, ancestor of temple servants under Zerubbabel, *Ezra 2:45*

LECAH, son of Er, clan leader in Judah, *1 Chr. 4:21*

LEMUEL, king named as author of Proverbs 31, *Pr. 31:1*

LETUSHIM, descendants of Abraham and Keturah, *Gen. 25:3*

LEUMMIM, descendants of Abraham and Keturah, *Gen. 25:3*

LEVI, son of Jacob and Leah, *Gen. 29:34*

2, ancestor of Jesus, *Lk. 3:29*

3, ancestor of Jesus, *Lk. 3:24*

4, *Mk. 2:14, see Matthew*

LEVIATHAN, sea monster, *Job 3:8*

LIBNI, son of Gershom, Levite clan leader, *1 Chr. 6:17*

2, great-grandson of Levi, *1 Chr. 6:29*

LIKHI, clan leader in Manasseh, *1 Chr. 7:19*

LINUS, Christian who greets Timothy, *2 Tim. 4:21*

LOIS, grandmother of Timothy, mother of Eunice, *2 Tim. 1:5*

LOT, son of Haran, nephew of Abraham, *Gen. 11:27*

LOTAN, Horite clan chief, *Gen. 36:20*

LOTHASUBUS, aide to Ezra, *1 Esd. 9:44*

LOZON, *1 Esd. 5:33, see Darkon*

LUCIUS, Roman consul, supporter of Jewish state, *1 Macc. 15:16*

2, from Cyrene, Christian prophet at Antioch, *Acts 13:1*

3, Christian, coworker of Paul, *Rom. 16:21*

LUD, son of Shem, *Gen. 10:22*

LUDIM, grandson of Ham, *Gen. 10:13*

LUKE, Christian physician, coworker of Paul, *Col. 4:14*

LYDIA, Christian from Thyatira, convert of Paul, *Acts 16:14*

LYSANIAS, tetrarch of Abilene, *Lk. 3:1*

LYSIAS, Syrian noble, attacked Judas Maccabeus, *1 Macc. 3:32*

LYSIAS 2, Roman commander, arrested Paul, *Acts 23:26*

LYSIMACHUS, brother of Menelaus, *2 Macc. 4:29*

2, translated book of Esther into Greek, *Ad. Est. 11:1*

M

MAACAH, nephew of Abraham, *Gen. 22:24*

2, concubine of Caleb, *1 Chr. 2:48*

3, wife or sister of Machir the Manassite, *1 Chr. 7:15*

4, wife of Jeiel, ancestor of Saul, *1 Chr. 8:29*

5, *1 Kg. 2:39, see Maoch*

6, father of one of David's 30 warriors, *1 Chr. 11:43*

7, father of an officer for David, *1 Chr. 27:16*

8, wife of David, mother of Absalom, *2 Sam. 3:3*

9, wife of Rehoboam, *1 Kg. 15:2*

MAADAI, left foreign wife, *Ezra 10:34*

MAADIAH, priest with Zerubbabel, *Neh. 12:5*

MAAI, musician, helped dedicate Jerusalem's walls, *Neh. 12:36*

MAASAI, *1 Chr. 9:12, see Amashsai*

MAASEIAH, Levite, played lyre before ark, *1 Chr. 15:18*

2, commander, helped depose Queen Athaliah, *2 Chr. 23:1*

3, officer under King Uzziah, *2 Chr. 26:11*

4, son of King Ahaz, *2 Chr. 28:7*

5, governor of Jerusalem for King Josiah, *2 Chr. 34:8*

6, father of Zephaniah 3, *Jer. 21:1*

7, father of Zedekiah 3, *Jer. 29:21*

8, doorkeeper in the temple, *Jer. 35:4*

9, father of Azariah 27, *Neh. 3:23*

10, priest, left foreign wife, *Ezra 10:18*

11, priest, left foreign wife, *Ezra 10:21*

12, priest, left foreign wife, *Ezra 10:22*

13, left foreign wife, *Ezra 10:30*

14, aide to Ezra, *Neh. 8:4*

15, Levite, taught the Law, *Neh. 8:7*

16, Jew in Jerusalem after the exile, *Neh. 11:5*

17, Benjaminite in Jerusalem, *Neh. 11:7*

18, priest, musician, *Neh. 12:41*

19, priest, musician, *Neh. 12:42*

20, sealed Nehemiah's covenant, *Neh. 10:25*

Isaiah's son Maher-shalal-hash-baz has the Bible's longest name.

MAASMAS, envoy for Ezra, *1 Esd. 8:43*

MAATH, ancestor of Jesus, *Lk. 3:26*

MAAZ, clan leader in Judah, *1 Chr. 2:27*

MAAZIAH, head of a division of priests, *1 Chr. 24:18*

2, priest, sealed Nehemiah's covenant, *Neh. 10:8*

MACCABEUS, *1 Macc. 2:4,* see Judas Maccabeus

MACHBANNAI, Gadite who joined David, *1 Chr. 12:13*

MACHBENAH, clan leader or town in Judah, *1 Chr. 2:49*

MACHI, father of spy for Moses, *Num. 13:15*

MACHIR, son of Manasseh, *Gen. 50:23*

2, ally of David, *2 Sam. 9:4*

MACCNADEBAI, left foreign wife, *Ezra 10:40*

MACRON, Syrian official, *2 Macc. 10:12*

MADAI, son of Japheth, grandson of Noah, *Gen. 10:2*

MAGDALENE, *Mt. 27:56,* see Mary Magdalene

MAGDIEL, clan chief in Edom, *Gen. 36:43*

MAGOG, son of Japheth, grandson of Noah, *Gen. 10:2*

MAGPIASH, sealed Nehemiah's covenant, *Neh. 10:20*

MAHALALEL, ancestor of Noah, *Gen. 5:12*

2, ancestor of returned exile, *Neh. 11:4*

MAHALATH, daughter of Ishmael, wife of Esau, *Gen. 28:9*

2, wife of King Rehoboam, *2 Chr. 11:18*

MAHALELEEL, *Lk. 3:37,* see Mahalalel 1

MAHARAI, one of David's 30 warriors, *2 Sam. 23:28*

MAHATH, Levite, ancestor of Heman the musician, *1 Chr. 6:35*

2, Levite under Hezekiah, *2 Chr. 29:12*

MAHAZIOTH, Levite, son of Heman the musician, *1 Chr. 25:4*

MAHER-SHALAL-HASH-BAZ, son of Isaiah, *Is. 8:1*

MAHLAH, great-grandson of Manasseh, *1 Chr. 7:18*

2, daughter of Zelophehad, *Num. 26:33*

MAHLI, grandson of Levi, *Ex. 6:19*

2, clan leader in Levi, *1 Chr. 6:47*

MAHLON, son of Naomi, husband of Ruth, *Ru. 1:2*

MAHOL, father (or guild) of four wise men, *1 Kg. 4:31*

MAHSEIAH, grandfather of Baruch, *Jer. 32:12*

MALACHI, prophet, *Mal. 1:1*

MALCAM, clan leader in Benjamin, *1 Chr. 8:9*

MALCHIAH, father of Pashhur, King Zedekiah's official, *Jer. 21:1*

MALCHIEL, grandson of Asher, *Gen. 46:17*

MALCHIJAH, ancestor of Asaph, *1 Chr. 6:40*

2, head of a division of priests, *1 Chr. 24:9*

3, priest, ancestor of returning exiles, *1 Chr. 9:12*

4, left foreign wife, *Ezra 10:25*

5, left foreign wife, *Ezra 10:31*

6, Rechabite, repaired Jerusalem's walls, *Neh. 3:14*

7, goldsmith, repaired Jerusalem's walls, *Neh. 3:31*

8, priest, musician, *Neh. 12:42*

9, aide to Ezra in reading Law, *Neh. 8:4*

10, sealed Nehemiah's covenant, *Neh. 10:3*

MALCHIRAM, son of King Jehoiachin, *1 Chr. 3:18*

MALCHISHUA, son of King Saul, *1 Sam. 14:49*

MALCHUS, slave whose ear Peter cut off, *Jn. 18:10*

MALLOTHI, Levite, son of Heman the musician, *1 Chr. 25:4*

MALLUCH, Levite, ancestor of Ethan, *1 Chr. 6:44*

2, priest with Zerubbabel, *Neh. 12:2*

3, left foreign wife, *Ezra 10:29*

4, left foreign wife, *Ezra 10:32*

5, priest, sealed Nehemiah's covenant, *Neh. 10:4*

6, sealed Nehemiah's covenant, *Neh. 10:27*

MALLUCHI, *Neh. 12:14,* see Malluch 2

MAMDAI, left foreign wife, *1 Esd. 9:34*

MAMRE, Amorite ally of Abraham, *Gen. 13:18*

MANAEN, Christian prophet, from Herod's court, *Acts 13:1*

MANAHATH, Edomite clan leader, *Gen. 36:23*

MANASSEH, son of Joseph, *Gen. 41:51*

MANASSEH 2, son of Hezekiah, king of Judah, *2 Kg. 20:21*

3, husband of Judith, *Jdt. 8:2*

4, left foreign wife, *Ezra 10:30*

5, left foreign wife, *Ezra 10:33*

MANIUS, Titus, Roman ambassador, *2 Macc. 11:34*

MANOAH, father of Samson, *Jg. 13:2*

MAOCH, father of King Achish of Gath, *1 Sam. 27:2*

MAON, clan leader in Judah, *1 Chr. 2:45*

MARA, *Ru. 1:20,* see Naomi

MARESHAH, son of Caleb, *1 Chr. 2:42*

2, clan leader in Judah, *1 Chr. 4:21*

MARK, John, coworker of Paul and Peter, *Acts 12:12*

MARSENA, Persian noble, adviser of Ahasuerus, *Est. 1:14*

MARTHA, sister of Mary and Lazarus, *Lk. 10:38*

MARY, mother of Jesus, *Mt. 1:16*

MARY 2, mother of James and Joseph, *Mt. 27:56*

MARY 3, sister of Martha and Lazarus, *Lk. 10:39*

4, wife of Clopas, *Jn. 19:25*

MARY 5, mother of John Mark, *Acts 12:12; see Mary 4, page 287*

6, Christian in Rome, *Rom. 16:6*

MARY MAGDALENE, disciple of Jesus, *Mt. 27:56*

Mary is the New Testament version of the Hebrew name Miriam; other than Moses' sister, only one Miriam is named in the Bible.

MASH, grandson of Shem, *Gen. 10:23*

MASIAH, ancestor of temple servants, *1 Esd. 5:34*

MASSA, son of Ishmael, *Gen. 25:14*

MATRED, mother-in-law of king of Edom, *Gen. 36:39*

MATTAN, priest of Baal, *2 Kg. 11:18*

2, official of King Zedekiah, *Jer. 38:1*

MATTANIAH, Levite, son of Heman the musician, *1 Chr. 25:4*

2, Levite, descendant of Asaph, *2 Chr. 20:14*

3, Levite under King Hezekiah, *2 Chr. 29:13*

4, *2 Kg. 24:17,* see Zedekiah 5

5, Levite with Zerubbabel, *Neh. 12:8*

6, grandfather of Levite under Nehemiah, *Neh. 13:13*

7, Levite musician, great-grandson of Asaph, *1 Chr. 9:15*

8, left foreign wife, *Ezra 10:26*

9, left foreign wife, *Ezra 10:27*

10, left foreign wife, *Ezra 10:30*

11, left foreign wife, *Ezra 10:37*

12, Levite, keeper of storehouses, *Neh. 12:25*

13, priest, helped dedicate Jerusalem's walls, *Neh. 12:35*

MATTATHA, grandson of David, ancestor of Jesus, *Lk. 3:31*

MATTATHIAH, *1 Esd. 9:43,* see Mattithiah 5

MATTATHIAS, ancestor of Jesus, *Lk. 3:26*

2, ancestor of Jesus, *Lk. 3:25*

MATTATHIAS 3, father of Judas Maccabeus, *1 Macc. 2:1*

4, Syrian envoy to Judas Maccabeus, *2 Macc. 14:19*

5, commander under Jonathan 16, *1 Macc. 11:70*

6, son of Simon 4, *1 Macc. 16:14*

In addition to Methuselah, six people lived more than 900 years.

MATTATTAH, left foreign wife, *Ezra 10:33*

MATTENAI, head of priestly family under Joiakim, *Neh. 12:19*

2, left foreign wife, *Ezra 10:33*

3, left foreign wife, *Ezra 10:37*

MATTHAN, grandfather of Joseph and ancestor of Jesus, *Mt. 1:15*

MATTHAT, ancestor of Jesus, *Lk. 3:29*

2, grandfather of Joseph and ancestor of Jesus, *Lk. 3:24*

MATTHEW, Levi, tax collector, apostle, *Mt. 9:9*

MATTHIAS, apostle who replaced Judas Iscariot, *Acts 1:23*

MATTITHIAH, Levite, played harp before ark, *1 Chr. 15:18*

2, Levite, sanctuary musician, *1 Chr. 25:3*

3, left foreign wife, *Ezra 10:43*

4, Levite, baker of temple bread, *1 Chr. 9:31*

5, aide of Ezra in reading Law, *Neh. 8:4*

MEBUNNAI, one of David's 30 warriors, *2 Sam. 23:27*

MEDAD, Israelite elder appointed by Moses, *Num. 11:26*

MEDAN, son of Abraham and Keturah, *Gen. 25:2*

MEHETABEL, wife of King Hadar of Edom, *Gen. 36:39*

2, grandfather of Shemaiah, a false prophet, *Neh. 6:10*

MEHIDA, ancestor of temple servants, *Ezra 2:52*

MEHIR, clan leader in Judah, *1 Chr. 4:11*

MEHUJAEL, descendant of Cain, *Gen. 4:18*

MEHUMAN, eunuch, chamberlain for Ahasuerus, *Est. 1:10*

MELATIAH, helped repair Jerusalem's walls, *Neh. 3:7*

MELCHI, grandfather of Shealtiel, ancestor of Jesus, *Lk. 3:28*

2, ancestor of Jesus, *Lk. 3:24*

MELCHIEL, father of Bethulia magistrate, *Jdt. 6:15*

MELCHIZEDEK, king of Salem, blessed Abraham, *Gen. 14:18*

MELEA, ancestor of Jesus, *Lk. 3:31*

MELECH, descendant of Saul and Jonathan, *1 Chr. 8:35*

MEMMIUS, Quintus, Roman envoy to Jews, *2 Macc. 11:34*

MEMUCAN, Persian noble, adviser of Ahasuerus, *Est. 1:14*

MENAHEM, assassin, king of Israel, *2 Kg. 15:14*

MENELAUS, high priest, *2 Macc. 4:23*

MENESTHEUS, father of Apollonius of Syria, *2 Macc. 4:4*

MENNA, ancestor of Jesus, *Lk. 3:31*

MEONOTHAI, son of Othniel the judge, *1 Chr. 4:13*

MEPHIBOSHETH, son of Saul and Rizpah, *2 Sam. 21:8*

MEPHIBOSHETH 2, son of Jonathan 3, *2 Sam. 4:4*

MERAB, daughter of King Saul, *1 Sam. 14:49*

MERAIAH, head of priestly family under Joiakim, *Neh. 12:12*

MERAIOTH, priest, ancestor of Zadok 1, *1 Chr. 6:6*

2, ancestor of priest under Nehemiah, *1 Chr. 9:11*

MERARI, son of Levi, *Gen. 46:11*

2, father of Judith, *Jdt. 8:1*

MERED, clan leader in Judah, *1 Chr. 4:17*

MEREMOTH, priest with Zerubbabel, *Neh. 12:3*

2, left foreign wife, *Ezra 10:36*

3, priest, helped weigh silver and gold, *Ezra 8:33*

4, priest, sealed Nehemiah's covenant, *Neh. 10:5*

MERES, Persian noble, adviser of Ahasuerus, *Est. 1:14*

MERIB-BAAL, *1 Chr. 8:34*, see Mephibosheth 2

MERODACH, Marduk, god of Babylon, *Jer. 50:2*

MERODACH-BALADAN, anti-Assyrian king of Babylon, *2 Kg. 20:12*

MESHA, clan leader in Benjamin, *1 Chr. 8:9*

2, son of Caleb, *1 Chr. 2:42*

MESHA 3, king of Moab, *2 Kg. 3:4*

MESHACH, companion of Shadrach and Abednego, *Dan. 1:7*

MESHECH, son of Japheth, grandson of Noah, *Gen. 10:2*

2, *1 Chr. 1:17*, see Mash

MESHELEMIAH, sanctuary gatekeeper, *1 Chr. 9:21*

MESHEZABEL, grandfather of one who repaired Jerusalem, *Neh. 3:4*

2, clan leader in Judah, *Neh. 11:24*

3, sealed Nehemiah's covenant, *Neh. 10:21*

MESHILLEMITH, ancestor of priest in Jerusalem, *1 Chr. 9:12*

MESHILLEMOTH, father of one who opposed enslaving Judahites, *2 Chr. 28:12*

2, *Neh. 11:13*, see Meshillemith

MESHOBAB, leader in Simeon under King Hezekiah, *1 Chr. 4:34*

MESHULLAM, clan leader in Gad, *1 Chr. 5:13*

2, clan leader in Benjamin, *1 Chr. 8:17*

3, grandfather of Shaphan, scribe of King Josiah, *2 Kg. 22:3*

4, father of Hilkiah 7, *1 Chr. 9:11*

5, overseer of temple work under King Josiah, *2 Chr. 34:12*

6, ancestor of the priest Maasai, *1 Chr. 9:12*

7, father of a Benjaminite after exile, *1 Chr. 9:7*

8, son of Zerubbabel, *1 Chr. 3:19*

9, Benjaminite, returned after exile, *1 Chr. 9:8*

10, head of priestly family under Joiakim, *Neh. 12:13*

11, head of priestly family under Joiakim, *Neh. 12:16*

12, gatekeeper in the time of Joiakim, *Neh. 12:25*

13, envoy of Ezra, *Ezra 8:16*

14, opponent of Ezra's reforms, *Ezra 10:15*

15, left foreign wife, *Ezra 10:29*

16, helped repair Jerusalem's walls, *Neh. 3:4*

17, helped repair Jerusalem gate, *Neh. 3:6*

18, helped in dedication of Jerusalem's walls, *Neh. 12:33*

19, aide of Ezra in reading Law, *Neh. 8:4*

20, priest, sealed Nehemiah's covenant, *Neh. 10:7*

21, sealed Nehemiah's covenant, *Neh. 10:20*

MESHULLEMETH, wife of King Manasseh, *2 Kg. 21:19*

METHUSELAH, son of Enoch, lived 969 years, *Gen. 5:21*

METHUSHAEL, descendant of Cain, *Gen. 4:18*

MEUNIM, ancestor of temple servants, *Ezra 2:50*

MEZAHAB, ancestor of Mehetabel, wife of Hadar of Edom, *Gen. 36:39*

MIBHAR, one of David's mighty men, *1 Chr. 11:38*

MIBSAM, son of Ishmael, *Gen. 25:13*

2, clan leader in Simeon, *1 Chr. 4:25*

MIBZAR, clan chief in Edom, *Gen. 36:42*

MICA, son of Mephibosheth 2, *2 Sam. 9:12*

2, *1 Chr. 9:15*, see Micaiah 4

3, Levite, sealed Nehemiah's covenant, *Neh. 10:11*

MICAH, Ephraimite who set up a private shrine, *Jg. 17:1*

2, Levite under David, *1 Chr. 23:20*

3, *1 Chr. 8:34*, see Mica 1

4, clan leader in Reuben, *1 Chr. 5:5*

MICAH 5, prophet, *Jer. 26:18; see Micah 2, page 295*

6, *2 Chr. 34:20*, see Micaiah 5

7, father of Bethulia magistrate, *Jdt. 6:15*

MICAIAH, *2 Chr. 13:2*, see Maacah 9

2, official of King Jehoshaphat, *2 Chr. 17:7*

MICAIAH 3, son of Imlah, prophet, *1 Kg. 22:8*

4, descendant of Asaph, *Neh. 12:35*

5, father of an official for King Josiah, *2 Kg. 22:12*

6, heard Baruch read Jeremiah's prophecies, *Jer. 36:11*

7, priest, helped dedicate Jerusalem's walls, *Neh. 12:41*

MICHAEL, clan leader in Issachar, *1 Chr. 7:3*

2, father of spy for Moses, *Num. 13:13*

3, father of an officer for David, *1 Chr. 27:18*

4, Manassite who joined David, *1 Chr. 12:20*

5, clan leader in Gad, *1 Chr. 5:14*

6, son of King Jehoshaphat, *2 Chr. 21:2*

7, clan leader in Gad, son of Abihail, *1 Chr. 5:13*

8, Levite, ancestor of Asaph, *1 Chr. 6:40*

9, clan leader in Benjamin after exile, *1 Chr. 8:16*

10, father of returning exile, *Ezra 8:8*

MICHAEL 11, angel, *Dan. 10:13*

MICHAL, daughter of Saul, wife of David, *1 Sam. 14:49*

MICRI, clan leader in Benjamin, *1 Chr. 9:8*

MIDIAN, son of Abraham and Keturah, ancestor of Midianites, *Gen. 25:2*

MIJAMIN, head of a division of priests, *1 Chr. 24:9*

2, priest with Zerubbabel, *Neh. 12:5*

3, left foreign wife, *Ezra 10:25*

4, priest, helped dedicate Jerusalem's walls, *Neh. 12:41*

5, priest, sealed Nehemiah's covenant, *Neh. 10:7*

MIKLOTH, Benjaminite ancestor of Saul, *1 Chr. 8:32*

2, army commander under David, *1 Chr. 27:4*

MIKNEIAH, Levite, played harp before ark, *1 Chr. 15:18*

MILALAI, Levite, helped dedicate Jerusalem's walls, *Neh. 12:36*

MILCAH, niece of Abraham, *Gen. 11:29*

2, daughter of Zelophehad, *Num. 26:33*

MILCOM, Ammonite god, *1 Kg. 11:5*

MINIAMIN, priest under Hezekiah, *2 Chr. 31:15*

2, priest with Zerubbabel, *Neh. 12:17*

3, priest, helped dedicate Jerusalem's walls, *Neh. 12:41*

MIRIAM, sister of Moses and Aaron, *Ex. 15:20*

2, daughter of Mered the Judahite, *1 Chr. 4:17*

MIRMAH, clan leader in Benjamin, *1 Chr. 8:10*

MISHAEL, kinsman of Moses, *Ex. 6:22*

2, *Dan. 1:6,* see Meshach

3, aide to Ezra in reading Law, *Neh. 8:4*

MISHAM, clan leader in Benjamin, *1 Chr. 8:12*

MISHMA, son of Ishmael, *Gen. 25:14*

2, clan leader in Simeon, *1 Chr. 4:25*

MISHMANNAH, Gadite who joined David, *1 Chr. 12:10*

MISPAR, Jewish leader with Zerubbabel, *Ezra 2:2*

MISPERETH, *Neh. 7:7,* see Mispar

MITHREDATH, treasurer of Cyrus, king of Persia, *Ezra 1:8*

2, Persian official, opposed Jerusalem rebuilding, *Ezra 4:7*

MITHRIDATES, *1 Esd. 2:11,* see Mithredath 1

2, *1 Esd. 2:16,* see Mithredath 2

MIZZAH, grandson of Esau, *Gen. 36:13*

MNASON, Christian from Cyprus, gave lodging to Paul, *Acts 21:16*

MOAB, son of Lot and his daughter, ancestor of Moabites, *Gen. 19:37*

MOADIAH, priest with Zerubbabel, *Neh. 12:5*

MOLECH, Ammonite god, *Lev. 18:21*

MOLID, clan leader in Judah, *1 Chr. 2:29*

MOLOCH, *Acts 7:43,* see Molech

MOOSSIAS, left foreign wife, *1 Esd. 9:31*

MORDECAI, Jewish leader with Zerubbabel, *Ezra 2:2*

MORDECAI 2, son of Jair of Benjamin, cousin of Esther, *Est. 2:5*

MOSES, lawgiver, led Exodus from Egypt, *Ex. 2:10*

MOZA, son of Caleb, *1 Chr. 2:46*

2, descendant of Saul, *1 Chr. 8:36*

MUPPIM, son of Benjamin, *Gen. 46:21*

MUSHI, grandson of Levi, *Ex. 6:19*

N

NAAM, son of Caleb, *1 Chr. 4:15*

NAAMAH, daughter of Lamech, descendant of Cain, *Gen. 4:22*

2, mother of Rehoboam, *1 Kg. 14:21*

NAAMAN, son or grandson of Benjamin, *Gen. 46:21*

NAAMAN 2, Syrian general healed by Elisha, *2 Kg. 5:1*

NAARAH, wife of Ashhur, leader of Tekoa, *1 Chr. 4:5*

NAARAI, *1 Chr. 11:37,* see Paarai

NAATHUS, left foreign wife, *1 Esd. 9:31*

NABAL, wealthy Calebite, opponent of David, *1 Sam. 25:3*

NABARIAH, aide of Ezra in reading Law, *1 Esd. 9:44*

NABOTH, owner of vineyard, killed by order of Jezebel, *1 Kg. 21:1*

NACON, owner of threshing floor, *2 Sam. 6:6*

NADAB, eldest son of Aaron, *Ex. 6:23*

2, kinsman of King Saul, *1 Chr. 8:30*

3, clan leader in Judah, *1 Chr. 2:28*

NADAB 4, son of Jeroboam, king of Israel, *1 Kg. 14:20; see* Nadab 2, page 314

5, nephew of Ahikar, *Tob. 11:18*

NAGGAI, ancestor of Jesus, *Lk. 3:25*

NAHAM, clan leader in Judah, *1 Chr. 4:19*

NAHAMANI, Jew with Zerubbabel, *Neh. 7:7*

NAHARAI, Joab's armor-bearer, one of David's 30 warriors, *2 Sam. 23:37*

NAHASH, king of Ammonites, *1 Sam. 11:1*

2, father of David's sisters, *2 Sam. 17:25*

NAHATH, grandson of Esau, *Gen. 36:13*

2, *1 Chr. 6:26,* see Tohu,

3, Levite under Hezekiah, *2 Chr. 31:13*

NAHBI, leader of Naphtali, spy sent into Canaan, *Num. 13:14*

NAHOR, Abraham's grandfather, *Gen. 11:22*

NAHOR 2, Abraham's brother, *Gen. 11:26*

NAHSHON, Aaron's brother-in-law, *Ex. 6:23*

NAHUM, prophet from Elkosh, *Nah. 1:1*

2, ancestor of Jesus, *Lk. 3:25*

NAIDUS, *1 Esd. 9:31,* see Benaiah 11

NAOMI, Ruth's mother-in-law, *Ru. 1:2*

NAPHISH, son of Ishmael, *Gen. 25:15*

NAPHTALI, son of Jacob and Bilhah, *Gen. 30:8*

NAPHTUHIM, son of Egypt, *Gen. 10:13*

NARCISSUS, head of household with Christians, *Rom. 16:11*

NATHAN, father of one of David's 30 warriors, *2 Sam. 23:36*

NATHAN 2, prophet, adviser of David, *2 Sam. 7:2*

3, father of officials for Solomon, *1 Kg. 4:5*

4, son of David, *2 Sam. 5:14*

5, clan leader in Judah, *1 Chr. 2:36*

6, envoy for Ezra, *Ezra 8:16*

7, left foreign wife, *Ezra 10:39*

NATHANAEL, ancestor of Judith, *Jdt. 8:1*

2, left foreign wife, *1 Esd. 9:22*

NATHANAEL 3, disciple of Jesus, *Jn. 1:45*

NATHAN-MELECH, official of King Josiah, *2 Kg. 23:11*

NEARIAH, leader in Simeon under King Hezekiah, *1 Chr. 4:42*

2, descendant of Zerubbabel, *1 Chr. 3:22*

NEBAI, sealed Nehemiah's covenant, *Neh. 10:19*

NEBAIOTH, first son of Ishmael, *Gen. 25:13*

NEBAT, father of King Jeroboam, *1 Kg. 11:26*

David's unwise adversary Nabal was aptly named "fool."

NEBO, ancestor of some who left foreign wives, *Ezra 10:43*

2, Babylonian god, *Is. 46:1*

NEBUCHADNEZZAR, king of Babylon, *2 Kg. 24:1*

NEBUCHADREZZAR, *Jer. 21:2,* see Nebuchadnezzar

NEBUSHAZBAN, Babylonian officer, *Jer. 39:13*

NEBUZARADAN, Babylonian general, *2 Kg. 25:8*

NECO, Pharaoh of Egypt, *2 Kg. 23:29*

NEBABIAH, son of Jehoiachin, *1 Chr. 3:18*

NEHEMIAH, Jewish leader with Zerubbabel, *Ezra 2:2*

NEHEMIAH 2, governor of Judah, *Neh. 1:1*

3, helped repair Jerusalem's walls, *Neh. 3:16*

NEHUM, *Neh. 7:7,* see Rehum 1

NEHUSHTA, wife of King Jehoiakim, *2 Kg. 24:8*

NEHUSHTAN, name given to bronze serpent, *2 Kg. 18:4*

NEKODA, ancestor of temple servants, *Ezra 2:48*

2, ancestor of unregistered Israelites, *Ezra 2:60*

NEMUEL, son of Simeon, *Num. 26:12*

2, descendant of Reuben, *Num. 26:9*

NEPHEG, Levite, brother of Korah, *Ex. 6:21*

2, son of David, *2 Sam. 5:15*

NEPHISIM, ancestor of temple servants, *Ezra 2:50*

NEPHUSHESIM, *Neh. 7:52, see* Nephisim

NER, grandfather of King Saul, *1 Chr. 8:33*

2, uncle of Saul 1 and father of Abner, *1 Sam. 14:50*

NERAIAH, *Bar. 1:1, see* Neriah

NEREUS, Christian in Rome, *Rom. 16:15*

NERGAL, Akkadian god of war, pestilence, and death, *2 Kg. 17:30*

NERGAL-SHAREZER, Babylonian official, *Jer. 39:3*

Noah is also a woman's name, given to one of Zelophehad's five daughters.

NERI, ancestor of Jesus, *Lk. 3:27*

NERIAH, father of Baruch and Seraiah, *Jer. 32:12*

NETHANEL, leader of Issachar under Moses, *Num. 1:8*

2, brother of David, *1 Chr. 2:14*

3, priest, blew trumpet before ark, *1 Chr. 15:24*

4, Levite, father of Shemaiah 6, *1 Chr. 24:6*

5, son of Obed-edom, sanctuary gatekeeper, *1 Chr. 26:4*

6, official of King Jehoshaphat who taught Law, *2 Chr. 17:7*

7, chief Levite under Josiah, *2 Chr. 35:9*

8, head of priestly family under Joiakim, *Neh. 12:21*

9, priest, left foreign wife, *Ezra 10:22*

10, Levite, musician, *Neh. 12:36*

NETHANIAH, son of Asaph 2, sanctuary musician, *1 Chr. 25:2*

2, Levite under King Jehoshaphat, *1 Chr. 17:8*

3, father of an official for King Jehoiakim, *Jer. 36:14*

4, father of Ishmael 5, *2 Kg. 25:23*

5, *1 Esd. 9:34, see* Nathan 7

NEZIAH, ancestor of temple servants, *Ezra 2:54*

NIBHAZ, Avvite god worshiped in Samaria, *2 Kg. 17:31*

NICANOR, Syrian general, *1 Macc. 3:38*

2, Christian leader, one of the seven, *Acts 6:5*

NICODEMUS, Pharisee who visited Jesus, *Jn. 3:1*

NICOLAUS, one of the seven, possible heretic, *Acts 6:5*

NIGER, *Acts 13:1, see* Simeon 7

NIMROD, son of Cush, *Gen. 10:8*

NIMSHI, grandfather or father of King Jehu, *1 Kg. 19:16*

NISROCH, Assyrian god, *2 Kg. 19:37*

NOADIAH, Levite under Ezra, kept temple treasure, *Ezra 8:33*

2, prophetess, opposed Nehemiah, *Neh. 6:14*

NOAH, builder of ark, *Gen. 5:29*

2, daughter of Zelophehad, *Num. 26:33*

NOBAH, Manassite who captured town, *Num. 32:42*

NODAB, ancestor of clan east of Jordan, *1 Chr. 5:19*

NOGAH, son of David, *1 Chr. 3:7*

NOHAH, son of Benjamin, *1 Chr. 8:2*

NOT MY PEOPLE, son of Hosea, *Hos. 1:9*

NOT PITIED, daughter of Hosea, *Hos. 1:8*

NUMENIUS, Jewish ambassador to Rome, *1 Macc. 12:16*

NUN, father of Joshua, *Ex. 33:11*

NYMPHA, Christian woman with house church, *Col. 4:15*

O

OBADIAH, clan leader in Issachar, *1 Chr. 7:3*

2, father of an officer for David, *1 Chr. 27:19*

3, Gadite who joined David, *1 Chr. 12:9*

OBADIAH 4, Ahab's chamberlain, *1 Kg. 18:3; see* Obadiah, page 329

5, official of King Jehoshaphat, *2 Chr. 17:7*

6, Levite under King Josiah, *2 Chr. 34:12*

7, descendant of Saul and Jonathan, *1 Chr. 8:38*

OBADIAH 8, prophet against Edom, *Ob. 1:1; see* Obadiah 2, page 329

9, clan leader with Zerubbabel, *Ezra 8:9*

10, gatekeeper under the high priest Joiakim, *Neh. 12:25*

11, Levite under Ezra, *1 Chr. 9:16*

12, priest, sealed Nehemiah's covenant, *Neh. 10:5*

13, descendant of Zerubbabel, *1 Chr. 3:21*

OBAL, descendant of Shem, *Gen. 10:28*

OBED, son of Ruth, grandfather of David, *Ru. 4:17*

2, one of David's 30 warriors, *1 Chr. 11:47*

3, grandson of Obed-edom 3, *1 Chr. 26:7*

4, clan leader in Judah, *1 Chr. 2:37*

5, father of ally of Jehoida, *2 Chr. 23:1*

6, *see* Ebed 2, *1 Esd. 8:32*

OBED-EDOM, keeper of the ark under David, *2 Sam. 6:10*

2, Levite, sanctuary gatekeeper, *1 Chr. 15:18*

3, Korahite Levite, sanctuary gatekeeper, *1 Chr. 26:4*

4, Levite under Amaziah, *2 Chr. 25:24*

OBIL, David's overseer of camels, *1 Chr. 27:30*

OCHIEL, *1 Esd. 1:9, see* Jeiel 8

OCHRAN, father of Pagiel, leader of Asher under Moses, *Num. 1:13*

ODED, father of Azariah 8, *2 Chr. 15:1*

2, prophet in Samaria, *2 Chr. 28:9*

ODOMERA, Arab slain by Jonathan the Maccabee, *1 Macc. 9:66*

OG, Amorite king of Bashan, *Num. 21:33*

OHAD, son of Simeon, *Gen. 46:10*

OHEL, son of Zerubbabel, *1 Chr. 3:20*

OHOLIAB, Danite craftsman under Moses, *Ex. 31:6*

OHOLIBAMAH, wife of Esau, *Gen. 36:2*

2, clan chief in Edom, *Gen. 36:41*

OLYMPAS, Christian woman at Rome, *Rom. 16:15*

OMAR, grandson of Esau, *Gen. 36:11*

OMRI, grandson of Benjamin, *1 Chr. 7:8*

2, David's officer over Issachar, *1 Chr. 27:18*

OMRI 3, king of Israel, *1 Kg. 16:16*

4, ancestor of returning exile, *1 Chr. 9:4*

ON, Reubenite rebel against Moses, *Num. 16:1*

ONAM, clan leader in Edom, *Gen. 36:23*

2, clan leader in Judah, *1 Chr. 2:26*

ONAN, son of Judah, *Gen. 38:4*

ONESIMUS, Christian slave, companion of Paul, *Col. 4:9*

ONESIPHORUS, Christian of Ephesus, *2 Tim. 1:16*

ONIAS II, high priest, father of Simon 2, *Sir. 50:1*

ONIAS III, son of Simon 2, high priest, *2 Macc. 3:1*

OPHIR, son of Joktan, descendant of Shem, *Gen. 10:29*

OPHRAH, clan leader in Judah, *1 Chr. 4:14*

OREB, Midianite prince defeated by Gideon, *Jg. 7:25*

OREN, clan leader in Judah, *1 Chr. 2:25*

ORNAN, *1 Chr. 21:15, see* Araunah

ORPAH, sister-in-law of Ruth, *Ru. 1:4*

OSNAPPAR, *Ezra 4:10, see* Ashurbanipal

OTHNI, grandson of Obed-edom, gatekeeper, *1 Chr. 26:7*

OTHNIEL, judge, nephew of Caleb, *Jos. 15:17*

OTHONIAH, *1 Esd. 9:28, see* Mattaniah 9

OX, grandfather of Judith, *Jdt. 8:1*

OZEM, clan leader in Judah, *1 Chr. 2:25*

2, brother of David, *1 Chr. 2:15*

OZIEL, ancestor of Judith, *Jdt. 8:1*

OZNI, descendant of Gad, *Num. 26:16*

P

PAARAI, one of David's 30 warriors, *2 Sam. 23:35*

PADON, ancestor of temple servants, *Ezra 2:44*

PAGIEL, leader of Asher under Moses, *Num. 1:13*

PAHATH-MOAB, ancestor of Jews with Zerubbabel, *Ezra 2:6*

2, sealed Nehemiah's covenant, *Neh. 10:14*

PALAL, helped repair Jerusalem's walls, *Neh. 3:25*

PALLU, son of Reuben, *Gen. 46:9*

PALTI, leader of Benjamin, spy sent into Canaan, *Num. 13:9*

PALTI 2, husband of Michal, *1 Sam. 25:44*

PALTIEL, leader of Issachar, helped divide land, *Num. 34:26*

2, *2 Sam. 3:15*, see Palti 2

PARMASHTA, son of Haman, Esther's enemy, *Est. 9:9*

PARMENAS, Christian leader, one of the seven, *Acts 6:5*

PARNACH, father of leader of Zebulun under Moses, *Num. 34:25*

PAROSH, head of family returning with Zerubbabel, *Ezra 2:3*

2, father of one who helped repair Jerusalem, *Neh. 3:25*

3, sealed Nehemiah's covenant, *Neh. 10:14*

PARSHANDATHA, son of Haman, *Est. 9:7*

PARUAH, father of one of Solomon's officers, *1 Kg. 4:17*

PASACH, clan leader in Asher, *1 Chr. 7:33*

PASEAH, clan leader in Judah, *1 Chr. 4:12*

2, ancestor of temple servants, *Ezra 2:49*

3, father of Joiada 1, *Neh. 3:6*

PASHHUR, father of official of King Zedekiah, *Jer. 38:1*

2, priest, clan leader, *Ezra 2:38*

3, ancestor of priest returning after exile, *1 Chr. 9:12*

4, official of Zedekiah, *Jer. 21:1*

God gave symbolic names to three of the prophet Hosea's children: Jezreel, Not my people, and Not pitied.

PASHHUR 5, priest who put Jeremiah in stocks, *Jer. 20:1*

6, priest, sealed Nehemiah's covenant, *Neh. 10:3*

PATROBAS, Christian in Rome, *Rom. 16:14*

PATROCIUS, father of Nicanor, a Syrian general, *2 Macc. 8:9*

PAUL, apostle, originally called Saul of Tarsus, *Acts 13:9*

PAULUS, Sergius, Roman proconsul on Cyprus, *Acts 13:7*

PEDAHEL, leader of Naphtali, helped divide land, *Num. 34:28*

PEDAHZUR, father of Gamaliel, leader of Manasseh under Moses, *Num. 1:10*

PEDAIAH, father of an officer for David, *1 Chr. 27:20*

2, father of Zebidah, mother of King Jehoiakim, *2 Kg. 23:36*

3, son of King Jehoiachin, *1 Chr. 3:18*

4, ancestor of returning exile, *Neh. 11:7*

5, helped repair Jerusalem's walls, *Neh. 3:25*

6, aide of Ezra in reading Law, *Neh. 8:4*

7, Levite under Nehemiah, *Neh. 13:13*

PEKAH, assassin of King Pekahiah, king of Israel, *2 Kg. 15:25*

PEKAHIAH, son of Menahem, king of Israel, *2 Kg. 15:22*

PELAIAH, Levite who translated for Ezra, *Neh. 8:7*

2, Levite, sealed Nehemiah's covenant, *Neh. 10:10*

3, descendant of Zerubbabel, *1 Chr. 3:24*

PELALIAH, ancestor of priest after exile, *Neh. 11:12*

PELATIAH, leader of Simeon against Amalekites, *1 Chr. 4:42*

2, Jerusalem leader seen by Ezekiel, *Ezek. 11:1*

3, descendant of Zerubbabel, *1 Chr. 3:21*

4, sealed Nehemiah's covenant, *Neh. 10:22*

PELEG, son of Eber, ancestor of Abraham, *Gen. 10:25*

PELET, clan leader in Judah, *1 Chr. 2:47*

2, Benjaminite who joined David, *1 Chr. 12:3*

PELETH, Reubenite, father of rebel against Moses, *Num. 16:1*

2, clan leader in Judah, *1 Chr. 2:33*

PENINNAH, wife of Elkanah, rival of Hannah, *1 Sam. 1:2*

PENUEL, clan leader in Judah, *1 Chr. 4:4*

2, clan leader in Benjamin, *1 Chr. 8:25*

PERESH, grandson of Manasseh, *1 Chr. 7:16*

PEREZ, son of Judah and Tamar, *Gen. 38:29*

PERIDA, *Neh. 7:57*, see Peruda

PERSEUS, last king of Macedonia, *1 Macc. 8:5*

PERSIS, Christian woman in Rome, *Rom. 16:12*

PERUDA, ancestor of temple servants, *Ezra 2:55*

PETER, apostle, *Mt. 4:18*

PETHAHIAH, head of a division of priests, *1 Chr. 24:16*

2, Jewish agent of Persian king, *Neh. 11:24*

3, Levite, left foreign wife, *Ezra 10:23*

4, Levite, led public confession, *Neh. 9:5*

PETHUEL, father of the prophet Joel, *Jl. 1:1*

PEULLETHAI, son of Obed-edom, sanctuary gatekeeper, *1 Chr. 26:5*

PHALARIS, tyrant of Agrigentum, *3 Macc. 5:20*

PHALTIEL, Jewish leader under Ezra, *2 Esd. 5:16*

PHANUEL, father of Anna the prophet, *Lk. 2:36*

PHARAKIM, ancestor of temple servants, *1 Esd. 5:31*

PHARAOH, title of Egyptian king, *Gen. 12:15*

PHARES, *1 Esd. 5:5*, see Perez

PHASIRON, ancestor of Bedouin clan, *1 Macc. 9:66*

PHICOL, Philistine general, *Gen. 21:22*

PHILEMON, Christian of Colossae, *Philem. 1:1*

PHILETUS, Christian heretic at Ephesus, *2 Tim. 2:17*

PHILIP II, king of Macedon, father of Alexander the Great, *1 Macc. 1:1*

2, V, king of Macedon, *1 Macc. 8:5*

3, Phrygian governor of Jerusalem, *2 Macc. 5:22*

4, courtier of Antiochus IV Epiphanes, *1 Macc. 6:14*

5, *Lk. 3:1*, see Herod Philip

6, first husband of Herodias, *Mt. 14:3*

PHILIP 7, apostle, *Mt. 10:3*; see Philip, page 356

PHILIP 8, the evangelist, one of the seven, *Acts 6:5*; see Philip 2, page 357

PHILOLOGUS, Christian at Rome, *Rom. 16:15*

Pochereth-Hazzebaim's name is a job description: gazelle binder.

PHILOMETOR, *2 Macc. 4:21*, see Ptolemy VI Philometor

PHILOPATOR, *3 Macc. 1:1*, see Ptolemy IV Philopator

PHINEHAS, son of Eleazar, grandson of Aaron, *Ex. 6:25*

2, son of Eli, brother of Hophni, *1 Sam. 1:3*

3, father of priest under Ezra, *Ezra 8:33*

PHLEGON, Christian in Rome, *Rom. 16:14*

PHOEBE, Christian deaconess at Cenchreae, *Rom. 16:1*

PHYGELUS, Christian who deserted Paul, *2 Tim. 1:15*

PILATE, Pontius, Roman governor, *Mt. 27:2*

PILDASH, nephew of Abraham, *Gen. 22:22*

PILHA, sealed Nehemiah's covenant, *Neh. 10:24*

PILTAI, head of priestly family under Joiakim, *Neh. 12:17*

PINON, clan chief in Edom, *Gen. 36:41*

PIRAM, Amorite king of Jarmuth, *Jos. 10:3*

PISPA, clan leader in Asher, *1 Chr. 7:38*

PITHON, grandson of Jonathan, *1 Chr. 8:35*

POCHERETH-HAZZEBAIM, ancestor of temple servants, *Ezra 2:57*

PONTIUS, *Lk. 3:1*, see Pilate

PORATHA, son of Haman, *Est. 9:8*

PORCIUS, *Acts 24:27*, see Festus

POSIDONIUS, Syrian envoy to Judas Maccabeus, *2 Macc. 14:19*

POTIPHAR, Egyptian official, bought Joseph, *Gen. 37:36*

POTIPHERA, Egyptian priest, father-in-law of Joseph, *Gen. 41:45*

PRISCA, wife of Aquila, coworker of Paul, *Rom. 16:3*

PRISCILLA, *Acts 18:2*, see Prisca

PROCHORUS, Christian leader, one of the seven, *Acts 6:5*

PTOLEMY IV PHILOPATOR, king of Egypt, *3 Macc. 1:1*

2, VI PHILOMETOR, king of Egypt, *1 Macc. 1:18*

3, *2 Macc. 10:12*, see Macron

4, VII PHYSCON, king of Egypt, *1 Macc. 15:16*

PUAH, *1 Chr. 7:1*, see Puvah

2, Hebrew midwife in Egypt, *Ex. 1:15*

3, father of the judge Tola, *Jg. 10:1*

PUBLIUS, chief official of Malta whose father Paul healed, *Acts 28:7*

PUDENS, Christian who greeted Timothy, *2 Tim. 4:21*

PUL, *2 Kg. 15:19*, see Tiglath-pileser III

PURAH, servant of Gideon, *Jg. 7:10*

PUT, son of Ham, grandson of Noah, *Gen. 10:6*

PUTIEL, father-in-law of Aaron's son Eleazar, *Ex. 6:25*

PUVAH, son of Issachar, *Gen. 46:13*

PYRRHUS, father of Sopater, companion of Paul, *Acts 20:4*

Q

QUARTUS, Christian in Corinth, *Rom. 16:23*

QUINTUS, *see Memmius, 2 Macc. 11:34*

QUIRINIUS, Roman governor of Syria, *Lk. 2:2*

R

RAAMA, *1 Chr. 1:9, see Raamah*

RAAMAH, great-grandson of Noah, *Gen. 10:7*

RAAMIAH, clan leader with Zerubbabel, *Neh. 7:7*

RACHEL, wife of Jacob, *Gen. 29:6*

RADDAI, brother of David, *1 Chr. 2:14*

RAGUEL, father of Sarah, cousin of Tobit, *Tob. 3:7*

RAHAB, prostitute of Jericho, *Jos. 2:1*

RAHAB 2, monster, enemy of Yahweh, *Job 9:13*

RAHAM, clan leader in Judah, *1 Chr. 2:44*

RAKEM, great-grandson of Manasseh, *1 Chr. 7:16*

RAM, ancestor of Elihu 1, *Job 32:2*

2, son of Hezron, ancestor of David, *Ru. 4:19*

3, clan leader in Judah, *1 Chr. 2:25*

RAMESES, king of Egypt for whom city is named, *Gen. 47:11*

RAMIAH, left foreign wife, *Ezra 10:25*

RAPHA, son of Benjamin, *1 Chr. 8:2*

RAPHAEL, archangel, *Tob. 3:7*

RAPHAH, descendant of Saul and Jonathan, *1 Chr. 8:37*

RAPHAIM, ancestor of Judith, *Jdt. 8:1*

RAPHU, father of spy for Moses, *Num. 13:9*

RAZIS, Jewish elder and martyr, *2 Macc. 14:37*

REAIAH, grandson of Judah, *1 Chr. 4:2*

2, clan leader in Reuben, *1 Chr. 5:5*

3, ancestor of temple servants, *Ezra 2:47*

REBA, king of Midian killed by Israel, *Num. 31:8*

REBECCA, *Rom. 9:10, see Rebekah*

REBEKAH, wife of Isaac, *Gen. 22:23*

RECHAB, assassin of Ish-bosheth, *2 Sam. 4:2*

RECHAB 2, ancestor of Rechabites, *2 Kg. 10:15*

3, father of Malkijah, who repaired Jerusalem, *Neh. 3:14*

REELAIAH, *Ezra 2:2, see Raamiah*

REELIAH, Jew who returned with Zerubbabel, *1 Esd. 5:8*

REGEM, clan leader in Judah, *1 Chr. 2:47*

REGEM-MELECH, emissary from Bethel, *Zech. 7:2*

REHABIAH, grandson of Moses, *1 Chr. 23:17*

REHOB, father of Hadadezer, defeated by David, *2 Sam. 8:3*

2, sealed Nehemiah's covenant, *Neh. 10:11*

REHOBOAM, son of Solomon, king of Judah, *1 Kg. 11:43*

Four angels are named in the Bible (including the Apocrypha): Gabriel, Michael, Raphael, Uriel.

REHUM, Jewish leader with Zerubbabel, *Ezra 2:2*

2, chief priest with Zerubbabel, *Neh. 12:3*

3, Persian official, *Ezra 4:8*

4, helped repair Jerusalem's walls, *Neh. 3:17*

5, sealed Nehemiah's covenant, *Neh. 10:25*

REI, friend of David, *1 Kg. 1:8*

REKEM, king of Midian, *Num. 31:8*

2, clan leader in Judah, *1 Chr. 2:43*

REMALIAH, father of King Pekah of Israel, *2 Kg. 15:25*

REPHAEL, grandson of Obed-edom 2, *1 Chr. 26:7*

REPHAH, clan leader in Ephraim, *1 Chr. 7:25*

REPHAIAH, grandson of Issachar, *1 Chr. 7:2*

2, descendant of King Saul through Jonathan, *1 Chr. 9:43*

3, clan leader in Simeon in King Hezekiah's time, *1 Chr. 4:42*

4, descendant of David, *1 Chr. 3:21*

5, helped repair Jerusalem's walls, *Neh. 3:9*

REPHAN, Babylonian planetary god, *Acts 7:43*

RESAIAH, *1 Esd. 5:8, see Raamiah*

RESHEPH, clan leader in Ephraim, *1 Chr. 7:25*

REU, descendant of Shem, ancestor of Abraham, *Gen. 11:18*

REUBEN, son of Jacob and Leah, *Gen. 29:32*

REUEL, *Ex. 2:18, see Jethro*

2, son of Esau and Basemath, *Gen. 36:4*

3, *Num. 2:14, see Deuel*

4, ancestor of returning exile, *1 Chr. 9:8*

REUMAH, concubine of Nahor, Abraham's brother, *Gen. 22:24*

REZIN, Aramean king of Damascus, *2 Kg. 15:37*

2, ancestor of temple servants, *Ezra 2:48*

REZON, king of Damascus, *1 Kg. 11:23*

RHESA, ancestor of Jesus, *Lk. 3:27*

RHODA, servant of Mary, mother of John Mark, *Acts 12:13*

RHODOCUS, Jew who betrayed Judas Maccabeus, *2 Macc. 13:21*

RIBAI, father of one of David's 30 warriors, *2 Sam. 23:29*

RIMMON, father of assassin of Ish-bosheth, *2 Sam. 4:2*

2, Syrian thunder god, *2 Kg. 5:18*

RINNAH, clan leader in Judah, *1 Chr. 4:20*

RIPHATH, great-grandson of Noah, *Gen. 10:3*

RIZIA, clan leader in Asher, *1 Chr. 7:39*

RIZPAH, concubine of Saul, *2 Sam. 3:7*

RODANIM, *1 Chr. 1:7, see Dodanim*

ROHGAH, clan leader in Asher, *1 Chr. 7:34*

ROMAMTI-EZER, Levite, son of Heman the musician, *1 Chr. 25:4*

ROSH, son of Benjamin, *Gen. 46:21*

RUFUS, son of Simon 11, *Mk. 15:21*

2, Christian in Rome, *Rome. 16:13*

RUTH, Moabite wife of Boaz, *Ru. 1:4*

S

SABBAIAS, left foreign wife, *1 Esd. 9:32*

SABTA, *1 Chr. 1:9, see Sabtah*

SABTAH, great-grandson of Noah, *Gen. 10:7*

SABTECA, great-grandson of Noah, *Gen. 10:7*

SACHAR, *1 Chr. 11:35, see Sharar*

2, son of Obed-edom 2, *1 Chr. 26:4*

SACHIA, clan leader in Benjamin, *1 Chr. 8:10*

SAKKUTH, Assyrian astral god, *Am. 5:26*

SALA, *Lk. 3:32, see Salmon*

SALAMIEL, ancestor of Judith, *Jdt. 8:1*

SALATHIEL, alternate name of Ezra, *2 Esd. 3:1*

SALLAI, ancestor of priestly family, *Neh. 12:20*

2, Benjaminite in Jerusalem after exile, *Neh. 11:8*

SALLU, priest with Zerubbabel, *Neh. 12:7*

2, Benjaminite under Nehemiah, *1 Chr. 9:7*

SALMA, founder of Bethlehem, *1 Chr. 2:51*

2, *1 Chr. 2:11, see Salmon*

SALMON, father of Boaz, *Ru. 4:20*

Jewish historian Josephus confirms the name of Herodias's daughter.

SALOME, unnamed daughter of Herodias, *Mt. 14:6*

SALOME 2, disciple of Jesus, *Mk. 15:40*

SALU, father of Zimri 2, *Num. 25:14*

SAMGAR-NEBO, name or title of Babylonian prince, *Jer. 39:3*

SAMLAH, king of Edom, *Gen. 36:36*

SAMSON, Israelite hero against Philistines, *Jg. 13:24*

SAMUEL, judge, priest, prophet, *1 Sam. 1:20*

SANBALLAT, Samaritan opponent of Nehemiah, *Neh. 2:10*

SAPH, Philistine giant slain by Sibbecai, *2 Sam. 21:18*

SAPPHIRA, wife of Ananias 5, *Acts 5:1*

SARAH, wife of Abraham, *Gen. 17:15*

SARAI, *Gen. 11:29, see Sarah*

SARAPH, Judahite who ruled in Moab, *1 Chr. 4:22*

SARASADAI, ancestor of Judith, *Jdt. 8:1*

SAREA, scribe for Ezra, *2 Esd. 14:24*

SARGON II, king of Assyria, *Is. 20:1*

SAROTHIE, ancestor of temple servants, *1 Esd. 5:34*

SARSECHIM, Babylonian official, *Jer. 39:3*

SATAN, the adversary, *1 Chr. 21:1*

SATHRABUZANES, *1 Esd. 6:3*, see Shethar-bozenai

SAUL, first king of Israel, *1 Sam. 9:2*

2, *Acts 7:58*, see Paul

SCEVA, father of seven Jewish exorcists, *Acts 19:14*

SEBA, great-grandson of Noah, *Gen. 10:7*

SECUNDUS, companion of Paul from Thessalonica, *Acts 20:4*

SEGUB, son of Hezron 2, *1 Chr. 2:21*

2, son of Hiel, builder of Jericho, *1 Kg. 16:34*

SEIR, ancestor of Horites, *Gen. 36:20*

SELED, clan leader in Judah, *1 Chr. 2:30*

SELEMIA, scribe for Ezra, *2 Esd. 14:24*

SELEUCUS IV PHILOPATOR, king of Syria, *1 Macc. 7:1*

SEMACHIAH, Levite leader of gatekeepers, *1 Chr. 26:7*

SEMEIN, ancestor of Jesus, *Lk. 3:26*

SENAAH, ancestor or home of returning exiles, *Ezra 2:35*

SENNACHERIB, king of Assyria, *2 Kg. 18:13*

SEORIM, head of a division of priests, *1 Chr. 24:8*

SERAH, daughter of Asher, *Gen. 46:17*

SERAIAH, brother of Othniel the judge, *1 Chr. 4:13*

2, clan leader in Simeon, *1 Chr. 4:35*

3, non-Israelite secretary for David, *2 Sam. 8:17*

4, official sent to arrest Jeremiah, *Jer. 36:26*

5, brother of Baruch the scribe, *Jer. 51:59*

SERAIAH 6, chief priest, executed by Nebuchadnezzar, *2 Kg. 25:18*

7, ally of Gedaliah the governor, *2 Kg. 25:23*

8, Jewish leader with Zerubbabel, *Ezra 2:2*

9, priest with Zerubbabel, *Neh. 12:1*

10, sealed Nehemiah's covenant, *Neh. 10:2*

11, priest in restored temple, *Neh. 11:11*

SERED, son of Zebulun, *Gen. 46:14*

SERGIUS PAULUS, *Acts 13:7*, see Paulus

SERON, commander of Syrian army, *1 Macc. 3:13*

SERUG, Abraham's great-grandfather, *Gen. 11:20*

SESTHEL, left foreign wife, *1 Esd. 9:31*

SETH, son of Adam and Eve, *Gen. 4:25*

SETHUR, leader of Asher, spy sent to Canaan, *Num. 13:13*

SHAAPH, son of Caleb by Maacah, *1 Chr. 2:49*

2, clan leader in Judah, *1 Chr. 2:47*

SHAASHGAZ, eunuch for King Ahasuerus, *Est. 2:14*

SHABBETHAI, Levite who aided Ezra's reform, *Ezra 10:15*

SHADRACH, companion of Meshach and Abednego, *Dan. 1:7*

The woman most named in the Bible is Abraham's wife, Sarah.

SHAGEE, father of one of David's 30 warriors, *1 Chr. 11:34*

SHAHARAIM, Benjaminite in Moab, *1 Chr. 8:8*

SHALLUM, grandson of Simeon 1, *1 Chr. 4:25*

2, clan leader in Judah, *1 Chr. 2:40*

3, father of one who opposed enslaving Judahites, *2 Chr. 28:12*

SHALLUM 4, king of Israel, *2 Kg. 15:10*

5, father of the high priest Hilkiah, *Ezra 7:2*

6, father of a temple doorkeeper, *Jer. 35:4*

7, uncle of Jeremiah, *Jer. 32:7*

8, husband of the prophet Huldah, *2 Kg. 22:14*

9, *1 Chr. 3:15*, see Jehoahaz 2

10, ancestor of temple servants, *Ezra 2:42*

11, Levite, left foreign wife, *Ezra 10:24*

12, left foreign wife, *Ezra 10:42*

13, chief temple gatekeeper, *1 Chr. 9:17*

14, with daughters helped repair Jerusalem, *Neh. 3:12*

15, helped repair Jerusalem gate, *Neh. 3:15*

SHALMAI, *Neh. 7:48*, see Shamlai

SHALMAN, destroyer of Beth-arbel, *Hos. 10:14*

SHALMANESER V, king of Assyria, *2 Kg. 17:3*

SHAMA, one of David's 30 warriors, *1 Chr. 11:44*

SHAMGAR, son of Anath, judge, *Jg. 3:31*

SHAMHUTH, commander under David, *1 Chr. 27:8*

SHAMIR, Levite clan leader under David, *1 Chr. 24:24*

SHAMLAI, ancestor of temple servants, *Ezra 2:46*

SHAMMA, clan leader in Asher, *1 Chr. 7:37*

SHAMMAH, grandson of Esau, *Gen. 36:13*

2, brother of David, *1 Sam. 16:9*

3, one of David's three chief warriors, *2 Sam. 23:11*

4, one of David's 30 warriors, *2 Sam. 23:25*

SHAMMAI, clan leader in Judah, *1 Chr. 2:28*

2, descendant of Judah through Caleb, *1 Chr. 2:44*

3, clan leader in Judah, *1 Chr. 4:17*

SHAMMOTH, *1 Chr. 11:27*, see Shammah 4

SHAMMUA, leader of Reuben, spy sent to Canaan, *Num. 13:4*

2, son of David, *2 Sam. 5:14*

3, ancestor of Levites, *Neh. 11:17*

4, head of priestly family under Joiakim, *Neh. 12:18*

SHAMSHERAI, clan leader in Benjamin, *1 Chr. 8:26*

SHAPHAM, clan leader in Gad, *1 Chr. 5:12*

SHAPHAN, grandfather of Gedaliah the governor, *2 Kg. 22:12*

2, father of idolator seen by Ezekiel, *Ezek. 8:11*

SHAPHAN 3, King Josiah's official who brought him the Law, *2 Kg. 22:3*

4, father of emissary of Jeremiah, *Jer. 29:3*

SHAPHAT, leader of Simeon, spy sent to Canaan, *Num. 13:5*

2, one of David's official herdsmen, *1 Chr. 27:29*

3, Levite clan chief, *1 Esd. 5:34*

4, father of the prophet Elisha, *1 Kg. 19:16*

5, clan leader in Gad, *1 Chr. 5:12*

6, descendant of Zerubbabel, *1 Chr. 3:22*

SHARAI, left foreign wife, *Ezra 10:40*

SHARAR, father of one of David's 30 warriors, *2 Sam. 23:33*

SHAREZER, son of King Sennacherib of Assyria, *2 Kg. 19:37*

2, emissary from Bethel, *Zech. 7:2*

SHASHAI, left foreign wife, *Ezra 10:40*

SHASHAK, clan leader in Benjamin, *1 Chr. 8:14*

SHAUL, son of Simeon, *Gen. 46:10*

2, king of Edom, *Gen. 36:37*

3, Levite, descendant of Kohath, *1 Chr. 6:24*

SHAVSHA, *1 Chr. 18:16*, see Seraiah 3

SHEAL, left foreign wife, *Ezra 10:29*

SHEALTIEL, son of King Jehoiachin, father of Zerubbabel, *1 Chr. 3:17*

SHEARIAH, descendant of Saul and Jonathan, *1 Chr. 8:38*

SHEAR-JASHUB, elder son of Isaiah, *Is. 7:3*

SHEBA, descendant of Ham, *Gen. 10:7*

2, descendant of Shem, *Gen. 10:28*

3, grandson of Abraham, *Gen. 25:3*

SHEBA 4, rebel against David, *2 Sam. 20:1*

5, clan leader in Gad, *1 Chr. 5:13*

SHEBANIAH, priest who trumpeted before ark, *1 Chr. 15:24*

2, Levite, aided Nehemiah's covenant renewal, *Neh. 9:4*

3, priest, sealed Nehemiah's covenant, *Neh. 10:4*

4, Levite, sealed Nehemiah's covenant, *Neh. 10:10*

5, Levite, sealed Nehemiah's covenant, *Neh. 10:12*

SHEBER, son of Caleb and Maacah, *1 Chr. 2:48*

SHEBNA, secretary of King Hezekiah, *2 Kg. 18:37*

SHEBNAH, *2 Kg. 18:18*, see Shebna

SHEBUEL, Levite, son of Heman the musician, *1 Chr. 25:4*

SHECANIAH, head of a division of priests, *1 Chr. 24:11*

2, priest under Hezekiah, *2 Chr. 31:15*

3, ancestor of exiles who returned with Ezra, *Ezra 8:3*

4, priest with Zerubbabel, *Neh. 12:3*

5, father of Shemaiah 25, *Neh. 3:29*

6, father-in-law of Tobiah 2, *Neh. 6:18*

7, descendant of Zerubbabel, *1 Chr. 3:21*

8, head of family returning with Ezra, *Ezra 8:5*

9, supported Ezra's reforms, *Ezra 10:2*

SHECHEM, son of Hamor, raped Dinah, *Gen. 33:19*

2, clan leader in Manasseh, *Num. 26:31*

3, clan leader in Manasseh, *1 Chr. 7:19*

SHEDEUR, father of leader of Reuben under Moses, *Num. 1:5*

SHEERAH, daughter of Ephraim, built three towns, *1 Chr. 7:24*

The third most common name in the Bible is Shemaiah.

SHEHARIAH, clan leader in Benjamin, *1 Chr. 8:26*

SHELAH, great-grandson of Noah, *Gen. 10:24*

2, son of Judah, *Gen. 38:5*

SHELEMIAH, sanctuary gatekeeper under David, *1 Chr. 26:14*

2, grandfather of official under King Jehoiakim, *Jer. 36:14*

3, father of official under King Zedekiah, *Jer. 37:3*

4, father of captain who arrested Jeremiah, *Jer. 37:13*

5, official sent to arrest Jeremiah, *Jer. 36:26*

6, father of one who repaired Jerusalem's walls, *Neh. 3:30*

7, left foreign wife, *Ezra 10:39*

8, left foreign wife, *Ezra 10:41*

9, temple treasurer under Nehemiah, *Neh. 13:13*

SHELEPH, descendant of Shem, *Gen. 10:26*

SHELESH, clan leader in Asher, *1 Chr. 7:35*

SHELOMI, father of leader of Asher under Moses, *Num. 34:27*

SHELOMITH, mother of a blasphemer, *Lev. 24:11*

2, *1 Chr. 23:18*, see Shelomoth 2

3, sanctuary treasurer under David, *1 Chr. 26:25*

4, son or daughter of King Rehoboam, *2 Chr. 11:20*

5, ancestor of family with Ezra, *Ezra 8:10*

6, daughter of Zerubbabel, *1 Chr. 3:19*

SHELOMOTH, Levite, descendant of Gershon, *1 Chr. 23:9*

2, Levite with David, *1 Chr. 24:22*

3, Levite, descendant of Eliezer, *1 Chr. 26:25*

SHELUMIEL, leader of Simeon under Moses, *Num. 1:6*

SHEM, son of Noah, *Gen. 5:32*

SHEMA, clan leader in Judah, *1 Chr. 2:43*

2, clan leader in Reuben, *1 Chr. 5:8*

3, clan leader in Benjamin, *1 Chr. 8:13*

4, aide of Ezra in reading Law, *Neh. 8:4*

SHEMAAH, father of two Benjaminites who joined David, *1 Chr. 12:3*

SHEMAIAH, clan leader in Reuben, *1 Chr. 5:4*

2, chief Levite under David, *1 Chr. 15:8*

3, Levite scribe under David, *1 Chr. 24:6*

4, son of Obed-edom 2, *1 Chr. 26:4*

SHEMAIAH 5, prophet against Rehoboam, *1 Kg. 12:22*; see Shemaiah, page 397

6, Levite teacher under King Jehoshaphat, *2 Chr. 17:8*

7, ancestor of a Simeonite under King Hezekiah, *1 Chr. 4:37*

8, Levite under King Hezekiah, *2 Chr. 29:14*

9, priest who distributed offerings under King Hezekiah, *2 Chr. 31:15*

10, kinsman of Tobit, *Tob. 5:13*

11, Levite descended from Asaph 2, *Neh. 12:36*

12, father of the prophet Uriah, *Jer. 26:20*

13, father of official of King Jehoiakim, *Jer. 36:12*

14, chief Levite under King Josiah, *2 Chr. 35:9*

SHEMAIAH 15, opponent of Jeremiah, *Jer. 29:24*; see Shemaiah 2, page 397

16, priest with Zerubbabel, *Neh. 10:8*

17, father of Levite under Nehemiah, *Neh. 11:15*

18, Jew who returned with Ezra, *Ezra 8:13*

19, envoy for Ezra, *Ezra 8:16*

20, priest, left foreign wife, *Ezra 10:21*

21, left foreign wife, *Ezra 10:31*

22, left foreign wife, *1 Esd. 9:34*

23, Levite after exile, *1 Chr. 9:14*

24, prophet hired to discredit Nehemiah, *Neh. 6:10*

25, helped rebuild Jerusalem's walls, *Neh. 3:29*

26, helped dedicate Jerusalem's walls, *Neh. 12:34*

27, Levite musician under Nehemiah, *Neh. 12:35*

28, priest, helped dedicate Jerusalem's walls, *Neh. 12:42*

29, priest, sealed Nehemiah's covenant, *Neh. 10:8*

30, descendant of Zerubbabel, *1 Chr. 3:22*

SHEMARIAH, Benjaminite who joined David, *1 Chr. 12:5*

2, son of King Rehoboam, *2 Chr. 11:19*

3, left foreign wife, *Ezra 10:32*

4, left foreign wife, *Ezra 10:41*

SHEMEBER, king of Zeboiim, ally of Sodom, *Gen. 14:2*

SHEMED, builder of towns of Ono and Lod, *1 Chr. 8:12*

SHEMER, ancestor of Ethan the musician, *1 Chr. 6:46*

2, owner of a hill that King Omri bought, *1 Kg. 16:24*

SHEMIDA, clan leader in Manasseh, *Num. 26:32*

SHEMIRAMOTH, Levite, played lyre before ark, *1 Chr. 15:18*

2, Levite under King Jehoshaphat, *2 Chr. 17:8*

SHEMUEL, grandson of Issachar, *1 Chr. 7:2*

2, leader of Simeon, helped divide land, *Num. 34:20*

SHENAZZAR, son of King Jehoiachin, *1 Chr. 3:18*

SHEPHATIAH, Benjaminite who joined David, *1 Chr. 12:5*

2, David's officer over Simeon, *1 Chr. 27:16*

3, son of David and Abital, *2 Sam. 3:4*

4, ancestor of temple servants, *Ezra 2:57*

5, son of King Jehoshaphat, *2 Chr. 21:2*

6, ancestor of returning exiles, *Ezra 2:4*

7, official of King Zedekiah, *Jer. 38:1*

8, ancestor of Jews under Nehemiah, *Neh. 11:4*

9, father of Benjaminite after exile, *1 Chr. 9:8*

SHEPHI, *1 Chr. 1:40*, see Shepho

SHEPHO, Horite chief in Esau's time, *Gen. 36:23*

SHEPHUPHAM, grandson of Benjamin, *Num. 26:39*

SHEPHUPHAN, *1 Chr. 8:5*, see Shephupham

SHEREBIAH, Levite with Zerubbabel, *Neh. 12:8*

2, Levite clan leader, temple servants, *Ezra 8:18*

3, Levite clan chief under Eliashib, *Neh. 12:24*

4, Levite, sealed Nehemiah's covenant, *Neh. 10:12*

SHERESH, clan leader in Manasseh, *1 Chr. 7:16*

SHESHAI, giant in Hebron, driven out by Caleb, *Num. 13:22*

SHESHAN, Judahite father of daughters, *1 Chr. 2:31*

SHESHBAZZAR, son of Jehoiachin, leader of first return from Babylon, *Ezra 1:8*

SHETH, ancestor of Moab, *Num. 24:17*

SHETHAR, Persian noble, adviser of King Ahasuerus, *Est. 1:14*

SHETHAR-BOZENAI, Persian official, *Ezra 5:3*

SHEVA, son of Caleb and Maacah, *1 Chr. 2:49*

2, *2 Sam. 20:25*, see Seraiah 3

SHILHI, grandfather of King Jehoshaphat, *1 Kg. 22:42*

SHILLEM, son of Naphtali, *Gen. 46:24*

SHILSHAH, clan leader in Asher, *1 Chr. 7:37*

SHIMEA, clan leader in Levi, *1 Chr. 6:30*

2, grandfather of Asaph the musician, *1 Chr. 6:39*

3, *1 Chr. 2:13*, see Shimeah 2

4, son of David, *1 Chr. 3:5*

SHIMEAH, Benjaminite, kinsman of Saul, *1 Chr. 8:32*

2, brother of David, *2 Sam. 13:3*

SHIMEAM, *1 Chr. 9:38*, see Shimeah 1

SHIMEATH, mother of official who killed King Joash of Judah, *2 Kg. 12:21*

SHIMEI, grandson of Levi, *Ex. 6:17*

2, clan leader in Levi, *1 Chr. 6:29*

3, clan leader in Simeon, *1 Chr. 4:26*

4, clan leader in Reuben, *1 Chr. 5:4*

5, clan leader in Benjamin, *1 Chr. 8:21*

6, Levite, grandfather of Asaph the musician, *1 Chr. 6:42*

7, brother of David, slew giant, *2 Sam. 21:21*

8, overseer of David's vineyards, *1 Chr. 27:27*

SHIMEI 9, Benjaminite who cursed David, *2 Sam. 16:5*

10, Levite, prophesied with lyre, *1 Chr. 25:3*

11, ally of Solomon against Adonijah, *1 Kg. 1:8*

12, officer of Solomon over provisions, *1 Kg. 4:18*

13, Levite under King Hezekiah, *2 Chr. 29:14*

14, Levite over treasury, *2 Chr. 31:12*

15, ancestor of Mordecai, *Est. 2:5*

16, brother of Zerubbabel, *1 Chr. 3:19*

17, Levite, left foreign wife, *Ezra 10:23*

18, left foreign wife, *Ezra 10:33*

19, left foreign wife, *Ezra 10:38*

SHIMEON, left foreign wife, *Ezra 10:31*

SHIMON, clan leader in Judah, *1 Chr. 4:20*

The Old Testament including the Apocrypha lists 3,137 names; the New Testament only 287.

SHIMRATH, clan leader in Benjamin, *1 Chr. 8:21*

SHIMRI, clan leader in Simeon, *1 Chr. 4:37*

2, father of one of David's 30 warriors, *1 Chr. 11:45*

3, Levite, sanctuary gatekeeper, *1 Chr. 26:10*

4, Levite under King Hezekiah, *2 Chr. 29:13*

SHIMRITH, mother of assassin of King Joash of Judah, *2 Chr. 24:26*

SHIMRON, son of Issachar, *Gen. 46:13*

SHIMSHAI, Persian scribe, opposed rebuilding Jerusalem, *Ezra 4:8*

SHINAB, king of Admah, ally of Sodom, *Gen. 14:2*

SHIPHI, father of Simeonite leader under King Hezekiah, *1 Chr. 4:37*

SHIPHRAH, Hebrew midwife in Egypt, *Ex. 1:15*

SHIPHTAN, father of leader of Ephraim under Moses, *Num. 34:24*

SHISHA, *1 Kg. 4:3*, see Seraiah 3

SHISHAK, king of Egypt, *1 Kg. 11:40*

SHITRAI, chief herdsman for David in Sharon, *1 Chr. 27:29*

SHIZA, father of one of David's 30 warriors, *1 Chr. 11:42*

SHOBAB, son of Caleb, *1 Chr. 2:18*

2, son of David, *2 Sam. 5:14*

SHOBACH, Syrian commander defeated by David, *2 Sam. 10:16*

SHOBAI, ancestor of temple gatekeepers with Zerubbabel, *Ezra 2:42*

SHOBAL, Horite chief, son of Seir, *Gen. 36:20*

2, clan leader in Judah, descended from Caleb, *1 Chr. 2:50*

SHOBEK, sealed Nehemiah's covenant, *Neh. 10:24*

SHOBI, prince of Ammonites, aided David, *2 Sam. 17:27*

SHOHAM, Levite, of the sons of Jaaziah, *1 Chr. 24:27*

SHOMER, great-grandson of Asher, *1 Chr. 7:32*

2, *2 Kg. 12:21*, see Shimrith

SHOPHACH, *1 Chr. 19:16*, see Shobach

SHUA, Judah's Canaanite father-in-law, *Gen. 38:2*

2, daughter of Heber the Asherite, *1 Chr. 7:32*

SHUAH, son of Abraham and Keturah, *Gen. 25:2*

SHUAL, clan leader in Asher, *1 Chr. 7:36*

SHUBAEL, Levite descendant of Amram, *1 Chr. 24:20*

2, Levite musician under David, *1 Chr. 25:20*

SHUHAH, clan leader in Judah, *1 Chr. 4:11*

SHUHAM, *Num. 26:42*, see Hushim 1

SHULAMMITE, heroine of Song of Solomon, *S. of S. 6:13*

SHUNI, son of Gad, *Gen. 46:16*

SHUPPIM, clan leader in Benjamin, *1 Chr. 7:12*

2, temple gatekeeper, *1 Chr. 26:16*

SHUTHELAH, son of Ephraim, *Num. 26:35*

2, descendant of Ephraim, *1 Chr. 7:21*

SIA, *Neh. 7:47*, see Siaha

SIAHA, ancestor of temple servants with Zerubbabel, *Ezra 2:44*

SIBBECAI, *2 Sam. 21:18*, see Mebunnai

SIDON, great-grandson of Noah, *Gen. 10:15*

SIHON, Amorite king of Heshbon, *Num. 21:21*

SILAS, coworker of Paul and Peter, *Acts 15:22*

SILVANUS, *2 Cor. 1:19*, see Silas

SIMEON, son of Jacob and Leah, *Gen. 29:33*

2, ancestor of Jesus, *Lk. 3:30*

3, great-grandfather of Judas Maccabeus, *1 Macc. 2:1*

4, *1 Macc. 2:65*, see Simon 4

SIMEON 5, Jewish prophet who met infant Jesus, *Lk. 2:25; see Simeon 2, page 400*

6, *Acts 15:14*, see Peter

SIMEON 7, called Niger, Christian prophet, *Acts 13:1; see Simeon 3, page 401*

SIMON, Chosamaeus, left foreign wife, *1 Esd. 9:32*

SIMON 2, son of Onias II, high priest, *Sir. 50:1; see Simon, page 401*

3, captain of temple under Onias III, *2 Macc. 3:4*

SIMON 4, brother of Judas Maccabeus, high priest, *1 Macc. 2:3; see Simon 2, page 402*

5, father of Judas Iscariot, *Jn. 6:71*

6, *Mt. 4:18*, see Peter

SIMON 7, apostle called the Zealot or Cananaean, *Mt. 10:4; see Simon 3, page 402*

8, brother of Jesus, *Mt. 13:55*

SIMON 9, Pharisee, invited Jesus to dinner, *Lk. 7:40; see Simon 4, page 403*

SIMON 10, leper, invited Jesus to dinner, *Mt. 26:6; see Simon 5, page 403*

SIMON 11, from Cyrene, carried Jesus' cross, *Mt. 27:32; see Simon 6, page 403*

SIMON 12, Samaritan magician, *Acts 8:9; see Simon 7, page 404*

SIMON 13, Christian tanner, host of Peter, *Acts 9:43; see Simon 8, page 404*

SIPPAI, *1 Chr. 20:4*, see Saph

SIRACH, father of Jesus, author of Ecclesiasticus, *Sir. 50:27*

SISERA, Canaanite general, *Jg. 4:2*

2, ancestor of temple servants, *Ezra 2:53*

SISINNES, governor of Syria in time of Zerubbabel, *1 Esd. 6:3*

SISMAI, clan leader in Judah, *1 Chr. 2:40*

SITHRI, cousin of Moses, *Ex. 6:22*

Men such as Sirach are known only as fathers of a famous son.

SO, king of Egypt, *2 Kg. 17:4*

SOCO, clan leader or town in Judah, *1 Chr. 4:18*

SODI, father of spy for Moses, *Num. 13:10*

SOLOMON, son of David and Bathsheba, king of Israel, *2 Sam. 5:14*

SOPATER, Christian from Berea, coworker of Paul, *Acts 20:4*

SOPHERETH, *Neh. 7:57*, see Hassophereth

SOSIPATER, captain under Judas Maccabeus, *2 Macc. 12:19*

2, Christian coworker of Paul, *Rom. 16:21*

SOSTHENES, synagogue ruler converted by Paul, *Acts 18:17*

SOSTRATUS, Syrian commander, *2 Macc. 4:28*

SOTAI, ancestor of temple servants, *Ezra 2:55*

STACHYS, Christian at Rome, *Rom. 16:9*

STEPHANAS, first Christian convert in Achaia, *1 Cor. 1:16*

STEPHEN, one of the seven, first Christian martyr, *Acts 6:5*

SUAH, clan leader in Asher, *1 Chr. 7:36*

SUBAS, ancestor of temple servants, *1 Esd. 5:34*

SUDIAS, *1 Esd. 5:26*, see Hodaviah

SUSANNA, wife of Joakim, in Babylon, *Sus. 1:2*

SUSANNA 2, disciple of Jesus, *Lk. 8:3*

SUSI, father of spy for Moses, *Num. 13:11*

SYNTYCHE, Christian woman at Philippi, *Phil. 4:2*

T

TABBAOTH, ancestor of temple servants, *Ezra 2:43*

TABEEL, father of intended puppet king of Judah, *Is. 7:6*

2, Samarian official, opposed rebuilding Jerusalem, *Ezra 4:7*

TABITHA, *Acts 9:36*, see Dorcas

TABRIMMON, father of King Benhadad of Syria, *1 Kg. 15:18*

TAHAN, son of Ephraim, clan leader, *Num. 26:35*

2, clan leader in Ephraim, *1 Chr. 7:25*

TAHASH, nephew of Abraham, *Gen. 22:24*

TAHATH, *1 Chr. 7:20*, see Tahan 1

2, clan leader in Levi, *1 Chr. 6:24*

3, clan leader in Ephraim, *1 Chr. 7:20*

TAHPENES, Egyptian queen in time of David, *1 Kg. 11:19*

TAHREA, *1 Chr. 9:41*, see Tarea

TALMAI, son of Anak, driven from Hebron by Caleb, *Num. 13:22*

2, king of Geshur, David's father-in-law, *2 Sam. 3:3*

TALMON, ancestor of temple gatekeepers, *Ezra 2:42*

2, temple gatekeeper under Ezra, *1 Chr. 9:17*

TAMAR, daughter-in-law of Judah, *Gen. 38:6*

TAMAR 2, daughter of David, *2 Sam. 13:1*

3, daughter of Absalom, *2 Sam. 14:27*

Assyrian king Tiglath-pileser is also called Tilgath-pilneser and Pul in the Bible.

TAMMUZ, Babylonian god of fertility, *Ezek. 8:14*

TANHUMETH, father of commander under Gedaliah, *2 Kg. 25:23*

TAPHATH, daughter of Solomon, *1 Kg. 4:11*

TAPPUAH, clan leader in Judah, son of Hebron, *1 Chr. 2:43*

TAREA, great-grandson of Jonathan, *1 Chr. 8:35*

TARSHISH, grandson of Japheth, *Gen. 10:4*

2, clan leader in Benjamin, *1 Chr. 7:10*

3, Persian noble, adviser of Ahasuerus, *Est. 1:14*

TARTAK, Avvite god in Samaria, *2 Kg. 17:31*

TATTENAI, Persian governor west of Euphrates, *Ezra 5:3*

TEBAH, nephew of Abraham, *Gen. 22:24*

TEBALIAH, Levite, sanctuary gatekeeper, *1 Chr. 26:11*

TEHINNAH, clan leader in Judah, founder of Nahash, *1 Chr. 4:12*

TELAH, ancestor of Joshua, clan leader in Ephraim, *1 Chr. 7:25*

TELEM, Levite, left foreign wife, *Ezra 10:24*

TEMA, son of Ishmael, *Gen. 25:15*

TEMAH, ancestor of temple servants, *Ezra 2:53*

TEMAN, grandson of Esau, *Gen. 36:11*

2, clan chief in Edom, *Gen. 36:42*

TEMENI, clan leader in Judah, *1 Chr. 4:6*

TERAH, father of Abraham, *Gen. 11:24*

TERESH, eunuch guard for Ahasuerus, *Est. 2:21*

TERTIUS, secretary for Paul, *Rom. 16:22*

TERTULLUS, lawyer who argued against Paul, *Acts 24:1*

THADDAEUS, apostle of Jesus, *Mt. 10:3*

THARRA, *Ad. Est. 12:1*, see Teresh

THASSI, *1 Macc. 2:3*, see Simon 4

THEODOTUS, plotted against Ptolemy IV Philopator, *3 Macc. 1:2*

2, Syrian ambassador to Judas Maccabeus, *2 Macc. 14:19*

THEOPHILUS, recipient of the books of Luke and Acts, *Lk. 1:3*

THEUDAS, leader of Jewish rebellion against Romans, *Acts 5:36*

THOMAS, apostle of Jesus, *Mt. 10:3*

TIBERIUS, Roman emperor, *Lk. 3:1*

TIBNI, fought Omri for throne of Israel, *1 Kg. 16:21*

TIDAL, king of Goiim, fought Abraham, *Gen. 14:1*

TIGLATH-PILESER III, king of Assyria, *2 Kg. 15:29*

TIKVAH, father of Shallum, husband of Huldah, *2 Kg. 22:14*

2, father of opponent of Ezra, *Ezra 10:15*

TILGATH-PILNESER, *1 Chr. 5:6*, see Tiglath-pileser

TILON, clan leader in Judah, *1 Chr. 4:20*

TIMAEUS, father of blind Bartimaeus, *Mk. 10:46*

TIMNA, daughter-in-law of Esau, *Gen. 36:12*

2, sister of a Horite chief, *Gen. 36:22*

3, clan chief in Edom, *Gen. 36:40*

TIMON, Christian leader, one of the seven, *Acts 6:5*

TIMOTHY, coworker of Paul, *Acts 16:1*

TIRAS, son of Japheth, grandson of Noah, *Gen. 10:2*

TIRHAKAH, king of Egypt, *2 Kg. 19:9*

TIRHANAH, son of Caleb and Maacah, *1 Chr. 2:48*

TIRIA, clan leader in Judah, *1 Chr. 4:16*

TIRZAH, daughter of Zelophehad, *Num. 26:33*

TITIUS JUSTUS, Christian in Corinth, *Acts 18:7*

TITUS, *2 Macc. 11:34*, see Manius

TITUS 2, coworker of Paul, *2 Cor. 2:13*

TOAH, Levite, ancestor of Samuel, *1 Chr. 6:34*

TOBADONIJAH, Levite under King Jehoshaphat, *2 Chr. 17:8*

TOBIAH, ancestor of Jews with Zerubbabel, *Ezra 2:60*

TOBIAH 2, opponent of Nehemiah, *Neh. 2:10*

TOBIAS, son of Tobit, *Tob. 1:9*

2, father of wealthy depositor in temple, *2 Macc. 3:11*

TOBIEL, father of Tobit, *Tob. 1:1*

TOBIJAH, Levite under King Jehoshaphat, *2 Chr. 17:8*

2, Jew who brought gold from Babylon, *Zech. 6:10*

TOBIT, Jew in Assyrian exile, *Tob. 1:1*

TOGARMAH, great-grandson of Noah, *Gen. 10:3*

According to legend, Thomas's unnamed twin was actually Jesus.

TOHU, Levite, ancestor of Samuel, *1 Sam. 1:1*

TOI, king of Hamath, friendly to David, *2 Sam. 8:9*

TOKHATH, *2 Chr. 34:22*, see Tikvah 1

TOLA, son of Issachar, *Gen. 46:13*

TOLA 2, judge from Issachar, *Jg. 10:1*

TOU, *1 Chr. 18:9*, see Toi

TROPHIMUS, coworker of Paul, *Acts 20:4*

TRYPHAENA, Christian woman at Rome, *Rom. 16:12*

TRYPHO, Syrian general and usurper, *1 Macc. 11:39*

TRYPHOSA, Christian woman at Rome, *Rom. 16:12*

TUBAL, son of Japheth, grandson of Noah, *Gen. 10:2*

TUBAL-CAIN, son of Lamech, descendant of Cain, *Gen. 4:22*

TYCHICUS, coworker of Paul, *Acts 20:4*

TYRANNUS, owner of hall in Ephesus where Paul taught, *Acts 19:9*

U/V

UCAL, symbolic name, subject of proverb, *Pr. 30:1*

UEL, left foreign wife, *Ezra 10:34*

ULAM, clan leader in Manasseh, *1 Chr. 7:16*

2, warrior clan leader in Benjamin, *1 Chr. 8:39*

ULLA, clan leader in Asher, *1 Chr. 7:39*

UNNI, played lyre before ark for David, *1 Chr. 15:18*

UNNO, Levite with Zerubbabel, *Neh. 12:9*

UR, father of one of David's 30 warriors, *1 Chr. 11:35*

URBANUS, Christian in Rome, *Rom. 16:9*

URI, father of Bezalel the craftsman, *Ex. 31:2*

2, father of governor of Gilead for Solomon, *1 Kg. 4:19*

3, Levite, left foreign wife, *Ezra 10:24*

URIAH, husband of Bathsheba, *2 Sam. 11:3*

URIAH 2, chief priest in time of King Ahaz, *2 Kg. 16:10*

3, priest used by Isaiah as witness, *Is. 8:2*

URIAH 4, a prophet executed by King Jehoiakim, *Jer. 26:20*; see Uriah 3, page 425

5, father of priest who weighed gold for Ezra, *Ezra 8:33*

6, aided Ezra in reading Law, *Neh. 8:4*

URIEL, Levite clan leader under David, *1 Chr. 6:24*

2, father-in-law of King Rehoboam, *2 Chr. 13:2*

URIEL 3, angel who appeared to Ezra, *2 Esd. 4:1*

UTHAI, Jew in Jerusalem after exile, *1 Chr. 9:4*

2, ancestor of temple servants, *1 Esd. 5:30*

3, Jew who returned with Ezra, *Ezra 8:14*

UZ, grandson of Shem, *Gen. 10:23*

2, nephew of Abraham, *Gen. 22:21*

3, Horite chief in Esau's time, *Gen. 36:28*

UZAI, father of one who helped repair Jerusalem, *Neh. 3:25*

UZAL, descendant of Shem, *Gen. 10:27*

UZZA, clan leader in Benjamin, *1 Chr. 8:7*

2, owner of garden where kings were buried, *2 Kg. 21:18*

3, ancestor of temple servants, *Ezra 2:49*

UZZAH, son of Abinadab, touched ark, *2 Sam. 6:3*

2, Levite clan leader in the time of David, *1 Chr. 6:29*

UZZI, grandson of Benjamin, *1 Chr. 7:7*

2, grandson of Issachar, *1 Chr. 7:2*

3, priest, descendant of Eleazar, *1 Chr. 6:6*

4, father of Benjaminite in Ezra's time, *1 Chr. 9:8*

5, head of priestly family under Joiakim, *Neh. 12:19*

6, Levite officer, descendant of Asaph, *Neh. 11:22*

7, Levite, helped dedicate Jerusalem's walls, *Neh. 12:42*

UZZIA, one of David's 30 warriors, *1 Chr. 11:44*

UZZIAH, father of a treasurer for David, *1 Chr. 27:25*

2, Levite clan leader, *1 Chr. 6:24*

UZZIAH 3, king of Judah, also called Azariah, *2 Kg. 15:13*

4, city magistrate of Bethulia in time of Judith, *Jdt. 6:15*

5, father of Judahite under Nehemiah, *Neh. 11:4*

6, priest, left foreign wife, *Ezra 10:21*

UZZIEL, grandson of Benjamin, *1 Chr. 7:7*

2, uncle of Moses and Aaron, *Ex. 6:18*

3, Levite, son of Heman the musician, *1 Chr. 25:4*

4, Levite under Hezekiah, *2 Chr. 29:14*

5, Simeonite captain, fought Amalekites, *1 Chr. 4:42*

6, goldsmith, helped repair Jerusalem's walls, *Neh. 3:8*

VAIZATHA, son of Haman, enemy of Esther, *Est. 9:9*

VANIAH, left foreign wife, *Ezra 10:36*

VASHTI, wife of King Ahasuerus of Persia, *Est. 1:9*

VOPHSI, father of spy for Moses, *Num. 13:14*

Z

ZAAVAN, Horite clan chief, *Gen. 36:27*

ZABAD, clan leader in Judah, *1 Chr. 2:36*

2, clan leader in Ephraim, *1 Chr. 7:21*

3, one of David's 30 warriors, *1 Chr. 11:41*

4, assassin of King Joash, *2 Chr. 24:26*

5, left foreign wife, *Ezra 10:27*

6, left foreign wife, *Ezra 10:33*

7, left foreign wife, *Ezra 10:43*

ZABBAI, father of one who repaired Jerusalem's walls, *Neh. 3:20*

2, left foreign wife, *Ezra 10:28*

ZABDI, grandfather of Achan, *Jos. 7:1*

2, clan leader in Benjamin, *1 Chr. 8:19*

3, David's overseer of wine cellars, *1 Chr. 27:27*

4, Levite, descendant of Asaph 4, *Neh. 11:17*

ZABDIEL, father of one of David's three chief warriors, *1 Chr. 27:2*

2, priest, division overseer, *Neh. 11:14*

3, Arab, beheaded Alexander Balas, *1 Macc. 11:17*

ZABUD, priest, adviser of Solomon, *1 Kg. 4:5*

ZACCAI, ancestor of clan with Zerubbabel, *Ezra 2:9*

ZACCHAEUS, officer of Judas Maccabeus, *2 Macc. 10:19*

ZACCHAEUS 2, tax collector, *Lk. 19:2*

ZACCUR, father of spy for Moses, *Num. 13:4*

2, Levite clan leader, *1 Chr. 24:27*

3, son of Asaph 2, leader of musicians, *1 Chr. 25:2*

4, clan leader in Simeon, *1 Chr. 4:26*

5, father of assistant temple treasurer, *Neh. 13:13*

6, Jew who returned with Ezra, *Ezra 8:14*

7, Levite, left foreign wife, *1 Esd. 9:24*

8, helped repair Jerusalem's walls, *Neh. 3:2*

9, Levite, sealed Nehemiah's covenant, *Neh. 10:12*

ZADOK, high priest for David and Solomon, *2 Sam. 8:17*

2, priest, descendant of Zadok 1, *1 Chr. 6:12*

3, grandfather of King Jotham of Judah, *2 Kg. 15:33*

4, priest, son of Meraioth 2, *1 Chr. 9:11*

5, scribe over temple treasures, *Neh. 13:13*

6, helped repair Jerusalem's walls, *Neh. 3:4*

7, priest, helped repair Jerusalem's walls, *Neh. 3:29*

8, sealed Nehemiah's covenant, *Neh. 10:21*

9, ancestor of Jesus, *Mt. 1:14*

ZAHAM, son of King Rehoboam, *2 Chr. 11:19*

ZALAPH, father of one who repaired Jerusalem's walls, *Neh. 3:30*

ZALMON, one of David's 30 warriors, *2 Sam. 23:28*

Only two letters long in English, Ir, Og, On, Ur, and Uz each have three letters in Hebrew.

ZALMUNNA, Midianite king defeated by Gideon, *Jg. 8:5*

ZANOAH, clan leader in Judah, *1 Chr. 4:18*

ZAPHENATH-PANEAH, name given to Joseph 1 by Pharaoh, *Gen. 41:45*

ZARIUS, brother of King Jehoiakim, *1 Esd. 1:38*

ZATTU, ancestor of exiles with Zerubbabel, *Ezra 2:8*

2, sealed Nehemiah's covenant, *Neh. 10:14*

ZAZA, clan leader in Judah, *1 Chr. 2:33*

ZEBADIAH, clan leader in Benjamin, *1 Chr. 8:15*

2, clan leader in Benjamin, *1 Chr. 8:17*

3, Benjaminite who joined David, *1 Chr. 12:7*

4, division commander under David, *1 Chr. 27:7*

5, Levite, sanctuary gatekeeper, *1 Chr. 26:2*

6, Levite under King Jehoshaphat, *2 Chr. 17:8*

7, leader in Judah under King Jehoshaphat, *2 Chr. 19:11*

8, head of clan returning with Ezra, *Ezra 8:8*

9, priest, left foreign wife, *Ezra 10:20*

ZEBAH, Midianite king defeated by Gideon, *Jg. 8:5*

ZEBEDEE, father of James and John, *Mt. 4:21*

ZEBIDAH, mother of King Jehoiakim, *2 Kg. 23:36*

ZEBINA, left foreign wife, *Ezra 10:43*

ZEBUL, governor of Shechem for Abimelech 3, *Jg. 9:28*

ZEBULUN, son of Jacob and Leah, *Gen. 30:20*

ZECHARIAH, *1 Chr. 9:37*, see Zecher

2, father of an officer for David, *1 Chr. 27:21*

3, clan leader in Reuben, *1 Chr. 5:7*

4, Levite musician, *1 Chr. 15:18*

5, priest, blew trumpet before ark, *1 Chr. 15:24*

6, Levite under David, *1 Chr. 24:25*

7, head of division of gatekeepers, *1 Chr. 26:2*

8, Levite gatekeeper, *1 Chr. 26:11*

9, official for King Jehoshaphat, *2 Chr. 17:7*

10, Levite whose son prophesied before King Jehoshaphat, *2 Chr. 20:14*

11, son of King Jehoshaphat, *2 Chr. 21:2*

ZECHARIAH 12, prophet, son of the priest Jehoiada, *2 Chr. 24:20; see Zechariah, page 430*

13, adviser of King Uzziah, *2 Chr. 26:5*

14, King Hezekiah's grandfather, *2 Kg. 18:2*

ZECHARIAH 15, son of Jeroboam II, king of Israel, *2 Kg. 14:29; see Zechariah 2, page 431*

16, served as witness for Isaiah, *Is. 8:2*

17, Levite musician under King Hezekiah, *2 Chr. 29:13*

18, Levite, temple overseer for King Josiah, *2 Chr. 34:12*

19, priest, temple administrator, *2 Chr. 35:8*

20, ancestor of a Jew under Nehemiah, *Neh. 11:4*

21, ancestor of priest, *Neh. 11:12*

22, ancestor of Judahite under Nehemiah, *Neh. 11:5*

ZECHARIAH 23, prophet, *Ezra 5:1; see Zechariah 3, page 431*

24, head of priestly family under Joiakim, *Neh. 12:16*

25, Jew who returned with Ezra, *Ezra 8:3*

26, Jew who returned with Ezra, *Ezra 8:11*

27, envoy for Ezra, *Ezra 8:16*

28, left foreign wife, *Ezra 10:26*

29, temple gatekeeper, *1 Chr. 9:21*

30, Levite, aided dedication of Jerusalem's walls, *Neh. 12:35*

31, priest, blew trumpet for dedication of wall, *Neh. 12:41*

32, aided Ezra in reading Law, *Neh. 8:4*

ZECHARIAH 33, father of John the Baptist, *Lk. 1:5; see Zechariah 4, page 431*

ZECHER, Benjaminite kinsman of Saul, *1 Chr. 8:31*

ZEDEKIAH, court prophet for King Ahab, *1 Kg. 22:11*

2, ancestor of Baruch, *Bar. 1:1*

3, prophet, opponent of Jeremiah, *Jer. 29:21*

4, son of King Jehoiakim, *1 Chr. 3:16*

ZEDEKIAH 5, son of King Josiah, king of Judah, *2 Kg. 24:17; see Zedekiah 2, page 432*

6, official of King Jehoiakim, *Jer. 36:12*

7, priest, sealed Nehemiah's covenant, *Neh. 10:1*

ZEEB, Midianite leader killed by Gideon, *Jg. 7:25*

ZELEK, one of David's 30 warriors, *2 Sam. 23:37*

ZELOPHEHAD, father of five daughters, *Num. 26:33*

ZEMIRAH, grandson of Benjamin, *1 Chr. 7:8*

ZENAS, coworker of Paul, *Tit. 3:13*

ZEPHANIAH, Levite, ancestor of Heman the musician, *1 Chr. 6:36*

ZEPHANIAH 2, prophet, *Zeph. 1:1; see Zephaniah, page 435*

ZEPHANIAH 3, priest, consulted Jeremiah for King Zedekiah, *2 Kg. 25:18; see Zephaniah 2, page 435*

4, father of returning exile, *Zech. 6:10*

ZEPHI, grandson of Esau, *Gen. 36:11*

ZEPHON, son of Gad, *Num. 26:15*

ZERAH, grandson of Esau, *Gen. 36:13*

2, son of Judah and Tamar, twin of Perez, *Gen. 38:30*

3, father of Jobab, king of Edom, *Gen. 36:33*

4, Levite clan leader, *1 Chr. 6:21*

5, son of Simeon, *Num. 26:13*

ZERAH 6, Ethiopian invader, *2 Chr. 14:9*

ZERAHIAH, ancestor of Ezra, *1 Chr. 6:6*

2, father of returning exile, *Ezra 8:4*

The most common biblical name is Zechariah; there are 32 in the Old Testament but only one in the New: John the Baptist's father.

ZERAIAH, *1 Esd. 8:34, see Zebadiah 8*

ZERDAIAH, *1 Esd. 9:28, see Aziza*

ZERESH, wife of Haman, enemy of Esther, *Est. 5:10*

ZERETH, clan leader in Judah, *1 Chr. 4:7*

ZERI, Levite, leader of sanctuary singers, *1 Chr. 25:3*

ZEROR, ancestor of King Saul, *1 Sam. 9:1*

ZERUAH, mother of King Jeroboam, *1 Kg. 11:26*

ZERUBBABEL, governor of Jerusalem, builder of temple, *1 Chr. 3:19*

ZERUIAH, David's sister, mother of Joab, Asahel, and Abishai, *1 Sam. 26:6*

ZETHAM, Levite, sanctuary treasurer for David, *1 Chr. 23:8*

ZETHAN, clan leader in Benjamin, *1 Chr. 7:10*

ZETHAR, eunuch, servant of King Ahasuerus, *Est. 1:10*

ZEUS, Greek god, *2 Macc. 6:2*

ZIA, clan leader in Gad, *1 Chr. 5:13*

ZIBA, servant of Saul's family, *2 Sam. 9:2*

ZIBEON, Horite chief, son of Seir, *Gen. 36:20*

ZIBIA, clan leader in Benjamin, *1 Chr. 8:9*

ZIBIAH, mother of King Joash of Judah, *2 Kg. 12:1*

ZICHRI, cousin of Moses, *Ex. 6:21*

2, father of Levite under David, *1 Chr. 26:25*

3, father of an officer for David, *1 Chr. 27:16*

4, Levite, son of Asaph 4, *1 Chr. 9:15*

5, clan leader in Benjamin, *1 Chr. 8:19*

6, clan leader in Benjamin, *1 Chr. 8:23*

7, father of commander under King Jehoshaphat, *2 Chr. 17:16*

8, father of army commander under the high priest Jehoiada, *2 Chr. 23:1*

9, clan leader in Benjamin, *1 Chr. 8:27*

10, warrior from Ephraim, killed King Ahaz's son, *2 Chr. 28:7*

11, head of priestly family under Joiakim, *Neh. 12:17*

12, father of overseer of Benjamin under Nehemiah, *Neh. 11:9*

ZIHA, ancestor of temple servants, *Ezra 2:43*

2, overseer of temple servants, *Neh. 11:21*

ZILLAH, wife of Lamech, descendant of Cain, *Gen. 4:19*

ZILLETHAI, clan leader in Benjamin, *1 Chr. 8:20*

2, Manassehite who joined David, *1 Chr. 12:20*

ZILPAH, concubine of Jacob, mother of Gad and Asher, *Gen. 29:24*

ZIMMAH, Levite clan leader, *1 Chr. 6:20*

2, father of Levite under King Hezekiah, *2 Chr. 29:12*

ZIMRAN, son of Abraham and Keturah, *Gen. 25:2*

ZIMRI, killed by Phinehas for adultery with Midianite woman, *Num. 25:14*

ZIMRI 2, assassin, king of Israel for one week, *1 Kg. 16:9*

3, *1 Chr. 2:6, see Zabdi 1*

4, descendant of Saul, *1 Chr. 8:36*

ZINA, *1 Chr. 23:10, see Zizah*

ZIPH, grandson of Caleb, *1 Chr. 2:42*

2, clan leader in Judah, *1 Chr. 4:16*

ZIPHAH, clan leader in Judah, *1 Chr. 4:16*

ZIPHLON, son of Gad, *Gen. 46:16*

ZIPPOR, father of King Balak of Moab, *Num. 22:2*

ZIPPORAH, wife of Moses, *Ex. 2:21*

ZIZA, son of Rehoboam, *2 Chr. 11:20*

2, clan leader in Simeon under King Hezekiah, *1 Chr. 4:37*

ZIZAH, Levite clan leader, *1 Chr. 23:11*

ZOBEBAH, clan in Judah, *1 Chr. 4:8*

ZOHAR, father of Ephron the Hittite, *Gen. 23:8*

2, son of Simeon 1, *Gen. 46:10*

ZOHETH, clan leader in Judah, *1 Chr. 4:20*

ZOPHAH, clan leader in Asher, *1 Chr. 7:35*

ZOPHAI, *1 Chr. 6:26, see Zuph*

ZOPHAR, Job's friend, *Job 2:11*

ZUAR, leader of Issachar under Moses, *Num. 1:8*

ZUPH, ancestor of Samuel, *1 Sam. 1:1*

ZUR, king of Midian killed by Israel, *Num. 25:15*

2, kinsman of King Saul, *1 Chr. 8:30*

ZURIEL, leader of Merari clan in Levi under Moses, *Num. 3:35*

ZURISHADDAI, father of leader of Simeon under Moses, *Num. 1:6*

CREDITS AND ACKNOWLEDGMENTS

The editors thank the following artists for the illustrations on the pages following their names:

Thomas Blackshear—pages 120, 264, 314, 315, 333; Blas Gallego—pages 34-35, 86, 92-93, 274-275, 366-367 (all copyright © 1994 Blas Gallego); Christopher Megadini—pages 65, 175, 198, 290; Joseph Miralles—title page and pages 6, 16-17, 38, 76-77, 81, 112, 150, 182-183, 195, 256-257, 311, 334, 384, 388-389, 407, 428 (all copyright © 1994 Joseph Miralles); Joan Pelaez—pages 41, 115, 141, 225, 321, 437 (all copyright © 1994 Joan Pelaez); Gabriel Picart—pages 53, 135, 158, 200, 230, 240-241, 250-251, 273, 352-353, 370, 404, 414, 434 (all copyright © 1994 Gabriel Picart) and Joe Le Monnier, for the maps on pages 17, 36, 78, 79, 142, 202, 211, 252, 304, 340, 341, 433.

Picture research by Carousel Research, Inc.

(**Key to abbreviations used** AR: Art Resource; AR/G: Art Resource/Giraudon; AR/JM: Art Resource/Jewish Museum; AR/L: Art Resource/Lessing; AR/N: Art Resource/Nimatallah; AR/S: Art Resource/Scala; AR/TG: Art Resource/Tate Gallery, London; AR/V&A: Art Resource/Victoria & Albert Museum, London; BSM: Bayerische Staatsgemaldesammlungen, Munich; BNP: Bibliotheque Nationale, Paris; BAL: Bridgeman Art Library; BL: British Library, London; BM: British Museum, London; KM: Kunsthistorisches, Museum, Vienna; NYPL: New York Public Library; RS/AAA: Richard Sheridan/Ancient Art & Architecture Collection; MMA: The Metropolitan Museum of Art, New York; V&A: Victoria & Albert Museum, London; ZR: Zev Radovan)

A 8 Guasparri di Bartolomeo Papini, after cartoon by Alessandro Allori, Biblioteca Apostolica Vaticana; 9 V&A; 10 RS/AAA; 11 Duomo, Monreale, AR/S; 12 David Teniers I, Rafael Valls Gallery, London, BAL; 13, James Joseph Jacques Tissot, Jewish Museum, NY, AR/JM; 14, Dura Europas, Synagogue, ZR; 18 Bassano, KM, Artothek; 20 ZR; 21 Raphael, Vatican, AR/S; 22 Jan Victors, Museum fur Bildende Kunste, Budapest, Artothek; 23 Johann Liss, Uffizi, Florence, AR/S; 24 San Vitale, Ravenna, AR/S; 25 National Gallery of Art, Washington D.C., Rosenwald Collection; 26 Church of the Madeleine, Vezelay, RS/AAA; 27 Museo del Duomo, Florence, AR/S; 28 Pol de Limbourg, Musee Conde, Chantilly, AR/G; 29 RS/AAA; 30 Johann Ramboux, Wallraf-Richartz Museum, Cologne, Artothek; 32 Domenico Beccafumi, Duomo, Siena, AR/S; 33 Herri met de Bles, Pinacoteca Nazionale, Bologna, AR/S; 37 Lysippus, Louvre, Paris, BAL; 39 Bibliotheque Municipale, Moulins, AR/G; 42 RS/AAA; 43 The Cleveland Museum of Art; 44 Nicholas von Hagueneau, Musee Unterlinden, Colmar, AR/G; 45 center RS/AAA; 45 left ZR; 45 right BM, Michael Holford; 46 top RS/AAA; 46 bottom RS/AAA; 47 Ephesus Museum, Turkey, BAL; 48 Church of St. Peter, Lowick, Northamptonshire, BAL; 49 BM, Michael Holford; 50 Vatican, AR/S;

B 52 ZR; 54 Giotto, Scrovegni Chapel, Padua, AR/S; 55 BL, BAL; 56 Museum Mayer van den Bergh, Antwerp; 57 Rembrandt van Rijn, RS/AAA; 58 Giovanni Andrea di Ferrari, Priv. Coll., BAL; 59 Al-Jazari, ZR;

C 60 Duccio di Buoninsegna, Cathedral of Siena, AR/S; 62 RS/AAA; 63 top Louvre, Paris, AR/SEF; 63 bottom RS/AAA; 64 Santi di Tito, Santa Croce, Florence, AR/S;

D 66 Bibliotheque Municipale, Dijon, AR/G; 68 Michelangelo Buonarroti, Sistine Chapel, Vatican, AR/S; 70 Louvre, Paris, Service Photographique, Reunion des Musees Nationaux; 71 Iran, AR/G; 73 Bartolommeo Bellano, MMA; 74 Lucas van Leyden, Royal Museum of Beaux-Arts, Antwerp, AR/S; 75 Rembrandt van Rijn, Louvre, Paris, AR/G; 79 ZR; 80 RS/AAA; 82 V&A, BAL; 83 BM, Michael Holford; 84 Staatliche Antikensammlungen und Glyptothek, Munich, Newsweek Books; 85 National Museum, Naples, AR/G;

E/F 88 John Singleton Copley, Wadsworth Atheneum, Hartford,; 89 Salomon de Bray, Musee de la Chartreuse, Douai, BAL; 90 Reginald Hallward, Christopher Wood Gallery, London, BAL; 91 Albert Moore, Bury Art Gallery and Museum, Lancaster, London, BAL; 94 A. Franchi, Duomo, Siena, AR/S; 95 Louvre, Paris, AR/G; 96 Bibliotheque de l'Arsenal, Paris; 98 top RS/AAA; 98 bottom Ford Madox Brown, V&A, BAL; 100 BM; 101 Jean Fouquet, Musee Conde, Chantilly, AR/G; 102 Albertinelli Mariotto, Uffizi, Florence, AR/S; 103 RS/AAA; 105

Peter Paul Rubens, Staatgalerie in Schloss Schleissheim, Artothek; 106 Andrea Castagno, Uffizi, Florence, BAL; 107 top Workshop of Nicholas of Verdun, MMA, The Cloisters Collection; 107 bottom Filippino Lippi, Musee Conde, Chantilly, BAL; 108 Lucas Cranach, KM, AR/N; 109 Raphael, Pitti Palace, Florence, BAL; 110 V&A, BAL; 111 Dura Europas, ZR; 113 BL;

G 116 Federico Barocci, Palazzo Ducale, Urbino, AR; 118 BL; 119 Bibliotheque Royale, Brussels; 121 German Church, BAL; 122 Johann Heinrich, KM, AR/L; 124 Guercino, Galleria Sabauda, Torino, AR/S; 125 Bible Society, London, AR/Bridgeman; 127 Musee Conde, Chantilly, AR/G; 128 Master of Flemalle (Robert Campin), Hermitage, St. Petersburg, BAL; 129 Klosterneuburg, Austria, AR/L; 130 ZR;

H 131 V&A, AR/V&A; 132 V&A, AR/V&A; 133 Nicolaes Maes, BSM, Artothek; 134 BL, AR/Bridgeman; 136 Louvre, Paris, AR/G; 137 top Rembrandt van Rijn, National Gallery, Edinburgh, Artothek; 137 bottom Louvre, Paris, AR/Josse; 138 Museo Gregoriano Etrusco, Vatican, AR/S; 139 top Basilica San Marco, Venice, AR/S; 139 bottom ZR; 143 Giovanni Pisano, Duomo, Pisa, AR/S; 144 top ZR; 144 bottom ZR; 146 Duccio di Buoninsegna, Cathedral, Siena, AR/S; 147 Benozzo Gozzoli, National Gallery of Art, Washington DC, BAL; 148 Elizabeth Sirani, Burghley House, Stamford, Lincolnshire, BAL; 149 BM, AR/L; 152 Donatello, Piazza della Signoria, AR/S; 153 MMA, The Cloisters Collection; 154 Caporali, Pinacoteca, Perugia, AR/S; 155 Bibliotheque Municipale, Rouen, AR/G; 156 top The Cleveland Museum of Art, Purchase; 156 bottom, BM, Michael Holford; 157 BL; 159 BL;

I 160 Andrea Mantegna, KM, AR/L; 162 MMA; 164 Jean-Baptiste Jouvenet, Musee des Beaux-Arts, Rouen, AR/G; 165 Raphael, Church of S. Agostino, Rome, AR/S; 166 Bibliotheque Municipale, Bourges, AR/G; 167 Pinturricchio, Vatican, AR/S; 168 Church of St. Pierre, Moissac, RS/AAA; 169 Pierpont Morgan Library, NY; 170 Mattia Preti, BSM, Artothek;

J/K 172 MMA; 174 Holburne Museum, Bath, BAL; 176 Giusto de Menabuoi, Baptistery, Padua, AR/S; 177 Raphael, Vatican, AR/S; 178 Rembrandt van Rijn, Gemaldegalerie, Kassel, BAL; 179 Goffredo da Viterbo, BNP,AR/S; 180 James Jacques Joseph Tissot, Jewish Museum, NY, AR/JM; 181 George Tinworth, Guards Chapel, BAL; 183 Luca della Robbia, Pazzi Chapel, S. Croce, Florence, AR/S; 184 Crusader Church, Nazareth, ZR; 185 Master of Trebon (Wittingau), Narodni Gallery Prague, AR/L; 186 RS/AAA; 187 Jacob's Chapel, Duomo, Pistoia, AR/L; 189 Staatsbibliothek zu Berlin, Preussischer Kulturbesitz; 190 Bibliotheque de l'Arsenal, Paris; 192 Edward Henry Corbould, Private Collection, BAL; 193 BM, Michael Holford; 196 Donatello, Museo dell'Opera del Duomo, Florence, AR/S; 197 Vatican Msueum, AR/S; 199 Rembrandt van Rijn, Rijksmuseum, Amsterdam, AR/S; **200** ZR; **203** Jean-Honore Fragonard, Ecole des Beaux-Arts, Paris, AR/G; **204** Cathedral, Chartres, BAL; **204** BL; **206** El Greco, Galleria Estense, Modena, AR/S; **207** Peter Paul Rubens, KM, AR/L; **208** top Musee Conde, Chantjlly, AR/G; **208** bottom Albrecht Durer, Uffizi, Florence, AR/S; **209** BNP, AR; **210-211** National Library, Athens, AR/L; **212** Konrad Witz, Musee d'Art et d'Histoire, Geneva, BAL; **213** Jan Sanders van Hemessen, Alte Pinakothek, Munich, Artothek; **214** top Museo Arcivescovile, Ravenna, AR/L; **214** bottom Armenian Museum, AR/G; **216** Meister Johann von Flandern, Museo del Prado, Madrid, Artothek; **217** RS/AAA; **218** V&A, AR/VA; **219** Master of the Heisterbacher Altar, BSM, Artothek; **220** Lorenzo Lotto, Louvre, Paris, AR/G; **221** Peter Paul Rubens, Alte Pinakothek, Artothek; **222** Nicolas of Verdun, Monastery, Klosterneuburg, AR/L; **223** Sir Charles Lock Eastlake, Cecil Higgins Art Gallery, Bedford, BAL **224** Church of San Isidoro, Leon, AR/G; **226** Strasbourg, Cathedral, RS/AAA; **227** Albrecht Durer, Stadelsch. Kunstinstitut, Artothek; **228** University Museum, University of Pennsylvania; **229** Alonso Berruguete, Choir, Todelo Cathedral, AR/S; **231** Louvre, Paris, Reunion des Musees Nationaux, Service Photographique; **232** BL, BAL; **233** Donatello, Museo Nazionale del Bargello, Florence, AR/S; **234** Musee Conde, Chantilly, AR/G; **235** Erhard Altdorfer, Museen der Stadt, Regensburg, Artothek; **237** Hans Memling, Memling Museum, Bruges, AR/S; **238** top ZR; **238** bottom ZR; **239** Nicolas of Verdun, Collection of the Abbey Church, Klosterneuburg, AR/L; **241** Staatsbibliothek, Bamberg; **242** BNP, BAL; **244** Museo del Bargello, Florence, AR/N; **245** Jean Adrien Guignet, Musee des Beaux-Arts, Rouen, BAL; **246** Agnolo Bronzino & Francesco Salviati, Palazzo Vecchio, Florence, AR/S; **247** Conrad von Soest, St. Nicholas Church, Niederwildungen, BAL; **248** Musee Conde, Chantilly, BAL/Giraudon; **249** top Benedetto Gennari, the elder, Burghley House, Stamford, Lincolnshire, BAL; **249** bottom B. Elkan, High Menorah in the Parliament Garden in Jerusalem, ZR; **253** Raphael, Vatican, AR/S; **254** Canterbury Cathedral, RS/AAA; **258** Musee Conde, Chantilly, BAL/Giraudon; **259** Autun Cathedral, AR/G; **260** RS/AAA; **261** Musee Conde, Chantilly, AR/G; **262** RS/AAA; **265** Sandro Botticelli, Sistine Chapel, Vatican, AR/S;

L **266** Jean Restout, Musee des Beaux Arts, Rouen, AR/G; **268** Richardson and Kailas Icons, London, BAL; **269** Dante Gabriel Rossetti, Tate Gallery, London, AR/TG; **270** ZR; **271** Lucas Cranach the elder, KM, Artothek; **272** box Peter Mabuse, KM, BAL;

M **276** Barna da Siena, Collegiata at San Gimignano, Siena, AR/S; **278** Walters Art Gallery, Baltimore; **279** Kupferstichkabinett, Staatliche Museen zu Berlin, Bildarchiv Preussischer Kulturbesitz, Berlin; **280** San Marco, Venice, AR/S; **281** V&A, AR/V&A; **282** Tintoretto, Alte Pinakothek, Artothek; **283** Carlo Maratta, KM, Artothek; **284** Dante Gabriel Rossetti, Tate Gallery, London, AR/TG; **285** Fra Angelico, Museo di San Marco Dell'Angelico, Florence, BAL; **286** Stadtbibliothek, Trier, Codex Egberti; **287** Piero di Cosimo, Galleria Nazionale d'Arte antica, Palazzo Barberini, Rome, AR/N; **288** Austrian School, Klosterneuberg, Austria, AR/L; **291** top North Porch, Cathedral, Chartres, RS/AAA; **291** bottom Masolino, National Gallery, London; **292** NYPL, Spencer Collection; **294** top Hessische Landes- und Hochschul- Bibliothek, Darmstadt; **294** bottom Andre Beauneveu, BNP, BAL; **295** ZR; **296** Treasury of San Marco, Venice, AR/S; **298** Edward Burne-Jones, Waterford, Herts., BAL; **299** Dura Europos, now Toda Iraq, ZR; **301** Lawrence Alma-Tadema, Private Collection, BAL; **302** Sandro Botticelli, Sistine Chapel, Rome, AR/S; **303** Domenico Fetti, KM, Artothek; **305** Museo Egizio, Turin, AR/S; **306** Saint Etienne du Mont, AR/G; **307** Musee Conde, Chantilly, AR/G; **308** Simon Vouet, Musee des Augustins, Toulouse, BAL; **309** Raphael, Vatican, AR/S; **310** Michelangelo Buonarroti, S. Pietro in Vincoli, Rome, AR/S ;

N/O **312** Jacob Savery II, private collection, BAL; **316** BNP, BAL; **317** Lambeth Palace Library, London, BAL; **318** RS/AAA; **319** Church of St. Lazare, Avallon, RS/AAA; **322** Michel Wohlgemuth, BAL; **323** Pietro da Rimini, Louvre, Paris, AR/S; **324** RS/AAA; **325** Emeterio the Monk, Cathedral of Gerona, AR/L; **326** top Italian School, Basilica of San Marco, Venice,; **326** bottom Cathedral San Matteo, Salerno, AR/L; **327** Louvre, Paris, AR/G; **328** Winchester Cathedral, Hampshire, BAL; **329** Domenico Beccafumi, Duomo, Siena, AR/S; **330** England, RS/AAA; **331** BL;

P/Q **336** Hans Holbein the Elder, BSM, Artothek; **337** Marx Reichlich, Alte Pinakothek, Munich, Artothek; **338** V&A, AR/L; **339** Cathedral, Monreale, AR/G; **341** England, RS/AAA; **342** after Raphael cartoon, Palazzo Ducale, Mantua, AR/S; **344** RS/AAA; **346** Museo Bargello, Florence, AR/N; **348** S. Apollinare Nuovo, Ravenna, AR/S; **349** Francisco Solibes, Private Collection, Hungary, Artothek; **350** Master of the Heisterbach Altar, BSM, Artothek; **351** Filippino Lippi, Chiesa del Carmine, Florence, AR/S; **354** Rembrandt van Rijn, Christie's, London, Artothek; **355** Hans Holbein the Elder, BSM, Artothek; **356** England, RS/AAA; **357** Nicholas von Hagueneau, Musee Unterlinden, Colmar, AR/G; **358** top Bayerische Staatsbibliothek, Munich; **358** bottom, BNP; **359** Duccio di Buoninsegna, Cathedral, Siena, AR/S; **360** Schottenmeister, Schottenstift, Vienna, AR/L; **362** Biblioteca Apostolica, Vatican; **363** BNP;

R **364** Laurent de La Hyre, Louvre, Paris, AR/G; **366** William Dyce Kunsthalle, Hamburg, Robert Harding Picture Library **368** Benozzo Gozzoli, S. Agostino, S. Gimignano, AR/S; **369** Bartolome Esteban Murillo, Museo del Prado, Madrid, Artothek; **371** Raphael, Vatican, AR/S; **373** West London Synagogue, BAL;

S **374** Armand Point Whitford & Hughes, London; BAL **376** Hans Gieng, Switzerland, RS/AAA; **377** Giovanni Francesco Barbieri Guercino, Sotheby's, London, BAL; **379** BNP, AR/L; **380** Chartres Cathedral, RS/AAA; **381** Raphael, Vatican, AR/S; **383** Adriaen van der Werff, BSM, Artothek; **385** Louvre, Paris, BAL/Giraudon; **386** box The Devil's Window, Fairford, England, RS/AAA; **387** Hugo van der Goes, KM, BAL; **388** Nicolas of Verdun, Klosterneuburg, Austria, AR/L; **390** Pierpont Morgan Library, NY; **391** Rembrandt van Rijn, Mauritshuis, The Hague, AR/L; **392** Lambeth Palace Library, London, BAL; **393** Jean Restout the elder Musee des Beaux-Arts, Rouen, AR/G; **394** Jean Colombe, Musee Conde, Chantilly, AR/G; **395** ZR; **396** Matteo Raverti, Ducal Palace, Venice, AR/Cameraphoto; **399** Karnak, Egypt, AR/L; **400** BL; **401** Rogier van der Weyden, Alte Pinakothek, Munich, BAL; **402** Strasbourg Cathedral, RS/AAA; **403** Duccio di Buoninsegna, Cathedral, Siena, AR/S; **408** ZR; **409** Eramus Quellin II, Musee des Beaux-Arts, Lille, BAL/Giraudon; **410** RS/AAA; **411** Domenico Ghirlandaio, Museum of Fine Arts, Budapest, BAL; **412** College Archives, Perugia, AR/S; **413** Anthony van Dyck, Alte Pinakothek, Munich, Artothek;

T **416** Duccio di Buoninsegna, Cathedral, Siena, AR/S; **419** Andrea del Verrocchio, Orsanmichele, Florence; **420** Louvre, Paris, AR/G; **421** BM, Michael Holford; **423** Michael Holford;

U/V **425** Royal Library, Copenhagen; **426** England, RS/AAA; **427** Filippino Lippi, Musee Conde, Chantilly, BAL;

Z **430** Michelangelo Buonarroti, Sistine Chapel, Vatican, AR/S; **432** Giovanni di Paolo, MMA; **435** V&A, BAL; **438** KM, AR/L; **439** BL; **440** Limbourg Brothers, Musee Conde, Chantilly.

INDEX

*Page numbers in **bold** type refer to main entry.*

317, 405-406, 429
heeds David's wish to destroy
Shimei, 398
kingdom, 35, 202, 279, 406, 410
mother Bathsheba, 11, 56, 80, 405
proverbs, 149
and queen of Sheba, 408, 409
renowned wisdom of, 408-409, 410
son Rehoboam, 31, 79, 199-200,
201, 202, 369-371, 397, 398, 410
temple at Jerusalem, 77, 79, 118,
134, 143, 151, 152, 406- 407,
425, 433, 436
Wisdom of Solomon, 271, 408
wives and concubines, 408
mentioned, 8, 12, 31, 40, 132, 196,
228, 238, 332, 385, 398
Stephen, 336-337, 353, **411-412**
Susanna, disciple of Jesus, 226, 287,
413
Susanna, wife of Joakim, **412-413**
Syrians
Maccabean revolt, 37, 52, 83, 84,
130, 241-242, 260-261, 275,
402, 410
mentioned, 78, 95, 101, 227

T

Tamar, daughter-in-law of Judah,
256, 331, 348, 367, **415**
Tamar, daughter of David, 26, 39, 80,
238, **415**, 429
Temple at Jerusalem
Herod the Great's renovation, 143
Jesus drives money changers from,
216-217, 269
Jesus with elders in, 283-284
Malachi's preaching, 277-278
purified by Judas Maccabeus, 260
repair funding, 188, 227, 254
Sheshbazzar's role in reconstructing
(second temple), 397, 398
Solomon's (first temple), 59, 79,
118, 143, 151, 152, 406- 407,
425, 433, 436
Zerubbabel's reconstruction (sec-
ond temple), 71, 111, 112, 133-
134, 143, 203, 398, 436- 437
mentioned, 45, 47, 255, 309, 318,
319, 361, 401, 425
Ten Commandments, 127, 306, 307
Terah, 16, 271, 382, **415**
Thaddaeus, 258, **416**, 418
See also Judas, son of James

Thomas, apostle, **417-419**
Three wise men, 138, 207, 208, 248,
405
Tiberius (Tiberius Julius Caesar Au-
gustus), 50, 147, 148, 274, 360,
363, **419-420**
Tiglath-pileser III (Tilgath- pilneser),
34, 41, 157, 158, 292, 293, 316,
347, 371, 372, 394, **420**, 425,
430
Timothy, 102, 156, 186, 270, 332,
342, 343, 358, 363, 399-400,
420-422, 422
Titus, emperor of Rome, 58, 85, 145
Titus, 46, 339-340, 342, 344, 421,
422
Tobiah, 121, 320-321, **422**
Tobias, 368, **422-423**, 423
Tobit, 367-368, 422-423, **423**
Tola, 10, 123, 161, 171, 181, 394, **424**
Torah. *See* Mosaic Law
Tower of Babel, 125-126, 323, 348
Tree of Jesse, 204
Tribes of Israel. *See* Twelve tribes of Is-
rael
Trinity, the, 153
Trophimus, **424**, 424
Trypho, 45, 46, 83, 242, 402, **424**
Twelve apostles/disciples, 212-213
fates of, 44
New Testament lists of, 55, 289, 402
See also specific names
Twelve tribes of Israel
apostles as renewal of, 44, 212
descent from Jacob's sons, 171,
176, 179, 247, 256, 316, 430
division into two kingdoms, 35,
103, 199, 202
genealogy, 24
inspection of Canaan, 62, 250
mentioned, 251, 333
See also Israelites; specific tribes
Tychicus, 102, 331, 346, **424**

U/V/W

Uriah, chief priest, 34, **425**
Uriah, husband of Bathsheba, 55- 56,
79, 225, 317, **425**
Uriah, prophet, 196, **425-426**
Uriel, 117, 297, **426**
Uzzah, 77, 330, **426**
Uzziah, 39, 165, 166, 168, 255, **426-
427**
Vashti, 33, 106, 107, 300, **427**

Vespasian, 85, 361
Virgin Mary. *See* Mary, mother of Je-
sus
Wise men. *See* Three wise men
Women disciples of Jesus, 212, 221,
226, 286, 287-288, 375, 413
Women prophets, 82

X/Y/Z

Xerxes I. *See* Ahasuerus
Yahweh
and Athaliah, 49-50
biblical use of, 126
and Jezebel, 32, 223-224
known as Baal, 51
Moabite Stone, 295, 395
See also God
Zacchaeus, 216, **429**
Zadok, 8, 11, 31, 77, 88, 317, 332,
405, **429**
Zebedee, 43, 44, 56, 144, 182, 184,
185, 186, 212, 233, 236, 340,
349, 350, 354, 404, **429-430**
Zebulun, 171, 269, 365, **430**
Zechariah, adviser to Uzziah, 427
Zechariah, father of John the Bap tist,
101-102, 117, 233, 382, **431-
432**
Zechariah, priest/son of Jehoiada,
227, **430-431**
Zechariah, prophet/son of Berechiah,
40, 133, 203, 217, 231, 278, 385,
431, 437
Zechariah, son of Jeroboam II, 41,
157, 292, 394, **431**
Zedekiah, court prophet, 297, **432**
Zedekiah, son of Josiah, 156, 188,
197, 198, 318, 319, 330, **432-
434**, 436
Zephaniah, prophet, **435**
Zephaniah, son of Maaseiah/high
priest, 397, **435-436**
Zerubbabel, 112, 128, 133, 143, 203,
204, 321, 385, 393, 398, 431,
436-437
Zeruiah, 14, 48, 225, **437-438**
Zeus, 45, 47, 84, 138, 260, 318, **438**
Zilpah, 49, 117, 132, 176, 269, **438-
439**
Zimri, king of Israel, 87, 331, 420,
439
Zimri, son of Salu, 64, 357, **439**
Zipporah, 64, 104, 120, 223, 302, **439**
Zophar, 59, 229, **440**